HONOR AMONG THIEVES

HONOR AMONG THIEVES

A Zooarchaeological Study of
Neandertal Ecology

MARY C. STINER

PRINCETON UNIVERSITY PRESS
PRINCETON, NEW JERSEY

Copyright © 1994 by Princeton University Press
Published by Princeton University Press, 41 William Street, Princeton, New Jersey 08540
In the United Kingdom: Princeton University Press, Chichester, West Sussex

Library of Congress Cataloging-in-Publication Data

Stiner, Mary C., 1955–
Honor among thieves : a zooarchaeological study of Neandertal
ecology / Mary C. Stiner.
p.   cm.
Includes biographical references and index.
ISBN 0–691–03456–7
1. Neandertals—Italy.   2. Paleolithic period—Italy.   3. Animal
remains (Archaeology)—Italy.   4. Hunting, Prehistoric—Italy.
5. Paleoecology—Pleistocene.   6. Paleoecology—Italy.
7. Italy—Antiquities.   I. Title.
GN285.S75   1994
937—dc20   93–45881

This book has been composed in Times Roman
Designed by Jan Lilly

Princeton University Press books are printed on acid-free paper
and meet the guidelines for permanence and
durability of the Committee on Production Guidelines for
Book Longevity of the Council on Library Resources

Printed in the United States of America

2 4 6 8 10 9 7 5 3 1

to my family

Contents

Figures

Tables

Preface

WHEN IT comes to published works on the Paleolithic, most of the juicy lines have been taken: Flower people, Hunters, Scavengers, Thick in every way, and Smarter than you think. No Haiku-master, the title of my book consists of a metaphor and a strand of keywords, alluding in turn to a theory about how coexisting predators evolve and an analytical means for testing ideas therefrom. Portions of this research have appeared elsewhere (e.g., Stiner 1990b, 1991a, 1991b, 1992, 1993b; Stiner and Kuhn 1992), though not in their entirety, and much of the work has not been published before. Only by gathering all of the substantive results in one place, complete with background and organized around the main questions about Neandertal adaptations, can the larger picture emerge. Far from the final word on anything, this book is about the process of getting closer to a definitive answer on the nature of Neandertals through a nontraditional approach. Because the study concentrates on how ancient hominid adaptations were structured, the research perspective and the information it yields are pertinent for all scientists interested in problems of human evolution. Because the methods deal with the analytical problems posed both by museum collections and newly excavated materials, the work is simultaneously an exercise in an analytical specialty (the study of animal bones) and the sociology and history of the science. Here, then, is an exposition of what the research is about and what it was intended to accomplish.

SCIENCE seems to operate with two currencies, particles and principles, and the success of any scientific endeavor can be measured by its capacity to surprise the people who undertake it. With these thoughts in mind, I am indebted to the following people for my education: Lewis Binford, Diane Gifford-Gonzalez, Henry Harpending, Steven Kuhn, Lawrence Straus, Erik Trinkaus, and Juan Villamarin. Special thanks goes to Steve, whose innovative work on technology and raw material economy in the Paleolithic is an inspiration.

I owe a great deal to my Italian colleagues, Aldo G. Segre, Eugenia Segre-Naldini (IIPU), Amilcare Bietti (U. Roma), Piero Cassoli (Museo Pigorini), Carlo Tozzi (U. Pisa), and Giorgio Manzi (U. Roma), who helped me in many, many ways. I also thank, posthumously, Alberto Carlo Blanc and Luigi Cardini, who excavated and documented many of the collections I studied. Thanks, too, to Daniella Cocchi (Museu A. C. Glanc in Viareggio), Antonio Radmilli (U. Pisa), Marcello Piperno (Museo Pigorini), and the folks at the Museo Zoologica di Roma for allowing me to study materials at their institutions. I remember well the kind assistance of Graeme Barker and the staff at the British School at Rome, and of Anna Maria Bietti-Sestieri, Fabio Parenti, Claudio Sorrentino, Tonino Tagliacozzo, Silvana Vitagliano, and Barbara Wilkinson during various phases of the project.

On the American side, I thank Gary Haynes (U. Nevada-Reno) for the use of his comparative collections on carnivore-damaged bone, Lee Lyman (U. Missouri) for thoughtful critiques along the way, and Thomas Smith (then of the New Mexico Department of Fish and Game) for his generous loans of kill and scat assemblages and behavioral data on mountain lions. Thanks also to Henk K. Mienis (Mollusk Collection Curator, Hebrew University, Jerusalem) for classifying the land snails from Grotta dei Moscerini and for bringing my knowledge of mollusk taxonomy a little closer to that of the twentieth century. Review comments by Paul Mellars, James O'Connell, Robert Whallon, and John Yellen were a great help for refining the book manuscript.

My research in Italy was made possible by grants

from the Institute of International Education (Fulbright Program), the National Science Foundation (BNS-8618410), the L.S.B. Leakey Foundation, and the Sigma Xi Scientific Research Society. The final year of dissertation writing, from which this work evolved, was supported by an Educational Foundation Fellowship (American Fellow) from the American Association of University Women.

HONOR AMONG THIEVES

1

The Research Problem

MUCH HAS been thought, said, written, and thought yet again about Middle Paleolithic lifeways in Eurasia. Neandertals were like modern humans in many respects, but the differences that we do find invariably surprise us. How can paleoanthropologists effectively recognize adaptational differences between two similar but apparently nonidentical human forms, one of which is extinct? It is clear from recent debates on these topics that answers will not come from simply gathering more of the same kinds of data. Some new ways of working with archaeological records are needed, as well as new perspectives on the data they yield.

This book presents a case study comparing faunal records created between 120,000 and 10,000 years ago by Neandertals,[1] late Upper Paleolithic humans, spotted hyaenas, and wolves in Italian caves. It shows in fairly simple terms how a study grounded on principles of niche theory can provide qualitatively new information about the antecedents of modern humans; I investigate variation in hominid foraging practices in one environment in Italy and, within this framework, examine possible evolutionary relationships between Neandertals and anatomically modern *Homo sapiens*. Because the habits of the sole living representative of our species cannot explain why archaic humans were different, I work from an interspecific point of view. Questions about ecological distance and directions of change between Neandertals and anatomically modern humans can be evaluated in terms of general predator ecology, including predator-prey relationships, behavioral tendencies, physiology, and principles of mammalian demography. Rather than working from the standpoint of what renders humans unique among mammals, this study traces adaptive change in accordance with some basic rules that regulate the lifeways of all large terrestrial predators.

In addition to its theoretical slant, this book pursues a number of methodological options for studying Pleistocene and Holocene human adaptations on the basis of faunal remains. A variety of taphonomic issues are addressed, including how the bone (and mollusk) assemblages were formed, the biotic agencies responsible for them, and potential distortions caused by preservation conditions and archaeologists' recovery practices. Behavioral questions about ancient people and carnivores are investigated with the aid of comparative data on modern social carnivores. Such comparisons help establish the potential significance of the zooarchaeological variables chosen for study, as well as some of the limits on what can be inferred from the archaeological patterns.

This study is based primarily on animal remains recovered from coastal caves in Italy, now in museum collections. The faunal assemblages have never been studied from the point of view outlined here and, in some cases, details about them have never been published. I make no attempt to cover the Middle Paleolithic in its entirety, nor do I document every corner of this vast topic. I concentrate instead on those approaches and analyses that gave the highest payoffs. Moreover, the study concentrates on cave sites exclusively—places to which resources had to have been brought. Three major

---

[1] All of the culturally derived faunas dating to between 120,000 and 35,000 B.P. are associated with Mousterian stone tool industries. There is little reason to doubt that faunas dating to before roughly 50,000 B.P. in west-central Italy were collected by Neandertals, based on the extant human fossil material. Because hominid fossil associations toward the end of the Middle Paleolithic in Italy are ambiguous, however, I prefer the term *Mousterian* or *Middle Paleolithic hominids* (see Chapter 3).

sets of questions about the lifeways of Mousterian hominids are addressed: (1) Did their subsistence adaptations, evident from patterns of animal exploitation, fall within the range of anatomically modern humans that lived in analogous environments? Taking changes in global climate into account, can one reject the null hypothesis that the ecological niche of Neandertals was essentially the same as that of late Upper Paleolithic hunter-gatherers in west-central Italy? (2) What was the nature and extent of variation in Mousterian foraging patterns in Italy? What were their solutions to local fluctuations in food supply? Is there a trend in the behavioral variation within this region and period, and, if so, why? (3) Finally, what economic relationships existed between Mousterian technology and game use at caves in the study area? Collaboration with Steven Kuhn (see also Kuhn 1990a, n.d.) provides some unique insights into the structure of Mousterian economies and patterns of territory use.

NEANDERTALS: PEOPLE LIKE US?

Few creatures are more intriguing to us than an obscure prehistoric variant of ourselves. Neandertals are widely recognized as populations of *Homo sapiens*, although they may have formed a relatively distinct breeding community in Eurasia from roughly 150,000 to 35,000 years ago. The possibilities of contemporaneity and interfertility with anatomically modern humans in the later part of this time range are matters of dispute, unthinkable to some researchers and a normal expectation to others. Ancestors or cousins, Neandertals are important keys for understanding the origins of modern humans.

Questions about the fate of the Neandertals are most often phrased in terms of a biocultural transition centering on roughly 35,000 years ago in western Europe (e.g., Mellars 1973, 1989; White 1982). Paleoanthropologists working in Europe and in Asia generally refer to the Middle to Upper Paleolithic transition, while those working in Africa talk about the Middle to Late Stone Age. In Europe, Neandertal skeletal traits and Mousterian technology gave way to modern human skeletal and technological traits at *roughly* the same time. The anatomically modern human phenotype was present in the Middle East as early as 100,000 years age, however, and perhaps the same time or earlier in Africa (e.g., Stringer and Andrews 1988). Thus, Mousterian and Middle Stone Age technologies persisted in Asia and Africa after the appearance of modern human skeletal traits.

Even in Europe the terms *Neandertal*, a subspecies designation based on human skeletal anatomy, and *Mousterian*, a Middle Paleolithic cultural designation based on stone tool assemblages, cannot be considered wholly equivalent in time or space. A Neandertal skeleton found in stratigraphic association with progressive (Castelperronian) tool industries at St. Césaire in France, and anatomically modern human remains associated with Middle Paleolithic industries dating to roughly 92,000 B.P. at Qafzeh (Tchernov 1981, 1984; Valladas et al. 1988) and Neandertal remains dating to roughly 55,000–60,000 B.P. at Kebara Cave in Israel (Bar-Yosef 1989; Valladas et al. 1987), together suggest that the transition was neither as sudden nor as geographically uniform as was once thought (see also Arensburg 1989; Bar-Yosef 1989; Stringer 1988; Valladas et al. 1987; Vandermeersch 1989). Although the general associations continue to be upheld fairly well in Europe (see J. D. Clark 1981; Howell 1984; Mellars 1989; F. H. Smith 1984; Stringer et al. 1984), the anomalies noted above suggest that the evolutionary relationships among human skeletal anatomy, stone tool types, and behavioral evolution were indirect.

The modern variant of *H. sapiens* (a.k.a. anatomically modern humans) may have originated in one region or, alternatively, in many regions at once. In either case, the prodigious geographic distribution of our genus is extraordinary among primates. But human beings are sophisticated predators, in strong contrast to their primate cousins, and humans' distribution is not unusual relative to other large predators such as bears, cats, hyaenas, and wolves. Populations of *H. erectus* expanded into relatively cold habitats, if only periodically, as early as the Middle Pleistocene (e.g., Turner 1984,

1986). Hominids' tenacity in very cold or very arid biomes may have increased only toward the Upper Pleistocene, concomitant with the appearance of *H. sapiens* (e.g., Bar-Yosef 1989; Gamble 1986; Soffer 1989; but cf. Roebroeks et al. 1992). Australia, a continent separated from all others by deep ocean trenches, was colonized by humans for the first time in the later Upper Pleistocene (e.g., R. Jones 1989; Lourandos 1987). Clearly, the transition and its many repercussions had a vast geographic scope, yet took place within a comparative instant of geologic time.

Two areas of paleoanthropological research—human skeletal biology and stone tool technology—have contributed the most to our impressions of what Neandertals were like. Strong phylogenetic affinity is apparent between the skeletons of Neandertals and anatomically modern humans, leading us to expect their behaviors to have been similar too. Yet a good knowledge of modern hunter-gatherers does not fully prepare us for what we encounter in Middle Paleolithic archaeological records (e.g., Bordes 1961a; Binford 1983:93–94). The ranges of tool types in Mousterian industries vary surprisingly little across large stretches of Eurasia, and industries are usually dominated by only two classes of tools—scrapers and denticulates. Certain other kinds of stone tools are known for this culture period, but they are rare and the array of forms is quite limited. The contents of Upper Paleolithic stone tool kits, in contrast, are more diverse and vary more between regions. In addition to a greater emphasis on blade core techniques, Upper Paleolithic (and Late Stone Age) tool kits may include stone projectile points, a wider range of tool edge forms, and a plethora of bone tools. Bone working represents a whole new dimension to Upper Paleolithic technological systems, including fittings for composite weapon heads, harpoons, wrenches, throwing boards, awls, and needles (e.g., Gamble 1986; Graziosi 1960). Apart from unadorned human burials and the use of red ocher as a pigment or a preservative for wood and hides, Middle Paleolithic and Middle Stone Age peoples contributed no material expressions of art and symbols to the archaeological record (e.g., Chase and Dibble 1987; Davidson and Noble 1989; Lindly and Clark 1990; Mellars 1973; White 1982)—a stark contrast to the practices of Upper Paleolithic and Late Stone Age cultures.

The relative homogeneity of Mousterian industries suggests two things about Middle Paleolithic lifeways. One is that the standard stone tool typologies, the usual means for classifying lithic artifacts, are not very sensitive to how Mousterian technology varied in response to different environmental conditions. The lack of variation in stone tool types could be partly due to the possibility that most were destined for processing tasks and fashioning softer materials, such as wood, into yet other tools. Mousterian stone tools were seldom directly engaged in food procurement activities. The lack of variation in Mousterian tool types is surprising, because the people who made these tools occupied a geographic range approaching that of Upper Paleolithic humans, the latter of whom used diverse implements in similar ecological settings. Limited variation in tool forms suggests that technology figured in Mousterian economies in a significantly different way than it does in modern hunter-gatherer systems, an important clue that Mousterian cultures were organized according to somewhat different rules than those of any Upper Paleolithic or later human culture (for related discussions see Binford 1983; Gamble 1986; Kuhn 1990a; Whallon 1989).

The role of faunal data in human evolution studies

Faunal (zooarchaeological) studies of Upper Pleistocene subsistence and modern human origins tend to focus on a chronological boundary set by shifts in Paleolithic tool industries. Faunal data do not define the Middle to Upper Paleolithic or Middle to Late Stone Age cultural transitions, nor have these data played a very significant role in debates about human evolution. One has only to flip through the many edited volumes on the topic of modern human origins (e.g., those edited by Farizy 1990; Mellars 1990; Mellars and Stringer 1989; Otte 1988–89; Trinkaus 1983a, but see 1989) to realize that this is generally true. The faunal perspective on the Paleolithic nonetheless has much potential to enrich the mix of ideas and operational concepts in human evolution research.

Although some differences between Middle and

Upper Paleolithic tool industries are vivid, the evolutionary significance of these differences is unknown. Tool characteristics were used to define the cultural transition simply because these qualities had been documented in roughly comparable ways for the two cultural periods. As surprising as it may seem from the student's point of view, faunal analysts have no a priori reasons for expecting evolutionary shifts in human game use in the later Pleistocene to coincide with tool industry types. Indeed, patterns of human game use and foraging, outlined against the backdrop of predator economics, are among the kinds of information that may not coincide with the 35,000-year boundary in Europe.

The heretofore peripheral role of faunal data in molding perceptions of change in the Paleolithic puts zooarchaeologists in a unique position to investigate human origins in alternative ways to the standards set by stone tools and human skeletal evidence. The scope of faunal studies has expanded recently to include a variety of experimental and cross-taxa approaches, transforming zooarchaeology into a powerful tool for paleoanthropological research. Furthermore, because the zooarchaeological perspective is about food, its footings in

resource economics are indisputable, and many sources of information about animal resources still exist in modern settings. Some well-developed biological theories are also available to faunal analysts. There may be more to the variation we see in resource use by Paleolithic hominids than is suggested or implied by simple economic models, but an explicitly economic point of view provides testable (potentially refutable) propositions about life in the past and therefore represents an excellent point of departure for studies of Paleolithic subsistence and resource niche. An economic perspective is also a community ecology perspective; the story of human origins is partly the story of one large predator evolving relative to others. Applying faunal data to questions about hominid ecology and evolution requires, however, extensive independent research on the meaning of variables chosen for study (Binford 1972, 1983). The weight of faunal evidence gathered over the past century argues strongly for an interspecific approach, especially the processes by which coexisting predators diversify, behaviorally and/or morphologically, to alleviate the pressures of interference competition.

THE LEGACY OF COEXISTENCE

Two very different kinds of information together have revolutionized fauna-based research on the origins of modern humans: (1) modern primates and carnivores as referents for modeling the evolution of the human resource niche; and (2) the contents of Pleistocene faunas which, more often than not, indicate overlapping resource interests of hominids and carnivores. Controlled comparisons of the social and foraging behaviors of modern nonhuman species help us shed our native conceits about what makes us modern and how we evolved. Although humans are primates, they are a highly predatory variant; hominid ecology diverged from that of all other primate genera and became more like that of unrelated carnivorous taxa. The process of ecological divergence began long ago (Binford 1981; Bunn 1981; Bunn et al. 1980; Isaac 1984; Isaac and

Crader 1981; Potts 1982, 1988) and, by Upper Pleistocene times, humans were accomplished predators. They consumed large prey on a regular basis and coexisted with other behaviorally complex carnivores in tropical, temperate, and eventually subarctic ecosystems.

The usual contents of Pleistocene archaeofaunas have meanwhile forced a separate but related realization in human evolution research. Bone assemblages in Pleistocene archaeological sites frequently present evidence of carnivore activities intermixed or alternated with that of human activities. Re-evaluations of species lists and, more recently, taphonomic approaches, have opened the eyes and imaginations of many researchers about how Paleolithic bone assemblages came into being.

The section on the "Legacy of Coexistence" is adapted from the 1993 article "Modern human origins—faunal perspectives," and is reproduced with permission from the *Annual Review of Anthropology*.

Primate and carnivore models

Nonhuman primates are rich and highly favored sources for developing hominid behavioral models (reviewed by Tooby and DeVore 1987). There is also much to be learned from the large carnivores— species that are not close relatives of humans but instead are neighbors in the food web. The heuristic potential of carnivore sources for human evolution studies was anticipated in the 1960s by Kortlandt (1965) and Schaller and Lowther (1969) and has since been explored by investigators from numerous schools (e.g., Binford 1981, 1984; Blumenschine 1986; Foley 1984a; Gamble 1983; Potts 1984a; Shipman 1984; Stiner 1990a; Turner 1984). Whereas nonhuman primates in modern situations offer insights about the beginnings of tool use behavior in early hominids (e.g., McGrew 1987 Teleki 1974; Wynn and McGrew 1989) and the rudiments of primate-style predation, carnivores offer the richest information on the evolution of the human resource niche and the forces shaping hominids' divergence from the primate template. In short, data on primates help us understand what it was that *H. sapiens* came from but not the kind of social predator that *H. sapiens* ultimately became.

Much has been made of chimpanzees and baboons hunting smaller mammals (e.g., Butynski 1982; Hamilton and Busse 1978; Harding 1973, 1974; Harding and Strum 1976; Hausfater 1976; Morris and Goodall 1977; Strum 1981:282–284; Wrangham 1977). These cases are fascinating but cannot undermine the larger fact that omnivorous primates are particle feeders, even when they are consuming small animals (Butynski 1982; Hamilton et al. 1978; Jolly 1970, 1972; Milton and May 1976; Strum 1981; Teleki 1975). *Homo sapiens* appears to retain this general foraging characteristic in the form of gathering, but humans are also predators of large game. Moreover, humans frequently move food around their territories in order to balance or enhance resource availability relative to immediate and longer-term needs. Nonhuman primates seldom carry food about, and they certainly do not move food in order to feed their offspring.

Predation by humans and carnivores is about much more than the act of killing. One sees among the carnivores highly developed strategies for obtaining small and large game that may include cooperative hunting, cooperative infant care, deliberate transport of large quantities of food over long distances, and extensive and highly effective bone- and meat-processing capabilities. Examining the social and tactical contexts of predation only heightens the contrast between humans and nonhuman primates further: chimpanzees and baboons occasionally kill other mammals, for example, but the behavior is not followed up by carcass processing beyond rough dismemberment, and food transport is minimal or nonexistent.

The lifeways of some carnivores (e.g., wolves and, perhaps, lions) may have changed somewhat between 200,000 and 10,000 years ago (Eisenberg 1981; Kurtén 1968; 1971:118–119), but not nearly as much as hominid lifeways. Evidence of overlapping resource use by humans and carnivores abounds in Pleistocene records, and the ecology of modern carnivores highlights the nature and the evolutionary forum of the competition once faced by meat-dependent hominids. The effects of interspecific competition on the evolutionary histories of animals in communities are not fully understood (compare, among others, Diamond 1989; Schoener 1982; Simberloff 1983; Vrba 1992). The main evolutionary problem is filling the species' resource needs while keeping conflict with other interested parties to a minimum—a problem for which there are many potential solutions. Interspecific competition probably is not a universal or continuous force in the structuring of animal communities (e.g., Vrba 1992; Wiens 1977, 1983). In the case of mammalian predators, however, recent studies indicate that interspecific competition *does* periodically play an important role in shaping the niches and, by extension, the evolutionary histories of coexisting taxa (e.g., Diamond 1975; Jaksić et al. 1981a, 1981b; Rosenzweig 1966; Roughgarden 1983; Dayan et al. 1989, 1991). We know from archaeological evidence that hominids of the later Middle and Upper Pleistocene ate a fair amount of large game (Bar-Yosef et al. 1992; Binford 1984; Chase 1986; David and Poulain 1990; Hoffecker et al. 1991; Jaubert et al. 1990; Klein 1979; Stiner 1990a), the same prey species eaten by coeval wolves, spotted hyaenas, lions, leopards, and other large carnivores. Using information on carnivore niches as baselines of comparison, it is possible to understand why the boundaries of the hominid predatory niche shifted in certain directions through time, and to clarify the circumstances of hominids' ecological divergence from the primate group.

Pleistocene records of hominid-carnivore interactions

Archaeologists have searched long and hard for pure, undisturbed records of humans' past—snapshots of prehistory, living floors, and smoking guns (Binford 1972, 1983). Archaeology is traditionally bounded by an interest in people, and, from this viewpoint, purely cultural deposits might seem the only appropriate cases for reconstructing prehistoric human lifeways. This ideal of purity is inconsistent, however, with the fact that hominids evolved as members of animal communities (Foley 1984a). Mixed or alternating layers of debris generated by hominids and carnivores are the rule rather than the exception in Paleolithic archaeofaunas. Indeed, the farther back in time one searches, the more hominid-associated faunas tend to be intermingled with bones collected and/or modified by nonhuman predators (Bar-Yosef et al. 1992; Binford 1981; Brugal and Jaubert 1991; David and Poulain 1990; Gamble 1983, 1986; Klein 1975; Lindly 1988; Pitti and Tozzi 1971; Stiner 1990a, 1991a; Straus 1982; and compare Binford 1988 and Vincent 1988 on Abri Vaufrey). Mixed depositional histories involving humans and carnivores are especially common in cave faunas, but they also occur in many open settings.

Re-evaluations of Upper Pleistocene archaeofaunas began with species lists during the late 1970s and early 1980s. Frequent occurrences of the remains of large carnivores in Paleolithic sites (especially canids, hyaenas, bears, and leopards) were downplayed in most earlier archaeological reports (e.g., Blanc 1940, 1961; de Lumley 1972; Piperno 1976–77). The presence of carnivore remains was clear enough from the species lists, but, because bone-collecting behaviors by social carnivores were not well known in modern contexts until fairly recently (Binford 1981; Brain 1981; Klein 1975), there was not much reason to take issue with the interpretations of the facts. Beginning with

Kurtén's (1976) formative work on cave bears, we have gradually come to recognize that many of the large carnivores represented in "Early Man" sites were not prey of hominids but were instead visitors to the same caves, presumably on different schedules.

By abandoning the a priori assumption that only humans could have collected bones at locations where stone tools were also found, it became clear that hominids' uses of places during the Pleistocene often differed from what we expected based on our knowledge of modern hunter-gatherers. Gamble's (1983, 1986) work is among the most provocative in this regard because of its explicitly biogeographic perspective. He shows that the proportion of *large* carnivores to herbivores in Paleolithic caves was high in many regions of Europe prior to roughly 20,000 years ago; variation in the ratios of large carnivore to ungulate remains is best explained by latitudinal and maritime-continental geographic clines. After this time, however, human components exclude the presence of large carnivores in the same sites to a significant extent, despite some notable oscillations in climate. Gamble's study provides strong indications that important shifts in hominid resource ecology occurred within the Upper Pleistocene. Especially provocative is his conclusion that the timing of these changes does not match the chronologies built on stone tool types and human skeletal morphology; certainly, the shifts do not coincide with the 35,000-year boundary dividing the European Middle and Upper Paleolithic. The question of carnivore influences on archaeological records has since been taken up in force by bone taphonomists (e.g., Binford 1981, 1984; Binford and Bertram 1977; Brain 1980, 1981; Brugal and Jaubert 1991; Bunn 1981; Bunn and Kroll 1988; Hill 1978, 1984; Potts 1982, 1984a; Stiner 1990a, 1991a). Taphonomic approaches have grown beyond the production of cautionary tales. They now are opening doors onto a much more interesting set of problems than we had to work with before (Behrensmeyer and Kidwell 1985; Binford 1981, 1983; Gifford 1981), not least of which is the legacy of coexistence between humans and other large predators.

To summarize, two sources of information, one from the present (the behaviors of modern mammals) and the other from the past (co-occurrences of human and carnivore records), help define the issues for this study of Neandertal ecology and the evolutionary history of *H. sapiens* more generally. Humans are a strange kind of ape that, in becoming more predatory, became increasingly subject to unique external constraints (for a primate) over the course of their evolutionary history. Contrary to the ways of all other primates, the human species was shaped, at least in part, by the forces promoting behavioral convergence and coevolution among predators. Because the need for resources imposes limits on predator populations irrespective of their phylogenetic histories (sensu Jaksić 1981), the problem of human origins must be considered outside a strictly human arena and outside a strictly primate one as well. Likewise, faunal records biased by carnivores are research assets rather than obstacles—they have revolutionized our perceptions of possible ecological relationships between hominids and their prey, and between hominids and other predators.

BARKING UP A GOOD TREE

Determining how and why modern humans supplanted archaics, the scope of this phenomenon, and the rates of change is a tall order. The issue in evolutionary terms is selection upon variation, meaning that we should ultimately be working toward an understanding of variation in hominid resource use across the full geographic range of the species (or subspecies) at any given time in the past (sensu Hutchinson 1957). From this point of view, no region is inherently more important than another when investigating human origins, except to the extent that its archaeological record is underdocumented. My reasons for working in Italy are as simple as that. I could not possibly hope to document Neandertal ecology throughout Eurasia. Alternatively, understanding Neandertal ecology in one Mediterranean province that has not been adequately studied from a zooarchaeological point of view is a reasonable goal for a fat book.

Questions about hominid game use in the Paleolithic are often phrased in terms of "What were hominids capable of?" and "How efficient was their foraging?" Yet archaic populations of *Homo sapiens* were widely distributed and highly successful for a longer time than the modern variant has been in existence since. Neandertals' brains were as large as ours and as costly to support, and we can assume that hominids used their brains, in addition to feeding them. Paleoanthropologists are simply unable to evaluate capability outside of the contexts in which the behaviors of note were expressed. We can, however, learn about what hominid foragers of a given period were ecologically predisposed to do in a diverse array of habitats; this is the role of regional studies. If evolution at the species and subspecies levels occurs through selection upon variation, understanding any evolutionary transition also requires documenting the ranges of variation in behaviors on either side of that transition. The Middle Paleolithic is invariably the lesser-known period.

It is relevant to consider here the magnitude of differences that might reasonably be expected to differentiate subspecies of *Homo sapiens*. Behaviors vary only subtly between modern subspecies of nonhuman taxa (sensu O'Brien and Mayr 1991), and thus we should not expect huge discontinuities among late Pleistocene hominid variants in the basic constituents of behavior. If hominid predatory adaptations (admittedly only one part of the subsistence repertoire) changed significantly during the Upper Pleistocene, the changes should not, for example, exceed the magnitude that normally distinguishes other large predators in modern animal communities. Although more robust and apparently stronger than moderns (e.g., Trinkaus 1983a, 1983b, 1986), Neandertals would have been subject to similar physiological limitations. They would have faced generally analogous problems in getting food and designing artifacts to gain a physical advantage, and they would have experienced similar needs for key nutrients in their diets. Differences between populations of anatomically modern humans and their immediate predecessors are unlikely to have involved the addition or loss of any of the most basic components of foraging and technology. Instead, evolutionary changes are most likely to have been manifest in how these basic components were integrated or organized as problem-solving strategies for living. Binford's (1978, 1980, 1987, 1990) and Gamble's (1984, 1986) concerns with how human adaptations vary, particularly in terms of economic structure, the rules of strategy combination, and patterns of coexistence with other predators have been especially stimulating in this regard.

Our impressions about archaic *Homo sapiens* (including Neandertals) and their cultures are based on just a few regional records, inadvertent heartlands of human evolution research. Regions of intensive study are of historic interest because the prevailing research questions in paleoanthropology have grown mainly from these experiences. But these heartlands of investigation tell us little about Neandertal biogeography (see also Tchernov 1992). A substantial gap in knowledge presently exists for southern and eastern Europe in particular, save the Iberian peninsula. Sensational human fossil and archaeological discoveries brought the Italian peninsula to the forefront of Paleolithic studies during the 1940s, but news of the Italian Mousterian has since quieted. We know that Italy possesses a rich and well-preserved Upper Pleistocene record, thanks to the extensive surveys and excavations conducted in provinces such as Latium and Tuscany. We do not know how the Italian cases would figure in the broader scheme of human evolution if examined with the benefit of recent analytical techniques and research orientations.

This study capitalizes upon the presence of faunal assemblages generated by hominids and large carnivores in the same caves of Italy. These faunas present an opportunity to learn something about a way of life that no longer exists. Resource relationships between humans and two other species, spotted hyaenas and wolves, are of especial interest in the west-central Italian case. Here lies an important arena for comparisons at the level of resource niche, because all of these species preyed upon the same ungulate taxa, depended upon natural shelters from time to time, and were intensely social.

WHY CAVES?

The Italian study sample comes from Upper Pleistocene deposits in shallow limestone caves. Natural shelters do not represent the full spectrum of places inhabited by Mousterian hominids in Italy, but most of the evidence of game use is restricted to these sites for reasons of preservation. Biased windows on the past, shelters nonetheless provide some interesting situations for studying food procurement and transport by hominids and other bone-collecting predators. Game and other resources had to have been obtained elsewhere, and so the contents of transported faunas reflect a variety of economic contingencies and decisions. Issues of bone decomposition must be dealt with before economic hypotheses can be addressed, but, as will be shown, the subject assemblages are appropriate for the second (behavioral) level of study.

The total sample represents a long and fairly continuous time span, dated by radiometric methods and geochronological studies. Extensive geological work on Quaternary sediments has been done for coastal Latium and Tuscany, at both the regional and local levels (e.g., Blanc and Segre 1953; Segre 1982, 1984; Sevink et al. 1984). Many of the stone tool industries associated with the faunas are documented according to the standard typologies (e.g., Laj Pannocchia 1950; Taschini 1970, 1979; Tozzi 1970). The faunal sample is derived from several cave sites, each with multiple bone-bearing levels. The caves are distributed within a small geographic area, and their geologic settings are fairly analogous; the caves are relatively shallow cavities extending horizontally into the limestone bedrock at low elevations, usually along the sea.

The cave excavations were sponsored by institutions devoted to Quaternary research (Chapter 3), including divisions in paleontology, geology, and archaeology. Excavation teams regularly included specialists in all of these areas, resulting in unusually favorable bone recovery practices. The Istituto Italiano di Paleontologia Umana, in particular, played a decisive role in fostering standardized and systematic excavation and recovery methods from the 1930s through the 1950s at sites such as Grotta Breuil, Grotta Guattari, Grotta dei Moscerini, and Grotta di Sant'Agostino. In addition to consulting field notes and photographic records of the excava-tions, I interviewed some of the surviving members of the excavation teams. New excavations at some of the caves (e.g., Grotta Breuil, Riparo Salvini) aid in assessing the earlier accounts and resolving am-biguities about sample quality and context.

OLD COLLECTIONS, NEW INFORMATION, AND SCALES OF STUDY

This study primarily uses museum collections, ex-cavated before I was born. Vertical proveniences were recorded at no finer scale than geological stra-tum or arbitrary cut. The only information on hori-zontal distributions of bones, shells, and artifacts are the trench placements. The excavations often represent arbitrary slices through thousands of years of deposition, and the faunal and tool assemblages from these slices may or may not correspond to discrete sedimentary or human behavioral events; the slices represent many behavioral episodes oc-curring over long periods of time. The collections fall well short of anyone's research ideal.

If archaeologists have learned anything about ex-cavation procedures and behavioral research since the 1930s and 1940s, faunal collections from these decades will appear flawed from the modern point of view. Regardless of one's broader perspective and analytical ideals, however, older collections weigh upon the modern scientific conscience. Ar-chaeologists are forever generating material whose future utility will require creative thinking, and it will most likely be analyzed by people better in-formed than we are. Any excavation campaign, old or new, is a destructive act, and there would be no justification for undertaking new excavations if to-day's archaeologists can glean nothing from old col-lections with the benefit of an altered perspective. The long-term utility of museum collections hinges on clear documentation of the procedures used and consistent application of those procedures through-out the recovery and conservation phases of the pro-ject; these are the connections between generations of thought and the materials upon which under-standing is built. Systematic procedures and (often-times) detailed excavation records are the saving grace of the Italian collections used for this study, practices that guaranteed the continued value and relevance of the collections for new kinds of research.

As for the scale at which the subject assemblages can inform us about life in the past, there are some advantages to the coarse grain of data they afford. It is a widely held assumption that the closer one looks at faunal remains the better. The point is fair enough for the primary phases of data collection, especially if one is not exactly sure what one needs to know, but the finest scales of observation are not neces-sarily appropriate for addressing hypotheses about human evolution. Certain facts seem obvious to us as we bend over and stare at bones, because we are biologically and culturally equipped to witness those facts. Certain scales of perception also come to us naturally; others are more difficult to visualize. One thing is clear, however: ancient archaeological re-cords are usually disappointing for their lack of de-tail; they are jumbled, mixed, or deflated. Should we rate their scientific potential strictly in these terms?

In fact, appropriate scales of study hinge upon the theoretical premises in use and a number of practi-cal matters as well. The most obvious ways to cate-gorize facts about faunal remains may not be the best ones for research on the evolution of human niche. Finer scales of observation certainly do not necessarily bring us closer to seeing ancient behav-iors as an adaptation or phenotype. Some ecological relationships between species, such as between co-existing predators and between predators and their prey, are only perceptible at broad scales of compar-ison, because the relationships are about the rates at which tactics, actions, and decisions are repeated. The coarse grain most typical of archaeological re-cords presents a viable match with many of the problems of behavioral ecology and human evolu-tion, particularly as more and more cross-site and cross-region comparisons become possible.

Although the analyses to follow vary tremendously in scale, depending on where each analysis fits in the progression of argument, the largest view is the one most pertinent to understanding Neandertal behavioral ecology and niche. In light of the histories of the subject collections and the research objectives, the data are presented in a format conducive to the purposes of this study and, in my opinion the most appropriate uses of these data more generally.

2

Theory and Organization

THIS IS A study of one predator genus evolving in the midst of others. Generally speaking, predators consume what they do not produce, and they tend to focus on the richest foods in nature's larder. What one predator harvests reduces the pool of potential harvests for all others, and, in this game of high stakes, the incentives for keeping abreast with the competition are considerable. Predators are like thieves that live together and, in this context, must arrive upon some version of a truce. With an eye to their own interests, they may keep the peace by avoiding direct competition with another, because it is a cheap solution. Competition avoidance, in turn, promotes diversity in the ways of making a living from the same resource populations. The rules governing the interactions of predator species are imposed by the textures of resources in time and space; the rules are insensitive to the interests of individuals and species.

THE THEORY OF NICHE

Some especially productive guidelines for evolutionary studies of human subsistence can be traced to a family of theories from population ecology: optimality theory, game theory, and niche theory. Reviewed most elegantly by J. Maynard Smith (1974, 1982; also see, among others, Moulin 1986; Pianka 1978; Stephens and Krebs 1986), these theories in some way call upon the power of economics, and they provide expectations about the relationships between foragers and their physical and social environment that are reasonable, provocative, and slightly simple-minded. Although the theories differ greatly in their scales of consideration (e.g., compare Rensch 1959; Mayr 1963), they model interactions within and between species that may ultimately shape the evolutionary pathways of those organisms.

Optimality and niche theories have come into use in anthropology in the past two decades (e.g., reviews by Durham 1981; Foley 1984a; Smith and Winterhalder 1981). They now also influence archaeological research on game use in the Paleolithic. This is not to say that archaeologists necessarily feel capable of testing hypotheses of optimality or niche directly in prehistoric situations; this would be like trying to run a car on petroleum-rich mud. The terms of the models' mathematical equations are unforgivingly precise, whereas zooarchaeological data on the Paleolithic are fuzzy in the best of circumstances. Theories of optimality and, alternatively, resource niche, nonetheless have promoted a more balanced view of what predation is really about at the evolutionary level. The discipline of zooarchaeology now includes research on the signatures and causes of variation in faunal assemblages thought to reflect food choices, handling, transport, and processing, as well as the potential arenas of competition between trophically linked predators. True to the nature of archaeological records and the archaeological data we collect from them, however, the tools for learning about extinct human lifeways are pretty crude—for one thing, we are always too late to witness what actually happened.

This study of prehistoric humans and carnivores is organized in terms of niche theory. Niche theory concerns the processes by which species are assembled into communities, and how conflicts of interest between coexisting species in the quest for resources are minimized through the formation and adjustment of niches within an ecosystem. Though suitable for human evolution research, the theoretical approach is borrowed from another field, and its founding definitions and premises merit review (e.g., Diamond 1975; MacArthur 1968, 1970; Mac-Arthur and Levins 1967; May and MacArthur 1972; Rosenzweig 1966; Roughgarden 1983; Schoener 1974, 1983; and others).

Definitions from community ecology

In outlining the theoretical perspective of this study, I discuss four ecological concepts: community, trophic level, guild, and niche. The research focuses primarily on niche differences among coexisting predators and between two kinds of hominids separated in time, but the niche concept is only one element in a larger hierarchy. Community, trophic level, guild, and niche all concern assemblages of coexisting species, but imply significantly different scales of relationship. Knowledge of the four concepts, their hierarchical relationships, and recent refinements in the ecological literature are important for understanding the general design and rationale of this study. *Community* refers to the full assemblage of species coexisting in a given place and time (e.g., Jaksić 1981:399), irrespective of their trophic characteristics and the probabilities of interaction. In considering questions about community structure, it is important to distinguish between the uncompromising products of nature and the convenience of research: the taxonomic content of a natural community is shaped by a combination of accidents and the forces of evolution, whereas human investigators (such as the author) delineate subsets of variable taxonomic breadth for the purposes of research. There is no complete information on community content in Upper Pleistocene Italy available for this study. There are only biased windows created by the feeding habits of predators that collected bones and mollusk shells in caves.

Trophic level refers to the broad tiers of consumers (animals and plants) through which energy is cycled in an ecosystem. The classic definition of

trophic level, common to many ecology textbooks, is a group of organisms with the same general feeding habits and food sources, such as producers, herbivores, or carnivores (Hardesty 1977:302). Although humans are omnivorous, they qualify as carnivores to the extent that they rely on game.

Guild is a more difficult concept, if only because it varies so much in its applied definition. The concept of the guild has been around for some time (e.g., Root 1967; incipient also in Rosenzweig 1966), but has undergone numerous refinements recently. A guild refers to a particular set of coexisting taxa that are closely bonded by the resource bases they partly or wholly share. Relations between these taxa can be benign or competitive, but may be fairly peaceful most of the time (Wiens 1977). This study follows the definition of guild reviewed by Jaksić (1981:399). Guilds consist of species that exploit an investigator-defined resource in a similar manner—the guild members must be identified through the research process rather than defined in advance. Guilds are assembled by nature, independently of phylogeny; they are of special evolutionary interest, specifically because species that are not genetically related may significantly affect one another through their use of the same kind of resource. Guild members usually subsist at the same trophic level, although resource interests may also converge in other ways such as on habitat structure preferences. Investigations of prehistoric guilds may be confined primarily to considerations of food resources, the remains of which may be preserved in archaeological or paleontological sites, but there is also some information about habitat structure needs, including the use of caves as shelter, common foraging substrates, and landscape features facilitating the capture of large game.

The guild concept is straightforward enough, but, because the pioneering work concerned simpler organisms such as insects, semantic difficulties arise with applications of the concept to behaviorally complex predators whose adaptations emphasize variable response. After all, "exploiting resources in the same way" says a lot more about a multitude of grasshoppers (e.g., Joern and Lawlor 1981) than it does about larger and intelligent predators; no one-trick ponies, humans and most of the carnivores possess many more strategies and utilize more kinds of foods (e.g., Jaskič et al. 1981). The original criteria for guild membership among simple organisms equate behavioral tendencies and biomechanical or locomotor characteristics, a fair assumption in the case of the praying mantis or grasshopper. Landres (1983:393) and others now argue that the original restriction of guild membership to species that exploit resources in a *behaviorally* similar way is too simplistic for studies of higher organisms, because it effectively limits comparisons to taxonomically related species rather than groupings based on behavioral ecology, and foraging regimes in particular. With refinement, then, the guild concept holds that coexisting species rely on the same general resource classes (MacMahon et al. 1981), but that species can use and emphasize those resources differently. Guild members might differ in how they capitalize upon habitat structure, their biological apparatuses for digesting foods, and their strategies and maneuvers for finding, capturing, and processing food.

Hunter-gatherer societies usually find themselves in the same guild as large carnivores such as wolves, large cats, spotted hyaenas, and/or bears. Ungulates and other large mammals often are central to human economies. Even in regions where these prey items are consumed sporadically or infrequently, ungulates may still form essential complements to other foods. Ungulates therefore serve as the hypothetical core for this investigation set in Upper Pleistocene Italy, where ungulate prey clearly were important to hominids and large carnivores. In investigating prehistoric predator guilds, it should be clear that there could be no such thing as a "scavenger guild" or "hunter guild," because guild is defined on the basis of resources used, not procurement tactics.

Finally there is the concept of *niche,* by now a relatively familiar concept in anthropology, though catholic in its definition. Of the four concepts, only niche is exclusive to species (or even finer levels of existence) in a given place and time. The hypothetical boundaries between niches in some way distinguish species' adaptations. Here, I follow Pianka's definition:

> [Niche is] the sum total of the adaptations of an organismic unit, or as all of the various ways in which a given organismic unit conforms to its particular environment. As with environment, we can speak of the niche of an individual, a population, or a species. The difference between an organism's environment and its niche is that the latter concept includes the organism's abilities at exploiting its environment and involves the ways in which an organism actually interfaces with and *uses* its environment. (Pianka 1978:238)

Although most ecologists agree that niche encompasses both the resources used and the life space occupied by a species, niche is most clearly identified with resource use. The words *adaptation* and *niche* are sometimes used interchangeably for the purposes of discussion in this study, but I acknowledge here that they are not wholly equivalent terms. A species' niche can vary somewhat by environment, whereas the limits on its ability to adjust to situations throughout its total geographic range better characterize the species' adaptive potential. As explained in Chapter 1, I consider the ranges of variation in foraging strategies to be an important key for comparing niches of coexisting predators and those that lived in similar environments separated only in time. The definition of niche employed here therefore incorporates Hutchinson's (1957) idea about ranges of tolerances across a broad geographical gradient. Of course, this study is confined to one small region of the world, but my approach is ultimately geared to understanding adaptive variation in *H. sapiens* across a larger area.

The premises of niche theory

According to the theory of niche, each species occupies a hypothetical space in the food web of an ecosystem, and the boundaries of niches conjoin to form a fairly compact whole. The notion that organisms evolve in response to external pressures is fundamental, although these forces may be as diverse as interspecific competition, community history, and random global or local events (e.g., Dayan et al. 1989; Jaksič et al. 1981a; Schoener 1982, 1983; Vrba 1992; Wiens 1977). The concept of limiting similarity, also known as mutual exclusion (MacArthur and Levins 1967), is about interspecific competition in particular and is of especial concern to this research on Upper Pleistocene predators:

basically, it states that no two species can occupy the same niche in a given environment. Many ecologists anticipate that niche boundaries shared by some sympatric species are shaped and maintained by competition for key resources, and that the evolutionary consequences of this process may affect one or all of the species involved. Competition avoidance appears to be an important force in the evolution of predators, more so than in other animals (see Chapter 1), perhaps because predators concentrate on some of the richest foods available. The history of community assembly is also important to this study, because it may condition the opportunities for change and the potential directions of change in any constituent species; *H. sapiens,* for example, entered a somewhat different trophic category than it occupied previously, a category already rife with potential competitors.

Animal communities are viewed as dynamic entities, and their structure and content can change a great deal with time. New species arrive via colonization or they arise through development of qualitatively new adaptations. In either case, the ways that species are recruited into communities are most easily understood at the level of resource guilds. Comprised of species that depend on the same categories of resources irrespective of their phylogenetic histories, resource guilds are thought to represent important arenas of evolutionary change (e.g., Pianka 1976, 1978; Root 1967, 1975; Rosenzweig 1966). Competitive exclusion may fix or stabilize the boundaries separating the niches of guild members (Walter et al. 1984). Because the niche spaces occupied by guild members are thought to be contiguous, knowing the dimensions of the space occupied by one can aid in mapping that of another. A guild that depends on ungulate populations is therefore an appropriate setting for formulating hypotheses about how Paleolithic hominid adaptations were structured relative to those of other large predators.

The relationships among guild members are modeled as bonds for which a limited range of unions or contiguous boundaries is possible. No doubt there were limits on the ways in which hominids could manage to become increasingly carnivorous over the course of the Middle-Upper Pleistocene—there had to have been an easy-in, a weak link ready to

open. Some of the bonds linking species together in communities are nearly inviolable, based on their persistence through time; others are less stable. Recruitment of species into guilds probably proceeds in a conservative fashion, with new species attaching themselves to weak links in the structure, seizing upon a preexisting gap, or quickly filling a temporary opening from which the population cannot be ousted later. Opportunities for addition do not occur entirely at random; they are governed by the contingencies of fit and, therefore, community history. Generalist feeders are thought to enter in the early stages of community formation, when fewer limitations exist in the niche spaces available. Specialists tend to enter later in the process and must evolve within a more stringent set of constraints. We are safe in assuming that hominids were relative latecomers to large predator guilds on all of the continents they inhabited. In becoming increasingly carnivorous, hominids had to evolve in relation to the niches already occupied by better established predators.

Niche theory anticipates that members of resource guilds respond to one another and to the limitations set by food supply. Both conditions are evidenced by the cave faunas generated by hominids and carnivores in Italy. Overlapping use of these resources implies close, though not always competitive, ecological and evolutionary relationships. Occupations of the caves by hominids, wolves, spotted hyaenas, and bears alternate, and all but bears subsisted on ungulates to a large extent. Felids also figured in ungulate guilds throughout most or all of the geographical range of humans, but they are not discussed much here because the remains of cats are rare or absent from the Italian cases examined. The faunas show that two general classes of resources—ungulates and natural shelters—bound some or all of these predators into a single resource guild during the Upper Pleistocene. Hence, the niche boundaries of the carnivores should be very useful for evolutionary studies of a neighbor, *Homo sapiens,* during this time range (see, among others, Foley 1984a; Turner 1984). Large carnivores also underwent phases of adaptive radiation, continuing to evolve even now, but most of the major changes in these taxa occurred during the Miocene or Pliocene (Eisenberg 1981; Kurtén 1971); their adaptations were *relatively* stable by the Middle or Upper Pleistocene. It is for this reason that many of the basic features of the niches occupied by these carnivores can be reconstructed from the habits of modern counterparts, thereby supplying a general framework for comparing the economic behaviors of modern and archaic *Homo sapiens*. The comparisons are conducted in several dimensions, usually in terms of the variables from foraging models developed in the field of ecology. These dimensions include the behavioral and environmental correlates of prey species choice, prey age choice, the influence of food distributions and food quality on the search, procurement, and transport of food, the processing strategies used, and the seasons of shelter occupations.

ANALYTICAL APPROACH

The foraging adaptations of sympatric predators (human and nonhuman) can be compared through the cumulative patterns they create in bone assemblages. Because hominids were not the only occupants of Upper Pleistocene caves in coastal Italy, however, the research must deal with three analytical issues successively. The first problem is to determine through taphonomic and related analyses how the bone assemblages came into being; specifically, whether the animal remains in a geological level were collected by hominids or some other kind of agency. The taphonomic analyses also assess the extent to which bone representation has been biased by in situ bone destruction. Establishing the authorship(s) of assemblages is only partial preparation, however; a secure understanding of what the zooarchaeological variables can tell us about behavior, ecology, and evolutionary processes is also needed. Nearly everyone recognizes the hominid lifeways changed over time, but there is less agreement about what the perceived changes might mean in evolutionary terms, how to measure them, and the selective forces behind those changes. Certainly, the information value of zooarchaeological variables is not self-evident and, hence, must be addressed as an integral part of the study. The final and most interesting issue for this research is what the faunas reveal about foraging behaviors of hominids and carnivores. The relationships between cause and effect are determined mainly from studies of nonhuman predators living in modern ecosystems, providing the essential background for interpreting the archaeological patterns. Together, modern ethological and archaeological data provide information about hominids' impact on prey populations compared to other predators, the ways that they searched for, procured, and consumed prey, the thresholds for switching among resources, and the nature of the competition.

The benefits of a cross-species approach for this study are considerable, extending beyond the obvious questions about resource economics. Information on variation in modern predator adaptations in many parts of the world, including traditional human societies and free-ranging carnivores from the arctic to the equator, is used to explore the relationships among food choices, foraging strategies, and food debris. Cross-species comparisons likewise permit reconsiderations of the magnitude of differences that might reasonably be expected to distinguish subspecies of *H. sapiens*. It will also become clear through the application of modern referents that some zooarchaeological variables help identify the bone collector, whereas others identify behavioral strategies more or less independently of predator type; no variable can be expected to do both. The scales of analyses vary from chapter to chapter (see below), and each major analytical segment offers distinctly different classes of results. The analyses shift from interspecific comparisons and back to humans again in an effort to gauge the ecological and evolutionary dimensions of resource use by hominids.

Volume structure and organization

Following description of the sites and faunal samples (Chapter 3), this book divides into four major analytical sections. The first section (Chapters 4, 5, 6, and 7) uses taxonomic representation and patterns of bone damage to address questions about the composition of mammalian communities in Italy during the Upper Pleistocene, authorship of the bone assemblages in the coastal caves, and the prey species consumed by hominids, hyaenas, and wolves. The second analytical section (Chapters 8 and 9) focuses on prey body part representation as a means for comparing the prey procurement and transport strategies of hominids and the other large predators. The third section (Chapters 10, 11, 12, and 13) deals with ungulate and carnivore mortality patterns, based on tooth eruption and wear data. Mortality patterns are used for a variety of purposes, from discerning prey age selection habits of the predators (Chapter 11) to evaluating the seasons of death in carnivores (Chapter 12) and ungulates (Chapter 13). The final analytical section (Chapter 14), co-written with Steven Kuhn, examines the relationships between game use and Mousterian technology and raw material economy in the study area. The comparisons provide new insights about the nature of variation in Mousterian resource and land use strategies, thereby setting human predatory tactics in broader perspective. Although results are summarized at the close of each major analytical section, and especially in Chapter 14, a broader synthesis is undertaken in Chapter 15. The remainder of this discussion outlines the structure of the study in more detail, explaining the role of each analysis for addressing the main research questions.

The methods and variables employed in the four analytical sections of this book are different. Each section therefore contains a presentation of its key methods, variables, and working assumptions. Basic to the analyses are certain quantitative variables, five of which play especially important roles in the study. N-taxa, MNI, MNE, NISP, and AGE (Table 2.1). One quantitative variable commonly used by zooarchaeologists, known as NSP, is not considered much in this study, because the histories of the collections prohibit its use; NSP refers to the total number of items, including unidentifiable bone and tooth fragments, and such unidentifiable material may have been selectively discarded by the archaeologists who excavated the Italian caves. The main quantitative variables, summarized in Table 2.1, refer to aspects of animal taxonomy, anatomy, and individual lifetimes, and may differ in the levels of observation or assumptions required to produce them. Bone and tooth counts are partitioned within

the data set, because bones and teeth represent two distinct kinds of skeletal materials possessing different taphonomic properties and potentials for preservation. Other quantitative and qualitative variables also appear in the chapters that follow; qualitative variables that describe the condition of bone items are crucial to understanding the taphonomic histories of the assemblages.

Species abundance and taphonomy, based on N-taxa and NISP

Chapter 4 begins with comparisons of species content in the Italian cave faunas along the Mediterranean coast to those from analogous geological contexts in Britain, another marine-regulated climatic province, and to Israel, a classic warm Mediterranean province. Unlike the situation in Italy, however, Britain experienced periodic encroachment of glacial ice during the Upper Pleistocene, and for this reason presents a useful set of geographic contrasts in which to examine shifts in animal community structure in west-central Italy between roughly 120,000 and 10,000 years ago. The comparisons reveal that Italy supported a relatively diverse fauna throughout the Upper Pleistocene sequence and that species deletions and additions were relatively uncommon, a pattern also found in Israel. These findings pull few surprises, but they are important for establishing some baseline facts about the content, texture, and stability of Italian ecosystems during the Upper Pleistocene.

Chapter 4 also examines species representation in the Italian cave faunas by geological or archaeological levels. The species abundance data provide a first indication of the potential array of bone collectors that may have played a role in the formation of each stratum. Knowing the identity of the bone collectors and modifiers is crucial to any further interpretation of the faunas. Several species of carnivore periodically used the subject caves as denning sites, and some of them (spotted hyaenas and wolves) are known to be avid bone collectors. Chapter 5 addresses how the large mammal assemblages were formed, the agencies responsible for producing them, and the extent of in situ bone decomposition. Patterns of damage (e.g., gnawing, burning, tool marks, fracture patterns, and weathering) and spe-

TABLE 2.1
The main quantitative variables

Variable name	Short definition, subvariables, and chapter (no.) where explained in detail
N-taxa	Number of taxa; usually equivalent to number of species, but can refer to more generic taxonomic categories in some of the anatomical analyses (4).

MNI	Minimum number of individual animals; method of determination varies with the purpose of analysis but is generally based on the most common portion of the most common anatomical (skeletal) element in an assemblage.
	    bone-based MNI (9)
	    tooth-based MNI (11)

MNE	Minimum number of skeletal elements; an estimation of the number of skeletal elements represented by specimens in an assemblage, based on the most common portion of the element considered.
	    bone-based MNE, raw counts[a] (9)
	    bone-based MNE, standardized OBS/EXP (9)
	    tooth-based MNE (11)

NISP	Number of bone/tooth specimens identifiable to taxon and/or anatomical region, depending on the purpose of the analysis.
	    bone-based NISP (4)
	    tooth-based NISP (4)
	    total (bone plus tooth) NISP (4)

AGE	Age of an individual animal at the time of death; determined from tooth development or the extent of occlusal wear (11, 12).

[a]Determinations of head MNE counts use bone material, not teeth.

Note: All of the variables listed above can be defined either from bones or teeth. In this research, bone- and tooth-based counts are partitioned within the data set, because the two kinds of skeletal tissues have different taphonomic properties and potentials for preservation.

cies representation are used to reconstruct the taphonomic history of each assemblage. The agencies responsible for large mammal accumulations are identified, and when two or more agencies were involved, their roles are ranked relative to one another.

In addition to large mammal bones, some of the Mousterian faunal assemblages contain the remains of small animals, principally marine shellfish, landsnails, tortoises, rodents, rabbits, and hares. Very little is known about small animal exploitation during the Mousterian of Europe. Chapter 6 investigates the taphonomic associations of small species to the activities of hominids and other predators in the caves and explores the circumstances of exploitation. I show on the basis of damage patterns that most of the terrestrial small species were prey of wolves, foxes, wild cats, hedgehogs, and some-

times avian predators. In contrast, most of the marine mollusks and reptiles were collected and consumed by Mousterian people. The patterns of shellfish exploitation at one cave (Grotta dei Moscerini) relate partly to subtle changes in sea level; the rise and fall of the Mediterranean over time affected the cave's proximity to the shoreline and the kinds of shellfish available immediately in front of it. This unusual glimpse of small animal exploitation in the Mousterian is important for understanding how hunting, gathering, and scavenging practices may have been integrated within their foraging adaptations. Grotta dei Moscerini is the first Mediterranean case for Middle Paleolithic shellfish exploitation ever documented from a taphonomic point of view.

Chapter 7 compares the diets of large predators on the basis of prey species abundance. The predators considered are Middle Paleolithic humans, late Upper Paleolithic humans, spotted hyaenas, and wolves. The question is whether the species consumed at the caves by each kind of predator can be explained by natural abundance, as opposed to preferences or differing niches. The dietary data are analyzed for both the ranges and the relative proportions of prey species associated with each consumer. The comparisons reveal few if any significant differences among the four predators, including the two noncontemporaneous variants of *H. sapiens*. Uniformity in prey species consumed in the study area shows that natural prey abundance exerted a powerful influence on predators' choices, despite obvious differences in their adaptations. The most important outcome of the analysis is its demonstration of close trophic and ecological relationships among Upper Pleistocene hominids, hyaenas, and wolves in Italy at the level of resource guild. Species consumed did not consistently distinguish these predators at the level of niche.

Body part representation, using bone-based MNE and MNI

The body parts transported to caves by predators may reflect their methods of procurement and the contexts of consumption. When anatomical analyses are supported by taphonomic data, they can represent a powerful means for diagnosing the foraging strategies of bone-collecting predators, especially humans, canids, and hyaenids. Chapter 8 begins this section on body part representation by outlining the problem and behavioral bases of food transport and formulating some expectations.

Chapter 9 is about ungulate body part representation in modern and Upper Pleistocene shelters. In addition to documenting basic patterns, this chapter explores how habitual procurement tactics, processing capabilities, and food quality affected predators' transport choices. Patterns of anatomical representation are examined in terms of the total quantity of skeletal parts transported per carcass source, and biases in skeletal composition relative to prey anatomy. The comparisons are organized according to small, medium, and large body size categories in ungulates. The skeletal patterns created by each kind of predator in shelters are used to

infer their main procurement methods, aided by observed carnivore strategies in modern situations from around the world. Counts of head parts are based exclusively on bony tissues of the cranium (not teeth) so that they can be compared to other sections of the prey anatomy. The ratio of crania to limbs proves effective for gauging the relative importance of hunting versus scavenging and, by implication, certain niche differences between the predator species. Of special interest are the ranges of variation displayed by the bone-collecting predators and the relative position of each predator's range within the analytical scheme. In coastal Italy, the foraging strategies of spotted hyaenas and Mousterian hominids were quite variable at the interassemblage level of comparison, placing strong emphases on both hunting and scavenging in the study area. Wolves and Upper Paleolithic hominids, in contrast, displayed much less variation in this regard, relying primarily on hunting. The comparisons demonstrate that anatomical representation in transported faunas is not diagnostic of predator species. Rather, these data distinguish broad classes of predatory strategies. The comparisons also suggest that the spatial distribution of carcasses on a landscape and the nutritional quality of body parts further limit a predator's emphasis on either class of foraging strategy.

Mortality patterns, based on tooth eruption-wear and MNI

Chapter 10 opens the third analytical section of this book by reviewing the theoretical role of predators in predator-prey relationships. This chapter explores the many links between mortality patterns and cause, and it takes a critical look at the potential of mortality data for interpreting the foraging strategies and niches of predators. Modern wildlife studies, principles of mammalian demography, and the life history characteristics of prey species are used to build an analytical framework for interpreting the prehistoric cases. The chapter also considers some of the seasonal and spatial correlates of mammalian mortality patterns in modern situations, outlining potential strengths and shortcomings of seasonality data from the archaeological perspective.

Chapter 11 is a comparative analysis of prey age

selection habits of modern and Pleistocene predators, based on eruption-wear frequency data for ungulate teeth. The analyses use three age categories:
juveniles, prime adults, and old adults. The age
groups are partitioned according to physiological
changes that naturally occur in prey throughout the
life course and associated changes in their inherent
nutritional value to predators. The analyses begin
by examining mortality patterns arising from nonviolent causes of death, followed by patterns resulting from the prey age selection habits of modern
carnivores (felids, canids, and hyaenids) and humans. Contrary to some previous claims, most
kinds of mortality patterns cannot be expected to
distinguish the causes of death in fossil assemblages, much less species or subspecies of predators. However, mortality patterns are effective for
distinguishing broad classes of predatory strategies
and predatory niches, provided that many assemblages are compared and each assemblage is firmly
attributed to the predator through independent taphonomic evidence. The findings on modern (and Holocene) predators are then used as a background for
comparing Mousterian and late Upper Paleolithic
cases from west-central Italy. Ungulate mortality
data indicate that Mousterian procurement techniques were considerably more diverse across assemblages than those of late Upper Paleolithic humans within the confines of the study area and among
modern human cultures more generally. The Mousterian data indicate a strong reliance on hunted ungulate prey in some sites, but on scavenged individuals of the same species in other sites. By contrast,
late Upper Paleolithic and later human cases invariably indicate a strong emphasis on hunted prey. The
geographic frame of this contrast is important to the
conclusions drawn.

Chapters 12 and 13 investigate the seasons and
durations of the cave occupations by carnivores and
hominids respectively. Carnivore age structures are
used as an alternative way to evaluate the hypothesis that wolves and spotted hyaenas denned in
some levels of the caves, because dens are places
where many young carnivores normally die. Tooth
eruption-wear stages for juvenile ungulates and the
relative incidence of adult deer antler are the bases
of seasonality determinations for common prey species. Antler and red deer canines relative to bone-

based cranial counts are used to evaluate sex ratios
in adult red deer. Although limited in scope, the
results on seasonality and sex ratios supplement
other kinds of zooarchaeological data in interesting
ways. The full cycle of seasons is represented in the
Mousterian sample as a whole, but the seasons of
occupations appear to vary by site. Some of the
Mousterian assemblages may have accumulated in
spring and/or summer, whereas others almost certainly represent fall-winter occupations. Seasonality data for the late Upper Paleolithic sample indicate primarily fall-winter shelter occupations in this
region of Italy.

*Relationships between Mousterian technology
and game use*

Most of this research on Neandertal ecology concerns the use of game. Chapter 14 turns to the economic relationships *between* technology and subsistence in the Mousterian of west-central Italy and
looks for possible trends in these data. This chapter
is also the first step toward synthesis in that it summarizes most of the main results on the faunas. The
lithic analyses (by S. Kuhn) emphasize technological variables expected to have been most heavily
influenced by people's food search and procurement
strategies, primarily core reduction techniques and
the reduction histories of stone tools. These qualities of Paleolithic systems are keyed to raw material
economy. While the arrays of tool types produced
by Mousterian hominids, and the mammalian prey
species that hominids consumed, stayed much the
same between 120,000 and 35,000 years ago, other
aspects of technology varied in concert with prey
mortality patterns, prey body part representation,
and the seasons of shelter use. Covariation in game
use and technology appears directional through
time when examined statistically with assemblages
ranked on an ordinal chronological scale. The trend
in the lithic and faunal data may be explained by
shifts in local habitat structure caused by a general
decrease in sea level between 120,000 and 35,000
years ago. The extent of variation, rather than its
vectored appearance, is perhaps the more broadly
significant result, as it clearly demonstrates great
variation in the responses of Mousterian hominids
to the world around them; this is very different from

how the makers of the Mousterian are commonly portrayed. Covarying patterns of game use and technology afford some extraordinary insights about Mousterian land use and the nature of the adaptive raw material already present in hominid behavioral repertoires of the Middle Paleolithic.

Synthesis

Chapter 15 synthesizes the results from a diverse series of analyses. The discussion returns to the main questions posed at the beginning of this book: Were Mousterians people like us? Did they occupy the same general ecological niche in west-central Italy as anatomically modern humans living under similar climate regimes during the late Upper Paleolithic? Taken together, the evidence shows that Mousterian foraging practices were organized according to a somewhat different set of rules than was true of modern humans and that some significant shifts occurred in the human resource niche sometime during the Upper Pleistocene. Because the Italian sample represents a relatively small geographic area, the greater range of variation in foraging strategies evident for Mousterians may indicate significant differences in the scale of territory use relative to later Upper Paleolithic peoples, a notion supported by the lithic data. Both varieties of hominid certainly were mobile foragers, but Mousterian responses may have been governed more by local, immediate exigencies than was true for Upper Paleolithic peoples. Some changes in hominids' economic practices suggest increasing specialization with time, or, at least, greater uniformity in the strategies for utilizing resources within an arbitrary geographic window some 70 km across. The timing of these changes remains unclear, although the mortality analyses show that some began in the later part of the Mousterian rather than at the Middle-Upper Paleolithic chronological boundary. This book concludes with a discussion relating the findings to broader issues in human evolution research, such as the much debated Middle-Upper Paleolithic transition in Eurasia and the implications of this research for future studies on modern human origins.

COPING WITH SMALL SAMPLES

I am about to embark on a detailed description of the sites and faunas from west-central Italy (Chapter 3). Hence, it will soon become clear that the sizes of the faunal assemblages used in this study vary tremendously, making numerical comparability an issue. Absolute minimums on sample size must exist for any comparison, although the boundaries differ with the purpose and procedures of the investigation. We have little or no a priori knowledge about where those boundaries lie; we try to find them when it becomes worth our while to do so. A number of techniques for assessing sample size biases have been developed (e.g., Grayson 1984), and, generally speaking, the simpler they are the better. Paleolithic faunal assemblages are often difficult to analyze because they tend to be small, and they are precious scientific resources because they are rare. The sparseness of some bone accumulations could have behavioral significance, because, for example, the human occupations at these places were relatively ephemeral.

There is more than one acceptable cost-benefit ratio for evaluating sample size biases. One point of view is merely conservative relative to a sampling ideal, whereas the other is conservative relative to what is available for study. The first approach usually involves plotting one quantitative variable against another in a simple two-dimensional format. The investigator identifies and eliminates all cases that appear potentially problematic by some predefined standard that may or may not be wholly appropriate. The a priori threshold for eliminating samples may be overly stringent, but it does not matter in a rich universe, because the investigator can afford to throw out many samples and find better ones. Borrowing a metaphor from population biology, this approach corresponds to an *r*-strategy for selecting samples.

An alternative approach for evaluating the impact of sample size biases involves cross-referencing patterns across multiple, causally independent (or partly independent) dimensions, an option frequently used in this study—life in a poor universe. Basically, this strategy assumes that any one pattern may be questionable due to sampling error, but consistent relationships among patterns derived from independent classes of data are likely to be significant. Sampling bias is assessed by looking for consistent relationships *between* large and small samples, and *across* distinct classes of zooarchaeological data. This is the *K*-strategy of sample bias assessment, because it invests more consideration in each potential case. By way of example, the authorship of faunal assemblages might be evaluated by first looking at species representation, followed by bone damage patterns, and finally by looking at carnivore age structure, if denning is suspected, or the presence and relative quantities of stone tools. Cross-referencing can be performed in as many dimensions as there are causally independent variables in the study. Even when cross-referencing yields a fuzzy answer, the procedure aids in refining the questions asked of the data and outlining new questions for investigation.

The *r* and *K* strategies for coping with sample size biases are not incompatible; I, for example, use both. The point is that there is no universal or absolutely correct threshold of statistical significance when trying to figure out if zooarchaeological patterns are explained by sample size. An investigator's decision to emphasize one strategy over the other is a question of research economy, a statistical issue that is not widely recognized among archaeologists. Human paleontologists, for example, are seldom willing to ignore a rare type of hominid fossil because doing so effectively eclipses segments of the human evolutionary sequence from scientific consideration. A generally similar argument applies to archaeological studies of the Lower and Middle Paleolithic; contra the situation for more recent phases of prehistory, where archaeologists can sometimes be choosier about samples, researchers working in earlier time frames cannot. Cross-referencing is especially germane to Paleolithic studies, because so little is known about the hominids responsible for these ancient archaeological records, bone preservation is a widespread problem, and the assemblages often are smaller than we would like them to be.

The Study Sample from Italy: Archaeology
in the Context of Quaternary Studies

THE PROVINCE of Latium has an extensive and colorful history of archaeological, geological, and paleontological work, though not very well known outside of Italy. Much of this history is about an integrated multidisciplinary program of Quaternary research by the Istituto Italiano di Paleontologia Umana. Here, I present the study sample and its history, along with information on radiometric dating, regional and local geology, and the associated technological and human fossil records.

THE LAND

A rich Paleolithic record lines the modern edge of Italy, along the Tyrrhenian branch of the Mediterranean Sea (Figure 3.1). Much of this record is assigned to the Middle Paleolithic period, based on the presence of Mousterian tool industries. The best-preserved sites typically occur in shallow caves in the limestone bedrock, although open sites are plentiful on the Pontine Plain to the north. Mousterian occurrences in the open are often widely scattered and thin, whereas certain shelters in the coastal cliffs contain thick accumulations. These caves were frequented by hominids time and time again, much like the strings of Mousterian and Upper Paleolithic sites along the Dordogne cliffs in France.

A substantial proportion of the Mousterian cave sites of Latium are concentrated at two points along the Tyrrhenian coast where large masses of uplifted limestone jut into the sea (Figure 3.2). Monte Circeo is the more famous of these localities, an isolated mountain of Cretaceous and Jurrasic limestone rising 514 m from the water and bordered by poorly drained coastal plain on its east and south sides. Another concentration of Mousterian caves occurs roughly 40 km to the south near the medieval town of Gaeta, where limestone cliffs again meet the sea.

Because they have undergone several major episodes of erosion due to sea level transgression, probably only a fraction of the former archaeological accumulations is preserved in the modern era. Many of the caves were scoured out by the high seas of the Last Interglacial, erasing virtually all deposits dating to before this time. Holocene sea transgressions subsequently destroyed some Upper Pleistocene deposits in low-lying caves. A few of the coastal sites nonetheless retain Paleolithic strata, locked either in flowstones lining the cave walls or in protected portions of cave interiors. Two important caves, Grotta Guattari and Grotta di Sant'Agostino, contain nearly intact cultural deposits due to their position several meters above modern sea level.

It is clear from the vertical thicknesses and artifactual richness of the remnant Middle and Upper Paleolithic strata that these shelters were used repeatedly by hominids. The full horizontal extent of each deposit usually cannot be known, but a single skirt of artifact-rich talus may have linked several of the contiguous shelters lining the base of Monte

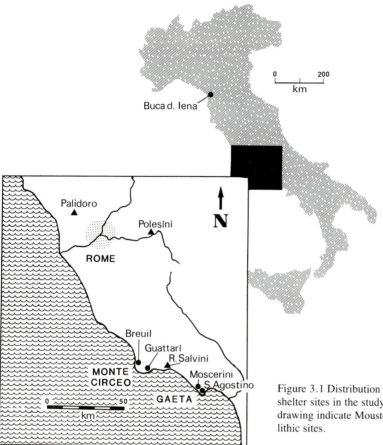

Figure 3.1 Distribution of Upper Pleistocene caves and shelter sites in the study sample from Italy. Circles in inset drawing indicate Mousterian sites; triangles, Upper Paleolithic sites.

Circeo (including Grotta Breuil, Grotta della Maga Circe, and Le Cinque Grotte; see Figure 3.2b). The time frame over which hominids used the caves is not fully known, much less the sizes of hominid social groups involved. The earliest preserved cultural sequences in the caves begin around 120,000 B.P., although hominids probably also used the caves prior to the Last Interglacial.

The rich archaeological accumulations at some localities give us cause to wonder what repeatedly attracted Mousterian hominids to these promontories by the sea. Karstic formations normally foster the preservation of bone to an extraordinary degree, and there is no question that this is the situation in west-central Italy. There is some evidence nonetheless for discriminating choices of caves by Paleolithic hominids, since few upland shelters (above 50 m), safely above the reaches of the highest sea

stages, contain substantial cultural deposits (Blanc and Segre 1947). Certain low-lying localities instead held some kind of long-term attraction for hominids. The natural juxtaposing of rich coastal plains and wetlands alongside abrupt rocky heights may provide a partial explanation; such conditions normally support considerable ecological diversity within a small area. The coast is also graced with a relatively mild climate tempered by sea-born winds, and the land seldom if ever freezes today, allowing tropical palms to colonize the rugged cliffs.

The bald southwestern face of Monte Circeo is vertical, craggy, and especially rich in Paleolithic sites (Figure 3.2), as are the cliffs near Gaeta. The spacious shallow caves orient to the southwestern sun, fully or partly protected from continental winds. The caves are cool in summer, while the surrounding plains are hot and humid. In autumn,

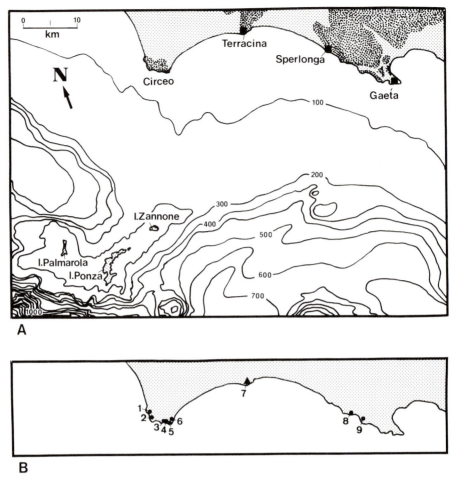

Figure 3.2 Topography of the Tyrrhenian coast of Latium (Italy) in the vicinity of Monte Circeo and Gaeta. (A) underwater contours (in m) of the continental shelf below modern sea level. (B) locations of coastal Paleolithic sites: (1) Grotta Breuil, (2) Grotta Maga Circe and Le Cinque Grotte, (3) Grotta del Fossellone, (4) Grotta delle Capre, (5) Grotta Barbara and Grotta Blanc, (6) Grotta Guattari, (7) Riparo Salvini, (8) Grotta dei Moscerini, (9) Grotta di Sant'Agostino. Heavy stippling indicates uplifted limestone massif.

the caves are warm or cool by day, depending on where one sits, and the outer walls radiate captured heat into the night. The geographic positions of these caves may have coincided with winter pastures of wild ungulates. Plant growth continues considerably longer in the coastal lowlands than in the mountainous interior. Herders of the nineteenth and twentieth centuries routinely took advantage of the high productivity of the marshy plains each winter, moving their stock into the area for the cold season (A. G. Segre, p.c.). Marine life abounds along the

littoral margin (despite recent pollution), exploited along with terrestrial resources from the Paleolithic through modern times.

While Mousterian records constitute the bulk of the deposits in the subject caves, early Upper Paleolithic through Mesolithic shelter occupations are also preserved in the coastal area (Figure 3.2B). Aurignacian components have been identified in Grotta Barbara (Mussi and Zampetti 1990–91; see also Caloi and Palombo 1990–91) and Grotta di Fossellone (Blanc and Segre 1953; Vitagliano and

Piperno 1990–91), and Mesolithic components in Riparo Blanc (Taschini 1964, 1968). A later Upper Paleolithic site is documented in Riparo Salvini, above the town of Terracina (Avellino et al. 1989; Bietti 1984; Bietti and Stiner 1992). Two other, more inland Upper Paleolithic shelters (see Figure 3.1) are of interest for this study: Grotta Palidoro northwest of Rome (e.g., Bietti 1976–77a, 1976–77b; Cassoli 1976–77) and Grotta Polesini at Ponte Lucano on the Aniene River (Radmilli 1974).

Long before the Romans: Regional History and Geology

Monte Circeo is the fabled home of La Maga Circe, the witch from the tales of Odysseus. This isolated mountain looks like an island from afar, but in reality forms the southern edge of the Pontine Plain. The plain, formerly called the Pontine Marshes, was a malarial zone, infamous in Roman times and impenetrable to permanent settlement until the twentieth century. As noted above, people used the area seasonally, moving their stock into the marshlands in autumn and exiting by spring to avoid "pestilence." It is not known just when these marches formed in prehistory, nor are the details of their expansion and contraction wholly understood relative to the glacial sequence (but see Sevink et al. 1984). Numerous programs were undertaken in historic times to drain these vast wetlands, beginning with the Romans. All attempts met with failure, however, until the *Bonificazione* campaign undertaken by Mussolini in 1930, after which the area was permanently settled for the first time in re-

corded history. The offshore islands of Ponza, Zannone, and Palmarola are visible on clear days 35 km west of Circeo (Figure 3.2A). Palmarola was an important source of obsidian to Neolithic and later seafarers of this region. At Terracina, where the limestone massif also touches the sea, is a famous gate along the Roman Via Appia. Above it lies the late Upper Paleolithic rockshelter called Riparo Salvini, and above that, the Roman Temple of Jupiter.

The land rises and flattens abruptly along the length of the Tyrrhenian coast, quick alternations of steep limestone and flat plains and basins. The low-lying areas are fed by inland rivers and mountain runoff. Water flow stopped short of the sea throughout most of the area, gathering in basins and creating extensive wetlands not only in the Pontine area, but also in lowlands between Circeo and Terracina and between Terracina and Sperlonga. Lines of Pleistocene dunes parallel the coast between Circeo and Terracina, forming natural barrier lagoons of

TABLE 3.1
Estimated distances (km) of Latium Mousterian caves from the shoreline, based on sea level regressions by 10-m increments

Site	Present	−10 m	−20 m	−30 m	−50 m	−100 m[a]
Breuil (Monte Circeo)	0.0	0.5	0.9	1.2	1.5	7.0
Guattari (Monte Circeo)	0.3	1.3	3.5	5.3	7.0	> 10.0
Moscerini (Gaeta)	0.0	0.5	0.8	1.3	1.7	8.5
Sant'Agostino (Gaeta)	1.0	1.5	1.8	2.3	2.7	8.0

Sources: Carta Geologica D'Italia, Foglio 170 (Terracina 1961), and Foglio 171 (Gaeta 1968).

[a]Sea regression at the last glacial maximum (ca. 18,000 years ago).

brackish water. The coastal plains are bounded on the east (inland) by the Volsci and Lepini Mountains.

Generally speaking, the coastal shelters were always situated fairly close to the shore when occupied by hominids (e.g., Segre 1976–77, 1982, 1984). However, even moderate changes in sea level would have had significant implications for accessibility of the caves (Blanc 1937c; Segre 1953), as well as their general appeal as shelters and foraging localities. Gradual regression of the sea over the course of the Upper Pleistocene would have resulted in considerable expansion of the coastal plain separating each cave from the shore, and most of the lagoon formations were eventually replaced by terrestrial habitats. Thus, any change in

global climate had a direct impact on the local shelter settings and the sequences of use by hominids and other large predators.

Table 3.1 estimates the breadth of coastal plain exposed in front of each of the four Mousterian caves at various hypothetical sea stages in the past (see also Blanc 1937c; Blanc 1957; Segre 1953). Some of the limestone beds of this area have undergone localized tectonic uplift, particularly at Monte Circeo (A. G. Segre, p.c.), so the reconstructions provide only a general idea of the settings for each cave during the period in question. Figure 3.2a shows the contours of the modern sea floor. The continental shelf drops away only 50 km west of Monte Circeo, forming a subaqueous basin more than 3000 m deep just west of the islands of Pal-

Figure 3.3 Scenes from the Sperlonga coast survey in 1947; (top) surveyors' craft at the entrance of Grotta della Scala, (bottom) rock samples being taken from inside Grotta dei Pipistrelli. (Courtesy of IIPU archives)

marola and Ponza. The contours of the shelf decline gradually to about 200 m from shore, however, permitting appreciable land expansion with any lowering of sea level. None of the four Mousterian caves was more than 7 km from the sea when occupied, probably much closer.

PALEOLITHIC RESEARCH IN LATIUM

Latium has been the subject of several ambitious research programs, beginning between the World Wars and continuing to this day. The Paleolithic of Latium gained international attention with the discovery of the Circeo I fossil, a nearly complete Neandertal cranium, in Grotta Guattari in 1939. The discovery spurred an intensive program of survey and excavation of Quaternary deposits in the 1940s, conducted mostly along the coast and producing many of the collections used for this study.

The regional programs directed by Alberto Carlo Blanc (see also Howell 1962) integrated work by archaeologists and paleontologists, including Luigi Cardini, Eugenia Segre-Naldini, Antonio Radmilli, and (later) Piero Cassoli, and geologist Aldo G. Segre. Deliberate combination of such expertise was inspired, at least in part, by Blanc's father, Gian Alberto Blanc, whose collaborations with Portis, Regalia, Forsyt-Mayor, Boule, Obermaier, and the Abbé Breuil on paleontological and paleoethnological research are well known (A. G. Segre 1967; E. Segre 1972). The projects directed by the Blancs (father and son) were organized through the Istituto Italiano di Paleontologia Umana (IIPU), founded in Florence and later transferred to Rome in 1954. Activities of this research group were published primarily in the journal *Quaternaria*, edited consecutively by A. C. and Elena Blanc, L. Cardini, Mariela Taschini, and finally A. G. Segre and E. Segre-Naldini.

Many projects were undertaken by the IIPU in Latium, including the 1936–38 surveys of the Latium coast between Rome and Terracina, and the 1947–49 survey between Sperlonga and Gaeta (Blanc 1935b, 1936, 1937b, 1938, 1939b, 1955a, 1955b; Blanc and Segre 1947, 1953). Both projects, conducted by (A. C.) Blanc and Segre, are of special importance for this study. The surveys were conducted by walking all accessible parts of the coast, and by using a small fishing craft to survey Quaternary deposits in sea caves (Figures 3.3 and 3.4). In addition to the concentration of sites on Monte Circeo, the section of coastline between Sperlonga and Gaeta is particularly rich in caves: 102 were recorded at elevations between 0 and 20 m above modern sea level, and 11 more (including Grotta di Sant'Agostino) between 30 and 100 m above sea level. Pontinian Mousterian chipped stone industries were found with fossil faunas in 6 of the caves. Faunas without industries were found in 4 other caves; many other caves contained resid-

Figure 3.4 Residual Upper Pleistocene sediments cemented to limestone bedrock at the entrance to Grotta Breuil (Monte Circeo), visible from the sea.

TABLE 3.2

Background information for Paleolithic sites in Latium and Tuscany

Cave or rockshelter	Cultural association	Excavator/ research group	Additional references
Polesini (L)	late UP (ca. 10,000 B.P.)	Radmilli	Radmilli 1974
Salvini (L)	late UP (ca. 12,500 B.P.)	Bietti	Bietti 1984 Avellino et al. 1989 Bietti and Stiner 1992
Palidoro (L)	late UP (ca. 15,000 B.P.)	IIPU	Bietti 1976–77a,b Cassoli 1976–77 Segre 1976–77
Buca della Iena (T)	late MP and spotted hyaena den (ca. 35,000–42, 000 B.P.)	Viareggio Group	Pitti and Tozzi (1971 Fornaca Rinaldi and Radmilli 1968
Sant'Agostino (L)	late MP (ca. 40,000–55,000 B.P.)	Tongiorgi	Laj Pannocchia 1950 Tozzi 1970
Breuil (L)	late MP (ca. 35,000–45,000+ B.P.)	Bietti	Bietti et al. 1988 Taschini 1970
Guattari (L)	earlier MP (ca. 51,000–78,000 B.P.)	IIPU	Blanc and Segre 1953 Piperno 1976–77 Taschini 1979
Moscerini (L)	earlier MP (ca. 60,000–120,000 B.P.)	IIPU	Vitagliano 1984

Note: (L) Province of Latium, (T) Province of Tuscany, (UP) Upper Paleolithic, (MP) Middle Paleolithic or Mousterian, (IIPU) Istituto Italiano di Paleontologia Umana research group.

ual Quaternary sediments only (Blanc and Segre 1947).

Excavations were conducted in several of the caves after the surveys were completed (Table 3.2), including a major campaign at Grotta dei Moscerini in 1949–50. Other excavation projects undertaken in the 1950s included the Upper Paleolithic site of Palidoro (Bietti 1976–77b; Cassoli 1976–77), along with additional testing at Grotta Guattari by Segre, Cardini, and finally Radmilli. Surface surveys of the Agro Pontino (Pontine Plain), the Fondi Basin to the south, and elsewhere in Latium were undertaken in the late 1960s (Bietti 1969; Mussi 1977–82; Tozzi 1970; Zei 1970; see also Cardini and Biddittu 1967). A large-scale survey was begun in 1979 by the Institut voor Prae- en Protostorie (IPP) of the University of Amsterdam, under the direction of A. Voorrips, S. Loving, and H. Kammermans (Loving et al. 1990–91; Voorrips et al. 1983), following completion of soil surveys of the same area (Sevink et al. 1984). The IPP archaeological survey employed a "nonsite" recording strategy, focusing on long-term changes in landscape use by humans. The project addresses a variety of archaeological issues having to do with regional sedimentation patterns, including deforestation in Neolithic times, and the distributions of exposed fossil beach deposits containing flint pebble sources so important in Paleolithic times. Many of the archaeological localities on this coastal plain would not be considered sites by conventional criteria, yet together constitute a vast, if spatially diffuse, record of prehistoric and historic human occupations.

PONTINIAN MOUSTERIAN INDUSTRIES: THE LOCAL SOLUTION TO RAW MATERIAL SCARCITY

The Mousterian stone tools of Latium, collectively termed the *Pontinian,* are best known for their small dimensions. Mousterian industries were first classified in the Dordogne region of France, where tools are often quite large. Pontinian tools are Lilliputian by comparison, yet display most of the classic Mousterian tool forms defined by Francois Bordes (e.g., 1961a, 1961b) for French industries of similar age. Pontinian industries were first described by Blanc (1937b; see also Blanc 1935c; Taschini 1972)

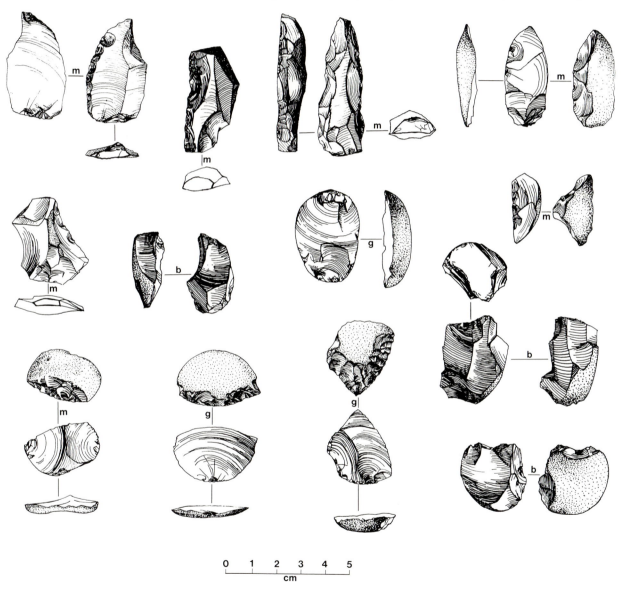

Figure 3.5 Examples of Pontinian Mousterian artifacts manufactured from local flint pebbles; specimens from Grotta dei Moscerini (m), Grotta Guattari (g), and Grotta Breuil (b).

at Canale Mussolini (renamed Canale delle Aque Alte). The tools were made almost exclusively on tiny flint pebbles obtained from Pleistocene beach deposits in the area (Figure 3.5). Similar industries were reported soon afterward in Grotta Guattari, Grotta del Fossellone, and other caves lining the coastal plains of Latium (e.g., Blanc and Segre 1953).

Most lithic analysts agree that the small sizes of Pontinian Mousterian tools, which average around 3 cm in maximum dimension (Kuhn 1990a:130), relate directly to the local scarcity of suitable larger raw materials (Bordes 1968:119; Piperno 1984:48; Taschini 1972:70–74; Tozzi 1970). There is somewhat less agreement about how this might affect the outcomes of tool manufacture itself.

Pandemic scarcity of raw material in coastal Italy also is evident from other aspects of the Mousterian record, including the occasional use of marine clam shells as simple scraping tools (e.g., Vitagliano

1984; Palma di Cesnola 1965; Kuhn 1989b). The economic problem of widely scattered, uniformly small raw materials was expressed in other ways during the Lower Paleolithic of this area: elephant bone was fashioned into handaxes at Castel di Guido (Mallegni et al. 1983; Radmilli et al. 1979) and Fontana Ranuccio (see Biddittu et al. 1979; Segre et al. 1987; also Segre and Ascenzi 1984 on associated remains of archaic *Homo*). The constraints imposed by the paucity of stone suitable for manufacturing tools creates an interesting situation for research on raw material economy in Paleolithic Latium. Kuhn (1990a, 1990–91a, 1991, n.d.) has completed a large-scale comparative study of this phenomenon for the Pontinian Mousterian, based on patterns of core reduction, tool reuse, and transport (summarized in Chapter 14). The study includes all assemblages from the subject caves, as well as material from the IPP Agro Pontino survey.

HUMAN FOSSILS FROM THE LATIUM CAVES

Latium is a rich source of Neandertal fossils (see review by Manzi and Passarello 1989). Two Neandertal crania were recovered from river gravels at Saccopastore (e.g., Blanc 1935a), and a parietal fragment, possibly Neandertal, at Casal de'Pazzi (Anzidei et al. 1984; see also 1989). Other Neandertal fossils, from the caves of Monte Circeo, occur in general association with Pontinian Mousterian artifacts. Three Classic Neandertal specimens were found in Grotta Guattari. A nearly complete cranium (Circeo I) and mandible (Circeo II) were discovered in 1939, lying among a scatter of ungulate and carnivore bones on the surface of the cave interior (Blanc 1939a, 1939b, 1939c; Sergi and Ascenzi 1974; Taschini 1979). The mandible may articulate with the cranium, based on assessments of individual age and some osteometric measurements (A. Ascenzi, p.c.), but the association cannot be confirmed because the ascending rami of the mandible are missing. A second mandible (Circeo III) was recovered from the breccia at the entrance of Guattari in 1951 (Sergi 1954, 1955).

A mandible fragment and three teeth of a Neandertal child were found in Grotta del Fossellone, a neighboring cave on Monte Circeo, between 1953

and 1954 (Blanc 1954). Probable Neandertal remains, consisting of a parietal fragment and two teeth representing two individuals, were recovered during new excavations at Grotta Breuil between 1986 and 1989. While efforts are being made to classify these specimens, their taxonomic identity presently is ambiguous (Manzi and Passarello 1990–91; and in Bietti et al. 1988).

Skeletal remains of anatomically modern humans are known from the late Upper Paleolithic sites of Riparo Salvini (Avellino et al. 1989) and Grotta Polesini (Radmilli 1974). Only a few teeth, probably from a young male, were found in Riparo Salvini. Human bone is more plentiful in Grotta Polesini, as is true for mammalian remains in general. Radmilli reports seventy-nine fragmentary specimens representing three adults (two males, one female?) and one juvenile individual, based on determinations by De Vecchis and Favati (Radmilli 1974:31–34).

Culturally derived faunas in the study sample are classified as Mousterian if associated with these kinds of industries. The makers of Mousterian tools were probably Neandertals, but not all assemblages contain the hominid fossil material needed to secure the cultural association. New radiometric dates indicate that the Guattari I cranium was deposited no later than 51,000 ± three thousand years ago (Schwarcz et al. 1991), suggesting that Mousterian stone tools deposited before this time are attributable to Neandertals; anatomically modern human remains known for the region as yet present no surprises with regard to the standard Paleolithic chronology. Human fossil associations for later Mous-terian assemblages are unclear, however. Ongoing excavations at Grotta Breuil, for example, yield human remains likely to date after 50,000, but, as noted above, none clearly diagnose subspecies. For this reason, I prefer the terms *Mousterian hominids* or *Middle Paleolithic hominids* as opposed to *Neandertals* when discussing the evidence from west-central Italy.

DATING IN ITALY

Prior to the radiometric work begun in coastal Latium in the late 1980s, all of the Middle Paleolithic sites were dated by geochronological associations, along with cultural and human *fossiles directeurs.* Virtually all credit for establishing geochronological sequences can be attributed to three individuals: G. A. Blanc, who worked primarily in Tuscany, and A. C. Blanc and A. G. Segre, who worked in Latium. Segre is perhaps best known for his geomorphic classifications and mapping of the coastal area for the Servizio Geologica d'Italia. Segre's geochronological studies of the Middle Paleolithic caves sites are based in large part on the relationships of sedimentary deposits to high sea stands and phases of volcanic activity in Latium (e.g., Blanc and Segre 1953; Segre 1953, 1982, 1984; Segre and Ascenzi 1984; Segre et al. 1987; see also Blanc 1937c). Fossil beaches containing shells of *Strombus bubonius* (Durante and Settepassi 1976–77) from the Last Interglacial (Hearty 1986), and the vertical extent of scars left by ancient colonies of lithodome mollusks (*Lithodomus* [= *Petricola*] *lithophaga*) marking past high sea lines, help define the earliest chronological limits of the cave sequences on the Tyrrhenian coast.

Lithodomes are rock-dwelling mollusks that bore symmetrical holes roughly 1 cm in diameter and up to 3 cm deep in sea-side limestones during life. The animals aggregate in colonies around the high tide line, forming honey-comb patterns in the rocks along the coast. The species has been common in the Mediterranean for a very long time, and scars from ancient colonies mark the vertical extent of various Middle and Upper Pleistocene sea stages. Lithodome scars on cave walls indicate that sea level rose approximately 12 m above the modern line during the Last Interglacial (120,000–125,000 B.P.). This means that the sedimentary sequences in caves near the modern shoreline had to have formed *after* the Last Interglacial (beginning with isotope stage 5e), the caves having been scoured clean by waves before that time. The earliest preserved deposition sequences commenced with sandy beaches, some containing reworked volcanic material (e.g., Blanc and Segre 1953). The limestone cliffs along the coast are products of uplift, however, and features within the rock were not always as high in altitude as they are today.

West-central Italy is the locus of considerable tectonic activity, particularly at Monte Circeo. Tectonic activity is manifest by the massive uplift of Cretaceous and older limestone beds throughout the area and by a line of volcanoes running northwest-southeast about 25 to 40 km inland of the coast. Eruptions of the Sabatino volcanic group north of Rome produced distinctive tuffs rich in black pumices; these tuffs are important geochronological markers for the Middle Pleistocene sequence of Latium. The Latiale eruptions (e.g., Blanc 1936b), along with smaller volcanoes in the Sacco-Liri River valleys, present a second set of well-dated markers for the Middle Pleistocene through Interglacial geological sequence in southern Latium, particularly in the large inland basins (e.g., Segre and Ascenzi 1984). Ashy sediments, apparently originating from portions of the Latiale volcanic group known as the Alban Hills (Colle Albani), were reworked by shore waves into Interglacial beaches at the base of the stratigraphic sequences in Grotta Guattari and Grotta dei Moscerini (Blanc and Segre 1953).

Pollen studies conducted in central Italy reveal a significant cold period after 55,000 years ago in the study area (discussed by Kuhn n.d., see especially Table 4.2 therein). This change in climate on the Italian peninsula is especially clear from the 250,000-year pollen record from the bed of the crater lake known as Valle di Castiglione, 20 km east of the city of Rome (Follieri et al. 1988). The later portion of the sequence is corroborated by the 60,000-year pollen record from Lake Vico, another crater lake in west-central Italy (Frank 1969). While

not the only cold phase that occurred in the Upper Pleistocene sequence of Italy, the shift toward colder temperatures around 55,000 years ago is very important to this research, because it is linked to changes in hominid land use, foraging, and technological practices in the study area.

The geochronological and pollen work in Latium provides the background needed for placing the Paleolithic cultural records in a general temporal and sedimentary framework. The data are not sufficiently fine-grained for linking the relative chrono-

TABLE 3.3
Radiometric dates for the Mousterian cave deposits

Site and vertical provenience	Dating technique	Material	Date and error range
Moscerini:[a]			
stratum 25 (M3)	ESR	red deer tooth	79,000 + —
26 (M3)	ESR	red deer tooth	67,000 + —
26 (M3)	ESR	red deer tooth	81,000 + —
33 (M3)	ESR	red deer tooth	89,000 + —
33 (M3)	ESR	red deer tooth	123,000 + —
35 (M3)	ESR	red deer tooth	66,000 + —
38 (M4)	ESR	red deer tooth	96,000 + —
38 (M4)	ESR	red deer tooth	106,000 + —
39 (M4)	ESR	red deer tooth	96,000 + —
39 (M4)	ESR	hippopotamus tooth	97,000 + —
Guattari:			
surface GO[b]	U/Th	stalagmite	51,000 + 3000
stratum G4	ESR	aurochs tooth	71,100 + 2760 (avr)
G5	ESR	aurochs tooth	77,500 + 9500 (avr)
Sant'Agostino:			
layer S1	ESR	aurochs tooth	43,000 + 9000 (avr)
S2	ESR	aurochs tooth	53,000 + 7000 (avr)
S3	ESR	aurochs tooth	55,000 + 11,000 (avr)
upper flowstone[b]	U/Th	stalagmite	112,000 + 14,000
lower flowstone[b]	U/Th	stalagmite	120,000 + 15,000
Breuil:			
capping flowstone[b]	U/Th	stalagmite	26,000 + 12,000
stratum 3/4	ESR	aurochs and horse teeth	36,600 + 2700 (avr)

Sources: Schwarcz et al. (1990–91), (1991).

[a]Strata are those identified by Segre in 1949 for the exterior sequence of Moscerini; designations in parentheses refer to level groups. Due to complete obstruction of the cave entrance in the 1970s, background dose rates for the ESR analyses were estimated using soil cemented to the tooth specimens and, hence, no error ranges are listed.
[b]Noncultural stratum.

Note: (ESR) electron spin resonance technique, with errors calculated on the basis of multiple slices of each sample using a linear uptake model, (U/Th) uranium series technique, (avr) averaged value based on more than one sample.

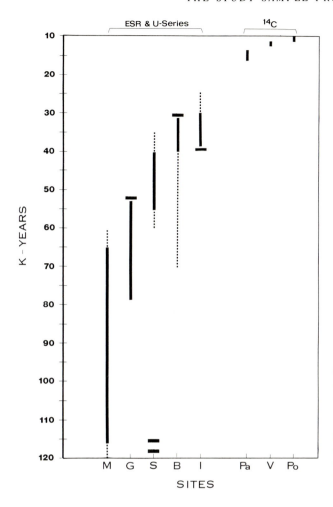

Figure 3.6 Chronologies of the Italian cave and rockshelter deposits. Solid vertical lines indicate ranges dated by ESR or ^{14}C technique; short horizontal bars represent uranium series dates on calcite flowstone layers; dashed lines indicate estimated but undated extent of range. (M) Moscerini, (G) Guattari, (S) Sant'Agostino, (B) Breuil, (I) Buca della Iena, (Pa) Palidoro, (V) Riparo Salvini, (Po) Polesini.

logies of the cave sequences together, however. With this problem in mind, radiometric analyses by uranium series (U/Th) and electron spin resonance (ESR) methods were begun in 1987 at Grotta Guattari, Grotta dei Moscerini, Grotta di Sant'Agostino, and Grotta Breuil (Table 3.3 and Figure 3.6). The analyses were performed by Henry P. Schwarcz, Rainer Grün, and co-workers then at McMaster University in Canada (Schwarcz et al. 1990–91). The samples for dating were collected by the author, Kuhn, and Schwarcz, with the logistical assistance of A. Bietti (U. Roma). The U/Th analyses were performed on calcite crusts (also known as horizontal stalagmites or flowstones) that cap or are intercalated with friable strata. The ESR analyses were performed on ungulate tooth enamel/dentin, pri-

marily from aurochs and horse. Red deer teeth were used only if samples from larger species were not available.

We originally hoped to obtain pairs of ESR and U/Th dates for targeted strata, or adjoining strata, to cross-check results obtained from the two methods. U/Th is considered a generally reliable source of chronological information elsewhere in the world and has the advantage of being fairly well-calibrated at some localities (e.g., Bischoff et al. 1988). U/Th analyses proved less useful than expected for dating the Latium cave deposits, because the parent limestone of this region is poor in uranium and the stalagmites, though common in coastal caves, often do not contain sufficient amounts of thorium for precise dating. Some notable exceptions are the calcite concretions covering bones on the surface of Grotta Guattari (G0) and the capping flowstone in Grotta Breuil (Schwarcz et al. 1990–91). Likewise, Fornaca Rinaldi and Radmilli (1968) obtained a U/Th date on a horizontal stalagmite in Buca della Iena, another coastal cave just north of Pisa (Figure 3.1). Tentative U/Th dates, centering around 115,000–120,000 B.P. were obtained for the flowstones underlying cultural deposits in Grotta di Sant'Agostino (Schwarcz et al. 1990–91).

Like uranium series methods, the ESR dating method uses carbonate-rich material. The ESR technique is based on one or more models of uranium uptake by an object following its burial in the soil. The technique at this stage shows considerable promise, especially with refinements in the last few years (e.g., Grün and Stringer 1991). It is theoretically sound, but some aspects of the uranium uptake models are still being tested and calibrated, as discussed by Grün (1988), Grün, Schwarcz, and Zymella (1987), Schwarcz and Grün (1993), and others. It is also clear that the means for controlling for sources of background radiation, particularly that introduced by percolating groundwater, and the rates of isotope uptake by various classes of material (e.g., tooth, bone, mollusk shell) require continued research. Tooth enamel/dentin was used for ESR dating of the Italian Mousterian assemblages. Tooth material is preferable to mammal bone or mollusk shell on grounds that teeth absorb uranium at a more predictable rate. Moreover, because ungulate molars typically contain multiple interior and exterior layers of enamel, interior and exterior doses may be compared; this procedure aids in checking the patterns of uranium absorption and transfer throughout the tooth specimen.

The ESR model of uranium uptake is based on the general observation that free uranium present in the surrounding soil replaces calcium in (for example) tooth enamel and dentin. As the specimen absorbs uranium, the level of radiation emitted from the specimen increases. Because the intrinsic radiation dose rate changes over time, one also needs to know the rates of change in order to adjust the accumulated dose for dating purposes. Two models of uranium uptake are currently under consideration in ESR research. The Early Uptake model assumes that the rate at which a specimen traps uranium is very high soon after burial, and decreases rapidly thereafter. The alternative Linear Uptake model instead assumes that a specimen will soak up uranium at a relatively continuous rate following burial, provided that it is not re-exposed by erosion (Grün 1988:39–40; Ikeya 1978). Results based on the Linear Uptake model so far prove more consistent with data obtained from alternative techniques, and these results therefore are used to construct the general ESR chronology for the Mousterian sample (Table 3.3 and Figure 3.6). The Early Uptake model, on the other hand, yields what may be considered minimum ages.

ESR analyses require background readings of ambient radiation, the same parameters required for thermoluminescence dating. Background doses were measured in various locations in each of the Italian sites, except Grotta dei Moscerini, by burying the dosimeter in sediment for predetermined lengths of time. We could not take readings in Moscerini because the site is completely buried by rocky fill. The background dose readings for the neighboring Grotta di Sant'Agostino (see Figures 3.1 and 3.2), complemented by soil samples adhering to clusters of bones and shell collected from Moscerini in 1949, were used to estimate the background dose for the Moscerini samples.

Table 3.3 shows that it is not possible to arrange the assemblages into precise chronological series due to considerable error ranges and the fact that a few samples are clearly out of order. However, the ESR results are quite useful for creating a relative, or floating, chronology for the sites. Two major chronostratigraphic sets can be discerned. The earlier series begins soon after the Last Interglacial and ends around approximately 55,000 B.P.; it includes the deposits of Grotta dei Moscerini and Grotta Guattari. The second series begins around 50,000–55,000 B.P. and ends at roughly 35,000, coinciding with the transition period between the Middle and Upper Paleolithic as defined elsewhere in Europe; this chronostratigraphic series includes the deposits of Grotta di Sant'Agostino and Grotta Breuil. Note that the capping stalagmites in Guattari (51,000 B.P.) and Breuil (30,000 B.P.), dated by the U/Th method, do not contain lithic industries.

Figure 3.6 summarizes the relative chronologies

of the Middle and Upper Paleolithic cave and shelter deposits in the study sample, including the U/Th-dated spotted hyaena den complex of Buca della Iena (Tuscany) and the radiocarbon-dated Upper Paleolithic rockshelters of Grotta Palidoro, Riparo Salvini, and (by association) Grotta Polesini. The total sample spans a time range beginning around 115,000 years ago and ending at about 10,000. All of the Mousterian sequences span substantial periods of time, Grotta dei Moscerini being the longest. The upper terminations of the Mousterian sequences are due primarily to filling of the shelters with sediment (Grotta Guattari, Grotta Breuil, and probably Grotta dei Moscerini), not necessarily because the geographic locations of the shelters were no longer useful to hominids.

The dates for Grotta dei Moscerini are for exterior level groups M3 and M4 exclusively and range between roughly 66,000 and 110,000 B.P. Geological and faunal associations suggest that the youngest strata in the exterior series are older than 55,000 B.P. ESR and U/Th results are available for Grotta Guattari and suggest that strata G0 through G5 formed quickly, consistent with Segre's earlier geochronological assessments (Blanc and Segre 1953, and p.c.). The temporal span of bone-bearing

layers in Guattari is approximately 78,000 to 51,000 B.P. (Schwarcz et al. 1990–91). The underlying beach deposit is not dated. The ESR dates for layers S0 through S3 of Grotta di Sant'Agostino indicate that the deposits formed fairly rapidly, and that the entire sequence (except S0) dates to the late Mousterian. The age of the oldest cultural layer in the series (S4) is not known, although the contents and condition of the S4 fauna are much like the overlying material and may postdate the 55,000 B.P. boundary as well.

Only the capping flowstone layer (U/Th) and in situ tooth material from provisional Stratum 3/4 of Grotta Breuil have been subjected to radiometric analyses. The flowstone cap dates to roughly 30,000 B.P., while the youngest set of Mousterian layers in Stratum 3/4 yields an averaged ESR date of 36,600 ± 2700 B.P. Together, these deposits form only the top of a thick cultural/stratigraphic sequence. The Breuil series is almost exclusively Middle Paleolithic, although there is limited evidence of use during the late Neolithic and possibly Upper Paleolithic periods. The age of the oldest cultural strata in the series is not known, but probably is not older than 70,000 B.P.

THE MOUSTERIAN SAMPLE: FAUNAS, SITES, AND STRATIGRAPHIES

Four stratified cave sites are central to this study of Mousterian foraging and shelter use in west-central Italy: Grotta Guattari and Grotta Breuil on Monte Circeo, and Grotta di Sant'Agostino and Grotta dei Moscerini near Gaeta. In addition to these deeply stratified human sites, the sample includes the spotted hyaena den complex of comparable age from Buca della Iena. Some ephemeral Mousterian occupations are evident in the upper levels of Buca della Iena, but virtually all bone collecting is attributable to spotted hyaenas (see Chapter 5). Table 3.2 summarizes background information on chronological and cultural associations of the sites and their respective histories of publication.

Late Upper Paleolithic rockshelter faunas from Grotta Palidoro, Riparo Salvini, and Grotta Polesini serve as points of comparison for evaluating variation in the Mousterian faunas. Ideally, such a comparative sample would also include early Upper Paleolithic material, but appropriate material is not available. Comparisons to the late Upper Paleolithic collections proved extremely productive despite the chronological gap that separates them from the Middle Paleolithic period (see Figure 3.6). Some modern carnivore control cases from North America, Asia, and Africa—usually den faunas—are brought to the analyses in later chapters. For the sake of clarity, these control cases are described in the chapters in which they first appear in an analytical context.

The faunal assemblages vary in size, usually between five hundred and four thousand identifiable bone specimens, and between three hundred and one thousand teeth. Table 3.4 presents a general inventory of *identifiable specimen* counts (NISP) for teeth and bones. Table 3.5 presents counts for

TABLE 3.4
Numbers of bone and tooth fragments (NISP) from the Upper Pleistocene caves

Site and taxonomic category	Bone NISP[a]	Isolated tooth NISP[b]	Isolated tooth and bone NISP[c]	Composite tooth count[d]
Moscerini (eMP):				
carnivores	134	33	—	62
ungulates	501	262	—	681
small mammals	359	—	—	—
reptiles/amphibians	108	—	—	—
marine bivalves	3100[e]	—	—	—
all taxa	4202	—	—	743
Guattari (eMP):				
carnivores	70	84	—	135
ungulates	660	665	—	1017
small mammals	19	—	—	—
all taxa (and *Homo*)	752	—	—	1152
Sant'Agostino (lMP):				
carnivores	409	64	—	120
ungulates	1222	1168	—	1390
small mammals	631	—	—	—
all taxa	2262	—	—	1510
Breuil (lMP):				
carnivores	18	40	—	48
ungulates	1111	332	—	390
small mammals	1	—	—	—
all taxa	1131	—	—	440
Buca della Iena (sh):				
carnivores	326	259	—	313
ungulates	390	194	—	229
small mammals	20	—	—	—
all taxa	736	—	—	542
Salvini (lUP):				
carnivores	—	—	6	—
ungulates	—	—	652	—
small mammals	—	—	2	—
all taxa	—	—	660	—
Polesini (lUP):				
carnivores				
ungulates	—	—	1561	—
small mammals	—	—	41,953	—
reptiles/amphibians	—	—	1511	—
all taxa (and 79	—	—	21	—
Homo)	—	—	45,125	—
Palidoro 1–8 (lUP):				
carnivores	—	—	28	—
ungulates	—	—	1270	—
small mammals	—	—	13	—
all taxa	—	—	1311	—

TABLE 3.4 (*Continued*)

Site and taxonomic category	Bone NISP[a]	Isolated tooth NISP[b]	Isolated tooth and bone NISP[c]	Composite tooth count[d]
Palidoro 33–34 (lUP):				
carnivores	7	1	—	1
ungulates	558	139	—	235
small mammals	—	—	—	—
all taxa	565	—	—	236

[a]Based exclusively on bone specimens.
[b]Based exclusively on isolated tooth specimens.
[c]Combined counts for isolated teeth and bone, as published in original source.
[d]Based on all teeth (isolated and articulated in whole or partial tooth rows).
[e]Marine shell fragments.

Note: (—) not applicable, (eMP) early Middle Paleolithic, (lMP) late Middle Paleolithic, (lUP) late Upper Paleolithic, (sh) spotted hyaena den complex.

TABLE 3.5
Mousterian lithic counts for the cave sites and the Agro Pontio survey collection

Site and provenience	Tools	Flakes	Cores	Debris	Total
Agro Pontino	151	43[d]	192	—	386
Moscerini M1[a]	11	9	3	22	45
M2	123	64	29	166	382
M3	131	46	24	123	324
M4	93	45	5	39	187
M5	39	19	11	58	127
M6	76	30	22	68	196
Guattari G0	0	2	0	0	2
G1	57	39	29	115	240
G2	98	66	86	202	452
G4	181	87	104	504	876
G5	92	47	98	245	482
S. Agostino S0	184[d]	10[d]	—	1[d]	2863
S1	475[d]	170[d]	126	24[d]	3138
S2	130	309	83	453	975
S3	73	110	25	243	451
S4	39	70	12	91	212
SX	0	0	0	0	0
Breuil Br[b]	329	428	159	2333	3249
Buca della I1–2[c]	14	20	1	0	35
Iena I3	17	16	0	0	33
I4	28	15	3	0	46

Sources: Kuhn (1990a), Pitti and Tozzi (1971), Taschini (1979), Tozzi (1970).

[a]Counts are for level groups of Grotta dei Moscerini. See text for explanation.
[b]The lithic sample is from the redeposited zone of Grotta Breuil.
[c]Flake counts include lithic debris (Pitti and Tozzi 1971).
[d]All values for Grotta Guattari, and possibly for Grotta di Sant'Agostino, are slightly underestimated relative to previous studies (see, for example, Taschini 1979).

Note: (—) Incomplete samples (see total); category is represented in the collection but was not sampled.

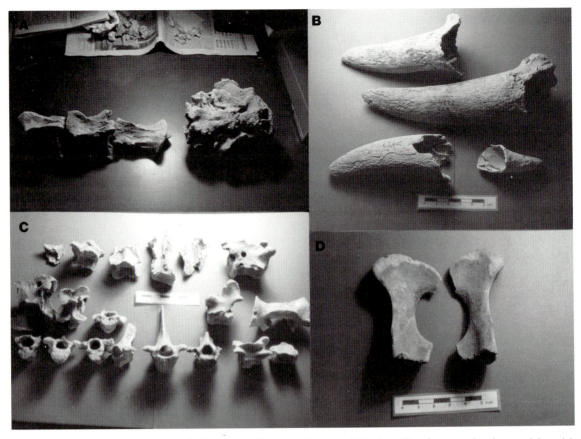

Figure 3.7 Delicate bone items from the Latium caves, illustrating the generally high quality of preservation due to calcium-rich sediment chemistries: (A) posterior section of red deer cranium (anterior gnawed away by hyaenas) and first three cervical vertebrae found in articulation in Grotta Guattari G0–1; (B) ibex horn cores and (C) roe deer vertebral elements from various layers of Grotta di Sant'Agostino; (D) unfused ischial segments of a juvenile cervid pelvis from INT 1 (level group M5) of Grotta dei Moscerini.

broad categories of Mousterian artifacts (tools, flakes, cores, and debris) associated with the faunas, listed by stratigraphic units (Kuhn 1990a). The Paleolithic faunal collections permit some kinds of analyses, while posing partial or absolute impediments to others. I discuss these issues in detail in the analytical chapters, but a few comments on the quality of bone preservation provide a useful introduction here.

The Italian faunal collections usually lack provenience information other than stratigraphic-geologic associations. Horizontal coordinates are limited to trench locations. This is not an ideal situation in which to explore all dimensions of behavioral analyses currently favored in Paleolithic

studies. Yet the collections prove remarkably informative in other respects. The geological characteristics of the Italian peninsula are especially well suited to preserving Pleistocene faunas, particularly in caves. The quality of bone preservation generally is very good—sometimes extraordinary—in the caves, due to carbonate-rich depositional environments (Figure 3.7). Many bones are damaged, but most destruction is attributable to biological agencies rather than geological or chemical causes. The only significant exception is Riparo Salvini, where bone preservation is only fair due to locally acidic soils and disturbance by humans during historic occupations of the site. The sites are discussed individually in the sections that follow, beginning with the most famous and best-published of the Mousterian-aged caves, Grotta Guattari.

Grotta Guattari

Grotta Guattari is located on the southeastern flank of Monte Circeo, roughly 100 m inland and less than 10 m above modern sea level. The cave interior extends some 15 m front to back, and 12 m at its widest cross-section. The space is dark, fully enclosed, and broken into multiple small side chambers (Figures 3.8 and 3.9). The ceiling is approximately 1.5 m at its highest point, but is considerably lower throughout most of the interior.

The entrance of Grotta Guattari was discovered by local workmen in 1939 while preparing the hillside for a vineyard planting, a procedure that often requires substantial modification of slopes, as well as deep plowing (Figure 3.10). At least three narrow tunnels lead into the cave, one of which was later greatly enlarged to accommodate tourists. The tunnels open into the largest chamber which, in turn, fans out into multiple smaller lobes or niches.

Few Paleolithic sites have so colorful a history as Grotta Guattari. The cave was sealed from the outside world by colluvium roughly 50,000 years ago, and opened again only in this century. This small

cave became widely known for the Neandertal cranium found there (Blanc 1939c, 1939d), as well as an unusual surface littered with animal bones. The cranium apparently was isolated from the main bone scatter, lying in a small chamber amid, as the story goes (e.g., Blanc 1958), an arc or ring of stones (Figures 3.11 and 3.12). A Neandertal mandible (Circeo II) was found within the bone scatter the same year, and another Neandertal mandible (Circeo III) was removed in 1950 from the breccia lining one of the cave entrances. The bones on the cave floor (G0) lay undisturbed for millennia, their upward faces blanketed by cauliflower-form calcite concretions of cave coral (also on the stones in Figure 3.12). The many fine layers of calcite, formation of which began around 51,000 years ago and ended about 13,000 years ago, are the basis for uranium series dates of the Guattari surface and the bones lying on it (Schwarcz et al. 1991).

From famous beginnings, Grotta Guattari grew into a somewhat notorious case, owing to claims of evidence for Neandertal ritual burial and possibly cannibalistic activities (Blanc 1958, 1961; Piperno 1976–77). The foramen magnum of the Circeo I cranium had been enlarged, and a disproportionate quantity of deer antler was noted among the animal remains. More than any other Neandertal site, it

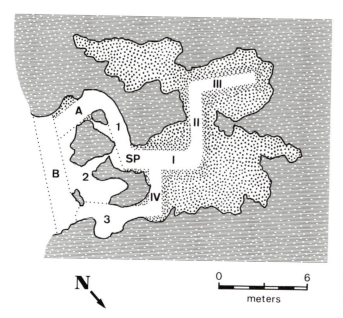

Figure 3.8 Plan view of the interior of Grotta Guattari, showing locations of trenches excavated by IIPU. (Stiner 1991a, adapted from Taschini 1979)

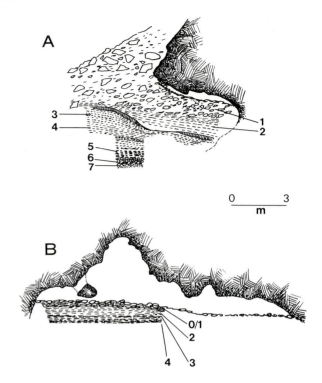

Figure 3.9 Longitudinal schematic views of the Guattari stratigraphy (A) at the cave mouth and (B) inside the central chamber. (Adapted from drawings by Segre, in Taschini 1979)

was Guattari that touched off a major and continuing debate about the humanness of Neandertals (see Blanc 1939d, 1940, 1961; and most recently, Marshack 1989): if truly attributable to Neandertals, the interment of the Circeo I cranium would represent some of the earliest evidence for ritual behavior in human prehistory.

The presence of hominid fossils and some spectacular claims about the cultural significance of the material riveted attention on the surface deposit, although four strata containing Mousterian industries and animal bones lie below it. With attention comes closer scrutiny, and there are, without a doubt, several shortcomings to the early interpretations of the Guattari case (Gamble 1986:176, 270; Chase and Dibble 1987:279–280). The surface

Figure 3.10 One of three original entrance tunnels leading into Grotta Guattari, approximately 0.6 m maximum diameter.

Figure 3.11 Luigi Cardini (left) and Alberto Carlo Blanc (right) posing before the arc of stones in the "Antro dell'Uomo" chamber of Grotta Guattari. Lighting is from artificial sources. (Courtesy of IIPU archives)

fauna includes many carnivore remains and hyaena coprolites (Blanc and Segre 1953; also listed in Cardini's inventory, published by Piperno 1976–77). And accounts of the exact position of the skull and the supposed arrangement of manuported stones around it are ambiguous at best, posing several contradictions to claims of ritual disposal of the hominid skull by fellow Neandertals. The ritualistic interpretation of the Guattari surface has since been falsified by Stiner (1991a) and White and Toth (1991). Taphonomic analyses of the faunal remains and hominid fossils, respectively, point to spotted hyaenas as the collectors of the bones on the Guattari surface, not hominids; the bases for these conclusions are described in Chapter 5.

The circumstances of the cave's discovery are worth reviewing, not so much from the published accounts, but from my interviews with Segre (IIPU). Much of the story he relates about the discovery and ensuing work at Guattari can also be found in published accounts by Blanc (e.g., 1939a, 1939b, 1940), but some details of Segre's personal account are relevant to reassessments of the surface fauna. The Circeo I Neandertal cranium was found by workmen, who removed it from the cave the same day. A. C. Blanc was notified soon thereafter and managed to visit the site within a few days. He questioned the workmen at the cave regarding the original position of the skull, hoping to recapture as much information as possible. In retrospect, Segre suggests that the excitement created an atmosphere unwittingly ripe for fiction and, though customary, it is probably significant that the interviewees were paid a gratuity for their trouble and cooperation. Segre believes that the general location of the skull on the surface within the *Antro dell'Uomo* chamber (area of Trench III in Figure 3.8) is accurate, but the exact placement of the cranium relative to the stone feature and accounts of its orientation may not be.

The stone feature, allegedly containing the cra-

Figure 3.12 The "arc" or "circle" of stones in Grotta Guattari; the Neandertal cranium allegedly was found inside this feature in 1939. (Courtesy of IIPU archives)

nium and variously described as a circle or an arc, is the weakest link in the chain of interpretations of this site. Figure 3.12 is a photograph of the original feature (as opposed to one of many interpretive renditions) and appears more like an arc than a full circle, consistent with the label in Italian on this IIPU archive photograph. Cardini's map of the surface accurately portrays the distribution of animal bones but records stones only at the location where the skull was found. Many otherwise identical stones litter the surface throughout the cave. Piperno (1976–77) and Taschini (1970) cite the presence of manuported stones on the surface as evidence for noneconomic or ritual use of the cave. Segre, a geologist by training, refers to the same stone pavement as cryoclastic limestone *éboulis* that spalled from the vault or related sources outside

of the cave, perhaps washing into the interior later (Blanc and Segre 1953:89, and p.c.).

Formal excavations began at Guattari the year of its discovery—first under the supervision of Blanc, and later under Cardini (Taschini 1979:181–182). Cardini excavated in thin, arbitrary units, while Blanc excavated by geological levels. Additional, limited testing was undertaken by Segre in 1950 to resolve questions about the stratigraphy. In all, IIPU members dug nine trenches (letters and numbers in Figure 3.8) outside and inside the cave. Based on his tests, Segre was able to unify the provenience data of Blanc and Cardini (Taschini 1979:184) into seven major geological levels of variable vertical and horizontal dimensions (Table 3.6). The strata are thickest at the front of the cave (Figure 3.9A), thinning toward the rear (Figure 3.9b). Levels G4

TABLE 3.6
Summary of Segre's descriptions of the Guattari sediments

Stratum	Description
1	partially cemented, concretion-covered angular blocks of limestone *éboulis* mixed with loose brown earth; includes the "surface"
2	loose, "incoherent" brown earth
3	compact brown earth, heavily cemented and containing numerous calcareous concretions and crusts
4	partially cemented fill with fossil and modern root casts
5	brown-violet sandy soil
6	cemented gray sand with fragments of marine mollusk shells
7	marine beach conglomerate of cemented sand, containing whole or nearly whole marine shells

Source: Taschini (1979).

and G5 are barely perceptible in the interior section.

The deposits in the interior are true cave soils, originating primarily from decomposition of the surrounding limestone bedrock. There is some evidence of thermoclastic activity toward the younger end of the sequence, indicated by limestone spall littering the surface (G0) and in level G1. The cryoclastic stone pavement in G0–1 led Segre to attribute these deposits to the very cold part of the Wurm II (Taschini 1979:247). Assessments of sediment composition also indicate that levels G1 through G5 accumulated fairly rapidly, consistent with the ESR dates (Schwarcz et al. 1991).

Lithic artifacts occur only in levels G1, G2, G4, and G5 (Table 3.5). Some in-filling by sediments originating outside the cave is evident at the front (Figure 3.9a); some of the Mousterian tools first deposited at the cave entrance (where lithic densities are highest) probably were later carried into the tunnels by slopewash. Mammalian remains are more widespread in the deposits, occurring on the surface (G0) as well as in the levels named above. Only one bone, an aurochs mandible fragment, was recovered from G7. Many of the lithic artifacts are burned, as are some small bone fragments accidentally retained by the excavators because they were mistaken for burned flint chips. However, no hearth features or discrete ash lenses are reported.

As noted by Segre, the surface deposit does not represent a truly discrete stratigraphic unit; some

large bones link G0 and G1 together into a single entity, and a few bone specimens also link G1 with G2. Bones spanning these vertical proveniences may be due to carnivore disturbances occurring well after the deposition of cultural material in G1 and G2 (see Chapter 5). Stratum 3 is a distinct sterile layer that ranges between 10 and 75 cm in thickness and unequivocally separates G4 and G5 from the overlying portions of the sequence.

Remains of a "warm" fauna were reported for G4 and G5, initially suggesting that these levels might have formed during the Wurm I–II (Brorup stadial). However, the association is problematic; the climatic interpretation is based largely on the presence of hippopotamus remains noted by Cardini in G3–4 (in Blanc and Segre 1953:92), but I could not find any such remains in the collections (see Chapter 4). Radiometric analysis instead indicates that levels G0–5 formed between 78,000 and 50,000 years ago, after hippopotamus is thought to have disappeared from this region (e.g., Blanc 1937a; Caloi and Palombo 1988).

Levels G6 and G7, the latter representing a Tyrrhenian beach deposit based on the malacofauna (Durante and Settepassi 1976–77), may have formed over a longer period of time. Stratum G6 probably precedes most biological activity in the cave, although a single aurochs mandible fragment was found at the top of G7. Stratum G7 is clearly a beach deposit containing volcanic ash and is thought to date to the end of one of several sea transgressions (possibly oxygen isotope stage 5a?) following the Riss/Wurm Interglacial, based on geochronology (Blanc and Segre 1953). Most of the information about the basal beach deposits of Guattari is from salvage excavations in front of the cave in 1941–42, when the landowners built the foundation for an underground pantry (Blanc 1955c:270): at roughly 5 m below ground, they encountered Mousterian material, including probable hearths, directly overlying a Tyrrhenian beach deposit full of marine shells (Durante and Settepassi 1976–77). Though I have not studied the mollusks, those shells on public display at the Museo Pigorini do not show evidence of human modification.

Most of the basic descriptive work on Guattari was not published until the 1950s and later. Blanc and Segre presented the stratigraphy and the general summaries of the faunal and industrial associations in 1953; only a presence-absence species list is provided for faunal remains from the surface and subsurface strata. Cardini also produced a detailed map of the bones lying on the surface and a full accounting of the contents of that assemblage. The results of this work were published by Piperno in 1976–77.

Taschini assumed the task of describing the Mousterian industries of Guattari following Blanc's death in 1960. Following Taschini's untimely death in 1975, Bietti completed the monograph on the lithic industries (Taschini a cura Bietti 1979), the first major work on Pontinian Mousterian industries to employ Bordes' stone tool typology. The Pontinian is generally considered to be a relatively homogeneous assortment of industrial facies from the typological point of view, although it is widely distributed in coastal Latium. However, Taschini and Bietti observed the strongest typological contrasts in the Pontinian as a whole *within* the Guattari series, between the assemblages from G1 and G2 and those from G4 and G5, based primarily on platform faceting and Levallois indices (see also Bietti and Kuhn 1990–91).

Grotta dei Moscerini

Blanc, Segre, and co-workers recorded many caves during their surveys of the coast between Rome and Gaeta. For the purposes of inventory, the caves were named for nearby towns, people, rocky promontories of historical note, fig trees, and so forth. The Mousterian cave known as Grotta dei Moscerini was named for the clouds of gnats that inhabited its interior, apparently an important feature of the discovery experience.

Grotta dei Moscerini is located at the base of the steep limestone flank of Monte Agmemone (Figures 3.13 and 3.14), between the towns of Sperlonga and Gaeta (see Figure 3.2). The cave entrance lies only 2 to 3 m above modern sea level, broadly equivalent to the topographic positions of Grotta Breuil and Grotta del Fossellone at the base of Monte Circeo. The site is no longer accessible due to massive rockfall caused by the construction of Via Flacca, a road and tunnel carved into the steep hillside above (Figure 3.15).

Grotta dei Moscerini is an exceptional Mousterian site in many respects. It contains a broader array of animal remains than any other cave in the study sample. It also contains the oldest cultural deposits in the time frame examined, dating to as early as 115,000 to 120,000 years ago. Like some Middle Stone Age sites on the coast of South Africa (e.g., Voigt 1973, 1982), Moscerini presents some of the earliest evidence of aquatic resource exploitation by hominids (marine clams and mussels, tortoises, and the odd fragment of monk seal) in the world. Moscerini is one of the larger cave excavations (see Figure 3.14); Segre documented over 8 m of stratigraphy at the cave entrance (Figure 3.16a–b and Table 3.7a–b), most of which contains Mousterian artifacts. The deposits may have once filled the cave to within a meter of the vault (Figure 3.17) and extended far outward from the entrance. Some of the talus has been undermined and carried away by rising Holocene seas. The cave interior (Figure 3.18) stretches back some 12 m, where it narrows into two small tubes.

The site was excavated during the summer of 1949 by Blanc, Segre, Naldini (now Segre-Naldini), Laj Pannocchia, and others members of the IIPU (Figure 3.19). The excavation campaign was part of a larger research program initiated in 1947 to test various Quaternary cave deposits found between Sperlonga and Gaeta. Two areas of Moscerini were trenched: a large area at the mouth of the cave (the exterior series) that revealed a strati-

Figure 3.13 Grotta dei Moscerini (top) at the base of the limestone cliffs near Gaeta, and (bottom) the sandy beach immediately in front of the cave. (Courtesy of IIPU archives, 1949)

graphic column 8.5 m thick (Figures 3.16 and 3.17A–B), and a smaller pit (the interior series) in the back of the cave (Figure 3.17G). The exterior trench followed the natural levels of the cave deposits. The interior excavation instead relied mainly on arbitrary stratigraphic units, because the available lighting was poor and natural divisions among the layers were less distinct. The bulk of the work at Moscerini was never published (but see Vitagliano 1984), despite an extensive field campaign.

Segre described 44 strata in the exterior stratigraphic series (Table 3.7 and Figure 3.16), commencing at the bottom with a Tyrrhenian beach deposit. Four major cryoclastic events are documented within this series: stratum 3, strata 8–9, strata 27–28, and stratum 38. A wave-cut notch and ancient lithodome scars in the north wall of the cave (Figure 3.18, Lt) are thought to mark the high sea stage of the Riss/Wurm Interglacial, presumably isotope stage 5e. The cave almost certainly was scoured out by wave action at that time, with deposition beginning anew soon thereafter. The lithodome scars occur at approximately the same height as strata 8–20, obviously preceding Upper Pleistocene soil deposition in the cave.

The quantities of artifactual material vary greatly

Figure 3.14 Grotta dei Moscerini toward the close of the 1949 excavation. (Courtesy of IIPU archives)

among strata. The exterior and interior stratigraphic series of Moscerini have been simplified for some of the analyses presented in later chapters (Table 3.8), primarily to bolster sample sizes and make inter-assemblage comparisons possible. While I have taken some liberties in lumping these strata, the six level groups are consistent with the general rhythm of sedimentation, including particle sizes and thermoclastic events. The boundaries separating lumped stratigraphic units also correspond to significant changes in the presence of temperature-sensitive mammals (e.g., hippopotamus, Chapter 4) and, to a lesser extent, cyclical alternations of marine mollusk species (Chapter 6). Subtle yet cor-responding shifts are evident in the contents of the lithic industries as well (Kuhn 1990a:155).

Grotta di Sant'Agostino

Grotta di Sant'Agostino is located 40 to 50 km south of Monte Circeo, near the town of Gaeta and only 2.5 km south of Grotta dei Moscerini (see Figures 3.1 and 3.2). The cave sits somewhat higher in the limestone cliffs than the other sites (Figure 3.20), at roughly 25 m above modern sea level (my assessment; cf. Tozzi 1970:3). Here the cliffs form a wide amphitheater, today overlooking a narrow strip of coastal plain. The cave is a single, gaping chamber 20–25 m across with a parabolic vault about 8 m high (Figure 3.21). The back of the chamber (18 m from the entrance) slopes abruptly downward. The entrance faces due south, and because of its relative shallowness and wide mouth, the cave is well illuminated throughout the day. The cave deposits are primarily a loose sandy fill. Two flowstone layers are exposed at the base of the east wall and the southwest corner near the entrance, below all visible bone-bearing deposits. Samples of the flowstones were taken for U-series dating (Figure 3.21, shaded patches; locations 1 and 2 refer to locations of background radiation dose readings) and yielded ages of 112,000 ± 14,000 and 120,000 ± 15,000 years respectively.

Grotta di Sant'Agostino was excavated in 1948 by Tongiorgi, Cardini, and co-workers (Tozzi 1970). They dug two trenches: one reportedly near the cave entrance and possibly adjacent to the exposed flowstone layers; and the other in the rear-center of the cave, under an active spring. The trench near the entrance was approximately 50 cm deep, rich in mammal remains but lacking lithic artifacts (provenience SX; see Table 3.5). The trench near the back of the cave was excavated to 2.5 m below modern ground level (layers S0–4) and was rich in both animal bones and lithic artifacts.

We found several depressions in the floor during our visit to the cave in 1987 (Figure 3.21). Some or all of the depressions may correspond to Tongiorgi's excavation units, although the accounts of trench placements are unclear, and the interior trench appears to have been enlarged by recent clandestine digging. Tongiorgi excavated the S0–4 series of the interior trench in five arbitrary layers (cuts), due to the absence of discernible geological strata. The excavated areas and thicknesses of these layers vary, as shown in Table 3.9. Layer S0 (my designation) contains a mixture of historic material from when the cave was a sheep pen, along with (rare) Upper Paleolithic and Middle Paleolithic tools; Mousterian lithics predominate. Layers S1–4 are attributable to the Middle Paleolithic exclusively. The deposits of the S0–4 series could not be related to the SX trench at the time of excavation, although they are certainly of Upper Pleistocene age. No in-

Figure 3.15 Grotta dei Moscerini with only the top of the vault visible in 1971. The cave was completely buried soon thereafter by scree from road tunnel construction uphill of the cave. (Courtesy of G. Barker)

tact hearth features or ash lenses were noted (Laj Pannocchia 1950; Tozzi 1970).

Laj Pannocchia (1950) published the first study of the lithic material from Sant'Agostino soon after the close of the excavations. Her investigation employed a novel approach for the time, emphasizing patterns of core reduction and flake production. The study did not extend beyond preliminary descriptions of the technology, however, prompting Tozzi (1970) to undertake a more complete study of both the lithic and faunal assemblages twenty years later. Tozzi's analyses of the lithic material follow Laj Pannocchia's approach to studying the flakes and flake blanks; he used a combination of Laplacian and Bordesian techniques for analyzing the

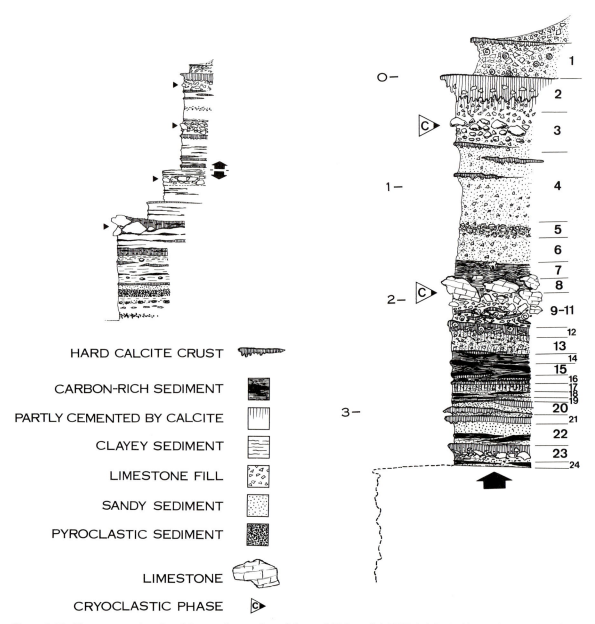

HARD CALCITE CRUST

CARBON-RICH SEDIMENT

PARTLY CEMENTED BY CALCITE

CLAYEY SEDIMENT

LIMESTONE FILL

SANDY SEDIMENT

PYROCLASTIC SEDIMENT

LIMESTONE

CRYOCLASTIC PHASE

Figure 3.16a The upper stratigraphy of the exterior trenches of Grotta dei Moscerini (EXT 1–24). Arabic numbers on the left denote meters below datum; cut numbers are on the right. Segre's sediment descriptions are listed in Table 3.7a. (Redrafted from Segre's 1949 unpublished drawing)

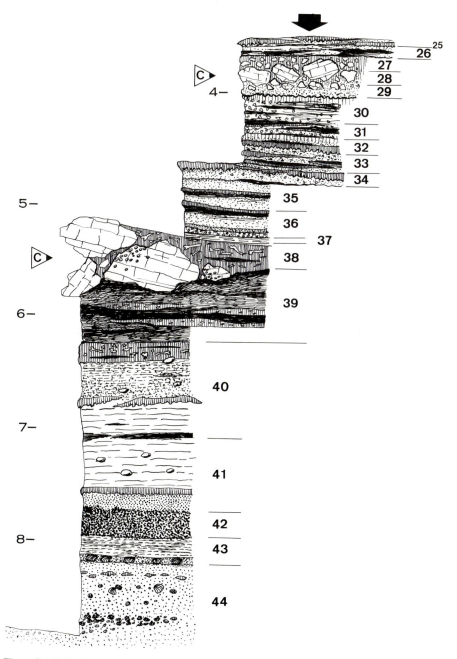

Figure 3.16b The lower stratigraphy of the exterior trenches of Grotta dei Moscerini (EXT 25–44). Arabic numbers on the left denote meters below datum; cut numbers are on the right. Segre's sediment descriptions are listed in Table 3.7b. (Redrafted from Segre's 1949 unpublished drawing)

3 - partly cemented talus containing medium-sized limestone rocks
4 - semibrecciated earth with nearly pure calcium carbonate lenses
5 - thin gray layer of breccia and large limestone fragments
6 - grayish-yellow soil
7 - brown earth, grading to black
8–10 - talus containing large limestone blocks, up to 60 by 100 cm but decreasing in size toward cut 10
11 - cemented breccia with "reticulated" stalagmitic deposits and charcoal
12 - crusty, cemented breccia grading into hard stalagmite, with some charcoal
13 - cemented earth and breccia
14 - black earth containing carbon and "indurated" ashy lenses
15 - black earth containing carbon
16 - calcium-cemented crusts and ash lenses, rare yellow pumice fragments
17 - hard, cemented stratum
18 - dark red sandy sediment containing thin crusts and carbon-rich lenses
19 - organic rich layer containing dark sands, carbon, and vegetable material
20 - carbonate lenses of sandy or earthy fill and concreted lenses
21 - thin stratum rich in stalagmites alternating with sandy lenses
22 - sandy or loamy stratum with carbon-rich lenses
23 - sandy or loamy stratum with hard stalagmite lenses
24 - thin series of loessic limestone, carbon-rich, and carbonate lenses

b. Segre's descriptions of the sediments of the exterior trenches of Moscerini

25–26 - thin series of loessic limestone, carbon-rich, and carbonate lenses
27 - talus containing small limestone blocks
28 - talus containing larger limestone blocks, cemented by yellow calcite
29 - yellow, powdery soil with yellow pumice fragments
30 - limestone fragment fill with carbon-rich horizons
31 - limestone fragment fill with carbon-rich horizons and carbonate lenses
32 - earth with carbon-rich lenses, cemented by calcium carbonate
33 - earth with crusts and carbon-rich lenses
34 - yellow earth with stalagmitic lenses
35–36 - burned earth, with "stalagmitized" ash lenses and white pumice
37 - light green-gray clay, spotted with manganese
38 - basal talus of large limestone blocks (with lithodome scars) and bone-rich breccia intercalated with yellowish earthy lenses, some charcoal
39 - thick carbon-rich layers (with some carbonized seeds) alternating with unburned fill, more gravel and crusting toward the bottom
40 - several distinct layers: top consists of purple stalagmitic fill and fine burned lenses, underlain by sandy-clay fill with few pebbles, and finally purple sand with concreted lenses
41 - several distinct layers: top consists of carbon-rich lenses, sandy-clay fill with pebbles, a hard stalagmite layer, and finally sandy fill
42 - compact dark green pyroclast sediment, possibly eroded at top
43 - brown clay containing some charcoal
44 - sandy sediments with several quasi-distinct layers: top is a thin cemented Tyrrhenian beach deposit rich in marine shells and some pumice, followed by loose sands containing fewer shells but more pumice and small concretion fragments, finally by sediments richer in both pumice and shells

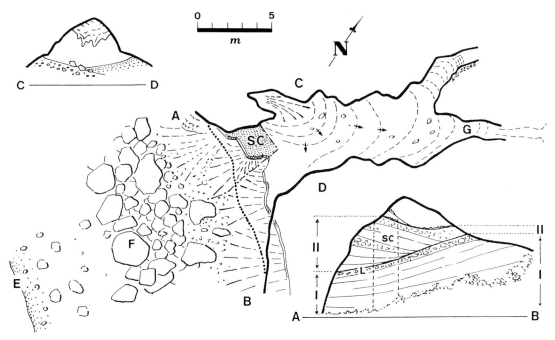

Figure 3.17 Plan and cross-sectional views of Grotta dei Moscerini: (A–B) cross-section at the modern dripline, (SC) location of the exterior excavation trench, (C–D) cross-section midway into the cave interior, (E) modern shoreline, (F) limestone blocks from mountainside above, (G) approximate location of the interior trench. (Adapted from Segre's 1950 unpublished drawings)

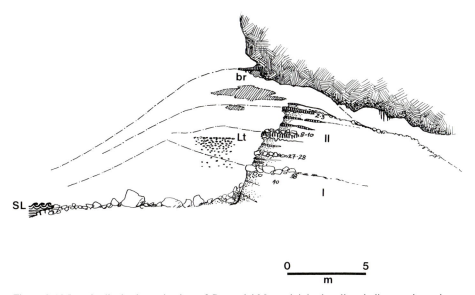

Figure 3.18 Longitudinal schematic view of Grotta dei Moscerini: broken lines indicate estimated extents of cultural deposits projected from horizontal flowstone layers, (I and II) discordance noted in cross-section "A–B" in Figure 3.17, (Lt) lithodome scars in north wall, (br) breccia/stalagmite marking uppermost fill line prior to erosion of the outer sediments, (SL) modern sea level. The drawing corresponds to cross-section "E–G" in Figure 3.17. (Adapted from unpublished drawing by Segre)

Figure 3.19 Scenes from the 1949 excavations at Grotta dei Moscerini:
(A) full view of the "exterior" strata; (B) detail of the lower portion;

(C) closeup view of the sediments; (D) workers screening excavated sediments
(Courtesy of IIPU archives)

TABLE 3.8
Major level groupings in Grotta dei Moscerini

Level group	Fine strata as defined by Segre in 1949	Description
M1	EXT 1–10	thick, sandy layers with few stalagmites or crusts, little evidence of fire
M2	EXT 11–20	thin strata with sandy or loamy fill and few well-developed stalagmites, numerous small ashy lenses
M3	EXT 21–36	thin layers with alternating stalagmites and sandy fill, extensive burned areas[a]
M4	EXT 37–43	thick sandy strata, extensive burned horizons in 39 and 41, charcoal lens in upper part of 40, some unworked flint pebbles in fill
T.B.	EXT 44	Tyrrhenian beach deposit with wave-worn marine shells, including *Strombus bubonius*
M5	INT 1, 1A–D, 2	no account
M6	INT 3–4	no account

[a]Some of the dark lenses identified as hearths may be a combination of burned material and decomposed organic products forming dark sheets of manganese phosphate.

Note: (EXT) exterior trench, (INT) interior trench.

retouched tools. Tozzi published equally exhaustive summaries of the faunas, including species and body part counts in NISP format and various osteometric measurements.

Grotta Breuil

Grotta Breuil is another cave documented during the IIPU surveys (Figure 3.22). It is named in honor of Abbé H. Breuil, who briefly accompanied Blanc during the 1936 survey of the northern Latium coast; the Abbé Breuil also participated in excavations at Grotta del Fossellone around that time. Grotta Breuil consists of a large, single chamber aligned generally west-east, but twisting northward and upward toward the rear (Figure 3.23). The cave opens directly onto the Mediterranean Sea and faces west-southwest. It lies approximately 2 km west of Grotta Guattari (see Figures 3.1 and 3.2). The entrance is about 12 m wide by 12 m high, and the main (anterior) segment of the chamber is about 18 m deep (Figure 3.24). The rear portion terminates into an active debris cone (Figure 3.23A), fed by decomposing limestone and, periodically, waste from bat colonies and swift nests in the upper vault. The

sheet of debris picks up archaeological materials (organic and inorganic) as it progresses down the 35° slope toward the sea. A second, smaller cave lies just north of the entrance to Grotta Breuil and preserves a series of Upper Pleistocene deposits cemented to its walls, lacking or poor in cultural material.

Access to Grotta Breuil today is hindered by its position only 3 m above sea level and a sheer cliff rising some 100 m above the opening. Its relative isolation has protected the cave from severe looting and has limited archaeological work there until recently (Bietti et al. 1988), although some minor test pits were excavated into the unstable slope deposits in 1938, 1953, and 1954 by members of the IIPU. The lithic artifacts recovered from the early tests indicated existence of two cultural components in grossly disproportionate quantities (Taschini 1970): a few tools of Upper Paleolithic character were identified, but most of the artifacts were assignable to the Pontinian Mousterian.

Nearly fifty years after the discovery of Grotta Breuil, members of the IIPU began large-scale excavations in the cave, directed by A. Bietti, with the support of the University of Rome. Work began

Figure 3.20 Grotta di Sant'Agostino (top) in the base of limestone cliffs north of Gaeta and (bottom) the flat coastal plain in front. (Courtesy of G. Barker, 1971)

with an exploratory trench during the fall of 1985 (Figure 3.23C). A 1 m by 1 m grid, oriented north-south and east-west, was installed in the cave vault, followed by larger excavations in July and September 1986 and each summer through the present.

A loose blanket of redeposited soils and artifacts covers a thick eroded face of intact strata in Grotta Breuil. The fill is excavated by arbitrary cuts, designed to keep track of the current proximity of loose material to adjacent intact strata. In situ material is excavated by geological level (subdivided into arbitrary 5 cm cuts) and piece-plotted in three dimensions. The material is rinsed by running sea water through plastic screens. Sea water appears to

be a sound preservation medium for the bone, as these Pleistocene deposits are already impregnated with salt. The macroscopic condition of the bone is very good, although some recrystallization has certainly occurred. Unlike the procedures used in previous decades, all lithic and bone fragments from Breuil are retained for study, also providing control information for assessing probable recovery biases in the older museum collections.

Once cleaned of the eroded blanket, approximately 7 m of intact strata are clearly visible in the Breuil series (Figure 3.24 and provisional levels X–XX in Figure 3.25). They are merely the remnant of a much larger site, representing perhaps one-quarter

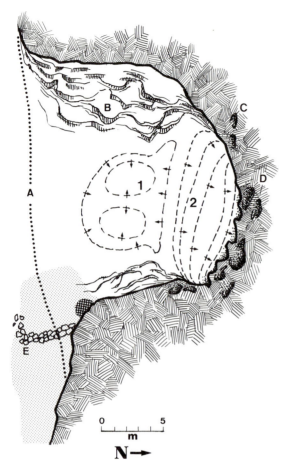

Figure 3.21 Plan view of Grotta di Sant'Agostino: (A) modern dripline, (B) rocky bench, (C) modern owl roost, (D) empty solution cavities in the upper walls, (E) recent dry-lain stone wall, (1,2) locations of background dosimeter readings taken inside the depressions of the old excavations. Light and dark shadings indicate flowstone layers; the older (dark) flowstones, lying below the deposit containing bones and sand, were dated by U-series method. (1987 field drawing by Stiner)

TABLE 3.9

Thicknesses and areal extents of arbitrary layers in the interior trench excavated by Tongiorgi in Sant'Agostino

Tozzi's provenience notation[a]	Stiner's provenience notation	Average thickness (cm)	Excavated area (m²)
A	S0	30	12.40
A1	S1	30	5.75
A2	S2	40	5.75
A3	S3	60	4.05
A4	S4	90	3.00

Source: Tozzi (1970).

[a]Exterior trench SX not included.

Figure 3.22 Grotta Breuil in the base of the western precipice of Monte Circeo, accessible today only from the sea. Visible equipment and persons are associated with current excavations (1985 to present).

or one-third of the original volume of material once preserved there (Figure 3.25, dashed line). Missing portions of the deposit were undermined by the sea during the Holocene, slowly crumbling downward and carried away during the worst winter storms. Massive limestone blocks protect the remaining deposits from the onslaught of sea waves. Most of the exposed strata in Grotta Breuil are rich in artifacts and bones, all originating from in situ strata. While the vault rises to a narrow dome in the back of the cave, we find no evidence of a chimney that could feed the debris cone from outside the cave. Virtually all of the stone tools recovered since 1985 are Mousterian, and, contrary to early reports, no unequivocal Upper Paleolithic artifacts have been identified. We encountered a very limited late Neolithic (?) occupation, however, atop the youngest Mousterian level in the rear south corner of the cave. Use of the cave in Neolithic times is evident from a few rough pot shards and two blades made on Palmarola obsidian obtained from the small offshore island by the same name (Figure 3.2A).

Three distinct high sea stands are evident from lithodome scars in the north wall of Grotta Breuil (Figure 3.24 illustrates only the highest stand). A lithified Tyrrhenian beach containing fossil mollusks is exposed at the cave mouth. Segre's geochronological assessments suggest that the earliest friable geological deposits in Breuil were formed after the Last Interglacial, probably following isotope stage 5a; forming a thick bed of sterile silty sands (below level XX in Figure 3.25).

The faunal assemblages from Grotta Breuil used in this study came from the 1987 and 1988 field seasons only, as indicated in the text and tables. The Grotta Breuil project is still quite new and these are the only samples that have been completely studied thus far (see also Bietti and Grimaldi 1990–91; Bietti et al. 1988, 1990–91; Kuhn 1990–91b; Lemorini 1990–91; Rossetti and Zanzi 1990–91; Stiner 1990–91). The samples represent two spatially discrete sources, the redeposited zone (Br) and the in situ deposits in provisional Stratum B3/4 (Figure 3.24, area 11). While generally referred to as redeposited material, the Br sample was taken from squares near the top of the strata column and clearly originated from these layers; thus, the Br material has undergone some reworking by erosion, but in a limited way.

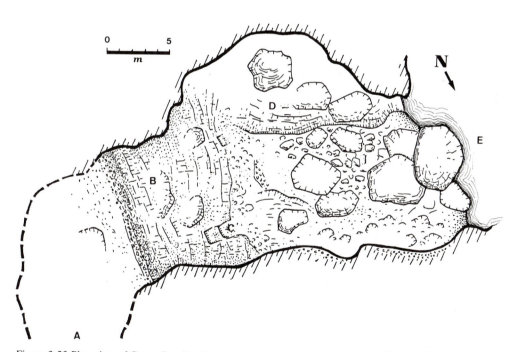

Figure 3.23 Plan view of Grotta Breuil: (A) estimated extent of the rear chamber, (B) eroded face of stratified cultural deposits, (C) early test units at base of the eroded strata column, (D) rocky bench in south cave wall, (E) modern sea edge. (Adapted from unpublished drawing by Segre)

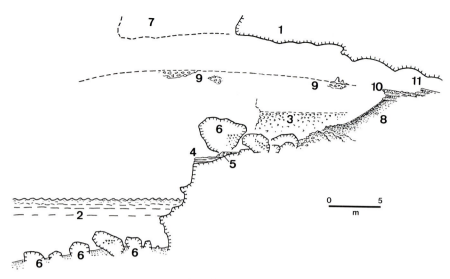

Figure 3.24 Longitudinal schematic section of Grotta Breuil: (1) extent of modern overhang, (2) modern sea level, (3) height of lithodome scars on north wall of cave, (4) lithified Tyrrhenian beach deposit, (5) limestone and lithified conglomerate from eroded strata above, (6) limestone blocks that fell from the vault, probably at the end of the Wurm I, (7) estimated extent of vault prior to collapsing, (8) eroded face of cultural strata, (9) line of cemented breccia indicating probable outward extent of cultural strata prior to Holocene erosion, (10) remnant horizontal stalagmites, (11) top of depositional sequence capped by youngest (U/Th 26,000 ± 12,000) horizontal stalagmite. (Adapted from Bietti et al. 1988)

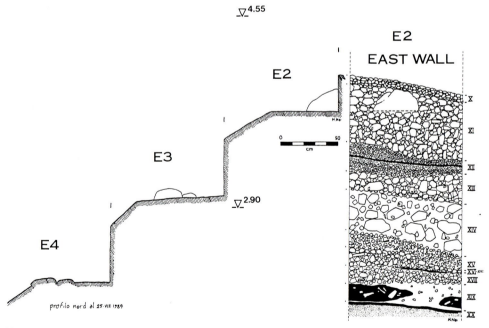

Figure 3.25 Cleaned, unexcavated stratigraphic section of the lower cultural levels of Grotta Breuil. Section shows provisional levels X–XX, corresponding to "(10)" and downward in Figure 3.24. (Drawing by Mei, 1989)

THE LATE UPPER PALEOLITHIC SAMPLE

The late Upper Paleolithic period in Italy, known as the Epigravettian, is considered relatively unique to southern Europe (for general reviews, see Barker 1981; Gamble 1986; for Italy, Bietti 1990). All of the rockshelter faunas associated with fully modern humans in the study sample are from this period, dating between 15,000 and 10,000 years ago. Examples of Upper Paleolithic lifeways for the purposes of this study, such hunter-gatherer economies nonetheless persisted in west-central Italy well after the appearance of Mesolithic cultural complexes in northern Europe (Barker 1981:47–51). Epigravettian lithic industries are defined by the conspicuous presence of backed points, backed blades, and bladelets; these technologies emphasized, among other things, elaborate haftings and composite weapons.

Grotta Palidoro

The Upper Paleolithic rockshelter of Grotta Palidoro was discovered in the 1950s during quarry operations in the Palidoro area (Figures 3.26 and 3.27) some 30 km northwest of Rome (see Figure 3.1). Fossilized mammal bones were reported at the locality as early as 1947 (Bietti 1976–77b). A. C. Blanc and V. G. Chiappella identified an Epigravettian cultural component at the Palidoro shelter when they surveyed the area in 1954 (Blanc 1955a, 1955b; Chiapella 1956, 1959, 1965). Now completely destroyed, the rockshelter site was found within a massive travertine formation, in an overhang etched by a small stream (Segre 1976–77). It contains a thick series of Upper Paleolithic strata, sealed from overlying Neolithic, Bronze Age, and

Figure 3.26 The Palidoro travertine quarry prior to its destruction by commercial mining in 1959. The late Upper Paleolithic shelter is hidden in the lower half of the hillside. (Courtesy of IIPU archives)

Figure 3.27 Cultural layers in the lower rear portion of Grotta Palidoro, exposed by the 1959 excavations and with about half of the surrounding travertine mass quarried away in the meantime. (Courtesy of IIPU archives)

Iron Age occupations by a collapse of blocks from the vault (Blanc 1955a, 1955b).

The shelter was the subject of a large-scale multidisciplinary study over the next two decades, excavated as the surrounding travertine quarry was mined away in the same years (Figures 3.27 and 3.28). Cassoli (1976–77) undertook the first major testing of the rockshelter in 1955. No stratigraphy could be discerned, and the deposits were dug in a series of eight arbitrary layers, each roughly 10 cm thick. Another excavation was undertaken by Chiappella from 1956 to 1959, with forty-five arbitrary cuts of variable thickness (10–20 cm each): the upper twelve cuts represent Neolithic through Bronze/ Iron Age occupations; cuts 13/14 through 20 are sterile and full of travertine blocks; and cuts 21/22 represent the youngest layers of the Upper Paleolithic series. The base of Cassoli's excavations (cut 8) corresponds to cut 34 in Chiappella's trench. Chiappella's excavation ended with a sterile layer in cut 45. Because the two excavations were not contiguous, no clear stratigraphic associations could be made between them (Bietti 1976–77b).

I undertook an intensive study of the faunal assemblages from Chiappella's cuts 33–34 only. These data, along with those reported by Cassoli for cuts 1–8 (1976–77:193–194), here serve as comparative samples from Grotta Palidoro. Figure 3.29 illustrates the condition and density of animal bones and teeth as they were excavated from Chiappella's cuts 34 and 37, respectively. The quality of bone preservation is very good and is more or less typical of Upper Pleistocene faunas found in travertine and limestone shelters in Latium and Tuscany. Nearly all broken edges of the bones visible in Figure 3.29 are green breaks, fractures that occurred when the bones were processed for food by humans.

Many radiocarbon dates on burned bones and bone collagen are available for the late Upper Paleolithic (Epigravettian) strata of Grotta Palidoro, both for the 1955 and 1956–59 excavations (Alessio et al. 1976–77). All of the dates fall between 14,300 and 15,900 B.P. The full late Upper Paleolithic sequence is bracketed by two major cryoclastic events, the latter of which (noted above) destroyed part of the shelter's overhang. The deposits are rich

Figure 3.28 Various phases of the 1959 excavations at Grotta Palidoro: (top) removing the extreme northeast portion of cut 7, (bottom) older strata exposed later in the project. (Courtesy of IIPU archives)

in lithic artifacts, many of which were manufactured on local flint pebbles. The analyses of stone tools (Bietti 1976–77a) and faunas (Cassoli 1976–77) reveal little if any variation through most of the stratigraphic sequence. Sediment analyses of the 1955 cuts by Palmieri (1976–77), along with Cassoli's data on the fauna, associate most of the depositional sequence with a wet, temperate oscillation in the Last Glacial, ending with a rather sudden shift to a cold, dry phase.

Riparo Salvini

Riparo Salvini, shown in Figure 3.30, is a small shallow rockshelter in the limestone cliffs above the town of Terracina (see Figure 3.2). This and other shelters, largely destroyed when the cliff was quarried for building stone, once formed a line of sites lying about 35 m above modern sea level and within 100 m of the shore. The position of Riparo Salvini may have conferred some strategic advantage for Paleolithic hunters, as it overlooks two segments of coastal plain, to the north and to the south, pinched to a narrow ribbon by the cliffs containing the site.

Riparo Salvini was first tested by Cardini in 1963. Formal excavations were begun in 1979 under the direction of Bietti and closed in 1990. The shelter has a long history of use by humans, culminating in a small shepherd's hut with a rough cobbled floor in the early part of the twentieth century. The historic occupations resulted in considerable damage to the uppermost prehistoric layers, which contain late Upper Paleolithic (late Epigravettian) industries and a moderately well-preserved fauna. The prehistoric cultural deposits are fairly homogeneous and have a high organic content (Avellino et al. 1989; Bietti 1984).

The late Upper Paleolithic deposit in Salvini yields a radiocarbon date of 12,400 ± 170 years B.P. (Bietti 1986), linking the human occupations to the putative colder oscillation of the Dryas II and the beginning of the evolved Epigravettian cultural phase. The site appears to have served as a residential camp from which hunting operations were

Figure 3.29 Animal remains and lithic artifacts exposed in cuts 34 (top) and 37 (bottom) of Trench "g" at Grotta Palidoro in 1959. The quality of bone preservation at Palidoro is typical for cave faunas in the study area. Virtually all visible breaks are green bone fractures. (Courtesy of IIPU archives)

Figure 3.30 Riparo Salvini in 1988. This late Upper Paleo-lithic shelter site also contains Roman period burial crypts and a shepherd's hut from the early twentieth century. Most of the late Upper Paleolithic material is from the deep depression in the foreground (bottom); the line of stone barricades was constructed by the excavators to prevent erosion.

undertaken and to which carcasses were brought, probably one or two at a time, for complete processing and consumption (Bietti and Stiner 1992). The faunal assemblage from Riparo Salvini used for this study consists of material recovered only during the 1988 excavations—from squares B1, C1, and C2, cuts 10 through 15 (2.7 to 3.0 m below datum). The cuts underlie those yielding the faunal sample studied by Cassoli and Guadagnoli (1987). Of the excavated layers, the 1988 sample from Salvini contains the best-preserved bone, which accumulated in a natural depression in the shelter (see Figure 3.30).

Grotta Polesini

Grotta Polesini is one of a group of shallow shelters in the travertine formations at Ponte Lucano, on the Aniene River near Tivoli (see Figure 3.1). The site overlooks the river's flood plain some 70 to 100 m above modern sea level, and the hills surrounding this narrow valley rise abruptly to 1100 m. Radmilli and co-workers excavated several of the sites at this locality between 1952 and 1956 (Radmilli 1974). The cultural material is preserved in a sandy and/or clay matrix created by periodic flooding of the river. The uppermost deposits, containing Neolithic, Eneolithic, Iron Age, and even some Roman burials, were disturbed by recent inundations. The underlying late Upper Paleolithic strata were largely intact at the time of the excavation, although saturated by underground springs. Confronted with an absence of discernible stratigraphy, Radmilli dug the Polesini shelter in twelve arbitrary layers, or cuts, each about 20 cm thick. Three stages are noted based on industrial facies (Radmilli 1974:70–75), but species content is essentially the same among the layers.

Like Riparo Salvini, the Polesini occupations are generally attributed to the evolved Epigravettian culture (late Upper Paleolithic, Barker 1981:51). Radmilli reports a substantial quantity of mobile art made on bone and shell from this site (1974). The animal remains are described by Cassoli (1976–77) as a typical cold phase Epigravettian fauna, including marmot, wild ass, and the rare wolverine. Associations to other rockshelters in the region suggest a fairly short chronology, spanning roughly 11,000 to 10,000 B.P.

The quantity of mammalian remains recovered from Grotta Polesini and the quality of preservation are extraordinary (over forty thousand specimens, see Table 3.4). Because I was interested in the faunas for comparative purposes, I studied only selected portions of this enormous collection. I used bone and tooth specimen counts (NISP) published by Radmilli (1974:27–31) for the taxonomic analyses, but collected my own data on tooth eruption-wear of ungulate teeth (Chapters 11 and 13). I also undertook complete zooarchaeological analyses of selected mammalian species—namely, roe deer, fox, badger, brown bear, and lynx—as examples of damage and part transport of ungulates and small carnivores by humans. I was especially interested in obtaining reliable information on patterns of modification on carnivore bones, since it is clear that these animals fell prey to the human occupants of Grotta Polesini. I also examined general patterns of bone damage on a fraction of the red deer remains (cut marks, fracture forms, and fracture locations) for comparative information on food processing by modern humans in Italy during the terminal Pleistocene.

CARNIVORE DENS FROM UPPER PLEISTOCENE ITALY

Carnivore den faunas from Buca della Iena are also brought to the comparisons. Buca della Iena is primarily a late Pleistocene spotted hyaena den complex from a small cave northwest of Pisa (Figure 3.1), documented by Pitti and Tozzi in 1971. The assemblages from this site serve as references, or control cases, for identifying spotted hyaena den components in other Italian cave sites. Buca della Iena is an especially valuable source of reference because its multiple occupational layers document some of the variation in bone-collecting activities of Pleistocene spotted hyaenas in this region. The stratigraphic sequence dates to the same period as the later Mousterian sites in the study sample, and it formed in a generally similar environmental and geological context.

Buca della Iena was excavated in 1964 and 1965 by the Museo Blanc research group of Viareggio (east of Pisa). The project involved testing at three small caves: Grotta dell'Onda, Buca della Iena, and Grotta del Capriolo. Parts of the larger karst system in coastal Tuscany, the caves occur within 100 m of one another. Level E (called I5 in this study) of Buca della Iena yields a U/Th date of approximately 40,000–41,000 B.P., indicating that most of the assemblages (except level F, or I6 by my designation) are somewhat younger (see Figure 3.6). The youngest strata probably formed before 35,000 B.P., based on the scant presence of Mousterian tools mixed with hyaena components in levels I1–4 (see Table 3.5).

Because I needed detailed information on skeletal representation and bone damage, I completely restudied the Buca collections, using Pitti and Tozzi's (1971) work as a guide for the taxonomic identifications. My criteria for identifiable versus unidentifiable bone produced somewhat higher NISP counts overall, but the relative proportions of various taxa are entirely consistent with the earlier study.

MODERN REFERENCE CASES

Working strictly from Upper Pleistocene analog cases is a dangerous way to make inferences about ancient formation processes. Obviously, one does not always have a choice, but a rich and sophisticated literature is available on the bone-collecting habits of modern hunter-gatherers and social carnivores (especially hyaenas and wolves). Because humans' and carnivores' responses vary with environment and season, no single case can typify any species' behavioral patterns in general. I therefore focus on variation among cases produced by the same (or closely related) species as a source of control information. Ranges of variation, in my opinion, represent the most appropriate format for using analog or control data on predator behaviors in general and what predators tend to do to bones in particular.

Data on bone collecting by modern carnivores are available from both wildlife and actualistic studies. The sources used for this study vary widely, depending on the purpose of each comparison made. Accounts of the sources and kinds of information drawn from modern reference cases are not undertaken here; Chapters 4, 7, 8, and 10 are devoted to this task. Both behavioral data and the resultant bone material were available for study in some of the modern reference cases. Three sources remain largely unpublished: (1) Lewis Binford's Alaskan wolf den collections and unpublished data on Kalahari spotted and brown hyaena dens, the latter collected with Gus Mills; (2) Gary Haynes' comparative collection of wolf-damaged bone and an unpublished hyaena den collection from Zimbabwe; and (3) my unpublished comparative study of modern mountain lion kills from New Mexico, and of scatological bone for various carnivorous taxa (free-ranging coyotes, foxes, mountain lions, and from owl pellets).

4

Animal Communities and the
Passage of Species

THIS CHAPTER presents basic data on mammalian species in the Italian shelter faunas. There are many ways of and reasons for examining species abundance, but here it is used to address just two questions: one about mammalian community structure in Upper Pleistocene Italy, and a second about the possible array of bone-collecting agencies responsible for each assemblage based on the behaviors of modern carnivores. Numbers of identifiable bone and tooth specimens (NISP) and numbers of species (N-taxa) describe the arrays of larger mammals, primarily ungulates and carnivores. Apart from presenting quantitative accounts, discussions of the small animals, including lagomorphs, reptiles, and mollusks, are postponed until Chapter 6.

The first analysis focuses on how and to what extent the structure of lowland mammalian communities in Italy, Britain, and Israel responded to interglacial–glacial climate cycles, by comparing the total numbers of mammalian species and relative proportions therein. Britain presents an interesting contrast because, like west-central Italy, local conditions were regulated by maritime winds to a significant extent. Unlike coastal Italy, however, Britain experienced periodic encroachment of large glacial ice masses. The comparisons reveal that Italy supported a relatively diverse animal community throughout the Upper Pleistocene, and that species deletions and additions were uncommon. This finding is important to later assessments of foraging choices by hominids and other predators, since the patterns of species utilization by predators are impossible to understand without also knowing about what there was to choose from.

In considering lowland mammalian community structure in Italy and possible shifts in that structure during the Upper Pleistocene, some inherent biases in cave faunas must be acknowledged. Few if any natural processes of bone accumulation produce nonselective assortments of species (e.g., Behrensmeyer 1976; Stuart 1982:94–96). Assemblages collected by large carnivores and hominids, for example, are biased because these predators concentrate on prey within certain body size ranges. Within a given size range, however, predators may not be very selective at all (e.g., Skinner et al. 1986), and considerable overlap in the species consumed can occur among predators living in the same environment, as modern wildlife studies attest (see Chapter 7 for a biological review of this point). Small predators are similarly affected by prey availability, but for smaller-sized prey (e.g., Eberhardt and Sargeant 1977).

Prey choice within size classes is most responsive to the relative abundance of prey species in the environment and the kinds of habitats that predators are physically equipped to search (e.g., water, forest floors or open lands, trees, and so on). The resident, living abundance of prey in turn relates to species-specific patterns of demographic recruitment, and therefore relative biomass, in an ecosystem (e.g., Sowls 1984:81). In sum, body size and natural abundance together explain far more about the taxonomic composition of prey death assemblages in a region than the preferences or tastes of predators. Within the general body size limits specified by predators' adaptations, predator-generated faunas can tell us quite a bit about the composition of mammal communities (e.g., Tchernov 1992).

Species representation also sets the stage for the taphonomic analyses: it is the first step toward establishing who the bone collectors were, based on the potential array of bone-collecting predators rep-

resented in each assemblage. Behavioral data for modern counterparts of the carnivore taxa found in the Italian caves are used to evaluate each species as a potential collector of bones; not all of them are.

TAXONOMIC CLASSIFICATIONS AND THE NISP VARIABLE

Taxonomic classifications of mammals and other animals in the study sample are based on comparative collections housed at the Italian Institute of Human Paleontology (IIPU, Rome), the Zoological Museum in Rome, and the University of Pisa. Taxa are identified to the level of species wherever possible; hence N-taxa is usually synonymous with number of species. The full array of mammalian species present in the cave assemblages is listed in Table 4.1. The analyses employ numbers of identifiable specimens (NISP) for bones and teeth, corresponding to the most basic catalog of identifiable fragmented and/or fully disarticulated units in each assemblage (see also Table 2.1). The definition and use of the NISP variable follow Grayson (1984) with some modifications.

Of the many counting units developed by zooarchaeologists, NISP is least prone to the pitfalls of data aggregation. NISP demands fewer assumptions about a data set, contra the variables derived from it, such as MNI (cf. Klein 1980a; Klein and Cruz-Uribe 1984). Although problematic when used as a measure of taxonomic abundance for isolated cases, NISP is well suited to interassemblage comparisons, provided the assemblages involve the same potential array of species and the degrees of bone fragmentation are generally comparable.

These criteria are met fairly well by the Italian sample. Moreover, the caves have similar ecological, topographic, and geomorphic settings, and the depositional environments in limestone caves are generally analogous (compare Blanc and Segre 1953; Pitti and Tozzi 1971; Segre 1982).

The extent of bone fragmentation and chemical decomposition varies somewhat among the assemblages (see Chapter 5), but neither of these phenomena is sufficient to drastically alter the relative abundances of taxa within major body size categories. Bone trabeculae, the most sensitive skeletal tissues to any destructive process, are distributed similarly in skeletons within mammalian groups. As for archaeologists' recovery practices, the contents of the older collections are biased in some important ways, but not from the standpoint of species representation. The excavation teams screened the excavated sediments and programmatically collected bones identifiable to species or genus. Indeed, the main purpose of collecting animal remains at that time was to monitor changes in species content across periods. Most axial elements are not diagnostic to species and many were therefore discarded, but the excavators clearly recognized the potential of cranial and appendicular bone (in addition to teeth) for studies of taxonomic representation.

COUNTING NISP AND ASSEMBLAGE COMPARABILITY

Aspects of how the NISP data are organized affect the way in which they should be read and interpreted. The smallest components of articulated skeletal units are counted as separate entities in this study, regardless of whether they are found together or apart. For example, three articulated segments of an ungulate foot found intact in a deposit are counted as three specimens. A distal radius with five carpals still attached is counted as six speci-

mens. A midsection of mandible in which two teeth remain fixed is counted as three specimens (teeth are counted as disarticulatable units just like bones). Anatomical segments often enter archaeological deposits in articulated states but become disassociated through a host of small-scale geological processes.

How best to count isolated versus articulated teeth may not be intuitively obvious in situations of good preservation and limited postdepositional dis-

TABLE 4.1

Italian Upper Pleistocene species, listed by small
mammal, carnivore, and ungulate categories

Common name	Latin name
SMALL MAMMALS:	
INSECTIVORA	
common mole	Talpa europaea
Roman mole	Talpa romana
mole	Talpa caeca
hedgehog	Erinaceus europaeus
CHIROPTERA	
—	Rhinolophus euryale
—	Rhinolophus ferrum-equinum
—	Myotis emarginatus
—	Myotis myotis
—	Myotis oxygnathus
—	Miniopterus schreibersii
—	Barbastella barbastella
LAGOMORPHA	
rabbit (European)	Oryctolagus cuniculus
hare	Lepus capensis/europeus
RODENTIA	
common hamster	Cricetus cricetus
common vole	Microtus arvalis
water vole	Arvicola terrestris
wood mouse	Apodemus sylvaticus
marmot	Marmota marmota
garden dormouse	Eliomys quercinus
dormouse	Muscardinius avellanarius
fat dormouse	Glis glis
rat	Epimys rattus
CARNIVORES:	
wolf	Canis lupus
red fox	Vulpes vulpes
brown bear	Ursus arctos
cave bear	Ursus spelaeus
polecat	Mustela putorius
weasel	Mustela nivalis
pine martin	Martes martes
wolverine	Gulo gulo
badger (European)	Meles meles
spotted hyaena	Crocuta crocuta
wild cat (European)	Felis silvestris
lynx	Lynx lynx
lion	Panthera leo
leopard	Panthera pardus
monk seal	Monachus monachus
UNGULATES:	
PROBOSCIDEA	
elephant	Elaphus antiquus

TABLE 4.1   (Continued)

Common name	Latin name
PERISSODACTYLA	
horse	Equus caballus
wild ass	Equus hydruntinus
rhinoceros	Dicerorhinus/Rhinoceros sp.
ARTIODACTYLA	
fallow deer	Dama dama
roe deer	Capreolus capreolus
red deer	Cervus elaphus
giant deer	Megaceros giganteus
aurochs	Bos primigenius
chamois	Rupicapra rupicapra
ibex	Capra ibex
wild boar	Sus scrofa
hippo	Hippopotamus amphibius

turbance, such as in the caves of west-central Italy. The Italian sample is comparatively unusual, however. In archaeological records of many other parts of the world, isolated teeth are the rule rather than the exception even if bone tissues surrounding the teeth are not destroyed. Teeth fall away from bone very easily, due to differential rates of tissue shrinkage, sediment shifting, and chemical alteration; counting each item as a separate unit is inescapable in these circumstances. For the sake of interassemblage comparability, the counting procedure mandated for the less well-preserved faunas must be extended to better-preserved material wherein some or all teeth are still nested in mandibular and maxillary bone. The proportions of isolated to articulated teeth in the Italian study sample vary among assemblages and even more among sites (Table 4.2). When calculated as the percentage of total teeth, values for isolated teeth range between 15 percent (mostly articulated, as in Moscerini M4) and 97 percent (mostly isolated, as in Buca della Iena I1). The macroscopic condition of bone is uniformly good in these assemblages, suggesting that (1) tooth disarticulation is due mainly to mechanical (e.g., digging) rather than chemical phenomena, and (2) tooth disarticulation can occur well in advance and somewhat independently of chemically induced bone attrition. Both the disarticulation of teeth from bone and processes of in situ bone attrition occur after deposition by biological

TABLE 4.2
Isolated tooth, articulated tooth, and bone NISP for carnivores and ungulates by site and provenience

GROTTA DEI MOSCERINI	M1	M2	M3	M4	M5	M6	TOTAL
CARNIVORES							
isolated teeth	·	·	·	·	32	1	33
articulated teeth	·	·	2	1	26	·	29
bones	·	2	1	1	128	2	134
UNGULATES							
isolated teeth	9	7	47	17	100	82	262
articulated teeth	·	9	147	98	104	61	419
bones	7	21	164	42	226	41	501

GROTTA GUATTARI	G0	G1	G2	G3	G4	G5	G7	TOTAL
CARNIVORES								
isolated teeth	27	46	8	1	2	·	·	84
articulated teeth	36	12	3	·	·	·	·	51
bones	45	22	2	·	1	·	·	70
UNGULATES								
isolated teeth	219	344	44	3	27	28	·	665
articulated teeth	195	102	32	·	8	10	5	352
bones	435	169	28	1	15	11	1	660

GROTTA DI SANT'AGOSTINO	S0	S1	S2	S3	S4	SX	TOTAL
CARNIVORES							
isolated teeth	26	5	1	6	6	20	64
articulated teeth	10	9	15	4	4	14	56
bones	65	91	90	56	26	81	409
UNGULATES							
isolated teeth	422	355	153	76	58	104	1168
articulated teeth	37	78	28	10	13	56	222
bones	285	319	168	74	63	313	1222

GROTTA BREUIL	B3/4	Br
CARNIVORES		
isolated teeth	30	10
articulated teeth	8	·
bones	7	11
UNGULATES		
isolated teeth	237	95
articulated teeth	40	18
bones	299	815

BUCA DELLA IENA	I1	I2	I3	I4	I5	I6	TOTAL
CARNIVORES							
isolated teeth	34	8	36	52	28	101	259
articulated teeth	4	·	·	6	9	35	54
bones	25	11	56	71	92	71	326

(*continued*)

TABLE 4.2 (*Continued*)

Buca della Iena	I1	I2	I3	I4	I5	I6	TOTAL
UNGULATES							
isolated teeth	31	4	8	10	13	128	194
articulated teeth	1	·	·	3	8	23	35
bones	55	14	28	64	81	148	390

Grotta Palidoro	cuts 33–34
CARNIVORES	
isolated teeth	1
articulated teeth	·
bones	7
UNGULATES	
isolated teeth	139
articulated teeth	96
bones	558

agencies, but their causes and respective thresholds differ.

Variation in the extent of tooth disarticulation in the Italian study sample underscores the issue of interassemblage comparability: if isolated teeth were counted as separate units and articulated teeth were not, then assessments of raw taxonomic abundance would depend, at least in part, upon the extent of postdepositional disturbance. Figure 4.1 (data in Table 4.2) shows that the relationship between composite (isolated and articulated) tooth NISP and bone NISP for ungulates is *linear* (or very close to linear at this level of comparison) and highly significant (Figure 4.1A, $r = .845$, $r^2 = .714$, N-cases = 26, $P \ll .001$). In contrast, the relationship between isolated tooth NISP and bone NISP is a *nonlinear* upwardly convex curve in Figure 4.1B, and also highly significant ($r = .852$, $r^2 = .726$, N-cases = 26, $P \ll .001$).[2] Two conspicuous outliers, Breuil Br and Palidoro 33–34, are excluded from the regression calculations, and it is not clear why they diverge so strongly from the main regression lines. As will be apparent in Chapter 7, hyaena- and wolf-generated cases appear no different in this regard from the Mousterian faunas.

Why does the graphed relationship between isolated ungulate tooth NISP and ungulate bone NISP have a profoundly curvilinear appearance when the relationship between composite tooth NISP and bone NISP does not? The answer is not altogether clear, but the observation is surprising. One widespread, traditional system for counting NISP assumes linearity, judging from the zooarchaeological literature. Certainly, bones disappear sooner than teeth overall, since teeth are harder and denser than bones, but it is significant for this study that tooth disarticulation varied greatly while the macroscopic quality of bone preservation is uniformly high among assemblages. Likewise, the extent of bone fragmentation is related to consumer type (Chapters 5 and 7), but interassemblage variation in tooth disarticulation is not.

Comparisons of isolated tooth NISP to articulated tooth counts and to bone NISP are instructive about the extent of postdepositional mechanical destruction. Such comparisons also show that isolated and articulated teeth should be counted by the same standard, preferably one in which the numerical relationship to bone NISP is linear, or close to linear. This procedure affords greater control over differing degrees of disarticulation among assemblages. The quantitative effect is no different from what geological processes so commonly enforce in archaeological records across regions and depositional settings.

[2] This curvilinear relationship is best described by the second order regression formula: $Y = -7.14 + 3.16(X) - .0064(X^2)$.

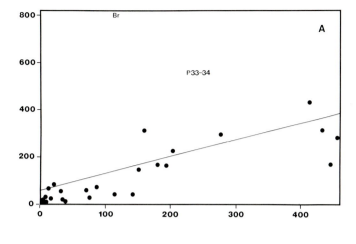

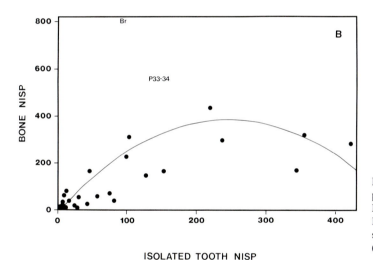

Figure 4.1 Plot of bone NISP to (A) composite tooth NISP and (B) isolated tooth NISP for ungulate remains in various Italian cave faunas (see text for regression statistics); outlier cases are Breuil (Br) and Palidoro (P33–34).

COMMUNITY COMPLEXES AND CLIMATE

The disappearance and/or replacement of animal species in assemblages over time usually imply changes in climate and corresponding shifts in local habitats. Because predators tend to eat prey species that they most often encounter in an environment, but within the general body size range specified by their adaptions, it is practical to examine some aspects of community structure in Italy using mammalian species in the cave deposits.

General factors that affect mammalian distributions in particular outline the kinds of climate-induced shifts in community structure that one can reasonably expect. Mammals are less likely to be influenced directly by climatic variation than lower vertebrates, because they regulate body temperature internally. The bigger the animal, the lower the chance that its geographic distribution will be determined by mean temperature, if for no other reason than higher body mass (which increases as a cube function) to skin surface area (a square function) enables them to conserve heat better. A related point concerns the food supplies of predatory mammals:

TABLE 4.3
Numbers of species (by Order) in mammalian faunas from British paleontological sites

Mammalian Order	Various Interglacials			Cold Stage			Modern (Warm)	
	W Runton[a]	*Swans-combe*[b]	*Joint Mitnor*[c]	*Wretton*[d]	*Tatter-shall*[e]	*Pickens Hole*[f]	*British Isles*	*NE France, Belgium*
Insectivora	7	1	·	·	·	·	5	7
Chiroptera	·	·	·	·	·	·	11	13
Primates	·	2	·	·	·	1	1	1
Lagomorpha	1	1	1	·	·	·	2	1
Rodentia	10	5	5	1	1	2	9	13
Carnivora	9	5	7	2	2	4	9	10
Proboscidea	1	1	1	1	1	1	·	·
Perissodactyla	2	3	1	2	2	2	·	·
Artiodactyla	7	6	6	2	2	3	4	5
N-taxa	37	24	21	8	8	13	41	50

Source: Stuart (1982:96).

[a] West Runton freshwater bed (Cromerian).
[b] Swanscombe lower gravel/loam (Hoxnian).
[c] Joint Mitnor (Ipswichian) trap site.

[d] Wretton (E-Devensian) river terrace deposit.
[e] Tattershall Castle (M-Devensian) fluviatile gravel.
[f] Picken's Hole 3 (M-Devensian) hyaena den site.

smaller prey tend to be more sensitive to mean (usually summer) temperature. This is why, among mammals, smaller taxa generally are better indicators of climate change than larger ones. In lieu of direct observations on small mammal biogeography, tracing changes in total number of species is a cruder but necessary alternative for monitoring this process (e.g., Stuart 1982:73; Tchernov 1992). Species distributions may also vary along clines grading between maritime and continental settings or across latitude. Describing regional vegetation, and the animals dependent upon it, strictly in terms of latitudinal bands can be deceiving, however. Levels of heterogeneity in vegetation and the scales at which heterogeneity is expressed can be critical determinants of species diversity in animal communities (see, for example, discussions in Batcheler 1960; Guthrie 1990:200–272; Terborgh 1983; also Cody 1986; Wilcove et al. 1986 on separate but related effects of habitat fragmentation due to human development).

In high-latitude environments of the Pleistocene, the number of mammalian species in animal communities was quite sensitive to large-scale oscillations in global climate. Stuart (1982:96), for example, observes a precipitous drop in the number of

mammalian species during cold periods in Britain relative to interglacial periods. Stuart's comparisons of species richness across time involve multiple glaciation and deglaciation cycles, from roughly 350,000 to 10,000 years ago, and are based on faunas from open localities and caves (Table 4.3). The greatest changes occur in the relative abundances of small mammals, because these species typically have higher reproductive rates and feed upon invertebrates and/or plants.

How might the numbers of mammalian species in coastal west-central Italy, a lower-latitude environment, reflect climate change between 120,000 and 10,000 years ago? Britain has always been a relatively cooler geographic province than west-central Italy, although weather in both regions presently is partly regulated by maritime winds (today being a warm phase in the earth's history). The presence of fallow deer, roe deer, aurochs, wild boar, hippopotamus, elephant (*Palaeoloxodon antiquus*), rhinoceros (*Dicerorhinus*), smaller mammals such as *Macaca*, wood mouse, and the red-backed vole (*Clethrionomys glareolus*), as well as the European pond tortoise (*Emys orbicularis*), signals warm interglacial conditions in Britain. In contrast, arctic fox, mammoth, reindeer, and muskox, among others, mark the coldest periods (Stuart 1982:171). The number of species present in Britain only during interglacial phases (including Cromerian, Hoxnian, Ipswichian, and the modern one) is broadly akin to that of Italy for nearly the entire Upper Pleistocene.

The Italian data, which represent only cave faunas and a shorter time frame than Stuart's sample, nonetheless span significant changes in sea stand (Blanc and Segre 1953; Segre 1984) and global temperature (oxygen isotope stages 5e through 3, following Shackleton and Opdyke 1973). Indeed, the Italian faunas cover all but the coldest phase centering on 18,000 years ago (see Figure 3.6). The member species of animal communities cannot be expected to have remained absolutely the same over the course of the Pleistocene, but levels of species richness (numbers of species) should wax and wane with glacial-interglacial cycles if substantial shifts in local temperature conditions took place.

Table 4.4 suggests that the number of mammalian species in west-central Italy was consistently high throughout the Upper Pleistocene, apart from the

TABLE 4.4

Number of species (by Order) in paleontological and archaeological faunas from the Italian caves

Mammalian Order	eMP	lMP	UP	lUP
Insectivora	4	2	?	2
Chiroptera	4	2	?	5
Primata	1	1	1	1
Lagomorpha	2	2	1	1
Rodentia	7	7	2	7
Carnivora	10	10	4	9
Proboscidea	1	1	.	.
Perissodactyla	2	3	2	2
Artiodactyla	8	6	5	6
N-taxa	39	34	16[a]	33

[a]The sample is small, and rare taxa are unlikely to be represented.

Note: (eMP) earlier Middle Paleolithic-aged faunas (120,000–55,000 B.P.) from Moscerini and Guattari; (lMP) late Middle Paleolithic-aged faunas (50,000–35,000 B.P.) from Sant'Agostino, Breuil, and Buca della Iena; (UP) Upper Paleolithic cultural deposits (15,000 B.P.) from Palidoro; (lUP) late Upper Paleolithic (late Epigravettian) cultural deposits (12,500–10,000 B.P.) from Polesini and Salvini.

short unsampled gap around 18,000 B.P. The values for the late Middle Paleolithic (circa 50,000–35,000 B.P.) and the late Upper Paleolithic (circa 12,500–10,000 B.P.) are quite similar. The value for the earlier part of the Middle Paleolithic (circa 120,000–55,000 B.P.) following the Last Interglacial is only slightly higher. Palidoro is isolated in Table 4.4 due to its chronological age. Although it appears to be an exception, the sample is small for this kind of analysis and easily accounts for the lower number of mammal species. The Palidoro faunas date to around 15,000 B.P. by ^{14}C method, roughly one thousand years into a global warming trend. Land temperatures are not thought to have increased markedly until around 13,000 years ago (e.g., Dennell 1983), but Palidoro almost certainly represents warmer conditions than Riparo Salvini (at 12,000–12,500 B.P.) and possibly Grotta Polesini (10,000–11,000 B.P.).

The small sample for Palidoro taken into account, all of the values for Upper Pleistocene Italy resemble the values for interglacial and modern-day Britain (Table 4.4) but contrast with Britain's glacial values. The lack of substantial variation in the number of mammal species in coastal Italy with time indicates stability in animal communities of this area; the rates of species additions-deletions in the community per accumulation time were relatively constant.

Another useful comparison of numbers of mammalian species can be made with Israel, a Mediterranean region lying southeast of peninsular Italy. Tchernov's (1981:95–96) account of species additions and deletions indicates minimal change in the total number of taxa throughout the Upper Pleistocene. Of twenty-seven larger mammalian species living in Israel during that time, only three are lost by the middle of the Mousterian. More changes are apparent among the twenty smaller mammal species. All told, however, four species are lost and five gained from the beginning to the close of the Upper Pleistocene; the total number of mammalian species, large and small, changes from forty-six to forty-seven.

We may conclude that community structure was fairly stable in coastal Italy, consistent with what is known for Upper Pleistocene Israel. The relative abundances of species may have waxed and waned during this time range, but few new taxa were added and permanent deletions were rare. Italy simply never witnessed the replacement or loss of whole suites of species apparent in the north. Some periods in Upper Pleistocene Italy were relatively cold in human terms, but weather was not grossly distorted by glacial ice masses. Mediterranean plant and animal communities may also have been structured differently as a rule, allowing more taxa with diverse habitat requirements and tolerances to coexist.

The beginning and the end of the Mousterian segment of the Upper Pleistocene sequence in Italy nonetheless are bracketed by the loss and gain of two large species—hippopotamus and wild ass, respectively. An indisputably warm-conditions taxon, the modern hippopotamus has a tropical to subtropical distribution, extending as far north as the Nile River Valley in historic times. Hippopotamus bones are found in interglacial riverine deposits of West Germany and parts of Britain and France, in addition to Italy. Its association primarily to interglacial deposits in these regions suggests genuine sensitivity to ambient temperature and/or dependency upon very high plant productivity for its survival (Stuart 1982:89–90). In the Italian sample, hippopotamus remains are found only in the lowermost levels of Grotta dei Moscerini (levels 39 and 40, level group M4); these levels are older than 110,000 B.P. (see Table 3.3) and therefore approach the interglacial boundary. Hippopotamus remains are also reported by Cardini (in Blanc and Segre 1953) for the lower levels of Grotta Guattari (G3 and G4), but I was not able to locate the specimens, and there is some doubt as to whether they exist.

The arid open-land or cold-adapted wild ass (the extinct *Equus hydruntinus*) appears around the middle of the Mousterian (see also Blanc 1937a; Caloi and Palombo 1988 for other sites). A substantial increase in ibex parallels the appearance of wild ass, along with other species considered indicative of relatively colder conditions, such as marmot and possibly chamois. Wolverine is known only from the enormous late Upper Paleolithic assemblages of Grotta Polesini (circa 10,000 B.P.). However, the wolverine's exclusive presence there is best explained by sampling bias, not climate, since the living counterpart is rare in intact portions of its range.

In considering the Italian faunal series, it is clear that many taxa could tolerate a variety of environmental settings. Red deer, brown bear, and wolf are distributed widely and are highly versatile consumers throughout their modern ranges. However, these Eurasian animals coexisted in Pleistocene Italy with taxa of African origin, such as the spotted hyaena; no overlap exists in their modern geographic ranges. It is remarkable just how many other species—ones thought to possess distinct habitat preferences—managed to coexist in Italy. We know, for example, that the local climate grew significantly colder after about 55,000 years ago, because tree pollen profiles give way to those of grasses, artemesias, and chenopods around this time (Follieri et al. 1988; Frank 1969). The few gains and losses of mammalian taxa by the ecosystems of coastal Italy during the Upper Pleistocene are dwarfed by the startling assortment that weathered all changes in global temperature. The forest-loving roe deer coexisted with aurochs, fallow deer, wild ass, ibex, horse, elephant, and rhinoceros. Ibex populations may have surged in the later part of the chronological sequence, but they were already present in the area. Fallow deer, often described as a "warm" species, were not affected by conditions favoring the appearance of steppic/forest animals, such as wild ass and marmot (Caloi and Palombo 1988; Cassoli 1976–77:190). And the spotted hyaena, now restricted to Africa, once lived alongside the wolf, a predator now occurring only north of the Sahara (Ewer 1973:384; Savage 1988:19). The frequencies of spotted hyaena and wolf in Pleistocene Italy may have been inversely correlated in the general sense, however; a negative relationship is suggested by paleontological records of this region but requires further study.

The difference in mean annual temperature between Britain and the Mediterranean during phases of the Pleistocene apparently fostered distinct grains—patch sizes and distributions—and levels of complexity in plant communities in the respective regions (sensu Davis 1969). These differences would have affected the assembly of mammalian communities accordingly. Prolonged coexistence of "warm," "cold," "openland," and "forest" species in Mediterranean regions specifically suggests considerable heterogeneity in the plant communities. This general quality appears to have been maintained throughout the Upper Pleistocene, although the relative sizes of plant stands, their distributions in space, and the absolute frequencies of plant species may have varied.

The use of cold and warm species to infer climate conditions has some validity, but the Italian data suggest that the implications of any one can change with latitude, especially when large animals are concerned. In northerly regions, the passage of species may correspond to shifting bands of relatively homogeneous biotypes, such as the latitudinal extent of boreal versus deciduous forests, or open steppe versus tiaga and tundra. However, plant communities closer to the equator are more complex and, holding altitude constant, the rules of animal community assembly change as a consequence of heightened plant diversity and the grain of patchiness.

Data on habitat relationships among three species of deer in modern environments of Britain provide some clues about how environmental heterogeneity affected patterns of species coexistence in the past. The climate of modern Britain resembles interglacial conditions. Batcheler (1960) finds that changing local abundances of sympatric roe, fallow, and red deer follow the natural stages of plant succession in forests to a large degree. Roe deer are usu-

ally most abundant in young forests where the average tree diameter is small, but their numbers decline with the more advanced stages of forest succession. Red deer are more abundant in intermediate to later stage forest growth, and fallow deer show a preference for climax stands. Batcheler argues that the greater the heterogeneity in the ages of tree stands within any one forest, the closer the balance in the relative numbers of the three deer species.

This case from modern Britain may generally describe the patterns of community assembly in Upper Pleistocene Italy. Plant stands may have simply fragmented internally rather than shifted northward or southward in homogeneous bands, so that the grain of patchiness might be altered without much loss in vegetal heterogeneity. The maritime conditions and high topographic relief of coastal Italy may have emphasized heterogeneity in plant distributions further.

The details of animal and plant community structure in west-central Italy are largely matters of speculation. The most important finding from the regional comparisons is that mammalian species richness in Italy was both relatively high and fairly continuous throughout the time frame considered. (The short gap corresponding to the early Upper Paleolithic may be an exception; it is not represented in the study sample.) These facts provide an essential constant for comparing hominid and carnivore patterns of game use in that time and place.

POTENTIAL BONE COLLECTORS IN THE ITALIAN CAVES

The following discussion undertakes three things in succession. First, it introduces the common predator species represented in the study sample. A review of modern behavioral data evaluates how their remains may accumulate in caves and the potential of each species as a collector of herbivore bones in these settings. Second, the arrays and relative abundances of large mammal species (based on NISP) are outlined by site and vertical provenience, with special attention to the carnivores. Finally, comparisons of large and small carnivore NISP to ungulate NISP and to total lithic artifact counts identify

the assemblages as *probably* hominid-collected, carnivore-collected, or seriously mixed, as preparation for the taphonomic analyses in Chapter 5. Statistical assessments of relative abundances of species in relation to sample size are not undertaken until Chapter 7.

The very presence of carnivore skeletal remains in shelter deposits suggests a possible role in assemblage formation: animals that use dens often die in them. The associations can be further refined with wildlife data for modern counterparts or closely related species. The presence of lithic artifacts, on the

TABLE 4.5
Summary of Mousterian lithic counts, large carnivore and ungulate NISP from the Italian caves

Site and provenience	Total lithics	Large carnivore NISP	Ungulate NISP	Large carnivore NISP: ungulate NISP
Moscerini M1	45	0	16	.00
M2	382	2	37	.05
M3	324	3	358	.01
M4	187	2	157	.01
M5	127	154	430	.36
M6	196	3	184	.02
Guattari G0	2	108	849	.13
G1	240	80	615	.13
G2	452	13	104	.08
G3	0	1	4	.25[a]
G4	876	3	50	.06
G5	482	0	49	.00
G6	0	0	0	.00
G7	0	0	6	.00
Sant'Agostino S0	2863	24	744	.03
S1	3138	26	752	.03
S2	975	7	349	.02
S3	451	16	160	.10
S4	212	24	134	.18
SX	0	82	473	.17
Breuil Br	3249	34	928	.06
B3/4	—	32[b]	576	.05
Buca della Iena I1–2	35	75	105	.71
I3	33	68	36	1.89
I4	46	106	77	1.38
I5	0	94	102	.92
I6	0	206	299	.69

[a] The bone sample is too small for the ratio value to be meaningful: one large carnivore bone to four ungulate bones.
[b] Value represents highly localized concentrations of large carnivore remains above Breuil B3/4.

other hand, unequivocally testifies to human use of a site, regardless of what else has taken place there, and represents a way to isolate human components independently of herbivore abundance. The total quantity of lithic artifacts (tools, flakes, cores, and debris) in each level also provides a coarse measure of occupational intensity or duration by hominids (Table 4.5). However, the stratigraphic association of animal bones and stone tools cannot exclude the possibility of carnivore activity unless large carnivore bones and gnawing damage are absent.

In making these comparisons, I assume that hominids discarded lithic artifacts in every shelter they used. This is reasonable because Paleolithic and many later technologies require continual manufacture and/or modification of stone, causing people to drop things wherever they went. I also assume that denning is the most likely cause of deposition of carnivore remains in the Italian caves, not their having fallen prey to hominids. As we will see in later chapters, this assumption seldom is contradicted by the patterns of bone damage (Chapters 5 and 6) and carnivore age structure (Chapter 12).

Bone collectors and noncollectors:
Modern behavioral evidence

Not all carnivores that use shelters collect bones in them. It is possible to separate predators that use shelters into two behavioral categories, bone collectors and noncollectors, based on what living representatives do in natural situations. Carnivores often fall prey to other carnivores and may become part of den assemblages for this reason. The general tendencies to investigate others' den sites and to tailgate the occupants while foraging greatly enhance the probability of inter- and intraspecific violence. Den defense behaviors are intended to keep strangers at bay, but general interest in shelter often brings a carnivore within the predatory range of another.

The arrays of carnivore taxa in the Italian cave faunas tend to be diverse, never monospecific. Shelters apparently had a more or less uniform appeal to all den-using predators or they appealed to none; the longer the time frame, the more carnivore species one can expect to find in the deposits. Coastal caves in Italy contain the remains of brown and/or cave bear, spotted hyaena, wolf, red fox, lion, leopard, wild cat, lynx, badger, polecat, pine martin, weasel, wolverine, and even monk seal (see Table 4.1). Carnivore frequencies in the faunal assemblages follow one of two basic patterns. The first pattern is carnivore-rich—generally some combination of bear (a hibernating omnivore), one large social carnivore (wolf or spotted hyaena), and a wider range of small carnivores (mostly red fox, wild cat, and badger). The carnivore-rich faunas are dominated by just one or two of the large predators (principally spotted hyaena or wolf) and bear. Some of these faunas are also associated with very sparse lithic scatters, but the hominid components are very ephemeral. The second kind of pattern is nearly devoid of large predator remains—except the occasional fragments of bear—but rich in lithic artifacts, accompanied by variable quantities of small carnivores. It is clear that *large* carnivore represen-

tation is pivotal to understanding human versus carnivore roles in collecting herbivore bones in the caves. Small carnivores can represent prey of either humans or large carnivores, or casualties in a den, but they generally are not gatherers of large herbivore bones.

The incidence of bear (usually brown bear [*Ursus arctos*], but sometimes cave bear [*U. spelaeus*]) is relatively constant throughout the carnivore-rich faunas, reinforcing my earlier assertion that all assemblages in this study are palimpsests of many events. In carnivore-poor faunas, bears are usually the only large species present. Interassemblage comparisons indicate that bear frequencies are neutral or independent with respect to herbivore abundance; the paleontological evidence suggests that bears contribute their own bones to cave faunas, but they are not regular collectors of ungulate bones. Bears may simply indicate gaps in the occupations of other predators (human and nonhuman), time windows large enough to make the shelter an attractive place to hibernate.

The significance of bear remains in caves is not widely understood by archaeologists (e.g., see discussion following Stiner 1991a). Although the cave bear is extinct, we may assume that these bears denned in order to hibernate, because this is the main reason why modern bear species use dens. They may be attacked by other predators (including humans) during this time (e.g., Mattson et al. 1992), but most bear bones in cave deposits represent nonviolent deaths. Bear remains are abundant in caves because mortality rates are high during and, especially, at the end of hibernation (e.g., Garshelis and Pelton 1980; Kurtén 1976; Rogers 1981, 1987; Stuart 1982:85). Some of the best research on the hibernation process and associated mortality has been done on the American black bear (*U. americanus*), because this species is still fairly common in the lower forty-eight states (U.S.A.) and makes for a relatively tractable subject (see, for example, Hellgren et al. 1990; Garshelis and Pelton 1980; Johnson and Pelton 1980; see also Watts and Jonkel 1988 on grizzly bears, and Watts et al. 1987 on polar bears). Although black and brown bears represent distinct species of the genus *Ursus*, they have much in common biologically, including most details of their hibernation behavior. Wildlife data on black bears in particular unlock some of the secrets of bear natural history relevant to brown bear accumulations in Pleistocene shelters (also see recent work on brown bears in Italy, Tassi 1983; in Spain, Clevenger 1990, 1991; Clevenger et al. 1987, 1988, 1992; Clevenger and Purroy 1991; and in North America, Watts and Jonkel 1988).

Starvation is the principal cause of death in modern bear cubs and yearlings in the areas where they have been studied extensively (e.g., Rogers 1987). The energetic cost of dormancy is relatively high and invariant (Watts and Jonkel 1988; Watts et al. 1987), whereas foraging conditions change all of the time. Bears are especially prone to malnutrition toward the end of hibernation following lean years. Starvation actually leads to a shortened hibernation period: the animal awakens early in a sometimes futile attempt to compensate for the energy that it could not gain the previous autumn. An undernourished bear may even emerge while the ground is still covered by snow, before spring forage is available. The bear responds to this dire situation by shortening the lengths of its forays from the den, resting and trying to outwait the lean period. These individuals often die inside or in the immediate vicinity (often the entrance) of their lairs.

Brown and black bears generally are not known to collect food debris in dens. This behavior conflicts with the need to reduce odors that might betray the sleeping bear's location to other predators. Bears are very vulnerable when torpid, as documented attacks by wolves, people, and other bears attest (e.g., Rogers 1987:53; Tietje et al. 1986). They appear furtive in their choice of den sites and avoid advertising the site. Black bears typically amass piles of vegetable bedding in hibernation dens, but not food. Likewise, Clevenger (1991) reports twigs and other plant material in abandoned dens of the Cantabrian brown bear, but no bones. The cave faunas of Italy show that brown and cave bears frequently made use of natural shelters in the past. Modern data indicate that bears do not collect herbivore bones in caves, although they will hibernate in caves if suitable ones are available (Clevenger and Purroy 1991:113–123). While ancient bear remains sometimes co-occur with the bones of other mammals, we have no reason to assume that

bears were responsible for bones other than their own.

The remains of large cats, lion (*Panthera leo*) and leopard (*P. pardus*), are present in some of the cave sites, but they are rare and represented only by the odd skull, mandible, and/or tooth fragment. Leopards are known to create bone assemblages in karst cavities in South Africa (Brain 1981) as they feed in trees near natural fissures or sinks. Leopard remains are common in many Upper Pleistocene cave records of Europe (e.g., in Hortus, de Lumley 1972), but there is little evidence of them in the study sample. The role of leopards as bone collectors cannot be absolutely excluded in this study (see exchange between Turner and Stiner, following Stiner 1991a), but the paucity of their remains and absence of felid scatological bone (Chapter 5) make it unlikely.

In contrast, spotted hyaenas (*Crocuta crocuta*) and wolves (*Canis lupus*) commonly occupied the Mousterian caves. Unlike bears, they are avid and deliberate collectors of bones at modern dens (e.g., Ballard et al. 1987; Binford 1981; Ewer 1973; Fentress and Ryon 1982; Henschel et al. 1979; Hill 1980a, 1980b, 1984; Kruuk 1972; Mech 1970; Mills 1984a; Mills and Mills 1977; Murie 1944; Rutter and Pimlott 1968; Sutcliffe 1970; Tilson et al. 1980). The bone-collecting habits of wolves and hyaenas come under fuller discussion in Chapters 8 and 9; here, it is sufficient to assert that wolves were prevalent in Italy until recently (e.g., Boscagli 1985), and they were important bone collectors in some caves along the west-central Italian coast (see also Stuart 1982:87 for Pleistocene Britain). Large social groups may occupy dens, either as parents and helpers (wolves), or because dens are used communally (spotted hyaenas). This fact, along with high reproductive and infant mortality rates, accounts for substantial accumulations of wolf or hyaena bones in den deposits (see Chapter 12).

Smaller carnivores, principally foxes, may also collect bones in shelters, but of smaller prey (Burton 1979; Ewer 1973). The European wild cat (*Felis sylvestris*) and lynx (*Lynx lynx*) are primarily hunters of lagomorphs in some areas, and elsewhere hunters of mice, shrews, and squirrels, supplemented by rabbits, hares, marmot, and occasionally young deer. The red fox (*Vulpes vulpes*) feeds primarily on lagomorphs and rodents, along with (especially ground-nesting) birds, insects, fruit, and carrion (Ewer 1973; Ozoga et al. 1982; Stuart 1982:84–86). Of the two, the wild cat tends to focus more on lagomorphs, whereas the fox is more likely to take smaller prey, particularly rodents (Burton 1979). Red foxes may den communally (Macdonald 1979) and are known to carry bones to dens to feed mates and young (Burton 1979). Like other canids, red foxes are diligent, deliberate bone collectors and cachers, often scavenging or pilfering from other predators. It is conceivable that foxes might scavenge bones of larger herbivores and carry them to dens, but it is unlikely that they would produce substantial accumulations of large mammals there.

The diet of the Eurasian badger (*Meles meles*) is more varied than those of foxes and wild cats, but also is restricted primarily to smaller prey. While badgers rely on natural or excavated shelters, they are not known to carry food to their dens. Burton (1979:113–125) provides a comprehensive account of the habits of this social species: many individuals may live in traditional den sites, called "setts," ringed by networks of well-worn trails. Den excavations are extensive, with multiple entrances and conspicuous piles of disturbed soil. Badger setts occur in wooded and hilly country where well-drained soils and some plant cover are available, including low sea cliffs where crevices and caves are common.

Badgers not only avoid carrying food back to dens; they actively clean these areas. Old nesting material is purged yearly, and they routinely defecate in open pit latrines some distance away. Badgers are not true hibernators, but, like raccoons, they may go into a reduced metabolic state in winter (Burton 1979; Ewer 1973) The diet is thoroughly omnivorous, and meat other than rodents is obtained mainly by scavenging; badgers are known to kill the young of larger mammals on occasion.

The basic badger social unit consists of a female and her young, but these units are organized into clans consisting of multiple reproducing females, juveniles, and a variable number of males. Only dominant males actively defend the home range, and bachelor clans, consisting exclusively of males, may form periodically (Kruuk 1978). Two, three, or more sows may occupy a sett; several setts may be incorporated within a communal range, with much visiting among them. Fidelity to den sites can span many generations of badgers, lasting decades or even centuries, creating a steady, ample rain of badger bones into the deposits.

Some of the Italian caves along the sea contain remains of monk seal (*Monachus monachus*), a small phocid once distributed throughout the Mediterranean (Eisenberg 1981:137). This shy species has received little study and is severely threatened throughout the remainder of its geographic range; less than five hundred individuals exist today. Certain features of its life history, extrapolated in part from what is known about a closely related cousin, the Hawaiian monk seal (*M. schauinslandi*), help explain the presence of Mediterranean monk seal bones in the Upper Pleistocene caves.

The monk seal is a shore-adapted species and relatively solitary in habit. Lone or small groups of pregnant females seek caves along the shore in which to give birth (Wirtz 1968). The female and her pup stay ashore for about five weeks, after which they leave the area. Infant mortality accounts for some seal deaths inside caves. The first few weeks of aquatic life are especially dangerous for monk seals; many pups die from accidents, exhaustion, and predator attacks. Those that perish at sea usually wash back to shore (Wirtz 1968:237–238). Scant remains of only two individuals (see below) are found in the Italian Mousterian caves—one individual in level group M5 of Grotta dei Moscerini and another in layer S2 of Grotta di Sant'Agostino. The animal represented in Moscerini may have perished in its own den, or it was killed or scavenged by terrestrial carnivores (M5 is rich in hyaena remains). Of the few seal bones in Sant'Agostino, the carpal is cut marked, indicating butchering by hominids. Because Moscerini and Sant'Agostino date to different segments of the Upper Pleistocene, one can assume that seals were present along the shores of this area throughout the Middle Paleolithic.

While birds of prey (mainly owls) are not the main subject of this chapter, they, too, contributed to the rodent faunas in some cases. Other birds, along with bats, roosted in the cave vaults and merely fell into the deposits as they died.

TABLE 4.6
Grotta dei Moscerini: NISP counts for large mammals by level group and taxon

Taxa	M1	M2	M3	M4	M5	M6	TOTAL
CARNIVORA							
red fox	·	·	·	·	15	·	15
brown bear	·	1	3	2	74	2	82
spotted hyaena	·	1	·	·	76	1?	77
wild cat	·	·	·	·	17	·	17
monk seal	·	·	·	·	4	·	4
carnivore total:	·	2	3	2	186	3	196
PERISSODACTYLA							
horse	·	·	1	·	14	·	15
rhino	2	·	2	1	·	·	5
ARTIODACTYLA							
fallow deer	2	2	13	8	67	28	120
roe deer	6	2	65	16	137	18	244
red deer	4	21	240	123	140	120	648
aurochs	2	·	4	·	22	8	36
ibex	·	·	15	5	5	·	25
wild boar	·	·	4	·	·	·	4
hippotamus	·	·	·	2	·	·	2
MU	·	12	14	2	45	10	83
ungulate total:	16	37	358	157	430	184	1182

Note: (·) not present; (MU) medium-sized ungulate; data are for specimens with provenience designations only.

Large mammal species arrays by site and level

Table 4.6 lists NISP for carnivore and ungulate species in the six level groups of Grotta dei Moscerini. The quantities of carnivore remains are very small, except in M5, where carnivores are abundant by contrast. Bear and spotted hyaena predominate among the carnivores in M5, accompanied by low frequencies of fox, wild cat, and monk seal. Some lithic artifacts are also present in M5, but in comparatively low frequencies. Of the carnivore remains, only those of brown and (rarely) cave bear occur throughout the level groups; they are much more common in M5, however, where they co-occur with other carnivore bones. The incidence of bear remains is least responsive to the presence of lithic artifacts in the Moscerini series. Because modern bears (of the genus *Ursus*) generally are not known to collect herbivore bones in dens, spotted hyaenas are the principal candidates as collectors of ungulates in M5.

In contrast to patterns of carnivore abundance, ungulate remains are present throughout the Moscerini series, with comparable NISP values in M3 and M5, and lower yet comparable values in M4 and M6. Red deer is the most common ungulate by a wide margin, followed by roe deer. Level group M5 represents an exception in that red deer and roe deer codominate. A variety of other ungulate taxa are also present in low frequencies, including horse, rhinoceros (tooth fragments only), hippopotamus (tooth fragments only), fallow deer, aurochs, ibex, and wild boar. Apart from M5, variation in total ungulate NISP can be explained by lithic artifact frequencies (see Table 4.5), suggesting that hominids were the principal bone collectors in level groups M2, M3, M4, and M6. On the other hand, ungulate NISP is highest in M5, suggesting longer accumulation times or greater food transport opportunities enjoyed by hyaenas. Ungulate NISP for M1 is 7—too small to merit discussion.

Each level group in Moscerini represents multiple occupational episodes, based on the amount of sediment buildup and the presence of multiple lenses therein. The generally negative relationship between the frequencies of carnivore remains and stone tools among level groups also indicates stratigraphic separation of hominid and spotted hyaena occupations in most of the sequence. As noted above, lithics and hyaena bones co-occur in level group M5, but lithics are fewer in relation to her-

bivore bones (below). Postdepositional disturbance by the hyaenas, rather than alternating occupations, may be the cause of mixed components in this case.

Table 4.7 lists NISP data for carnivore and ungulate species from the preserved surface (G0) and in the seven subsurface levels (G1–7) of Grotta Guattari. Levels G3 and G6 are essentially sterile horizons; the few bones in G3 are probably intrusions from the levels above. The quantities of both ungulate and carnivore bones are much greater in G0 and G1 than in the lower levels, decreasing from G2 downward. Spotted hyaena is the dominant species

TABLE 4.7
Grotta Guattari: NISP counts for large mammals by level and taxon

Taxa	*G0*	*G1*	*G2*	*G3*	*G4*	*G5*	*G7*	*TOTAL*
CARNIVORA								
wolf	3	1	·	·	·	·	·	4
fox	·	+	+	·	+	·	·	·
cave bear[a]	10	1	·	·	+	·	·	11
spotted hyaena	91	77	13	1	3	·	·	185
leopard[b]	4	1	·	·	·	·	·	5
polecat	·	·	·	·	+	·	·	·
carnivore total:	108	80	13	1	3	·	·	205
PRIMATA								
Neandertal	3	·	·	·	·	·	·	3
PROBOSCIDEA								
elephant	3	+	+	·	·	·	·	3
PERISSODACTYLA								
horse	65	60	3	2	5	+	·	135
rhino (*R. merckii*)	1	+	·	·	+	·	·	1
ARTIODACTYLA								
fallow deer	90	17	13	+	12	+	·	132
roe deer	48	5	13	+	+	2	·	68
red deer	406	349	33	+	16	10	·	814
giant deer	1	·	·	·	·	·	·	1
aurochs	202	156	20	1	16	37	6	438
ibex	·	+	+	·	·	·	·	·
wild boar	33	28	22	1	1	·	·	85
hippopotamus	·	·	·	+	+	·	·	+
ungulate total:	849	615	104	4	50	49	6	1677

[a]Classification as cave bear is based on Cardini's identification (Blanc and Segre 1953).
[b]One specimen previously noted as leopard (posterior section of skull) is probably lion.

Note: (·) not present, (+) species appears in Cardini's provisional list of species presence-absence published in Blanc and Segre (1953), but I found no evidence of it in the collection; values are for specimens with provenience designations only.

among carnivores, averaging around 90 percent. Bones of cave bear, wolf, leopard, and probably lion are present but rare in G0–1.

The prevalence of spotted hyaena remains on G0 and in G1 leaves little reason to doubt that they were largely if not wholly responsible for bone accumulations there. About 12.5 kilos of hyaena coprolites were also recovered from these levels (a few from G2). Hyaenas played a role in creating the assemblage in G2 as well, but the presence of many lithic artifacts (N = 452) also indicates a strong hominid component in this level.

Red deer is the most common ungulate species in the hyaena-associated levels G0 and G1, followed by aurochs, and much lower frequencies of roe deer, fallow deer, wild boar, and horse. Scant remains of elephant, rhinoceros, and giant deer

(*Megaceros* sp.) are also present. The sample sizes for levels G2 through G5 are quite small, yet some relatively rare species persist, and aurochs appears more common.

Carnivore NISP and artifact counts in Guattari show a strongly negative relationship through the strata, but there is no clear relationship between carnivore NISP and ungulate NISP. Differences in preservation cannot account for this pattern, because the condition of bone specimens is good throughout the levels in which bones are found. Mousterian lithics are present in level G1, but are more common in G2, G4, and G5, where they number 400 or more per level (see Table 4.5).

Table 4.8 lists NISP data for carnivore and ungulate species in the six layers of Grotta di Sant'Agostino. Each layer contains Mousterian

TABLE 4.8
Grotta di Sant'Agostino: NISP counts for large mammals by layer and taxon

Taxa	S0	S1	S2	S3	S4	SX	TOTAL
CARNIVORA							
wolf	10	21	3	11	21	76	142
red fox	54	54	62	31	10	29	240
brown bear	13	4	3	3	1	6	30
weasel	1	·	·	·	·	·	1
pine martin	·	·	·	4	·	·	4
badger	1	2	1	1	·	·	5
wild cat	21	22	36	14	2	3	98
lynx	·	1	·	·	·	·	1
leopard	1	1	·	2	2	·	6
monk seal	·	·	1	·	·	1	2
carnivore total:	101	105	106	66	36	115	529
PERISSODACTYLA							
horse	9	21	6	2	4	·	42
wild ass	·	1	1	1	·	·	3
rhino (*Rhinoceros* sp.)	9	10	2	·	·	·	21
ARTIODACTYLA							
fallow deer	138	118	47	23	15	10	351
roe deer	146	106	52	28	32	211	575
red deer	246	283	162	69	30	26	816
aurochs	51	72	16	7	5	4	155
ibex	74	73	33	17	40	221	458
wild boar	71	68	30	13	8	1	191
ungulate total:	744	752	349	160	134	473	2612

Note: (·) not present; NISP counts may not be in complete agreement with those presented in Tozzi (1970) due to slightly different criteria of bone identifiability.

tools and debris (see Table 4.5), with the exception of the separate, shallow unit called SX. Lithic artifacts are most abundant in S0, S1, and S2; those in S0 are mostly Mousterian (Laj Pannocchia 1950; Tozzi 1970; and Kuhn [1990a] estimates that 80 percent of all tools are Mousterian), whereas the other levels contain Mousterian artifacts exclusively. Ungulate remains likewise are most abundant in layers S0 and S1, but ungulates also are fairly abundant in SX, where stone tools are absent.

A wide variety of predator taxa are represented in Sant'Agostino, including wolf, fox, wild cat, brown bear, weasel, pine martin, badger, leopard, and rarely, lynx or monk seal. A quick scan of Table 4.8 reveals the strong presence of wolf, fox, and wild cat. Wolf is most common in layers SX (no lithics), followed by S4 (lithics = 212) and S1 (lithics = 3138). It is significant that fox and wild cat are most abundant where wolf is less so, suggesting some measure of mutual exclusion for as yet undetermined reasons. Of the rarer species, bear, badger, and leopard are the most widely, if thinly, scattered among the layers. The fact that lithic artifact frequencies and total carnivore NISP do not segregate very well in the S0–4 series (excluding SX) implies complex histories of assemblage formation at this site.

In the upper layers of Sant'Agostino (S0, S1, S2, and S3), red deer predominate among ungulates, followed by roe and fallow deer. The situation is quite different in layers S4 and SX, where roe deer and, especially, ibex are more abundant. Ibex NISP is linked to wolf NISP, whereas red deer NISP increases with lithic artifact abundance. Rare ungulate taxa in Sant'Agostino include the wild ass (*Equus hydruntinus*), whose appearance in S2 (and S1, as reported by Tozzi 1970) is the earliest in the study sample (ESR 53,000 ± 7000 B.P.). Wild ass co-occurs with remains of marmot, horse, fallow deer, aurochs, and wild boar. Lynx, probably the southern or pardel variant[3] (Burton 1979:147), oc-

curs only in low frequencies in layer S1 (and in SX, as reported by Tozzi 1970).

Tozzi (1970) attempted to trace climate shifts based on differing frequencies of three deer species, wild ass, and ibex among the layers of Sant'Agostino. While the presence of wild ass and marmot might reflect cooler conditions, most or all differences in species abundance in this site are better explained by the relative frequencies of wolf NISP to lithic artifacts. The latter comparisons suggest that hominids were the primary bone collectors in S0, S1, S2, and S3, even if assemblage formation processes were complicated by other factors. Wolves appear to be the foremost collectors of ungulate bones in S4 and the sole collectors in SX.

Table 4.9 lists NISP data for carnivore and ungulate species in the uppermost in situ deposit and from the redeposited material (Br) of Grotta Breuil. Level B3/4 averages around 36,600 ± 2700 years old by ESR technique, representing the youngest documented Mousterian cultural deposits in the cave and for Latium as a whole. Ungulate remains are abundant in Breuil, but carnivores are rare. A highly localized concentration of carnivore remains, including wolf, bear, and spotted hyaena (and one hyaena coprolite), is identified at the back of the cave; this concentration postdates the cultural material in B3 and accounts for virtually all large carnivores in excavated portions of the site. The concentration of carnivore remains may represent minor den components beginning when the cave was nearly filled by sediment, after Mousterian hominids stopped using the cave.

Red deer and ibex dominate the ungulate remains from Breuil B3/4. Ungulate remains in Br (an amalgam of material originating from contiguous unexcavated strata below B3) are dominated by red deer, followed by roe deer, aurochs, and ibex, and much lower quantities of other ungulate species. Rare remains of wild ass and probably chamois occur in B3/4 and Br, and elephant (tooth fragment only) and rhinoceros remains were recovered from Br.

[3] Opinions vary on the proper classification of the pardel lynx (Burton 1979:147). Two or more populations of lynx may be distinguished in the Old World based on general appearance, body size, and habitats occupied. The classic form (*Lynx lynx*) occurs throughout the boreal forests of Europe and North America. The southern or pardel variant was native to the Mediterra-

nean region until roughly A.D. 1500 and may have occupied an ecological niche analogous to that of the American bobcat (*L. rufus*) and the caracal (*L. caracal*). Both the boreal and pardel lynxes today inhabit dense woodlands; the boreal variant lives in pine forests and the pardel variant in Mediterranean-type scrub oak forests.

TABLE 4.9
Grotta Breuil: NISP counts for large mammals by level
and taxon

Taxa	B3/4	Br
CARNIVORA		
wolf	22	9
red fox	5	9
brown bear	10	1
spotted hyaena	2[a]	.
wild cat	6	2
carnivore total:	45	21
PRIMATA		
Neandertal (?)	.	3
PROBOSCIDEA		
elephant	.	1
PERISSODACTYLA		
horse	8	13
wild ass	1	1?
rhino (*Rhinoceros* sp.)	.	6
ARTIODACTYLA		
fallow deer	9	2
roe deer	14	35
red deer	112	168
aurochs	22	40
ibex	184	22
chamois	1?	?
wild boar	.	1
SU	5	108
MU	206	415
LU	14	116
ungulate total:	576	928

[a]Includes one hyaena coprolite.

Note: (·) not present, (SU) small ungulate, (MU) medium ungulate, (LU) large ungulate.

Table 4.10 lists NISP data for carnivore and ungulate species in the six levels of Buca della Iena. This site is primarily a spotted hyaena den complex, first described by Pitti and Tozzi (1971) and the source of "soft" control cases for this study. Buca della Iena was excavated more recently than most of the other caves, and the excavators saved all bone and tooth material, including the unidentifiable fragments. Buca della Iena lies approximately 300 km north of the Latium caves, but, like them, is situated in uplifted limestone near the Mediterranean coast. Ephemeral use by Mousterian hominids is evident from the few lithic artifacts in levels I1 through I4, totaling 114 pieces (see Table 4.5).

Identifiable bones (NISP) are not bountiful in any level of Buca della Iena, and carnivore frequencies approach those for ungulates. Spotted hyaenas and brown bears dominate the carnivore fractions, and their presence is fairly consistent from one level to the next. Badgers are present in levels I3 through I5, where they constitute substantial proportions of the carnivore remains. Bones of wolf, fox, polecat, wild cat, lynx, and leopard are found in some levels, but they are rare. High hyaena NISP values throughout and very low lithic artifact counts in levels I1–4 suggest that hominids had little influence in the bone accumulations in this site.

Ungulate species frequencies in Buca della Iena present some subtle but interesting contrasts to the Latium cave faunas. Red deer and horse codominate, and aurochs is the next most common species in most levels. Horse, in particular, tends to be comparatively rare in the Latium caves. Roe deer are rare in Buca della Iena, and fallow deer, ibex, and wild ass are entirely absent.

The radiometric dates for level I5 (U-series, between 41,000 and 51,000 years ago) suggest that the dens of Buca della Iena are roughly coeval with the cultural deposits of Grotta di Sant'Agostino and Grotta Breuil. The presence of marmot (see Chapter 6) in Buca della Iena may be linked to a general global cooling trend, consistent with the faunas of Sant'Agostino and Breuil. Rare fragments of elephant and rhinoceros demonstrate that these taxa persisted in west-central Italy into late Mousterian times, perhaps later. The relatively great abundance of horse and scarcity of roe deer, however, is more likely due to local differences in environment; more open terrain may have existed around Buca della Iena.

The next four tables present data for Upper Paleolithic faunas from lowland rockshelters in Latium. Grotta Palidoro (near Rome) and Riparo Salvini (at Terracina) are located on or near the coast, while Grotta Polesini lies inland on the Aniene River. Another source of soft controls, the carnivore and ungulate remains in these faunas are largely or wholly attributable to humans, although very low levels of carnivore modification of human food debris are apparent in some cases (Chapter 5).

TABLE 4.10
Buca della Iena: NISP counts for large mammals by level and taxon

Taxa	*11*	*12*	*13*	*14*	*15*	*16*	*TOTAL*
CARNIVORA							
wolf	·	·	1?	5	3	4	13
red fox	2?	1	·	·	·	·	3
cave bear	26	4	32	75	40	53	230
polecat	·	·	·	1	·	·	1
badger	3	·	23	22	30	1	79
spotted hyaena	32	13	33	25	48	149	300
wild cat	·	·	·	·	6	·	6
lynx	·	1?	1?	·	·	·	2?
leopard	·	·	2	1	2	·	5
carnivore total:	63	19	92	129	129	207	639
PROBOSCIDEA							
elephant	·	·	·	·	1	1	2
PERISSODACTYLA							
horse	30	4	2	8	14	119	177
rhino (*Rhinoceros* sp.)	4?	·	·	·	5	7	16
ARTIODACTYLA							
roe deer	2	1	2	13	10	7	35
red deer	19	3	6	15	17	82	142
giant deer	·	·	2	1?	·	11?	14?
aurochs	11	1	2	4	7	27	52
wild boar	1	·	2	3	10	3	19
MU	6	3	12	17	16	15	69
LU	14	6	8	16	22	27	93
ungulate total:	87	18	36	77	102	299	619

Note: (·) not present, (MU) medium ungulate, (LU) large ungulate; cave bear is listed here in accordance with identifications by Pitti and Tozzi (1971:225). They also report both leopard and lion, but I was able to find only leopard.

Table 4.11 lists NISP data for carnivore and ungulate species from arbitrary cuts 1 through 8 of the 1955 excavations at Grotta Palidoro (data from Cassoli 1976–77), and for cuts 33 and 34 of Chiappella's 1956–59 excavations at the same rockshelter (my data). Both sets of assemblages are roughly contemporaneous, dating to around 15,000 years ago by ^{14}C technique. Carnivore remains are rare throughout and, of these, badger is most notable. Red deer is the most common ungulate species, but not by a large margin; wild ass and aurochs are nearly as abundant. Horse, roe deer, and wild boar occur in much lower frequencies, and ibex is especially rare. The most conspicuous contrasts to Middle Paleolithic faunas are the relatively higher incidence of both aurochs and wild ass in Palidoro and the paucity of carnivores, roe deer, and ibex. The high frequencies of wild ass and aurochs may suggest larger expanses of open grass zones in the local environment around 15,000 years ago.

Table 4.12 lists NISP data for carnivore and ungulate species in cuts 10 through 15 of Riparo Salvini, excavated by Bietti in 1988 (see also Bietti and Stiner 1992) and dating to about 12,000 to 12,500 years ago by ^{14}C technique. Small carnivore (fox and wild cat) remains are comparatively rare, and large carnivores are absent. Red deer dominate the ungulate fraction, more so than in Palidoro, although wild ass and horse are also fairly common. Aurochs, roe deer, chamois, and ibex are present but rare. Occurrences of chamois bones in lowland sites are considered by some researchers to signal

TABLE 4.11
Grotta Palidoro: NISP counts for large mammals by level and taxon

Taxa	1	2	3	4	5	6	7	8	TOTAL	33–34
CARNIVORA										
wolf	1	·	1	·	1	·	·	1	4	·
red fox	·	·	·	·	·	·	·	1	1	·
badger	·	·	2	1	5	3	7	4	22	8
lion	·	·	·	·	·	1	·	·	1	·
carnivore total:	1	·	3	1	6	4	7	6	28	8
PERISSODACTYLA										
horse	4	5	3	·	7	3	32	19	73	25
wild ass	24	12	42	9	98	48	86	33	352	100
ARTIODACTYLA										
roe deer	·	1	1	·	4	1	·	5	12	1
red deer	16	27	42	19	140	68	143	77	532	245
aurochs	24	25	32	4	71	17	50	12	235	185
ibex	1	·	·	·	·	·	·	·	1	1
wild boar	7	11	7	5	10	1	15	9	65	19
MU	·	·	·	·	·	·	·	·	·	127
LU	·	·	·	·	·	·	·	·	·	90
ungulate total:	76	81	127	37	330	138	326	155	1270	793

Source for cuts 1–8: Cassoli (1976–77), avian fauna omitted.

Note: (·) not present, (MU) medium ungulate (LU) large ungulate.

cooler climatic conditions, but the few chamois remains in the late Mousterian and late Upper Paleolithic sites could also be interpreted as rare game acquisitions, taken in a remote area and carried back to the shelters by human hunters.

Table 4.13 lists NISP data for carnivore and ungulate species in cuts 1 through 12 of the late Upper Paleolithic site of Grotta Polesini (data from Radmilli 1974). Polesini is thought to date to around 10,000 years ago, with the assemblages forming relatively quickly, based on industrial (Epigravettian) and mobile art associations to other sites. An enormous quantity of material was found in this rockshelter, but the deposits lack discernible stratigraphy. Red deer is the most common ungulate species (averaging 71 percent overall), whereas all other ungulate species are relatively uncommon: horse, wild ass, roe deer, aurochs, chamois, ibex, and wild boar.

There is little variation in taxonomic representation among the cuts of the Palidoro shelter. Carnivore remains are relatively uncommon, although several smaller taxa are represented due to the large sample sizes available. Red fox is most abundant by far, followed in descending order by badger, wild cat, and wolf. Remains of brown bear, weasel, pine martin, wolverine, and lynx are present but rare. The novel addition of wolverine to the array is best explained by a large sample size, because species that are rare in modern ecosystems (always true for wolverines) tend to be "invisible" in small, non-selective samples (e.g., Fisher et al. 1943). Today, wolverines are found primarily in boreal forests, but they are not restricted to these habitats (Stuart 1982:86).

Summary: Lithic artifact counts versus carnivore NISP

The relationships among carnivore, ungulate, and lithic artifact frequencies are evaluated below, using ungulate NISP as the baseline for the comparisons. Examining the data in this way illuminates fundamental contrasts within the Italian sample, es-

TABLE 4.12

Riparo Salvini: NISP counts for large mammals from the 1988 excavations

Taxa	Cuts 10–15
CARNIVORA	
red fox	1
wild cat	1
MM	4
carnivore total:	6
PERISSODACTYLA	
horse	13
wild ass	37
ARTIODACTYLA	
roe deer	9
red deer	98
aurochs	4
chamois	1?
ibex	4
SU	43
MU	368
LU	75
ungulate total:	652

Source: Bietti and Stiner (1992).

Note: (·) not present, (SU) small ungulate, (MU) medium ungulate, (LU) large ungulate, (MM) medium-sized mammal.

sentially distinguishing probable hominid-collected faunal assemblages from those collected by large carnivores. The contrasts previewed here using species and artifact abundances are upheld to a large extent by the results of taphonomic analyses in Chapter 5. Table 4.14 summarizes the frequency relationships between small *or* large carnivore NISP and ungulate NISP in the site levels discussed. Two ratios—small carnivore NISP/ungulate NISP and large carnivore NISP/ungulate NISP—are calculated. The small carnivore category potentially includes wild cat, lynx, fox, badger, and other mustelids. The large carnivore category potentially includes bear, wolf, spotted hyaena, leopard, and lion. The predator species are partitioned into the two size categories on the assumption that small carnivores are far more likely to represent prey of other predators, including humans. Large carnivores also may, at times, fall prey to their fellows and to humans, but the natural history characteris-

tics of these species indicate that denning is the most likely cause of carnivore bones in cave deposits.

Table 4.14 shows much variation in the relative frequencies of small and large carnivores to ungulates among sites. Small carnivores are completely absent from the level groups of Moscerini, except M5 where they are uncommon; likewise the ratio for large carnivores (mainly hyaena and bear) is very low except in M5 (36%). Small carnivore remains are absent from Guattari, although Cardini reported a few fragments of fox and polecat (in Blanc and Segre 1953). Large carnivore ratio values are highest in G0 through G3, varying between 8 percent and 25 percent and dropping to 6 percent in G4 and then to 0 percent (note that sample size also decreases markedly, however).

Small carnivores are more common in Sant'Agostino and Buca della Iena. Small carnivore NISP ranges between 10 percent and 31 percent of ungulate NISP in Sant'Agostino S0–3, and is lowest in S4 (9%) and SX (7%), where wolves are abundant. The incidence of small and large carnivore remains is negatively related, if only weakly. In Buca della Iena, both small and large carnivores are abundant relative to ungulate NISP, and their frequencies, if anything, appear to track one another. The assemblages from Breuil and all of the late Upper Paleolithic sites display very low ratios for both small and large carnivores; small carnivores persist at around 1 percent to 3 percent of ungulate NISP.

Figure 4.2 is a plot of the ratio of *large* carnivore NISP to ungulate NISP for Mousterian and like-aged assemblages (see Table 4.5), including those from Buca della Iena. Late Upper Paleolithic faunas are not plotted, but closely follow the ungulate NISP (horizontal) axis without exception. We can expect a priori that the amounts of herbivore bone collected by denning large carnivores varied with immediate foraging conditions, because we know that these animals adjust their strategies to feeding opportunities in modern settings. Points representing den assemblages therefore should be fairly high on the carnivore NISP (vertical) axis as total mammal NISP increases, but their distributions may vary greatly with respect to the ungulate (horizontal) axis. Hominid-generated faunas should hug the ungulate axis because, while hominids may have

TABLE 4.13
Grotta Polesini: NISP counts for large mammals by cut and taxon

Taxa	1	2	3	4	5	6
CARNIVORA						
wolf	7	11	6	15	21	20
red fox	72	67	36	117	199	85
brown bear	.	.	.	.	2	.
weasel	.	.	.	.	1	.
pine martin	.	.	.	2	1	.
badger	26	20	19	38	71	17
wolverine	.	.	.	.	.	.
wild cat	16	25	14	28	43	27
lynx	6	3	1	5	7	4
carnivore total:	127	126	76	205	345	153
PRIMATA						
modern human	3	1	3	8	20	9
PERISSODACTYLA						
horse	159	46	67	101	134	86
wild ass	238	95	139	177	243	221
ARTIODACTYLA						
roe deer	206	217	263	372	678	334
red deer	2126	1411	2526	2931	4825	3324
aurochs	96	43	60	71	154	92
chamois	61	32	58	64	103	47
ibex	32	14	22	25	52	39
wild boar	373	267	278	334	561	396
ungulate total:	3291	2125	3413	4075	6750	4539

Taxa	7	8	9	10	11	12	(1–12) TOTAL
CARNIVORA							
wolf	29	26	18	10	4	13	180
red fox	85	65	74	20	12	40	872
brown bear	.	1	.	.	.	.	3
weasel	.	.	.	.	.	.	1
pine martin	.	.	1	.	.	.	4
badger	11	16	6	8	2	7	241
wolverine	1	1	.	1	.	.	3
wild cat	20	13	9	6	3	4	208
lynx	2	9	4	3	.	5	49
carnivore total:	148	131	110	48	21	69	1561
PRIMATA							
modern human	6	2	8	3	4	.	(R = 12) 79
PERISSODACTYLA							
horse	138	135	158	119	23	84	1250
wild ass	255	210	290	220	46	128	2262

TABLE 4.13 (*Continued*)

Taxa	1	2	3	4	5	6
ARTIODACTYLA						
roe deer	277	300	191	108	25	196	3167
red deer	3038	2577	3002	1942	502	1581	29,785
aurochs	110	116	92	84	25	37	980
chamois	68	46	64	90	11	50	694
ibex	26	31	51	41	3	26	362
wild boar	318	254	247	195	48	182	3453
ungulate total:	4230	3669	4095	2799	683	2284	41,953

Source: Radmilli (1974).

Note: (·) not present, (R) human bone specimens lacking provenience data.

TABLE 4.14
Small or large carnivore NISP to ungulate NISP ratios by site and provenience

Site and ratio	Provenience							
Moscerini	M1	M2	M3	M4	M6	M5		total
sc/ung	.00	.00	.00	.00	.00	.07		.03
lc/ung	.00	.05	.01	.01	.02	.36		.23
Guattari	G0	G1	G2	G3	G4	G5	G7	total
sc/ung	.00	.00	.00	.00	.00	.00	.00	.00
lc/ung	.13	.13	.08	.25	.06	.00	.00	.12
Sant'Agostino	S0	S1	S2	S3	S4	SX		total
sc/ung	.10	.10	.28	.31	.09	.07		.13
lc/ung	.03	.03	.02	.10	.18	.17		.07
Breuil		B3/4			Br			total
sc/ung		.02			.01			.01
lc/ung		.06			.01			.03
Buca della Iena	I1	I2	I3	I4	I5	I6		total
sc/ung	.06	.11	.67	.30	.34	.003		.14
lc/ung	.67	.94	1.89	1.38	.92	.69		.89
Palidoro		1–8 (1955)			33–34 (1956–59)			total
sc/ung		.02			.01			.01
lc/ung		.004			.00			.002
Salvini		10–15 (1988)						
sc/ung		.00						
lc/ung		.01						
Polesini		1–12						
sc/ung		.03						
lc/ung		.004						

Note: (sc/ung) small carnivore NISP/ungulate NISP, (lc/ung) large carnivore NISP/ungulate NISP. Small carnivores include badger, wild cat, lynx, fox, and mustelids. Large carnivores include bear, wolf, spotted hyaena, leopard, and lion.

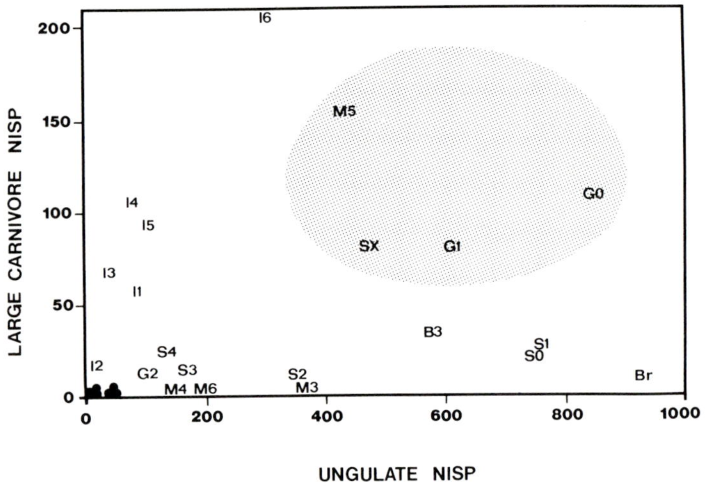

Figure 4.2 Plot of ungulate NISP to large carnivore NISP for various Italian cave faunas of Mousterian age. (B) Breuil, (G) Guattari, (I) Buca della Iena, (M) Moscerini, (S) Sant'Agostino; cases occurring within the shaded area are unlikely to have been collected by hominids; unmarked points near the graph intercept include G3, G4, G5, G7, M1, and M2.

killed large carnivores from time to time, they were not great predators of them. All that we can justifiably seek in this interassemblage comparison is a general threshold, below which lie strong candidates for hominid collecting activities, and above which lie candidates for carnivore collecting activities.

The assemblages from the hyaena den complex at Buca della Iena clearly follow the carnivore (vertical) axis as predicted. The majority of Mousterian-associated assemblages closely follow the ungulate (horizontal) axis as one would hope. Isolated in the middle zone (shaded area) are four assemblages—Moscerini M5, Sant'Agostino SX, and Guattari G0 and G1—very strong candidates for carnivore-collected den faunas, rich in both herbivore and predator bones. Unmarked points near the graph intercept (G3, G4, G5, G7, M1, and M2) are too small to be evaluated in this way.

Figure 4.3 presents a related comparison of large carnivore NISP/ungulate NISP to the total number of lithic artifacts associated with each faunal assemblage (data in Table 4.5). Again, only a threshold separating groups of cases is sought, because (1) the amounts of food that carnivores transport to dens can vary, and (2) while only hominids made stone tools, postdepositional mixing of occupational horizons is likely in some cases. The vertical axis is logged to exaggerate the differences among low large carnivore NISP/ungulate NISP values, enhancing the visibility of each case in the distribution. Ratio values greater than 0.1 here are considered significantly biased toward carnivore collectors (shaded area), although the control cases from Buca della Iena are closer to 1.0. Moscerini M5, Guattari G0, G1, and G3 (NISP = 5!), and Sant'Agostino SX and S4 all occupy the lower part of the shaded area and are isolated from all other cases. The distribution of the other faunas is better explained by the lithic (horizontal) axis, including Guattari G4 and G5. Breuil B3/4 is not plotted because complete lithic counts are not yet available; Br follows the horizontal axis, but lies off the graph (lithics = 3249). Only Guattari G3 and G7 and Moscerini M1 are too small to be informative in this preliminary evaluation.

CONCLUSIONS

Species arrays provide important information about the structure of lowland Mediterranean ecosystems during the Upper Pleistocene, in terms of both taxonomic diversity and the magnitude of changes therein. In contrast to regions to the north, few mammalian species made a novel entrance or a permanent exit from the community of coastal west-central Italy between 120,000 and 10,000 years

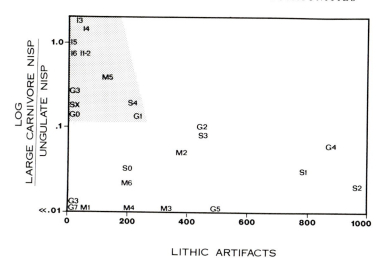

Figure 4.3 Plot of total lithic artifact counts to (log) large carnivore NISP/ungulate NISP for various Italian cave assemblages of Mousterian age. Symbols as in Figure 4.2; cases occurring within the shaded area are unlikely to have been collected by hominids.

ago. The number of mammalian species was high and relatively constant throughout the Middle and Upper Paleolithic, suggesting considerable heterogeneity within the plant community; this is not surprising given the latitudinal placement and great topographic relief of the west-central Italian coast. Changes in global temperature may have altered the grain of plant patches locally, but not enough to prevent mammals with diverse habitat requirements from coexisting.

Analyses of species arrays also assess the potential range of bone collectors in the coastal caves. Behavioral accounts show that spotted hyaenas and wolves routinely collect ungulate bones in modern dens. Foxes and, to a more limited degree, wild cats represent potential accumulators of small mammal bones. In contrast, bears and badgers seldom if ever transport food to dens, but often contribute their own remains to shelter deposits through natural mortality. Remains of large cats are rare in the Italian caves, suggesting little if any role as bone collectors there. The high incidence of spotted hyaena remains in Moscerini M5 and in Guattari G0 and G1, on the other hand, strongly implicates these animals as the primary agencies of bone accumulation. Other proveniences of Moscerini (M2, M3, M4, and M6) and Guattari (G4 and G5) more probably represent hominid bone collecting activities. Wolves appear to have been the sole bone collectors in layer SX and possibly the main collectors in S4 of Sant'Agostino. Because small carnivores do not kill

ungulates nor transport scavenged ungulate parts to any significant degree, the S0, S1, S2, and S3 faunas from Sant'Agostino suggest hominid activities. Carnivore remains (especially large species) are rare and highly localized in Breuil, suggesting that hominids were the main bone collectors there, akin to the situation for the late Upper Paleolithic assemblages.

One large social predator (human or nonhuman) dominated bone collection activities in each cave assemblage. Where carnivore remains are abundant, social predators greatly exceed all solitary species except bear. The prevalence of spotted hyaenas or wolves in some levels probably is due to (1) communal denning behavior (hyaenas, occasionally foxes) or cooperative parenting (wolves) and (2) the amount of time spent in dens per annum. Communal denners, especially spotted hyaenas, may cache several litters in the same shelter simultaneously. This behavior leads to a higher input of remains into the deposits because many individuals are present, den occupations are long, and juvenile mortality is high (e.g., Kruuk 1972). Wolves are social breeders, but a pack usually produces only one litter per year (e.g., Packard and Mech 1980; Van Ballenberghe 1983). While the denning season of wolves is short, many individuals maintain close contact with the den during that period and thereby elevate the probability of attritional death in the vicinity of the den. Large litter sizes and high juvenile mortality likewise contribute to the pattern.

Bear remains are relatively ubiquitous in shelter deposits of west-central Italy. Modern behavioral accounts indicate that death during or just after hibernation is the most likely reason for the presence of bears in cave faunas. Hibernation is linked to elevated mortality in bears, governed primarily by food supplies of the previous summer and fall.

Stone tools sometimes occur alongside evidence of carnivore denning activities (e.g., hyaena bones, latrines, gnaw marks, etc.), so that they are spatially associated with one another in the final and literal senses. However, taphonomic research (the topic of Chapter 5) shows that archaeological and paleontological records should not be read literally, because behavioral and sedimentary processes do not operate at the same rates, and the former can play havoc with the latter. The apparent mixing of lithic artifacts with remains of bears, wolves, and other carnivores in some levels reinforces impressions of alternating use of the Italian shelters by these species. The possibility of rotating use within years would have been restricted to hominids and those carnivores with short denning periods, if it happened at all. Wolves, for example, use dens intensively for up to two months, after which the den is visited only sporadically or abandoned completely (Ballard et al. 1987; Ewer 1973:308–309). In contrast, spotted hyaenas and badgers may use dens for extended periods, minimally one year and usually longer (Kruuk 1972; Burton 1979). Rotating occupations by hominids, spotted hyaenas, and/or badgers therefore require longer time cycles, so that each kind of occupant might dominate larger segments of a sedimentary sequence.

Summary comparisons of large and small carnivore NISP to ungulate NISP, and the proportions of these skeletal remains to stone artifact frequencies, isolate the probable agencies of bone collection in the Italian caves. Using ungulate abundance as the baseline for interassemblage contrasts, comparisons of *large* carnivore NISP to lithic counts are as enlightening as they are simple: they are a strong first step toward understanding the histories of the bone assemblages.

As a related point concerning carnivore body sizes and relative abundances, carnivore components in pre-35,000-year-old faunas incorporate many large predator remains, whereas the post-15,000-year-old faunas are poorer in carnivores and confined primarily to small species. These findings are consistent with those of Gamble (1983, 1986) for Eurasia more generally and suggest differences in the nature of coexistence between hominids and carnivores between the two periods.

The comparisons of carnivore, ungulate, and artifact frequencies may also have implications for the intensity of hominid occupations. If hominids reused a site year after year and/or for relatively long periods in any given year, carnivore remains should be rare unless they represent prey of human hunters. If, on the other hand, people only occasionally used a shelter, and only for short periods, large carnivore components may be more common. The latter situation need not imply strong interspecific competition for shelters in the study area, just a different context of use by hominids. Sparse lithic material in Buca della Iena I1 through I4, and possibly in Moscerini M2, M3, M4, and M6 suggest ephemeral occupations by hominids. In contrast, the late Middle Paleolithic occupations at Sant'Agostino (S0, S1, S2, and S3) and Breuil may have been more intense and prolonged, not unlike the late Upper Paleolithic cases in the study sample.

Large Mammal Taphonomy and the Agencies of Bone Collection

IDENTIFYING the bone collectors and modifiers responsible for each assemblage is critical to any behavioral interpretations of the Italian faunas. Bones of nonhuman predators are present in the caves of coastal Latium, along with human artifacts. Spotted hyaenas and wolves are especially important candidates as bone collectors in strata where their own remains are common, because these large predators are known to collect bones at modern dens.

This chapter focuses on how the large mammal assemblages were formed and the agencies responsible for producing them, less on the details of how each predator processed food. Analyses of the large mammal remains begin with considerations of recovery, preservation, and fragmentation biases, followed by quantification of damage types by site and vertical provenience. Damage type frequencies are then summarized across assemblages, along with qualitative observations, to identify the collectors and/or modifiers of each assemblage. The chapter closes with discussions of some general issues, including the problem of distinguishing feeding sequences in which more than one type of consumer was involved, implications of tool marks and burning, interior space preferences of hominids and carnivores, and, finally, refutation of the hypothesis that Grotta Guattari was a Neandertal ritual chamber. Because taphonomic concerns shift with each major dimension of zooarchaeological analysis, some of the issues raised here are rekindled in chapters to come.

TAPHONOMY IS A BAD DOG

Ambiguity and self-doubt are inherent to the field of taphonomy. The ways that we are forced to go about observing and interpreting faunas make hypothesis testing especially challenging, and, certainly, there are safer realms of inquiry for preserving one's good reputation. I privately think of taphonomic problems the way I think about a mean dog, at night, on the same side of a locked gate as I. There is no escape, and doubt continually nips at the heels of a study, even if the dog is small. Answers that ring of "absolutely" and "absolutely not" are hard to find, and even "probably" can turn on you. Three things are reasonably certain, however: (1) taphonomic analyses demand both a substantial capacity for analogy and a steady pair of reins on the same imagination; (2) being careful is important, but being meticulous is no substitute for rigorous methods nor does it cause an investigator to hatch useful ideas; and (3) simple hypotheses are always better, if only because the possible outcomes are few and separable (sensu Jefferys and Berger 1992). Clearly, there is only one way to arrive at the conclusion that Paleolithic and other faunas were collected and modified by none other than *Homo sapiens,* and that is to avoid the subject of taphonomy completely.

In prefacing this chapter, it is useful to step back for a moment and consider the job of taphonomists —what taphonomic studies are really intended to accomplish in archaeology, and the balance be-tween knowledge gained and the cost of doing. We learn very quickly in life that virtually everything is biased by something else. In the case of fossil faunas, the processes responsible for assemblage formation will also, with time, distort assemblage contents in significant and hopefully predictable ways. The signatures of processes that create fossil faunas may be cumulative, but short-term observa-tions of modern events may not fully describe the long-term consequences of the same processes. Controlled observations in modern settings there-fore must be translated and scaled according to the terms stipulated by ancient faunal records. Repeti-tion of events, their frequency and magnitude, gov-ern the nature of most kinds of patterns that zoo-archaeologists and paleontologists encounter; most accumulations do not represent discrete, instan-taneous events.

The existence of carnivore components in Paleo-lithic localities is not universally recognized in our field even now, making comparisons across sites and regions difficult. Whereas only people make elaborate stone tools, many animals collect and modify bones and may inhabit the kinds of places that people also find congenial. Faunal assemblages accumulate piece by piece, and there is consider-able potential for several agencies to play roles in creating an assemblage, as illustrated by the works of Brain (e.g., 1980, 1981), Binford (1978, 1981), Andrews (1990), and others. We can try to assess the complete history of bone assemblage formation, thereby offering an assessment of "whodunit" for analytical purposes, but the reality is almost never neat (Bar-Yosef et al. 1992; Binford and Bertram 1977; Gamble 1983, 1986; Gifford 1981; Lindly 1988; Stiner 1991a; Straus 1982). As a concession to this fact, it is necessary to cross-reference alter-native classes of taphonomic data. Only in this way can taphonomists avoid the "shopper" effect when trying to test hypotheses.[4]

METHODOLOGY

Many of the primary observations in taphonomic studies are, as it turns out, made in vain. Taphon-omy is an exciting but relatively undeveloped area of research, possessing few concrete working prin-ciples. What principles we have are borrowed from other sciences and are, as yet, incompletely inte-grated with problems in archaeology (see Gifford 1981). It is partly for this reason that observations about presence-absence of, or two-way contrasts within, damage classes continue to be among the most enlightening about how bone assemblages were formed. Simple is beautiful in research de-sign, and this is doubly true in the case of taphon-omy. Even when the problem cannot be brought to elegance, simplicity renders the potential outcomes of an investigation controllable and logically divisible.

Presence-absence or two-way-difference obser-vations in taphonomy are usually about things like burning, gnawing, cut marks, weathering, and so on. We then try to complement presence-absence information with size or damage intensity data, along with qualitative observations about form, ap-pearance, and whatever else strikes the eye. One runs a parallel risk of becoming buried beneath heaps of minutiae when doing this kind of work. Suffice it to say, one of the greatest challenges in taphonomic reporting is keeping the reader's face off the printed page.

Many of the types of observations I made over the course of this research do not inform anyone about much of anything; while important information about human behavior certainly lies in bone damage patterns, it is far easier to generate a great deal of noise. Here, I try to remove as much chaff as possi-ble, focusing instead on the things that distinguish agencies of bone collection and modification in rel-atively straightforward terms. The basic geological conditions in the Italian cave sites are described in Chapter 3: it is clear that soil chemistry and the stable environment afforded by karstic systems in coastal Latium tend to preserve bone well.

The principal bone accumulators and modifiers in

---

[4] In the parlance of this author, the "shopper" effect refers to situations in which only data supporting a preferred view are presented and contradictions apparent for the same case or group of cases are ignored. Potential contradictions might include con-flicting information or, more commonly, how data are aggre-gated in time and space.

Upper Pleistocene Italy can be narrowed to mammalian predators: hominids, large carnivores, and small carnivores. The possible carnivore inhabitants are outlined in Chapter 4, based on the relative abundances of their remains to stone tools in the deposits. The presence of a carnivore species known to collect bone does not prove action, however: carnivore remains could also represent prey of other predators, including hominids. Factors such as in situ bone attrition may also have taken a toll on the bones once gathered inside the caves. My objective is to understand the impact of major biasing factors in relation to the kinds of behavioral phenomena at issue, and then, to answer three questions: (1) Which agencies played major roles in bone accumulation? (2) Which assemblages are wholly or largely attributable specifically to hominid economic behaviors? (3) What was the sequence of agencies in the case of assemblages with more complex taphonomic histories?

Bone modification patterns, along with species frequencies and behavioral information from Chapter 4, identify the agencies of collection through the process of elimination. The possibility that carnivores (especially hyaenas and wolves) collected the bones is addressed first. Because the responses of modern predators vary greatly with context, multiple cases for each class of agency are needed to anticipate the potential variation in taphonomic signatures. Using information on gnawing, burning, tool marks, fracture patterns, weathering, and other criteria, I compare the Mousterian cave faunas to the modern and Upper Paleolithic (soft) control cases. Damage frequencies are expressed as percentages of total *bone* NISP (the latter is defined in Chapter 4). Comparisons concerning bone preservation instead employ minimum numbers of individual animals (MNI).

With the exception of the next section, the analyses focus on damage on *bones,* not teeth. Bone has the potential to reflect a more complete record of destructive factors. With the notable exception of burning damage, this is not true of teeth. I approach the taphonomic questions on multiple fronts, cross-referencing results wherever possible. This strategy is necessary, because clues may be lightly scattered among the items in an assemblage, and the assemblages often are small.

TESTS OF ATTRITION

Three more or less distinct phenomena potentially distort our perceptions of anatomical representation in archaeofaunas. These are the recovery practices of archaeologists, in situ bone decomposition due to soil chemistry (preservation), and bone fragmentation in relation to thresholds of specimen identifiability. The three phenomena can act together or alone. Questions about anatomical biases in transported faunas are not simply problems of counting what is there: we also need to explain why certain animal body parts are missing. The difference between bones never having arrived and those reduced to invisible forms after arrival is crucial. The problem is to figure out which of these factors exerted significant biasing effects in the Italian shelter faunas, and if so, to what extent.

Recovery biases

Interviews of surviving IIPU members, their field notes, and my interassemblage comparisons of the old collections to those from new excavations at neighboring caves reveal a priori that the study sample is limited by recovery practices employed between 1939 and 1955. Refined for their time, IIPU recovery procedures nonetheless sacrificed many axial (vertebra and rib) and limb midshaft fragments, because small broken specimens from these regions of the skeleton are not well suited for taxonomic studies. Most of the collections in the study sample are from earlier decades, though complemented with material from modern excavations in which bone recovery was complete.

The recently excavated assemblages from Grotta Breuil (MP), Riparo Salvini (IUP), and Buca della Iena (primarily spotted hyaena dens) here serve as points of reference. They are keys for understanding what could be missing from the earlier collections as the result of archaeologists' recovery practices. The faunal assemblages from Breuil, Salvini, and Buca della Iena suggest that, while some vertebral and rib elements were saved during the earlier work at other caves (e.g., Figure 3.7), recovery for these kinds of items was not always systematic. Apart from limb-shaft fragments, however, recovery of limbs and cranial specimens was thorough. The same was true for antler, skull, and upper neck bones. The question of long bone counts in the absence of limb-shaft fragments is addressed by referring to the completely recovered assemblages, but this discussion is postponed until the anatomical study in Chapter 9, where it is most relevant. Some kinds of axial specimens were carefully sought and retained by the IIPU excavators but are confined primarily to rib heads, atlas, axis, and acetabulum fragments. The analyses of anatomical representation and bone damage in the Italian study sample therefore must concentrate primarily on the head region and the appendicular anatomy. In fact, these body parts yield a great deal of information from taphonomic and economic perspectives.

Because recovery biases in the Italian collections center on the axial anatomy of mammals, their impact on anatomical representation overlaps with patterns of bone loss expected to occur from in situ decomposition (e.g., Binford and Bertram 1977; Lyman 1984a, 1985). Bones possessing comparatively low tissue densities, particularly spongy bone (trabeculae), generally are the same ones that cannot be easily or reliably identified to species.

As for assessing the influence of in situ decomposition, Lyman (1985, 1991b), in particular, offers an innovative and practical set of tests contrasting skeletal part representation and food utility (e.g., from Binford 1978) for the same array of parts (implemented, for example, by Hoffecker et al. 1991). Lyman (1991b:126) recognizes, as do others, that the consequences of bone decomposition can overlap with the kinds of damage caused by humans or carnivores while feeding (described, for example, by Binford and Bertram 1977; Brain 1969, 1981; Gifford 1980; Speth 1991; Yellen 1977). The overlap is explained by the nature of bone structure itself: trabecular tissue is soft and it is edible. Elegant in the right circumstances, Lyman's procedure nonetheless assumes complete recovery of bone from archaeological deposits, a condition not met by the early excavations in Latium, Italy. Likewise, Brain (1981), Bunn (1983), Villa and Mahieu (1991), and others offer a variety of approaches for

ascertaining agencies of bone collection and modification on the basis of fragment sizes, fracture forms, or overall shapes of broken specimens. These, too, require complete recovery in order to be fully effective.

Having isolated the recovery problem for the subject assemblages, I present below some alternative approaches to evaluating bone attrition caused by decomposition and fragmentation. Designed specifically to circumvent the problems posed by recovery biases in the 1939–55 collections, the tests are equally useful alternatives for analyzing material recovered from modern excavations.

Fragmentation: Modifiers versus identifiability thresholds

Several classes of phenomena that destroy bone are worth distinguishing at the conceptual level, even if we cannot always separate their effects in real archaeological situations. In particular, I refer to fragmentation and chemical decomposition. Weathering was not a serious factor for the Italian faunas (see below), because the assemblages formed inside caves with moist atmospheres, and most of the bones were buried quickly. Fragmentation and decomposition, on the other hand, are important concerns; either may reduce the potential for identifying bones.

Fragmentation can help identify agencies of bone collection and modification despite the damage it causes overall. Mean fragment lengths and size ranges for completely recovered (identifiable and nonidentifiable) bone from Breuil, Salvini, and Buca della Iena vary greatly (Table 5.1). Alternative sources of information on assemblage origins have yet to be presented, but it is fair to note that the first two sites were created by hominids and the third by hyaenas. The mean fragment sizes are most important, because they are least sensitive to idiosyncratic differences among the assemblages; maximum sizes may describe many or just a few specimens. Some postdepositional machination may also have occurred in each site, but the differences are largely behavioral in origin, with hyaena-collected material from Buca della Iena showing greater variation in fragment sizes and a higher mean. The results are consistent with contrasts observed by Brain

TABLE 5.1
Degree of fragmentation of identifiable and nonidentifiable bone from three cave excavations involving complete recovery

	Riparo Salvini (lUP)	*Grotta Breuil (lMP)*	*Buca della Iena (spotted hyaena dens)*
N observations	421	391	1210
mean length	2.3 cm	3.0 cm	6.1 cm
minimum length	1.0 cm	1.0 cm	1.0 cm
maximum length	8.3 cm	9.5 cm	27.9 cm

Note: Samples from Salvini and Breuil are from selected proveniences only, but are representative of total excavated material (Stiner 1990a:253); data for Buca della Iena are samples from all levels (I1–6) combined.

(1981:279–284, 310–311) and Bunn (1983) for modern hyaena den assemblages and human refuse faunas; fragment sizes in hyaena-accumulated faunas tend to be larger.

Figure 5.1 shows variation in fragment sizes for large mammal bones from the Italian caves. Variation among assemblages, in terms of both ranges and means, is considerable, yet difficult to interpret because tiny pieces were not kept by IIPU excavators unless they could be identified to species. The reference assemblages from Salvini (V), Breuil (B3), and Buca della Iena (I1–I6) are shown at the top of the illustration, separated from the 1939–55 IIPU collections by a dashed line. Mean sizes for the older collections are either higher or equivalent to the cases involving complete bone recovery. The graph suggests that the IIPU recovery system amplified mean size values overall, making it necessary to upscale the expected contrasts between hominid-modified and carnivore-modified faunas. Mean fragment size values for Guattari G4, G1, and G0 and for Moscerini M5 and M1 are conspicuously elevated relative to the other cases, suggesting that hyaenas could have been partly or wholly responsible for bone modification in these levels.

Preservation bias by a universal measure

Questions about biases due to bone attrition (decomposition and/or advanced fragmentation) versus selective transport to caves by ancient consumers can be addressed by contrasting MNI counts based

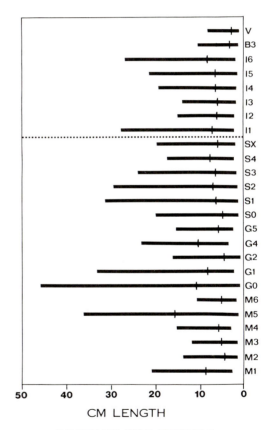

CM LENGTH

IDENTIFIABLE BONE SPECIMENS

Figure 5.1 Minimum, maximum, and mean lengths of bone specimens from the Italian collections. (V) Salvini, (B) Breuil, (I) Buca della Iena, (S) Sant'Agostino, (G) Guattari, and (M) Moscerini. Assemblages shown above the dashed line involved a complete bone recovery system; those below, a more selective, species-oriented recovery system.

on teeth versus cranial bone. Standardized element counts (Chapter 9) based strictly on bone show that head parts are among the most common skeletal remains in the Upper Pleistocene shelter assemblages. Such comparisons demand, however, that the identifiability potentials of both classes of skeletal material have been exhausted, and that the bone-based and tooth-based counts are mutually exclusive. The identifiability potential of bone is sometimes overlooked by analysts, either because their research priorities lie elsewhere or because of inexperience. Many landmarks on the bony cranium and mandible are as valuable for identifying species and numbers of individual animals (MNI) as are teeth. Tooth-based and bone-based counts nonetheless should be partitioned in data bases in recognition of the differing material properties and susceptibilities that they embody (see also Figure 4.1 and associated discussion of NISP).

If these analytical conditions are fulfilled, as they are in this study, we can expect MNIs derived from mammal cranial bones versus teeth to be roughly equivalent wherever preservation is good and specimen identifiability thresholds have not been seriously undermined by fragmentation. In situations of poor preservation, we can expect tooth-based and cranial bone-based MNIs to diverge significantly. Values derived from bone should decline faster than those based on teeth,[5] because bone tissues generally are softer and suffer greater attrition as decomposition and/or fragmentation progresses. The relatively smaller size of teeth also contributes to their higher probability of being preserved.

A simple test for attrition can be constructed from the idealized expectation of equivalence between bone-based and tooth-based cranial MNIs. The comparison must be conducted within the head region, not across the entire skeletal anatomy. It is important to appreciate that cross-element comparisons confuse the potential effects of two separate processes that may operate on transported faunas: (1) loss by decomposition and fragmentation, and (2) transport decisions made by consumers. One does not even know, a priori, where legs and other zones of the anatomy were segmented in advance of portage, nor can it be assumed that a carcass was

partitioned at the joints (see below). Confining comparisons of bone-based and tooth-based MNIs to the cranium effectively avoids these ambiguities, and the results can be generalized (with caution) to the assemblage as a whole.

The head region is comprised of diverse skeletal materials, ranging from dense, vitreous teeth to paper-thin bone, within a single transportable food unit. The probability that teeth will be separated from head bone by consumers at acquisition sites is quite low, unless processing, and the immediate discard that normally accompanies it, take place at the procurement site. The probability that teeth will be separated from bone greatly increases at the final destination of the transport trajectory, due both to processing and postdepositional phenomena.

Figure 5.2 models several slopes, which together describe the range of possible relationships between cranial bone-based MNI and tooth-based MNI. Each slope is a function of identifiability loss due to fragmentation or decomposition. The modeled relationship is linear—close enough to reality for the purposes of this comparison. All conceivable archaeological conditions are portrayed so that the quality of preservation for the Italian assemblages can be ranked in global terms.

In plotting bone-based MNI against tooth-based MNI, we can only expect a strong positive relationship; this is a given, not a revelation. Two other aspects of this comparison are of greater analytical interest: (1) Do the arrays of plotted taxa from each site share the same slope? (2) How steep is the slope of each?

Assuming that head parts are present in assemblages, the most common situations worldwide are represented by slopes A and B, where tooth-based MNIs are significantly higher than those for cranial bone. This means that decomposition has occurred in place and/or fragmentation has reduced much of the bone to nonidentifiable pieces. Teeth will also eventually disappear as attrition advances, but their higher densities and generally smaller sizes slow the effect. Slope C, in contrast, represents the ideal situation (slope = 1, *x-y* intercept = 0) in which MNIs based on bone are about as high as MNIs based on teeth. Slope C emulates a situation in

[5] Even the presence of relatively fragile deciduous teeth should not damp the general expectations posed here.

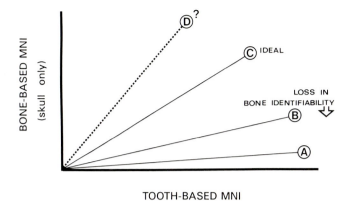

Figure 5.2 Modeled relationships between tooth-based MNI and bone-based cranial MNI as a function of identifiable bone loss from decomposition or fragmentation.

which little if any loss of identifiable bone has occurred, allowing the analyst to perceive more or less equal MNI values from the different classes of skeletal material. Slope D represents what may be an impossible situation ("?") in which bone-based MNI consistently overtakes tooth-based MNI. Slope D contradicts the founding premise that teeth are more resistant to destruction than bone, but special circumstances might exist, and it is wise to be generous.

Because this scheme compares only the features of the mammalian skull, its implications may not be wholly generalized to skeletal elements comprised of spongy (trabecular) bone. My purpose is to evaluate how tissue density affects the preservation of cranial versus postcranial parts that contain signifi-

cant amounts of cortical bone tissue, especially limb elements. At least one epiphysis of every limb bone, and all carpals, tarsals, and phalanges, contain cortical bone; hence the comparison of cranial skeletal tissues may be generalized to them. This kind of assessment is not as effective with regard to preservation of the vertebral column.

Having outlined the expectations about how bone-based MNIs and tooth-based MNIs could relate to one another for cranial remains in assemblages, let us now turn to real faunas. Figure 5.3 is a plot of cranial bone- and tooth-based MNIs for large mammalian taxa from Moscerini, Guattari, Sant'Agostino, and Buca della Iena. Values are summed by taxon and across levels in each site (Table 5.2). Although the comparisons are confined

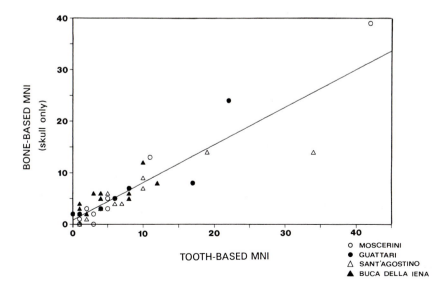

Figure 5.3 Tooth-based MNI bone-based cranial MNI for large mammals from Moscerini, Guattari, Sant'Agostino and Buca della Iena (slope = .784, y-intercept = .606). Assemblages are lumped by site with each point representing one taxon.

TABLE 5.2
Tooth- and bone-based MNIs by taxon and site

Taxon	Moscerini		Guattari		Sant'Agostino		Buca d. Iena	
	B	T	B	T	B	T	B	T
leopard	·	·	2	0	·	·	2	1
bear	5	5	2	1	4	7	6	8
hyaena	2	3	7	8	·	·	8	12
fox	2	3	·	·	8	12	·	·
wild cat	1	1	·	·	6	5	2	2
seal	1	1	·	·	0	1	·	·
wolf	·	·	2	1	7	10	4	1
badger	·	·	·	·	·	·	6	4
red/fallow deer	39	42	24	22	14	34	12	10
roe deer	13	11	·	·	14	19	6	3
aurochs	3	5	8	17	6	5	5	4
ibex	3	2	·	·	9	10	·	·
wild boar	0	1	3	4	6	5	3	1
horse	1	1	5	6	4	6	5	8
wild ass	·	·	·	·	1	2	3	4
rhinoceros	0	3	·	·	·	·	·	·
hippopotamus	0	1	·	·	·	·	·	·

Note: (·) species not present, (B) bone-based MNI, (T) tooth-based MNI. Only sites yielding multiple assemblages are listed, and MNIs are summed across levels. Taxa include large mammals only, and some very rare species are omitted from consideration. Bone MNI uses the most common bony portion of the most common skeletal element for the species in each assemblage; values often are highest for elements from the head region, but are *never* based on teeth. Tooth MNI, in contrast, uses the most common deciduous or permanent tooth element, upper or lower, across fifteen possible age classes in each assemblage; an MNI value may be higher than or equal to that presented in the mortality analyses in Chapter 11, where only one type of tooth element is targeted for comparison. For elements that naturally occur in pairs, right and left sides are summed and divided by 2. This averaging procedure is intended to counteract aggregation errors across levels.

to large mammals, the arrays of taxa span a wide range of body sizes. The cases represent differing circumstances of accumulation; ungulate heads were carried as food by one collector agency or another, whereas many of the carnivore heads represent animals that lived and died inside the caves.

The four series plotted in Figure 5.3 appear to share a single slope, suggesting that conditions affecting bone and tooth identifiability were similar among the sites, irrespective of collector; outlier points are rare exceptions to the general pattern. The relationship is both positive and strong ($r = .889$, $P \ll .001$), enforced by the mathematical basis of the comparison. More important is the angle of the slope, which approaches the ideal value of 1 (slope = .784, y intercept = .606). Teeth tend to yield slightly higher MNIs overall, but bone MNIs come fairly close. This result is consistent with my general observation that the Italian cases formed under good preservation conditions, and that, apart

from the recovery biases outlined above, loss of identifiable bone via fragmentation or decomposition is comparatively low.

The above comparison of bone-based and tooth-based cranial MNIs sets the Italian shelter faunas in broader perspective, documenting relatively high levels of bone preservation and specimen identifiability relative to archaeological records in other parts of the world. While the collections suffer from recovery biases against the axial skeletal anatomy, surprisingly little bone identifiability has been lost in the head region and, probably, the appendicular anatomy (see Chapter 9) to decomposition and fragmentation (see also, the condition of the cranial specimen in Figure 5.4F).

The findings are especially encouraging in the case of Grotta dei Moscerini, where the ungulate faunas are extraordinarily biased toward head parts, to the exclusion of nearly every other kind of skeletal element (see also Chapter 9). Table 5.3 shows

TABLE 5.3
MNIs for large mammals in Moscerini, based on cranial and mandibular bone versus teeth and listed by level group

Taxon	M1 B	M1 T	M2 B	M2 T	M3 B	M3 T	M4 B	M4 T	M5 B	M5 T	M6 B	M6 T
bear	·	·	1	0	1	1	1	1	1	2	1	1
hyaena	·	·	·	·	·	·	·	·	2	3	·	·
red fox	·	·	1	0	·	·	·	·	1	3	·	·
wild cat	·	·	·	·	·	·	·	·	1	1	·	·
monk seal	·	·	·	·	·	·	·	·	1	1	·	·
red/fallow deer	1	2	1	3	15	12	8	8	7	9	7	8
roe deer	1	1	1	0	4	3	2	2	4	4	1	1
aurochs	1	0	·	·	0	2	·	·	1	2	1	1
ibex	·	·	·	·	1	1	0	1	1	0	1	0
wild boar	·	·	·	·	0	1	·	·	·	·	·	·
horse	·	·	·	·	·	·	·	·	1	1	·	·
rhinoceros	0	1	·	·	0	1	0	1	·	·	·	·
hippopotamus	·	·	·	·	·	·	0	1	·	·	·	·

Note: (·) species not present, (B) bone-based MNI, (T) tooth-based MNI. Bone MNI uses the most common bony portion of the most common skeletal element for the species in each assemblage. Tooth MNI, in contrast, uses the most common deciduous or permanent tooth element, upper or lower, across fifteen possible age classes in each assemblage; an MNI value may be higher than or equal to that presented in the mortality analyses in Chapter 11, where only one type of tooth element is targeted for comparison. For elements that naturally occur in pairs, right and left sides were summed and divided by 2.

that tooth-based MNIs are equal to or only marginally exceed bone-based MNIs across level groups and taxa, indicating that most potentially identifiable cranial bone specimens (some of which are quite fragile) were not lost to decomposition or fragmentation. The head-biased faunas of Moscerini (and Guattari G4–5) cannot be explained away by bone attrition.

As a caution for applying this method to archaeological circumstances more generally, variation in human processing practices, which can bring about different patterns of postdepositional destruction, must be taken into account. In his study of the modern !Kung, Yellen (1991b) observes that processing procedures strongly affect the relative probabilities that various skeletal elements of game will be preserved in identifiable forms, more so than subsequent gnawing by local carnivores. Likewise, Brain (1981:21–24) found that goat mandibles lasted exceptionally well in the Hottentot village dumps, but in this case people did not open the mandibles for marrow (pp. 17–18), instead discarding them whole and unmarred. All ungulate head parts in the Italian Paleolithic situations were thoroughly processed and smashed, encouraging postdepositional destruction and identifiability loss in principle. This fact about the predepositional state of the skulls indicates that the postdepositional environment was a very good preservation medium; this is why bone-based MNIs are nearly as high as those for teeth.

DAMAGE FREQUENCIES: METHODS AND VARIABLES

In the site-by-site presentation to follow, I compare the frequencies of bone damage types on carnivore and ungulate remains in relation to total bone specimen counts (NISP) by taxonomic category and vertical provenience. Although part of the original data collection scheme, information on the intensity of each type of damage is not presented, except where directly relevant to another point of fact. The analyses of bone damage begin with situations in which I have a somewhat better idea about who created the assemblages and the behaviors involved. These cases are soft controls or references, because they occurred in the past, and the actual events leading to their formation could not be observed. The reference cases are from the stratified spotted hyaena den complex known as Buca della Iena (first reported by Pitti and Tozzi 1971) and from two Upper Paleolithic rockshelters, Grotta Palidoro (see also Bietti 1976–77a, 1976–77b; Cassoli 1976–77) and Grotta Polesini (see also Radmilli 1974). The hyaena dens and Upper Paleolithic cases from west-central Italy help outline and refine expectations of difference between hominid and carnivore components in the Mousterian caves of Latium.

Damage patterns in relation to prey anatomy also merit some introduction. Holding agency constant, some faunas may contain more evidence of certain types of damage simply because they are rich in limb bones. Most classes of bone damage are differentially distributed across the skeletal anatomy of prey, partly because soft tissues, marrow, and hard structures are distributed unevenly. Inter-assemblage variation in body part profiles in the Italian cave faunas ranges from head-dominated to rich in all major elements, including limb bones. Cut marks and damage caused by marrow processing are most evident on long bones, meaning that hominid-generated assemblages rich in limb elements will also tend to have higher frequencies of cut marks, cone fractures, and related processing damage.

Archaeologists' perceptions of damage frequencies can also be affected by how much of the non-identifiable fraction of a bone assemblage was retained during excavation. Much of the processing damage on limb elements occurs on the cortical surfaces surrounding the medullary cavities. With fragmentation, many of these traces are isolated from identifiable bone features (a.k.a. landmarks). Shaft fragments were not systematically retained in the earlier excavations, so we can expect the frequencies of hominid-caused damage to be somewhat lower in the 1939–55 collections than in the completely recovered faunas from Breuil and Salvini or modern ethnoarchaeological cases (e.g., Binford 1978). Evidence of carnivore damage, in contrast, is most evident on epiphyseal portions of limb bones although it is not confined to them. Damage frequencies therefore can be artificially elevated by species-oriented recovery procedures. Old recovery practices sometimes make the job of distinguishing hominid- and carnivore-collected faunas more difficult, heightening the significance of whatever contrasts can be found.

A number of bone damage variables appear in the site-by-site comparisons. Some of the variables are widely documented and in common use, whereas others arise directly from my observations of the Italian faunas. The damage variables are defined and illustrated below.

Burning refers to specimens that are partly carbonized, wholly carbonized, or calcined. The degree of burning damage to specimens is summarized only where essential for discussion.

Abrasion refers to the rounding of natural and broken edges of bones, caused by rubbing against fine particles in a soil matrix. Abrasion may indicate the amount of traffic inside a site (trampling) or geological rolling. Little if any of the abrasion was due to sieving by the archaeologists.

Chemical pitting refers to irregular holes in bone surfaces, probably from localized concentrations of acidic compounds. In Grotta Guattari, the pits were almost certainly caused by water dripping from the cavern ceiling during periods of karstic activity. Chemical pitting differs from carnivore digestive erosion (which is rare on large mammal remains) in that the pits are large and usually isolated on one part of a bone specimen. The pits, which often have a shallow, basin-like form, also differ from gnawing marks, in that they are not accompanied by the polished appearance characteristic of digested or mouthed (a.k.a. salivary rounding) bone fragments.

Bipolar impact fracture or crushing occurs when force is applied simultaneously to opposing surfaces of a bone, creating symmetrical damage (Figure 5.4B,C). Bipolar damage may occur from the jaws of a large carnivore, but it more often results from hominids placing bones on a hard anvil and striking them with a stone hammer. Bipolar damage is rare overall, but when present, it is often associated with cone fractures (see below).

A *transverse dent* refers to a relatively linear indentation, oriented perpendicularly to the long axis of a long bone or mandible. Transverse dents may occur from jaw pressure exerted through the car-

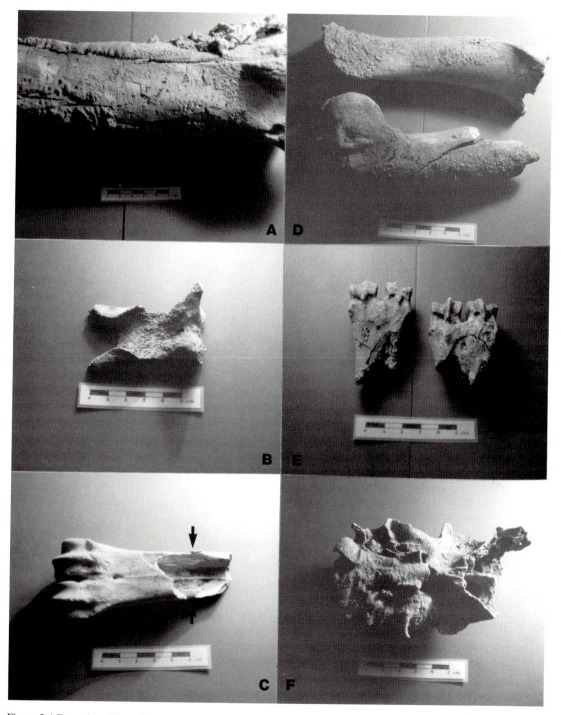

Figure 5.4 Examples of bone damage types in the Italian cave faunas: (A) Geological scratches on aurochs tibia from the Guattari surface deposit (G0). Damage on this specimen superficially resembles grooves from juvenile carnivore teeth, but the striae are very straight, with consistently V-shaped cross-sections. (B) Bipolar crushing/fracture on horse phalanx from Moscerini M5, probably by spotted hyaena. (C) Bipolar cone fractures on deer metapodial from Moscerini M5, probably from hyaena. (D) Partly destroyed red deer humeri from Guattari G0–1, damaged by spotted hyaenas. Note incompletely detached spiral fracture on lower specimen, damage often associated with cortical "stripping" by large carnivores. (E) Crushed distal metapodials of ibex from Sant'Agostino SX, damaged by wolves. Note puncture from carnassial tooth on specimen on left. (F) Posterior section of roe deer skull (ventral aspect) from Moscerini M5, with anterior section gnawed away. Specimen also exemplifies the generally high quality of preservation of bones in the site.

nassial molars of a carnivore or from hominids striking a bone with a heavy tool or against a pointed anvil. This type of damage is not common in carnivore den assemblages. In contrast, it is very common in the Upper Paleolithic reference faunas (Polesini and Palidoro), usually part of a complex of damage resulting from sectioning or shearing limb bones through shaft diaphyses (see later discussions; also Binford 1978:63).

The term *cone* refers to the preserved scar (usually one-half) of a Hertzian cone fracture (Figures 5.4C and 5.5D,G), analogous to those commonly observed on cryptocrystalline and glassy substances (e.g., Speth 1977) and on high-fired ceramics. Cone fractures are caused either by direct pressure from large carnivore teeth, especially hyaenas', or impact by hominids' tools. Either way, the force must be concentrated through a small point of contact, and the bone surface must be relatively dense in order for a cone fracture to occur. Cone fractures on skeletal material are usually confined to cortical bone, and their frequencies are linked to the presence of limb elements, prey body size, and the processing methods of the consumers. Cones are directly associated, for example, with marrow processing of limb bones in Binford's (1978) ethnoarchaeological collections from Nunamiut camps. Both carnivores and humans can produce cone fractures on bone (e.g., Brain 1981:141–142; Potts 1982), and the average diameters of cones created by tools versus hyaena teeth overlap completely. However, cones are significantly more common in human-generated faunas; thus, the relative frequencies of cones are of interest, not simply presence-absence.

Crushing is a relatively amorphous category of damage, sometimes associated with gnawing by large carnivores (e.g., Figure 5.4E) and, in other cases, with marrow processing by hominids, especially of mandibles and phalanges.

Split through epiphysis refers to linear sectioning of a long bone end, such as on radii and metapodials (Figure 5.5E,F). The frequency of split epiphyses depends on both the relative abundance of long bones in an assemblage and the agency of bone damage. Both carnivores and hominids may split epiphyses in order to extract marrow from the medullary cavities of long bones. Holding prey limb frequencies constant, split epiphyses are more common in hominid-generated assemblages than in carnivore-generated assemblages. Split specimens also differ in the details of fracture form, location, and associated damage, depending on the modifier.

Geological scratching refers to fine linear striae, usually occurring in aligned arrangements on prominent or flat bone surfaces (Figure 5.4A). Because stone tools and natural stones in sediments can produce similar traces on bone, the positions of the striae in relation to skeletal anatomy are important for their definition. Geological striae may or may not follow the distribution of muscle or ligament attachments, whereas the majority of cut marks should (e.g., Binford 1978). Geological scratching tends to occur in patches and often coincides with localized abrasion.

Cut marks refer to fine linear traces on bone surfaces caused by stone tools. On long bones, cut marks may be aligned three ways relative to the main axis of the element: diagonally to (Figure 5.5A,B), perpendicularly to, or with the axis (Figure 5.5C). It is not possible to make a positive identification of cut marks in every case, regardless of whether traces are studied with the naked eye or through image enhancement techniques; judgment is required in either situation. However, certain characteristics, such as placement on the skeletal anatomy and details of form, permit a high level of certainty. Dubious cases are classified as geological scratches. In this study, cut marks (and suspected tool marks) were examined in strong light with the aid of an (10X) optical microscope.

Gnawing refers to any of several kinds of damage caused by carnivore teeth and salivary enzymes. Gnawing damage includes punctures in trabecular bone, crenelation of break edges, salivary rounding, grooves, and related tooth drag marks. The average diameters of deep tooth punctures in trabecular bone are discussed later in an attempt to assess the body sizes of the gnawing carnivores. No evidence of gnawing by human teeth was found.

The quantitative account of bone damage by site and vertical provenience considers ungulate and carnivore remains separately. Damage patterns are evaluated in two steps: (1) frequencies of each type of damage; and (2) summary comparisons of key damage types, primarily gnawing, cut marks, and burning.

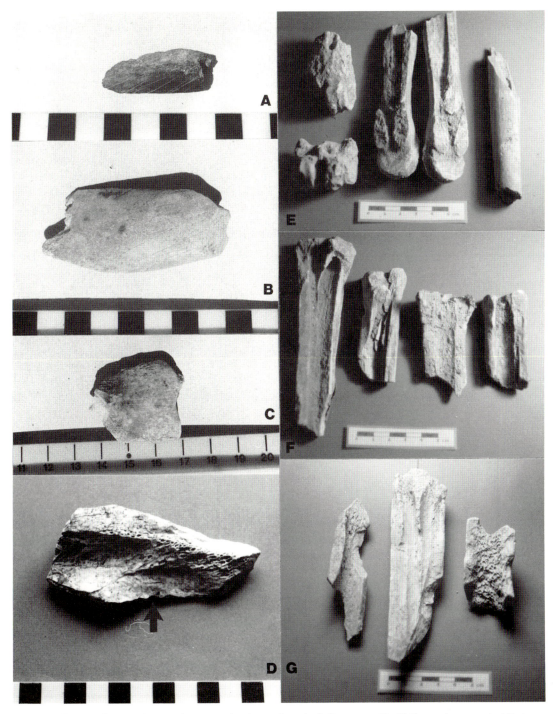

Figure 5.5 Fracture forms and cut marks on ungulate bones from the Italian caves: (A–B) Cut marks on cortical limb shaft fragments from Breuil, oriented diagonally to main axis of bone. (C) Tool scrape marks on cortical limb shaft fragment from Breuil, following main axis of bone. (D) Cone fracture on cortical limb shaft fragment from Breuil. Arrow shows point of impact, originating from exterior surface. (E) Split distal metapodial (center) of red deer from Guattari G1, damaged by spotted hyaena. (F) Split proximal metapodials of red deer from Guattari G1–4, possibly damaged by hominids. (G) Cortical limb shaft fragments with cone fractures from Buca della Iena, damaged by spotted hyaenas.

QUANTITATIVE ACCOUNT OF BONE DAMAGE BY SITE AND VERTICAL PROVENIENCE

Buca della Iena is a Pleistocene spotted hyaena den complex from Tuscany (Pitti and Tozzi 1971). The cave also contains some brown bear and badger components, but neither of these species is known to collect bone at dens in modern contexts (Chapter 4). Buca della Iena also contains some very ephemeral Mousterian hominid occupations, evident from the small quantities of stone tools in levels I1–4. Most of the ungulate skeletal material, on the other hand, comes from levels I5–6, and spotted hyaena bones and coprolites are common in all levels.

Table 5.4 shows the relative frequencies of each type of bone damage on ungulate and carnivore remains by level (I1–6). None of the ungulate bones

TABLE 5.4

Buca della Iena: Percentages of ungulate and carnivore bone NISP with burning, abrasion, weathering, and fracture damage by level

Damage type	I1 %	I2 %	I3 %	I4 %	I5 %	I6 %
a. ungulates:						
burning	·	·	·	·	·	·
abrasion	53	100	100	89	63	56
weathering	13	·	3	6	11	15
chemical pitting	2	·	·	·	·	1
fractures:						
bipolar impact/crushing	·	·	·	·	·	·
transverse dent	·	·	·	·	·	1
cone (1/2)	2	·	·	·	5	1
crushing	4	·	31	11	4	8
split through epiphysis	4	7	·	·	1	·
geological scratching	2	·	·	1	2	1
cut marks	·	·	·	·	·	·
total ungulate bone NISP	55	14	28	64	81	148
b. carnivores						
burning	·	·	·	·	·	·
abrasion	100	100	73	80	27	85
weathering	16	·	2	1	8	13
chemical pitting	·	·	·	·	·	·
factures:						
bipolar impact/crushing	·	·	·	·	·	·
transverse dent	·	·	·	·	·	·
cone (1/2)	·	·	·	·	·	·
crushing	4	·	·	·	2	8
split through epiphysis	·	·	·	·	1	·
geological scratching	·	·	2	·	1	·
cut marks	·	·	·	·	·	·
total carnivore bone NISP	25	11	56	71	92	71

Note: Percent values represent frequencies of each damage class relative to total ungulate or carnivore bone NISP (shown at the base of each column).

are burned or have cut marks on them. The incidence of abrasion is high (53–100%) in all levels, probably due to trampling and/or digging by the hyaenas, bears, and badgers inside the shelter. Geological scratches on bone surfaces are uncommon, but occur in most levels. Weathering damage occurs in low but significant frequencies on both the ungulate and carnivore bones, perhaps reflecting slower rates of burial in I1 and I6. Only slight through moderate weathering stages (following Behrensmeyer 1978) are represented, however, and the damage usually is restricted to one side of a specimen. The incidence of weathering in Buca della Iena is generally consistent with observations of modern carnivore dens in that bones often lie about the entrance or interior chambers for some time before becoming buried (e.g., Brain 1981; Hill 1984:117; Skinner et al. 1980; and my observations of Binford's Alaskan wolf den collections).

Of the various types of fracture damage, crushing is especially common in the Buca della Iena assemblages. Some cone fractures are present, in both the levels containing small quantities of stone tools (I1–4) and those where tools are completely absent (I5–6). The frequency of cone fractures ranges between 0 and 5 percent. Split long bone epiphyses range from 0 to 7 percent, and large spiral cracks leading away from breaks range from 0 to 3 percent. The frequencies of abrasion and weathering damage on carnivore remains (Table 5.4b) are entirely consistent with those for ungulates. However, cones, split epiphyses, and large spirals are rare or absent on carnivore bones. Their absence relates in part to the differing dimensions and textures typical of carnivore bones, since most are considerably smaller than ungulate bones and slightly less dense overall. Although hyaenas certainly chewed carnivore bones along with those of ungulates, significant differences in the quantities of marrow available from fresh carnivore and ungulate skeletons also may have affected consumers' interest in and methods for processing them differently.

Table 5.5 presents frequencies of gnawing damage in Buca della Iena. Gnawing marks are prevalent throughout the site, and on carnivore and herbivore remains alike. The incidence of gnawing among levels averages 21 percent for carnivore remains and 35 percent for ungulates, but can be as high as 100 percent. The frequency of gnawing is not affected by the existence of minor hominid components in levels I1–4.

Generally speaking, the intensity of gnawing damage by hyaenas normally exceeds that produced by all other carnivores, including wolves. Hyaena damage is unmistakable, provided that assemblages are large enough to warrant taphonomic comparisons, because all hyaenids are adapted to consume bone and digest it thoroughly (e.g., Owens and Owens 1985; Sutcliffe 1970). The consequences of this behavior are clearly evident on the bones in Buca della Iena, in both the frequencies of gnawing and the obvious nature of the damage (see below). Intensive gnawing by hyaenas, which typically occurs at dens, can lead to the selective deletion (total destruction via consumption) of smaller bones and/or less dense bones. The extent to which bone deletion occurs varies greatly with context, and especially with the availability of good (see Chapter 8).

Grotta Polesini is a late Upper Paleolithic (Epigravettian) rockshelter that yielded an enormous quantity of animal bone. For practical reasons, only certain species (small carnivores and roe deer) were studied for damage patterns (Table 5.6). Polesini represents a typical shelter fauna for this cultural period in Italy. Previous research on this site indicates that it was a residential camp from which multiple hunting operations were undertaken (Bietti and Stiner 1992). Most parts of prey carcasses were brought back to the shelter for processing and consumption.

The small carnivore and bear remains in Polesini provide some useful examples of bone modification by humans. Virtually all of the lynx, badger, and fox remains in the site represent humans' prey. Some carnivore bones show distinctive types of damage that can be tied to processing and, in some cases, consumption by humans. Burning is equally prevalent on the small carnivore and roe deer remains of Polesini; this damage often is restricted to one epiphysis when it occurs on long bones. Three fox femora, for example, are burned on the proximal condyle only, indicative of roasting. Cone fractures are absent from the small carnivore remains,

TABLE 5.5
Buca della Iena: Percentages of bone NISP with gnawing damage by taxon and level

Taxon	I1 %	I2 %	I3 %	I4 %	I5 %	I6 %	Total bone NISP
wolf	·	·	100	0	100	33	9
red fox	0	0	·	·	·	·	3
cave bear	9	0	15	13	18	19	99
polecat	·	·	·	0	·	·	1
badger	·	·	21	17	11	·	65
spotted hyaena	0	28	14	17	18	51	139
wild cat	·	·	·	·	20	·	5
lynx	·	0	0	·	·	·	2?
leopard	·	·	·	100	0	0	3
							(mean = 21%)
elephant	·	·	·	·	0	0	2
horse	64	50	·	0	28	100	50
rhinoceros	0	·	·	·	100	67	11
roe deer	50	100	0	40	17	40	26
red deer	67	100	50	54	37	70	86
giant deer	·	·	·	0	·	40	6?
aurochs	100	100	100	100	67	65	40
wild boar	·	·	0	100	0	·	7
							(mean = 35%)

Note: Damage values are expressed as percent of bone NISP by taxon. Total NISP for taxon (last column) is for all levels combined; this value is not the basis for calculating the percentage of specimens damaged in each level, but instead provides general information on the total quantities of material involved. The mean damage frequency (mean) is for all carnivores or all ungulates respectively.

TABLE 5.6
Polesini: Percentages of lynx, badger, fox, and roe deer bone NISP with burning, abrasion, weathering, and fracture damage

Damage type	Lynx %	Badger %	Fox %	Roe deer %
burning	8	4	2	7
weathering	·	·	·	·
fractures:				
cone (1/2)	·	·	·	< 1
split through epiphysis	·	·	·	3
gnawing	3	·	·	< 1
cut marks	·	4	< 1	< 1
total bone NISP	35	139	590	1216

Note: Data are for all cuts (1–12) combined. Percent values represent frequencies of each damage class of total bone NISP for each taxon (shown at the base of each column).

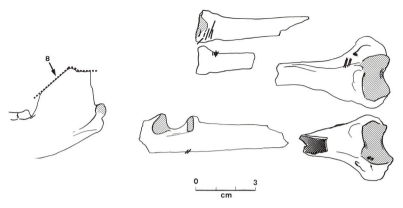

Figure 5.6 Cut marks and associated damage on badger bones from Polesini. Locations and forms of transverse breaks on limb shafts are typical. Damage on mandible occurs on eight specimens. Shading denotes an articular surface.

and cones are rare (< 1%) on roe deer remains. Cones are more common on larger ungulate prey (not shown), however, indicating that interassemblage comparisons of cone frequencies are meaningful only if considered for prey of comparable body size.

Polesini is unequivocally a human-generated fauna, yet a small fraction (< 1% overall, but lynx = 3%) of the small carnivore and roe deer bones were gnawed by carnivores. The gnawing damage appears to be from canids, almost certainly scavengers of humans' garbage at this site. All conceivable stages of human-caused processing damage are evident on roe deer (and other) ungulate remains. Many of the carnivore bones were modified similarly by humans (but see below).

Cut marks are relatively common on badger (4%), but rare on fox (< 1%) and roe deer (< 1%). Figure 5.6 illustrates cut marks on badger forelimbs and mandibles, coinciding with muscle and ligament attachment areas. Some of the cut marks may relate to skinning procedures, but the animals may have been eaten as well; the marrow cavities of the limb bones were opened. Consumption of badgers by humans generally is not common, but there are reports that badgers were considered good eating in Scotland in historic times (Burton 1979:116). Badger mandibles from Polesini were severed just below the condyle-coronoid area, a damage pattern that occurs on all of the mandibles (8 specimens) and is exclusive to this species. In describing the

morphology of the badger cranium, Burton notes that the jaw is locked to the skull by bony flanges (1979:114, also true of other mustelids) and must be severed or broken in order to detach it from the skull; hence the damage on the Polesini specimens.

The human residents of Polesini also ate parts of at least one bear. Bear bones are rare in this site, but one femoral fragment displays multiple cut marks (Figure 5.7) on the anterior aspect, just below the proximal head. The hind limb was detached from the pelvis in the manner routinely used for ungulate carcasses at this site—broken just below the femoral head rather than separated at the joint. Ethnographic accounts of human predation on bears are thinly distributed in the ethnographic literature on traditional Native American societies, yet suggest opportunistic killing of bears during the early stages of hibernation (e.g., Rogers 1981:69). This practice may be echoed in prehistoric situations, such as at Polesini and elsewhere (e.g., Bárta 1989, Slovakian Mesolithic).

Figure 5.8 illustrates cut mark frequencies (percent of sampled NISP), common locations of clean transverse breaks (usually oriented perpendicularly to the long axis), and split epiphyses on a randomized sample of limb elements of red deer. Only limb bones were sampled; hence, the head and axial regions are shaded-out in the drawing. Many of the cut marks occur midshaft (up to 30%), especially on the femur, tibia, and scapula. Nearly every red deer long bone was severed transversely, usually at the

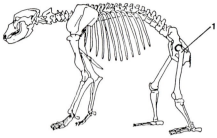 

Figure 5.7 Cut marks and associated damage on proximal bear femur from Polesini. Shading denotes an articular surface.

same location. The transverse fractures would have exposed a minimum of the medullary cavity of each bone, suggesting that the damage relates to early steps in the butchering process and/or that marrow was rendered by heating the bones and collecting the fat in liquid form. Deer scapulae from Polesini are never whole; the breaks are irregular on thin flat portions of the element, owing to its natural fragility. The high incidence of clean transverse breaks through limb bones is interesting, although the purpose of this processing procedure is unclear. The

limbs were almost certainly processed for marrow, and nearly all phalanges were broken open to expose the medulla (not quantified).

Grotta Palidoro is an Upper Paleolithic (early Epigravettian) rockshelter. Here, ungulate remains only from cuts 33 and 34 (Chiappella's 1956–59 excavations) are considered for comparative purposes (Table 5.7). Grotta Palidoro may have been used by human foragers in a manner similar to Grotta Polesini (e.g., Bietti 1976–77a; Cassoli 1976–77). Burning, weathering, and chemical pitting occur on 2 percent of all bone specimens. Geological scratching is rare. Transverse dents (5%), cone fractures (7%), and crushing (12%) are relatively common, and this assemblage is somewhat

Figure 5.8 Common locations of transverse fractures on limb bones, split epiphyses, and cut marks on the appendicular skeleton of red deer from Polesini. Cut mark frequencies are expressed as fractions of MNE; no data are available for trunk, neck, and head elements. Side of anatomy is not significant in this illustration.

TABLE 5.7
Palidoro 33–34: Percentages of ungulate bone NISP with burning, abrasion, weathering, and fracture damage

Damage type	%
burning	2
weathering	2
chemical pitting	2
fractures:	
bipolar impact/crushing	.
transverse dent	5
cone (1/2)	7
crushing	12
split through epiphysis	.
geological scratching	< 1
cut marks	5
total ungulate bone NISP	558

Note: Percent values represent frequencies of each damage class of total ungulate bone NISP (shown at base of each column).

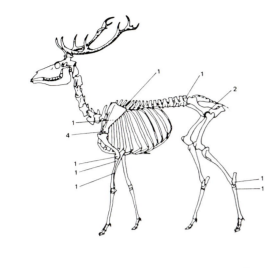

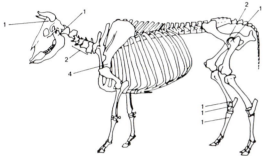

Figure 5.9 Locations and numbers of cut marks observed on red deer postcrania and all parts of large ungulates (aurochs and horse) from Palidoro. Side of anatomy is not significant in this illustration.

also found on the acetabular rims of the pelvis, lumbar vertebrae (probably those near the iliac crest), thoracic vertebrae (possibly those behind the proximal scapula), ventral sides of the cervical vertebrae, mandible, and the anterior horn base (the latter on aurochs). Observations for ribs are best considered missing, because these elements are uncommon in the collections and may have been overlooked by the excavators.

Table 5.8 summarizes the distributions of gnawing damage and cut marks in the Palidoro assemblages by species. As at Polesini, some of the Palidoro bones have been gnawed by carnivores (averaging 2%). Gnawing damage shows no consistently negative relationship to cut mark frequencies. The treatment of ungulate remains by humans, including the relatively high incidence of cut marks (mean = 5%, up to 14% on horse) and limb-sectioning practices, suggests that humans had complete access to all choice tissues of prey, and that gnawing occurred after humans discarded the material at the site. Note that the frequency of gnawing on badger remains is higher than for other species; this may be a sampling problem, since only seven specimens of badger were found in cuts 33–34. The fact that cut marks tend to be found on common prey and not on rare prey also may be explained by differing sample sizes.

Grotta Breuil is a late Middle Paleolithic cave on

more fragmented than the Polesini faunas. Nearly all of the fractures occurred while the bones were fresh, however, and the edges have a clean, unmarred appearance. The practice of shearing limb bones noted for the Polesini ungulates is also evident on those from Palidoro, but marrow processing resulted in greater destruction of long bone shafts at Palidoro. The relatively higher incidence of impact cones on the Palidoro ungulates also supports this observation.

The frequency of cut marks at Palidoro averages 5 percent of ungulate NISP. Figure 5.9 shows the distribution of cut marks on various skeletal elements, including the axial and head regions. The distribution of cut marks on limb bones is consistent with the Polesini red deer sample. Cut marks were

TABLE 5.8
Palidoro 33–34: Percentages of bone NISP with gnawing damage and cut marks by taxon

Taxon	Gnawing %	Cut marks %	Total bone NISP
badger	14	·	7
horse	·	14	7
wild ass	2	7	59
roe deer	·	·	1
red deer	5	9	146
aurochs	3	7	125
ibex	·	·	1
wild boar	9	·	11
	(mean = 2%)	(mean = 5%)	

Note: Damage values are expressed as percent of bone NISP by taxon. The mean damage frequency (mean) is for all carnivores or all ungulates respectively.

Monte Circeo. As explained above, the faunal material was recovered with the benefit of modern excavation methods. Both the identifiable and unidentifiable bone fractions have been studied and partitioned in the data set. Here, damage frequencies are presented only for the *identifiable* fraction from provisional stratum B3/4 (Table 5.9) to ensure comparability to the IIPU collections from the other sites.

Burning damage is relatively rare (1%—but see section on burning) on identifiable bones from Breuil 3/4, abrasion is minimal (< 1%), and there is no evidence of geological scratching. Weathering damage also is rare and restricted to the earliest stages when present. These data suggest that postdepositional destruction was minimal. Most fracture types are rare or absent with the notable exception of cones (16%). The high frequency of cone fractures, in concert with limited evidence of postdepositional damage, indicate that most fragmentation was due to marrow processing by hominids. Likewise, gnawing damage is especially rare (< 1%) in the B3/4 faunal assemblage. Cut marks

TABLE 5.9
Breuil B3/4: Percentages of ungulate and carnivore bone NISP with burning, abrasion, weathering, and fracture damage

Damage type	Ungulate %	Carnivore %
burning	1	·
abrasion	1	·
weathering	2	·
chemical pitting	·	·
fractures:		
bipolar impact/crushing	·	·
transverse dent	1	·
cone (1/2)	16	·
crushing	1	·
split through epiphysis	?	·
geological scratching	·	·
gnawing	< 1	·
cut marks	3	·
total bone NISP	299	7

Note: (w) wolf bone. Percent values represent frequencies of each damage class of total ungulate or carnivore bone NISP (shown at the base of each column).

TABLE 5.10
Breuil B3/4: Percentages of bone NISP with cut marks by taxon

Taxon	%	Total bone NISP
wolf	·	5
brown bear	·	2
	(mean = 0%)	
horse	·	3
fallow deer	·	2
roe deer	·	4
red deer	17	35
aurochs	14	7
ibex	13	23
	(mean = 3%)	

Note: Damage values are expressed as percent of bone NISP by taxon. The mean damage frequency (mean) is for all carnivores or all ungulates respectively.

occur on 3 percent of all ungulate specimens (Table 5.10); cut mark frequencies are higher for common prey taxa in the assemblage, occurring on 17 percent, 14 percent, and 13 percent of red deer, aurochs, and ibex bones respectively. Similar cut mark frequencies are observed at the late Upper Paleolithic shelters. Interspecific differences in cut

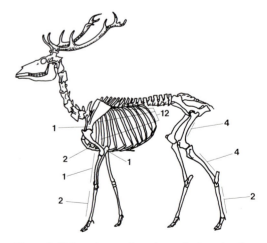

Figure 5.10 Locations and numbers of cut marks observed on red deer postcrania from Breuil Br. Many of the cut marks occur on long bone shafts rather than on epiphyses. Side of anatomy is not significant in this illustration.

mark frequencies within assemblages may be explained by prey body size: soft tissue attachments are stronger in larger prey; hence humans' greater reliance on tools during the butchering process, regardless of the procedural details.

Figure 5.10 illustrates the distribution of cut marks on red deer bones from another Breuil assemblage, the redeposited (Br) zone excavated in 1987. This assemblage is derived from a limited array of intact strata below B3/4 that collapsed recently (see

Chapter 3). The Br sample is much larger than the in situ B3/4 assemblage and thus is better suited for comparisons to the late Upper Paleolithic faunas from Palidoro and Polesini. The frequencies of cut marks on the Br ungulates are in complete agreement with the observations for the Upper Paleolithic shelter faunas. Moreover, all processing stages are in evidence, including carcass disarticulation, defleshing, and opening virtually all limb and mandible medullary cavities for marrow. Considerable ev-

TABLE 5.11

Sant'Agostino: Percentages of ungulate and carnivore bone NISP with burning, abrasion, weathering, and fracture damage by layer

Damage type	S0 %	S1 %	S2 %	S3 %	S4 %	SX %
a. ungulates:						
burning	3	3	6	1	·	·
abrasion	10	11	10	7	6	3
weathering	15	29	28	44	32	40
chemical pitting	·	1	3	1	·	< 1
fractures:						
bipolar impact/crushing	·	< 1	·	·	·	·
transverse dent	3	3	1	1	1	2
cone (1/2)	7	6	6	4	5	·
crushing	2	3	3	4	2	1
split through epiphysis	7	8	8	9	·	8
geological scratching	·	1	2	3	1	< 1
cut marks	4	7	5	3	8	·
total ungulate bone NISP	285	319	168	74	63	313
b. carnivores:						
burning	1-b	1-w	·	·	·	·
abrasion	9	8	8	5	4	2
weathering	9	14	10	23	23	6
chemical pitting	·	·	·	·	·	·
fractures:						
bipolar impact/crushing	·	·	·	·	·	·
transverse dent	·	·	·	·	·	·
cone (1/2)	·	·	1-f	·	·	·
crushing	·	·	1-f	·	·	·
split through epiphysis	1-f	·	1-f	·	·	·
geological scratching	·	·	·	·	·	1-f
cut marks	·	1-b	1-s	·	·	·
total carnivore bone NISP	65	91	90	56	26	81

Note: (b) bear, (w) wolf, (f) fox, (s) seal. Percentage values represent frequencies of each damage class for total ungulate or carnivore bone NISP (shown at the base of each column). None of the ibex bones are burned. Weathering damage is slightly more advanced on bones from SX.

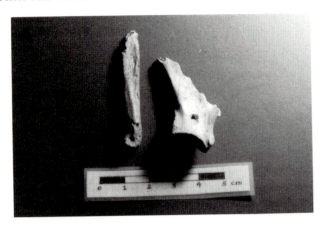

Figure 5.11 Gnawed remains of (A) wild cat from Moscerini M5 and (B) foxes from Sant'Agostino S0–4.

idence of defleshing and some sectioning scores are found on the rib cage.

Grotta di Sant'Agostino is one of the late Middle Paleolithic caves near Gaeta. As concerns ungulate remains, the major agencies of bone collection to be distinguished in this site are Mousterian hominids and wolves. Sant'Agostino differs in this regard from the other Middle Paleolithic caves (Moscerini, Guattari), where hominid occupations alternated primarily with spotted hyaenas (although some wolf remains are present in Moscerini M5).

The patterns of bone damage on the Sant'-Agostino faunas suggest a complex taphonomic history, involving both hominids and carnivores during the formation of each assemblage except in the case of SX. Table 5.11a shows that ungulate remains from every level display a wide array of damage types. Some damage is directly attributable to hominids, but a quick comparison of Tables 5.12 and 5.13 suggests an amalgam of events. For example, some wolf (innominate fragment), bear (first phalanx), and monk seal (carpal) bones from layers S0, S1, and S2 are burned or cut marked (Table 5.11b), but gnawing damage is frequent in all layers (Table 5.13). With the exception of SX, there is no stratigraphic separation of bone damage patterns according to biological agencies; hominids and canids (foxes in some layers, wolves in others) participated in creating and altering the very same assemblages. The analysis of Sant'Agostino therefore must address the sequence of modifying events and the possibility of contemporaneous effects by hominid and carnivore consumers.

Of the carnivore taxa represented in the

Sant'Agostino deposits, wolves are of especial concern, because their diet includes large prey, they are social, and they are avid bone collectors. Layer SX is very rich in wolf bones and lacks stone tools. Wolf remains are present in some of the tool-bearing layers, but wolves are much less common there, except in S4. Red fox and wild cat remains occur in all layers, regardless of whether stone tools are present and most show evidence of gnawing by other small carnivores (Figure 5.11B) or by wolves. Because foxes are, as a rule, diligent pilferers and scavengers, they also must be considered potential modifiers at Sant'Agostino, regardless of who brought the bones to the site. Foxes are most common where wolves are rare (see Chapter 4), suggesting that human presence exerted a stronger negative effect on the abundance of wolf remains than fox

remains. In other words, there is less evidence of human-avoidance by foxes than by wolves.

Table 5.11a shows that burning is relatively common on ungulate bones in S0 through S2, less common in S3. No burning is evident on ungulate bones in S4, although some stone tools are present (see Table 4.5). None of the bones in SX are burned, where lithic artifacts are completely absent. Abrasion is common on bones in most layers, but drops noticeably in the wolf-associated and spatially separate deposit SX. Weathering damage is relatively common throughout the site, ranging between 15 and 44 percent, but only the earlier stages of weathering damage are represented. Weathering damage is slightly more advanced in SX. Evidence of geological scratching is also relatively common at Sant'Agostino. All three types of damage (abra-

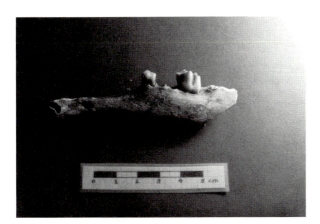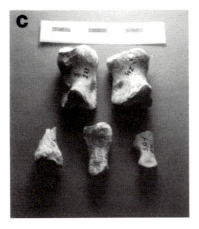

Figure 5.12 Examples of cut marks on herbivore bones from Sant'Agostino: (A) deer mandible from S0, (B) horse vertebra from S1, (C) wild boar phalanges from S0–S3, and (D) aurochs proximal metatarsal from S1.

sion, weathering, and scratching) are more likely to occur with prolonged exposure of bones on the ground surface. This may also be relevant for understanding why so much gnawing damage occurs in conjunction with human modification in layers S0 through S4. The frequencies of geological striae may be slightly inflated due to my conservative system for assessing possible cut marks. However, the forms attributed to geological scratching in the Sant'Agostino faunas are distinct from those classified as cut marks (Figure 5.12).

Virtually all fracture forms indicate that the bones were broken while fresh. Cones and dents are common in S0–4 (especially the upper layers), but absent from SX. Split long bone epiphyses are relatively abundant, always on the lower limb bones, especially metapodials. Most of the splits appear to have been made by hominids, although some fragments were subsequently gnawed by canids. Large spirals and bipolar impact/crushing are rare.

Cut marks on carnivores are infrequent and, as noted above, confined to one bear (Figure 5.13, Tables 5.11b and 5.12) and one monk seal (a rare species). No other carnivore remains have cut marks despite relatively high numbers of the former in some layers. Cut marks are common on ungulate

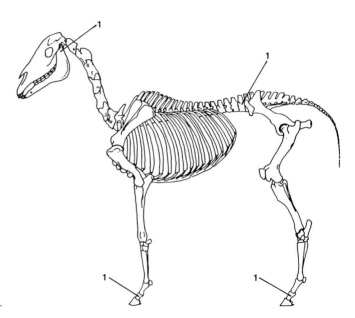

Figure 5.13 Locations and numbers of cut marks on horse and brown bear from Sant'Agostino. Side of anatomy is not significant in this illustration.

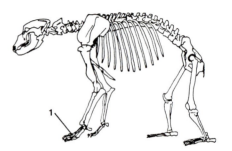

TABLE 5.12
Sant'Agostino: Percentages of bone NISP with cut marks by taxon and level

Taxon	S0 %	S1 %	S2 %	S3 %	S4 %	SX %	Total bone NISP
wolf	0	0	0	0	0	0	100
red fox	0	0	0	0	0	0	199
brown bear	0	33	0	0	.	0	15
weasel	0	.	.	.	.	.	1
pine martin	.	.	.	0	.	.	4
badger	0	0	0	0	.	.	5
wild cat	0	0	0	0	0	0	77
lynx	.	0	.	.	.	.	1
leopard	0	0	.	0	0	.	6
monk seal	.	.	100	.	.	.	1
							(mean < 1%)
horse	0	28	.	0	100	.	11
wild ass	.	.	0	.	.	.	1
rhinoceros	.	.	.	.	.	.	.
fallow deer	13	3	8	11	0	0	97
roe deer	2	6	3	0	12	3	352
red deer	1	5	6	4	17	0	330
aurochs	5	14	0	0	0	0	59
ibex	0	0	0	0	0	0	257
wild boar	10	10	9	0	20	0	115
							(mean = 4%)

Note: Damage values are expressed as percent of bone NISP by taxon. Total NISP for taxon (last column) is for all levels combined; this value is not the basis for calculating the percentage of specimens damaged in each level, but instead provides general information on the total quantities of material involved. The mean damage frequency (mean) is for all carnivores or all ungulates respectively.

remains from layers S0–4 of Sant'Agostino, as shown in Table 5.12. In contrast, only a few possible cut marks occur on roe deer bones in layer SX; none of these can be firmly attributed to tools as opposed to geological scratching. If the SX assemblage is removed from consideration, the incidence of cut marks on ungulates exceeds the averages for any other Paleolithic site in the study sample. The anatomical distributions of cut marks on red deer, fallow deer, aurochs (Figure 5.14), wild boar, and roe deer (Figure 5.15) reflect complete, primary access by hominids to the richest tissues of these prey. Ungulate limbs in layers S0–3 often were sheared transversely through the bone by hominids, partly or wholly defleshed, and the marrow cavities invariably opened. The situation is quite different in wolf-rich layer SX, where prey limb bones and mandibles often were not opened or, if so, incompletely (see below).

Evidence of carnivore gnawing, shown in Table 5.13, introduces some confusion to what heretofore seemed a fairly straightforward separation of hominid (S0–3) and wolf (SX) occupations. Gnawing damage is prevalent on ungulate and carnivore bones from all layers, averaging 19 percent on carnivore remains and 12 percent on ungulate remains for the site as a whole. Resolving the contradictions posed by human-caused tool marks, burning, and carnivore gnawing warrants a temporary retreat to more secure ground. First, wolves are prevalent in SX where tools are absent, SX is a discrete excavation area, and ungulate remains show no clear signs of hominid modification. We may conclude, therefore, that SX is a wolf den fauna. Second, evidence of hominid modification is prevalent on ungulates only in layers that also contain Mousterian tools (S0–3), where wolf remains are present but greatly outnumbered by foxes (see Table 4.8).

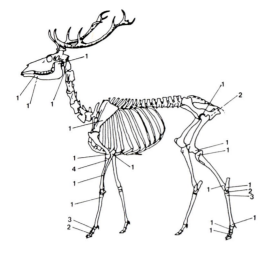

scavanging was possible for many months. The Sant'Agostino ungulates from S0–3 therefore appear to represent situations in which human-generated refuse attracted scavenging carnivores, particularly canids and possibly bears. Pilfering of certain skeletal elements from the refuse middens would seem likely in this situation, but, as will be shown in Chapter 9, was confined primarily to axial elements, if it happened at all. Most carnivore remains in the tool-bearing layers (S0–3) certainly represent prey of hominids; many soft tissues of foxes may simply have been left to scavangers; cut marks and burning damage on carnivores from the tool-bearing layers are scarce relative to gnawing damage. Gnawing damage to the SX fauna occurred in a different context; these bones were collected by

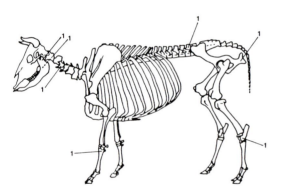

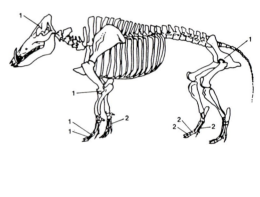

Figure 5.14 Locations and numbers of cut marks on red/fallow deer and aurochs from Sant'Agostino. Side of anatomy is not significant in this illustration.

The faunas from layers S0–3 of Sant'Agostino provide the only clear cases of contemporaneous damage by hominid and carnivore agencies in the entire study sample; it is significant that the overlap is confined to hominid-canid interactions. While examples of damage overprinting on specimens are uncommon at Sant'Agostino (see below), they invariably point to hominids as the primary consumers in S0–3 and canids as the secondary modifiers. It is not clear if gnawing by the canids took place while hominids were using the site or after they left. Certainly, the weathering data indicate that many of the bones lay exposed for some time before becoming buried in the sand and suggest that

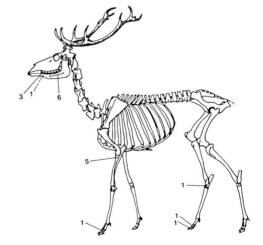

Figure 5.15 Locations and numbers of cut marks on wild boar and roe deer from Sant'Agostino. Side of anatomy is not significant in this illustration.

TABLE 5.13
Sant'Agostino: Percentages of bone NISP with gnawing damage by taxon and level

Taxon	S0 %	S1 %	S2 %	S3 %	S4 %	SX %	Total bone NISP
wolf	20	25	0	0	14	36	100
red fox	14	23	20	19	33	10	199
brown bear	25	0	0	100	.	20	15
weasel	0	.	.	.	.	.	1
pine martin	.	.	.	0	.	.	4
badger	0	0	0	0	.	.	5
wild cat	20	9	7	17	0	33	77
lynx	.	0	.	.	.	.	1
leopard	0	0	.	50	0	.	6
monk seal	.	.	0	.	.	.	1
							(mean = 19%)
horse	0	0	.	100	0	.	11
wild ass	.	.	100	.	.	.	1
rhinoceros	.	.	.	.	.	.	.
fallow deer	8	3	8	0	20	0	97
roe deer	7	14	19	17	18	16	352
red deer	11	6	13	4	0	0	330
aurochs	10	3	0	33	0	0	59
ibex	7	36	15	12	30	18	257
wild boar	8	2	24	10	0	0	115
							(mean = 12%)

Note: Damage values are expressed as percent of bone NISP by taxon. Total NISP for taxon (last column) is for all levels combined; this value is not the basis for calculating the percentage of specimens damaged in each layer, but instead provides general information on the total quantities of material involved. The mean damage frequency (mean) is for all carnivores or all ungulates respectively.

denning wolves (see also Chapter 12 on wolf age structure).

Wolf remains in SX accumulated as the result of natural age-dependent mortality in the context of denning (Chapter 12). Because of the season and brief duration of den use by wolves in any given year, it is at least possible that alternations between hominids and wolves took place in rapid succession, in contrast to hyaena-hominid alternations at some of the other caves. The situation in S4 is problematic; damage to ibex bones resembles that on wolf-collected material from SX, but some of the bones of horse, deer, and wild boar have cut marks on them. The S4 assemblage appears to be a palimpsest of human and wolf occupations of the cave, wherein wolf effects predominate.

Grotta dei Moscerini is a deeply stratified Middle Paleolithic site. While ungulate remains and Mousterian stone tools occur in all six major level groups

(as defined in Chapter 3), only those faunas from the upper part of the interior excavation (level group M5) are rich in carnivore remains (Table 5.14) and display high levels of gnawing (Figure 5.11A and Table 5.15). The lower part of the interior excavation (M6), and most of the deep exterior sequence (especially M2, M3, and M4), yield faunas of a distinctly different character: bones seldom are gnawed, stone tools and burning damage are common, and carnivore remains are rare. The origin of the exterior M1 fauna is more ambiguous, due to small sample size, but this level group may correspond to the carnivore-dominated component in the interior group M5.

Table 5.14 summarizes bone damage data for ungulate and carnivore remains by level group in Moscerini. Burning damage is especially common on ungulate remains in M2 (52%) and M3 (32%), less so in M4 (7%) and M6 (7%). Burned bones are rare

TABLE 5.14

Moscerini: Percentages of ungulate and carnivore bone NISP with burning, abrasion, weathering, and fracture damage by level group

Damage type	M1 %	M2 %	M3 %	M4 %	M5 %	M6 %
a. ungulates:						
burning	·	52	32	7	2	7
abrasion	·	5	6	9	5	22
weathering	·	9	19	21	18	36
chemical pitting	·	·	·	·	·	·
fractures:						
bipolar impact/crushing	·	5	12	12	6	27
transverse dent	14	9	11	5	9	36
cone (1/2)	·	5	7	5	3	5
crushing	·	19	38	42	10	63
split through epiphysis	·	·	1	·	2	17
geological scratching	·	·	·	·	·	·
cut marks	·	·	·	·	< 1	·
total ungulate bone NISP	7	21	164	42	226	41
b. carnivores:						
burning	·	·	·	·	·	·
abrasion	·	·	·	·	9	·
weathering	·	·	100	·	16	·
chemical pitting	·	·	·	·	·	·
fractures:						
bipolar impact/crushing	·	·	·	·	·	·
transverse dent	·	·	·	·	·	·
cone (1/2)	·	·	·	·	·	·
crushing	·	·	·	·	1	·
split through epiphysis	·	·	·	·	·	·
geological scratching	·	·	·	·	·	·
cut marks	·	·	·	·	1	·
total carnivore bone NISP	0	2	1	1	128	2

Note: Percent values represent frequencies of each damage class for total ungulate or carnivore bone NISP (shown at the base of each column).

in carnivore-associated M5 (2%), and absent from the small sample from M1. The prevalence of burning in M2 and M3 is unusual compared to other Mousterian caves in the study sample; it probably indicates that the excavations at Moscerini cut through a series of hearth-centered activity areas. Segre describes burn features for these level groups in his 1949 field notes, but detailed spatial information is not available. The incidence of burning on mollusk remains (Chapter 6) follows the same distribution, whereas burned artifacts are common throughout the many levels of Moscerini (see below).

Abrasion damage is moderately frequent throughout the Moscerini site, usually ranging between 5 and 9 percent, but up to 22 percent in M6. Weathering is fairly common in all level groups (9–36%), again highest in M6, but nearly all weathering damage is confined to the earliest stages (following Behrensmeyer 1978). Higher frequencies of abra-

TABLE 5.15
Moscerini: Percentages of bone NISP with gnawing damage by taxon and level group

Taxon	M1 %	M2 %	M3 %	M4 %	M5 %	M6 %	Total bone NISP
red fox	·	·	·	·	17	·	6
brown bear	·	0	0	0	11	0	57
spotted hyaena	·	0	·	·	7	0	55
wild cat	·	·	·	·	7	·	14
monk seal	·	·	·	·	0	·	2
							(mean = 9%)
horse	·	·	0	·	0	·	11
rhinoceros	·	·	·	·	·	·	·
fallow deer	0	0	0	0	0	0	40
roe deer	25	0	0	14	3	0	143
red deer	·	0	0	0	55	3	211
aurochs	0	·	0	·	17	·	16
ibex	·	·	0	·	20	·	13
wild boar	·	·	0	·	·	·	1
hippopotamus	·	·	·	·	·	·	·
							(mean = 7%)

Note: Damage values are expressed as percent of bone NISP by taxon. Total NISP for taxon (last column) is for all levels combined; this value is not the basis for calculating the percentage of specimens damaged in each level group, but instead provides general information on the total quantities of material involved. The mean damage frequency (mean) is for all carnivores or all ungulates respectively.

sion and weathering damage in M6 may suggest slower rates of burial. Transverse sectioning, impact crushing, and cone fractures are prevalent on ungulate remains, except in M5 where these kinds of damage are significantly less common (Table 5.14a). These data are consistent with the fact that level groups M2, M3, M4, and M6 are far richer in burned bones and stone tools (see Table 4.5). Only level group M5 contains large quantities of carnivore remains (see Table 4.6) and high frequencies of gnawing damage (Table 5.15). Roe deer bones from M1 and M4 also display elevated frequencies of gnawing, but the roe deer samples are very small, and other mammal remains in these level groups do not show gnawing. Cut marks are virtually nonexistent in the Moscerini faunas; the only fully convincing cut mark is, ironically, on a bear (second) phalanx in M5.

The near absence of cut marks in the Moscerini assemblages from M2, M3, M4, and M6 is surprising in light of abundant burning damage, stone tools, and fractures (see below) that normally point to hominid feeding activities. The scarcity of cut marks on ungulate bones in the tool-bearing level groups can be explained by the fact that so few limb elements are represented; the ungulate faunas in the cultural levels of Moscerini are dominated by head parts (documented in Chapter 9). Given the paucity of limb bones, the frequencies of cone fractures are relatively high in M2, M3, M4, and M6 (5–7%), also indicating hominid processing activities. Cones are rarer in M5 (3%), where carnivore remains, gnawing damage, and ungulate limb bones are prevalent.

In sum, damage frequencies indicate that the agencies responsible for bone collection and modification in M5 (and possibly M1) differed from those responsible for the other level groups. Cones, burning, and transverse fractures (especially on ungulate mandibles; see below) link the bones directly to hominid activities in level groups M2, M3, M4, and M6. The faunas in M5 instead appear to represent a mixture of hominid and carnivore components, dominated by spotted hyaena bone-collecting activities. Faunal remains in level group M1 are too few to evaluate.

Grotta Guattari is a stratified Middle Paleolithic cave site. The circumstances surrounding the discovery of three Neandertal cranial fossils there (one nearly complete cranium and two mandibles) have made Guattari the subject of considerable debate (Stiner 1991a). Two of the hominid fossils occur in association with carnivore and herbivore remains on the most recent cave floor (G0), but only the subsurface levels contain stone tools (G1, G2, G4, and G5; see Table 4.5). Nonhuman mammalian remains occur both on the preserved surface and in most subsurface levels. As explained in Chapter 4, hyaena and other carnivore remains, and hyaena coprolites, are particularly abundant in G0 and G1.

Most of the bones from the surface of Guattari (G0) are partially covered by a thick calcium coating or cave coral. Roughly 40 percent of each bone is obscured by these concretions, making identification of subtle damage types (cut marks, abrasion, and geological scratching) difficult for the G0 fauna. Some specimens from G1 also display thinner coverings of the same material, but most types of damage are discernible. Bones in the levels below G1 are not covered with calcium concretions. The distributions of the concretions on bones are more or less random with respect to mammalian skeletal anatomy; the coatings merely reduce the size (amount of observable bone surface area) of the sample with regard to subtle damage types, such as cut marks. The presence of concretions on bones from G0 and G1 does not significantly bias observations of the more spectacular damage classes, such as gnawing by hyaenas.

Table 5.16 summarizes bone damage frequencies on ungulate remains in Guattari by level. None of the identifiable specimens are burned. The absence of burning damage may be deceiving, however, since a number of small carbonized cortical bone chips were found among the lithic collections from G2 and G4–5. These unidentifiable burned bone fragments were mistaken for lithic debris, the only reason why they were retained. While no information on the relative proportion of burned specimens in the unidentifiable fraction is available, this serendipitous sample shows that hearths once existed in levels G2, G4, and G5.

Abrasion and weathering damage occur in comparatively high frequencies wherever ungulate re-

mains are present, particularly in the larger assemblages of G0 through G2. Weathering damage is evident, although confined to the early stages. Both kinds of damage suggest that the bones in the upper levels were subjected to some trampling or digging by carnivores and that the bones often lay exposed for some time prior to burial in cave sediments. Some of the ungulate bone specimens from Guattari display a distinctive chemical pitting caused by acidic compounds; the pits are quite large, are irregular in circumference, and have smooth basins. While gnawing damage is pervasive (Table 5.17), the pits were not caused by carnivore digestive acids; they are from some other (nonbiological) factor unique to this cave.

The types of fracture damage most often associated with human butchering and marrow-processing are rare or absent from the faunas of G0–2 (Table 5.16). Cones are present, but they are relatively uncommon if compared to hominid-associated faunas of other sites. The small sample from G5 shows a high incidence of cone fractures (9%), well above the frequencies noted in the hyaena reference cases from Buca della Iena. The incidence of split epiphyses and large spirals is also noticeably higher in G4 and G5, suggesting a different agency than those dominating bone accumulation and modification in G0–1. The situation in G2 is less clear-cut. Hominid presence nonetheless is evidenced in levels G1, G2, G4, and G5 by stone tools. However, only the faunas of G4 and G5 can be linked to hominids on the basis of bone damage frequencies.

Geological scratching is rare in G0–1, and absent in all other levels. Figure 5.4a is an example of scratching on the shaft of an aurochs tibia from the surface (G0); the scratches in this case closely resemble grooves caused by the milk dentition of juvenile carnivores, but the striae are very straight and have angular rather than U-shaped cross-sections. They certainly are not cut marks. In fact, no definite cut marks were found on any of the ungulate remains in Guattari, although four possible cases on fallow deer are shown in Figure 5.16; excavated well after the main field campaigns, the prevenience of these remains is unclear. The general condition and degree of fossilization of the fallow deer bones suggest that they came from a very different part of the site than the earlier excavated material, pos-

TABLE 5.16
Guattari: Percentages of ungulate and carnivore bone NISP with burning, abrasion, weathering, and fracture damage by level

Damage type	G0 %	G1 %	G2 %	G3 %	G4 %	G5 %	G7 %
a. ungulates:							
burning	·	·	*	·	*	*	·
abrasion	20	29	32	·	13	·	·
weathering	21	12	18	·	13	·	·
chemical pitting	8	9	·	·	·	9	·
fractures:							
bipolar impact/crushing	·	·	·	·	·	·	·
transverse dent	·	·	·	·	·	·	·
cone (1/2)	1	2	3	·	·	9	·
crushing	4	1	3	·	·	·	·
split through epiphysis	4	3	·	·	7	9	·
geological scratching	< 1	1	·	·	·	·	·
cut marks	·	·	·	·	·	·	·
total ungulate bone NISP	435	169	28	1	15	11	1
b. carnivores:							
burning	·	·	·	·	·	·	·
abrasion	24	4	·	·	·	·	·
weathering	15	4	·	·	·	·	·
chemical pitting	7	4	·	·	·	·	·
fractures:							
bipolar impact/crushing	·	·	·	·	·	·	·
transverse dent	·	·	·	·	·	·	·
cone (1/2)	·	·	·	·	·	·	·
crushing	13	·	·	·	·	·	·
split through epiphysis	·	·	·	·	·	·	·
geological scratching	·	·	·	·	·	·	·
cut marks	·	·	·	·	·	·	·
total carnivore bone NISP	45	22	2	·	1	·	·

Note: Burning damage is not apparent on identifiable bone specimens (*), but twenty-nine small carbonized cortical fragments were found in the Guattari lithic collections. Percent values represent frequencies of each damage class of total ungulate or carnivore bone NISP (shown at the base of each column).

sibly from semibrecciated sediments near the cave mouth.

The total number of Mousterian artifacts increases as hyaena remains decrease through the strata sequence of Guattari, with G0 containing no more than two flints and plenty of hyaena bones. Given the large quantities of spotted hyaena and other carnivore remains in G0–1, the absence of cut marks on ungulate remains in the upper levels is not surprising (Table 5.16a).

Sample sizes are small for the faunas of G4 and G5, posing serious problems for interpretation. However, these levels are rich in artifacts, several of the burned bone chips come from here, and cone fractures are abundant in G5. The absence of cut marks in these cases could be explained by anatomical representation, since the faunas are biased toward cranial elements (documented in Chapter 9). Only one hyaena specimen is present in G4 (6% of that faunal assemblage), none in G5.

TABLE 5.17
Guattari: Percentages of bone NISP with gnawing damage by taxon and level

Taxon	G0 %	G1 %	G2 %	G3 %	G4 %	G5 %	G7 %	Total bone NISP
wolf	0	0	.	.	.	.	.	2
fox	.	+	+	.	+	.	.	.
cave bear	50	0	.	.	+	.	.	7
spotted hyaena	32	26	50	.	0	.	.	56
leopard	75	0	.	.	.	.	.	5
polecat	.	.	.	.	+	.	.	.
								(mean = 33%)
elephant	33	+	+	.	.	.	.	3
horse	42	37	100	100	25	+	.	58
rhinoceros	0	+	.	.	+	.	.	1
fallow deer	39	40	0	+	0	+	.	47
roe deer	30	0	0	+	+	0	.	64
red deer	58	47	62	+	20	0	.	335
giant deer	0	.	.	.	.	.	.	1
aurochs	52	45	100	.	0	14	0	137
ibex	.	+	+	.	.	.	.	.
wild boar	37	25	0	.	.	.	.	14
hippopotamus	.	.	.	+	+	.	.	+
								(mean = 44%)

Note: (+) This species appears in Cardini's provisional list of species published in Blanc and Segre (1953). I find many discrepancies between the 1953 list and my own counts, and am convinced that the former should be disregarded; also significant, level G3 is described as nearly sterile, yet several of the "missing" taxa are alleged to have come from here. Damage values are expressed as percent of bone NISP by taxon. Total NISP for taxon (last column) is for all levels combined; this value is not the basis for calculating the percentage of specimens damaged in each level, but instead provides general information on the total quantities of material involved. The mean damage frequency (mean) is for all carnivores or all ungulates respectively.

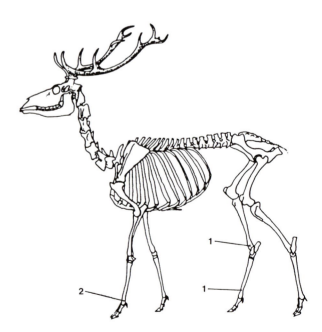

Figure 5.16 Locations and numbers of possible cut marks on unprovenienced fallow deer bones from Guattari. Side of anatomy is not significant in this illustration; all cut mark diagnoses are questionable.

Table 5.17 lists the frequencies of gnawing by species and level in Guattari. Gnawing damage is especially prevalent on ungulate remains from G0 through G2, decreasing though significant in the lower levels, G4 and G5. The incidence of gnawing damage in G0–2 is comparable to the frequencies of gnawing observed in the spotted hyaena dens of Buca della Iena. Crushing is common (13%) on specimens from the surface (Table 5.16), but, unlike human-caused damage, is irregular, localized, and clearly related to gnawing.

Grotta Guattari Is Not a Neandertal Ritual Chamber

The frequencies and intensities of gnawing damage on mammal bones are positively correlated to the abundance of spotted hyaena skeletal remains and coprolites in Guattari (Stiner 1991a). Hyaena remains are especially abundant in G0 and G1, as is evidence of their latrines. Data on species representation, coprolites, and bone damage for these upper levels unequivocally point to hyaenas as the primary bone collectors and modifiers. Mortality patterns for the hyaenas (Chapter 12) also support this conclusion. Hyaenas appear to have been solely responsible for the surface assemblage (G0), despite the presence of three hominid fossils and a few remains of leopard. Leopards are known to aggregate prey bones in some modern circumstances, mainly through their habit of stashing carcasses in trees that grow above natural karst fissures or traps (e.g., Brain 1981). Leopards also were a factor in bone collection in some Upper Pleistocene caves in Europe (see exchange between Stiner and Turner, in Stiner 1991a), but leopard bones are quite rare in the Latium sites, confined primarily to severely gnawed head parts. Fecal bone indicative of felid digestion is completely absent. Only two stone tools were found on G0, probably brought to the surface by postdepositional disturbance. Some of the larger bone specimens actually poke through the surface from G1, possibly linking them into one semicontinuous depositional unit.

The gnawing damage on ungulate bones in Guattari G0–1 resembles that from Buca della Iena (Figure 5.17, compare B–G) and gnawing damage by modern spotted hyaenas documented, for example, by Sutcliffe (1970). Because they are adapted to eat bone tissues, hyaena gnawing typically results in severe crenelation and salivary rounding of break edges, large punctures, tooth drag marks, and one or both ends (epiphyses) of long bones literally eaten away (e.g., Guattari specimens in Figure 5.4D). However, complete destruction of both epiphyses of long bones by carnivores is rare in the Italian caves; usually only one end is destroyed, the other left intact.

The Neandertal skull (Circeo I) from Guattari displays no clear signs of cut marks, but may have gnaw marks (White and Toth 1991). One or both of the Neandertal mandibles are gnawed on the ascending rami (also my observations), following a pattern found on large mammal head parts more generally. Figures 5.17F and 5.18 illustrate gnawing destruction on spotted hyaena skulls by other hyaenas, characteristic of what these predators do to any thick-walled skull. Anterior portions of the snout, orbital region, and zygomatic area have been destroyed on the right side of the hyaena cranium from G0, shown in Figure 5.17F. Similar damage occurs on cranial elements of bear and on one lion skull. The composite pattern of destruction, illustrated on an articulated hyaena skull in Figure 5.18, is not unlike that noted by White and Toth (1991) on the Neandertal cranium (Circeo I) and on the coronoid-condyle area of the Neandertal mandibles (Circeo II and III). The damaged zones, shaded in Figure 5.18, together show how hyaenas disarticulate the jaw from the cranium during prolonged episodes of gnawing. Comparable damage patterns are documented by Horwitz and Smith (1988) on human and carnivore head parts recovered from modern striped hyaena dens in Israel.

We conclude that the Neandertal fossils in Guattari were collected by spotted hyaenas primarily because they are spatially associated with unequivocal hyaena den material. The lack of unambiguous carnivore damage on the Neandertal cranium in no way contradicts its inferred association to the hyaena-collected fauna of Guattari G0, however: tapho-

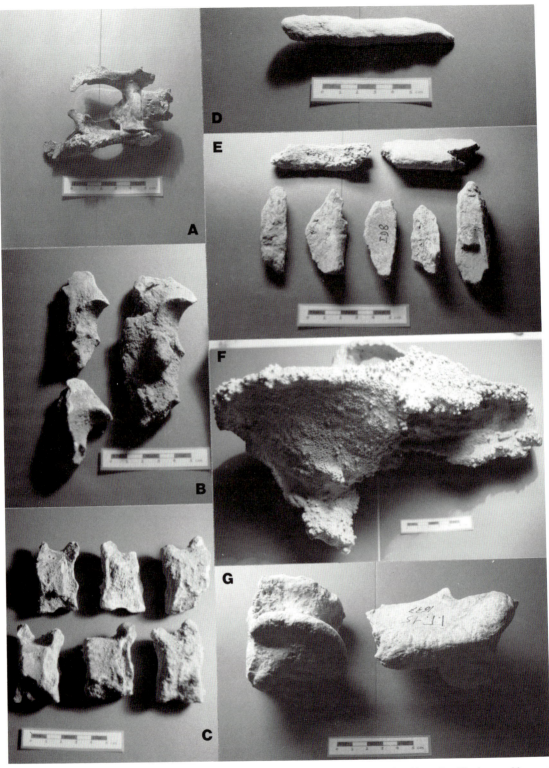

Figure 5.17 Examples of gnawing damage by carnivores: (A) Gnawed fox pelvis from Sant'Agostino S2, damaged by small carnivores, probably other foxes. (B) Gnawed red deer ulnae from Guattari G0–1, damaged by spotted hyaenas. (C) Gnawed deer astragali from Guattari G0–1, damaged by spotted hyaenas. (D) "Mouthed" cortical bone fragment from Guattari G1, rounded from salivary enzymes and gnawing by spotted hyaenas. (E) "Mouthed" cortical and flat bone fragments from Buca della Iena, rounded from salivary enzymes and gnawing by spotted hyaenas. (F) Spotted hyaena skull from surface (G0) of Guattari, damaged by other hyaenas. Note destruction of nasal and zygomatic regions, and calcite concretions covering upper portion of specimen. (G) Horse astragalus and calcaneum from Buca della Iena, gnawed by spotted hyaenas.

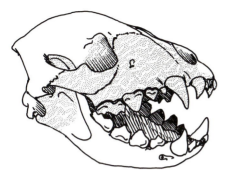

Figure 5.18 Areas on hyaena skulls (shaded) from Guattari G0–1 most commonly destroyed by other hyaenas. (From Stiner 1991a)

nomic analyses depend on large samples in which specific kinds of bone damage are repeated. Only half of the bones on the surface display evidence of gnawing, and the hominid fossils constitute a subsample of 3 in a total of 336 large mammal specimens. On the other hand, the presence of the hominid fossils amidst a den fauna does not necessarily mean that the Neandertals (MNI = 2?) were killed by spotted hyaenas. Human remains, scavenged from shallow graves, occasionally turn up in spotted, brown, and striped hyaena dens in the Middle East and Africa today (e.g., Skinner et al. 1980; Horwitz and Smith 1988).

Spotted hyaenas also dominate bone collections in G1 and, to a lesser extent, G2. However, the presence of lithic artifacts testifies to considerable hominid activity in these subsurface levels as well, especially in G2 (see section on mandible processing below). The faunas of G1 and G2 are separated from earlier cultural material by semisterile level G3. As noted above, the origins of the assemblages in levels G4 and G5 are more difficult to evaluate because the assemblages are small. One spotted hyaena phalanx exists in the G4 assemblage, and no carnivore remains occur in G5. Gnawing is apparent on some ungulate bones from G4 and G5, but it is less common than in the upper levels of Guattari. Stone tools and abundant cone fractures (9% in G5) suggest, but do not prove beyond all reasonable doubt, that hominids were the principal bone collectors and modifiers in the lower levels.

The taphonomic observations on the Guattari faunas lead to a radically different assessment of the cultural significance of this well-known cave site. The best-known interpretations of the surface assemblage—which still appear in many textbooks —cite the hominid and animal remains as evidence of Neandertal ritual burial, possibly cannibalized (Blanc 1958, 1961; Piperno 1976–77). Combined information on species representation and bone damage refutes this hypothesis, showing the surface fauna and most of G1 to be typical of hyaena lairs (see also Chapter 12). Level G2 represents some mixture of hyaena and (predominantly?) hominid activities, whereas the smaller assemblages of levels G4 and G5 appear to be the products of hominid activities.

Grotta Guattari is an interesting case from both a scientific and historic point of view. Sensational and controversial, the case of the Guattari surface (G0) nagged at paleoanthropologists' conceptions of what Neandertals were like. Oddly, Blanc (1939b:492) was the first to acknowledge the possibility of hyaena dens in the uppermost deposits of Guattari (G0, G1). In the year of the site's discovery, he suggested that alternating occupations by Neandertals and spotted hyaenas accounted for the associations of hyaena bones and coprolites with hominid cranial fossils there. His account implies, however, that only hominids would have introduced human skeletal material into the cave, citing "intentional" fracturing of bones, burned material, and Mousterian industries as proof that this was so. Blanc (1954:171) suggested a similar situation for several layers of Grotta del Fossellone, where abundant infant hyaenas (see Chapter 12) and coprolites were discovered in general association with the hominid cranial material (two adult teeth and one Neandertal child's mandible), and, among other bones, those of horses, pachyderms, and whale (one vertebra). We now know that some of Blanc's criteria for distinguishing hominid versus hyaena occupations of these caves are invalid, yet he and his co-workers— most notably L. Cardini—recognized the existence of significant hyaena den components in these caves long ago. Only later were these facts pushed aside or de-emphasized in favor of a more thoroughly humanistic explanation for anomalies in the G0 and G1 faunas (Blanc 1958, 1961; Piperno 1976–77).

Reinterpretation of Guattari is made possible primarily by recent innovations in the area of taphonomy and a more extensive knowledge base about the nature and signatures of human cannibalism (see White and Toth 1991). Such information was not available to researchers fifty years ago, a time when, instead, the widely influential works of Weidenreich, Chardin, and the Abbé Breuil asserted that early hominids at Zhoukoudien Cave in China were cannibals (Richards 1987:277; see also Binford 1981; Binford and Ho 1985). The Guattari case thus has served as a special focus point for research on the Middle Paleolithic, upon which analytical techniques are sharpened, new methods developed, and research questions refined over five decades. It is also an example of the perennial conflict between gaining knowledge for its own sake and the obvious market value of fleeting impressions for a wider, hungry audience, a problem that may never disappear from human evolution research.

SUMMARY OF KEY DAMAGE CLASSES, LITHIC ARTIFACTS, AND UNGULATE-CARNIVORE ABUNDANCE

Table 5.18 summarizes lithic artifact counts, ratios of large carnivore to ungulate bone NISP, and percentages of ungulate bones with cone fractures, burning, cut marks, and gnawing damage. Generally speaking, cone fractures are more frequent where large carnivore remains and gnawing frequencies are lower, despite the fact that carnivores are physically capable of producing cone fractures. Burning and cut marks are negatively related to the abundance of large carnivore remains in the assemblages.

While burning, cut marks, and high cone frequencies all may be considered indicative of hominid activities, these signatures do not necessarily show a clear numerical correspondence among the hominid-generated faunas. This is to be expected, given the wide array of foraging contexts in which bone damage by humans can arise. The fact that human effects can vary underlines the importance of using multiple damage signatures, not one alone, to evaluate and segregate the influences of hominids, carnivores, and other agencies. Assuming that all of one's criteria are equally appropriate, crossreferencing permits more rigorous taphonomic assessments.

Figure 5.19 is a scatter plot of the percent of ungulate bones gnawed (% NISP) and the ratio of large carnivore NISP to ungulate NISP. The assemblages from Sant'Agostino are removed from consideration, because overprinting of hominid and carnivore damage unique to this site would confuse the comparison (instead see next section on feeding sequences). Here, two distinct criteria of large carnivore influence are used together to assess carnivore roles in assemblage formation. Only large predator species are included in the carnivore-ungulate NISP ratio, because only they are known to collect ungulate bones in quantity. A high value on either axis of Figure 5.19 suggests increasing carnivore influence, but, because either measure can vary greatly with foraging circumstances (e.g., Kruuk 1972; Mills 1984a, 1984b; Henschel et al. 1979; Tilson et al. 1980), it is better to approach the question on two fronts simultaneously. Allowing that variation can occur on either axis, the expectation is that carnivore-generated cases should fan widely outward from the graph intercept. Hominid-generated cases should, instead, hug the intercept of the graph, forming a cluster of low values relative to both axes (unless damage overprinting is a problem, as at Sant'Agostino).

Many of the cases previously identified as cultural do, in fact, center on the intercept (filled circles) in Figure 5.19, including Moscerini M2, M3, M4, and M6, Breuil B3/4 (Br not plotted), and Palidoro 33–34 (the only lUP case plotted). Guattari G4 and G5 co-occur with hominid-generated assemblages from other sites. The hyaena den reference cases from Buca della Iena are widely scattered on the graph, high on one or both axes. The same is true for Guattari G0 and G1. The situation for Moscerini M5 and Guattari G2 is less clear, although they are well removed from the x-y-intercept; the frequency of gnawing damage is higher in G2, while the proportion of large carnivore remains is higher in M5. The intermediate po-

TABLE 5.18

Lithic counts, large carnivore to ungulate NISP, and percent of ungulate bone NISP damaged in the Italian faunas

Site and level	Lithics total	Ungulate NISP	Cones %	Burning %	Cut marks %	Gnawing %	Large carnivore NISP: ungulate NISP
Moscerini:							
M1	45	16	0	0	0	14	.00
M2	382	37	5	52	0	0	.05
M3	324	358	7	32	0	0	.01
M4	187	157	5	7	0	2	.01
M5	127	430	3	2	<<1	15	.36
M6	196	184	5	7	0	2	.02
Guattari:							
G0	2	849	1	0	0	50	.13
G1	240	615	2	0	0	44	.13
G2	452	104	3	*	0	28	.08
G4	876	50	0	*	0	0	.06
G5	482	49	9	*	0	7	.00
Sant'Agostino:							
S0	2863	744	7	3	4	8	.03
S1	3138	752	6	3	7	9	.03
S2	975	349	6	6	5	15	.02
S3	451	160	4	1	3	11	.10
S4	212	134	5	0	8	19	.18
SX	0	473	0	0	<<1	17	.17
Breuil:							
B3/4	—	576	16	1	3	<<1	.05[a]
Buca della Iena:							
I1	}35	87	2	0	0	44	.67
I2		18	0	0	0	28	.89
I3	33	36	0	0	0	11	1.89
I4	46	77	0	0	0	22	1.38
I5	0	102	5	0	0	18	.92
I6	0	299	1	0	0	52	.69
Palidoro:							
33–34	—	793	7	2	5	2	.00

[a]All large carnivore remains are from a highly localized concentration at the top of B3/4, in the rearmost portion of the cave.

Note: (*) Burned bone chips are present, but relative frequencies are not known. All percent damage values are of total ungulate bone NISP for designated level or level group.

sition of M5 and G2 suggests the mixed influences of hominid and carnivore agencies. It is interesting that, while carnivore damage is quite rare in some Paleolithic cases, common in others, gnawing is never completely absent from human-generated cave faunas in Italy. Refuse dumps created by mobile peoples, modern or ancient, typically are surface accumulations: bones may lie about before becoming buried, often attracting the attention of scavenging predators, and low-level gnawing is nearly inevitable.

Figure 5.20 illustrates a generally negative relationship between the frequencies of cone fractures and gnawing damage in the Italian shelter faunas.

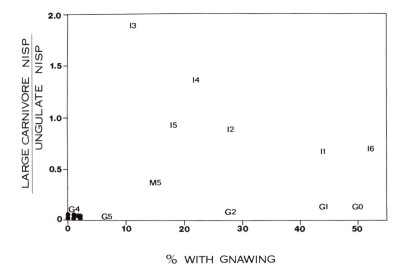

Figure 5.19 Identifiable ungulate bones with gnawing damage (% NISP) and the ratio of large carnivore NISP to ungulate NISP. Filled circles are M2, M3, M4, M6, B3/4, and P33–34; the plot excludes the Sant'Agostino assemblages.

Because any bone specimen may show either kind of damage, the two damage criteria are not autocorrelated, and plotting percentages of one against the other is permissible. Of the potential carnivore agencies, hyaenas are definitely known to produce cone fractures on cortical bone (e.g., Brain 1981:141–142), and wolves probably do so. However, humans will tend to generate many more cones with their stone hammers while processing bones for marrow (e.g., Binford 1978). Ignoring cases in which cones are completely absent (I2, I3,

I4, and SX), the incidence of gnawing in the Italian assemblages increases as the frequency of cones decreases, and the relationship is significant ($r = -.683$, $r^2 = .466$, N = 20, $.02 < P < .05$). The distributions of what are inferred to be hominid-collected versus hyaena-collected assemblages (including the Buca della Iena reference cases) intergrade within the area of 3 to 5 percent on the cones (x) axis. Otherwise the assemblages separate well, with hyaena-generated cases on the high end of the slope and hominid-generated cases on the low end.

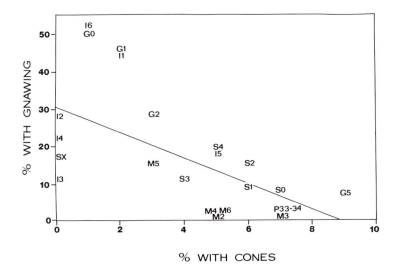

Figure 5.20 Percent identifiable ungulate bone NISP with cone fractures versus gnawing.

On Distinguishing Hominid-Carnivore Feeding Sequences

I have for the most part dichotomized damage criteria according to two distinct groups of collector-modifier agencies: hominids and carnivores. It also would be useful to know which taxa among the carnivores were most active in creating and damaging bones at each site. Were they, for example, all large species, or some combination of large and small? And do the diameters of tooth punctures vary with prey body size? Spotted hyaenas or wolves are implicated in several cases. The signatures of hyaenas have been discussed in detail above. What, then, does canid-caused damage look like? Sant'Agostino is the case in point, since substantial quantities of fox and/or wolf remains are represented in some layers. I suggested on the basis of species abundance that wolves were the main collector-modifiers in SX, and that they probably played a role in S4. Sant'Agostino also presents intriguing examples of contemporaneous overprinting of hominid and canid activities. Foxes, wolves, and possibly bears visited human refuse middens during the formation of assemblages in S0 through S3. Nearly ignored in the previous summary, the Sant'Agostino faunas receive special consideration here, focusing first on tooth puncture diameters and then presenting detailed accounts of damage superposition on individual specimens and on an assemblage-wide scale.

Puncture diameters and carnivore body size

Table 5.19 lists means and ranges for the diameters (mm) of carnivore tooth punctures in trabecular bone by site and species consumed. Only relatively deep punctures are considered, in an attempt to avoid superficial impressions caused by larger, pointed teeth. The data separate carnivore agencies into two general body size groups, large and small, and do not distinguish hyaena from wolf, or wild cat from fox.

Large punctures are found primarily on large carnivore and ungulate remains (e.g., Figure 5.4E), averaging 3.0 mm or more in diameter. The associated patterns of damage on ungulate and large carnivore bones also are similar; compare, for example, modern bison femurs gnawed by captive wolves (Figure 5.21F) to wolf long bones gnawed by Upper Pleistocene wolves at Sant'Agostino (Figure 5.21E). Large punctures are found on bones of smaller mammals, too (see fox pelvis in Figure 5.17A). Small puncture diameters, on the other hand, are confined to small taxa (e.g., other small carnivores, Figure 5.11; see also rabbits and hares in Chapter 6), except at late Upper Paleolithic Palidoro (domesticated dogs?, circa 15,000 B.P.).

The puncture marks are less than definitive in terms of who made them, but they are valuable indicators of dietary separation between small and large carnivores in the study sample. The data show that carnivores often scavanged or killed other carnivores of equivalent size, including conspecifics. Any small mammal could fall prey to a large carnivore, whereas small carnivores fed almost exclusively on small mammals. Carnivore deaths are common in denning contexts, from both nonviolent attritional mortality and territorial conflict (see Chapter 12), and these carcasses are routinely consumed by other carnivores. The frequency and intensity of interspecific violence tend to be high in the vicinity of dens (see Chapter 4), regardless of whether the den is actually in use or merely defended as part of the territory held by a group of social predators.

Very few carnivore remains, large or small, represent prey of Mousterian hominids in the Italian study sample. Exceptions were the occasional brown bear (at Moscerini), monk seal, or wolf (at Sant'Agostino). It is not known whether these individuals were hunted or scavenged by Mousterian people, nor how they made use of them, but evidence of burning or cut marks is confined to the paws of a bear and a wolf, and one seal flipper, respectively.

Superposition of damage types

The taphonomic history of Sant'Agostino is exceptionally complex, involving contemporaneous activities of hominids and canids in layers S0 through S3. Both agencies modified some of the same bones

TABLE 5.19

Puncture diameters in trabecular bones of ungulates and carnivores, listed by
site, provenience, and species

Taxon	N-observations	Mean (mm)	Range (mm)
Palidoro (33–34):			
wild ass	1	(4.0)	—
red deer	6	3.2	2.5–4.0
aurochs/horse	4	2.5[a]	2.0–3.0
Buca della Iena (I1–6):			
rhinoceros	18	6.2	3.8–10.5
horse	8	4.5	3.3–5.6
aurochs	13	4.8	2.0–7.8
red deer	8	4.8	4.1–7.2
roe deer	2	4.0	2.0–6.0
brown bear	12	5.2	4.2–6.4
spotted hyaena	20	4.7	3.1–7.0
wolf	1	(5.6)	—
wild cat	3	5.2	4.3–6.0
badger	3	3.9	3.4–4.8
Sant'Agostino (mostly from SX):			
aurochs	1	(6.9)	—
fallow deer	1	(6.8)	—
ibex	12	4.5	2.7–6.8
wild boar	6	5.5	4.7–6.7
roe deer	19	4.9	2.8–9.2
brown bear	4	4.7	3.5–6.0
leopard	1	(3.8)	—
wolf	20	3.5	3.1–9.0
fox	39	2.5[a]	1.6–4.0
wild cat	10	2.3[a]	1.7–4.3
Moscerini (M5):			
roe deer	5	5.2	3.5–7.6
spotted hyaena	4	4.9	4.0–5.6
wild cat	1	(3.4)	—
Guattari (G0–1):			
aurochs	5	4.8	3.1–5.9
red deer	25	5.3	2.8–6.4
fallow deer	10	3.8	2.8–4.3
brown bear	5	6.9	6.1–7.3
leopard	1	(2.2)[a]	—
spotted hyaena	5	6.6	3.9–7.7

[a]The average diameter is especially small.

Note: ( ) only one data point is available, not an average. Samples include punctures in
trabecular or flat bone weak enough to allow full penetration of a carnivore tooth.

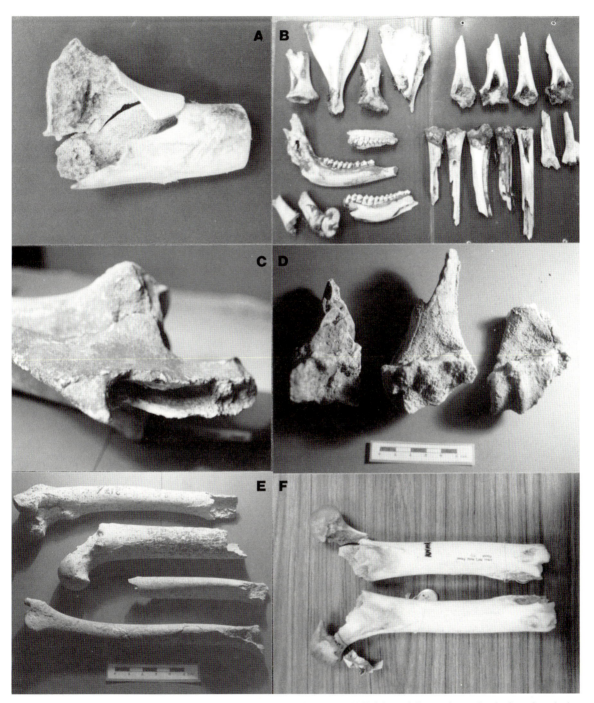

Figure 5.21 Examples of gnawing damage by wolves and spotted hyaenas: (A) Epiphyseal destruction and stripping of cortical shaft to access marrow cavity of moose humerus, damaged by modern wild free-ranging wolves on Isle Royale (opposite end cut with a saw). (Haynes' collection) (B) Assortment of deer limb and mandible parts damaged by modern captive wolves. Note ragged breaks, stripping of cortical shafts, and irregular bow-like forms of mandible specimens. (Haynes' collection) (C) Proximal aurochs radius-ulna from surface (G0) of Guattari, damaged by spotted hyaenas. (D) Distal red deer humeri from Guattari G0–2, damaged by spotted hyaenas. (E) Gnawed wolf femurs and tibiae from Sant'Agostino SX and S4, damaged by other wolves. Note ragged stripping damage on shafts. (F) Gnawed bison femurs, damaged by modern captive wolves. Note damage to proximal epiphyses and ragged stripping on opposite ends. (Haynes' collection)

while fresh. I claimed above that canids made use of bones previously discarded by hominids, not the other way around. Wolves were the sole collectors and modifiers of bones in SX, apparently in the context of denning (see also Chapter 12 on wolf mortality patterns). Layer S4 may represent some mixture of noncontemporaneous wolf and hominid components; clear instances of overprinting are few in S4, and most bone collecting appears to have been done by wolves, especially of ibex.

A fuller evaluation of the Sant'Agostino cases is possible from qualitative observations of bone damage. Figure 5.22D–E shows a series of sectioned and split deer metapodials from layers S0–3. Most of the break edges are clean and unmarred, and many have large cone fractures on them; a fraction thereof were subsequently gnawed by canids (specimens on the right in Figure 5.22D,E). Transverse sectioning of limbs, typical of human processing activities in late Upper Paleolithic shelters in Italy, also is common in the S0–3 assemblages (Figure 5.22F); some of these, too, were later gnawed by canids (Figure 5.22C).

The split deer metapodials from Sant'Agostino S0–3 present a strong contrast to the ragged, unsplit lower limb bones of deer gnawed by modern captive wolves (Figure 5.22B, lower right portion of photograph). The modern wolves in Haynes' experiments did not produce long clean splits on metapodials, nor straight transverse breaks across long bone shafts. The softer epiphyses of long bones were often completely destroyed instead (e.g., Binford 1981; Haynes 1982, 1983a, 1983b), and portions of cortical limb shafts were peeled and chipped away to expose the marrow cavity (detail in Figure 5.21A). Large carnivores, such as wolves and hyaenas, are capable of creating transverse fractures across limb shafts of large prey by biting them cross-wise and shearing them through. But carnivores do so only occasionally, whereas hominids did so routinely. Parenthetically, I did not find cone fractures in the modern Alaskan wolf den assemblages I examined, although wolf skull architecture suggests that they are able to generate them (Lopez 1978:25–26).

Both carnivores and hominids may create long spiraling fractures when opening long bone cavities to obtain marrow. Humans do so by direct or indirect percussion and are more proficient at opening bones instantly and completely. Carnivores, in contrast, work in a more gradual fashion, leaving a very different composite signature, including incomplete destruction of bone tubes and ragged edges, often accompanied by partly detached bone chips (see also Bunn 1983), tooth marks, and rounding from salivary and gut enzymes.

Damage overprinting analogous to that found at Sant'Agostino is documented for a variety of modern human situations, such as Binford's study of Nunamiut Eskimo camps in Alaska (1978; also my observations of the same collections), Brain's (e.g., 1981) studies of bone refuse at Hottentot villages in South Africa, and Binford and Bertram's (1977) study of Navajo residential dumps in the southwestern United States. The Nunamiut, for example, keep dogs and live in close ecological proximity to wolves and foxes. These relationships lead to considerable damage overprinting on bones in rubbish dumps and in dog-yards where valued animals are fed a combination of unprocessed prey parts and some processed leftovers. Superpositioning of human and canid damage takes a generally analogous form on goat and sheep bones from a historic midden at Zuni Pueblo, New Mexico (author's research, Figure 5.22A), where local dogs and free-ranging coyotes scavenged unburied refuse. Zuni people sectioned the limb bones of goats and sheep transversely with metal axes and consumed the soft tissues; only afterwards were some of the bones gnawed by canids at the community dump.

There is no evidence of domesticated dogs in the Italian Middle Paleolithic, but patterns of damage overprinting analogous to those described above certainly can result from wild canids (and other carnivores) that scavenge concentrated human garbage. Humans are uniquely adapted to transport food (Chapter 8) and, as a result, may concentrate impressive quantities of refuse at certain places. The refuse scatters in turn become resource magnets for other predators, wild or tame (e.g., Binford 1978, 1981; Gifford-Gonzalez 1990). Carnivores' strong interest in humans' garbage is as old as the inception of food transport behavior in the evolutionary history of humans. Wildlife studies con-

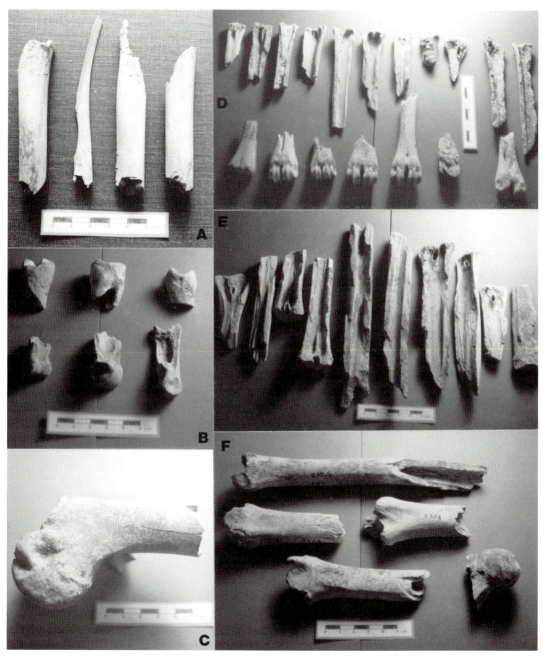

Figure 5.22 Examples of human-caused transverse fractures, splits, and cones on ungulate limb bones, some subsequently gnawed by carnivores: (A) Scored transverse fractures on sheep and goat limb bones from historic midden at Zuni Pueblo, New Mexico. Bones were either prescored and snapped or struck through with a metal ax. Note subsequent gnawing by canids. (B) Ibex phalanges from Sant'Agostino S1–4 opened for marrow by Mousterian hominids. (C) Distal humerus of red deer from Sant'Agostino S4. Note clean transverse fracture on shaft, and epiphysis gnawed by canids. (D) Deer metapodials from Sant'Agostino S0–3. Note transverse fractures on lower ends of shafts and split proximal epiphyses, many with cone fractures. Five specimens on right subsequently were gnawed by canids. (E) Split proximal deer metapodials from Sant'Agostino S0–3, many with cone fractures. Some specimens on right subsequently were gnawed by canids. (F) Distal ibex tibiae from Sant'Agostino S2, S4, and SX. Compare long spiral break on specimen at top (from SX) to perpendicular transverse fractures on other tibiae and transverse fracture on femoral fragment just below the proximal condyle. Transverse fractures are very common in hominid-generated faunas, but wolves and other large carnivores also produce them on occasion (as on specimen marked "XSAX").

ducted near developed areas testify to free-ranging carnivores' frequent use of dumps as sources of food in modern situations, even to the point of re-adjusting their territorial movements to fully exploit rich ones (e.g., Garrott et al. 1983; Danner and Smith 1980; Rogers 1987). It is very likely that carnivores, especially bears, hyaenas, and canids, tracked human activities in Paleolithic times as well, making the most of garbage opportunities in addition to whatever they caught for themselves.

Contrasts of ethnoarchaeological and Paleolithic cases show that gnawing damage does not by itself specify the context of food consumption by carnivores. Archaeologists can and should expect to find some gnawing damage in virtually any human-generated fauna, no matter how strong or weak the indications of human activity are. Gnawing is especially likely at the bone dumps of mobile peoples, because the dumps are not defended much; moving away only expands opportunities to rob the heap or modify bones in place. It is conceivable that robbing would leave its own set of anatomical biases (e.g., Marean et al. 1992 on axial bones), but the Italian cases generally do not fulfill such expectations for head or limb parts, the bases of anatomical comparisons in Chapters 8 and 9. Damage overprinting might also arise from situations in which hominids scavenged carnivore kills, the evidence of sequential processing thereby reversed. However, I find no convincing cases of this in the study sample: it might have occurred from time to time, but there

are no readily detectable signatures of this kind of reversed feeding sequence.

The possibility that carnivore gnawing can occur in more than one context, such as when carnivores scavenge human refuse, feed at dens, or a reversed situation in which hominids scavenge carnivore kills, begs the question of who were primary diners and who were secondary at any Pleistocene site. The feeding methods of carnivores and humans differ in fundamental ways, and these facts about their behavioral tendencies are pivotal for discerning the sequence of consumers from bone damage patterns. Indeed, bone modification data, alone, are not powerful means for reconstructing what transpired, much less why it happened. The full potential of bone modification data is unlocked by parallel considerations of spatial associations with other kinds of archaeological materials, species representation, and the behavioral ecology of modern predators. It is clear from behavioral studies, for example, that bears and badgers are not significant bone collectors in caves, even though their own skeletal remains often accumulate in dens. Small carnivores, such as foxes, were active in several of the Mousterian caves, but taphonomic and modern behavioral evidence indicate that they normally collect only small prey (see also Chapter 6). The late Upper Paleolithic cases present a notable contrast in this regard: most small carnivores were prey of humans, as evident from bone damage and anomalous mortality patterns (see Chapter 12).

TOOL MARKS AND TOOL SIZES

Tool marks, especially cut marks, have as much human appeal as arrowheads—seemingly unequivocal evidence of human activity. Yet human processors do not always leave tool marks on bones, and not every scratch can be shown to be from human tools. Many ambiguities surround the identification and interpretation of cut marks in archaeological contexts (Binford 1981; Bunn and Blumenschine 1987; Lyman 1987a; Shipman 1986; Turner 1989). Few studies, scattered across many decades, specifically address what cut mark data—forms, frequencies, and anatomical placements—might mean with regard to human economics (e.g., Bin-

ford 1978, 1981; Frison 1970; Guilday et al. 1962; Henri Martin 1907–10; Todd 1983). It remains unclear, for example, why cut marks are common in one apparently human-generated fauna and rare in another.

The paucity of cut marks in some of the Middle Paleolithic cave faunas of Latium is therefore a problem of broader analytical interest: cut marks are strangely lacking in what otherwise appear to be hominid-collected faunas at Moscerini, but common at other caves such as Sant'Agostino and Breuil. As explained above, the relative abundance of cut marks is certainly affected by variation in anatomical representation of prey. Another factor in west-central Italy in particular—the nature of raw material availability—may also have affected the frequencies, forms, and sizes of cut marks on bones. All Pontinian Mousterian and most late Upper Paleolithic tools in this region were made on small flint pebbles, obtained locally and averaging between 3 and 4 cm in diameter (Kuhn 1990a:130). Small tools, with short working edges and little weight behind them, are less likely to inflict noticeable marks on fresh bone. Pontinian tools, in particular, may have decreased the probability that Mousterian hominids would leave cutting traces while processing prey, given that we have no indications that tools or flakes were hafted to increase leverage. What cut marks are found on bones tend to be short, light, and difficult to see (e.g., Figure 5.12). In contrast, the sizes and visibility of cut and hack marks on bones from other Mousterian caves in Italy (Grotta di Gosto, Tozzi 1974) and elsewhere (La Quina, Henri Martin 1907–10) are much greater, and these cases associate with larger pieces of locally available stone and significantly larger tools.

Cut marks on ungulate bones from the late Upper Paleolithic shelter of Palidoro (circa 15,000 B.P.) range from 0.6 to 2.3 cm in length, but most are 2.0 cm or greater. Cut marks on ungulate bones from the Mousterian sites of Sant'Agostino range between 0.5 and 1.0 cm in length with few exceptions (illustrated in Figure 5.12); although cut marks are less frequent on the bones of small taxa, no significant differences in cut mark lengths relative to prey body size exist. The length range for cut marks from Sant'Agostino is noticeably less than that for the Upper Paleolithic site of Palidoro, although defleshing activities are indicated at both sites. The difference between the average cut mark lengths may be explained by the fact that the Pontinian Mousterian industries were made almost exclusively on local pebbles, while territorial movements of late Upper Paleolithic peoples at Palidoro covered areas containing larger raw materials in addition to small pebbles (e.g., Bietti 1976–77a).

The late Upper Paleolithic shelter of Riparo Salvini (circa 12,000–12,500 B.P.) instead lies well within the raw material-poor zone (Chapter 3), as do the four Mousterian caves. The occupants of Riparo Salvini carried in some larger tools and flakes made from raw materials obtained more than 70 km away, but relied most heavily on small local pebbles (Bietti and Stiner 1992). The range of cut mark lengths at Salvini nonetheless is closer to that observed at Palidoro (0.3 to 2.5 cm), most exceeding 2.0 cm. While more and larger samples from the study area are needed to evaluate this contrast rigorously, the perceived difference in cut mark frequencies and sizes between the late Upper Paleolithic and Mousterian sites on the raw material-poor coastal plain may be a question of tool hafting, a factor that ultimately affects the visibility of the cut marks produced. Small lithic elements are known to have been hafted into composite tools during the late Upper Paleolithic of this area. In contrast, hafting practices appear to have been minimal in the Mousterian (e.g., Kuhn 1990a). Corresponding differences in tool leverage therefore may be reflected by the cut mark data across the two cultural periods.

Because human food processing procedures vary with the portion of the animal anatomy involved (e.g., head, axial column, limbs), the chances that archaeologists will find cut marks in a culturally associated bone assemblage also depends on what parts hominids actually carried to the shelters. Much of the intersite variation in cut mark frequencies *within* the Mousterian is almost certainly explained by differing food transport agendas (documented in Chapter 9). As is the case for cone fractures, cut marks are relatively common at Grotta di Sant'Agostino and Grotta Breuil, because limb elements are more common. This is not simply a problem of whether limb shaft fragments are conserved in collections, although their inclusion in samples can further amplify cut mark and cone frequencies (as at Grotta Breuil). Cut marks are rarest in the Mousterian faunas from Grotta dei Moscerini (M2, M3, M4, and M6) and Grotta Guattari (G4–5), yet transverse impact dents and other distinctive fractures (see below) from heavier stone tools or anvils are fairly common, and many items are burned. More to the issue, these assemblages are dominated by head parts, and are poor in ungulate limb bones. The absence of cut marks in these cases does not indicate an absence of hominid influence.

Some Distinctive Processing Signatures of Hominids versus Large Carnivores

Fracture data have analytical advantages over cut marks in that bones must be broken to access marrow, whereas cut marks may or may not occur due to the delicacy, skill, or procedures of the processor, as well as the weight and size of a stone tool. Some fracture forms produced by one type of predator can mimic those of another (e.g., Haynes 1982, 1983a, 1983b on wolf damage; Brain 1981, Potts 1982 on cone fractures by spotted hyaenas; see also Lyman 1984b), but other kinds of fractures can, in fact, diagnose agency to a significant degree. Oftentimes, it is a complex of damage that creates a diagnostic form or progression as feeding intensifies (e.g., Binford 1981; Brain 1981). These fracture complexes can be evaluated qualitatively, if not quantified.

I have encountered several distinctive damage complexes in my study of the Paleolithic and control assemblages that merit description, either because they have not been fully outlined in other studies, or they are especially prominent in this data set. The discussions that follow primarily concern the mandible and limb elements of ungulates and large carnivores. All of the fracture complexes are attributable to differing methods for extracting bone marrow by hominids, wolves, and hyaenas.

The mandible: Ragged bows versus angular splits

Schematic differences in progressive damage to ungulate mandibles by humans and carnivores are illustrated in Figures 5.23 and 5.24, respectively.

Humans (modern and, apparently, Mousterian hominids) typically opened the marrow cavities of ungulate mandibles by breaking them transversely into segments and splitting the base of the horizontal ramus away from the tooth row. The fractures tend to be clean and relatively straight, resulting in a series of pieces with generally squared contours. Evidence of localized crushing often occurs at the point of impact on basal and transversal splits (Figure 5.25C). The coronoid usually is broken (or cut?) away from the rest of the mandible. The condyle is split vertically from the anterior portion of the ascending ramus, possibly as the mandible is separated from the skull (e.g., to remove the tongue). The kinds of fragments that commonly

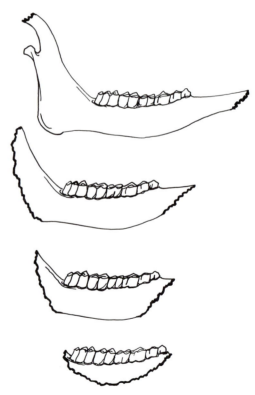

Figure 5.24 Schematic diagram of progressive damage to ungulate mandible by spotted hyaenas and wolves. Note that the base of the horizontal ramus is destroyed only in the final stages of the progression.

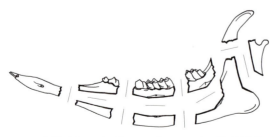

Figure 5.23 Schematic diagram of progressive damage to ungulate mandible by humans. Note that base of horizontal ramus is separated away early in the progression.

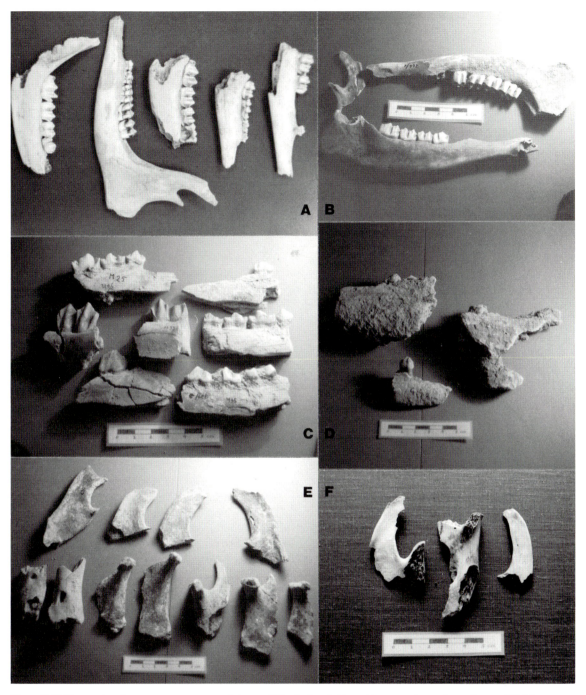

Figure 5.25 Contrasting damage patterns on ungulate mandibles by hominids and large carnivores in modern and Pleistocene contexts: (A) Deer mandibles gnawed by modern captive wolves. Note ragged contours of all breaks and bow-like forms of two specimens. (Haynes' collection) (B) Roe deer mandibles from Moscerini M5, gnawed by carnivores. (C) Red deer mandible segments from Moscerini M2 and M3, damaged by hominids. Note clean perpendicular relationship between transverse breaks and splits. Localized crushing, transverse dents, and light burning are evident on some specimens. (D) Aurochs mandible segments from Guattari G0–2, damaged by spotted hyaenas. Note crenelated, yet rounded edges, and generally bow-like form of the two specimens. (E) Characteristic breaks on condyle and coronoid fragments of red deer mandibles from Sant'Agostino S0–3 damaged by hominids. (F) Characteristic breaks on condyle and coronoid fragments of sheep and goat mandibles from historic midden at Zuni Pueblo, New Mexico, damaged by modern humans; one specimen (center) subsequently gnawed by canids.

Figure 5.26 Red deer cranium and upper neck section from Guattari G0–1. Anterior portion of the cranium was eaten away by hyaenas.

result from these procedures are illustrated in Figure 5.25C,E,F.

Carnivores may also extract marrow from the mandibles of large prey, especially after transporting the parts to dens or rest sites. Progressive gnawing damage on mandibles by carnivores usually begins at the margins of the coronoid and on the anterior region. Early stages of the progression are exemplified by the largest wolf-gnawed deer mandible from Haynes' modern comparative collection (Figure 5.25A) and the gnawed roe deer mandibles from Moscerini M5 (Figure 5.25B). Because the skull of a prey animal is an articulated unit at the outset, consisting of cranium and jaws, a carnivore may begin by chewing away the snout and anterior mandible together (Figure 5.26, also Figure 5.17F). The outer corner of the mandible may also be damaged at this time (e.g., Binford 1981:62–63). Continued gnawing of the mandible progresses from the anterior end and/or proximal ascending ramus toward the midsection containing the cheek teeth (Figure 5.24). The damage advances in essentially the same way for ungulate and large carnivore mandibles (Figure 5.27). In situations of extensive gnawing, spotted hyaenas and wolves tend to create a ragged bow form, preserving much or all of the tooth row and the bony rim that holds the teeth in place (Figure 5.25A,D; see also Brain 1981:70, 80). The base of the mandible may be destroyed in extreme cases, and the damaged areas will tend to have irregular edges, even when tooth marks are absent. Of course, no single specimen can diagnose the history of an entire assemblage (Brain 1981:140–142), but repetition of distinctive fracture complexes, such as those on mandibles, effectively distinguishes hominid from carnivore effects. The fracture complexes can be especially enlighten-ing in analyses of assemblages with complex formation histories.

Gnawing damage is common in assemblages from Sant'Agostino S0–3, but ragged bows on mandibles are rare. In contrast, ragged bows are relatively common in wolf-dominated SX. Figure 5.27A shows examples of wolf mandibles from Sant'Agostino, gnawed by other wolves; most of them occur in SX, where associated ungulate mandibles are damaged in a similar way. Figure 5.27B shows an analogous damage complex on red deer mandibles gnawed by spotted hyaenas in Guattari G0–1; the condition of these mandibles presents a marked contrast to those processed by Mousterian hominids in Moscerini M3–4 (Figure 5.28A–B) and Sant'Agostino S0–3 (Figure 5.28C).

Interestingly, many of the ungulate mandibles from Guattari G4 and G5 display damage complexes attributable to hominids, as do some from G1–2 (Figure 5.28D). The problem in G1–2 is that, while these levels contain Mousterian tools, they also contain ample evidence of spotted hyaena activity, including hyaena skeletal remains, coprolites, and severe gnawing. I find no evidence of damage overprinting by hominids and carnivores in G1 and G2; they appear to represent situations of postdepositional mixing of hominid-generated and carnivore-generated debris—mixed in the geological sense, rather than because of contemporaneous actions of different biological agencies.

As a final note on damage to the head region of prey, severed axes (the second cervical vertebra behind the skull) are common in several of the Paleolithic assemblages. Only the anterior-ventral portion of the axis is usually preserved, and the pattern is observed on red deer, fallow deer, roe deer, horse, and even one rhinoceros. Figure 5.29 shows six

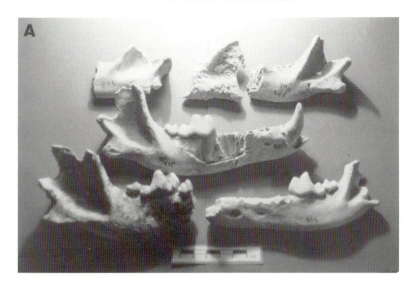

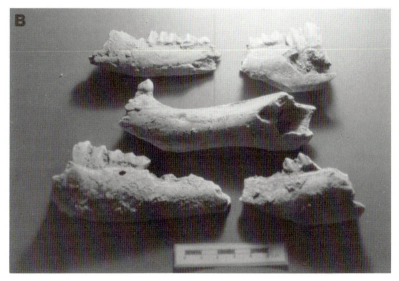

Figure 5.27 Wolf mandibles from Sant'Agostino gnawed by other wolves (A), and deer mandibles from Guattari G0–1 gnawed by spotted hyaenas (B). Note that bases of horizontal rami are intact.

anterior-ventral axis fragments from Guattari G1–2. It is not clear how this damage arises, nor, at this point, that it necessarily could diagnose agency. I found no such damage on ungulate axes in the modern carnivore control assemblages I examined, but axes are few and far between in these samples. In Italy, some level of hominid presence is indicated wherever anterior-ventral axis fragments occur, but most often in situations where Mousterian hominid

components are mixed with hyaena activity, a finding that is both frustrating and intriguing. Few if any of the axis specimens show evidence of gnawing; they were merely ripped or severed while fresh. Three specimens with forms identical to those in Figure 5.29 exist in the Palidoro (33–34) collection and are clearly associated with Upper Paleolithic human activities. Analogous severing of ungulate axes is also evidenced in Paleolithic faunas of other

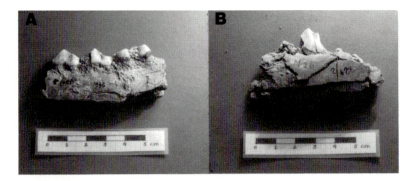

Figure 5.28 Deer mandibles processed by hominids from (A–B) Moscerini M3–4 and
(C) Sant'Agostino S0–3, and (D) mandibles probably processed by hominids from
Guattari G1–5.

Figure 5.29 Anterior-ventral portions of red deer axes from Guattari G1–2.

Mediterranean regions such as at Hayonim Cave in Israel (my current research; see also Bar-Yosef 1991; Belfer-Cohen and Bar-Yosef 1981; Tchernov 1992).

Oddly, it is the anterior (cranial) end of the axis bone that is represented most often in the cave assemblages, if axes are present at all. The damage pattern may reflect simultaneous removal of the head and the large bib of soft throat and neck tissues from the torso in situations where the animals are in relatively fat condition (see Chapter 8). My experiences of butchering deer with stone tools show that a more perfect separation of the skull from the upper neck is easy: cut away the neck muscles just below the skull and twist at the joint of the atlas-axis—no bones broken. But this procedure frees only the head and was not always the desired effect in the prehistoric Italian situations. In some cases, consumers consistently aimed slightly lower, shearing or splitting the axis.

Limb and toe bone processing

In his ethnoarchaeological study of the Nunamiut Eskimo, Binford (1978) describes two basic procedures for partitioning carcasses into smaller units. These relate, at least in part, to the state of the carcass: still warm, or frozen by cold or rigor mortis. Butchering practices varied accordingly, so that carcass partitioning was done at joints or by hacking through the bone. In the Italian Paleolithic, sectioning limbs through bone was a common procedure

and usually resulted in clean, perpendicular breaks across limb shafts, as illustrated by the specimens in Figures 5.22C,F from Grotta di Sant'Agostino (S0–3). Some detachment of limb elements at the joints may have taken place as well, but it was less common at Sant'Agostino (MP), Breuil (MP), Polesini (lUP), and Palidoro (lUP), perhaps because butchering was delayed. However, none of these observations can be extended to hominid-collected faunas in Moscerini or Guattari, because limb elements are rare.

Large carnivores are physically capable of producing shear transverse breaks across ungulate limb shafts, but seldom do so on larger prey. Hyaenas and wolves instead tend to produce ragged breaks as they access the marrow cavity of long bones by gnawing away one or both epiphyses. In the Italian caves, large carnivores often left bone shafts or tubes intact or partly intact, apparently moving on to other food items rather than completely destroying any one. Hominids' procedures for extracting marrow resulted in much more bone fragmentation, but without obliterating the harder long bone epiphyses. To the extent that limb shafts are preserved in cultural faunas, however, shear transverse fractures are common.

Paleolithic faunas rich in limb elements contain much evidence of marrow processing, almost as a matter of course. These practices extend to the first, second, and often third phalanges of ungulate prey (especially deer and aurochs), which hominids

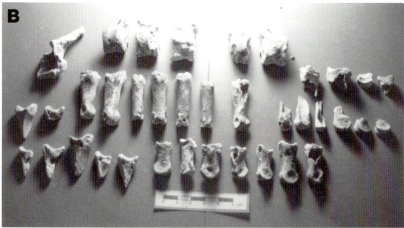

Figure 5.30 Hominid-processed deer phalanges from (A) Sant'Agostino S0–3, and (B) wolf-gnawed astragali and phalanges from the SX den. Note impact scar associated with break on hand-held specimen in (A) and that most of the gnawed phalanges from SX are not opened (B).

opened systematically. Phalanges (toe bones) were split at almost any angle, but consistently display clean break edges. A very different situation is found in modern and (inferred) Upper Pleistocene carnivore den faunas: small holes were occasionally produced by progressive gnawing, but most phalanges were not opened at all. Figure 5.30 contrasts hominid-damaged and wolf-damaged deer phalanges from Sant'Agostino S0–3 and SX respectively. Transverse impact dents, localized crushing,

or tiny cones are apparent on many of the toe bones opened by Mousterian hominids (Figure 5.30A). Deer toes in SX are heavily gnawed, but only a small fraction are opened.

Patterns of marrow extraction and the arrays of parts actually transported to shelters by humans may have implications for the seasons of procurement. The marrow of ungulates is not equally nutritious throughout the year (e.g., Binford 1978; Speth 1987). Wildlife studies conducted in the temperate zone (see Chapters 8 and 10) show that the fat levels in marrow are highest in adult ungulates during the fall, declining to a minimum by late spring. Thorough extraction of limb marrow by hominids at Sant'Agostino, Breuil, and late Upper Paleolithic sites suggests procurement during seasons when these tissues were worth eating: sometime between early fall and winter (see Chapter 13). This may not have been true for assemblages in Moscerini M2–4 and M6 or in Guattari G4–5, where only head parts are common (Chapter 9).

THE BEHAVIORAL SIGNIFICANCE OF BURNED BONE

Large gaps exist in our understanding of the differences between bone damage resulting from purposeful human actions and accidents that occur during or after the fact. It is especially difficult to recognize the difference in the case of burned bone. Because bone may be transformed through a series of distinct events, however, deliberate and accidental burning ultimately informs us about human space use inside shelters and the rates of reuse relative to sediment accumulation.

Archaeologists are very interested in burning damage because, like cut marks, it may diagnose human activity (see James 1989, and comments ff.). Of course, bones may be burned in a wider variety of circumstances, including cooking, cleansing an area for reuse (Binford 1978:461; also my observations, Navajo cache area preparation, New Mexico), spontaneous combustion of dry organics in cave deposits, or natural large-scale brush fires. Thankfully, fire is one signature that carnivores never leave. Most burning of bones in cultural contexts is not a direct result of food preparation, but instead occurs when garbage is thrown into fires or when new fires are built atop old material (Brain 1981:54; Walters 1988:218).

Burned bones are securely associated with hominid occupations of the Italian caves. However, there is no simple correspondence to cooking activities in these assemblages. Stone artifacts are burned as or more often than bones, evidenced by Kuhn's unpublished data for Mousterian industries shown in Table 5.20. Indeed, burned lithics provide a more uniform demonstration that fires were regular occurrences in all four sites: we have little information about intact fire features in the caves, but many lithic tools, flakes, cores, and debris are burned. Apart from the occasional practice of heat-treating flint raw material, there is no reason to burn stone artifacts deliberately. Likewise, mollusk shell fragments in Moscerini are burned in excess of the practical requirements of cooking (see Chapter 6). Note, in contrast, that ungulate bones in Moscerini M1 and M5 and in Sant'Agostino S4 show comparatively low frequencies of burning within their respective strata series, concomitant with the facts that lithic artifacts (Table 3.5) are less common and large carnivore remains more so (see Chapter 4).

Differing frequencies and intensities of burning on bones relative to fragment size may be the product of a site's horizontal structure over the long term (e.g., Rosen 1989; Stiner et al. n.d.), a possibility worth exploring in the Italian sites to the extent that recovery practices allow. While burning of large mammal bones is generally less common than burning of lithic artifacts, the incidence of burned bone increases dramatically below a certain size threshold (for related observations see Gifford 1978; O'Connell 1987; Rosen 1989; Schiffer 1983). The intensity of burning in the Italian faunas also increases as fragment size decreases: smaller specimens usually are fully carbonized or partly calcined, whereas larger specimens show only localized, light burning; fully calcined bones are rare.

It is significant that most small fragments in completely recovered faunal assemblages fall in the nonidentifiable bone category. Thus, frequencies of burning damage are highest within this fraction. Nonbone materials in the Mousterian levels also display higher frequencies of burning damage because they tend to be small (< 2.0 cm). Only in situations of complete bone recovery is the incidence of burning on lithics comparable to that on nonidentifiable bone fragments. These observations underscore the conceptual importance of fragment size, not material type, for explaining variation in burning frequency and intensity. The variation is

TABLE 5.20
Percentages of burned ungulate bones and lithic artifacts in the Italian
Mousterian caves

Site and provenience	of Ungulate bone NISP	of Lithic artifacts			
		Tools	Flakes	Cores	Debris
Grotta dei Moscerini:					
M1	0	18	22	33	18
M2	52	42	30	38	44
M3	32	53	39	58	42
M4	7	32	18	40	41
M5	2	41	26	18	67
M6	7	41	17	41	32
Grotta Guattari:					
G1	—	11	0	3	15
G2	*	5	0	11	11
G4	*	12	3	9	27
G5	*	8	12	9	27
Grotta di Sant'Agostino:					
S0	3	11	—	—	—
S1	3	10	13	14	25
S2	6	14	12	14	28
S3	1	12	8	4	16
S4	0	8	6	0	22
Grotta Breuil:					
Br	2	20	14	16	24
B3/4	1	—	—	—	—

Source: Kuhn, unpublished data.

Note: (—) no data, (*) burned bone chips are present, but relative frequencies are not known. Percentage values are calculated relative to total items in each level and artifact category as listed in Table 3.5.

primarily an outcome of disposal practices and interior space use rather than of cooking.

Two sites, Grotta Breuil (MP) and Riparo Salvini (lUP), represent situations in which bone fragments of all sizes were systematically collected by the excavators, permitting a simple test of the stated relationships among burning frequency, fragment size, and bone identifiability. Table 5.21 lists summary statistics, including *t* test results, on the frequency of burning as a function of bone specimen length. Each sample combines identifiable and nonidentifiable fractions from selected proveniences of Breuil and Salvini, respectively. The data indicate very significant differences in specimen length between burned and unburned bones in both sites, with the majority of burned specimens coming from

the nonidentifiable fractions. The results are entirely comparable between the two sites, although they are from different cultural periods and associated with different variants of *Homo sapiens*.

The results presented in Table 5.21 also show that the overall percentage of burning in any faunal assemblage will appear significantly higher if nonidentifiable bone fractions are considered alongside identifiable bone. Total burn frequencies are as high as 29 percent in Riparo Salvini and 11 percent in Breuil. Localized concentrations of burned bones in horizontal space should be expected, because excavation trenches may or may not cut through hearth areas. These features were not always intact in the Latium caves, but preliminary testing in Breuil suggests that some hearths may be partially preserved

TABLE 5.21

Summary statistics for bone fragment size (cm) relative to the frequency of burning on identifiable and nonidentifiable bone from Breuil and Salvini

Not burned		*Burned*	
Grotta Breuil sample:[a]			
N-observations	347	N-observations	44
minimum length	1.0	minimum length	0.2
maximum length	9.5	maximum length	3.3
mean length	3.0	mean length	1.4
standard deviation	1.5	standard deviation	0.7

Statistical significance of length differences between burned and unburned bone specimens:

t–statistic = 6.636   probability < .001

Riparo Salvini sample:[b]			
N-observations	297	N-observations	124
minimum length	1.0	minimum length	0.4
maximum length	8.3	maximum length	5.0
mean length	2.3	mean length	1.4
standard deviation	1.0	standard deviation	0.6

Statistical significance of length differences between burned and unburned bone specimens:

t–statistic = 8.731   probability < .001

[a] Breuil sample consists of all piece-plotted specimens and unplotted material from screen bags #350 and #397, excavated from Square E0, Stratum 3/4 in 1988.
[b] Salvini sample is from square C1, subsquare d, arbitrary layer XII, excavated in 1988.

there. Segre's field observations of fine levels in Moscerini M2 and M3, along with burning data on lithics (see Table 5.20) and shells (see Chapter 6) from the same level groups, suggest a similar situation there.

It is not clear whether small pieces of bone are burned because they were small to begin with or, conversely, because burned bones are more likely to crumble. This question would be better addressed with the aid of experimental data (see Stiner et al. n.d.), but it is significant in the Italian cases that, while fully blackened fragments are common, calcined specimens are rare. I would expect calcined fragments to be more common as the influence of heat-caused breakdown increases. In contrast to the prevalence of burning damage on small bone chips,

burning on larger bone specimens is rare, light, and highly localized on individual pieces (Figure 5.31). Some of this damage occurs on articular surfaces of limb bones and is indicative of roasting. Other bones may simply have come in contact with stray coals. Suffice it to say, roasting damage involves, at most, minimal burning of bone: the presence of soft tissues on roasted body parts prevents the flames from reaching bone surfaces, except where they have been exposed by the butchering process (e.g., Gifford 1977; Gifford et al. 1980; Yellen 1977).

While originating from the same prey carcasses, small nonidentifiable bone fragments evidently became separated from larger bones at some point during assemblage formation in the Italian cases. The burning data link the small, *nonidentifiable* bone fraction most closely to the depositional history of lithics and mollusk shells, and to loci of repeated fire building. In other words, small bone fragments remained in the vicinity of hearth areas, whereas large ones often did not. Small bone, shell, or stone fragments simply do not affect the comfort or utility of an occupied surface as much as do large pieces. This is especially true in confined spaces, such as inside shelters, where hearths may be superimposed time after time, level upon level (Walters 1988).

Hence the intensity of burning damage refers as much or more to relationships between successive events as it does to the activities comprising any one depositional event (Stiner *et al.* n.d.). Burning on bones and stones as a function of fragment size may reflect, for example, differing intensities of activity area maintenance relative to rates of sediment buildup.[6] The more frequently shelters are revisited and the longer the stays, the greater the need to move—or just shove—larger, angular garbage away from favored activity spaces (Deal 1985; Hayden and Cannon 1983; Kramer 1982:109; Siegel and Roe 1986; see also review by Rosen 1989). More and more of the tiny fragments left behind may become burned over the lengthy history of a fire feature (Stiner *et al.* n.d.). In this study, small burned fragments effectively signal the remains of hearths, cross-cut by IIPU excavation units. The burning data present a potential, albeit crude,

---

[6] The process may be complicated by the effects of natural sheet burning of organic materials.

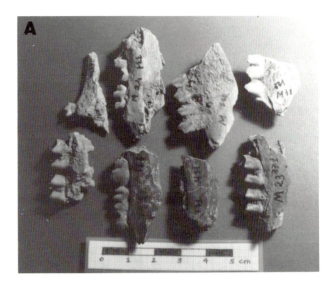

Figure 5.31 Deer (A) mandible and (B) maxilla
segments from Moscerini M3 and M4 that were
broken and burned by Mousterian hominids.

means for learning about site structure in the absence of recognizable or fully intact hearth features.
Patterns of burning relative to item size, in particular, reflect some basic physical responses of humans
in their living space.

INTERIOR SPACE USE AND OCCUPATION SEQUENCES BY HOMINIDS AND CARNIVORES

When it comes to shelter, humans and carnivores
clearly have different needs and preferences, stem-
ming from fundamentally divergent physiologies
and patterns of locomotion. There are two spatial
dimensions of cave occupations worth discussing
for the Italian material: (1) the rate at which tenant
changes occurred through vertical strata sequences;
and (2) the differing uses of cave interiors by the
respective tenants in any given level. The time scale
of tenant alternations relates in part to the natural
history cycles of the carnivores, as well as to the
intensity of hominid use of shelters independently
of carnivores' needs. The second phenomenon, interior space preference, is expressed in terms of the
horizontal plans of caves and the ceiling height at
any given time in the past. While the Italian data are
less than optimal for spatial analyses, details of the
cave interiors and Order-specific behavior patterns
may explain some changes in the horizontal distributions of bones in the caves, and why some shel-

ters were eventually abandoned by hominids, the tallest predators.

In Grotta dei Moscerini (interior series) and Grotta Guattari, spotted hyaenas monopolized the shelters during the final stages of soil accumulation. While generally rare in Grotta Breuil, large carnivore remains are abundant in the rear-most area of the final level. Cultural deposits comprise the earlier portions of the same sequences. Some mixing is apparent at vertical transitions between human and hyaena components in Guattari and the interior series of Moscerini. It is not clear if the mixed components represent multiple alternations over many years, or merely postdepositional scrambling by digging carnivores; modifying and re-excavating cave interiors is an important part of den preparation.

Eventual takeover of a cave by spotted hyaenas may have been inevitable in some deposition sequences, because the space between floor and ceiling was reduced, and because of the ways that shelters normally figure in the life history of this species. The large accumulations of bone in the hyaena components of the Latium caves suggest that the caves served mainly as maternity dens rather than natal dens (e.g., Kruuk 1972:57; Mills and Mills 1977; Sutcliffe 1970; Skinner and van Aarde 1991). Occupations at hyaena maternity dens can last up to two years for each new generation of cubs. Because dens may be used communally by adult females and birthing in modern populations is aseasonal, litters of different ages may be housed at the same den, thereby extending the period of use. Some dens are used by hyaena clans across generations; the dens may be vacated periodically to escape parasites, especially fleas, but may be continuously defended as part of the clan's territory. Hyaena dens are marked with strong olfactory signatures, such as dense latrines in side-chambers and near the entrances, a pattern also evident in Guattari G0–1 and Buca della Iena I1–6 (see also Chapter 6 on canid fecal bone in Sant'Agostino). It stands to reason that such intense and long-term use of shelters by hyaenas would render these places less attractive to other prospective tenants, further expanding the cycles of alternation with other species such as humans.

Like Guattari and the interior sequence of Moscerini, Buca della Iena exhibits some evidence of alternating use by hominids, spotted hyaenas, bears, and badgers. Pitti and Tozzi (1971:239–240) report very small quantities of Mousterian lithic artifacts in levels I1 through I4 (see Table 4.5), showing that hominids did use the cave, if only sporadically. In contrast, occupations by hyaenas are evidenced throughout the sequence, based on the presence of hyaena skeletal remains, coprolites, and extensive gnawing on herbivore and carnivore bones.

It is interesting that, while hyaena use of shelters corresponds to low-intensity use by hominids, hominids were not completely excluded from the sequences. The possibility of anything more than ephemeral use by hominids appears to have been greatly reduced by hyaenas' interest in the caves, yet gaps in hyaena presence were sufficient at times to allow hominids to use the caves, too. The ephemeral character of the hominid occupations is a recurring theme for these sites, as shown in the chapters to follow. The possibility that carnivore disturbance rather than a multiple–palimpsest situation was the cause for mixed cultural and hyaena components is difficult to exclude in the broadly unidirectional tenancy shifts of Guattari and the interior sequence of Moscerini. All of the nonhuman carnivores discussed are avid diggers and may scoop massive quantities of soil away to improve bedding areas, thereby modifying the contours of chambers to their needs. However, the occupational sequence in Buca della Iena clearly involved many alternations between hominids, hyaenas, brown bears, and badgers. The gradations in their respective effects are not simply from postdepositional mixing of thick and once discrete strata; many things transpired during the formation of each level.

Final takeovers by spotted hyaenas in the Italian cave sequences most probably relate to geologically induced changes in the available living space. Significant changes in usable space include the overall shape of the interior, its absolute dimensions, and the amount of illumination at the entrance (also see Straus 1979). As the caves filled with sediment, the area within and around the cave gradually became less useful to hominids and, meanwhile, increasingly suitable for denning bears, spotted hyaenas, and wolves. Increasing carnivore presence in the later portions of the stratigraphic sequences probably does not signal direct competition between hominids and carnivores for shelters. It is more likely to represent situations in which each kind of tenant responded opportunistically to the prospect of clean, empty shelters of suitable dimensions and setting. Each would have avoided caves already taken up by other predators, the cheapest strategy in a landscape full of holes.

Significant differences in the *horizontal* distributions of carnivore and hominid occupations also are apparent in Grotta Guattari, Grotta dei Moscerini, Grotta Breuil and, possibly, in Grotta di Sant'-Agostino. The horizontal distributions of faunal material in Guattari illustrate this point fairly well. Figures 3.8 and 3.9 show the interior plan of the cave, which consists of multiple chambers, and Figure 3.10 shows what was probably the largest entrance, a constricted hole roughly one meter across. The scale of the Guattari interior is much smaller than those of the other Circean and Gaetan caves; the space is crowded and fully enclosed.

Table 5.22 lists bone NISPs for ungulate plus carnivore remains from G0–2 and G4–7 by trench location (see Figure 3.8). The data are grouped horizontally from front to back; Trench III cross-cuts the location where the Neandertal skull (Circeo I) was found (Blanc 1958). The quantities of material are far less in G4–5, yet there are noticeable differences to G0–2 in the percentages of material in front of the cave versus the interior. Recall that the faunal remains in levels G4–5 are primarily associated with Mousterian hominids, while the faunas of G0–1,

and to a lesser extent G2, are primarily associated with spotted hyaenas. Trench B is situated outside the entrance, and Trench A leads into the largest of the three openings. Most of the faunal remains in levels G4–5 occur in Trench B, spilling into the entrance tunnels of the cave. Entrances 1, 2, and 3 are *cuniculi*, the Italian word for tunnels; prior to modifications for tourists, all were narrow passages feeding into the main chamber. *Sotto ponte* (under the bridge) is a small bridge-like formation where Cuniculo 1 meets Trench I. Most of the faunal material in levels G0–2 occurs in the entrance tunnels and Trench IV inside the cave.

Horizontal segregation of hominid and carnivore activities is more pronounced in Moscerini. This cave is a large, elongated chamber (15 m) that narrows into two small tunnels at the back. The entrance was about 5 m across prior to recent burial by construction scree, based on Segre's drawings (see Figures 3.17 and 3.18). Carnivore occupations of the cave associate almost exclusively with the interior excavation trench at the back of the chamber (see Figure 3.17G), whereas most (not all) of the cultural debris comes from the excavation units at the cave entrance.

Predator occupations of Sant'Agostino primarily involved hominids and wolves. Sant'Agostino is a large open cave, approximately 20 m across at the entrance, with a grand, parabolic vault (see Figure 3.21). Flowstone formations are extensive on the southern end of the cave entrance, forming large shelves hidden in sand. This may have been the location of the SX wolf den (soft sediment and a hard roof). The exact location of the wolf occupations at Sant'Agostino is difficult to reconstruct, however, due to poor information on the horizontal placement of the excavation units (see discussion by Tozzi 1970:3).

Rapid alternations in cave use are more feasible in principle between hominids and carnivores with short denning periods (wolves, foxes, and wild cats) than between hominids and hyaenas. Hence, a rather different pattern of alternation may be proposed for Sant'Agostino than for the Mousterian caves discussed previously. The denning season of modern wolves is both predictable and short in any given year (probably February–April in Italy; see Chapter 12). Because of the brief duration of den

TABLE 5.22
Gross horizontal and vertical distributions of large mammal bones in Guattari

Exterior (Trenches A–B)	Entrances (Trenches 1–3)	Interior chambers (Trenches I–IV)
Levels G0–2:		
.11	.69	.20
Levels G4–5:		
.48	.40	.11

Note: Comparisons are based on fractions of total large mammal bone NISP; counts do not include teeth. Data are for material from trenches, and exclude items from unexcavated zones of the surface deposit and specimens removed from the calcareous outcrop at the cave entrance.

use, wolves may not create the formidable latrines typical of hyaena dens, although there certainly was some buildup at Sant'Agostino (see Chapter 6).

The interior of Breuil resembles Sant'Agostino in both scale and general contours. The anterior portion of the cave is spacious and, even filled with deposits, is well lit. Unlike Sant'Agostino, however, the vertical dimensions of the Breuil chamber constrict suddenly and upwardly toward the back, where the space above the youngest stratum is dark and close (see area 11 in Figure 3.24). This area is an uncomfortable place to excavate today, and it is only here that we have encountered concentrations of wolf and brown bear remains (along with one hyaena coprolite).

The horizontal distributions of hominid-collected and carnivore-collected material inside the shelters contrast in predictable ways. Human debris accumulated most conspicuously near the cave entrances, probably because hominids require light to carry out manufacturing and processing activities and fire is not always a practical source. The hominid occupations of limestone shelters in coastal Latium suggest a preference for shallow caves with wide entrances, often oriented south or southwest, a pattern that includes both the Middle and Upper Paleolithic (e.g., at Salvini and Polesini). Data on

spotted hyaena and brown bear dens in this part of the world indicate preferences for smaller, tighter quarters. Modern wildlife studies reinforce this observation for bears (e.g., Clevenger and Purroy 1991; Rogers 1981, 1987), wolves (e.g., Mech 1970; van Ballenberghe 1983), and striped hyaenas (e.g., Skinner et al. 1980, 1986; Skinner and van Aarde 1991).

While the interspecific comparisons reveal a common interest by predators in shelters as well as food, the biological bases of shelter use are not equivalent between humans and carnivores. Wolves, bears, and hyaenas are attracted to caves as places to den—facilities that enhance their reproductive success by providing protection from the elements and other carnivores. Humans, on the other hand, might have enjoyed some of the same basic benefits from shelters, but the rules governing their uses of caves probably were organized quite differently—and independently—of those of carnivores (see also Gamble 1986:320–321). The sequences of shelter occupations and interior space requirements help outline some important interspecific differences in resource use, as well as provide useful expectations for archaeologists who excavate caves.

Conclusions

Some of the collections that form the basis of this study of Neandertal foraging and economics are biased in significant ways, primarily by the recovery practices of excavators working between 1939 and 1955. The recovery biases are easily identified and surmountable, however, and do not compromise the main objectives of this research. The geological conditions are similar among the sites, and bone preservation ranges between good and extraordinary, because of the favorable chemistry of the cave soils.

As for the biological agencies of bone collection and modification, it is clear that both hominids and a variety of bone-gathering carnivores used the caves of Latium. This situation calls for careful evaluation of who collected what, not to mention the contributions or deletions by pilferers and scavengers. It

also must be accepted that there are few purely cultural or purely carnivore assemblages in the study sample. Instead, one normally encounters differences in the degree of influence by a host of biological agencies, but where one usually is the primary player. This observation reflects a general and very ancient relationship between humans and nonhuman predators, manifested somewhat differently through time (Gamble 1983, 1986), but universal nonetheless (e.g., Binford 1981; Brain 1981; Lindly 1988; Stiner 1986, 1991e, Straus 1982). The quest for purity in the taphonomic histories of archaeofaunas may be a false hope, as there is no ecological basis for this expectation in research on mobile human societies.

Because the taphonomic analyses here concern several sites and many bone assemblages, the conclusions about formation histories must be synthe- sized in a simple format for the benefit of all chap- ters to follow. The taphonomic assessments are based on multiple damage categories, some of which are exclusive to hominids or carnivores. Other damage categories distinguish agencies only on the basis of relative frequency: damage is more common in assemblages generated by hominids or by carnivores along a single continuum of difference.

Figure 5.32 presents a matrix of evidence for hominid versus carnivore dominance in the forma- tion of the large mammal bone assemblages. The matrix combines mutually exclusive and frequency- dependent criteria. In this way, distinct classes of information are cross-referenced for a final assess- ment of who dominated bone-collecting activities in each assemblage, ignoring, for the moment, the po- tential roles of secondary modifiers.

We have already seen that not every criterion an- swers for every assemblage: a criterion can be very informative about some cases, but in other instances may be completely silent. Eleven in all, the taph- onomic criteria are weighted equally in the matrix; each is defined and summarized in Table 5.23. Six are exclusive criteria, three for hominids and three for large carnivores. Only one class of agency —hominids or large carnivores—is able to produce an exclusive signature, a question of presence- absence. Present but rare is further qualified in the matrix by using a smaller symbol. Exclusive signa- tures of hominid activities are (1) burned ungulate bones, (2) cut marks, and (3) lithic artifacts. Exclu- sive signatures of large carnivore activities are (9) gnawing damage, (10) latrines evident from con- centrations of hyaena coprolites or canid fecal bone (data from Chapter 6), and (11) elevated frequen- cies of infants and juveniles among the carnivore remains (borrowing data from Chapter 12). Because virtually any archaeofauna will show some evi- dence of gnawing, frequencies must exceed 10 per-

TABLE 5.23
Criteria for the evidence summary of hominid versus carnivore roles in assemblage formation in Figure 5.32

Criterion code	*Hominids*	*Hominids or carnivores*	*Carnivores*
criteria exclusive to hominid role:			
1	BURNED BONE	—	—
2	CUT MARKS	—	—
3	LITHIC ARTIFACTS	—	—
frequency-dependent indicators of hominid versus carnivore roles:			
4	(> 6%)	CONES	(≤ 5%)
5	(low)	MEAN FRAGMENT LENGTH	(high)
6	(angular splits, toes usually opened)	FRACTURE COMPLEXES	(ragged bows, toes usually unopened)
7	(light, open)	INTERIOR SPACE USE	(dark, cramped)
8	(≤ 10%)	LARGE CARNIVORE NISP: UNGULATE NISP	(> 10%)
criteria exclusive to large carnivore role:			
9	—	—	GNAWING (> 10%)
10	—	—	LATRINE
11	—	—	CARNIVORE YOUNG

Note: Frequency-dependent criteria are evaluated in terms of a predetermined threshold, usually expressed as percent of ungulate bone NISP. Evidence of carnivore latrines includes spotted hyaena coprolites and digested (fecal) bone from wolf scats (presented in Chapter 6). Carnivore young refers to large carnivore age structures that are significantly biased toward neonates and juveniles (presented in Chapter 12). Interior space use refers to gross horizontal distributions of material relative to cave vault shape and dimensions, assuming that denning carnivores generally prefer smaller spaces and that hominids prefer larger spaces.

	hominids (exclusive)			hominids or carnivores (frequency-dependent)					carnivores (exclusive)		
	1	**2**	**3**	**4**	**5**	**6**	**7**	**8**	**9**	**10**	**11**
M1	•	•	▬	–	□	–	–	–	□	•	•
M2	■	•	■	■	■	■	■	■	•	•	•
M3	■	•	■	■	■	■	■	■	•	•	•
M4	■	•	■	■	■	■	■	■	•	•	•
M5	▬	▬	▬	□	□	□	□	□	□	□	□
M6	■	•	■	■	■	■	■	■	•	•	•
G0	•	•	•	□	□	□	□	□	□	□	□
G1	•	•	▬	□	□	□	□	□	□	□	□
G2	■	•	■	□	■	▣	▣	■	□	□	•
G4	■	•	■	–	–	■	■	■	•	•	•
G5	■	•	■	■	■	■	■	■	•	•	•
S0	■	■	■	■	–	■	–	■	•	•	•
S1	■	■	■	■	–	■	–	■	•	•	•
S2	■	■	■	■	–	■	–	■	«□»	•	•
S3	■	■	■	■	–	■	–	■	«□»	•	•
S4	•	■	▬	■	–	□	–	□	□	□	□
SX	•	•	•	□	–	□	□	□	□	□	□
B3	■	■	■	■	■	■	■	■	•	•	•
Br	■	■	■	■	■	■	■	■	•	•	•
Salvini	■	■	■	■	■	■	■	■	•	•	•
Palidoro	•	■	■	■	–	■	■	■	•	•	•
Polesini	■	■	■	■	–	■	■	■	•	•	•
I1	•	•	▬	□	□	□	□	□	□	□	□
I2	•	•	▬	–	□	□	□	□	□	□	□
I3	•	•	▬	–	□	□	□	□	□	□	□
I4	•	•	▬	–	□	□	□	□	□	□	□
I5	•	•	•	□	□	□	□	□	□	□	□
I6	•	•	•	□	□	□	□	□	□	□	□

Evidence of hominid activities is ■ strong; or ▬ present, but comparatively scant. Evidence of large carnivore activities is □ strong; or ▣ suggests equal mix with that of hominids. • No significant presence in the case of exclusive criteria; – no answer in the case of frequency-dependent criteria. «»Overprint damage, see text.

Figure 5.32 Cross-referenced evidence for hominid and carnivore roles in bone assemblage formation based on mutually exclusive and frequency-dependent criteria (see Table 5.23 for criteria descriptions). (1) burned ungulate bones, (2) cut marks, (3) lithic artifacts, (4) cone fractures, (5) mean bone fragment length, (6) fracture complexes, (7) interior space use, (8) large carnivore bone NISP to ungulate bone NISP, (9) gnawing damage, (10) carnivore latrines, (11) juvenile-dominated carnivore mortality patterns.

cent of ungulate bone NISP to suggest collection by large carnivores; more growing takes place at dens than most other places that carnivores feed (discussed in Chapter 8). The significance of an elevated juvenile fraction among the carnivore remains is documented in Chapter 12, but, in essence, it connotes denning activities, places to which wolves and hyaenas typically bring the bones of prey.

Frequency-dependent criteria, pointing to hominid activities at one end of the continuum and to large carnivores at the other, are as follows: (4) cone fractures, (5) mean bone fragment length, (6) distinctive fracture complexes involving the treatment of ungulate mandibles and toe bones, (7) interior space use, and (8) the ratio of large carnivore bone NISP to ungulate bone NISP. The fracture complexes contrast the relative incidence of angular splits versus ragged bows on ungulate mandibles and the extent to which toe bones were fully opened to extract marrow. I acknowledge that the nutritional value of marrow, and thus the incentive for any predator to open bones, is mediated by season of death, food supplies, and prey health. Taking this into account, however, the basic contrast between what hominids and large carnivores do to mandibles and toe bones is generally upheld.

The results presented in Figure 5.32 should be read by row, beginning with the assemblage name in the first column. Reference cases from late Upper Paleolithic and hyaena den sites in Italy are provided in the lower part of the figure, illustrating the expected visual appearances of assemblages collected by humans as opposed to hyaenas and other large carnivores. A row dominated by filled squares argues for hominid collectors, whereas a row full of open squares argues for large carnivore collectors. The composite taphonomic indications are not always clear-cut, sometimes showing significant influence by both classes of agencies. Equivocal

results reflect either postdepositional mixing of hominid and carnivore components (e.g., Guattari G2, Sant'Agostino S4) or, alternatively, contemporaneous damage overprinting (e.g., Sant'Agostino S2 and S3). Dots indicate absence in the case of exclusive criteria, whereas fine dashes indicate no information in the case of frequency-dependent criteria.

The matrix in Figure 5.32 identifies the following faunas as suitable for analyses of Mousterian foraging practices in the Italian study sample:

(a) Grotta dei Moscerini, level groups M2, M3, M4, and M6
(b) Grotta Guattari, levels G4 and G5
(c) Grotta di Sant'Agostino, arbitrary layers S0, S1, S2, and S3
(d) Grotta Breuil, B3/4 and Br

TABLE 5.24
Summary of principal and secondary agencies of assemblage formation in the Latium caves

Site & assemblage	Dominant	Mixed with	Overprint
GROTTA DEI MOSCERINI:			
M1	carnivores (?)	hominids	—
M2	hominids	—	—
M3	hominids	—	—
M4	hominids	—	—
M5	spotted hyaenas	hominids and wolf?	—
M6	hominids	—	—
GROTTA GUATTARI:			
G0 (surface)	spotted hyaenas	—	—
G1	spotted hyaenas	hominids	—
G2	hominids	spotted hyaenas	—
G4	hominids	spotted hyaenas (?)	—
G5	hominids	—	—
G7	hominids (?)	—	—
GROTTA DI SANT'AGOSTINO:			
S0	hominids	—	canids
S1	hominids	—	canids
S2	hominids	—	canids
S3	hominids	—	canids
S4	wolves	hominids	(?)
SX	wolves	—	—
GROTTA BREUIL:			
Br	hominids	—	—
B3/4	hominids	—	—

The matrix identifies the following assemblages as primarily carnivore-collected:

(e) Grotta dei Moscerini, level group M5, principally spotted hyaenas

(f) Grotta Guattari, levels G0 and G1, principally spotted hyaenas

(g) Grotta di Sant'Agostino, layer SX, wolves

(h) Buca della Iena, levels I1, I2, I3, I4, I5, and I6, spotted hyaenas

Mixed cases from Guattari G2 and Sant'Agostino S4 are problematic, although qualitative assessments point more strongly to hominids in the former and to wolves in the latter. All assessments are further summarized in Table 5.24 according to principal and secondary agencies and include information on mixing and overprint damage.

6

Small Animal Exploitation

CAVE FAUNAS of Mousterian age in Italy sometimes include the remains of small animals, principally shellfish, tortoises, rabbits, and hares, in addition to the bones of large mammals. Little is known about small game use by Mousterian hominids in Europe, yet these data are essential for understanding how practices of hunting, gathering, and perhaps scavenging were integrated within Middle Paleolithic foraging adaptations. Here, small species are examined from taphonomic, zooarchaeologic, and biogeographic perspectives, in an effort to link their remains to hominid or other predator activities in the caves. Results include the first clear demonstration of shellfish exploitation by humans in the Mediterranean region as early as 115,000 years ago (Stiner 1993b).

HUNTING BY GATHERING

For reasons of preservation, most direct evidence of Paleolithic subsistence is restricted to animal remains, not plants. Of these materials, however, large mammal bones are the bases for virtually all inferences about hunting and land use practices of Paleolithic peoples. Whereas ungulate remains are, without question, the most conspicuous and abundant taxa in archaeofaunas across Eurasia, studies of modern hunter-gatherers show plants and other potentially gatherable foods to be essential to most human economies. Only a small leap of faith is required to impose the same general expectation upon hominid lifeways of the past. The use of plants and that of small animals have much in common tactically because these resources are stationary gatherable particles, often scattered in time and space. These characteristics generally set plants and small prey apart from large game.

Small prey may be considered sessile in habit either because they are truly immobile (as are plants), or because their territories are so small that the effect is one of immobility from the human point of view. Small prey may also require different, sometimes incompatible, search and procurement tactics from what is typical of large game hunting. Small animals are protein-rich, sometimes fat-rich, and represent potential sources of limiting nutrients that humans must consume regularly. Because most kinds of small prey are easily gathered, they are accessible to a wider variety of persons (ages and sexes) in social groups, and obtaining them is less likely to conflict with the demands of child care (Bigalke and Voigt 1973:259; Blurton Jones et al. 1989; Hawkes 1987, 1991; Meehan 1982, 1988).

That small animal remains should turn up in the cultural refuse of caves is significant because transport by humans is implied—never mind how far. Alternatively, the paucity of small animal remains in hominid-associated faunas overall would imply that transport of these foods was relatively uncommon, although they probably were not ignored during the search for food. Here lies an important eco-

The portions of this chapter concerning tortoises and marine shellfish are reworked from the 1993 article entitled "Small Animal Exploitation and Its Relation to Hunting, Scavenging, and Gathering in the Italian Mousterian," in *Hunting and Animal Exploitation in the Later Palaeolithic and Mesolithic of Eurasia*, Archaeological Papers of the American Anthropological Association, no. 4, with permission of the American Anthropological Association, Washington, D.C.

nomic distinction: tiny food packages may not have been worth carrying to shelter except under some special circumstances, but they may have been well worth eating where encountered. While much less abundant in Middle Paleolithic records, small animal remains offer unique clues about the ordinarily mute side of subsistence. They potentially inform us about the contingencies of food transport, how search and procurement tactics may have been organized, and the contexts of site use.

Not all small animal remains found in Paleolithic caves actually represent foods eaten by hominids, however. Spatial association does not, after all, ensure a behavioral connection, and thus the analyses of small animal remains must begin with taphonomy. Can the remains of small animals be attributed to human economic activities at the cave or were they collected by other bone- and shell-gathering agencies? Three major categories of small animals are considered (Table 6.1): mollusks, tortoises, and mammals. Wave action, for example, could account for the presence of marine shellfish in Grotta dei Moscerini, whereas tortoises might have been attracted to the soft sediments inside the cave as places to hibernate, some subsequently perishing

there. The analyses of damage patterns presented below eliminate these possibilities, firmly linking the marine shells and tortoise bones to human foragers. Bone damage tells a very different story for the small terrestrial mammals; most were brought to the caves by denning canids. Bats and birds are present in some deposits, but equivalent or greater abundances in sterile strata imply no significant link to hominid or carnivore occupations of the caves.

Evidence of small animal exploitation in the coastal Mousterian caves centers on water-dwelling rather than terrestrial species, especially marine clams and mussels. I therefore concentrate on the aquatic component of the small animal assemblages in later analyses, effectively narrowing the discussion to the deep stratigraphic series of Moscerini. I investigate the conditions in which the hominids brought these foods to the cave, variation in the kinds of small prey that were transported, and the scale of exploitation. The implications of these data for the contexts of foraging by Mousterian peoples are considered at the end of the chapter and compared to the practices of certain modern human groups that occupy littoral landscapes.

METHODS: TAXONOMY AND TAPHONOMY

The cave deposits include substantial Mousterian cultural components, but their histories of formation are more complex (Chapter 5). In addition to hominids, several species of bone-collecting carnivore periodically used the shelters as den sites; the impact of carnivore activities varies greatly among the caves and levels therein, however. Damage patterns and related phenomena are used to determine how small animal remains entered the deposits. For the ease of presentation, the analyses are organized according to whether small species were terrestrial or aquatic in habit.

Taxonomic classifications of the small mammals, reptiles, and mollusks are based on comparative skeletal and shell collections of the Istituto Italiano di Paleontologia Umana (IIPU) and the Università di Pisa. Because species diversity is great in marine communities of the Mediterranean, and taxonomic research on mollusks spans many centuries and gen-

erations of natural historians, two or more Latin synonyms often exist for the same animal. My identifications primarily follow Durante (1974–75; see also Bucquoy et al. 1882; Canavari 1916; Durante and Settepassi 1972; Leonardi 1935) for sand clams, mussels, scallops, limpets, and other marine species, but I defer whenever possible to the nomenclature used in the widely accessible *Simon and Schuster's Guide to Shells* (Feinberg/Sabelli 1980). The classifications emphasize genus-level taxonomy, because they rely on shell forms in absence of soft parts. Older generic synonyms are also provided if relevant. The terrestrial gastropods (land snails) were identified by Henk K. Mienis (Mollusk Collection Curator) of Hebrew University; ecological descriptions are provided for most of these taxa by Kerney and Cameron (1979) and Settepassi and Verdel (1965).

The analyses employ two types of specimen

TABLE 6.1
Small animal species in the Italian caves

Common name	Latin name
SMALL MAMMALS:	
INSECTIVORA	
common mole	*Talpa europaea*
Roman mole	*Talpa romana*
mole	*Talpa caeca*
hedgehog	*Erinaceus europaeus*
CHIROPTERA	
—	*Rhinolophus euryale*
—	*Rhinolophus ferrum-equinum*
—	*Myotis myotis*
—	*Myotis oxygnathus*
—	*Miniopterus schreibersii*
LAGOMORPHA	
rabbit	*Oryctolagus cuniculus*
hare	*Lepus capensis/europeus*
RODENTIA	
common hamster	*Cricetus cricetus*
common vole	*Microtus arvalis*
water vole	*Arvicola terrestris*
wood mouse	*Apodemus sylvaticus*
marmot	*Marmota marmota*
garden dormouse	*Eliomys quercinus*
dormouse	*Muscardinius avellanarius*
fat dormouse	*Glis glis*
rat	*Epimys rattus*
OTHER TAXA:	
REPTILES:	
European pond tortoise	*Emys orbicularis*
spur-thighed tortoise	*Testudo graeca*
COMMON MARINE MOLLUSKS:	
mussel (rock-dwelling)	*Mytilus galloprovincialis*
clam (sand-dwelling)	*Callista (Meretrix) chione*
clam (sand-dwelling)	*Glycymeris (Pectunculus)* sp.
cockle (sand-dwelling)	*Cardium tuberculatum, Cerastoderma edule*
RARE MARINE MOLLUSKS AND SPONGES:	
limpet	*Patella caerulea, P. ferruginea*
scallop	*Pecten jacobaeus*
edible oyster	*Ostrea edulis*
conch	*Choronia lampas?*
one-toothed turbin	*Monodonta turbinata*
turret shell	*Turritella* sp.
worm shell	*Vermicularia?* sp.
vongola clam	*Venus gallina*
sponge	(taxon unknown)

TABLE 6.1 *(Continued)*

Common name	Latin name
TERRESTRIAL MOLLUSKS:	
—	*Pomatias elegans*
—	*Murella signata*
—	*Oxychilus* sp.
—	*Pupa* spp.
—	*Retinella* spp.
—	*Rumina decollata*
—	*Poiretia dilatata*

counts: (1) bone or shell NISP, and (2) mollusk shell hinge counts. NISP refers to the number of identifiable specimens (Chapter 4) assignable to species or a more generic level, and in the case of mollusks (shell NISP), refers to any sort of shell fragment. Hinge refers to an anatomically unique hard structure of the shell useful for estimating the number of animals (MNI). In bivalves, such as clams, mussels, and scallops, the hinge is the location where the two valves articulate in the living animal. The internal coil (columbella) serves the same purpose for marine and terrestrial gastropods, and the apex of the shell is counted in place of a hinge for limpet-like gastropods. Hinge counts are an important reference point for comparing the degree of breakage in the assemblages and, when divided by two for bivalve species, represent the number of individual animals (hinge/2 = MNI). Hinge counts for gastropods correspond directly to MNIs (hinge = MNI).

The frequencies of damage on shells or bones are expressed as fractions of total NISP by taxon. Several classes of damage may be considered, depending on the type of material. The bones of small mammals and tortoises are examined for tool marks, distinctive fracture patterns (e.g., green breaks, impact cones, and impact depressions), burning damage, and for evidence of gnawing, crushing, abrasion, and digestive etching by carnivores. Weathering damage is practically nonexistent and therefore is not discussed. Digestive etching refers to the chemical erosion or polishing that occurs on bones while in the carnivore mouth or gut (or owl crop, e.g., Andrews 1990; Brain 1981). Digestive etching varies in appearance and intensity according to the type of predator involved (Stiner, unpublished comparisons for canids, felids, hyaenids, and owls). Marine shells are examined for beach polish (sand abrasion) and fractures associated with wave action, based on modern examples. Evidence of modification by humans includes burning damage, fracture forms, and the relative freshness of break edges. The shellfish assemblages also include a small number of specimens that were retouched into tools (Vitagliano 1984). Land snails are examined for crushing, burning, and punctures from the teeth of small mammalian predators, principally hedgehogs and foxes.

SMALL ANIMAL SPECIES BY SITE AND ASSEMBLAGE

Basic quantitative data for small species in the Middle and late Upper Paleolithic cave faunas are presented first. It is clear from Table 6.2 that Grotta dei Moscerini yields most of the small animal assemblages in the Mousterian study sample, including insectivores, lagomorphs, rodents, tortoises, marine and terrestrial mollusks, and even marine sponges. On the basis of quantity alone, the long and complex sequence of Moscerini is the most interesting for examining small game use in west-central Italy. Small animal collections from Grotta Guattari (Table 6.3) are sparse by contrast. The small animal components of Grotta di Sant'Agostino are more substantial, although strictly confined to mammals (Table 6.4). Rabbits, hares, water voles, and fat dormice are especially common among the

TABLE 6.2
Grotta dei Moscerini: NISP for small animals by level group and taxon

Taxa	M1	M2	M3	M4	M5	M6	TOTAL
INSECTIVORA							
Roman mole	1	1	.	.	.	.	2
mole	.	2	.	.	.	.	2
hedgehog	2	.	.	.	9	1	12
CHIROPTERA							
Rhinolophus euryale	.	.	.	.	1	.	1
Rhinolophus ferrum-equinum	.	.	.	.	4	.	4
Myotis myotis	.	.	.	.	2	.	2
Miniopterus schreibersii	.	1	.	.	1	.	2
LAGOMORPHA							
rabbit	.	.	.	.	1	.	1
hare	4	2	.	.	47	1	54
RODENTIA							
common vole	.	.	.	.	2	.	2
water vole	.	.	.	.	1	.	1
wood mouse	8	159	.	.	10	2	179
dormouse (*Muscardinius*)	.	12	.	.	.	.	12
fat dormouse	.	2	.	.	58	8	68
rat	.	.	.	.	16	.	16
rodent (?)	.	1	.	.	.	.	1
subtotal	15	180	.	.	152	12	359
REPTILIA/AMPHIBIA							
pond tortoise	.	.	.	.	15	10	25
spur-thighed tortoise	.	.	.	.	52	29	81
toad	.	1	.	.	1	.	2
subtotal	.	1	.	.	68	39	108
MARINE MOLLUSKS AND SPONGES							
mussel	.	1091	348	98	.	.	1537
Callista and *Glycymeris*	.	89	1062	89	166	92	1498
Cardium and *Cerastoderma*	.	7	31	4	1	9	52
conch	.	12	17	14	15	3	61
limpet	.	5	4	7	4	.	20
scallop	1	2	5	.	4	4	16
oyster	.	4	8	.	.	1	13
turbin	.	12	7	3	4	3	29
turret shell	.	.	.	1	.	.	1
worm shell	.	.	.	1	.	.	1
vongola clam	.	.	.	.	1	.	1
sponge	.	3	34	1	1	.	39
subtotal	1	1225	1516	218	196	112	3268

TABLE 6.2 (*Continued*)

Taxa	M1	M2	M3	M4	M5	M6	TOTAL
TERRESTRIAL MOLLUSKS							
Pomatias elegans	45	22	46	·	486	26	625
Murella signata	90	38	56	4	181	11	380
Oxychilus sp.	·	·	·	·	5	·	5
Pupa spp.	1	3	1	1	4	·	10
Retinella spp.	1	2	1	1	36	·	41
Rumina decollata	·	·	·	·	11	1	12
Poiretia dilatata	2	·	·	·	24	1	27
subtotal	139	65	104	6	747	39	1100

small mammal remains and will receive the most attention in the taphonomic analyses below. Only one hare tibia was recovered from the tool-bearing levels of Grotta Breuil by 1989 (Table 6.5). Remains of bats, swallows, owls, and regurgitated owl pellets occur in sterile deposits there, part of the normal biological rain from the cave vault (material under study; see also Stiner in Bietti et al. 1988; Kotsakis 1990–91). Small mammals are present in the hyaena-dominated faunas of Buca della Iena (Table 6.6), but they are rare relative to large mammal abundance (cf. Table 4.10).

Small animal remains occur in the late Upper Paleolithic sites of Grotta Palidoro (Table 6.7) and Grotta Polesini (Table 6.8), and samples from the latter site are large. Only one hare bone exists in the Riparo Salvini collection from 1988 (Bietti and Stiner 1992) and nothing more can be said about it. The data on small animals from Palidoro and Polesini are taken from others' work (Cassoli 1976–77, and Radmilli 1974, respectively), and no taphonomic information is available. Brown hare and water vole are most abundant throughout the twelve cuts of Polesini. The hares were probably human food, but the site's location on a river meander calls the prevalence of water vole into question. The bat remains probably originated from colonies inhabiting the shelter vault.

TABLE 6.3
Grotta Guattari: NISP for small animals by level and taxon

Taxa	G0	G1	G2	G3	G4	G5	G7	TOTAL
INSECTIVORA								
common mole	·	·	·	·	+	·	·	·
LAGOMORPHA								
brown hare	·	+	·	·	+	·	·	·
RODENTIA								
water vole	·	5	·	·	+	4	·	9
wood mouse	·	·	·	·	4	·	·	4
fat dormouse	1	1	2	·	+	2	·	6
subtotal	1	6	2	·	4	6	·	19
REPTILIA/AMPHIBIA								
turtle	·	·	·	+	+	·	·	+
toad	·	+	·	·	·	·	·	·

Note: (+) Reported as present by Cardini (in Blanc and Segre 1953), but not found in the collection.

TABLE 6.4
Grotta di Sant'Agostino: NISP for small animals by arbitrary layer and taxon

Taxa	S0	S1	S2	S3	S4	SX	TOTAL
INSECTIVORA							
Roman mole	4	·	2	·	·	2	8
hedgehog	·	8	·	4	·	·	12
CHIROPTERA							
Rhinolophus ferrum-equinum	·	·	·	1	1	·	2
Myotis oxygnathus	·	9	8	15	2	2	36
LAGOMORPHA							
rabbit	10	6	2	1	·	175	194
hare	17	13	4	3	4	·	41
RODENTIA							
common hamster	·	2	·	1	1	·	4
common vole	·	6	4	3	3	·	16
water vole	18	33	31	22	11	3	118
wood mouse	3	6	2	4	1	3	19
marmot	6	3	1	1	8	14	33
garden dormouse	·	·	3	2	1	1	7
fat dormouse	15	62	37	14	6	7	141
total	73	148	94	71	38	207	631

TABLE 6.5
Grotta Breuil: NISP for small animals by provenience
and taxon

Taxon	B3/4	Br
LAGOMORPHA		
hare	·	1

TABLE 6.6
Buca della Iena: NISP for small animals by level and taxon

Taxa	I1	I2	I3	I4	I5	I6	TOTAL
INSECTIVORA							
hedgehog	·	3?	4	·	·	·	7
LAGOMORPHA							
brown hare	·	1?	·	1	1	·	3
RODENTIA							
water vole	·	·	2	2	4	1	9
marmot	·	1?	·	·	·	·	1?
total	·	5	6	3	5	1	20

TABLE 6.7
Grotta Palidoro 1–8: NISP for small animals by taxon

Taxa	1	2	3	4	5	6	7	8	TOTAL
LAGOMORPHA									
brown hare	·	1	·	·	1	2	1	·	5
RODENTIA									
water vole (?)	1	·	·	·	·	·	·	6	7
garden dormouse	·	·	·	·	·	·	·	1	1
total	1	1	·	·	1	2	1	7	13

Source: Cassoli (1976–77).

TABLE 6.8
Grotta Polesini: NISP for small animals by arbitrary layer and taxon

Taxa	1	2	3	4	5	6
INSECTIVORA						
Roman mole	2	1	1	6	1	2
hedgehog	1	2	1	1	4	·
CHIROPTERA						
Rhinolophus euryale	·	·	·	1	3	4
Rhinolophus ferrum-equinum	·	·	·	1	·	·
Myotis emarginatus	1	·	3	41	50	23
Barbastella barbastella	·	·	·	2	·	1
Miniopterus schreibersii	·	·	·	·	·	·
LAGOMORPHA						
brown hare	27	18	34	37	69	43
RODENTIA						
common vole	·	·	2	6	2	2
water vole	74	25	24	52	69	63
wood mouse	1	3	3	9	15	8
marmot	2	·	·	1	·	4
garden dormouse	·	·	·	5	11	8
fat dormouse	·	·	·	·	3	·
rat	·	1	1	1	1	·
subtotal	108	50	69	163	228	158
REPTILIA/AMPHIBIA						
European pond tortoise	·	·	·	2	·	·
spur-thighed tortoise	2	1	1	1	·	1
common toad	7	·	1	·	3	2
subtotal	9	1	2	3	3	3

TABLE 6.8   (Continued)

Taxa	7	8	9	10	11	12	1–12 Total
INSECTIVORA							
Roman mole	·	1	·	1	5	1	21
hedgehog	·	1	1	·	·	·	11
CHIROPTERA							
Rhinolophus euryale	1	·	·	·	1	6	16
Rhinolophus ferrum-e.	·	·	·	·	·	1	2
Myotis emarginatus	6	7	12	·	15	41	199
Barbastella barbastella	·	2	1	·	·	4	10
Miniopterus schreibersii	·	·	·	·	·	1	1
LAGOMORPHA							
brown hare	33	25	28	20	9	22	365
RODENTIA							
common vole	5	3	5	1	1	11	38
water vole	59	42	59	42	52	114	675
wood mouse	1	3	5	4	2	47	101
marmot	1	1	·	·	·	1	10
garden dormouse	·	1	2	·	5	19	51
fat dormouse	1	1	1	·	·	·	6
rat	1	·	·	·	·	·	5
subtotal	108	87	114	68	90	268	1511
REPTILIA/AMPHIBIA							
European pond tortoise	·	·	·	·	·	·	2
spur-thighed tortoise	·	·	·	·	·	·	6
common toad	·	·	·	·	·	·	13
subtotal	·	·	·	·	·	·	21

Source: Radmilli (1974).

RABBITS AND HARES—AND CANIDS

Taphonomic analyses normally focus on the repetition of key damage types on items in an assemblage and, to a lesser extent, spatial associations among distinct classes of materials. Substantial quantities of bone usually are required to test hypotheses about the causes of assemblage formation. Scarcity eliminates many cases in the Italian study sample from serious consideration; one can speculate about how these small animal assemblages formed, but little more. Only two of the four Mousterian caves, Moscerini and Sant'Agostino, yield samples sufficiently large for reliable taphonomic assessments. Of the terrestrial species therein, hares (*Lepus europeus*),

rabbits (*Oryctolagus cuniculus*), and a few species of rodent are most common, and thus merit the most attention.

Lagomorphs occur primarily in levels that are also rich in carnivores, especially wolves (see Tables 4.6 and 4.8). A wolf den component is identified in layer SX of Sant'Agostino (see Chapters 5 and 12), where rabbit bones are exceptionally abundant (Table 6.9a). A mixed carnivore den series, dominated by spotted hyaenas but including foxes and wild cats, occurs in level group M5 of Moscerini. Here, hares are abundant (Table 6.9b). Owls represent another potentially important contributor

TABLE 6.9
Damage data for lagomorph remains from Sant'Agostino and Moscerini

a. Rabbits and hares from Sant'Agostino

| | | | | | | Punctures | |
| | | | | | | --- | --- |
Vertical provenience	Bone NISP	Fraction with cut marks	Fraction burned	Fraction gnawed	Fraction digestive polish	N	Average diameter (mm)
rabbits:							
S0	10	.	.	.	.70	.	.
S1	6	.	.	.50	.33	2	2.0
S2	2	.	.	.	.50	.	.
S3	1	.	.	.	.	.	.
S4	.	.	.	.	.	.	.
SX	175	.	.	.19	.39	28	2.2
hares:							
S0	17	.	.	.06	.29	4	4.1
S1	13	.	.	.31	.	2	1.3
S2	4	.	.	.	.	.	.
S3	3	.	.	.	.	.	.
S4	4	.	.	.25	.	.	.
SX	.	.	.	.	.	.	.

Note: Fractions represent the proportion of total NISP exhibiting the type of damage specified in each column.

b. Hares from Moscerini

Vertical provenience	Bone NISP	Fraction with cut marks	Fraction burned	Fraction gnawed	Fraction digestive polish
hares:					
M1	4	.	.	.	.
M2	2	.	.	.	.
M5	47	.	.	.11	.02
M6	1	.	.	.	.

to small mammal assemblages in caves, but in the cases of Sant'Agostino and Moscerini, damage on the rabbit and hare bones is consistent with canid agencies, not owls.

The tendencies of canids to collect bones in dens and to create latrines nearby are well known (e.g., Ballard et al. 1987; Ewer 1973; Fentress and Ryon 1982). Lagomorphs are a typical food of wolves while denning because the alpha female and helpers are less mobile during this period. Wolves often resort to small territorial game while tending infants, supplemented by what other pack members bring back to the den, including hard parts of large

prey and soft tissues that can be regurgitated if needed (e.g., Peterson et al. 1984:21; see also Rogers et al. 1980). Red foxes and wild cats, also represented in the Italian caves, are known to feed on lagomorphs (Burton 1979; see Chapter 4). However, the size of digested rabbit and hare bones and the tooth punctures evident on some specimens in the Sant'Agostino sample from SX exceed the dimensions expected for fecal and punctured bone from foxes and wild cats.

Rabbit and hare bones in Sant'Agostino and Moscerini show no indications of burning or cut marks from stone tools (Table 6.9). All but the smallest bone elements are broken, displaying fracture patterns and superficial damage characteristic of control samples from modern wild canids. Many of the lagomorph bones have tooth punctures preserving the outline of a canine or premolar (Figure 6.1C,D) and/or are polished by digestive acids. Table 6.9 suggests that carnivore tooth punctures generally increase with lagomorph NISP. Gnawing is observed on undigested (Figure 6.1) and digested (cf. Figures 6.2 and 6.3) bones, the latter of which is attributable to canids based on the quality and degree of digestive polish.

Juxtaposing the Italian fossil specimens to lagomorph bones from modern coyote scats reveals striking similarities in all aspects, a surprise that is not confined to the Middle Paleolithic. Figures 6.2 and 6.3A contrast lagomorph bones from canid (probably coyote) scats recovered from floor surfaces and the sterile fill just above floors of Basketmaker pithouses in Arizona (marked by black ticks) with examples from modern control samples from latrines of free-ranging coyotes in Chaco Canyon, New Mexico (Stiner 1986). The three other photographs (Figure 6.3B–D) show rabbit and hare bones from Sant'Agostino in Italy. Consistent with the situation for Basketmaker period material from North America, the Upper Pleistocene specimens from Italy can be matched piece for piece with bones from the control sets on the bases of break forms and locations, the resultant shapes, and the appearance of the digestive polish. Wolves are bigger than coyotes in all of the relevant dimensions, foxes smaller, and the bone fragments in their scats vary accordingly. The damage is the same in every other way, however. Digested rabbit bone fragments in the wolf den of layer SX in Sant'Agostino and hare bones in the M5 den complex of Moscerini therefore appear to represent canid latrines, a typical olfactory marker of dens and other parts of modern canid territories. Ungulate remains in Sant'Agostino SX, especially ibex and roe deer, also display damage typical of wolves and meanwhile show no indications of hominid activity, nor associations with stone artifacts (Chapters 4 and 5).

Bones of the European wild cat, and occasionally other felids, are present among the carnivore remains from Sant'Agostino and Moscerini, but I do not find evidence of felid digestive damage on

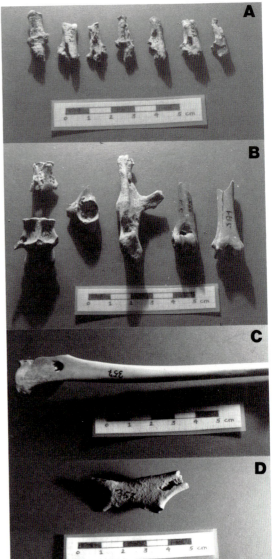

Figure 6.1 Canid-gnawed and canid-punctured (A) rabbit and (B) hare bones from Sant'Agostino and (C, D) hare bones from Moscerini.

lagomorph or other mammal remains. Etching damage to bones passing through the felid digestive tract tends to be more severe than is true for canids. Consider, for example, the specimens from modern mountain lion scats from the Guadalupe Mountains of New Mexico, shown in Figure 6.4, noting especially the condition of cortical bone fragments in the

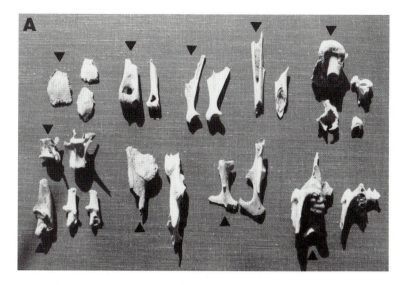

Figure 6.2 Comparisons of canid-digested (A) hare, rabbit, and (B) rodent bones from Basketmaker pithouse sites in Arizona (indicated by black ticks) and from modern coyote scat control samples collected by the author in Chaco Canyon, New Mexico.

bottom photograph. Such erosion occurs in the digestive tracts of all cats.

Spotted hyaenas are the most abundant carnivore species in Moscerini M5, and the associated ungulate bones display much evidence of damage by hyaenas. But hyaenas generally do not leave leftovers when eating small prey; they swallow all of the parts and digestion is complete. In contrast, many fragile bones of hares and rodents are preserved in M5, and some display the subtle traces of digestive polish from canids (Table 6.9b). Whether the bones represent fecal matter from wolves or foxes is not clear.

Explaining the moderate quantities of lagomorphs in layers S0 and S1 of Sant'Agostino is a more complicated problem, because bone fragments apparently originating from canid scats (Table 6.9a)

occur alongside ungulate bones unequivocally modified by humans and sometimes by canids thereafter. Sant'Agostino is a fascinating case in that canid gnawing of ungulate bones appears to have taken place after hominids had finished with the same food items (Chapter 5). The succession of damage, from butchering and marrow processing by humans to gnawing by foxes and wolves, grossly resembles the damage sequences documented by Binford (1978, 1981; collections that I also examined) for caribou bones in Eskimo camps where sled dogs were kept. Wolf-like in physiognomy, Eskimo dogs are often tethered and eat what they are given, whereas the canids at Sant'Agostino certainly were wild and made considerable, if unlicensed, use of ungulate bones discarded by Mousterian hominids during the formation of layers S0 through S3.

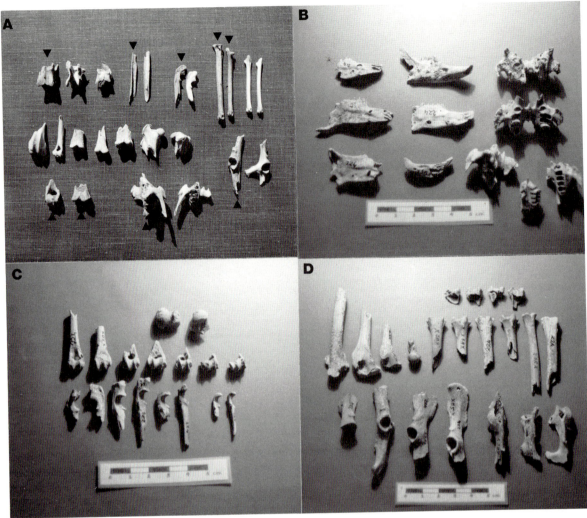

Figure 6.3 Canid-digested hare and rabbit bones from (A) Basketmaker pithouse sites in Arizona (indicated by black ticks) and from modern coyote scat control samples from New Mexico, and (B–D) hare bones from the Middle Paleolithic cave of Sant'Agostino.

In reviewing evidence of canids' impact on human refuse dumps, it is significant that modern canids normally defecate a prior meal at the location of the next one. This is more than a matter of digestive convenience, since the behavior serves to mark places in canid territories. Slightly elevated, well-ventilated, and already odorous landmarks are preferred. Human-generated garbage dumps are classic targets because they fulfill every condition. Marking by defecation may go a long way toward explaining canid-digested small mammal bones found alongside large mammal remains modified by hominids in Sant'Agostino. This phenomenon plays havoc with archaeofaunal records the world over, yet testifies to the close relationships between humans and canids long before domestication.

To summarize, bone damage on lagomorph remains reinforces many of the associations to carnivore agencies noted in Chapters 4 and 5. Most, perhaps all, rabbit and hare bones were introduced into Sant-Agostino by canids. The accumulations of hare remains in Moscerini likewise are attributable to canids, probably red foxes although wolves cannot be wholly excluded.

Figure 6.4 Digested bones from mountain lion scats, Guadalupe Mountains, New Mexico: (A) sample #25 contains bone fragments of ground squirrel, porcupine, and mule deer; (B) sample #47 contains bone fragments of a mule deer fawn and an adult. These are two of fifty samples collected from latrines of free-ranging lions (my current research). The study of scat and kill assemblages was done with the cooperation of Thomas Smith (lion biologist), then of the New Mexico Department of Fish and Game. Attributions of scat samples to lions by Smith are based on lion hair content (ingested while grooming) and, in some cases, direct observations.

LAND SNAILS IN MOSCERINI

Eliminating terrestrial mammals from the list of hominid foods effectively narrows consideration to one Mousterian cave in the study area, Grotta dei Moscerini. This cave contains a long stratigraphic sequence of thirty fine cultural levels in the exterior section and a more compressed series in the interior (Figure 3.16 and Table 3.7). Most of the levels contain Mousterian tools, mammals, marine and/or terrestrial mollusks, tortoises, and even some marine sponges. The complexity of the Moscerini series makes it especially interesting from the standpoints of both human foraging practices and site formation processes. It is best to begin, however, by discussing the snails.

The land snails in Moscerini were not eaten by people. Snail densities instead supply important information about shifts in cave microclimate, particularly humidity and karstic activity (e.g., G. Ruffo

172

CHAPTER SIX

and in the exterior levels EXT 1–11. Both stratigraphic segments correspond to relatively low occupational intensities by hominids, based on lower quantities of lithic artifacts. A brief lull in hominid activity is also suggested by relatively high snail counts and low artifact frequencies in EXT 26–29.

The horizontal and vertical distributions of snails in Moscerini differ markedly from those of marine shellfish and artifacts. The relative isolation of land snails from cultural material is not surprising in light of snails' habitat requirements: they generally prefer dark damp places above or below ground, preferably where they will not be crushed. Snails are most common in the dark interior and in the final (youngest) levels at the cave mouth when the space between ground and vault had narrowed and lost much of its former illumination. Whereas the carnivores and land snails made greatest use of the cave interior, hominid activities at Moscerini were oriented toward the cave mouth (Chapter 5). The increasing prevalence of land snails toward the end of

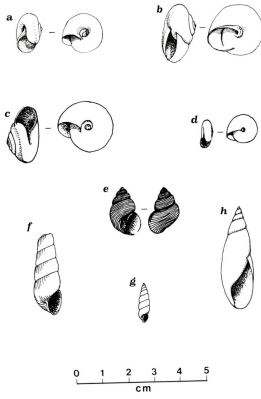

0 1 2 3 4 5
cm

Figure 6.5 Shell forms of terrestrial gastropods commonly found in Moscerini: (a,b) two forms of Helicidae including *Murella signata*, (c) *Retinella* spp., (d) *Oxychilas* sp., (e) *Pomatias elegans*, (f) *Rumina decollata*, (g) *Pupa* sp., and (h) *Poiretia dilatata dilatata*.

in M. Ruffo and Zarattini 1990–91). The land snails also are informative, if less directly, about hiatuses in human and carnivore uses of the cave and its increasingly inland position with time as the result of regressing seas. The shell forms of the terrestrial snail genera from Moscerini are illustrated in Figure 6.5. *Murella signata* (Fèrussac, 1821) and *Pomatias elegans* (Müller, 1774) are most abundant, accompanied by low frequencies of *Pupa* sp., *Retinella* spp., *Oxychilas* sp., *Rumina decollata* (Linnaeus, 1758), and *Poiretia dilatata dilatata* (Philippi, 1836). Where one snail taxon occurs in significant quantities, others are also likely to be found. Table 6.10 shows that snails are most common in the interior levels of Moscerini, especially INT 1–2 (level group M5) where carnivore remains are abundant,

Figure 6.6 Terrestrial snail shells from Moscerini punctured by the teeth of a small carnivore or insectivore.

TABLE 6.10
Shell MNI for terrestrial snails in Moscerini

Level	Pomatias	Murella	Pupa	Retinella	Oxychilus	Rumina	Poiretia
EXT 1	·	10	·	·	·	·	·
EXT 2–3	22	10	·	·	·	·	·
EXT 4–6	2	17	·	·	·	·	2
EXT 7–11	21	53	1	1	·	·	·
EXT 12	·	2	·	·	·	·	·
EXT 13	3	11	1	·	·	·	·
EXT 14	2	11	1	1	·	·	·
EXT 15	8	7	1	1	·	·	·
EXT 16	5	4	·	·	·	·	·
EXT 17	2	1	·	·	·	·	·
EXT 18	1	·	·	·	·	·	·
EXT 19	1	1	·	·	·	·	·
EXT 20	·	1	·	·	·	·	·
EXT 21	·	1	·	·	·	·	·
EXT 22	·	·	·	·	·	·	·
EXT 23	1	1	·	·	·	·	·
EXT 24	1	1	·	·	·	·	·
EXT 25	·	1	·	·	·	·	·
EXT 26	14	25	·	·	·	·	·
EXT 27	12	15	1	1	·	·	·
EXT 28	1	·	·	·	·	·	·
EXT 29	10	7	·	·	·	·	·
EXT 30	4	2	·	·	·	·	·
EXT 31	3	·	·	·	·	·	·
EXT 32	·	1	·	·	·	·	·
EXT 33	·	·	·	·	·	·	·
EXT 34	·	·	·	·	·	·	·
EXT 35	·	2	·	·	·	·	·
EXT 36	·	1	1	1	·	·	·
EXT 37	·	3	·	·	·	·	·
INT 1	122	92	·	8	·	2	18
INT 1A	65	13	·	1	·	2	2
INT 1B	6	8	·	·	·	·	·
INT 1C	120	29	3	7	3	5	2
INT 1D	100	17	1	2	2	1	1
INT 2	73	22	·	18	·	1	1
INT 3	26	11	·	·	·	1	1
INT 4	·	·	·	·	·	·	·

Note: Most specimens are whole or nearly whole shells. For terrestrial snails (and gastropods in general), MNI is determined from central spirals. Level groupings include the following fine levels: M1 (EXT 1–10), M2 (EXT 11–20), M3 (EXT 21–36), M4 (EXT 37–43), M5 (INT 1–2), M6 (INT 3–4).

the sequence corresponds to a time when Moscerini may have been as far as 1.5 km from the sea (see Table 3.1).

The snail shells tend to be whole or nearly whole, despite their fragility, and show no signs of burning. Some taxa (e.g., *Pomatias, Pupa*) are specifically adapted to wet limestone substrates, and colonies formed inside the cave. Other snails, especially of the genus *Murella,* instead fell prey to hedgehogs or foxes. Figure 6.6 shows whole *Murella* shells with tiny punctures, damage common on this genus but rare on the shells of other snails in the cave deposits. The hedgehog is an important snail predator throughout Europe (Evans 1972:105; Stuart 1982:73–74) and is known to collect quantities of shells in the backs of caves and crevices (C. Hunt, p.c.; Jenkinson 1984). Hedgehog remains are relatively few in Moscerini, but their distributions coincide with the highest frequencies of terrestrial gastropods; Table 6.2 shows that hedgehog bones are present in exterior level group M1 (EXT 1–10) and in interior level groups M5 (INT 1–2) and M6 (INT 3–4). Remains of red fox, another predator of snails (Burton 1979:36), also coincide with elevated quantities of snail shells and with small carnivore remains more generally (see Table 4.6).

TORTOISES IN MOSCERINI

While uncommon in the deposits overall, most or all of the aquatic and land tortoises in Moscerini were obtained and processed by humans. Tortoise remains are confined to the interior series of the cave (levels 1A–D to 4, or level groups M5 and M6, Table 6.2). Level group M5 is primarily a carnivore den complex, but also contains small quantities of flint artifacts. Level group M6 lacks significant evidence of carnivore activity but does contain signs of human presence, clearly the tail-end of a larger cultural deposit that thickens toward the cave mouth.

Two species of tortoise, one land-dwelling and one aquatic, occur in the deposits (Pritchard 1967; Street 1979). The land-dwelling variety is a species

TABLE 6.11

NISP, MNI, and damage data for tortoise remains in Moscerini by fine level and level group

a. Damage frequencies as fractions of total tortoise NISP

Fine level (and level group)	Spur-thigh NISP	Pond NISP	Total NISP	Fraction burned	Fraction impact cones or dents	Fraction with crushing	Fraction gnawed
Interior 1A–D (M5)	49	14	63	.05	.05	.05	.03
Interior 2 (M5)	3	1	4	.	.	.	.
Interior 3 (M6)	17	6	23	.22	.09	.09	.
Interior 4 (M6)	12	4	16	.12	.12	.06	.

Note: Value represents the proportion of total NISP exhibiting the type of damage specified in each column.

b. Impact cones and dents or crushing on carapace fragments relative to tortoise MNI

Fine level (and level group)	Total tortoise MNI	NISP with impact cones or dents	NISP with crushing
Interior 1A–D (M5)	6	3	3
Interior 2 (M5)	2	.	.
Interior 3 (M6)	2	2	2
Interior 4 (M6)	3	2	1

Note: The force of impact always originated from outside of the shell, pushing inward. Tortoise MNI is determined from the most common portion of the most common limb element, using information on side and species, in each vertical provenience.

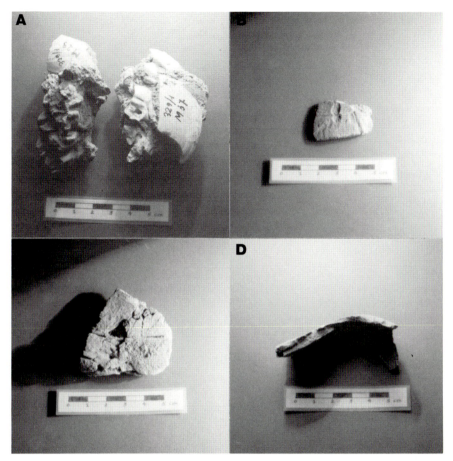

Figure 6.7 Small animal remains from Moscerini: (A) shell fragments of sand clam (*Callista chione*) cemented to red deer maxilla and mandible fragments, and (B–D) tortoise carapace and plastron fragments displaying green bone fractures, crushing, and impact depressions.

of *Testudo,* probably the mediterranean spur-thighed tortoise (*T. graeca*). It is more abundant, comprising 76 percent of total tortoise NISP and occurring in generally similar proportions throughout the interior level series (Table 6.11a). The European pond tortoise (*Emys orbicularis*) is an aquatic species, inhabiting still or slow-moving waters of ponds, lakes, and rivers (Stuart 1982:71–72). In coastal Latium, this tortoise is also found in brackish water habitats such as barrier lagoons. Both tortoise species hibernate in soft or disturbed sediments during the winter in Italy and, because of this behavior, whole fossilized specimens are frequently preserved in fine-grained alluvial sediments dating to the Pleistocene. Archaeological sites in

west-central Italy often contain soft sediments because of their association with hydrological settings. Tortoises seeking suitable hibernation spots may be attracted to these places, a possibility that must be addressed in the case of Moscerini.

Tortoise remains in the Moscerini deposits include limb bone, carapace, and plastron (belly plate) fragments. All but the smallest elements are broken and many display green bone fractures (conservatively, 46 percent of total NISP) akin to the kinds of damage found on large mammal bones in the same levels. The shells of the tortoises were opened while fresh, and the break edges seldom are abraded. Impact cones or, more often, impact depressions (Figure 6.7B–D) occur on the outside surfaces of carapace fragments, on or very near break edges (Table 6.11a). The tortoise shells appear to have been struck with a hard, blunt object, such as a rock hammer. As best as can be determined from this small sample, the incidence of cones or impact dents with associated crushing on carapace fragments in M6 equals tortoise MNI (Table 6.11b), as if only one or two blows were required to open the carapace of each animal. Fewer of these fracture types are represented relative to tortoise MNI in the predominantly carnivore den components of M5.

Of the sixty-three tortoise bones from 1A–D and 2 (level group M5), 3 percent were gnawed by large carnivores and 5 percent were burned (Table 6.11a). The mixing of specimens with carnivore- or human-inflicted damage in M5 testifies primarily to slower sedimentation rates in the back of the cave. Carnivores dominated ungulate bone-collecting activities in this level group (Chapter 5), and it is significant that gnawing and burning damage do not co-occur on the same specimens. In levels 3 and 4 (level group M6)—vertical units linked to hominid activities exclusively on the bases of damage on large mammal remains, lithic artifacts, and near absence of carnivore remains (Chapter 4)—tortoise bones are fewer in number (39 specimens). There is no evidence of gnawing by carnivores, however, and burning is more frequent at 12 to 22 percent of NISP. Thus, where taphonomic and archaeological evidence from large mammal remains and tool frequencies point only to hominid activities, evidence of burning on tortoise remains also increases.

The kinds of damage on tortoise carapace and plastron fragments from Moscerini are very different from that seen on naturally fossilized specimens from Latium. The latter display much fine abrasion from surrounding sands or silts and, to the extent that fragmentation occurs, breaks tend to follow the suture lines joining the bony plates of the shell. Green, spiraling, or cone fractures are virtually

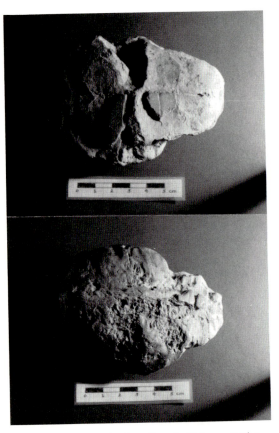

Figure 6.8 Fossil tortoise from Torre in Pietra preserving some of plastron and most of shell endocast. This kind of fossil results from tortoise deaths during hibernation in soft fluvial sediments.

nonexistent in these cases. Figure 6.8 shows a naturally fossilized tortoise from Pleistocene river sediments of Torre in Pietra (see also Caloi and Palombo 1978; Piperno and Biddittu 1978; Segre and Ascenzi 1984); the specimen shown retains a portion of the plastron and most of the endocast. In these situations, carapace and plastron fragments may eventually break away from the endocast when the sediments are disturbed.

SHELLFISH EXPLOITATION IN THE PALEOLITHIC: PROBLEMS AND PROSPECTS

Shells of marine mollusks are reported for several Mousterian caves lining the Mediterranean Sea (e.g., Blanc 1958–61; Palma di Cesnola 1965) and for roughly contemporaneous Middle Stone Age caves on the shores of South Africa, (e.g., Thackeray 1988; Voigt 1973, 1982). Five Mediter-

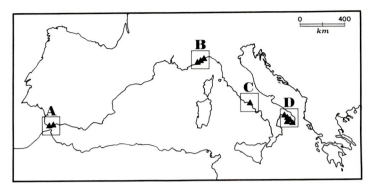

Figure 6.9 Northern Mediterranean localities where shellfish remains have been reported in Mousterian caves. (A) Gibraltar: Gorham's Cave, Devil's Tower. (B) Northern Italian Riviera (Liguria): Costa dei Balzi Rossi, Riparo Mochi, Barma Grande. (C) Gaeta (Latium): Grotta dei Moscerini. (D) Southern Italy (Puglia): Grotta dell'Alto, Grotta del Cavallo, Grotta Uluzzo C, Grotta Mario Bernardini, Grotta dei Giganti.

ranean localities have been noted in particular (Figure 6.9): the Gibraltar caves (Garrod et al. 1928; Baden-Powell 1964), the Balzi Rossi or Grimaldi caves in Liguria (Blanc 1958–61; Leonardi 1935; and my current research), the Moscerini and Breuil caves in Latium (Vitagliano 1984; Stiner 1990a, 1993b), several coastal caves in Puglia, southern Italy (Palma di Cesnola 1965, 1969), and at Haua Fteah in Cyrenaica, North Africa (McBurney 1967; Klein and Scott 1986). It is not clear if hominids were the shell collectors at the Gibraltar caves (Freeman 1981), but attributions to humans are credible in some of the Italian cases. Given the potential implications of shellfish exploitation in the Mousterian—in essence, the earliest evidence of marine resource use by land-bound hominids in Europe—this archaeological phenomenon is seriously under-reported. Whereas several probable cases have been recognized since the 1920s and 1930s, no systematic taphonomic inquiry relating these faunas to human diet has been done. Lack of documentation creates a false impression that Middle Paleolithic peoples simply did not exploit aquatic foods (e.g., Straus 1990:287–291). The only exception in Italy is Vitagliano's (1984) study of *Callista* shell tools from Moscerini, which covers one relatively specialized aspect of shell modification. Virtually nothing is known about other types of damage on shells in the coastal Mousterian sites.

Two competing explanations could account for how marine mollusk shells accumulated in the coastal caves. The first explanation would cite wave action and littoral drift acting in concert with natural mortality in shellfish communities: as animals died, their vacant shells were gradually concentrated in shoreline crags by waves and currents. The alternative explanation would cite humans, who gathered live shellfish for food (also as ornaments in Upper Paleolithic times), inadvertently accumulating shell debris at the places of consumption. Ideally, the appearance of shells—including patterns of abrasion, breakage, burning, and so on—gathered by geological forces as opposed to human hands should differ greatly. The Latium caves lay slightly inland when occupied by Mousterian hominids, protected from storms by banks of rocky talus or, in some cases, wide ribbons of dunes. There is little reason to anticipate that wave collection and human collection of shells operated simultaneously in any of the caves—a fact that greatly simplifies the task of analysis. Generally speaking, one should find evidence of one process or the other, not both.

Marine beach deposits containing wave-worn shells formed in many of the coastal caves of west-central Italy during or just after the Last Interglacial (e.g., Guattari and Breuil, Chapter 3). These beach deposits may be friable or silicified, depending on local geological conditions. Shells of the large conch-like gastropod *Strombus bubonius,* shown in Figure 6.10, are considered *fossile directeurs* in Italy, dating the ancient Tyrrhenian beach deposits to roughly the warm Interglacial period (e.g., Durante 1974–75; Durante and Settepassi 1972, 1976–77; Blanc and Segre 1953; Segre 1982, 1984). The distribution of *S. bubonius* is sensitive to changes in global temperature: it was prevalent along the Tyrrhenian coast of peninsular Italy 120,000 years ago, but disappeared from these waters soon thereafter (see Hearty 1986). Today, *S. bubonius* is confined primarily to warmer waters of the North African coast.

The arrays of molluskan taxa found in Mediterra-

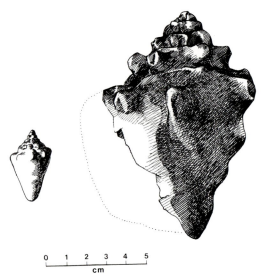

Figure 6.10 Upper Pleistocene examples of juvenile and adult *Strombus bubonius* from Italy. The body whorl of the adult specimen is missing, its original outline indicated by the dotted line.

nean Mousterian caves vary from east to west. Illustrated in Figures 6.11 through 6.15, these marine faunas are dominated by mussels (*Mytilus galloprovincialis, M. edulis*) and limpets (*Patella caerulea, P. ferruginea*) in the Gibraltar and Balzi Rossi cases, and by mussels and two genera of marine clam (*Callista* [= *Meretrix*] *chione* and *Glycymeris* [= *Pectunculus* = *Axinea*] spp.) in the west-central and southern Italian cases. One-toothed turbins, the marine gastropod *Monodonta turbinata*, also were eaten by Middle and Upper Paleolithic peoples in Italy. Human-caused damage on turbin shells is characteristic in all sites: usually a portion of the shell wall was sheared away by a sharp clean blow (Figure 6.15) or the shell was simply cracked like a nut.

All of the bivalve species named above can be found somewhere in the infralittoral zone of the modern Mediterranean Sea; most display a *Lusitanian* geographic range, which includes the entire Mediterranean and the Atlantic shores of Spain,

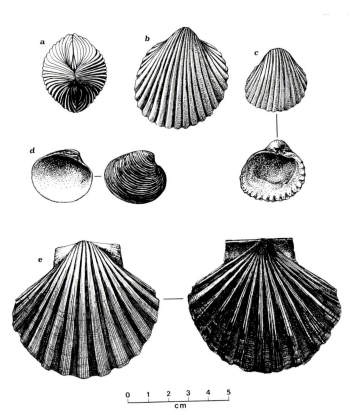

Figure 6.11 Ridge-shelled marine cockles *Cardium tuberculatum* (a,b) and *Cerastoderma edule* (c); Venus shells *Venus galina* (d); and scallop shells *Pecten jacobaeus* (e).

Portugal, and Morocco. Distributions of shellfish populations at a finer scale are regulated primarily by currents and the availability of preferred substrates such as soft sediments, hard rock or coarse gravels, and coral. Some species native to the Mediterranean are also sensitive to ambient temperature and/or salinity and therefore are confined to certain sea branches therein. Although not as diagnostic as *S. bubonius,* the presence of these taxa in Pleistocene deposits can inform us about climate and/or habitat structure along the littoral margin.

The habitats along the west-central Italian coast varied with time, principally through cycles of formation and destruction of barrier islands. Barrier systems greatly affect local evaporation potentials and patterns of water circulation from saline and

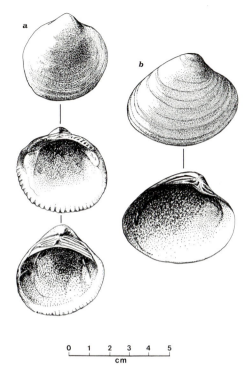

Figure 6.12 Smooth-shelled marine sand clams: (a) two-hinge form variants of *Glycymeris (=Pectunculus=Axinea)* spp.; and (b) *Callista (=Meretrix) chione.*

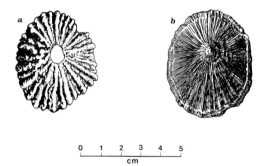

Figure 6.13 Marine limpets: (a) *Patella ferruginea* with damaged apex; and (b) complete shell of *P. caerulea.*

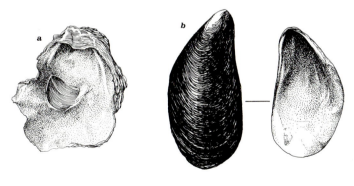

Figure 6.14 The edible marine oyster *Ostrea edulis* (a), and the Mediterranean mussel *Mytilus galloprovincialis* (b).

fresh sources. The presence of *Callista chione* (Figure 6.12b) along the Tyrrhenian coast during the Upper Pleistocene is ecologically significant because today it is found only along Adriatic shores, and no longer on the Tyrrhenian side of Italy. During the Upper Pleistocene, *Callista* coexisted with a variety of other sand clams (*Glycymeris, Cerastoderma,* and *Cardium*), whereas only the latter three are found there now. The disappearance of *Callista* from the Tyrrhenian coast apparently signals widespread loss of barrier lagoon habitats, warm shallow waters made more saline by high rates of evaporation. Their eventual disappearance is somehow keyed to gradual lowering of the sea over the course of the Upper Pleistocene (A. G. Segre, p.c.; Blanc and Segre 1953). We can be certain that *Callista* disappeared late, however, because small quantities of them have been found in the terminal Mousterian layers of Grotta Breuil (B3/4, ESR-dated to around 37,000 B.P.).

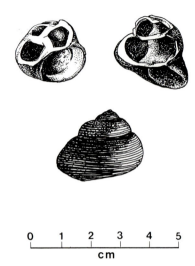

0   1   2   3   4   5
cm

Figure 6.15 One-toothed turbins, the marine gastropod *Monodonta turbinata,* (top) broken open by humans and (bottom) complete.

MARINE SHELLFISH IN MOSCERINI

Marine shells occur in thirty of the fine exterior levels of Moscerini and throughout the interior series. The most common species in the cave deposits are bivalves which can be grouped into two categories according to their substrate preferences. Most abundant are the rock-adhering mussel (*Mytilus galloprovincialis*) and two genera of silt- or sand-dwelling clams, *Callista chione* and *Glycymeris* spp. (Table 6.12). Shell fragments of *Callista* and *Glycymeris* are difficult to distinguish if lacking the hinge. Table 6.13 provides frequency breakdowns on the basis of hinges alone and shows that, of the smooth-shelled clams, *Callista* is concentrated in EXT 21–26, whereas *Glycymeris* is more evenly distributed through the exterior sequence. A variety of other marine bivalves and gastropods are represented in lower frequencies, including sand-dwelling cockles with corrugated shells, such as *Cardium tuberculatum* and *Cerastoderma edulis* (Figure 6.11a–c). Cockles co-occur with other sand clams in the deposits (Table 6.12). Conches (*Choronia lampas?*), limpets (*Patella caerulea* and *P.*

ferruginea), scallops (*Pecten jacobaeus*), marine sponges (taxon not known), one-toothed turbins (*Monodonta turbinata*), oysters (*Ostrea edulis*), Venus shells (*Venus gallina*), turret shells (*Turritella* sp.), and worm shells (*Vermicularia?* sp.) also occur in very low frequencies (Tables 6.14 and 6.15). All of these species can be collected from littoral habitats without diving in deep water or using water craft.

The circumstances of shell accumulation changed greatly through the exterior strata sequence of Moscerini, beginning with wave-accumulated material in sandy beach deposits, but soon shifting to anthropogenic material. Changes in the agencies of accumulation can be traced both from associations with Paleolithic stone tools and, more important, from patterns of damage on the shells themselves.

The entrance of Moscerini today lies just beyond the reach of the winter sea storm line (see Figure 3.13). Had the cave entrance not been entirely blocked by recent rockfall, one could walk outward

TABLE 6.12
NISP, hinge, and burn counts for common marine bivalves in Moscerini

Level	Callista chione and Glycymeris				Cardium and Cerastoderma				Mytilus galloprovincialis			
	NISP	NISP BURN	HINGE	HING BURN	NISP	NISP BURN	HINGE	HING BURN	NISP	NISP BURN	HINGE	HING BURN
EXT 13	·	·	·	·	·	·	·	·	5	1	1	1
EXT 14	5	1	·	·	·	·	·	·	386	42	88	13
EXT 15	9	2	3	·	2	·	1	·	510	85	126	30
EXT 16	13	10	·	·	1	·	·	·	63	21	13	5
EXT 17	24	7	2	1	·	·	·	·	35	11	9	5
EXT 18	16	7	4	2	·	·	·	·	4	·	1	·
EXT 19	10	6	2	·	·	·	·	·	2	1	·	·
EXT 20	12	11	3	2	4	·	·	·	86	33	23	10
EXT 21	259	123	29	16	6	3	1	·	45	18	7	4
EXT 22	271	176	37	20	7	4	1	·	10	9	·	·
EXT 23	165	90	22	11	8	2	1	·	2	·	1	·
EXT 24	106	44	23	11	1	·	·	·	3	·	1	·
EXT 25	96	40	17	9	2	1	·	·	3	·	·	·
EXT 26	100	23	21	11	2	2	·	1	5	2	·	·
EXT 27	4	·	1	·	1	·	·	·	·	·	·	·
EXT 28	12	4	1	·	·	·	·	·	6	3	1	·
EXT 29	·	·	·	·	·	·	·	·	4	2	1	·
EXT 30	7	2	·	·	3	2	·	·	128	61	27	17
EXT 31	6	2	2	·	·	·	·	·	71	30	9	3
EXT 32	12	4	1	·	1	·	·	·	12	·	2	·
EXT 33	5	3	·	·	·	·	·	·	39	15	7	3
EXT 34	3	·	·	·	·	·	·	·	19	9	3	·
EXT 35	9	2	2	1	·	·	·	·	1	·	·	·
EXT 36	7	·	1	·	·	·	·	·	·	·	·	·
EXT 37	32	1	7	·	4	·	·	·	26	4	9	2
EXT 38	15	1	3	·	·	·	·	·	35	11	6	2
EXT 39	30	2	3	·	·	·	·	·	31	16	5	4
EXT 40	·	·	·	·	·	·	·	·	·	·	·	·
EXT 41	2	·	·	·	·	·	·	·	6	·	2	·
EXT 42	·	·	·	·	·	·	·	·	·	·	·	·
EXT 43	10	·	3	·	·	·	·	·	·	·	·	·
BEACH	85	·	85	·	20	·	20	·	·	·	·	·
INT 1	65	1	24	·	·	·	·	·	·	·	·	·
INT 1A	15	·	5	·	·	·	·	·	·	·	·	·
INT 1B	7	2	1	·	·	·	·	·	·	·	·	·
INT 1C	22	2	5	·	·	·	·	·	·	·	·	·
INT 1D	16	1	3	·	·	·	·	·	·	·	·	·
INT 2	41	3	10	·	1	·	·	·	·	·	·	·
INT 3	71	1	28	·	2	·	·	·	·	·	·	·
INT 4	21	1	7	1	7	·	·	·	·	·	·	·

Note: (NISP) total shell fragment count, (NISP BURN) number of shell fragments burned, (HINGE) hinge count, (HING BURN) number of hinges burned. For bivalves, MNI estimates require dividing the number of hinges by 2. Level groupings include the following fine levels: M1 (EXT 1–10), M2 (EXT 11–20), M3 (EXT 21–36), M4 (EXT 37–43), M5 (INT 1–2), M6 (INT 3–4).

TABLE 6.13
NISP, hinge, and burn counts for *Callista chione* and
Glycymeris in Moscerini

	Callista		Glycymeris	
Level	*HINGE*	*HINGE BURN*	*HINGE*	*HINGE BURN*
EXT 15	·	·	2	·
EXT 16	·	·	5	·
EXT 17	·	·	1	1
EXT 18	·	·	1	·
EXT 19	1	·	·	·
EXT 20	1	·	3	·
EXT 21	25	9	3	·
EXT 22	31	15	4	3
EXT 23	19	8	3	3
EXT 24	18	8	3	·
EXT 25	19	7	·	·
EXT 26	21	11	1	·
EXT 28	·	·	2	1
EXT 31	2	·	·	·
EXT 32	·	·	2	·
EXT 33	·	·	1	1
EXT 35	1	·	1	·
EXT 36	1	·	·	·
EXT 37	4	·	1	·
EXT 38	1	·	1	·
EXT 39	2	·	4	·
EXT 43	·	·	3	·
BEACH	·	·	85	·
INT 1	12	2	7	·
INT 1A	2	·	3	·
INT 1B	2	1	·	·
INT 1C	4	1	2	·
INT 1D	1	·	4	·
INT 2	5	1	6	1
INT 3	7	·	19	·
INT 4	3	1	6	·

Note: MNI estimates require dividing the number of hinges by 2.
   Level groupings include the following fine levels: M1 (EXT
   1–10), M2 (EXT 11–20), M3 (EXT 21–36), M4 (EXT 37–
   43), M5 (INT 1–2), M6 (INT 3–4).

from it and, with only a minor accident, land face-down on wet sand if not in the water itself. The cave was scoured clean by the sea during the Last Interglacial, and the oldest sediments in the exterior sequence clearly postdate this high sea stand. Not long after 120,000 years ago, however, waves and littoral drift began depositing sands in the mouth of

the cave (see Figure 3.16). The stratigraphic sequence thus begins with beach sands (EXT 43–44), containing whole or nearly whole sand clam valves and, rarely, fragments of *S. bubonius* (not available for study but recorded in Segre's field notes). Most of these clam shells display damage characteristic of surf action (Table 6.16), including extensive polishing by sands and punched-out umbos. Circular umbo fractures, illustrated in Figure 6.16A, are usually caused by collisions with shoreline rocks or other shells as the waves carry the shells laterally along the coast to their final resting place. Some may also have resulted from predation by other mollusks (see below). Upper Paleolithic and Mesolithic peoples living along the Mediterranean occasionally took advantage of these fractures for stringing shell ornaments, but the fractures are from natural causes (e.g., at Riparo Mochi). This kind of damage is confined to clam umbo structures and generally contrasts with the more randomly placed beveled holes that Natacid predatory snails drill into the shells of their victims (Feinberg and Sabelli 1980; Leonardi 1935; and my comparative collections). All varieties of damage on shells from the ancient beach deposit of Moscerini EXT 43–44 match examples found on beaches in the region today.

Continued regression of the Mediterranean Sea following the Last Interglacial left the entrance of Moscerini permanently clear of the surf line. The cave was situated only slightly farther inland, but enough so that sediment formation involved terrestrial and aeolian phenomena exclusively. Humans began visiting Moscerini around 115,000 or 110,000 B.P. and occupations recurred there for 50,000 years, ending around 65,000 B.P. Within this time frame, evidence of surf polish on shells drops to nearly zero. The left portion of Figure 6.17 illustrates the decline in surf-polished specimens. Three averaged ESR dates (Schwarcz et al. 1990–91) are shown on the stratigraphy axis; because of the problems with dating this site (Chapter 3), the relative gaps between the dates are probably more informative than the absolute values.

Shellfish remains occur in every tool-bearing level of Moscerini, but the quantities are low and represent few individuals, as indicated by hinge counts in Tables 6.12 through 6.15. In contrast to the whole valves found in the sterile beach level,

TABLE 6.14
NISP, hinge, and burn counts for conch, limpet, scallop, and sponge in Moscerini

Level	Conch NISP	Conch NISP BURN	Conch HINGE	Limpet NISP	Limpet NISP BURN	Limpet HINGE	Scallop NISP	Scallop NISP BURN	Scallop HINGE	Sponge NISP
EXT 8	·	·	·	·	·	·	1	·	·	·
EXT 13	4	·	1	·	·	·	·	·	·	·
EXT 14	2	·	1	2	·	2	·	·	·	·
EXT 15	2	·	·	1	·	1	·	·	·	·
EXT 16	2	·	·	·	·	·	·	·	·	·
EXT 17	2	·	·	·	·	·	1	1	·	·
EXT 18	·	·	·	·	·	·	·	·	·	·
EXT 19	·	·	·	·	·	·	·	·	·	1
EXT 20	·	·	·	2	·	2	1	1	1	2
EXT 21	·	·	·	2	·	2	1	1	·	5[a]
EXT 22	·	·	·	·	·	·	·	·	·	15
EXT 23	4	1	1	·	·	·	·	·	·	9
EXT 24	1	1	1	·	·	·	·	·	·	3
EXT 25	·	·	·	·	·	·	1	·	·	1[a]
EXT 26	·	·	·	·	·	·	3	1	·	1
EXT 27	·	·	·	·	·	·	·	·	·	·
EXT 28	·	·	·	·	·	·	·	·	·	·
EXT 29	·	·	·	·	·	·	·	·	·	·
EXT 30	·	·	·	·	·	·	·	·	·	·
EXT 31	8	1	·	2	·	2	·	·	·	·
EXT 32	2	·	1	·	·	·	·	·	·	·
EXT 33	2	·	·	·	·	·	·	·	·	·
EXT 34	·	·	·	·	·	·	·	·	·	·
EXT 35	·	·	·	·	·	·	·	·	·	·
EXT 36	·	·	·	·	·	·	·	·	·	·
EXT 37	7	·	1	3	·	3	·	·	·	1
EXT 38	7	·	1	3	·	2	·	·	·	·
EXT 39	·	·	·	1	·	1	·	·	·	·
INT 1	4	·	1	2	·	2	2	·	·	·
INT 1A	2	·	·	·	·	·	1	·	·	·
INT 1B	2	·	1	·	·	·	·	·	·	·
INT 1C	·	·	·	·	·	·	·	·	·	1
INT 1D	3	·	·	·	·	·	1	·	·	·
INT 2	4	·	1	2	·	2	·	·	·	·
INT 3	3	·	1	·	·	·	3	1	1	·
INT 4	·	·	·	·	·	·	1	·	·	·

[a]One specimen is burned.

Note: (NISP) total shell fragment count, (NISP BURN) number of shell fragments burned, (HINGE) hinge count. Hinge here refers to the structures at which the two valves are joined in bivalves. MNI estimates require dividing the number of hinges by 2. Level groupings include the following fine levels: M1 (EXT 1–10), M2 (EXT 11–20), M3 (EXT 21–36), M4 (EXT 37–43), M5 (INT 1–2), M6 (INT 3–4).

TABLE 6.15
NISP, hinge, and burn counts for turbin, oyster, vongola, turrit, and worm shell in Moscerini

Level	Turbin[a]			Oyster			Vongola	Turret shell	Worm shell
	NISP	NISP BURN	HINGE	NISP	NISP BURN	HINGE	NISP	NISP	NISP
EXT 13	4	1	2	·	·	·	·	·	·
EXT 14	1	·	·	1	1	·	·	·	·
EXT 15	·	·	·	2	1	·	·	·	·
EXT 16	·	·	·	1	·	·	·	·	·
EXT 19	2	1	·	·	·	·	·	·	·
EXT 20	5	2	·	·	·	·	·	·	·
EXT 21	4	1	1	1	·	1	·	·	·
EXT 22	·	·	·	1	·	1	·	·	·
EXT 24	·	·	·	2	1	2	·	·	·
EXT 30	·	·	·	4	1	4	·	·	·
EXT 32	2	1	1	·	·	·	·	·	·
EXT 33	1	·	1	·	·	·	·	·	·
EXT 37	2	1	·	·	·	·	·	1	·
EXT 38	1	·	·	·	·	·	·	·	1
EXT 39	·	·	·	·	·	·	·	·	·
INT 1	2	1	·	·	·	·	1	·	·
INT 1B	1	·	·	·	·	·	·	·	·
INT 1D	1	·	·	·	·	·	·	·	·
INT 3	2	2	·	·	·	·	·	·	·
INT 4	1	1	·	1	1	·	·	·	·

[a]All turbin specimens are broken open, and break edges are clean and unabraded.

Note: (NISP) total shell fragment count, (NISP BURN) number of shell fragments burned, (HINGE) hinge count. Hinge here refers to the structures at which the two valves are joined in bivalves. MNI estimates require dividing the number of hinges by 2. Level groupings include the following fine levels: M1 (EXT 1–10), M2 (EXT 11–20), M3 (EXT 21–36), M4 (EXT 37–43), M5 (INT 1–2), M6 (INT 3–4).

shells associated with flint tools in EXT 13 through 41 are highly fragmented. Figure 6.17 illustrates this fact using the ratio of hinges to total bivalve NISP (hinge/tNISP). The degree of fragmentation varies, but falls within a restricted range throughout the exterior strata series. Nearly all break edges on the shell fragments are clean, square, and fresh-looking (Figure 6.16B); they were not abraded by trampling (or waves) to any significant extent yet were broken into many pieces. Surf polish is rare by contrast (Figure 6.17); sedimentological evidence does not indicate that the shells were washed in by waves after the beach (EXT 43–44) was formed, hinting that other agencies were responsible for the occasional wave-worn specimens in EXT 13 through 41. Ethnoarchaeological accounts of mod-

ern people suggest that gathering errors often account for the introduction of both rare nonedible taxa and otherwise inexplicable matter into shell middens (e.g., Bigalke and Voigt 1973:258–259).

Burning damage is completely absent from shells in the beach levels at the base of the Moscerini sequence. In contrast, burning damage is prevalent on shells from all of the levels that contain stone tools. The frequency of burning on shells varies greatly (Figure 6.17, and Tables 6.12–6.15), more so than the degree of fragmentation. Burning tends to be light; blackened or calcined specimens are rare. In levels where shells are burned, they are also fragmented, although the absolute frequencies of each class of damage do not parallel one another closely. The burned shells in EXT 13 through 39

TABLE 6.16
Beach polish on common marine bivalves in Moscerini

Level	Callista chione and Glycymeris		Cardium and Cerastoderma		Mytilus galloprovincialis	
	NISP	NUMBER POLISHED	NISP	NUMBER POLISHED	NISP	NUMBER POLISHED
EXT 13	·	·	·	·	5	·
EXT 14	5	·	·	·	386	·
EXT 15	9	·	2	·	510	·
EXT 16	13	1	1	1	63	·
EXT 17	24	3	·	·	35	·
EXT 18	16	·	·	·	4	·
EXT 19	10	·	·	·	2	·
EXT 20	12	2	4	4	86	·
EXT 21	259	·	6	·	45	·
EXT 22	271	·	7	·	10	·
EXT 23	165	·	8	·	2	·
EXT 24	106	·	1	·	3	·
EXT 25	96	·	2	·	3	·
EXT 26	100	·	2	·	5	·
EXT 27	4	·	1	·	·	·
EXT 28	12	·	·	·	6	·
EXT 29	·	·	·	·	4	·
EXT 30	7	·	3	·	128	·
EXT 31	6	·	·	·	71	·
EXT 32	12	·	1	·	12	·
EXT 33	5	·	·	·	39	·
EXT 34	3	3	·	·	19	·
EXT 35	9	·	·	·	1	·
EXT 36	7	1	·	·	·	·
EXT 37	32	·	4	4	26	·
EXT 38	15	1	·	·	35	·
EXT 39	30	4	·	·	31	·
EXT 40	·	·	·	·	·	·
EXT 41	2	·	·	·	6	·
EXT 42	·	·	·	·	·	·
EXT 43	10	7	·	·	·	·
BEACH	85	85	20	20	·	·
INT 1	65	·	·	·	·	·
INT 1A	15	·	·	·	·	·
INT 1B	7	·	·	·	·	·
INT 1C	22	·	·	·	·	·
INT 1D	16	·	·	·	·	·
INT 2	41	·	1	·	·	·
INT 3	71	·	2	·	·	·
INT 4	21	·	7	·	·	·

Note: Level groupings include the following fine levels: M1 (EXT 1–10), M2 (EXT 11–20), M3 (EXT 21–36), M4 (EXT 37–43), M5 (INT 1–2), M6 (INT 3–4).

Figure 6.16 Contrasting patterns of damage on marine bivalves in (A) Moscerini EXT 43–44, where shells tend to be whole, are beach-worn, and umbos are broken; and in (B) EXT 13–41, where shells are always fragmented, break edges are fresh, and many are burned.

clearly signify human activities in Moscerini and suggest that the mollusks were processed and/or discarded in the vicinity of fires. Because the incidence of burning on shell is akin to that on lithic artifacts (see Table 5.20), however, burning damage is not necessarily the direct result of cooking. Several superficial burn features were noted by the excavators in 1949 (Segre's unpublished notes), and light to mild burning of the shells may have been caused by new fires built atop old debris (see Stiner et al. n.d.).

The times, the place, and the people are far removed from Upper Pleistocene Italy, yet Goodale's (1971:169–172; see also 1957) accounts of roasting and baking procedures for cockles by the modern Tiwi of Melville Island (Australia) suggests a plausible, if generalized, thermomechanical explanation for the pattern of burning on shells in the Mousterian. Tiwi women and children gather mollusks,

turtles, turtle eggs, crabs, and other small animals along the shore, often bringing them to a nearby camp to be cooked and eaten. The women's methods for cooking cockles elevates the probability that the shells will become burned for two reasons. First, cockles are roasted briefly in or over a bed of coals to open them. Second, the shells from previous meals sometimes are deliberately piled into the fire to create a bed of hot shell and ash for roasting the next batch of fresh cockles. Fragments no doubt also find their way into the sediments around and below the firebeds. Sometimes shells are completely destroyed, other times not, apparently depending on the use-life of the hearth. Information on Mousterian fireplaces in Moscerini is limited, but the field accounts indicate very shallow ash and charcoal lenses, suggesting simple short-lived fires. The ephemeral nature of these hearths may explain why shell fragments, though invaria-

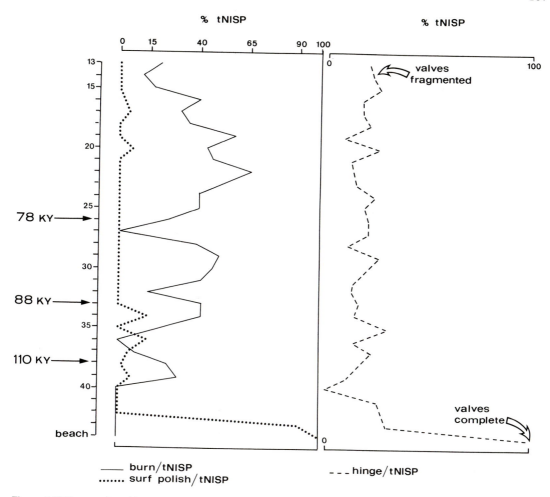

Figure 6.17 Frequencies of key damage types on marine shells from the exterior strata sequence of Moscerini: (left) surf polish and burning damage expressed as percent of tNISP, and (right) the degree of valve fragmentation expressed by the hinge/tNISP ratio. Three averaged ESR dates are shown on the stratigraphy axis.

bly fragmented, are seldom completely blackened or calcined.

Hominids brought shellfish into Moscerini primarily for alimentary reasons, but a small fraction of the shells also served as raw material for tool making (see also Vitagliano 1984), akin go the practices of certain modern maritime hunter-gatherers (e.g., Goodale 1971; Gusinde 1961). Valve fragments of *Callista chione* sometimes were retouched unifacially to make simple scraper tools (Figure 6.18), a phenomenon also reported for other coastal Mousterian caves in Italy (Palma di Cesnola 1965). Difficulties of species identification notwithstand-

ing, hominids apparently preferred *Callista* for this purpose; deliberate retouch is not reported for *Glycymeris,* the other bivalve genus common in the deposits and possessing a dense, smooth porcelain-like shell. Claims by Palma di Cesnola (1965) and Vitagliano (1984) that Mousterian people fashioned highly expedient tools from clam shells appear to be well-founded, even if some of the specimens from Moscerini previously identified as "retouched" are ambiguous (Kuhn, p.c.). Evidence of retouch on *Callista* shells occurs only on the inside lip (Figure 6.18), and shell tools are rare relative to total *Callista* NISP. Because of the natural curvature of the

Figure 6.18 Unifacial scrapers made of *Callista* shells from the Mousterian levels of Moscerini: (top) real specimens and (bottom) drawings adapted from Vitagliano (1984:159).

shell, it is only feasible, however, to produce such retouch by striking or pressing inwardly from the outside surface of the valve. As nature would have it, trampling might also produce marginal chipping on the inside edge of valves if they happen to be lying in the correct position. In contrast, any force applied from the inside outward would generally result in square-edged breaks. Mousterian hominids undoubtedly knew the best ways to modify shells into tools, but shell structure limited the orientation of deliberate retouch to one direction, not people. Thus, unifacial retouch in itself might not effectively distinguish deliberate tool-making from accidental trampling of *Callista* shells. More convinc-

ing is the stark presence-absence contrast between continuously retouched edges of shell tools and all other margin fragments: tools are retouched along the full length of natural lip fragments, whereas all other fragments are hardly chipped at all. This contrast exists despite uneven cave floors and universal fragmentation of bivalve shells throughout the cultural levels. Moreover, if marginal retouch were caused simply by trampling, the same kind of damage should be more evenly distributed on lip fragments of all clams possessing analogous valve morphologies; this is not the case for smooth-shelled *Glycymeris* specimens.

Shellfish and tortoises associated with Mous-

terian lithic artifacts in Moscerini show every indication of having been brought into the cave and
processed there by humans. Yet only one of the four
seaside caves in the Latium sample—Grotta dei
Moscerini—contains appreciable evidence of shellfish exploitation. New excavations at Grotta Breuil
have yielded a few *Callista* and *Patella* fragments,
but shell material is too sparse relative to mammal
remains to be considered economically significant
there. Each of the four caves lies within 1 km of the
modern shoreline, and short stretches of sandy
beach and rocky shore are, and always were, within
a short walk of all.

AQUATIC RESOURCES AND HOMINID FORAGING STRATEGIES

Smooth-shelled clams and mussels are the most
common types of shellfish in Moscerini. The relative proportions of these taxa vary greatly among
the cultural levels, however. This fact could be of
tactical significance, because the nutritional values
of the Mediterranean mussels, clams, and oysters
discussed here are roughly equal in both food mass
and content—at least according to recent summaries and dietary recommendations published in Italy
(*Corriere Salute* 1992)—but these species differ
greatly in their substrate requirements. Today, the
clam species inhabit sandy sediments exclusively,
whereas the mussels and oysters prefer rocky surfaces. Mussel colonies also may occur on softer
substrates, but they thrive best on hard ones, as
documented at Porto di Civitavecchia near Rome by
Taramelli et al. (1977). Mussels are also somewhat
more versatile than sand clams with regard to water
salinity and depth below the high tide line. And, of
the clams, *Callista* appears to be the most sensitive.
Because the substrate requirements of sand clams
and mussels do not overlap much, their relative frequencies in the archaeological deposits specify
which littoral habitats human foragers emphasized
while gathering these foods. Few other kinds of
prey reflect locational sources to this extent.

Variation in the frequencies of clams and mussels
in the exterior strata series of Moscerini is most
easily explained by subtle changes in sea level that
would, in turn, have altered shoreline habitats immediately surrounding the cave. The variation
probably does not reflect choosiness on the part of
human foragers. Both sand-dwelling clams and
rock-dwelling mussels are represented wherever
shells are found in the cultural deposits: one class is
merely more abundant than the other where samples
are large. Figure 6.19 compares sand clam and mussel counts in the exterior strata, based on total shell
NISP for each shellfish category. The graph reveals
an either/or situation in levels where shells are
abundant: sand clams dominate or mussels dominate, even though their frequencies are not negatively correlated in a straightforward way. The lack
of a simple or directly negative correlation is not
surprising. There is no reason to assume that selection criteria or foraging radii of Mousterian hominids should precisely match the spatial distributions
of live shellfish patches on rocky outcrops or in
sandy beds. We only know that, when hominids
collected more shellfish at Moscerini, they tended
to concentrate on species from one kind of substrate
or the other. Indeed, a regression in which samples
are weighted by size produces a significant negative
correlation ($P < < .01$).

Other, rarer shellfish taxa also may follow the
substrate alternations apparent for common bivalves. Limpets and oysters typically require firm
substrates, usually rocks and, as would be predicted, their frequencies follow rock-dwelling mussels in the exterior levels of Moscerini (cf. Tables
6.12, 6.14, and 6.15). Sponges are highly localized
in the exterior sequence, spanning only the largest
frequency pulse for sand clams (Table 6.12) and
with *Callista chione* in particular (Table 6.13). Turbin shells are not common in Moscerini, but all of
them were opened by humans. Turbins are known to
have been an important food species during later
cultural periods in Latium (e.g., at Riparo Blanc,
Taschini 1964; Riparo Mochi, my research) and
elsewhere on the Mediterranean (e.g., J. Shackleton 1988b). If anything, turbin frequencies in the
exterior sequence of Moscerini are highest at the

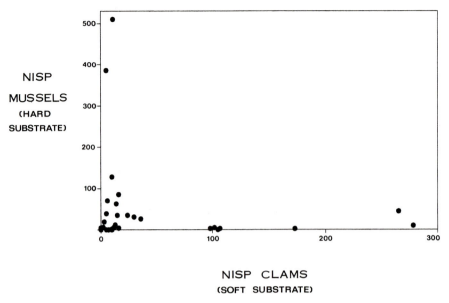

Figure 6.19 Scatter plot contrasting the relative frequencies of smooth-shelled sand clams and mussels in the exterior strata sequence of Moscerini. Values are shell NISP counts for each bivalve category, representing soft-substrate (sandy bottom) and hard-substrate (rocky surfaces and gravel) habitats respectively.

transitions between rock-dwelling mussels and sand-dwelling clams. The observation is intriguing, if data-poor; perhaps turbins were an alternative food species used at the locality when bivalve habitats in front of the cave were in the midst of change.

Figure 6.20 compares clam and mussel frequencies by fine levels in the exterior Moscerini sequence. The three averaged ESR dates are shown on the stratigraphy axis and, as noted above, the beach deposit at the base of the sequence was formed around the close of the Last Interglacial. The stratigraphic sequence culminates at or before the cold snap around 55,000 years ago, based on local pollen sequences (Follieri et al. 1988; Frank 1969) in Latium (see Chapter 3). Alternating frequency pulses are apparent for rock-dwelling mussels and sand-dwelling clams. The larger pulses display unidirectional tails, gradually increasing with time and then suddenly dropping to nothing. These pulses are evident both from shell NISP (illustrated) and hinge counts (consistently around 10 percent of NISP). The unidirectional pulses are not explained by differing degrees of shell fragmentation and/or mechanical sorting by size among the levels; fragmen-

tation patterns show no such trend (cf. Figures 6.17 and 6.20).

Rather than displaying smoothly opposed transitions, the mussel pulses track catastrophic declines in sand clam frequencies. The alternations span thousands of years, however, and therefore do not reflect short-term situational responses by human foragers. The time frame encompassed by the exterior strata sequence of Moscerini coincides with a general trend toward cooler climatic conditions, but incorporates several minor oscillations in global temperature and sea level. Local topography dictates that even relatively subtle changes in sea stand could alter the proportion of exposed rocky surfaces to sandy beach formations in the immediate vicinity of Moscerini. The sequence began long ago with warm temperatures and a soft beach out front, and, for the first time since the Last Interglacial, Holocene climate has once again raised the sea margin nearly to the altitude of this ancient beach. Sand may have eroded away or built up during certain phases of sea regression, periodically revealing new configurations of limestone bedrock along the littoral margin. The relative abundances of mussels and clams living at this locality would have shifted accordingly. Why the declines of either bivalve category in the Moscerini sequence are so sudden remains a mystery, but a geological explanation is likely. The Gaetan coast where Moscerini is situated is underlain by limestone, capped here and there by loose sediments easily worked by water and wind. Sediment movement under these conditions can be rapid once the process is set into motion. Colonization of the new local habitats by animals waits only for opportunity, and the rise of shellfish populations typical of one substrate or the other can take place within an instant of geologic time. Hominids may have simply responded by collecting what was available near the cave.

The above comparisons show that hominids were willing to eat bivalves of either substrate class. Their choices of which shellfish to bring into Moscerini appear to have been guided foremost by loca-tional convenience: one kind of shellfish patch, on rock or in sand, may have been closer to the cave entrance at any given time in the past. The case of Moscerini, contrasted with the lack of much evidence for shellfish exploitation at neighboring Mousterian caves only slightly farther inland, indeed suggests the influence of this simple energetic principle. Assuming that transport distance is generally limited by the relatively low caloric yield of these bivalves, regardless of substrate source, hominids may have been willing to carry the shellfish to shelter only from the closest patches before eating them. Otherwise, hominids might have preferred to eat the shellfish where they found them. This is not to say that Mousterian people were not choosy about which shellfish species they ate; certainly, they did not eat every nonpoisonous shellfish taxon to be found in coastal Latium. Rather, the point is that, of the taxa normally eaten, mussels and sand

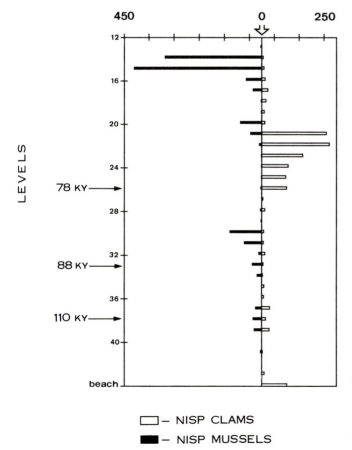

Figure 6.20 Bar chart contrasting the relative frequencies of smooth-shelled sand clams and mussels in the exterior strata sequence of Moscerini. Values are shell NISP counts for each bivalve category, representing soft-substrate (sandy bottom) and hard-substrate (rocky surfaces and gravel) habitats respectively. Three averaged ESR dates are shown on the stratigraphy axis.

☐ – NISP CLAMS
■ – NISP MUSSELS

clams were more or less equal in nutritional value. Hominids ate shellfish collected from soft or firm substrates, depending on foraging conditions. The alternating pulses of sand- and rock-dwelling bivalves in Moscerini cannot be related, for example, to short-term targeting of a single species.

It is significant, by contrast, that Mousterian hominids never brought small terrestrial prey to any of the four caves. They may well have eaten a variety of small prey elsewhere. The data only indicate that Mousterian hominids did not normally transport any kind of small prey to shelter unless obtained from concentrated patches close by. A small difference in distance from shore, on the order of a few hundred meters, and the tendency of the bivalves to form colonies, apparently determined whether shellfish would be carried to a cave at all. Local distributions of substrate-specific shellfish patches, on the other hand, determined which of these species would be deposited by foragers inside Moscerini over time. Thus, the economic rules governing food transport may have been the same for aquatic and terrestrial sources of small prey.

ON THE QUESTION OF SPECIES CHOICE

In the analyses above, I asked whether alternating frequencies of sand clams and mussels reflected deliberate food species selection by hominids or just opportunistic feeding in the contexts of changes in mollusk habitats around one cave. The data indicate that Mousterian foragers responded directly to local abundances of mussels and certain sand clams while inhabiting Grotta dei Moscerini. People did not carry the shellfish far before eating them, although the shellfish may have been cooked on fires. A key point to this discussion is the apparent nutritional equivalence between the mussels and sand clams in both food volume and content. Shells were discarded by Mousterian foragers in the cave only because the cave was adjacent to the food patches.

The question of whether hominid foragers were choosy about which species of mollusks to harvest is interesting above and beyond the case of Moscerini or the Middle Paleolithic more generally. Choosiness is an important issue in foraging studies, and the ways of setting up and testing hypotheses in archaeological situations merit special discussion. Propositions that human foragers make choices about which species to eat and to transport within a larger array of potentially edible species should be pitted against natural patterns of abundance within the confines of a given landscape and/or season.

The simplest proposition about food choice is an explicit version of the null hypothesis: people were not choosy within a specified array of foods, time frame, and foraging radius. Defining the edible food array is, of course, important here, as well as the relative value of each kind of food item therein; items may or may not be equivalent in volume or, alternatively, nutritional content. People may take a direct hand in determining which foods are to be eaten and which foods to move to another place prior to consumption, but not without reason. Though an apparently sensitive point in the literature on human origins, choice in opposition to natural availability is not an unequivocal tag of modernity from an evolutionary perspective. The value of being choosy is wholly dependent upon context, and being choosy oftentimes is not an intelligent or adaptive way to behave.

Choosing foods to transport to another place may be cause for greater deliberation by foragers. Food transport behavior is a classic and long-established way that humans can alter food distributions in response to the needs of social groups. Transport decisions and item choices can be phrased separately, even if one is a precondition of the other. In the Mousterian case, the null hypotheses were that (1) hominids did not choose between mussel and smooth-shelled sand clams because these species are nutritionally and volumetrically equivalent, instead taking whichever of these that they encountered in the infralittoral zone, and (2) hominids ate these kinds of shellfish pretty much where they found them. Assessments of the second statement are less secure, but nothing about the Moscerini case contradicts either hypothesis as presented. One may conclude that human use of marine mussels and clams was in keeping with natural abundances within the confines of the site locality. Rather than altering the distributions of shellfish by collecting and moving them to places where a larger number of individuals might convene, the Mousterian people generally moved to the shellfish patches. They did not graze indiscriminately on every non-poisonous molluskan taxon in Latium; Mousterians were after certain kinds and probably certain sizes of shellfish. When it came to mussels or clams, however, they were satisfied by what they encountered. In agreement with the Mousterian pattern, ethnoarchaeological accounts of three modern Bantu-speaking groups that routinely collect shellfish along the Transkei coast of southern Africa indicate that species choice within the potential edible array responds most directly to local differences in natural abundance and, to a lesser extent, dietary taboos by a person's age or sex (Bigalke and Voigt 1973:258). The biasing effects of dietary taboos would be further reduced as the debris from one foraging bout is piled on top of another because the foraging parties represent diverse age groups. Contra the Mousterian harvesting pattern as interpreted above, these modern people may carry fresh shellfish up to several kilometers before consuming them. In her study of the Anbarra of coastal Australia, on the other hand, Meehan (1982, 1988) reports that certain shellfish beds acted as magnets for foraging hubs, day camps to which people also brought other resources obtained from land or sea in this vicinity. The Anbarra people clearly prefer certain mollusk species, but, within that edible array, were not so choosy provided living shellfish beds were large or concentrated. It is the great time spans of prey species substitutions in the Mousterian case of Moscerini that leads me to discount the possibility of extensive transport of shellfish. In many regards, the Moscerini case best resembles the latter kind of situation—basically a foraging hub to which diverse resources were brought if convenient.

The question of species choice and preferential transport has been addressed in some studies of later prehistoric peoples living on the Mediterranean, most notably by J. C. Shackleton (1983, 1988a, 1988b). The cases from Moscerini contrast with harvesting tactics inferred by Shackleton for the Mesolithic occupations at Franchthi Cave, a site on the eastern Greek Peloponnese. Shackleton suggests that the human occupants sometimes traveled several kilometers to obtain preferred shellfish taxa and then transported them back to the cave. The interpretations are based on a chain of inferences involving shoreline reconstructions between 11,000 and 8,000 B.P. and projected fine-scale habitat distributions suited to the types of mollusks that occur in the site deposits. Shackleton's argument is impressive, but, as she admits, troubled by several sources of ambiguity. The apparent contrast between the Mousterian pattern of shellfish exploitation in Italy and that for the Greek Mesolithic and its relation to shoreline morphology at the local level nevertheless are worth considering, if only to refine questions for the benefit of future work.

The geographic setting of Moscerini during various phases of the Upper Pleistocene can be reconstructed to some extent. Although the cave now lies buried beneath construction scree, a small sandy beach is preserved just meters in front of where the entrance would be and another small beach lies just north of it, separated by a narrow rocky pinnacle. My census of shells cast onto these beaches in the summer of 1987 revealed a predominance of sand-dwelling clams and few mussels, averaging five to one respectively. Prevalence of *Glycymeris*, in particular, is consistent with the ancient beach deposits that formed at Moscerini soon after the Last Interglacial. The land is very steep where it descends into the sea at this locality (see Figure 3.13), but the subaqueous topography is more irregular, and minor episodes of sea regression almost certainly would have caused significant changes in mollusk habitats. Many subtle oscillations in sea level occurred between 115,000 and 65,000 years ago (N. J. Shackleton and Opdyke 1973), and the alternating frequencies of sand clams and mussels probably register these minor oscillations. At approximately 80,000 B.P., for example, EXT 33 of Moscerini is dominated by mussels and may correspond to a cold snap in Oxygen Isotope Stage 5b/5c. The peak abundances of *Callista* are found in EXT 21–26. Level EXT 26 dates to roughly 78,000, and lagunal formations may have been most prevalent in the area around this time and shortly thereafter.

HARVESTING INTENSITY AT MOSCERINI: SHELLFISH VERSUS TERRESTRIAL RESOURCES

Another interesting aspect of Mousterian use of marine resources at Moscerini is the intensity of harvesting. Here, intensity is considered only in the vaguest sense because the sizes of hominid foraging parties at the cave and the frequencies of site reuse are not known. One can only compare the rates of shellfish accumulation to those of sediments and other materials in the stratigraphic sequence. Although the site was revisited over many thousands of years, Mousterian hominids collected little more than an armload or two of mollusks per area excavated in each level. The frequency pulses in the exterior strata sequence were created over thousands of years (Figure 6.20), contain few individual animals per stratum (Tables 6.12, 6.14, and 6.15), and are associated with substantial sediment accumulations. The site was not fully excavated, but substantial areas of the talus and entrance were sampled (see Figure 3.19). Certainly, the hominids were not amassing surpluses of shellfish nor generating thick pavements of discarded shells, suggesting very short stays and/or that hominids' foraging agendas did not center on shellfish alone.

Moscerini does not contain the sort of dense shell middens that are classical for some later cultural periods. The assemblages from Moscerini contrast, for example, with the relatively dense shell beds in certain Mesolithic shelters in Italy, such as Riparo Blanc (Taschini 1964, 1968) and Grotta della Porta (Radmilli and Tongiorgi 1958; Tozzi 1976). Mesolithic occupations of coastal Spain (e.g., G. A. Clark 1983) and Denmark (e.g., Rowley-Conwy 1981) also resulted in fairly massive accumulations of shell. Ortea (1986) reports relatively dense shell debris in the Solutrean levels of La Riera in northern Spain. Likewise, terminal Pleistocene/early Holocene examples worldwide (Bailey 1978; Barker 1981; Dennell 1983; Rowley-Conwy 1981) and modern Australian examples (Bailey 1975; Meehan 1983) often suggest rapid rates of shell accumulation per unit time.

Comparisons of shell accumulation rates on a large geographic scale are made difficult by variation in sedimentary environments and climate conditions. Mousterian exploitation of marine mollusks in Italy nonetheless seems to have differed from that of later periods in the intensity of debris generation per unit of sediment volume. A parallel contrast is suggested between Middle Stone Age and Later Stone Age coastal sites in South Africa, although difficult to confirm on account of the inconsistent recovery procedures by the archaeologists (E. Voigt, p.c.). Why were earlier hominids so light on sea resources? Deacon (1984) argues that exploitation of marine species during the Late Stone Age in southern Africa was more efficient than in MSA times, based on Voigt's (1973) and Klein's (1976) descriptions of the earlier material. Whereas harvesting by LSA peoples does appear to have been conducted on a larger scale than during the MSA, nothing about these data clearly communicates changes in foraging efficiency. The differences in harvesting intensity in the MSA sites and in the Italian Mousterian more likely reflect differences in lengths of stays at sites and tactics for offsetting one kind of food resource with others.

Figure 6.21 lends additional perspective on mollusk harvesting at Moscerini by comparing the relative frequencies of ungulate bones, chipped stone artifacts, shellfish, sponges, and land snails in the exterior strata sequence. The horizontal axes are scaled by material type to facilitate the comparisons, and ESR dated strata are noted on the stratigraphy axis. Using total lithic artifact counts as a guide to hominid presence in the sequence, snail counts peak where hominid associations are rare or absent (i.e., the youngest levels, EXT 1–16). Another peak in land snail frequencies centers on EXT 26–27, dating to roughly 78,000 years ago and corresponding to a noticeable if brief hiatus in the deposition of all types of cultural materials. The lack of spatial correspondence to cultural material was expected for land snails based on previous discussion, but the loose spatial relationships among materials that unequivocally represent human food and tools are somewhat surprising. Ungulate bones and shells generally co-occur with lithic artifacts, the latter being indisputable markers of human presence, yet their frequencies do not strictly parallel one another at a fine vertical scale. Where one class

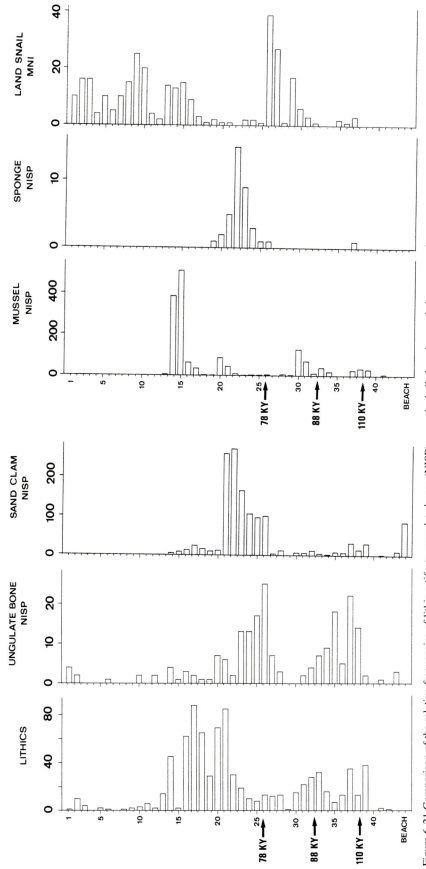

Figure 6.21 Comparison of the relative frequencies of lithic artifacts, ungulate bones (NISP), smooth-shelled marine sand clams, mussels, sponges, and common land snails (*Pomatias and Murella* MNI) in the exterior strata sequence of Moscerini.

of culturally derived material is found, others will certainly be found, but there is no straightforward positive correspondence in abundance. The lack of numerical agreement across the fine levels of Moscerini may indicate that hominids' emphases on ungulates, shellfish, and flint raw materials were not entirely interdependent. Hominids clearly had varied procurement agendas while occupying this cave.

Although the Mousterian pattern of shellfish harvesting at Moscerini and the MSA cases in South Africa appear to differ from some shell midden faunas of the later Upper Pleistocene and early Holocene, the modern case of the Anbarra "dinnertime camp" on the north coast of Australia (Meehan 1982, 1988) may undermine any simple interpretation citing evolutionary change. Archaeological comparisons of cultural periods must be qualified with care: Meehan's ethnoarchaeological study shows, for example, that some of the more impressive shell middens are created by the Anbarra people at certain shoreline foraging hubs, which are not necessarily home bases. The foraging hubs are centralized with respect to food sources, often on a daily basis, and the array of species exploited shifts with circumstance and season. Meehan's assertions about species diversity in middens at foraging hubs versus home bases are not based on statistical analyses, however, specifically those concerning the effects of sample size on relative abundance. While some of her conclusions must be taken with a grain of salt, it is significant that certain localities contain shellfish beds prized by the Anbarra. These beds may be rich in any of several mollusk species within the preferred array and are magnets for foraging hubs, places to which people may return again and again. Shellfish harvesting at these beds is normally augmented by a wider variety of aquatic and terrestrial resources. Short-term variation in species exploited therefore can be great. Also interesting is the fact that nearly all of the resources brought to this kind of hub are relatively small food packages, usually obtained nearby. Meehan's case of the Anbarra raises some important questions about site function at locations such as Moscerini, independent of culture period. Addressing these questions ultimately begs for Mousterian samples from more than one site, regardless of how many assemblages any one of them contains. The data in Figure 6.21 are provocative; whether they indicate a seaside foraging hub or a home base at Moscerini is unclear, but the data strongly indicate relatively ephemeral occupations, time and again. Evidence of scavenging of ungulates throughout the Moscerini sequence, presented in Chapter 9, makes these observations even more intriguing (Chapter 14).

POSSIBLE SEASONS OF SHELLFISH HARVESTING AT MOSCERINI

Seasonal factors almost certainly influenced hominids' interest in marine resources while occupying Moscerini. Mollusk exploitation by Mesolithic peoples in northerly provinces of Europe, for example, took place in every season but generally centered on late winter through spring (e.g., Deith and Shackleton 1986; Rowley-Conwy 1984; and, in Japan, Koike 1979). Shellfish presumably were used to supplement or weather periodic shortages of other kinds of foods. It is quite possible that Mousterian hominids were responding in a similar way to seasonal hardships in coastal Italy. Stable isotope (^{18}O) analyses of a limited number of *Glycymeris* and *Callista* shells from Moscerini suggest that these individuals died in late spring. The analyses were performed on material taken from the insides of shells near the hinge line by H. P. Schwarcz and coworkers at McMaster University. The results are very preliminary, however, and too few samples have been analyzed to exclude harvesting in other seasons.

The important point here is that marine mollusks may contain certain key (limiting) nutrients that drew hominids' interest to them when terrestrial sources were scarce and/or of poor quality. Although the total caloric value of marine mollusks tends to be low (e.g., Yesner 1981), nutrition is a relative phenomenon, especially for an omnivore. The bivalves discussed above are not rich in fats, but they are not so poor either; they are comparable in cholesterol, for example, to domestic chicken or turkey meat. Seasonal changes in the food values of molluskan species relative to terrestrial resources require additional research before some of the questions about seasonal use by humans can be effectively addressed. What dietary information is available on the Mediterranean mollusks is best considered against that for the large mammals, comparisons that therefore must be postponed until Chapters 13, 14, and 15.

CONCLUSIONS

When I first set out to study the Italian collections, I expected to find evidence for small animal exploitation by Mousterian hominids—lots of it. I figured that these components of hominid diet had been largely ignored in subsistence research and their economic value underestimated. Whereas the general assertion is true, I now count the demonstrable paucity of small animal food debris in the Italian caves among my first discoveries.

In abstracting the results of this chapter, it must be acknowledged that some of the findings represent firm conclusions, while others mainly refine hypotheses to be tested in other archaeological circumstances. It is clear from the taphonomic evidence that Middle Paleolithic foragers made use of marine resources at Moscerini. That peoples of the Mediterranean region consumed shellfish as early as the Mousterian has been suspected for some time (e.g., Leonardi 1935; Palma di Cesnola 1965), but the Moscerini case is the first taphonomic demonstration of this economic phenomenon. Marine bivalves were the main small prey group eaten, but other marine invertebrates, tortoises (land and water), and the occasional fragment of monk seal (Sant'Agostino S2) were also consumed by Mousterian hominids in Italy. With the application of modern methods, more Mousterian cases of shellfish harvesting are bound to emerge (e.g., Riparo Mochi in the Balzi Rossi, Liguria). Shellfish exploitation at Moscerini is generally consistent with cases dating to roughly the same time range in South Africa (e.g., Voigt 1973, 1982). Whether procuring shellfish, tortoises, or seals, Middle Paleolithic and Middle Stone Age hominids appear to have limited their forays to what could be obtained in littoral habitats, not from the deeper waters beyond (for South African cases, see Binford 1984; Marean 1986; Thackeray 1988; Voigt 1973, 1982).

It is interesting that small animal use by Mousterian people at the Latium caves is confined to aquatic species and, further, that these resources apparently were transported to shelter only when available in the immediate vicinity. Remains of small terrestrial mammals are abundant in some levels of both Moscerini and Sant'Agostino, but the taphonomic data associate them with carnivore collectors, not humans. Patterns of damage on the lagomorph bones, in particular, indicate that they fell prey to canids. Other small animals (hedgehogs, bats, and birds) apparently entered the caves by choice. Hominids may have eaten small terrestrial mammals when foraging away from caves, but they evidently did not bring small terrestrial or avian prey to the caves before doing so.

The economic rules governing the transport of shellfish to shelters may have been the same as those for terrestrial species. Hominids' limited willingness to transport small prey to shelters is evident not so much from the fact that they consumed clams and mussels at Moscerini as from the patterns of species alternation in the mollusks represented across thirty cultural layers and several thousand years of deposition. Variation in the frequencies of sand-dwelling clams and rock-dwelling mussels can be explained by subtle changes in sea level that in turn altered the extent of rocky versus sandy habitats near the cave entrance: hominids carried to Moscerini only the kind of shellfish that was closest at any given time in the past. The few wave-worn specimens that co-occur with shells processed by hominids were probably collected by accident, mixed with other things. The rare but persistent presence of wave-worn specimens in nonlittoral sediments suggests that the entrance of the cave was never far from the shore. In the times that the caves were occupied by people, Moscerini was always closer to the sea than Guattari, Breuil, and Sant'Agostino, though never by very much; yet appreciable shellfish accumulations occur only in Moscerini.

The Mousterian pattern of shellfish exploitation

in Italy may differ from many later human cases in both the intensity (or scale) at which it was practiced and in the companion tactics for utilizing large terrestrial animals. Comparatively low rates of shell accumulation to sediment volume at Moscerini hint that the economic focus of these Mousterian occupations was on other classes of resources, a point that can only be properly documented by juxtaposing information on large mammal use and technology (Chapters 14 and 15). The Mousterian pattern of small animal exploitation appears to differ from late Upper Paleolithic and Mesolithic foragers of the same region in Italy; all of these cultures utilized shellfish and ungulates, but Mousterians' economic emphases varied more by site (e.g., Chapters 9 and 11).

More information from other sites and regions is needed to fully address the question of how small game use coincided with the use of ungulate prey. The available data permit, however, some important refinements of hypotheses about contrasting modes of Paleolithic subsistence. Specifically, later peoples seem to have transported small terrestrial mammals and birds to every shelter they occupied, always in concert with relatively heavy exploitation of ungulates. Mousterian cases from Breuil and Sant'Agostino are thick with ungulate bones, but these faunas lack evidence of small game use. Bone accumulations in Moscerini and hominid-associated levels of Guattari are sparse relative to the rates of tool accumulation and other discrete measures (Chapter 14), and only Moscerini contains evidence of any kind of small game use, virtually all of it from aquatic sources. The Mousterian pattern suggests some fundamental differences from later cultures in the contexts of site use, mobility, and the strategies for offsetting humans' continuous needs for key but seasonally scarce nutrients such as protein and energy-sustaining fats or carbohydrates.

Use of small animals by archaic humans has been proposed as a sort of gateway in the evolution of predatory adaptations (e.g., Jones 1984). We still know little about Middle Pleistocene and earlier situations, but it is clear that no such transition took place between the Mousterian and Upper Paleolithic in Pleistocene Italy. The ways that Mousterian and later humans exploited small game instead appear to represent differing expressions of how people of these periods used foraging territories and their strategic solutions for balancing foraging opportunities with need. Gathering practices continue to be among the most poorly understood facets of Middle Paleolithic adaptations. This is partly because we have few opportunities to investigate gathering directly, but an overglorified and rather vague view of the ecological ramifications of large game hunting in human evolution is equally to blame. Gathering is about basic economics and foraging logistics, and from a scientific standpoint, evidence relating to gathering behavior warrants more attention than it currently receives in archaeological research. In addition to the demonstration that hominids exploited marine resources as early as 115,000 B.P. in Europe, the perspective gained from the case of Grotta dei Moscerini is important for a broader understanding of food search tactics in the Middle Paleolithic, including the economic context of hunting and scavenging. Small animal use is less conspicuous in Paleolithic records than large mammal procurement and certainly less sensational. However, small animal use implies some kind of gathering behavior, the otherwise invisible side of prehistoric foraging systems (Yellen 1991a:21–25; 1991b). As seen from the case of Moscerini, gathering practices are keys to how ancient subsistence systems were organized, keys for which there are no substitutes.

Species Use and Predator Guild

SPECIES "CHOICE" by modern predators is constrained by prey body size and the kinds of habitats that predators occupy, but only in a general way. Within these capacious boundaries, the menu is governed more by what is available than by outright preferences of predators. This is why the diets of modern carnivores of similar body size so often converge upon the same prey species in any given area. There are many instances in which a hungry (unsatiated) predator cannot afford to ignore an opportunity immediately at hand. Life is not that certain.

Have humans broken free of this apparent rule at some point in their evolutionary history, or do the species eaten form the arena wherein adaptational changes among predators occur? Finding out requires a baseline expectation about what a nonselective sample of species from the resource pool should look like, an aspect of animal community structure independent of time. Normally, a predator responds on the basis of encounter to taxa that it recognizes as food, but the rates of encounter may be conditioned by the ranging patterns the predator uses to locate its food. A predator may elect to ignore one prey animal, focusing instead upon another (sensu Rosenzweig 1966), but it is unlikely to ignore an entire species of the appropriate body size. Constructing tests about prey species use by predators boils down to an interesting family of sampling problems, which, as it happens, are much the same for biologists who census living species and for predators looking for food. At this level of consideration, one is confronted with two competing concerns: (1) how that organism takes or records the various taxa that

are really out there, and (2) the biasing influences of spatial distributions and sample size on numbers of species sighted or bagged nonselectively.

This chapter evaluates patterns of prey species use by Middle and late Upper Paleolithic hominids in Italy by comparing them to a wider array of predators (Stiner 1992). I begin with a review of wildlife data on modern carnivores, followed by comparisons of the diets of Mousterian hominids (presumed Neandertals), late Upper Paleolithic humans, spotted hyaenas, and wolves in Upper Pleistocene Italy. Diets are determined from food debris left in the caves, linked to each kind of predator by taphonomic assessments (Chapters 5 and 6). The analyses of species abundance in the predators' diets commence with a regression approach to taxonomic richness (N-taxa to total NISP). It is clear from the first step that many of the samples are small—too small—for classic diversity analyses. But the value of the classic approach is limited for addressing behavioral questions anyway, because differences in slope tend to reflect only the most extraordinary differences among species, essentially differences in trophic level (as defined in Chapter 2). Comparisons therefore turn to predators' relative emphases on common species, using a modified index of dissimilarity, and, finally, the numbers of resource classes utilized by the predators according to prey body size, habitat preferences, and functional characteristics.

The prey species data indicate nearly complete overlap in the large mammals consumed by Middle and late Upper Paleolithic hominids and spotted hyaenas in the study area. This finding documents

This chapter is reworked from the 1992 article entitled "Overlapping Species 'Choice' by Italian Upper Pleistocene Predators," *Current Anthropology* 33.

close ecological relationships between hominids and certain large carnivores throughout the Upper Pleistocene at the level of resource guild, but does not distinguish the niches of these predator species. Uniformity in species consumed represents a powerful constant, against which patterns of prey age selection, food transport, and processing strategies of hominids and sympatric social carnivores are compared in later chapters. The respective niches of hyaenids, canids, and hominids in west-central Italy articulated in evolutionarily meaningful ways throughout the time period considered, justifying the application of more general principles of predator-predator and predator-prey dynamics to this comparative study of humans.

On the Meaning of Taxonomic Abundance

As early as the 1940s work on species sampling of living animal communities elucidated a mathematical relationship between the number of taxa represented in nonselective samples and the number of individuals actually collected from an environment. Whether butterflies of the Malaysian lowlands (Fisher et al. 1943), or Andean birds along a topographic gradient (Terborgh 1977), rare species seem rarer or even invisible in small samples (see also Cody 1986). The same general relationship holds for the number of taxa (N-taxa) and the number of bones identifiable to taxon (NISP) preserved in fossil faunas (Grayson 1981, 1984). In archaeological and paleontological contexts, however, the first issue is obtaining samples that are representative of what the biotic agency (human or otherwise) collected from a living community long ago—essentially, sampling a sample without introducing a second generation of numerical biases. For archaeologists, then, eliminating the possibility of sampling bias due to recovery practices and assemblage sizes is only half the battle. We ultimately want to know what people were eating and how their choices of foods responded to the standing (but immeasurable) content of animal communities in the past.

Most zooarchaeological analyses of taxonomic abundance implicitly or explicitly assume that the species eaten will reveal important features of human ecology and evolutionary changes therein—once over the hurdle of numerical sampling effects. This expectation is valid in general terms, but at what level does it apply in the animal community structure? One frequently encounters an assumption in literature on the Paleolithic that the prey species consumed by hominids should change with time because hominids became more "able" or skillful hunters, not simply because species present in animal communities changed. We in fact know very little about what species abundance data mean with regard to the process of human evolution. Given the many levels at which species may interact in ecosystems, the most pressing question is about the scale(s) at which species in human diets are informative about human ecology.

This is not a strictly empirical issue; it has an important theoretical component as well. Specifically, can predatory adaptations be distinguished on the basis of the species consumed, or do humans and other predators respond directly to abundance within a shared set of boundaries? This question has been addressed many times by community ecologists in modern settings. More often than not, data on mammals and birds testify to the overwhelming influence of natural abundance on prey species selection *within* major trophic levels, such as among frugivores, insectivores, or carnivores (e.g., Schoener 1982; Skinner et al. 1986; Terborgh 1977; but see recent review by Rosenzweig 1992), despite most studies having been directed to finding differences (e.g., Bertram 1979; Eisenberg 1990; Koehler and Hornocker 1991; Leopold and Krausman 1986; Major and Sherburne 1987). Predators may vary in their relative emphases on certain prey species within a shared array, but there is much overlap even so. The overlap is especially pronounced between predators of similar body size, such as African lions and spotted hyaenas or leopards and cheetahs (Bertram 1979; Ewer 1973; Kruuk 1972; Schaller 1972).

There are more ways for predators to partition the environment and the resources it contains than by simply feeding on different species. The potential for interspecific competition among trophically linked predators can be reduced, for example, through spatial segregation within habitats (Koehler and Hornocker 1991), differing biological apparatuses for processing and digesting food (Van Valkenburgh 1989), and/or different strategies and maneuvers for locating and capturing food (Gautier-Hion et al. 1980; Holmes et al. 1979; Jaksić et al. 1981a, 1981b; Landres 1983; Schoener 1982; Terborgh and Diamond 1970; and references cited above). Resource use may also be partitioned in time, especially by season, and, when competition occurs over a resource, it tends to be periodic rather than continuous (e.g., Ballard 1982; Koehler and Hornocker 1991). Different predators have been observed to alternate their emphases under these circumstances, shifting away from a resource temporarily prized by another (due to, for example, reproductive season), then back when the pressure is reduced (Wiens 1977). Thus, even where differences in prey species use by predators are found, it remains to be established that the variation is not the product of short-term resource switching. Switching behavior is common among higher organisms; local or short-term diversification is merely an adjustment to temporary scarcity (for general reviews, see Kitchener 1991:98–105; Schoener 1982).

We know without a shadow of a doubt that modern predators are different from one another. The animals they eat simply do not provide a very sensitive measure of adaptive variation or niche; species consumed is about a more general level of relationship between certain species that coexist in an ecosystem. Many archaeologists nonetheless have turned to species representation in faunal assemblages to evaluate hypotheses about foraging specialization as opposed to generalist strategies (for an analytical review, see Grayson 1984:131–151). And in archaeological research on early populations of *Homo sapiens,* apparent uniformity in taxa consumed has been called upon to support a variety of arguments about foraging adaptations across the Middle to Upper Paleolithic transition in Eurasia (e.g., Clark and Lindly 1989a, 1989b; Mellars 1989). Other researchers meanwhile look to climatic stability (e.g., Tchernov 1981, 1989, 1992), or geographic isolation (Baryshnikov 1989) for explanations of the same general phenomenon.

Studies of niche separation between contemporaneous taxa living in the same ecosystem and between populations of the same genus separated in time (but in the same place) are not entirely equivalent problems. They are close enough, however, that it is relevant to ask what taxonomic abundance data really mean in the evolutionary history of human beings. The question is most germane to comparisons of hunter-gatherers because they usually do not produce any of their own food, consistent with the adaptations of the carnivores. Here, I examine the problem of species consumed and its ecological significance by looking at the diets of hominids, wolves, and spotted hyaenas while using shelters. If species consumed could detect subtle changes in the niches of hominid subspecies through time, then the same criterion certainly should be capable of distinguishing hominid adaptations from those of other ungulate predators in the same ecosystems. If, on the other hand, species consumed do not distinguish human from nonhuman predatory adaptations, then taxonomic abundance data are not really telling us about niche at all but, rather, about a more general level of relationship higher in the food chain called the "guild"— the very sort of constant needed for a study of predator coevolution.

Sample and Methods Review

The full array of animal species represented in the Upper Pleistocene caves of coastal west-central Italy is described in Chapters 4 and 6, with the exception of birds. Most species were present in the area throughout the Upper Pleistocene. Like modern Mediterranean-type environments worldwide (Cody 1986), lowland ecosystems of Upper Pleistocene Italy supported comparatively high levels of species diversity in the time periods considered by this study. Animals with distinct habitat preferences existed alongside one another through all but perhaps the coldest oscillation in climate (the last glacial maximum). Exceptions are hippopotamus and certain species of Chiroptera, whose food supplies are especially sensitive to temperature. Spotted hyaenas and pachyderms may have disappeared from the region very late in the sequence.

The presentation below considers all species initially, primarily ungulates, carnivores, and small mammals. Ungulates were principal resources for the four predators, however, and therefore receive the most attention once the analyses narrow to comparisons of predator diets. Ungulate remains were deliberately carried into the caves by one predator or another, whereas the other species sometimes arrived by their own means, the usual situation for bears and insectivores (bats, moles, and hedgehogs). Mousterian hominids were the principal bone collectors in Moscerini M2, M3, M4, and M6, Sant'Agostino S0–3, Breuil Br and B3, and probably Guattari G4–5. Only the SX assemblage from Sant'Agostino is attributable to denning wolves exclusively, although a wolf den occupation mixed with some Mousterian cultural material occurs in layer S4. Faunas gathered primarily by denning spotted hyaenas are from level group M5 of Moscerini, levels G0–1 of Guattari, and I1–6 of Buca della Iena. The uppermost levels of Buca della Iena also contain scant quantities of Mousterian tools, but hominids' contribution to the overall character of the faunas was very minor. Late Upper Paleolithic faunas are from Grotta Palidoro (data for cuts 1–8, Cassoli 1976–77), Grotta Polesini (cuts 1–12, Radmilli 1974), and Riparo Salvini.

A few of the assemblages in the comparison are especially small, making assessments of their taphonomic origins problematic. This is less of a problem, however, for hyaena-collected cases than for those thought to have been collected by hominids. Faunas attributed to hyaenas, even the small ones of Buca della Iena I1–4, typically display extensive and pervasive gnawing damage, accompanied by an abundance of coprolites. Attributing small assemblages to hominid activities is more difficult, because evidence of modification tends to be more lightly scattered among the bones. Guattari G4 and G5 are cases in point, and one would want to view them with caution; they have been accepted as Mousterian because evidence of carnivore modification is rare, whereas other kinds of damage point to hominid activities (see also Stiner 1991a).

Assemblages whose taphonomic histories appear severely scrambled (Sant'Agostino S4, Guattari G2), or too scant to assess (Moscerini M1, Guattari G3 and G7), are dropped from consideration following the first analytical step below.

The extent of variation embodied by the study sample is appreciable. Three species of predator and two subspecies of one of them (*H. sapiens*) are considered, contrasting ecologically dedicated hunters (late Upper Paleolithic humans and wolves) and hunter-scavengers (spotted hyaenas) with Mousterian hominids. The amount of accumulation time for each assemblage also varies, however: the Middle Paleolithic sample was collected over roughly eighty thousand years, whereas some of the late Upper Paleolithic faunal assemblages are quite large but formed in a comparatively short time. Other qualities of the study sample lend unusual strengths to this comparison of predator diets; the faunas are from the same region, and so they shared generally analogous climatic regimes and analogous geological and topographic settings. All are from caves situated at low elevations, usually near the sea; Grotta Polesini is the only exception in this regard, lying inland on the Aniene River. Obviously, hominids and other predators could have eaten any number of species while away from shelters; the cave faunas merely represent elements of predator diets filtered through the contingencies of transport, perhaps including only those resources sufficiently large or close by to make portage worthwhile. The caves appear to have served as residential or foraging hubs for the human occupants, and as dens for spotted hyaenas and wolves.

The methods for quantifying species are discussed in Chapter 4 and are only briefly reviewed here. N-taxa refers to the number of species for all animals except shellfish, which are compared at the level of genus instead. The analyses employ identifiable specimen counts (NISP) for bones, teeth, and shells. NISP gauges the relative importance of food species transported to shelters by each predator. The NISP variable is preferred for analyzing taxonomic abundance because it demands fewer assumptions about a data set and avoids errors resulting from data aggregation. NISP is especially suitable for inter-assemblage comparisons, providing the communities from which species derive and the degrees of bone fragmentation are roughly comparable. These criteria are met by the Italian study sample (Chapter 5).

The components of skeletal parts are counted as separate NISP units, regardless of whether they are articulated or isolated when found by archaeologists. Tooth NISP, for example, combines counts of articulated and isolated teeth (see Chapter 4); hence the term *composite tooth NISP*. This approach to counting NISP is warranted by two facts about the study sample. First, the relative proportion of isolated to articulated teeth varies across assemblages

and even more across sites. Second, the approach avoids, or at least reduces, distortions in the relative proportions of species within assemblages arising directly from a traditional system wherein only those teeth isolated from bone are counted. The distortions have nothing to do with agency-caused biases.

The above claims may surprise some analysts, but they can be demonstrated in the subject faunas. Figure 7.1 repeats two graphs from Chapter 4, but now the assemblages are labeled according to the

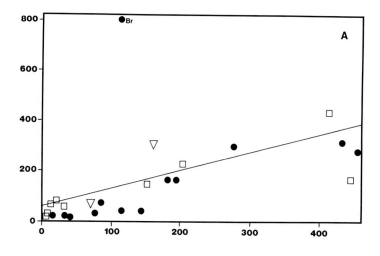

ALL TOOTH NISP

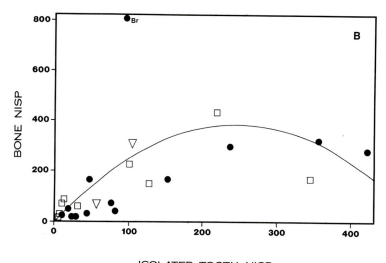

ISOLATED TOOTH NISP

▽ WOLF
☐ SPOTTED HYAENA
● MP HOMO

Figure 7.1 Plot of bone NISP to (A) composite tooth NISP and (B) isolated tooth NISP for ungulate remains from the Italian caves, marked according to collector agency. This figure repeats the distribution shown previously in Figure 4.1, but here specifies the identities of the predators responsible for the assemblages. In addition to showing that the relationship is close to linear for composite tooth NISP and curvilinear for isolated tooth NISP, the graphs demonstrate that the distributions are not explained by collector agency or by differing preservation conditions among sites.

CHAPTER 7

TABLE 7.1
NISP and N-taxa (species) counts for ungulates, carnivores, and small mammals in the Italian cave sites,
listed by agency of collection

Site and assemblage	Agency	Ungulates				Carnivores				Small mammals	
		NISP		N-taxa		NISP		N-taxa		NISP	N-taxa
GUATTARI:											
G0	sh	(414)	849	(5)	9	(63)	108	(3)	4	1	1
G1	sh	(446)	615	(6)	6	(58)	80	(1)	4	6	2
G2	mp/sh	(76)	104	(6)	6	(11)	13	(1)	1	2	1
G3	?	(3)	4	(3)	1	(1)	0	(1)	0	0	0
G4	mp	(35)	50	(5)	4	(2)	3	(1)	1	4	1
G5	mp	(38)	49	(2)	3	(0)	0	(0)	0	6	2
G7	?	(5)	6	(1)	1	(0)	0	(0)	0	0	0
SANT'AGOSTINO:											
S0	mp	(459)	744	(8)	7	(36)	101	(4)	7	73	7
S1	mp	(433)	752	(9)	7	(14)	105	(4)	7	148	10
S2	mp	(181)	349	(8)	7	(16)	106	(4)	6	94	10
S3	mp	(86)	160	(8)	7	(10)	66	(4)	7	71	12
S4	w/mp	(71)	134	(7)	7	(10)	36	(4)	4	38	10
SX	w	(160)	473	(5)	6	(34)	115	(4)	4	207	8
BREUIL:											
Br	mp	(115)	928	(9)	10	(10)	21	(2)	3	no data	
B3/4	mp	(277)	576	(8)	9	(38)	45	(5)	2	no data	
MOSCERINI:											
M1	?	(9)	16	(4)	3	(0)	0	(0)	0	15	4
M2	mp	(16)	37	(2)	4	(0)	2	(0)	2	180	8
M3	mp	(194)	358	(7)	7	(2)	3	(1)	1	0	0
M4	mp	(115)	157	(6)	3	(1)	2	(1)	1	0	0
M5	sh(+)	(204)	430	(5)	6	(58)	186	(5)	5	152	12
M6	mp	(143)	184	(4)	3	(1)	3	(1)	2	12	4
BUCA DELLA IENA:											
I1	sh	(32)	87	(5)	7	(38)	63	(3)	3	0	0
I2	sh	(4)	18	(2)	6	(8)	19	(2)	4	5	3
I3	sh	(8)	36	(5)	6	(36)	92	(4)	5	6	2
I4	sh	(13)	77	(5)	8	(58)	129	(4)	6	3	2
I5	sh	(21)	102	(6)	9	(37)	129	(5)	6	5	2
I6	sh	(151)	299	(7)	9	(136)	207	(4)	3	1	1
RIPARO SALVINI:											
1988	up		652		7		6		2	no data	
PALIDORO:											
P33–34	up	(235)	793	(5)	9	(1)	8	(1)	1	no data	
P1	up		76		6		1		1	1	1
P2	up		81		6		0		0	1	1
P3	up		127		6		3		2	0	0
P4	up		37		4		1		1	0	0
P5	up		330		6		6		2	1	1
P6	up		138		6		4		2	2	1

TABLE 7.1 (*Continued*)

Site and assemblage	Agency	Ungulates		Carnivores		Small mammals	
		NISP	*N-taxa*	*NISP*	*N-taxa*	*NISP*	*N-taxa*
PALIDORO:							
P7	up	326	5	7	1	1	1
P8	up	155	6	6	3	7	2

Sources: Stiner (1990a) and, for Palidoro 1–8, Cassoli (1976–77).

Note: NISP counts for teeth are listed separately (in parentheses) and together with large mammal bone wherever possible (exceptions are data taken from other published studies). NISP counts for bone therefore can be derived by subtracting tooth NISP from the total NISP value in this table. Two values also are provided for N-taxa of ungulates and carnivores, the first derived from teeth only (shown in parentheses) and the second derived only from bone. The arrays of taxa represented by the two counting methods overlap completely yet were derived independently. The higher of the two N-taxa values is used for the analyses. Agencies are (sh) spotted hyaenas, (mp) Middle Paleolithic humans, (up) late Upper Paleolithic humans, (w) wolves, (+) also smaller carnivores. In seriously mixed cases, major and minor agencies are separated by a slash. The main collector seldom accounts for bear and may not account for small mammal remains.

agency of bone collection on the basis of taphonomic evidence. Figure 7.1A illustrates a more or less linear relationship between bone NISP and composite tooth NISP (isolated plus articulated tooth specimens) that is significant at the .001 level of probability. In contrast, a conspicuously nonlinear relationship is evident between bone NISP and isolated tooth NISP in Figure 7.1B, also significant at the .001 level of probability. The observed differences stem from how tooth NISP is counted and are independent of biological agency. General differences in the degree of bone fragmentation (Chapter 5), on the other hand, depend on biotic agency to an appreciable extent.

While the presentation emphasizes comparisons of *total* NISP (composite tooth count plus bones), the analyses include parallel considerations of *bone* NISP alone: this is done as an internal check for sampling biases, because considering bone NISP alone effectively reduces each assemblage by half. Table 7.1 shows composite tooth NISP in parentheses alongside total NISP; subtracting the first value from the second yields bone NISP. N-taxa counts based exclusively on teeth are also shown in parentheses, with N-taxa based exclusively on bone beside them. A quick inspection of these data reveals that N-taxa is about as high on the average for bones as for teeth. Though determined independently of one another, the arrays of species in each assemblage based on these distinct classes of skeletal material overlap completely with few exceptions.

Analytical strategy

Potential biases due to numerical sampling are evaluated first by simple regression analysis of taxonomic richness (sensu Grayson 1984) for ungulates, carnivores, and small mammals. Broad patterns apparent from plotting N-taxa against log NISP are discussed in terms of expectations for hypothetical nonselective sampling. The procedure explores the potential influence of sample size biases and affords a preliminary look at whether species consumed by any of the four predators diverges from the overall slope of the distribution.

Comparisons then turn to the question of relative emphases on the most common prey species (ungulates), an approach that shows promise for elucidating shifts in human foraging ecology and land use in other studies (e.g., Grayson 1991). The statistical methods chosen here specifically respond to sample size problems exposed by the regression plots; differences in ungulates consumed by the predators are evaluated using a modified Robinson Index (Robinson 1951), also known as the Brainerd–Robinson distance coefficient (discussed in Cowgill 1990). This kind of analysis circumvents most problems caused by differing assemblage sizes in the study sample because: (1) the comparison concerns variation only among common prey taxa; (2) the assemblages associated with each predator are lumped by site, greatly increasing NISP in most instances; and (3) the index of difference employs percentage values. Because it is possible that the Upper Pleistocene predators partitioned common resources according to phylogenetic characteristics above the species level, the final analytical step compares the

numbers of resource classes—including mollusks, reptiles, and small mammals—represented in predators' diets.

Taxonomic Richness: Relationships Between N-taxa and NISP

The first step is to see if the Upper Pleistocene bone assemblages from the Italian caves conform to expectations about the mathematical relationship between taxonomic richness and sample size and whether any predator diets diverge from the main regression slope. Figures 7.2 and 7.3 are plots of N-taxa and log total NISP for the two dominant mammalian groups, ungulates and carnivores respectively, based on data in Table 7.1. The Polesini faunas are excluded from consideration because they are vastly larger than the other assemblages (Table 7.2). The upper graphs in Figures 7.2 and 7.3 identify the data points by site and the lower graphs identify them according to the main agency of accumulation. Question marks indicate assemblages whose origins are unknown or too scrambled to warrant further consideration (G2, G3, G7, S4, and M1). The N-taxa (vertical) axis is not logged because the ceiling values for mammalian subsets are relatively low (maximum ungulate species = 10, maximum carnivore species = 7).

Regression statistics in Table 7.3 indicate very significant relationships ($P < .001$) between N-taxa and total NISP for both the ungulate and the carnivore remains, and there are no obvious outliers. The plots show that much of the variation in numbers of species in these faunas *could* be due to numerical sampling bias—at least when compared in this way. This conclusion is not surprising; the Mousterian (and other) faunal assemblages tend to be small, an unfortunate fact of life. It is interesting that substantial differences in chronology have no consistent effect on the distributions. The cave deposits that yield the assemblages represent disparate amounts of accumulation time (see Figure 3.6), varying by site and by predator. Assemblages from Palidoro (UP), Riparo Salvini (UP), Breuil (MP), and the Sant'Agostino wolf den (W) from layer SX probably each formed within a thousand years, whereas

each level group in the Moscerini series (MP) formed over several thousand years.

Because four bone-collecting predators are represented in the sample, and human beings are more omnivorous as a rule, one might expect biases in species choice to emerge as the result of differing foraging practices, possibly expressed as different slopes. Visual inspection of Figures 7.2 and 7.3 does not support this expectation, however; all four predators emphasized ungulate prey and occasionally other large mammals, such as one another. To the extent that their diets included meat, humans apparently behaved like classic carnivores in the proportions of game species they consumed.

The regression comparisons nonetheless obscure one interesting fact about species in the study sample. While the total number of carnivore species does not diverge much between the Middle and late Upper Paleolithic periods in the Italian caves, the body sizes of carnivore species present and the relative abundances of carnivore to herbivore remains certainly differ. As predicted by Gamble (1983, 1986), the hominid- and carnivore-collected faunas dating to the Mousterian period display many more large carnivores, whereas those in late Upper Paleolithic shelters are nearly all small species and are uncommon relative to herbivores. Although taphonomic information segregates most carnivore remains from cultural components in Mousterian-aged faunas on the graphs, Gamble's basic contrast between the Middle and late Upper Paleolithic holds; time sharing of caves by large carnivores and hominids, so common in Mousterian times, all but ceased by the late Upper Paleolithic. Bears and wolves were still plentiful in the region by the later period, but apparently used different caves if and when they needed them.

Some subtle variation among predators series may also exist in relation to the main distribution for

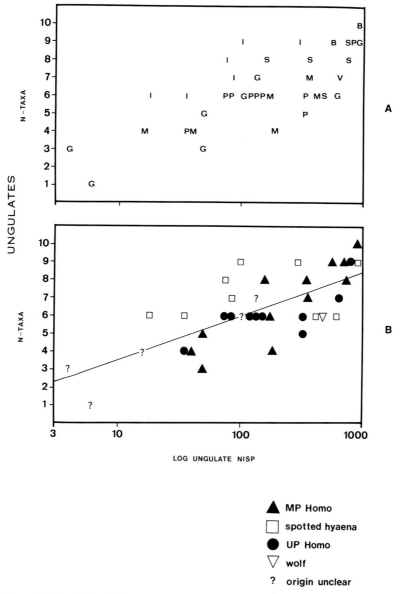

Figure 7.2 The relationship between ungulate NISP (logged) and ungulate N-taxa in the Italian Upper Pleistocene cave faunas, marked by (A) site name and (B) main agency of bone collection. (B) Breuil, (G) Guattari, (I) Buca della Iena, (M) Moscerini, (P) Palidoro, (S) Sant'Agostino, (V) Riparo Salvini. (From Stiner 1992)

ungulate remains, shown in Figure 7.2B. Spotted hyaena den faunas tend to fall on the high side of the line, Upper Paleolithic faunas occur on or below the line, and Middle Paleolithic faunas are more widely scattered. Such variation is not apparent for carni-vore remains from the same sites (Figure 7.3B). The differences are not statistically significant within the format considered, but a few thoughts pertaining to future research on this topic deserve mention. Be-cause spotted hyaenas may scavenge as often as

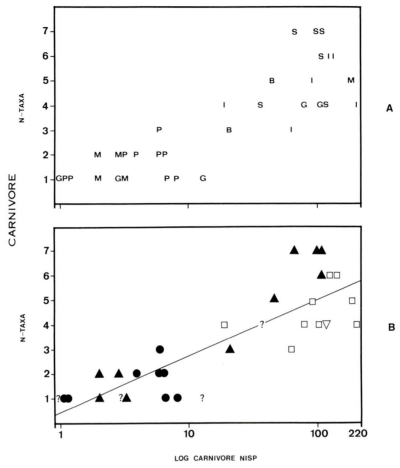

Figure 7.3 The relationship between carnivore NISP (logged) and carnivore N-taxa in
the Italian Upper Pleistocene cave faunas, marked by (A) site name and (B) main
agency of bone collection. Symbols as in Figure 7.2. (From Stiner 1992)

they hunt, it might be tempting to suggest that scavenging will increase species richness in shelter faunas in general. While probably true for hyaenas, the expectation is not borne out in the Middle Paleolithic assemblages. Species richness values for scavenged ungulate faunas in the Middle Paleolithic, interpreted on the basis of anatomical (Chapter 9) and mortality (Chapter 11) data, tend to be lower (Guattari and Moscerini, Figure 7.2) in relation to the regression line that those representing hunting (Breuil and Sant'Agostino). Perhaps scavenging opportunities exploited by hominids were more situationally (spatially or temporally) limited than those capitalized upon by hyaenas. Among

modern predators that scavenge, there are certainly contextual differences, the consequences of which merit continued exploration.

Also of interest is the observation that carnivore species richness associated with spotted hyaena dens and wolf dens in Figure 7.3B tends to be lower relative to the regression line than hominid-collected faunas overall. Exclusionary behavior associated with den defense may be responsible for this difference, but, if real, it is quite subtle and does not qualify as a compelling signature of denning behavior at the time scales considered here. High levels of interspecific violence, as documented in modern denning situations for the same kinds of

TABLE 7.2

NISP and N-taxa (species) counts for ungulates, carnivores, and small mammals in Grotta Polesini

Assemblage	Agency	Ungulates		Carnivores		Small mammals	
		NISP	*N-taxa*	*NISP*	*N-taxa*	*NISP*	*N-taxa*
1	up	3291	8	127	5	108	7
2	up	2125	8	126	5	50	6
3	up	3413	8	76	5	69	8
4	up	4075	8	205	6	163	13
5	up	6750	8	345	8	228	11
6	up	4539	8	153	5	158	10
7	up	4230	8	148	6	108	9
8	up	3669	8	131	7	87	11
9	up	4095	8	110	6	114	9
10	up	2799	8	48	6	68	5
11	up	683	8	21	4	90	8
12	up	2284	8	69	5	268	12

Source: Radmilli (1974).

Note: Assemblages are from arbitrary layers 1–12. Agencies of collection for small mammals may differ from that for ungulates and carnivores.

TABLE 7.3

Regression statistics for plots (N-taxa to total NISP) of ungulate and carnivore remains from all sites and proveniences

Taxa group	Sites and proveniences	r value	r^2	N-cases	P
ungulates	all	.733	.537	37	$< .001$
carnivores	all	.843	.711	32	$<< .001$

TABLE 7.4

Regression statistics for plots (N-taxa to total NISP) of various ungulate, carnivore, and small mammal assemblages by site (not illustrated)

Site	Vertical proveniences	r value	r^2	N-cases	P
Buca d.Iena	I1–6	.784	.615	17	$.01 > P > .001$
Guattari	G0–7	.902	.814	16	$<< .001$
Moscerini	M1–6[a]	.769	.591	15	$.05 > P > .01$
Sant'Agostino	S0–4, SX	.641	.411	18	$.1 > P > .05$[b]
Salvini and Palidoro	all cuts	.948	.899	25	$<< .001$
Polesini	all cuts	.277	.077	36	$>> .1$[b]

[a] Listed by level group.

[b] Relationship is not significant.

predators (e.g., Kruuk 1972; Schaller 1972), may work against the formation of monospecific or species-poor carnivore faunas over the long term; most paleontological records are palimpsests of many occupational events.

The potential effect of numerical sampling biases can also be explored at a finer level, such as by site. Table 7.4 lists regression statistics for all mammals

(not graphed) in caves yielding multiple assemblages. The results are consistent with the general pattern described above. Only a weak relationship is found for Sant'Agostino, however, perhaps because the assemblages are larger than most. As expected, the immense samples from Polesini show no relationship between N-taxa and total NISP at all.

RELATIVE EMPHASES ON COMMON PREY SPECIES BY PREDATORS

Let us now examine variation in the diets of the four predators by focusing on the relative frequencies of the most common prey taxa, first through a visual comparison and then by statistical analysis. Table 7.5 presents the full array of species consumed by each predator, based on total NISP and groomed

with the benefit of taphonomic information. The diet of each predator is compiled by site, greatly enlarging the units of comparison. Assemblages whose taphonomic origins are ambiguous now are dropped from consideration, with the exception of Middle Paleolithic Guattari G4–5. Only data for

TABLE 7.5
Dietary data (total NISP) for the four predators in Italian Upper Pleistocene shelters

Food species by descending body size	Middle Paleolithic humans				Wolves
	MOSC M2–4, 6	GUAT G4–5	SAGO S0–3	BREUIL Br, 3/4	SAGO SX
aurochs	14	54	146	188	4
horse	1	5	38	25	0
red/fallow deer[a]	574	38	1086	793	36
wild ass	0	0	3	3	0
ibex	20	0	197	325	221
wild boar	4	1	182	1	1
chamois	0	0	0	1	0
roe deer	105	2	332	162	211
Subtotal	718	100	1984	1498	473
elephant	0	0	0	1	0
hippopotamus	2	0	0	0	0
rhinoceros	3	0	21	3	0
monk seal	0	0	1	0	1
marmot	0	0	0	0	14
hare	0	0	0	1	0
rabbit	0	0	0	0	175
small rodents	0	0	0	0	0
reptiles/amphibians	40	0	0	0	0
birds[b]	0	0	0	0	0
shellfish	613	0	0	0	0
Subtotal	658	0	22	5	190
Total NISP	1375	100	2006	1503	663

TABLE 7.5   (*Continued*)

Food species by descending body size	Spotted hyaenas			Late Upper Paleolithic humans		
	MOSC M5	GUAT G0–1	BUCA II–6	PAL all	POL 1–12	SALV 10–15
aurochs	22	358	97	503	980	14
horse	14	125	225	98	1250	78
red/fallow deer[a]	245	863	225	902	29785	458
wild ass	0	0	0	411	2262	37
ibex	5	0	0	2	362	12
wild boar	0	61	19	84	3453	1
chamois	0	0	0	0	694	4
roe deer	137	53	35	13	3167	49
Subtotal	423	1460	601	2013	41,953	653
elephant	0	3	2	0	0	0
hippopotamus	0	0	0	0	0	0
rhinoceros	0	1	16	0	0	0
marmot	0	0	1	0	10	0
hare	0	0	0	5	365	2
rabbit	0	0	0	0	0	0
small rodents	0	0	0	0	0	0
reptiles/amphibians	0	0	0	0	0	0
birds[b]	0	0	0	25	514	?
clams/mussels	0	0	0	0	0	0
Subtotal	0	4	19	30	889	2
Total NISP	428	1464	615	2043	42,842	655

[a] The red/fallow deer category contains mostly red deer and only small quantities of fallow deer. Rare remains of *Megaceros* are also present in the Middle Paleolithic sites of Moscerini, Guattari, and possibly Buca della Iena.

[b] Avian species accepted as probable food in this study are ground- or rock-dwelling species: gray partridge, quail, and doves.

Note: Data are based on bones, teeth, and shells and are groomed on the basis of taphonomic evidence.

ungulates are analyzed in detail, because their remains predominate in the faunal assemblages. Pachyderms are excluded on grounds that they may not have been present in Italy by late Upper Paleolithic times.

Figure 7.4 summarizes the percentages of ungulate species consumed by each predator at all cave sites. It suggests that the proportion of ungulate species eaten by Mousterian hominids, late Upper Paleolithic humans, and spotted hyaenas at shelters were similar. Red deer was the principal prey species, supplemented by smaller quantities of large and small ungulates. The prey profile for spotted

hyaenas appears to be slightly weighted toward the large-bodied end of the scale, indicating a somewhat higher dependence on horse and aurochs. Conversely, the Mousterian prey profile is slightly weighted toward the smaller end of the ungulate size scale. None of these differences are substantial, however.

Only the dietary profile for denning wolves at Sant'Agostino (SX) shows a significant departure from the general red deer pattern. Although one of a kind in the study sample, the wolf den assemblage introduces a valuable dimension to the comparisons. The denning period of modern wolves often

NISP

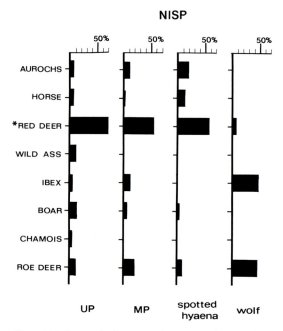

Figure 7.4 Composite frequency data on ungulate species (% of total ungulate NISP) in predator diets, listed in descending body size order. (*) The red deer category also includes a small percentage of fallow deer in most cases. (From Stiner 1992)

corresponds to a temporary drop in average prey size (Peterson et al. 1984). Ungulates are vital resources for unencumbered wolves, and, being aware of this, tend to avoid places where wolves concentrate for any amount of time (Mech 1977; Rogers et al. 1980). Because denning imposes spatial restrictions on the food quest (see also Harrison and Gilbert 1985 on coyotes), small prey, incapable of adjusting to wolf densities by moving away, become short-term staples; this point is relevant to the discussion of resource specialization below. The wolf den assemblage SX is entirely consistent with the expectations of denning, as the wolves focused on marmots and rabbits (see Chapter 6). They also fed on ibex and the highly territorial roe deer in Latium; ibex, for example, are important prey of modern nonreproducing wolves in other habitats with broken topography (e.g., Schaller 1977:140, on wolves in Afghanistan). Decreases in average prey body size are not apparent in spotted hyaena dens of Pleistocene Italy nor in modern spotted hyaena dens. This is because of hyaenas' digestive

capabilities and a rather different suite of foraging behaviors and transport objectives leading to bone accumulations in dens (e.g., Kruuk 1972). Young hyaenas may occupy dens over periods of many months, making the switching tactics practiced by reproducing wolves less feasible overall.

The comparison portrayed in Figure 7.4 suggests similar emphases on ungulate species by at least three of the predators, less so in the case of denning wolves. The similarities among the three other predators could be an oversimplification, however. The lumping of several the assemblages generated by each predator to create the bar chart might obscure heterogeneity at the interassemblage level. This is a just concern, because other lines of evidence indicate that the ways in which Mousterian hominids procured ungulate resources varied across sites, much more than was typical of Upper Paleolithic foragers in the same region. The question is whether uniformity in the relative emphases on ungulate prey species is upheld at a finer level than is compared in the bar chart, here examined statistically by predator and by site (as partitioned in Table 7.5).

Table 7.6 contrasts ungulate species representation among predators and sites using a variant of the Robinson Index of dissimilarity (Robinson 1951). Results for bone NISP (derived from Table 7.1) and total NISP (Table 7.5) are presented; no substantial discrepancies are found between the two versions of the matrix. The index is calculated by summing the differences in the percentage of each ungulate species for each pair of assemblage groups without regard to sign. Values vary between 0 (identical) and 200 (maximally different). Both versions of the matrix reveal fairly consistent levels of dissimilarity in the pairings for all predators except wolves. Although only one wolf den assemblage is represented, the distances from other predators are consistently great (e.g., varying between 116 and 179); distances between other predators at most reach only the lower limit of those from wolves. The fact that the wolf case is a solitary example does not fully account for its isolation from all other predator cases.

Relative emphases on ungulate taxa certainly vary among the other assemblages and predators, but this occurs within a narrower range, largely in-

TABLE 7.6
Robinson coefficients of dissimilarity for assemblage group pairs by site and agency

a. Bone NISP only

	Mosc MP	Guat MP	SAgo MP	Breu MP	SX w	M5 sh	G0–1 sh	I1–6 sh	Pal UP	Pol UP	Salv UP
Mosc MP	0										
Guat MP	109	0									
SAgo MP	52	96	0								
Breu MP	46	83	47	0							
SX w	138	175	124	138	0						
M5 sh	48	93	43	58	108	0					
G0–1 sh	60	52	70	35	172	65	0				
I1–6 sh	96	38	80	71	174	81	36	0			
Pal UP	105	67	85	80	185	90	55	55	0		
Pol UP	37	101	67	56	171	72	51	85	80	0	
Salv UP	38	84	81	54	170	69	43	71	85	21	0

b. Total NISP

	Mosc MP	Guat MP	SAgo MP	Breu MP	SX w	M5 sh	G0–1 sh	I1–6 sh	Pal UP	Pol UP	Salv UP
Mosc MP	0										
Guat MP	116	0									
SAgo MP	49	100	0								
Breu MP	63	92	32	0							
SX w	148	179	129	118	0						
M5 sh	47	103	39	55	116	0					
G0–1 sh	68	59	55	57	174	58	0				
I1–6 sh	108	77	89	85	170	96	62	0			
Pal UP	104	60	82	80	179	91	41	73	0		
Pol UP	36	107	49	69	166	56	54	96	79	0	
Salv UP	37	105	63	67	164	56	52	84	81	22	0

Note: (MP) Middle Paleolithic, (w) wolf, (sh) spotted hyaena, (UP) late Upper Paleolithic. Distance metric varies between 0 (identical) and 200 (maximally different).

dependent of time (see Figure 3.6). Palidoro, for example, is rather different from Moscerini (MP, 104), but Moscerini is also different from Guattari (MP, 116). In short, Middle Paleolithic assemblage groupings are about as different from one another as each is from various spotted hyaena den faunas and late Upper Paleolithic faunas. The results are not explained by differing assemblage sizes; total ungulate NISP for Guattari G4–5 is only 100, whereas NISP for most other samples ranges between roughly 400 and 2000, and just under 42,000 for Polesini.

The distances in the matrixes can be summarized in a straightforward way by focusing on the ranges and medians. These statistics are presented first by predator (Table 7.7) and then between predator pairs (Table 7.8), excluding wolves. Low, high, and median distances are remarkably similar, given the range of the distance metric, showing that none of the three predators diverges significantly from the others in terms of relative emphasis on ungulate species, regardless of whether bone NISP or total NISP counts are considered. The predator-paired results (Table 7.8) are of greater interest, because they involve a larger set of comparisons. Here, ranges and medians are even more alike, and there are no substantial differences in results between the bone NISP subsample and total NISP. With the

TABLE 7.7
Differences in distance between assemblage
groups by predator

a. Bone NISP only

Distance	MP human	Spotted hyaena	UP human
minimum	46	36	21
median	67	65	80
maximum	109	81	85

b. Total NISP

Distance	MP human	Spotted hyaena	UP human
minimum	34	58	22
median	77	62	79
maximum	115	96	81

Note: Distance metric varies between 0 (identical) and 200 (maximally different). Wolf is excluded from consideration because only one assemblage is available for comparison.

TABLE 7.8
Differences in distance between assemblage groups
between predator pairs

a. Bone NISP only

Distance	MP-sh	MP-UP	UP-sh
minimum	35	37	43
median	59	73	69
maximum	96	105	90

b. Total NISP

Distance	MP-sh	MP-UP	UP-sh
minimum	39	36	41
median	63	68	56
maximum	108	107	96

Note: (MP) Middle Paleolithic, (UP) late Upper Paleolithic, (sh) spotted hyaena. Distance metric varies between 0 (identical) and 200 (maximally different). Wolf is excluded from consideration because only one assemblage is available for comparison.

exception of the wolf case, then, the amount of difference among faunas collected by one kind of predator is about the same as between predators, irrespective of time and assemblage size. Ungulate species utilized do not distinguish the foraging niches of later Upper Paleolithic humans, Middle Paleolithic hominids, and spotted hyaenas in the context of cave occupations along the west-central coast of Italy.

RESOURCE CLASSES CONSUMED BY PREDATORS

Somewhat more variation is apparent in the use of *small* prey by the four predators at coastal caves, if only because Mousterian hominids sometimes used shellfish and tortoises, wolves ate marmots, rabbits, and hares, and late Upper Paleolithic people took some ground-dwelling birds. Taking into account inequities of body size, small animals constituted relatively minor fractions of the total food volume carried into shelters by the predators (Table 7.5) or, in the case of wolves, defecated there (see Chapter 6). On the other hand, the small species in the study sample certainly represent a more diverse array of habitats, and significantly different behaviors may have been required to obtain these small animals. Because modern sympatric predators often diverge with respect to habitats exploited, small game is quite interesting from the perspective of how the four Pleistocene predators supplemented their diets with alternative resources.

Food species are divided into ten classes in Table 7.9 on the assumption that prey body size, anatomical and locomotor characteristics, and/or habitat preferences affected their accessibility and nutritional value to consumers. Dietary profiles are lumped by predator, combining all food species in assemblages from all cave sites to create a complete dietary profile. The comparison considers both the number of resource classes represented and the number of species per class. From this perspective, the overall Mousterian diet at shelters is somewhat more diverse than the diets of the other predators, despite the fact that huge quantities of material are available for some of the late Upper Paleolithic cases. The Mousterian diet appears the least narrow

TABLE 7.9
Number of species in each resource class in the diets of the four predators

Resource classes by descending body size	Middle Paleolithic humans	Denning wolves	Denning spotted hyaenas	Late Upper Paleolithic humans
pachyderms (3)	3	0	2	0
large ungulates (2)	2	1	2	2
medium ungulates (5)	5	3	4	4
small ungulates (3)	3	2	2	3
phocids (seal) (1)	1	0	0	0
lagomorphs (2)	1	2	0	1
rodents (1)	0	1	1	1
reptiles (2)	2	0	1	—
birds (4)	0	0	0	4
marine mollusks (7)	7	0	0	0
Total species	24	9	12	15
Total classes	8	5	6	6

Note: Value inside ( ) indicates the maximum number of species possible (total = 30) for total combined food array. Pachyderms include elephant, rhinoceros, and hippopotamus; large ungulates include horse and aurochs; medium ungulates include red deer, fallow deer, giant deer, ibex, and wild ass; small ungulates include roe deer, chamois, and boar; the rodent category includes marmot only. In the case of Polesini, small quantities of tortoise are reported by Radmilli (1974:29), but these individuals may have perished underground during hibernation rather than having fallen prey to humans. Taphonomic evidence shows that some individual carnivores were also eaten by the four predators considered (e.g., hominids ate bears and foxes at Polesini and some bears at Moscerini). Carnivores representing prey are not included in the dietary profiles because of the potential for confusing isolated instances of predation with deliberate entry into caves by the same species.

with regard to prey carried to caves, followed by that of the late Upper Paleolithic, spotted hyaenas, and, finally, wolves. All but two resource classes are represented in the Mousterian diet, and the total number of species (24) is high relative to the maximum potential value (30) for the study sample as a whole. The diets of denning spotted hyaenas and late Upper Paleolithic humans display fewer resource classes and are more similar to one another. The wolf den assemblage shows the fewest resource classes of all, consistent with foraging restrictions imposed by the reproductive strategies of this species and possibly also the fact that only one assemblage is considered.

Data grouped by resource class appear more useful than unstructured comparisons of N-taxa for distinguishing the adaptations of the four predators. Even here the differences are not very pronounced, however, and their significance may be further re-

duced by ambiguities inherent in the sample. The total Mousterian profile spans a much longer time range than those for the other predators—more time for rare species to be recruited into the community-wide pool. Even so, Mousterian and late Upper Paleolithic diets diverge from those of the nonhuman predators only in the presence-absence of one or two small prey classes. For example, it is apparent from a small quantity of gnawed remains in Moscerini M5 that hyaenas also ate tortoises on occasion (see Chapter 6). The Mousterian differs from the Upper Paleolithic primarily in the mollusks and tortoises found at Moscerini and possibly also in the disappearance of pachyderms from the coastal Italian ecosystems by the later cultural period. The late Upper Paleolithic shelters under discussion were probably farther from the Mediterranean shore when visited by people, and truly littoral occupations and associated evidence of mollusk harvesting may now be inundated by the sea (for related discus-sions on Middle and Late Stone Age caves in South Africa, see Klein 1980a; Voigt 1982). Indeed, the Middle through Upper Paleolithic faunal sequence in Riparo Mochi, one of the Grimaldi caves on the northern Mediterranean coast near the Italian-French border, provides ample evidence of mollusk harvesting throughout the two cultural periods (my current research).

The data presented above expand the hypotheti-cal boundaries of Neandertal foraging. The Middle Paleolithic of Europe has been depicted as generally lacking evidence of aquatic exploitation or use of species that normally inhabit rocky uplands (e.g., Straus 1987, 1990). New information from Italy shows that Mousterian hominids clearly appreci-ated the benefits of gatherable aquatic prey and were wholly capable of hunting ibex (see Chapters 9 and 11), though seldom in quantity. Hominids living in west-central Italy prior to 50,000 years ago were certainly Neandertals, based on new dates for the Circeo I fossil cranium from Guattari (Schwarcz et al. 1991; see Chapter 3). Hominids thereafter, up to roughly 35,000 to 40,000 years ago, probably also were Neandertals, but verification is not currently possible (see, nonetheless, Manzi and Passarello on probable Neandertal remains from Breuil, in Bietti et al. 1988). If anything, Neandertals had the most diverse diet of the predators considered, but not by a large margin. The fact that birds, small mammals, and deep water aquatic prey are missing from Mousterian cave faunas does not undermine this pattern.

OVERLAPPING SPECIES USE: EXPRESSIONS OF COMMON INTEREST

The study sample holds region, topography, envi-ronment, and depositional context more or less con-stant, and predator diets are reconstructed from many assemblages (except for wolves) on the basis of taphonomic evidence. From the standpoint of a simple regression analysis (plots of N-taxa and log total NISP), nearly all variation in taxonomic rich-ness among the Italian cave assemblages could be explained by sample size effects. The slopes of the predator distributions are about the same as well: at least three of the predators tended to utilize the same number of prey species, regardless of whether they were human or nonhuman, hunting or scavenging, fully carnivorous or omnivorous.

Finer level comparisons circumvent sample size problems by focusing on the relative emphases on common ungulate species and on total numbers of resource classes represented in diets. These com-parisons clearly demonstrate that all predators ex-cept denning wolves took similar ranges of prey, in very similar frequencies. The results obtained for bone NISP, representing only half the data set, serve as an internal check for sampling error, and it is significant that the results are entirely consistent with those obtained for total NISP. Had this sub-stantial reduction in total sample size been enough to undermine its suitability for the analyses, chances are that we would have seen deterioration (less consistent, more aberrant cases) of the results relative to those observed for the total sample. I conclude, then, that the total sample is plenty big enough for what the analyses are intended to accom-plish here.

The bigger picture is one of uniform species choice among predators. More than anything, the results show that spotted hyaenas and Middle and late Upper Paleolithic hominids in coastal Italy op-erated not only within the same trophic level, but also in the same resource guild (see also Turner's [1984] discussion of biogeographic relationships between hominids and hyaenas in Middle Pleisto-cene Britain). Obviously, the hominid member of the guild changed at some point from Neandertals to anatomically modern humans. That species collec-tions in dens by spotted hyaenas, in turn, was a direct response to abundance is documented in modern situations (e.g., Skinner et al. 1986). Like the large carnivores around them, hominids ate what was common within the desired prey size cate-gories: in environments of Upper Pleistocene Italy, their economies focused primarily on red deer, with smaller numbers of aurochs, horse, ibex, roe deer, and other species.

To understand what similarity or difference in

prey taxa consumed might mean for archaeological studies, it is important to recognize that predators may interact with their environment at more than one scale. Of special interest are the ecological concepts of guild and niche, two distinct levels in the hierarchy of resource relationships thought to structure animal communities. As explained in Chapter 2, niches are occupied by species, the hypothetical boundaries of which distinguish the adaptations of species to a large extent. Common interest in certain resources, such as ungulates, unites some predators into a single guild, intensifying interspecific interactions in ways that can ultimately affect the evolutionary histories of these species. The range of taxa consumed tells us who the guild members are (as in this analysis), whereas the details of exploitation set members apart.

Understanding the difference between guild and niche concepts is essential for isolating and developing appropriate measures of adaptive difference in human evolution research. Neandertal diet in Italy resembled that of modern humans, but then so did the diet of spotted hyaenas. We know very well that humans were different from spotted hyaenas in a multitude of other ways; humans were probably far more omnivorous, had technology, lacked spots, and so on. The data on prey species consumed by those predators merely provide evidence of ecological commonality at a higher level. Beyond the issue of sampling bias, similarities in the ranges of species consumed by different predators in Italy were a product of the linking of these predators in a guild focusing primarily on ungulate prey. Guilds are of great interest for evolution research because unrelated taxa can affect one another through their use of the same resource. Humans have existed in the same guild as many large carnivores for as long as they have relied in any way upon ungulates for food.

SPECIES CONSUMED AS MEASURES OF EVOLUTIONARY CHANGE

Taxonomic abundance in death assemblages is interesting only in the context of knowledge about animal community structure and content, and it is important to distinguish between prey availability in the environment and selectivity on the part of predators. In Italy, the four predators responded in large part to the natural abundances of various ungulate species. The evidence specifically argues against using continuity in species consumed by hominids as support for evolutionary continuity across the Middle to Upper Paleolithic transition in Eurasia (cf. Clark and Lindly 1989a; 1989b:664). In other words, finding *no difference* in species exploited across time does not exclude the possibility of *no change* in hominid adaptations. Species data do not appear to be up to the task of negating the possibility of significant shifts in the human niche during the Pleistocene, because, after all, they cannot distinguish between Mousterian (or late Upper Paleolithic) hunters and spotted hyaenas. Alternatively, species data are very valuable for identifying guild relationships among hominids and certain other large predators, an important baseline for this study.

While somewhat tangential to the main subject of this chapter, the findings presented also have implications for studies of resource specialization. There are many reasons that humans and other large predators might appear to concentrate on a resource. Because of the unique way in which shelter figures in the life history of wolves, for example, prey taxa emphasized while using dens may be poor descriptors of wolves' dietary profile overall. The single wolf den assemblage from Sant'Agostino SX—the only case showing a significant departure in species use—is a case in point. Site occupations by mobile peoples can also be relatively short-term events. Though hardly an issue in the Italian study sample, nearly monospecific faunas are known in certain other Middle and Upper Paleolithic sites (e.g., Chase 1987; Mellars 1989; Kozłowski 1990; Rolland 1990; Straus 1987, 1990). Food may be brought in from the immediate vicinity or from farther away, depending on what is going on at that place as opposed to what generally goes on within a larger territory. Regardless of which other behaviors might interest us, the possibility of short-term adjustments to food supply—not the evolution of specialized hunting—is foremost among *behavioral* explanations for variation in taxonomic abundance. Any evidence that occupations were short-term (i.e., seasonal) as a matter of principle reduces the likelihood that a monospecific fauna (or one species therein) represents ecologically specialized hunting. It is at least as likely to reflect the response of a generalist forager to a situation or locality in which few prey species are available.

Questions about evolutionary shifts in hominid niche require both many cases for comparison and scaling of the archaeological data against something that can be ascertained independently about animal community structure. We can never know the absolute composition of ancient communities, since all records of them are biased in some way, but there are alternatives. One can set the archaeological evidence against longer-term climate-induced cycles in animal community content (e.g., Miracle and Sturdy 1991 in Herzegovina; Tchernov 1981, 1989, 1992 in Israel) or against what is known about animal biogeography (e.g. Gamble 1983, 1986 on hominid-carnivore cave use across Pleistocene Eurasia, and Grayson 1991 on the late Prehistoric period in the Great Basin) or, as in this study, against what other consumers with similar resource interests ate in the same situations. As for the problem of mapping shifts in the human niche, however, there are better places to look, such as in the ways that hominids sought, obtained, and processed the very same classes of foods through time.

SUMMARY

This chapter concludes the first major analytical segment of this research focusing on species representation in the Italian caves. By exploring patterns of species abundance and bone damage, the assemblages are tied to specific agencies, often with considerable certainty. The data on species consumed at shelters demonstrate close trophic linkages among hominids, wolves, and spotted hyaenas in Italy during the Upper Pleistocene. Consistent with the general argument posed by Gamble (1983, 1986), prey species representation is most informative about the nature of hominid-carnivore coexistence in this region and about predator guild in particular. The variety of taxa represented in the Italian cave faunas does not distinguish predator adaptations within the guild centering on ungulate prey in this region. This is because foraging behaviors, and the definition of resource niche more generally, are not simply problems of the species eaten by a predator, nor disparity in the kinds of sources exploited. Niche boundaries of coexisting large predators are better described by qualitatively different access procedures involving the same prey species, necessitated in part by the nature of interspecific or intraspecific competition. Through the processes of natural selection, coexisting predators have arrived at different and sometimes complementary ways of exploiting the same prey species. These solutions will be explored in terms of predators' strategies of searching, procuring, transporting, and processing food and seasonal use in the chapters to follow.

8

On Food Transport Behavior

THE KINDS OF prey body parts that predators carry to shelters potentially reflect the food choices they make, their tactics of procurement, and the contexts of consumption. Assuming that the problems posed by in situ bone attrition in archaeofaunas can be surmounted, the anatomical contents of shelter faunas are potentially powerful means for learning about the foraging systems of prehistoric humans. Owing to the complexity of food transport questions, some introduction to the general characteristics of bone assemblages collected by predators is needed to appreciate what prey body part profiles can reveal about predator behavior.

This chapter concerns the ecological bases of food transport behavior in social predators. I consider animals' economic motivations for transporting food in the context of their physical and social environments. The themes to be developed are: (1) how transported food volume declines as a simple distance function; (2) the role of food transport behavior in reducing interference competition and enhancing processing opportunities; (3) the relationship between food distributions and predators' emphases on hunting and scavenging; and (4) predators' decisions about which parts to carry away based on carcass state (age at death, extent of decomposition or ravaging) and the relative nutritional payoffs of various body parts.

While the discussion includes data on modern humans, it centers on food transport phenomena common to nonhuman social predators. An impressive body of ethnoarchaeological data has accrued in the past two decades and has greatly enriched our knowledge about hunter-gatherer lifeways. Without undermining the contributions of these works, it must be understood that the data they yield are often complicated by the recent acquisition of metal containers and other nondegenerative tools by the subject societies. Containers, especially those made from metal, enable people to boil foods for prolonged periods, and such crockery wears out only very slowly. The incorporation of these implements in technological systems adds a new dimension to humans' capabilities to extract fats, proteins, and minerals from animal bones (e.g., Brain 1981; Gifford-Gonzalez 1977, 1989; Speth 1991; Yellen 1977). As I argue elsewhere, the kinds of technical support that exist in any cultural system for processing foods greatly affect humans' decisions about which and how many prey body parts to carry away from procurement sites.

We simply do not know the extent to which novel processing equipment acquired by traditional societies of the modern era interferes with our use of these cases in research on prehistoric economies. We only know that such items of technology were once absent. Because the earlier periods in human evolution are least understood as a rule, ethnoarchaeological cases cannot be used uncritically in our efforts to understand how Pleistocene cultures differed through time. Humans are unique among primates in that they regularly transport food about and oftentimes share. Humans are not unique among mammals in this regard, however. The ecological ramifications of food transport behavior need to be established in a wider context before we can assign elaborate social meanings or technological advantages to this basic fact about human ecology.

Here, I cast the net widely as a way to set questions about food transport behavior in evolutionary perspective, considering only the most fundamental constraints on these behaviors among large preda-tory species. What follows is a four-part discussion of theories about and apparent goals of food trans-port behavior, a review of some wildlife and anthro-pological accounts of transport behavior, body part choice models based on nutritional characteristics of large mammals, and, finally, a formulation of some archaeological expectations pertinent to this study of Pleistocene predators in Italy.

It will not be possible to learn the absolute dis-tances over which carcass parts were moved by for-agers in the past, nor always the condition of the prey items when procured (alive and whole, dead and whole, decayed, or ravaged). Moreover, dis-cussion of prey body part profiles in shelters here concerns only the ultimate products of food trans-port trajectories. Attempts to tie anatomical patterns in archaeofaunas to processes operating in the pre-sent without the aid of contextual information (e.g., taphonomy, seasonality, mortality patterns) invaria-bly come up against problems of equifinality—a big word for the possibility that separate processes may leave the same kind of signature. My purpose is to lay out some of the more important parameters of transport behavior, to find some consistent relation-ships between pattern and cause, and to narrow down the ranges of possible explanations for any given pattern. No perfectly stringent or clear-cut predictions will come forth from this discussion; some of the questions I raise were, in fact, provoked by my archaeological experiences in Italy and, in any case, interpreting prey body part profiles re-quires the integration of other kinds of skeletal evi-dence and reference data.

THE PROBLEM OF FOOD TRANSPORT

The fact that people move food over substantial distances has long fascinated archaeologists. In-deed, food transport behavior is highly developed in humans, and, in routinely moving food, whatever the purpose, we resemble the social carnivores more than we resemble our closest relatives, the apes (see Chapter 1). Though Tooby and DeVore's (1987) essay on primate models is insightful on many fronts, it overlooks this crucial point about the ecology and evolution of human beings. Transport behavior is the point of clearest contradiction in primate-based comparisons: modern people are great porters of food. Chimpanzees and baboons sometimes pick up a piece of meat and move it from one spot to another, but these transport episodes are a pale contrast to what we see—hands or no hands—among humans, wolves, dholes, wild dogs, and hyaenas (e.g., Bertram 1979; Ewer 1973; Kruuk 1972; Mech 1970). Nothing in primate-based models could predict this quality in humans, whereas models based on the social predators cer-tainly would. The high rates of food transport and the volumes moved by humans and some carnivores underline the existence of convergent "structural" features of their foraging adaptations. These trans-port activities are not fluke occurrences that ob-servers must travel widely and wait years to see; they reflect behavioral tendencies that characterize the species in question. Best known among bone-gathering predators are the hyaenas, the larger ca-nids, and humans. Archaeological deposits thick with bones (e.g., Bar-Yosef et al. 1992; Binford 1984; Bunn et al. 1980; Chase 1986; Stiner 1990a, 1991b; Klein 1976, 1980a, 1987; Potts 1984b, 1986) indicate that hominids' tendencies to actively manipulate resource distributions emerged long ago.

An important and closely related side of human predation is food processing (Binford 1978; Binford and Bertram 1977; Brain 1981; Gifford-Gonzalez 1989; Metcalfe and Barlow 1992; Speth 1991; Yellen 1977, 1991a), the procedures for which can be elaborate, even cooperative. None of the carni-vores is a cooperative processor, but some species frequently move food to gain processing time and adult canids will vomit partly digested meat to feed hungry puppies. Here, again, humans must be paired ecologically with the carnivores rather than with their primate relatives. Hunting is a male-dominated activity in modern human societies—at least where large game is concerned—but transport and processing investments by other persons in the social group may occur subsequent to the hunting episode, and portions of a large kill may be dispersed accordingly. Hunting by nonhuman primates also tends to be a male-dominated activity (Strum 1981:296–297; Butynski 1982), but so is eating the spoils, and processing is nothing more than the simplest and most immediate acts of feeding. Carnivores, in contrast, are very effective processors of soft and hard animal tissues.

It is no coincidence that transport and processing costs are essential elements of the classic foraging models in population biology (e.g., Charnov 1976; Maynard Smith 1974). Working from real-life observations and energetic principles, these theoretical equations allow subsequent handling and processing costs to be as important as or more important than the act of capture. It also is clear that carcass transport and processing can be major investments in modern human cultures (e.g., Binford 1978; Yellen 1977; see also Metcalfe and Barlow 1992), and not without interest, much of that labor

may be afforded by women and other nonhunting members of human social groups. We do not know exactly when and how labor came to be divided between the sexes in prehistoric societies, but part of the answer must lie in evidence of game processing and the transport behaviors that make thorough processing feasible. Food transport is now a subject of intense investigation in modern situations and in the Paleolithic. Questions about food processing and changes in humans' technological backing for doing so have received relatively less attention (see also Gifford-Gonzalez 1993), yet both classes of behavior represent ways that a predator may exploit the same kind of resource differently from other species with whom it might compete in an ecosystem. Both classes of behaviors are therefore potentially important descriptors of resource niche and foraging adaptations in predators, including humans.

Why Do Predators Move Food? Observations from Life

Debates about the nature of archaic hominid adaptations often center on the *motives* behind food transport. The phenomenon of food transport lies at the heart of many reconstructions of Pleistocene hominid sociality. Until fairly recently, however, researchers assumed that food was transported so that it could be shared (e.g., Isaac 1971, 1978; Lovejoy 1981; also see review by Speth 1990). The rise and fall of the "home base" hypothesis (Isaac 1978 versus Potts 1982, 1984b; Binford 1981:294–296) reflect a newly found discomfort with the use of modern hunter-gatherer systems as direct behavioral analogs for premodern hominids. Even if ancient peoples did transport food expressedly to share it, we can only find out by first assuming the simplest of economic incentives—ones that humans have in common with other predatory species—and then by trying to exclude this possibility. There are some nearly universal constraints on what can be gained by moving food across a landscape—basically, the cost of work (e.g., Metcalfe and Barlow 1992)—and it is likely that some foraging activities of social carnivores and humans could lead to bone accumulations of similar anatomical content for this reason alone.

Transport behavior is widely documented for modern predator species, particularly canids, hyaenids, and humans, but the reasons that they move food are difficult to ascertain because several conditions may operate simultaneously. We find that food may be taken to residential places or foraging hubs (1) to monopolize it, (2) to gain a processing advantage, (3) to provision dependents, (4) to share with other capable adult foragers to reduce risk (sensu Winterhalder 1986; Binford 1991), or (5) to improve upon one's choice of mates. Hyaenas certainly fulfill the first and second conditions, sometimes the third (e.g., Hill 1980a; Kruuk 1972; Mills 1984b; Sutcliffe 1970). Wolves and other large canids fulfill all of the first three conditions (e.g., Fentress and Ryon 1982; Mech 1970), and possibly the fourth if den helpers are taken into account (Moehlman 1989). Modern humans, as a species, clearly fulfill all five conditions (e.g., Binford 1978; Kaplan and Hill 1985; Metcalfe 1989; Metcalfe and Barlow 1992; Yellen 1977). Although modern humans' reasons for carrying food can range from venality to largess, the more banal motives for carrying food to residences or foraging hubs are not necessarily eclipsed by the fact that the food is sometimes shared (see also Speth 1990). It is fairly clear that any social predator may move food simply to maintain sole access to it and to process the food more thoroughly. Only some species also carry food to feed their young, and, among them, only humans may share transported food outside contexts directly linked to parenting. It is conceivable that each succeeding transport condition of the four or five listed above could represent an outgrowth of the former in an evolutionary lineage.

As for the contingencies of food transport behavior, predators' responses are products of both their neurological and anatomical makeup and the external constraints that influence the availability and quality of food. Because carnivores usually eat as much as they possibly can at a procurement site, the take-away options from ungulate carcasses are limited by prey body mass, the proximity of soft tissues to each major bone element, and how many other individuals are feeding alongside that predator (e.g., Mills 1989). Holding the number of consumers constant, a bigger carcass will yield a greater variety and quantity of leftovers (e.g., Blumenschine 1986; Haynes 1980).

Carnivores frequently must cope with feeding interference from conspecifics and other predatory species. Taking food to a place relatively free of envious fellows is a common solution. The intensity of theft and conflict generally increases as food dispersion in the environment decreases (e.g., Mills 1989; Tilson et al. 1980; Tilson and Hamilton 1984). If prey body parts are not soft enough to be ingested immediately, and hunger is still an issue, wolves and spotted hyaenas may try to move parts away from the primary feeding area (Haynes 1980; Henschel et al. 1979; Kruuk 1972; Mills and Mills 1977). In these circumstances, the body parts are almost certainly carried to dens or rest sites to reduce feeding competition. The parts most likely to be moved are those requiring extra processing effort, because they cannot, after all, be easily bolted. Brown hyaenas (Mills and Mills 1977; Mills 1984a) and striped hyaenas (Skinner et al. 1980) differ from spotted hyaenas in that they are more solitary and more actively provision their young with solid foods, but all hyaenas are known to transport prey body parts away from the places of encounter. The playful removal of leftovers from kills

by wolves (e.g., Binford 1981; Fentress and Ryon 1982) and spotted hyaenas (e.g., Henschel et al. 1979) is an individual feeding strategy that appears to be especially important among juveniles and is most prominent in species that do not normally provision dependents with *undigested* food (e.g., spotted hyaenas, Kruuk 1972; Mills 1984a). Smaller terrestrial scavengers engage in pilfering strategies similar to those of juvenile spotted hyaenas; the principle is much the same in that a subordinate competitor moves food to lower the risk of feeding interference. The ungulate anatomy is comprised of a meaty torso and bony extremities, and consumers that enjoy primary access generally begin eating the bulky center and work outward. The pieces left over and therefore most often available to be taken away are the head and the lower limbs (e.g., Blumenschine 1986:36; Haynes 1980:82–83).

While food monopolization is the proximate motivation in most transport episodes, some predatory species ultimately share some or all of the food they move. Provisioning dependents at dens or rendezvous sites is well documented in canids, particularly wolves and wild dogs (Ewer 1973; Fentress and Ryon 1982; Ballard et al. 1987). As is true of food monopolization, provisioning effectively reduces feeding interference at the primary feeding site, but the advantages are conferred to closely related individuals too young to compete in the normal fray of adults, or to travel with them. Provisioning may extend even farther across the social network in canids to include nursing mothers and/or subadult helpers. Provisioning introduces more stringent spatial constraints on food transport tactics than does transport for the purpose of monopolization, because dependents wait in a fixed location (maternity den, rest site, or hunter-gatherer base camp), and food procurement locations vary tremendously.

One of the most interesting lessons from the social canids is that, because food need not always be transformed into milk by the mother, other (nonlactating) individuals in the social group potentially can participate in raising young other than their own. Labor is partitioned in many canid societies, and not wholly according to gender. Most or all participation in infant care probably can be explained by degrees of genetic relatedness; broadening of the ways that related individuals may supplement juvenile survivorship simply evens out the work load and pools the risks in situations in which these strategies are advantageous. The more broadly defined the sharing network, the greater the array of potential ties that bind the social group. In the case of humans, provisioning clearly supports division of labor within the social group, differing from the social canids only by degree (Moehlman 1989).

It is interesting that the existence of provisioning behavior in a species does not distinguish social hunters (wolves and modern humans) from obligate scavengers (brown and striped hyaenas). However, the arrays of body parts normally carried away from procurement sites do differ between them. The richest foods given to dependents by social hunters, other than those transformed directly into milk, are soft tissues carried in the stomach of the provisioner, to be regurgitated at the den. Transport by mouth instead involves hard parts, often corresponding to lower food values per item; the takeaway choices *tend to be* somewhat richer for subordinates spiriting away items from a kill made by their group than for other species scavenging what is left. Provisioning among wolves, African wild dogs, and Asiatic dholes most often involves regurgitation by adults of high-quality soft tissues (Fentress and Ryon 1982; Bertram 1979; Fox 1984), whereas older juveniles often transport solid items for themselves. In contrast, provisioning of dependents by brown and striped hyaenas at maternity dens first involves nursing and later the transport of unprocessed hard parts (Mills 1984a; Skinner et al. 1980) scavenged from disparate sources. There is no regurgitation to speak of, and, where transported hard parts are concerned, the choices are narrower and the quantities of food smaller.

Incentives to monopolize food for oneself and one's offspring hinge primarily on the risk of thievery. Few predators go about their business without another in the tail-wind (e.g., Paquet 1992), and, hence, monopolization is no small concern in carnivore and hunter-gatherer subsistence systems. Equally important, carnivores and humans can greatly increase the nutritional yields of animal parts by taking them to safe places or processing facilities at a foraging hub, especially if that hub is not far away. The processing implements of carnivores are built into their anatomies, always staying with the consumer. Humans use tools, implements that can be heavy or awkward to gather in times of need but can be stowed at preordained places. Humans often find it more economical to move food to these facilities than to move the implements to the food. Moreover, other members of the human social group might already be situated at foraging or residential hubs, individuals whose work and/or child-care agendas more readily accommodate the processing tasks required (e.g., Blurton Jones et al. 1989; Hawkes 1987, 1991). Food transport also has implications for patterns of land use (also see Binford 1984:261), a point exemplified below for spotted hyaenas and humans in particular.

Lessons from the spotted hyaena

Spotted hyaenas display some intriguing parallels to hominids because, until late in the Last Glacial, their geographic ranges were more or less coterminus in Europe (Turner 1984). The bone-collecting habits of spotted hyaenas are especially helpful for building models of food transport by hominids because both species are social, both possess extensive bone-rendering capabilities (hyaenas with their dentitions and digestive systems, humans with their tools), and both may have routinely alternated between hunting and scavenging to obtain meat.

The arrays of skeletal parts found in spotted hyaena dens vary greatly across environments, as does the quantity of material transported per carcass source (documented in Chapter 9). Clearly, no single case can serve as a general model for the consequences of searching strategies and transport behaviors of spotted hyaenas; the variation testifies to the versatile responses of this animal in the many environments it inhabits. Variation in bone assemblages collected by spotted hyaenas is brought about by at least two inter-related factors. The first factor, noted above, is the intensity of feeding competition at kill or find sites, which, at its worst, greatly encourages subordinate individuals to run off with whatever they can grab. The second factor is food abundance, how it varies with season and more immediate conditions such as carcass size and the average distances between feeding opportunities and the den.

Hyaenas respond to these conditions by, among other things, altering their emphases on hunting and scavenging. It may be impossible to tease apart the influences of the two factors on prey body part representation in den faunas. From a broader perspective, however, the anatomical patterns of prey that turn up in dens reflect the ways that hyaenas *habitually* exploit a resource fabric and the absolute spatial and temporal limits on their abilities to do so.

Much variation in the foraging behaviors of modern spotted hyaenas is documented across the African continent. The hyaenas adjust their tactics to local exigencies of food supply, and their responses reveal the powerful influence of food distributions and quality. Greater resource dispersion generally results in less food carried to dens and a stronger bias toward peripheral body parts that accumulate there. In South Africa and Botswana, for example, modern hyaena dens can be relatively poor in bone; few items are transported per carcass source, and the assemblages often contain high proportions of horns and/or heads, along with other relatively non-nutritious items (Mills and Mills 1977; Tilson et al. 1980; Binford's 1981 field notes). Mills (1984b, 1989) and Tilson et al. (1980) also report a greater reliance on scavenged food by spotted hyaenas in southern Africa, especially in areas where interspecific conflict is relatively infrequent and/or these hyaenas form the top of the local predator hierarchy. Highly scattered foraging opportunities relative to the location of the den translate to pandemic scarcity. And dispersal of the food base and the hyaenas dependent upon it in turn results in relatively sparse bone accumulations in dens *per unit time* and a strong bias toward peripheral prey body parts collected there (see Chapter 9).

The dens of spotted hyaenas in modern East Africa (Potts 1982; Hill 1978, 1980b, 1983), and Pleistocene Europe (e.g., Stiner 1991a on Italy; Stuart 1982 on British Isles), are considerably richer in limb elements and the overall quantities of bones transported per carcass source. Modern ecological accounts suggest that higher ungulate biomass is the primary factor behind the richness of bone material in the East African dens. Spotted hyaenas rely more heavily on hunted food in the Ngorongoro and Serengeti ecosystems than they do in southern Africa (compare Kruuk 1972; Mills 1984b, 1989; Tilson et

al. 1980). Food is relatively more concentrated and reliably positioned in space in these East African ecosystems, at least during some seasons. The likelihood of feeding interference at procurement sites is also higher in these situations (e.g., Blumenschine 1986; Kruuk 1972; Schaller 1972) and encourages juveniles to carry off pieces of food. More bone material may be introduced into dens by hyaenas wherever food is concentrated and/or ungulate biomass is high.

One may surmise from these accounts that the total number of prey body parts moved from procurement sites to dens should decline as a function of increasing average distances between procurement spots and the den. In circumstances in which food is dispersed (and/or packages are uniformly small), the predator's biggest problem is locating the food; the consumer must cover a lot of ground in order to eat regularly (e.g., Tilson and Hamilton 1984). In circumstances in which food is concentrated into relatively large, dense patches, one of the predators' biggest problems is dealing with competitors (e.g., Frank 1986 on interspecific competition and dominance hierarchies at feeding sites). Animals living in the latter conditions will move more food to dens or rendezvous sites to alleviate the pressures of interference; this is feasible because dens can be located near the areas where procurement most often takes place.

Intragroup strife at kill or find sites is unlikely to have been as much of an issue for archaic *Homo sapiens* as it is for spotted hyaenas and other social carnivores. Spotted hyaenas' responses to resource conditions nonetheless are helpful for interpreting the spatial contexts of food procurement and the benefits of alternating between hunting and scavenging tactics on a seasonal or longer-term basis.

Humans, preeminent porters and processors

Modern humans are extraordinary for their ability to move large amounts of unprocessed food: they are bipedal and have hands, and, pound for pound, they can outcarry virtually any other large predator on a long haul. The enormous quantities of bone refuse in hominid cave sites attest to the early appearance of this ability in the evolutionary sequence. Certain other qualifications of humans' capacities are also in order here. In contrast to the ways of spotted hyaenas, wolves, wild dogs, and dholes, people may delay much of their food consumption until they have reached a foraging or residential hub (e.g., Binford 1978 on the Nunamiut Eskimo; O'Connell and Marshall 1989 on the Alyawara; Bunn et al. 1988, O'Connell et al. 1988a, 1988b, 1990 on the Hadza; Yellen 1977, 1990a, on the !Kung). The procurers are not above filling their own stomachs at the kill or find site (e.g., Binford 1978; O'Connell et al. 1989). If the food package is large, however, they are often ready, or soon can get help, to move vastly more food than any person could eat in one sitting. Nonhuman predators represent the opposite situation, generally transporting considerably less than what they can ingest at the procurement site, even among those species that provision their young.

Humans are skillful and efficient bone processors, probably more so than any other predator save the hyaena, and a substantial proportion of humans' time and technology may be devoted to these activities. With the aid of tools, people can thoroughly render the nutritional value of hard and soft animal tissues alike, and this fact alone can greatly amplify the incentives to move food to a hub. Marrow and other soft tissues contained within the bones of prey are potentially rich sources of fats and minerals. However, skeletal tissues, and trabeculae in particular, present the greatest demands on humans' extraction capabilities. People may prefer to move marrow-rich or structurally complex items to base camps, where rendering facilities (deep hearths, firewood, anvils and hammers, or containers) are stowed and personnel more conveniently mustered to retrieve the full nutritional benefits of carcass parts. Today, we see among many hunter-gatherers a phenomenon best called "carrying for the cooking pot," concomitant to the widespread introduction of metal cookwares. No such technology existed in Paleolithic systems to the best of our knowledge, and we can expect that transport decisions of the earlier cultures differed in the absence of these tools.

The fact that processing and transport capabilities are highly developed in *Homo sapiens* greatly complicates questions about food sharing. It is clear from ethnographic accounts that food transport can greatly improve the chances of keeping food away from other pilfering species and that nutritional returns of many prey body parts can be enhanced through labor-intensive processing techniques. Sharing is an interesting and significant element of human subsistence systems, but it is unclear what advantages sharing adds above and beyond those gained by monopolizing food and processing it intensively. From the four-legged perspective, taking prey body parts to dens, rendezvous spots, or base camps may not be driven as much by a desire to share as the possibility that the cost of food transport is outweighed by the anticipated benefits of effective processing (see also Metcalfe and Barlow 1992). From the evolutionary perspective, transport decisions presently have more reliable connections to the nature of food supply and technology than to social premeditations. These connections can be further qualified by considering the inherent nutritional contents of ungulate body parts.

The nutritional bases of transport decisions

Because humans are omnivorous, the nutritional worth of any food item is relative rather than absolute; its value hinges upon what else is available within a reasonably immediate time frame. The greater the level of omnivory in a species, the greater its options for rounding out deficiencies in one kind of food with complementary sources. Foragers must consume nutrients according to a biologically determined schedule and in set proportions. It is for these reasons that predators' responses to food *scarcity* describe important characteristics of their foraging niches.

Food scarcity in environments usually is cyclical. If the cycles are not prolonged, humans and other predators may try to out-wait scarcity by turning to alternative food sources on a short-term basis. If the scarcity is persistent, they also may reorganize their preferences within the resource choice hierarchy; predators that depend on large mammalian prey, for example, may adjust how they treat various body parts within the usual prey. To develop this point, I focus on hunter-gatherers' prey body part transport and consumption choices in the context of the availability of two key nutrients, protein and food energy (sensu Speth and Spielmann 1983). Arctic and tropical habitats are presented as more or less opposing ecological conditions, although the biogeography of the human species is more complicated in reality. Within this simplified framework, human responses appear to follow certain rules about what to eat— and what to avoid—in lean times, not unlike the carnivores.

Protein is a relatively rare nutrient in environments overall. Its scarcity is fairly continuous, whereas food energy sources (fats and carbohydrates) undergo profound cycles of scarcity and abundance. The availability of carbohydrates is especially problematic in environments in which the amplitude of the seasons is great, because plant production slows or ceases for significant periods each year and foragers must find other sources of energy. Animal fats represent seasonal energy sources in temperate and arctic environments; fats are concentrated and abundant in prey from early fall through part of the winter, and become increasingly rare from late winter to spring (e.g., DelGiudice et al. 1991 for Yellowstone wapiti; Cederlund et al. 1991 for moose in Sweden). In many xeric (arid) environments and in tropical forests, fat scarcity may be chronic rather than seasonal, and opportunities to obtain fats may be widely scattered in time and space. Ungulates in xeric and tropical biomes generally do not build up the extensive fat reserves that typify high-latitude species (Speth 1991). Yet animal fat, by nature's design, outlasts plant sources of food energy in any seasonal environment, because mammals store fat in the body in anticipation of nutritional and/or water stress.

Humans and other omnivorous predators tend to rely more heavily on animal sources of food energy when plant productivity ceases, but there is also a spatial element to the problem. Although bears may sleep when plants are dormant, their diet immediately following the emergence from hibernation dens is instructive, because they are desperate for food energy before it is widely available. Brown bears in Spain, for example, frequently turn to scavenging of winter-killed ungulates at this time. Little rerouting of their foraging movements may be required because carcasses and new plant shoots emerge together along the line of retreating snow in spring (Clevenger 1991; Clevenger and Purroy 1991). Scavengable carcasses are not necessarily concentrated in patches, but their availability is somewhat concentrated by season; carcasses accumulate over the course of winter, preserved in ice until the thaw.

Though primarily hunters of ungulates, wolves scavenge them too. In regions where cumulative winter snow cover is great, wolves may turn to scavenging most often at the beginning and close of the snow season. During five winters in the Canadian province of Alberta, Huggard (1993) observed that scavenging was most profitable for wolves when snow was present on the ground but the cover relatively thin (cf. Fuller 1991, Minnesota). Wolves were able to range widely in these circumstances because travel was not inhibited much by the snow. This was also true for their longer-legged prey, and hence the rates of encounter of shallowly buried carcasses increased. Freezing halts decomposition, so the numbers of carcasses in existence at any time build up when the weather is cold. The availability of temporarily abundant carcasses hinges, however, on wolves being able to locate them and get at them without working too hard. Thin snow cover may be an optimal condition for scavenging in colder biomes, regardless of whether thin snow forms an even coating on the land or merely a line of retreat during the spring thaw.

It is clear in the case of humans that the distribution of fat-rich resources in time and space exerts a strong influence on their transport and processing decisions (e.g., Binford 1978; Speth and Spielmann 1983; Yellen 1977, 1991a). Animal fats are, in the absence of carbohydrates, required to obtain caloric energy and to physiologically assimilate proteins (e.g., Speth and Spielmann 1983). Animal fats are also important for neurological (prenatal and postnatal) development in children. Because fats are limiting nutrients for humans, subcutaneous and marrow fat reserves in prey are excellent parameters for studies of human subsistence tactics. The status of fat reserves in adult ungulates may explain, for example, variation in the transport and use of limb elements by humans. In seasons when food is plentiful, the richest and most easily rendered fats of mammalian prey are to be found in the layers just below the skin and the marrow encased in the limb shafts. Both are the focus of predators' feeding patterns in times of plenty; peripheral body parts generally become more important when food is scarce. Humans and a host of other predators are, in reality, preoccupied with head and axial parts of prey in many foraging contexts (e.g., Binford 1978; O'Connell et al. 1988a, 1990; Yellen 1977).

Humans' decisions about which animal parts to carry to residential sites range from whole bodies to some fraction thereof. For prey taxa that naturally store fat in quantity, humans' transport decisions are thought to follow a hierarchical formula that balances carcass size and the processing and transport costs of each part relative to net food gain (e.g., Binford 1978; Bunn et al. 1988; Metcalfe 1989; Metcalfe and Barlow 1992; O'Connell and Marshall 1989; O'Connell et al. 1988a, 1988b, 1990; Speth 1987). Several researchers have developed or refined indexes of carcass part values in order to understand human subsistence decisions and, in some cases, to interpret the function of archaeological sites. These studies generally focus on marrow fat and muscle mass as encompassing measures of carcass value, which in turn have become central to published prey body part choice models (Binford 1978, 1981; Lyman 1985; Lyman et al. 1992; Jones and Metcalfe 1988; Metcalfe and Jones 1988; Speth 1987, 1989).

Limb marrow indexes can be somewhat misleading if they are the only basis for estimating total carcass value. The first clue that something is missing from models strictly based on marrow indexes is a fundamental division that often arises in foragers' rankings of body parts in real-life situations (e.g., Binford 1978; O'Connell et al. 1988a, 1988b, 1989). Skeletal elements located within or near the torso are associated with high proportions of soft tissue to bone mass, although people sometimes cut the soft tissues away at the procurement site. Upper limb bones, to which large muscle masses are attached, may also contain fat-rich marrow and be moved along with the meat or stripped on site. In contrast, bone elements most peripheral to the torso—head and lower limbs—are associated with lower proportions of soft tissue, but may contain significant quantities of fat. A basic division line frequently emerges in transport trajectories between the torso proper and all other parts, primarily head and lower limb elements. The division seems to reflect differences of fat content in relation to mass

in each region of the body. Not only do head parts fall in the same general class as marrow-rich lower limb bones; head parts may also be ranked higher by foragers in many situations.

Speth (1987) presents one of the more explicit hierarchical models of part transport behavior by hominids (but also see Binford 1984; Potts 1984b, 1988). The model assumes that fat was a limiting resource and that reserves of mobilizable fat in ungulate prey fluctuate with season; both assumptions are well supported by the wildlife literature. Speth reasons that human foragers should favor bulky parts in periods of food abundance but avoid lean meat during periods of carbohydrate/fat scarcity, because the costs of digesting and assimilating these foods are too high in the latter situation (see also Speth and Spielmann 1983). In seasonal environments, human foragers should therefore be relatively more selective about which animal parts they consume during spring, or during the dry season in tropical environments. Because fat depletion in mammals generally begins with torso reserves and only later depletes those in more peripheral areas of the body, Speth predicts the following human responses under stressful conditions:

> body parts that are least susceptible to fat depletion are systematically selected while other parts are abandoned at the kill. Fat mobilization in ungulates proceeds in a relatively fixed sequence, beginning with the back fat, then proceeding to the deposits in the body cavity, and culminating with the marrow fat. . . . Thus, the particular body parts that are selected should change in a systematic manner over the course of the period of stress, with greatest selectivity being exercised in late spring or even early summer (late dry season or early rainy season).
>
> Marrow fat in the lower limbs (and possibly also the mandible) is the last deposit to be depleted, and in a severely stressed animal may be the only remaining portion of the carcass retaining sufficient fat to be worth eating. (Speth 1987:20)

The general logic of Speth's model is basic to this study of Italian cave faunas, but, in the form outlined above, does not effectively account for the unique value of head parts (but see Speth 1989:337; also Lyman 1992) and hence requires some modifications. Permanent, or *structural*, fat cells of the head and spinal cord represent a relatively continuous and high fat value in both healthy and starved prey, because the fat is a permanent feature of the myelinated nerve tissues. My concern with this problem began with anomalies I encountered in skeletal part representation in the Italian Mousterian faunas. The skeletal patterns will not be documented until the next chapter; suffice it to say, there is an extraordinary bias toward head parts in the cultural layers in some of the caves. The bias cannot be explained by differential preservation or archaeologists' recovery practices (see Chapter 5). It was only upon review of the physiological data on mammals that the universal relevance of structural (as opposed to metabolizable) fats to body part choice models became apparent. The archaeological cases, as well as den assemblages collected by certain modern carnivores, suggest that the distribution of fat tissues in the ungulate anatomy is more complex than marrow fat indexes predict. A closer look at the nature and physiological distributions of fat-bearing tissues in the prey anatomy reveals why this should be so.

The two types of fat tissues, here termed *metabolizable* and *structural* fats, exist in the mammalian system, and they have distinct physiologic properties. Metabolizable fat is unstable in the living animal, because it is built up and later drawn off by the metabolism in accordance with food availability. The quantities of metabolizable fats in prey vary with season, age, and species. Cervids, suids, and some bovids appear to be especially adapted to store fat in the body when food is abundant. The potential for storing fat is always greatest in adults of any population because the process of growth and development is completed. When abundant in the body, metabolizable fat reserves are concentrated just below the skin and within the medulla of the long bones and mandible and, in these states, are easiest to render from the consumer's point of view. The most important contrast between metabolizable and structural fats is that structural fat is stable; once built into the body's system, it never goes away during the lifetime of the animal. The contrast between metabolizable and structural fats is manifest in human foraging decisions.

Three characteristics of head parts and, to a lesser extent, axial tissues make them unique sources of

food to predators and, hence, contribute to the definition of structural fat here. First, neurological tissues are permanent cellular structures that retain maintenance priority in the body, even in the face of starvation. Structural fats are more constantly available to foragers because, with the exception of the mandibular marrow cavity, the food value of the cranial and upper neck region is most similar in healthy and starved prey. Starved carcasses may offer less total usable food to scavengers or hunters once the metabolizable reserves are gone, but the head and spine will retain most of their value as food sources, provided the predator is able to process them. The second unique characteristic of head parts is that myelinated nerve fibers are concentrated in the brain, the fine sensory tracts of the facial organs (tongue, nose, and lips), and the spinal cord. Myelinated nerve fibers (white matter) are proteinaceous cells sheathed in fat, whereas non-myelinated nerve fibers (gray matter) are not (Kimber et al. 1961). Modern humans living under conditions of chronic fat scarcity (e.g., in the tropical and subtropical latitudes) may take considerable pains to transport and process head and spinal elements, as shown by O'Connell et al.'s (1988a, 1990) study of the Hadza and Yellen's (1977; 1991a:18–20) of the !Kung. These modern groups possess metal cooking pots, making the boiling of trabeculae—one of the few effective ways to process the bones of the spine—feasible. Because fat storage is less pronounced in tropical ungulates overall, human foragers living in these environments are more consistent about rendering structural fats, in addition to whatever metabolizable fats are available from the prey carcass. The final characteristic that makes head parts unique concerns their processing requirements. Head and spinal elements require greater processing effort than most other body parts as a rule (e.g., Yellen 1977; see also Speth 1991), so that their attractiveness to foragers varies with the abundance of alternative sources. However, of heads and spinal bones, heads and ventral neck tissues are significantly easier to detach from the carcass and render for their food content in the absence of sturdy fireproof containers and/or groundstone tools. The physical arrangements of soft and hard tissues around the vertebral column are complex and require more labor and technological support to prepare for human consumption.

The unique food value of head organs to predators can be demonstrated by comparing head to other soft body tissues in domesticated adult cattle, using the ratio of total fat to total protein. Domesticated cattle here serve as the paradigm, because complete nutritional data are available for this taxon. The fat depletion sequence for postcranial soft tissues generally corresponds to marrow fat loss, although the schedules of depletion vary somewhat (Speth 1990:152). Domesticated cattle are selectively bred to produce more fat—wild prey tend to be leaner as a rule—but the basic relationships among the different classes of tissues are analogous in other species for reasons of basic organ function. The cattle example effectively approximates the relationship between (a) the potential buildup and loss differential for metabolizable fats in postcranial tissues in ungulates and (b) stable fats in the head and adjacent tissues in all mammals.

Table 8.1 illustrates the opposing nutritional states—fat and starved—by comparing the fat/protein ratio in cattle muscle cuts trimmed to .5 inch of existing fat (rich) as opposed to those completely trimmed (lean) of all visible fat (U.S.D.A. 1986; N.L.S.M.B. 1988). The fat/protein values in postcranial muscle mass range from a high of 134 percent to a low of 30 percent. To keep things in perspective, estimated levels in captive white-tailed deer (DelGiudice et al. 1990) in well-fed and undernourished states change from 63 to 10 percent respectively (see also DelGiudice et al. 1991 on elk). The fat/protein values for three kinds of soft head and upper neck tissues in cattle (brain, thymus, and tongue) occur on the high side of the differential for muscle fat. Of the torso organs, only the pancreas displays fat levels equivalent to head organs, but this level would be maintained only in the well-fed state. Not all fat is equal, however. The second column of Table 8.1 reveals that the brains of cattle (and large mammals in general) are extraordinarily rich in cholesterol, approximately 18 times higher within the fat fraction than for any other soft tissue of the body. Although some amount is needed, it is

TABLE 8.1

Fat and protein content of soft cranial and postcranial tissues
of adult domesticated cattle per 100 g unit

Soft tissue type	Nutrient Ratios	
	Total fat:protein	*Cholesterol:total fat*
head and upper neck organs:		
brain	.95	.18
thymus	1.67	.01
tongue	1.08	.005
muscle cuts, with and without fat:[a]		
lean plus fat	1.34	.003
lean	.30	.009
torso organs:		
liver	.19	.09
pancreas	1.18	—
spleen	.16	.09

Sources: United States Department of Agriculture (1986); National Live Stock and Meat Board (1988).

[a] Composite data on standard retail meat cuts are for muscle mass and associated metabolizable fat tissues (such as round, chuck, ribs, and brisket) and do not include head or torso organ meats. "Lean" denotes muscle tissue from which all separable fat has been cut away. "Lean plus fat" denotes muscle cuts retaining 0.5 in of visible fat layer.

difficult to find reliable estimates of humans' need for cholesterol in traditional diets, much less in what chemical form, partly because of the programmatic downplay of this nutrient in sedentary, high-stress lifestyles of industrial societies.

A handful of studies of modern hunter-gatherers provide thorough accounts of carcass part transport from procurement to residential (or foraging hub) sites, and the above observations about head parts are supported in the context of large game use. Hunter-gatherers living in warm, even xeric, environments often carry all parts of large prey to residential sites for processing and consumption, including the vertebral column, even if the soft tissues have already been removed (e.g., O'Connell and Marshall 1989 on the Alyawara; Bunn et al. 1988, O'Connell et al. 1988a, 1988b on the Hadza; Yellen 1977, 1991a on the !Kung). The practice also occurs in agrarian and/or herding economies such as among the Navajo (Binford and Bertram 1977). People eat absolutely everything they can from each carcass in these circumstances.

Nunamiut Eskimo of the Arctic Circle and Great Plains hunter-gatherers of the historic period contrast with human situations in warm ecosystems in that Eskimo and Plains hunters' transport and processing decisions seem to vary more *across sites*. Binford (1978:87–90) reports that Nunamiut strategies for utilizing caribou (and wild sheep) carcasses are quite variable and may be staged across places; bone discard patterns differ accordingly. Procurement sometimes involves mass harvesting and storage, with many parts discarded at kill-butchering sites, especially if the hunters are killing animals to meet anticipated consumption needs for many months to come. The best (richest) body parts usually receive preferred treatment under these conditions, whereas peripheral (less valuable without intensive processing) elements, such as heads, antlers, lower limb, axial, and neck parts, may be abandoned or ignored, depending on the season of procurement (Binford 1978:60–61, 77). Even the kill of a single animal can result in abandonment of the head if it occurs during the "fat" time of year (i.e., fall and early winter). Likewise, the caribou body parts that the Nunamiut Eskimo choose to eat vary conspicuously with season (Binford 1978:77–84). In the fall and winter, Nunamiut concentrate on the richest fat stores of the metabolizable type, along with muscle tissues. By spring, the marrow reserves in living caribou are seriously depleted, and foragers' attentions shift to include head parts, a second-class food item only a few months before. Heads of juveniles and adult females are preferred in these circumstances, and the tongue is considered especially desirable. Nunamiut people may ignore the marrow cavity of the mandible in spring, yet show great interest in the soft tissues of the nose and brain (Binford 1978:149–151).

Nunamiut food preferences during lean periods, when fat is scarce, better resemble tropical foragers' body part selection habits overall than do Nunamiut preferences during the bountiful months of the arctic year. The Nunamiut usually turn to head parts when fat becomes rare, whereas tropical peoples are more consistent consumers of cranial (and axial) parts as a rule. These contrasts represent very different tactical responses to food distributions and depend to a large extent on prey adaptations to cold and food stress. At the extreme limits of fat depletion in times of food scarcity, humans' part preferences appear to converge on a single theme, not unlike that of the carnivores. Species that often scavenge, for example, usually carry head parts away from carcasses because heads are among the most common leftovers, but the predators may also favor these parts because of their stable food value, moving them because the food value takes time to extract.

EXPECTATIONS FOR TRANSPORTED ARCHAEOFAUNAS

Some generalizations and analytical conditions may be offered regarding the relationships between anatomical profiles in shelter faunas and the processes responsible for them. A large scale of comparison is implied in the discussion to follow, consistent with the nature of most Pleistocene faunal records. Moreover, it must be understood that only some patterns of body part representation in shelters are relevant to the foraging habits of predators. Other patterns are best explained by the fragility of spongy bone tissues in mammalian skeletons, which tend to decompose faster than cortical bones and teeth (e.g., Lyman 1984a, 1985). Surprisingly similar patterns of bone loss may arise from carnivores feeding on them (e.g., Binford and Bertram 1977; Blumenschine 1986) and from archaeological recovery practices once oriented toward taxonomic questions rather than economic ones. An assemblage full of mammal tooth fragments but poor in bone, for example, probably is not dominated by head parts because ancient foragers chose only to transport heads of prey to the site; the pattern is most likely a product of unfavorable preservation conditions. Alternatively, some well-preserved faunas, wherein fragile bone materials are intact, may be biased because foragers made them that way. Only by controlling for in situ attrition, differences in prey body size, and carnivore ravaging is it possible to learn about predators' foraging tactics from archaeofaunas. Having stipulated this, the potential impact of foraging conditions on body part transport decisions can be discussed in terms of spatial issues, prey anatomy, and predators' body part transport choices as a function of nutritional yield and processing techniques.

Spatial issues

Four spatial issues emerge from the above discussion of food transport: transport pathways, bone accumulations representing multiple forays (palimpsests), distance decay phenomena, and the role of caves in humans' use of a landscape. The first issue concerns the degree to which transport pathways or trajectories are linear. The history of archaeology is such that our earliest perceptions of transport behavior in humans centered on stone tools and raw material. The pathways of bone transport often differ from those for items of technology, the latter of which can be quite convoluted. The transport of food tends to be unidirectional, probably because the use-life of food is relatively short. Food transport trajectories begin where food is obtained and end, almost invariably, at safe places, residential sites, or foraging hubs. Some contradictions to the generalization of linearity may exist in

societies in which tribute is paid or expensive rituals practiced, but most of these conditions do not apply to hunter-gatherer situations. Though unidirectional, food transport pathways may be complex if food is cached or stored, or if food undergoes staged preparation. Pathways involving game nonetheless permit the use of relatively simple spatial models wherein the quantities of food moved decline as transport distances increase. The individual histories of stone implements and cores may be nonlinear and more complex by contrast, because stone and wood are not nearly as perishable as foodstuffs, and the utility of tools and raw materials in hand declines through use or when better sources of raw material are encountered.

The second spatial issue, palimpsest effects in long-term accumulations, here concerns the practice of pooling foods at hub sites and the faunal signatures that this behavior may create in archaeofaunas. We can be certain that humans' choices of which prey body parts to transport away from procurement sites vary across foraging episodes. The extent to which small-scale (e.g., daily) variation in human foraging returns is reflected in faunal accumulations depends on whether the final destinations also vary according to the decisions that foragers make, or, alternatively, if everything is brought to the same place. One day or foraging bout in the life of any hominid is not very interesting from an evolutionary perspective; as with focusing upon a dot in a pointilist painting, a lone event says little about its importance or context within the foraging adaptation as a whole. This is just as well, because most archaeofaunas—especially the large assemblages that we find comfortable to work with from a statistical point of view—cannot represent daily vignettes of human life. In archaeological records in which palimpsests are commonplace, we may only theoretically distinguish between places where the products of diverse treatments of a particular kind of prey are pooled and places where the products of uniform treatment accumulate.

Transport sequences by modern hunter-gatherers range from being internally diverse and highly conditional for a particular kind of game animal (e.g., Binford 1978:87–90 on the Nunamiut Eskimo; O'Connell et al. 1988a, 1990 on the Hadza) to those that are the same time after time (e.g., O'Connell and Marshall 1989, Binford 1978:87–90 on the Al-yawara of Australia; Yellen 1977, 1991a on the !Kung). Binford relates the level of diversity in transport strategies for large prey to whether human groups are responding to anticipated long-term needs or just meeting immediate consumption requirements. And the strategies involved do seem to result in gross differences in anatomical patterns, apparently in accordance with special-purpose and multipurpose sites. The transport decisions among the Hadza of tropical arid East Africa also vary and are not explained by season (O'Connell et al. 1990), but it is significant for this discussion that the products of variation observed in humans' decisions are subsequently blended in the refuse dumps of hub sites. The degree of variation in anatomical content *across sites* within a region can be interesting for comparisons of land use by culture in analogous ecosystems, even if the full implications of the variation in the respective cultures are not perfectly clear.

The third spatial issue is the cost of moving food units as a function of distance, not simply from find spot to home base, but the average distances separating the food packages taken in a longer time frame. Predators may respond to food dispersion by increasing their emphasis on scavenging, apparently because the search tactics appropriate for finding food packages in conditions of high dispersal make scavenging increasingly economical. As different as they are, however, food dispersion and prey body size exert roughly similar effects on the quantities of food transported by foragers: fewer body *parts* may be moved as either factor increases. Clearly, any attempt to learn about the effects of one factor requires controlling the potential effects of the other, of which prey body size is far more tractable. The simple predictions of a distance decay model may also be undermined somewhat in den situations, because more bones of smaller taxa may be ingested subsequent to their arrival in a shelter, thereby distorting the appearance of the transported assemblage. For all of these reasons, prey body size must be held constant in anatomical comparisons to limit the potential confusion caused by carnivore ravaging, and so that food dispersion effects may be considered.

The fourth spatial issue concerns the functional implications of shelters as opposed to other places on a landscape, specifically with regard to food transport trajectories. Can kill sites and residential sites be distinguished, for example, on the basis of anatomical content or do the geophysical characteristics of the places where they occur tell us more about site function? Because food procurement generally takes place in the open, we can assume (barring geological trap situations) that human-associated faunas in natural shelters represent food that was carried in by foragers, even if we do not know the portage distances involved.

Ethnoarchaeological studies suggest that assemblages dominated by peripheral skeletal parts reflect very different things if found in the open as opposed to inside shelters. In the case of the Nunamiut, Binford (1978:60–62) notes three intergrading types of anatomical patterns in caribou assemblages that may form at kill-butchering sites, places that we normally call "special use" sites. One type of anatomical pattern at kill-butchering sites is the product of truncated transport operations due to, for example, unexpected changes in the weather. The other two types of anatomical patterns at kill-butchering sites are more standard products of traditional Eskimo economies, containing only heads or antlers, or some combination of heads, antlers, axial, and lower limb elements. All of these assemblages are dominated by low-utility parts, discarded at the procurement locality—out in the open on an arctic landscape—*not* chosen for transport to and processing at another location.

Some archaeologists have tried to use the predominance of low-utility elements in an assemblage to identify hunting camps in Paleolithic records and to explain them in terms of Binford's (1980, 1982) "collector" model of hunter-gatherer mobility (e.g., Bietti 1986; Donahue 1988). The Eskimo-based model was developed for open sites, however, and many of the places in which Paleolithic faunal assemblages occur are not (Bietti and Stiner 1992). Similar patterns of anatomical representation in open and shelter sites have vastly different implications about the human activities that brought them into being. Apart from vertical trap situations, one of the most useful parameters supplied by cave sites is that we may assume that the food was obtained elsewhere. In regions of the world where caves are plentiful, it is at least conceivable that a shelter was situated so near to the location of game procurement that people simply moved the butchering operation inside. While some shelters might well have been adjacent to locations of procurement, we may assume that this is a rare situation.

Archaeologists always must come to terms with the fragment of ancient landscapes their study sample represents. There is no need to assert, however, that open sites are inherently superior to cave sites for the information they offer, nor the opposite. Any kind of window on the past possesses both biases and strengths. The strength of cave sites is that they nearly always represent the receiving ends of transport trajectories; their contents have been filtered through the contingencies of human economic and social decisions.

Heads versus limbs: Prey condition and body size

When it comes to foragers' choices of body parts to transport, the most consistent division of the ungulate skeletal anatomy is between the torso and all other regions. Anatomists likewise may speak of axial and appendicular zones of the body, wherein the skull might as well be considered the terminal cervical vertebra. The position of the head is the only major contradiction between the two classification systems; the head is normally grouped with the axial (torso) skeleton from an anatomical point of view, but is remote to the torso from economic and taphonomic perspectives.

This research on body part representation will emphasize the appendicular skeleton and the head only, because most of the confusion that normally arises in anatomical analyses centers on the pelvis, vertebrae, and ribs. More can happen over time to trabecular and delicate flat-bone tissues, the main bony structures of the spine and rib cage, because they are less resistant to virtually every destructive agency, less easily identified to species, and less likely to have been conserved by excavators working in earlier decades. Variation in the frequencies of vertebrae and ribs should be interesting in principle, but because it is so difficult to get a reliable grasp on these data, it often is necessary to work around them. Certainly, this is true for the Italian cave faunas from west-central Italy, where the qual-

ity of bone preservation is relatively good, but recovery biases make observations on axial representation other than the head region unreliable. Many of the Italian collections also lack limb shaft fragments, a problem that can inhibit accurate limb counts, but, as I will show later, is controllable.

Although both head and limb bones are peripheral to the torso and possess comparatively high preservation potentials, the relative proportions of heads to upper and lower limb parts in the Italian cave faunas vary greatly. Comparisons of modern predators indicate that this contrast could be a product of the foraging tactics used, especially hunting and scavenging; the anatomical patterns do not distinguish predator agencies from one another, because nearly all predators hunt and scavenge to some extent. These facts are established in Chapter 9, but it is useful to note in advance that head parts are the most common elements in all of the cave assemblages even though head counts are based exclusively on bone material, not teeth. The frequencies of limb bones, in contrast, vary between being in anatomical balance with head counts to nearly absent. Consequently, the assemblages differ from one another in the total number of skeletal elements per individual carcass source, that is, the average amount of food transported per foray. Because these patterns cannot be explained by differential preservation or archaeologists' recovery methods, investigations of prehistoric behavior may proceed.

Food dispersion in an environment may contribute to a predator's inclination to scavenge, but the biochemical process of decay and the predominant causes of death (see Chapters 10 and 11) play especially important roles in predetermining the character of scavenging opportunities and what scavengers carry home. So strong are these effects that the prey body part profiles generated by terrestrial scavengers oftentimes converge on a single transport pattern. Predators that normally kill their own food enjoy the choicest transport opportunities on the average, if for no other reason than the high rate of primary access to whole, fresh carcasses. Scavengers that seldom kill for food have fewer transport choices on the average, both in the quantity of food and the types of parts available to them; they may get lucky, but not often. A heavy reliance on food obtained by nonconfrontational scavenging, as opposed to aggressive displacement of hunter-consumers, should therefore result in fewer parts per carcass carried to shelter sites and a bias toward the dregs most commonly available at find sites: head parts and/or lower limbs. Because both microbes and carnivores tend to ravage carcasses from the center of the body outward, peripheral parts have a higher probability of remaining intact for a longer time than parts closer to or within the torso. These predictions describe the average condition, of course, and some deviations from the main expectations are normal.

Prey body size and prey species may also affect the transport contingencies faced by humans and other bone-collecting predators. As explained above, it is imperative to hold prey body size constant in analyses of anatomical profiles. The larger or more complete the carcass, the wider the array of body parts to choose from, regardless of the procurement tactic. There also is some evidence that modern humans will do more field processing for larger prey (e.g., O'Connell et al. 1989, 1990). As for the cumulative record of transport decisions in relation to prey body size, we can expect predators' strategies to be most finely tuned to the prey species and body sizes that are common in the environment (Chapter 7). Ungulate taxa in the medium body size range fulfill this role in many parts of the world. Medium-sized ungulate remains also dominate virtually every archaeological and modern assemblage used for this study and display the greatest variation in body part representation in shelters. Medium-sized ungulates therefore are bound to be the most interesting prey size class from a coevolutionary perspective.

Part choice in response to fat depletion

Because human beings have considerable need for fats, many of the soft tissues of the prey cranium are always good food. Equally important, fatty tissues of the cranium are partly or wholly encased in bone, as is true of limb marrow. The contents of head parts may take time to prepare for eating, but, from a technical perspective, are relatively easy to extract without the benefit of grinding tools or crockery, in contrast to the situation for processing fat-rich trabeculae of the spine (e.g., Binford

1978:150–151; Yellen 1977:291–292; 1991a; Speth 1989, 1991). Head parts should therefore be valued by foragers if prey animals are in poor physical condition at the time of death, or in any situation in which fat is seasonally or chronically scarce. Moreover, because heads are resistant parts and require considerable processing time, there is much incentive to move them to protected locations, providing that people intend to eat them at all. The spinal region of prey carcasses also potentially presents a stable food source but poses different challenges to processors, depending very much upon the context of procurement and the technology available. Heads are relatively easy to separate from an ungulate carcass under all circumstances, whereas the cost of pulling and processing the axial column may or may not be. The spinal region is often fully exposed during the butchering of fresh carcasses and can easily be carried away by hunters if needed. In situations of scavenging of whole carcasses (e.g., winter-killed), however, the spine is embedded in tissues that themselves may not be worth eating; the cost of extracting the spinal column may be too high in the face of diminished returns and/or in the absence of appropriate technology.

In formulating a hierarchical model of prey body part transport choices by prehistoric foragers in response to the availability of energy-rich foods, we may assume that stressed prey do not offer as much food value as healthy animals but that the remaining value never declines to zero. Because the ratio of fat to protein in the cranium, upper neck, and spinal cord is relatively constant, irrespective of an animal's nutritional state, these anatomical regions offer balanced food even when other anatomical parts do not. Here, balanced food means that the extant proportions of fat and protein are in keeping with humans' metabolic ability to assimilate them. The food packages represented by the head and spine are comparatively small, however. Accepting the argument that hominids should be choosier about parts to consume (and transport) when fat is in short supply, hominids lacking elaborate processing tools should selectively focus on the head and lower limbs when fat is fairly scarce, and perhaps only on heads when fat is profoundly scarce. If grinding and/or intensive boiling technologies are present in the cultural system (e.g., Yellen 1977:291–294), we can expect people to be interested in the trabeculae of the spinal column as well, but significantly less so during most of the Paleolithic.

To summarize, patterns of bone transport by predators potentially reflect the environmental contexts of food acquisition, procurement tactics, and land use strategies. The appropriateness of anatomical data for addressing these questions about prehistoric human behavior depends, however, on whether postdepositional sources of anatomical bias can be brought under control and on recognizing the fundamental contextual differences embodied by caves and open sites. The contingencies of transport are complex and oftentimes inseparable in real-life situations. Body part analyses usually only succeed in narrowing the range of possible explanations, and behavioral interpretations of these data require cross-referencing with other information such as mortality patterns and seasonality. While the potential of anatomical patterns for behavioral studies is quite good, their implications are about strategies common to many predator species. Body part data should not be used in attempts to distinguish between predatory agencies responsible for fossil faunas; this is the job of taphonomy.

By making comparisons at the interspecific level, anatomical biases in shelter faunas may describe the main tactics of predators, important dimensions of their foraging niches. Though not the only scale at which comparisons of transport behaviors might be interesting, interspecific and intersite levels of comparison best reflect the *habitual behaviors* of hominids and coexisting predators, including the economic contexts of hunting and scavenging.

Predators' responses to resource distributions in modern contexts can provide a valuable framework for investigating the adaptations of extinct variants of *Homo sapiens* and more archaic hominid forms. Because hominids, wolves, and spotted hyaenas shared a strong interest in ungulates and shelters in Upper Pleistocene Italy, the prey bones that they carried to caves represent a common ground for comparing the foraging habits and resource niches of these sympatric predators. While the physiological and behavioral adaptations of large predators vary greatly, they face similar ecological problems wherever they depend on the same food supplies (e.g., Foley 1984a; Turner 1984). The ways that predators cope with spatial and temporal fluctuations in food availability and quality are clues to how their behavioral adaptations are organized. And, in going about their business, predators must work around one another to some extent. Not even dominance in a local predator hierarchy excuses a species from this basic concern, because dominance has never put an end to thievery. Moreover, a predator responds to how another most often behaves, because this aspect of another's disposition is predictable. The average condition is therefore a viable currency for studies of predator coevolution.

The most basic tactical elements of adaptations probably do not set species apart from one another, but the ways that tactics are habitually combined certainly can. These issues are investigated in the next chapter through comparisons of anatomical representation in Upper Pleistocene and modern shelter faunas collected by hominids, hyaenas, and wolves.

9

Bone Transport, Foraging Strategies, and Predator Niches

THIS CHAPTER investigates ungulate procurement strategies and skeletal part transport habits of a variety of social predators in order to test the hypothesis that Middle and late Upper Paleolithic hominids in Italy were ecologically similar (Stiner 1991b, 1993a). The analysis focuses on the anatomical composition of faunal assemblages in shelters and assumes that these places represent the final destinations of transport trajectories. Cross-species comparisons of modern predators document strong links between skeletal representation in transported faunas and the modes of procurement, principally hunting versus scavenging. Differences in transport choices associated with each class of foraging strategy stem from the combined influences of differential persistence of skeletal parts at procurement sites, fat-protein contents of certain prey body parts (particularly the cranium), and the spatial and seasonal characteristics of food supply. The scales at which the strategies are combined in time and space distinguish predator adaptations to a large extent. The fossil cave faunas from Italy are then compared in this framework, revealing significant niche separation between Mousterian hominids and later Upper Paleolithic peoples in the study area.

ANALYTICAL APPROACH

Food transport decisions are, in some sense, expressions of how foragers balance constraints imposed by food supply with methods of acquisition, social relationships, and the number of consumers present at procurement or residential sites. Humans and other social predators are great movers of food and stashers of young, often carrying food to gain a feeding and/or reproductive advantage (Chapter 8). The ecological rules of food transport in modern humans and other social mammals are poorly understood, however, making inferences about transport behavior in earlier hominids all the more difficult. Many paleoanthropologists now suspect that the social and economic adaptations of premodern *Homo* differed significantly from those of anatomically modern humans. Investigating possible differences from the perspective of food transport habits requires a comparative scope extending beyond the human species alone, one that effectively provides independent measures or standards for assessing ecological distance and adaptive change between noncontemporaneous hominid populations.

Ecological information on modern carnivores suggests that the distribution of food in space—seasonally regulated or otherwise—is a strong conditioner of the quantities of food transported per carcass source and the payoffs of one kind of search strategy versus another. Food transport decisions no doubt are tempered by the distance between a food source and shelter, but they also reflect the general

A version of this chapter first appeared in the 1991 article entitled "Food Procurement and Transport by Human and Non-human Predators," the *Journal of Archaeological Science* 18.

degree of uncertainty in locating food patches, ultimately affecting search requirements for getting food. That most large terrestrial predators both hunt and scavenge is a given fact, but these tactics can be combined in a multitude of ways. It is the patterns of tactical combination used to cope with spatial and temporal characteristics of food supplies that describe an important dimension of foraging niche in predatory species.

My approach to investigating the food transport habits of Mousterian hominids was prompted by some rather extraordinary patterns of skeletal variation that I encountered in my studies of the Latium cave faunas. Some aspects of this Middle Paleolithic record are anomalous when compared to what we see in Upper Paleolithic and later human sites in the same region. Other aspects of the Middle Paleolithic record are easily recognized as the products of hunting. My knowledge of Upper Paleolithic shelter faunas from Italy and elsewhere in Europe simply did not prepare me for the full extent of variation evidenced in the Mousterian cases.

Here, I investigate the relationship between Mousterian hominids' strategies for obtaining ungulate prey and the skeletal parts that they carried to shelters. Rather than working from the standpoint of what rendered humans unique relative to other mammals, I frame the problem in terms of some basic rules affecting all large terrestrial predators. Only some predators *deliberately* collect bones in shelters, however—a criterion that includes humans, canids, and hyaenids, but generally excludes the cats (even leopards). The comparisons consider faunal remains from Upper Pleistocene caves and modern dens of southern Europe, Africa, and North America. Exclusive focus on assemblages from natural shelters, combined with taphonomic data, for the Upper Pleistocene cases (Chapter 5) ensures that the faunas represent transported food and can be assigned to one type of predator. It will be apparent that anatomical patterns in shelter faunas cannot distinguish one variety of predator from all others. Instead, the patterns reflect the predominant foraging strategy employed, apparently in response to the quality and abundance of food during the time that a shelter was used. Anatomical representation in shelter faunas is examined using two kinds of information: (1) the total quantity of anatomical parts per carcass source; and (2) biases in the skeletal composition. Interpretations about procurement strategies are aided by reference to modern carnivore control cases of known authorship and ecological context.

THE MNE VARIABLE: NUMBERS OF SKELETAL ELEMENTS

The analysis of anatomical part transport uses minimum number of skeletal element counts (*bone MNE*) based on bone material, not teeth. Animal bones in archaeological assemblages usually have been smashed to bits for reasons beginning more or less with the processing habits of people, followed by any of a wide array of other destructive phenomena. In using MNE, zooarchaeologists try to reconstruct the full, minimum array of whole animal bones on the basis of many fragments. This is possible because most kinds of whole bones have distinctive features ("portions" or "landmarks") that inform us about which skeletal element the fragments came from, as well as how many whole bones the fragments may represent.

In this study, bone MNE is derived from the most common portion of each skeletal element and represents the sum of right and left sides for elements that naturally occur in pairs. Just which portion or landmark determines the MNE count is not decided in advance; instead, the most common portion or landmark is allowed to emerge from the data. Because a wide variety of portions and landmarks were recorded for each category of skeletal element in this research, it is possible to maximize MNE counts even when bones are highly fragmented. The MNE counts for limb bones employ unique landmarks on or near the articular ends, and any of a variety of distinctive bony features for axial elements and the cranium and mandible. Counting skulls may employ, for example, details such as the petrous, occipital condyle, incisive, mandibular condyle, or bony architecture of the maxilla or mandible behind the cheek tooth row if relatively complete. The MNE counts used for this analysis deliberately exclude carpals, most tarsals, and all teeth, because

TABLE 9.1
Crania and mandible MNEs determined from ungulate bones
versus teeth from Moscerini

Taxon	Tooth MNE		Bone MNE	
	Cranium	Mandible	Cranium	Mandible
red/fallow deer	40	48	38	74
roe deer	4	4	7	11
aurochs	2	4	—	—
ibex	4	6	2	2

Note: Hominid-collected faunas are from level groups M2, M3, M4, and M6 combined. Bone-based cranial and mandible MNEs are based on the most common bony portion of each skeletal element in any given assemblage. Tooth-based cranial and mandible MNEs are based on the most common tooth element, uppers and lowers considered separately, across fifteen age classes in each assemblage.

the uniformly dense structure of these elements tends to inflate their relative abundances in archaeological contexts, and they may arrive as non-nutritious riders on more substantial food-bearing elements. The study instead focuses on relatively large bones that, in principle, might represent the minimum transportable parcels that genuinely attract foragers, thereby influencing foragers' decisions to transport them.

Teeth, in particular, can seriously distort (amplify) head counts *relative to* postcrania wherever preservation conditions are less than ideal. This point is very important for understanding the anatomical comparisons, for which comparability in the face of differential preservation is crucial. Interestingly, bone-based MNE counts for head parts are higher than or balanced to tooth-based counts in most of the cave assemblages: Table 9.1 contrasts bone- and tooth-based MNE counts for ungulate crania and mandibles from Grotta dei Moscerini. Head parts often dominate the graphed profiles of anatomical representation, despite the exclusion of teeth.

MNE counts: Problems and strengths

In the case of limb elements, an analyst's choice of landmarks for determining limb MNE could affect the numbers perceived (Bunn and Kroll 1988; Turner 1989), although it is not universally true for any of the bone assemblages considered here. My use of epiphysis-based MNE counts for limbs is conditioned by the fact that the Italian study sample includes assemblages from old excavations along with material from current projects. The recovery procedures of earlier excavators artificially delimit the array of anatomical landmarks that can be used for determining MNE overall (discussed in Chapter 5). In particular, limb shaft fragments were not retained, while articular ends of all species—from rodents to pachyderms—were collected by the excavators in a systematic fashion. Comparable data for both old and new collections were needed; hence counts based on articular landmarks were used to create the MNE counts.

The pivotal concern in this MNE counting scheme is whether limbs in the deposits might disappear faster than heads due to in situ bone attrition or may have been lost due to archaeologists' recovery biases. Because the head counts are based strictly on bone and most large limb elements possess at least one very hard epiphysis (with the possible exception of the femur), neither phenomenon should seriously undermine head to limb ratios in this data set. All of the key bony portions and landmarks used to derive MNEs are diagnostic to species or genus, and, by the excavators' accounts, therefore were carefully retrieved. It is possible, of course, that the upper and lower portions of a given skeletal element might part ways long before a shelter is in sight, but, for the most part, differential transport of portions of elements does not appear to have confounded the investigation as here designed. The extent to which missing midshaft fragments in the old collections might have undermined limb MNEs merits additional discussion, however.

Bunn and Kroll (1988) have argued that landmarks on long bone shafts can produce more accurate MNE estimates than procedures that rely exclusively on features on articular ends (see also Marean and Spencer 1991 on captive hyaena experiments). Their data on the FLK *Zinjanthropus* site fauna from East Africa suggest, for example, that significant differences in MNE counts could arise between the two criteria in faunas that have been ravaged by large carnivores. Turner's (1989) discussion of the impact of recovery biases on anatomical representation in the Klasies River Mouth faunas also provides grounds for caution.

My choices about how to determine MNE were limited by what excavators chose to retain in the older Italian collections, raising concern about possible weaknesses in the data. In recognition of the potential impact of how MNE was determined in the study sample, I conducted controlled comparisons of the relative frequencies of epiphyseal landmarks versus midshaft foraminae (and certain muscle attachment scars) for faunas recently excavated from three cave sites in west-central Italy, each involving complete recovery of bone. The ramifications of the comparisons are limited, but it was possible to assess the general relevance of these issues to the Italian study sample. The faunal assemblage from Riparo Salvini is attributed to late Upper Paleolithic humans, the Grotta Breuil faunas to Mousterian hominids, and the Buca della Iena faunas (levels I1–6) principally to spotted hyaenas. All identifiable specimens and all unidentifiable macromammal bone specimens 1.0 cm or larger are retained in each collection, including all limb shaft fragments.

Table 9.2 compares MNE counts for long bone elements in terms of two sets of identification criteria: one set is based on landmarks on shafts, especially nutrient foraminae; the other is based on land-

TABLE 9.2
Limb MNE based on shafts[a] versus articular ends[b] for ungulate remains
from three cave excavations involving complete recovery of bone

Long bone element	Riparo Salvini MU		Grotta Breuil MU		Buca della Iena MU		LU	
	Shafts	Ends	Shafts	Ends	Shafts	Ends	Shafts	Ends
scapula	1	5	0	1	0	0	1	2
humerus	6	8	4	4	1	2	4	5
radius	1	3	3	3	2	3	4	5
femur	3	7	2	3	1	1	1	3
tibia	5	7	5	4	2	3	6	6
humerus/femur[c]	(4)	—	—	—	—	—	—	—
MNE total	20	30	14	15	7	9	16	21

Degree of fragmentation for all bone:[d]			
N-observations	421	391	1210
mean length	2.3 cm	3.0 cm	6.1 cm
minimum length	1.0 cm	1.0 cm	1.0 cm
maximum length	8.3 cm	9.5 cm	27.9 cm

[a] Shaft-based MNE counts use nutrient foraminae and certain midshaft grooves (fossa) or muscle attachments, depending on which is more common.

[b] End-based MNE counts use unique landmarks on or just above the epiphyses.

[c] The humerus and femur could not always be distinguished on the basis of foraminae, but foraminae (as opposed to other landmarks on shafts) provided the highest MNE for shafts in this case.

[d] Fragment size data combine identifiable and unidentifiable bone in each sample (see also Chapter 5).

Note: (MU) medium ungulates, (LU) large ungulates.

marks on or near articular ends. Specimens preserving the entire element, or substantial portions thereof, contribute to both sets of counts. Because an element's susceptibility to attrition relates primarily to tissue density (e.g., Binford and Bertram 1977; Lyman 1984a) and most skeletal elements incorporate more than one tissue type, we can expect the two counting techniques to produce roughly equivalent values only if significant attritional or spatial biases have *not* been introduced by preservation conditions and/or consumption habits of predators at shelters. One cannot expect absolute agreement between the two counting methods under any circumstance, however, due to the vagaries of sampling.

The total MNE values in all bone samples presented in Table 9.2 are fairly low, yet the data are sufficient to show that shaft-based counts yield either comparable or lower values than epiphysis-based counts, regardless of whether the bone collectors were hominids or spotted hyaenas. The counts are likewise unaffected by the degree of bone fragmentation (data repeated from Chapter 5). It is interesting that shaft landmarks did not yield superior counts for the hyaena den faunas (Buca della Iena), despite this species' tendency to gnaw epiphyses. The data show that shaft-based MNE criteria are not universally preferable to epiphysis-based ones. The comparisons of shaft-based and epiphysis-based limb MNE counts in the three control cases also justify application of the latter criteria to the older collections. I was not able to conduct such comparisons for the head-dominated faunas from Moscerini or Guattari, because these cases are represented only in certain older collections. The possibility of purely methodologically caused anatomical biases is directly contradicted, however, by the facts that

ungulate mortality patterns (Chapter 11) and technological data (Chapter 14) parallel the distinctions apparent from anatomical composition.

One possible explanation for roughly equivant limb bone MNEs based on shafts versus ends in Buca della Iena may be that bones arrived in the Italian hyaena dens faster than they could be fully processed. Figure 9.1 shows several gnawed bone specimens from hyaena-dominated levels G0–1 of Grotta Guattari. Many of the items are composed primarily of trabecular tissue and, while gnawed, they still can be identified to element and species. Comparatively fragile juvenile mammal remains, both from carnivores and ungulates (see Chapters 12 and 13, respectively), are abundant in these carnivore-collected faunas as well. Of course the few examples shown in Figure 9.1 and elevated juvenile abundance cannot account for the fate of every specimen that might have been deposited in these sites. The examples do suggest, however, that destruction of trabeculae-rich skeletal items by spotted hyaenas may not have been very thorough at Buca della Iena or at Guattari, where bones are in similar condition. The state of the illustrated items appears consistent with the equivalency of MNE counts based on bone ends and shafts observed in Buca della Iena (see Table 9.2). I conclude that observations that MNE counts can differ due to epiphysis-based versus shaft-based counting methods are cautions worth considering. It is decidedly premature, however, to assert that epiphysis-based counts are, as a matter of course, inferior to midshaft counts in all carnivore-ravaged assemblages, much less in all archaeological assemblages. Predators respond to food supply in part by adjusting their food-processing agendas.

ANALYTICAL PROCEDURES AND ANATOMICAL INDEXES

The procedures for this study of anatomical representation in ungulate prey include visual comparisons of *standardized* anatomical bar charts, regression analyses using anatomical indexes, and pair-wise (Kruskal–Wallis ANOVA) statistical comparisons of ranked data. To create the standardized bar charts, raw MNE counts are collapsed

into *nine anatomical regions*, illustrated in Figure 9.2. The nine regions are (1) horn/antler, (2) head, (3) neck, (4) axial column below the neck including the pelvis, (5) upper front limbs, (6) lower front limbs, (7) upper hind limbs (femur only), (8) lower hind limbs, and (9) feet. The rationale for these divisions is fairly straightforward, if slightly arbi-

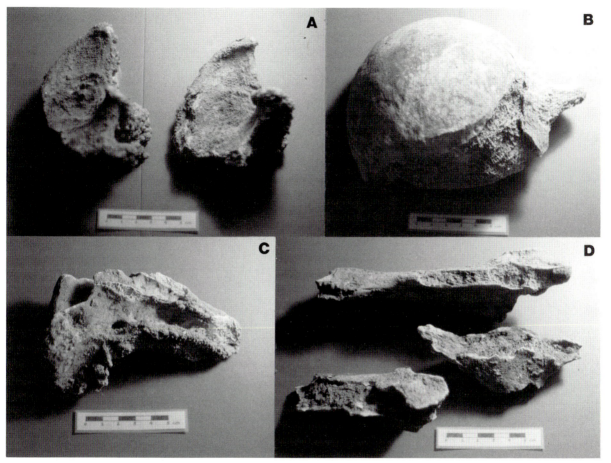

Figure 9.1 Hyaena-gnawed mammal bones from Guattari G0–2: (A) posterior segments of carnivore mandibles, (B) elephant femur head fragment, (C) ungulate sacrum, and (D) acetabulum fragments from red deer innominates. Note that, while all are partly destroyed, even items consisting of large amounts of trabecular bone tissue can be identified. Although modern captive hyaenas may destroy more trabecular bone than cortical bone in some circumstances, ancient free-ranging hyaenas did not necessarily do so at den sites in Italy. The extent to which bones are damaged at modern dens varies greatly, primarily in response to food availability.

trary. There is some room for debate about where to place the pelvis (axial or upper hind) in this scheme; my decision to count it with the axial region is a compromise based on transport habits of both humans and carnivores. As regards the head region, some researchers argue on the basis of archaeological (Binford 1984) and actualistic (Blumenschine 1986) studies that transport and processing of mandibles versus crania could vary according to the context of procurement; specifically, crania should greatly exceed mandibles if head parts were scavenged from carnivore kills. Crania and mandibles are grouped together in this study, only because I

found more or less equivalent frequencies, or an excess of mandibles, in the Italian Upper Pleistocene faunas. If anything, Table 9.3 shows that mandibles sometimes outnumber crania, not the other way around.

In the first analysis to be presented, the MNE counts for each anatomical region are *standardized*, using the expected values listed in Table 9.4. This produces a bone-based MNI estimate for each of the nine regions, the highest of which also serves as the estimated number of carcass sources from which food was obtained and carried to shelters. The data are plotted in bar graphs, and, because the values

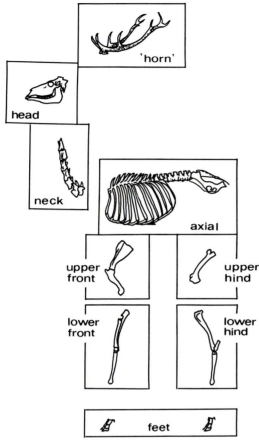

Figure 9.2 The ungulate skeleton divided into nine anatomical regions. (From Stiner 1991a)

four indexes: (1) anatomical completeness, representing the quantity of substantial bony parts transported relative to the average number of carcass sources (tMNE/MNI); (2) the proportion of horn/antler parts to all limb parts above the foot (HORN/L); (3) the proportion of head parts to limb parts above the foot (HEAD/L); and (4) the sum of horn/antler and head parts relative to limb parts above the foot ([H + H]/L).

For ease of reference, Table 9.5 summarizes the ratio definitions and presents expected values for complete artiodactyl prey. The tMNE/MNI ratio is obtained by dividing the total number of bony skeletal elements (tMNE) for a species in an assemblage by the minimum number of individual animals (MNI) represented. The ratio represents the *average* quantity of substantial bony parts transported to shelters per carcass source, where it is assumed that hunters have more take-away options from carcasses than do scavengers (see Chapter 8). The second ratio, called (H + H)/L, is the sum of horn/antler and head MNE counts for a species in an assemblage, divided by the MNE for all major limb bones above the phalanges. The (H + H)/L ratio accounts for roughly 50 percent of the variation observed in the faunas collected by all of the predators considered (demonstrated below). While biasing effects of bone attrition on anatomical representation cannot be wholly excluded in these comparisons, the ratio effectively circumvents most sources of ambiguity by avoiding the axial regions of the skeleton. HORN/L and HEAD/L are used to compare probable or documented scavenging cases attributable to hyaenas and hominids. A regression of (H + H)/L against tMNE/MNI traces the relationship between hunting and scavenging strategies as expressed by the dominant anatomical parts in the shelter faunas. Finally, (H + H)/L values are subjected to a rank order comparison to evaluate just how unique each predator is on the basis of these criteria.

are standardized, complete anatomical representation would be indicated by bars of equal height, as exemplified in Figure 9.3. The procedure makes imbalances or biases in anatomical frequencies very easy to spot in a visual comparison.

Unstandardized, or raw, MNE counts are used in subsequent analyses where the comparisons focus on key anatomical regions that account for most of the variation among faunas (see note in the Appendix for extracting raw MNEs). The analyses employ

ENIGMATIC MOUSTERIAN FAUNAS

Two distinct patterns of anatomical representation are apparent for medium ungulate remains collected by Mousterian hominids in the Latium caves. One

type of pattern, occurring in the cultural levels of Grotta Breuil and Grotta di Sant'Agostino, tends toward anatomical completeness (a.k.a. meaty),

TABLE 9.3
TABLE 9.3
Comparison of bone-based MNEs for selected skeletal elements of small, medium,
and large ungulates from the Italian shelters

Assemblage and (taxon)	Cranium	Mandible	Carpal[a]	Metacarpal	Tibia	Tarsal[b]	Metatarsal
Head-dominated faunas collected by Mousterian hominids:							
M3 (roe)	5	8	1	1	—	1	1
M4 (roe)	2	3	—	—	—	—	—
M2 (r)	1	3	—	—	—	—	1
M3 (r,f,i)	18	40	—	2	—	1	5
M4 (r,f)	13	16	—	—	—	—	1
M6 (r,f)	8	17	1	2	1	—	6
G2–3 (r,f)	4	7	—	1	1	1	1
G4–7 (r,f)	1	3	—	1	—	1	—
G2–3 (h,a)	—	2	1	—	—	1	—
G4–7 (a)	2	5	—	—	—	—	1
Meaty faunas collected by Mousterian hominids:							
S0 (roe)	3	6	2	4	—	1	2
S1 (roe)	1	5	3	3	—	—	—
S3 (roe,wb)	3	2	2	3	—	2	2
B3/4 (su)	2	2	—	1	1	2	2
S0 (r)	2	6	2	1	3	2	5
S1 (r,f,i)	7	12	3	7	11	6	7
S2 (r,f,i)	4	6	—	5	5	6	4
S3 (r)	1	4	1	—	1	1	1
B3/4 (mu)	2	2	2	2	4	2	4
S1 (a)	1	3	—	1	3	1	1
B3/4 (lu)	—	3	1	—	4	—	1
Meaty faunas collected by late Upper Paleolithic humans:							
Palidoro (wb)	—	2	—	—	1	—	—
Salvini (roe)	1	1	1	—	1	1	1
Palidoro (r,wa)	17	18	2	8	14	7	7
Salvini (r,i)	7	3	4	5	7	7	7
Palidoro (h,a)	2	8	5	4	5	4	2
Faunas collected by spotted hyaenas:							
M5 (roe)	7	9	1	5	1	2	2
G0 (wb)	1	1	—	—	1	—	—
I1–6 (r)	3	11	1	2	5	3	4
M5 (r,f)	8	23	1	6	3	5	14
G0 (r,f)	11	43	1	18	8	10	13
G1 (r,f)	5	19	2	8	6	3	6
I1–6 (h,a)	—	—	2	5	14	9	5
M5 (h,a)	—	—	—	1	3	3	1
G0 (h,a)	5	12	3	5	10	4	10
G1 (h,a)	6	5	2	—	—	3	—

(*continued*)

TABLE 9.3 *(Continued)*

Assemblage and (taxon)	Cranium	Mandible	Carpal[a]	Metacarpal	Tibia	Tarsal[b]	Metatarsal
Faunas collected by wolves:							
SX (roe)	4	13	—	8	1	7	7
S4 (i)	—	2	1	4	—	2	3
SX (i)	1	4	1	10	10	5	3

[a] Carpal value is an average for four elements within the carpal complex, rounded to the next highest whole number.
[b] Tarsal value is an average for the astragalus and calcaneous only, rounded.

Note: (a) aurochs, (f) fallow deer, (h) horse, (i) ibex, (r) red deer, (roe) roe deer, (wa) wild ass, (wb) wild boar, (su) small ungulates, including roe deer, wild boar, and rarely in UP cases, chamois; (mu) medium ungulates, including red deer, fallow deer, ibex, and rarely megaceros or wild ass; (lu) large ungulates, including aurochs and horse. All MNE values are based exclusively on bone, including head elements; data are taken directly from the Appendix. Only the main agency of bone collection is listed. Origins of assemblage G2 are ambiguous, perhaps dominated by the products of MP hominid collecting activities.

TABLE 9.4
Expected MNE values by skeletal element and by anatomical region
for carnivores, artiodactyls, and perissodactyls

By anatomical element				By anatomical region			
	CARN	ARTIO	PERISSO		CARN	ARTIO	PERISSO
horn/antler	·	2	·	HORN	·	2	·
1/2 mandible	2	2	2	HEAD	4	4	4
1/2 skull	2	2	2				
atlas	1	1	1				
axis	1	1	1	NECK	7	7	7
cervical vertebra	5	5	5				
thoracic vertebra	13	13	13				
lumbar vertebra	7	7	7				
sacral vertebra	1	1	1	AXIAL	49	49	49
innominate	2	2	2				
rib	26	26	26				
scapula	2	2	2	UPPER FRONT	4	4	4
humerus	2	2	2				
radius	2	2	2				
ulna	2	2	2	LOWER FRONT	14	6	6
metacarpal	10	2	2				
femur	2	2	2	UPPER HIND	2	2	2
tibia	2	2	2				
calcaneum	2	2	2	LOWER HIND	16	8	8
astragalus	2	2	2				
metatarsal	10	2	2				
1st phalanx	20	8	4				
2nd phalanx	20	8	4	FEET	60	24	12
3rd phalanx	20	8	4				
tMNE	156	106	92	tMNE	156	106	92

rNote: (·) not applicable, (CARN) carnivora, (ARTIO) artiodactyla, (PERISSO) perissodactyla. Horn/antler value is not used for artiodactyla lacking these structures. Horse serves as the anatomical model for perissodactyls.

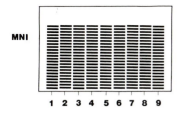

MNI

1 horn-antler
2 head
3 neck
4 axial
5 upper front
6 lower front
7 upper hind
8 lower hind
9 feet

1 2 3 4 5 6 7 8 9

Figure 9.3 Hypothetical example of complete skeletal representation using standardized MNE scheme for nine anatomical regions. Complete skeletal representation in an assemblage will be indicated by bars of equal height. The standardized MNE value for each region corresponds to bone-based MNI.

approximating the natural proportion of legs to head parts in the ungulate body. The other type, found in cultural levels of Grotta dei Moscerini and Grotta Guattari, is dominated almost exclusively by head parts. The cave sites have similar topographic settings, yet the anatomical patterns consistently sort by site.

Several lines of evidence indicate that the dichotomous anatomical patterns observed for the Italian Middle Paleolithic are not simply the product of sampling biases, archaeological recovery procedures, or in situ bone attrition (Chapter 5). The head

TABLE 9.5
Expected ratio values for complete artiodactyl carcasses

Ratio	Description	Expected value
(H + H)/L	Horn MNE + head MNE divided by all limbs MNE (excluding foot bones)	.30
tMNE/MNI	Anatomical completeness index: total MNE (from Table 9.4) divided by standardized MNI	106
HORN/L	Horn/antler MNE divided by all limbs MNE (excluding foot bones)	<.10[a]
HEAD/L	Head MNE divided by all limbs MNE (excluding foot bones)	.20

[a] Expected value will be less than .10 due to individual age in horned species and to a combination of age, sex, and season in cervids.

Note: All ratios employ unstandardized MNE counts.

counts are based on bony parts rather than teeth, bone preservation is uniformly good, and, apart from the axial skeletal regions, recovery procedures should not have resulted in these differences. Moreover, carnivore-collected assemblages in the same sites often display different patterns of anatomical representation for the same prey species (primarily hyaena-collected M5 in Moscerini, and G0–1 in Guattari; see below, and also the Appendix). Mortality data represent especially compelling contradictions to the idea that the biases are due primarily to postdepositional phenomena: the age structures of the head-dominated ungulate faunas are consistently and significantly biased toward old adult prey, whereas the meaty faunas display prime-dominated or nonselective age profiles (Chapter 11). The patterns of Mousterian stone artifact transport, reduction, and rates of discard associated with each of the two kinds of faunal patterns likewise indicate behaviorally distinct contexts of site occupation and mobility (Chapter 14; see also Kuhn 1990a, 1991).

Both carnivores and hominids process bone for food, however, and it is not always possible to distinguish parts carried to shelters from parts destroyed following arrival. I attempt to minimize the potential impact of differential loss by processing damage in the data set by focusing on the more resistant portions of prey skeletal anatomy in the later stages of the analysis. Indeed, most of the variation in anatomical representation involves horns/antlers, heads, and limbs (see also MNE frequency comparisons of carpals, tarsals, and adjoining large limb elements in Table 9.3).

The two distinct patterns of anatomical composition in the Mousterian caves involve the same prey species and are most conspicuous for medium-sized ungulates, principally red deer, fallow deer, and ibex. Figure 9.4 shows skeletal MNE representation for common ungulate species in Sant'Agostino S0–3, collected by Mousterian hominids. Standardized values for head parts appear balanced with respect to limb representation. The same is true for the common ungulate taxa in Breuil (Figures 9.5 and 9.6). Figure 9.6 contrasts MNE identifications made at the level of species versus more generic taxonomic criteria (undetermined medium ungulate) and is of some methodological interest: the

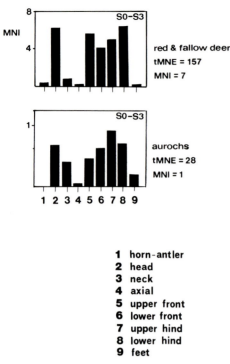

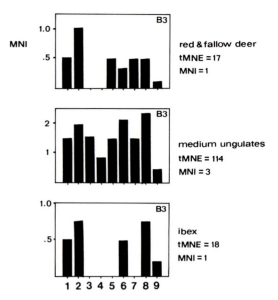

1 horn-antler
2 head
3 neck
4 axial
5 upper front
6 lower front
7 upper hind
8 lower hind
9 feet

Figure 9.4 Anatomical representation for red and fallow deer and aurochs collected by Mousterian hominids at Grotta di Sant'Agostino S0–3.

Figure 9.6 Anatomical representation for red and fallow deer, undetermined medium ungulate remains, and ibex collected by Mousterian hominids at Grotta Breuil (B3/4); codes as in Figure 9.4.

Figure 9.7 Anatomical representation for red deer collected by late Upper Paleolithic humans at Riparo Salvini (V); codes as in Figure 9.4.

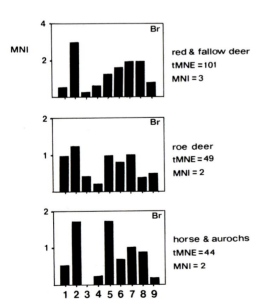

Figure 9.5 Anatomical representation for red and fallow deer, roe deer, and horse and aurochs collected by Mousterian hominids at Grotta Breuil (Br); codes as in Figure 9.4.

excavations at Breuil involve complete bone recovery, and perceived axial representation increases significantly in this case. Overall, the hominid-collected assemblages from Sant'Agostino (S0–3) and Breuil (Br, B3) display anatomical profiles that verge on anatomical completeness, apart from problematic counts for the axial skeleton and an apparently genuine scarcity of toe bones. The anatomical patterns in these Mousterian faunas closely resemble patterns in later Upper Paleolithic shelters in the study area, such as Riparo Salvini (Figure 9.7).

The other kind of anatomical profile found in cave faunas collected by Mousterian hominids consists almost exclusively of head parts. Figure 9.8

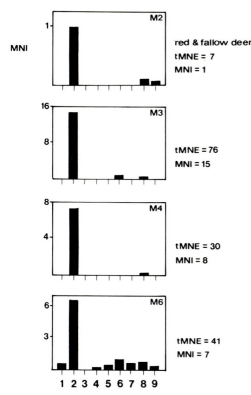

Figure 9.8 Anatomical representation for red and fallow deer collected by Mousterian hominids at Grotta dei Moscerini (M2, M3, M4, and M6); codes as in Figure 9.4.

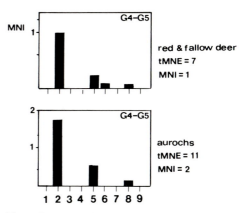

Figure 9.9 Anatomical representation for red and fallow deer and aurochs collected by Mousterian hominids at Grotta Guattari (G4–5); codes as in Figure 9.4.

shows a series of red and fallow deer assemblages from Moscerini, where the head-dominant pattern consistently associates with exploitation of marine shellfish (Chapter 6). In all cases, adult head parts are extraordinarily abundant, while antlers are completely absent or very rare, suggesting that the prey were females and/or individuals taken during seasons when antlers were absent or in early growth (and therefore not preserved). Limb elements occur in very low proportions, dwarfed by the abundance of head parts. All of the specimens in these assemblages are in a very good state of preservation; the examples presented throughout Chapter 5 (e.g., Figures 5.25C, 5.28A–B, and 5.31) are typical. The assemblages from G4–5 also appear to be dominated primarily by head parts (Figure 9.9), but the samples are very small.

Taken together, preservation and recovery biases fall far short of explaining the existence of the dichotomous Mousterian pattern sets, suggesting that

the patterns are the result of hominid transport choices. Yet I find no clear match for the contrasts observed in the Italian Mousterian among ethnoarchaeological studies of modern human beings. In raising this point, I emphasize that the level at which the archaeological differences are expressed is much coarser in time and space than scales of observation commonly used in ethnoarchaeological research. The Mousterian patterns of variation become apparent only by comparing many archaeological assemblages from several sites; each cave fauna represents debris from many foraging events mixed together at the end of transport trajectories.

Collapsing various ethnoarchaeological data sets might seem the obvious solution for bringing them in line with the archaeological problem. It would be necessary for the purposes of this study, however, to compile all Nunamiut (e.g., Binford 1978), or Aka (Hudson 1990), or Hadza (e.g., O'Connell et al. 1988a, 1988b; Bunn et al. 1988), or !Kung data (e.g., Yellen 1977) into just a handful of cases. Such a procedure meanwhile would obscure a diverse array of ecological contexts and habitat-specific foraging strategies across the world without providing, at this stage of knowledge, any meaning to the madness it would create. There is little information, for example, on hunter-gatherer economies of the temperate zone. In lieu of synthetic information on how human adaptations (and their archaeological consequences) should vary with environment, I turn to the carnivores.

The Comparative Sample for Six Social Predators

The analyses concern only the *final products* of food transport and feeding by predators. Most cases represent cumulative products of multiple procurement events, as indicated by bone-based prey MNIs greater than 1. In this way, the archaeological problem dictates the scale for designing experimental surveys of what other kinds of predators do. The purpose is to isolate some general rules about variation in patterns of anatomical part transport for a variety of social carnivore species that might help account for the full extent of variation found in the Italian Mousterian. Assemblages collected by six social predators are compared: striped hyaenas (*Hyaena hyaena*), brown hyaenas (*Hyaena brunnea*), spotted hyaenas, wolves, and Middle and Upper Paleolithic humans. All assemblages are from shelters or excavated dens at which the transported products of many procurement events were jumbled together.

In keeping with the archaeological problem, multiple cases are considered for each bone-collecting predator. The modern carnivore den faunas are from all over the world; the rest are from Upper Pleistocene Italy. Reference cases are derived from a variety of published and unpublished sources; Table 9.6 provides background information for those outside of Italy. Some very good information is available on the causes of variation in the foraging habits of nonhuman predators by environment and proves quite useful for later interpretations.

The faunal assemblages from striped (Israel, Skinner et al. 1980) and brown hyaena dens (southern Africa, Mills and Mills 1977; Binford, unpublished data) are of modern origin exclusively. Faunas from spotted hyaena dens (various regions of Africa, Bearder 1977 cited in Brain 1981; Binford, unpublished data; Haynes, unpublished collection; Henschel et al. 1979; Potts 1982) and wolf dens (Alaska, Binford, unpublished collections and data; see also 1978, 1981) are from both modern contexts and Upper Pleistocene Italian caves. My inclusion of red deer from Sant'Agostino S4 in the wolf den sample here is somewhat problematic (see Chapters 5 and 6); ibex is certainly permissible. The Middle and Upper Paleolithic hominid cases are from the four Latium caves. Late Upper Paleolithic cave faunas from northern Spain (La Riera, Altuna 1986; see also Straus 1986), a region with a similar climate, are used to bolster the array of Upper Paleolithic cases from west-central Italy. A few Span-

TABLE 9.6
Data sources for faunas from Spain, Israel, North America, and Africa

Case name (and agency)	Geographical location	Time frame	Principal data source	Additional bibliographic information
La Riera 1–30 (1UP Homo)	Spain	UP–Mesolithic (ca. 20,500–7,000)	Altuna 1986	Straus 1986
Zimbabwe (SH)	s. Africa	modern	Haynes (n.p.)	—
Natab (SH)	"	modern	Henschel et al. 1979	—
Kalahari 1981 (BH,SH)	"	modern	Binford (n.p.)	—
Kalahari 1977 (BH)	"	modern	Mills and Mills 1977	—
Timbavati (SH)	"	modern	Brain 1981	Bearder 1977
Amboseli (SH)	e. Africa	modern	Potts 1982	Hill 1984 Potts 1988
Arad Cave (STRH)	Israel	modern	Skinner et al. 1980	—
WD1–3 (W)	Alaska	modern	Binford (n.p.)	Binford 1978, 1981

Note: (n.p.) unpublished data, (lUP) late Upper Paleolithic humans, (SH) spotted hyaenas, (BH) brown hyaenas, (STRH) striped hyaenas, (W) wolves.

ish Mesolithic cases are grouped with the Spanish late Upper Paleolithic series, on grounds that all represent hunter-gatherer societies. I have deliberately restricted the geographical distribution of the hominid-generated cases to coastal Mediterranean habitats in order to control for variation in environment as much as possible; this procedure narrows the potential array of factors that could account for differences in hominid foraging responses; the main subject of the comparisons.

Each "case" used in the anatomical comparisons represents one (or two similar) prey species from an assemblage: a level or level group in archaeological contexts, and usually surface collections from modern carnivore dens. Pleistocene cases representing a thorough blending of the activities of different species were excluded from the comparison. Pleistocene cases involving both human and carnivore activities in which one was clearly dominant are included on grounds that low frequencies of gnawing (1–2% of total NISP) are evident in every hominid-associated fauna (including those of late Upper Paleolithic age), and, conversely, a few stone tools sometimes occur in what are without question primarily carnivore den faunas. Some minor amounts of mixing are unavoidable, because hominids coexisted with other predators and shared numerous resource interests with them.

Medium-sized ungulate prey receive the most attention in this presentation because they are most abundant in the assemblages, although analogous comparisons are made for smaller and larger prey whenever possible. Carcass size is known to influence the transport decisions of humans (e.g., Binford 1978, 1981; Bunn et al. 1988; Gifford 1977, 1980; O'Connell et al. 1988a, 1988b; Yellen 1977, 1991a) and large carnivores (e.g., Haynes 1980, 1982, 1983a, 1983b; Binford 1981; Blumenschine 1986, 1987), and it is significant that the medium body size range corresponds to the greatest variation in anatomical representation in shelter faunas created by large bone-collecting predators (see also discussions by Klein 1975, 1989b; Potts 1988:109–110).

For the southern European assemblages, the medium ungulate size category includes red deer, fallow deer, and ibex. North American cases involve caribou (a.k.a. reindeer, *Rangifer tarandus*). In the African and Middle Eastern cases, the medium size category includes Class II and III bovids as defined by Brain (1981:275) and occasionally other taxa, such as domesticated donkey. A full accounting of the anatomical data for Mousterian faunas is provided in the Appendix. Small ungulates from Italy are roe deer, wild boar and, in the Upper Paleolithic, chamois, whereas modern control cases include various Class I bovids and warthog. Large ungulates from Italy are aurochs and horse, and the modern control cases include various Class IV bovids, zebra, and camel. The analyses by necessity cross taxonomic boundaries in both predators and their prey.

VARIATION IN SHELTER FAUNAS COLLECTED BY SIX SOCIAL PREDATORS

Figure 9.10 presents a simple two-dimensional arrangement of anatomical bar graphs for medium-sized ungulate cases, based on standardized MNE data for the nine anatomical regions. The horizontal axis corresponds to predator species, and the vertical axis describes the dominant anatomical region represented (pattern type). More cases exist in the sample than are illustrated; the chart emphasizes the range of variation associated with each predator. Though complex, the figure effectively makes a few important points about broad patterns in the data, to be discussed and qualified below.

Much of the variation in anatomical representa-

tion is explained by the proportion of head and/or horn parts to leg parts above the foot. The relationship between these groups of anatomical regions is sufficiently strong to result in a more or less diagonal arrangement of cases across the chart. In contrast, vertebrae, ribs, and foot bones tend to be under-represented throughout the comparative sample. As noted earlier, the absence of axial elements may be due to their relatively great susceptibility to in situ destruction processes or recovery practices, rather than their being discarded at procurement sites; no clear answer is available on this point. In contrast, the comparatively dense structure of foot

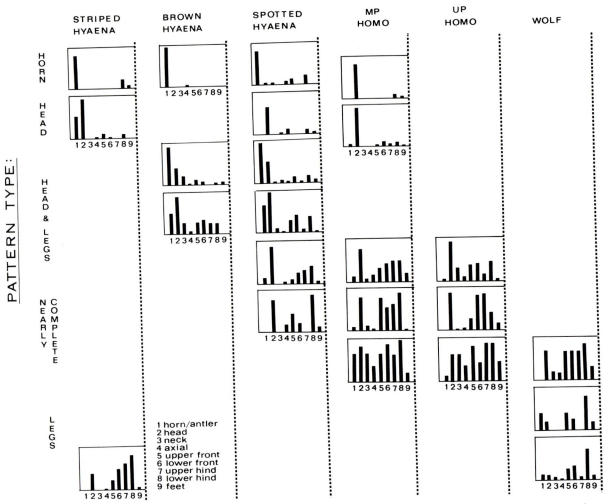

Figure 9.10 The full extent of variation in anatomical patterns in medium ungulate remains collected at shelters by the six types of predators based on standardized MNE data for nine anatomical regions. (From Stiner 1991b)

bones (phalanges) suggests that many of them never reached the shelters.

The distribution of modern carnivore control cases in Figure 9.10 corresponds to the *predominant* means for obtaining ungulate prey. The two series on the left in the chart (striped hyaena and brown hyaena) denote scavenging, while those on the extreme right (lUP *Homo* and wolf) represent primarily hunted sources. None of the predator species would refuse a good scavenging opportunity; the differences between series relate to how often they hunted as opposed to scavenged while using a particular shelter.

The arrangement of cases in the chart and the ecological circumstances behind their formation may be summarized by predator. Striped hyaena den faunas (N-cases = 3) from arid lands of the Middle East and brown hyaena den faunas (N-cases = 3) from arid environments of southern Africa represent assemblages collected by obligate scavengers. The assemblages are dominated by horn and/or head parts, and all other body parts are relatively rare. Considerable variation exists among these cases, but they tend to be distributed toward the top of the chart. One exceptional striped hyaena case, located at the bottom of the first column, represents an experimental situation in which the observers provisioned the animals with whole donkey carcasses near the den (Skinner et al. 1980:100). The striped hyaenas clearly preferred to remove limbs when confronted with artificially rich feeding opportunities, but did not do so in natural situations involving medium ungulates or, in one case, dogs.

The third column of Figure 9.10 shows cases from a variety of spotted hyaena dens (N-cases = 11). The fact that this species both hunts and scavenges is well known (e.g., Kruuk 1972). The relative emphasis on each strategy varies with environmental conditions, and, generally speaking, southern African populations scavenge more often than do East African populations (compare Mills 1984a, 1984b; Tilson et al. 1980; Kruuk 1972; Schaller 1972). The range of variation exhibited by the spotted hyaena series is extensive and continuous. The cases are distributed according to the environment of origin, and appear to follow differences in ecosystem richness as measured by ungulate biomass and the degree of food dispersion. The cases in the upper part of the column are from modern southern Africa and are dominated by head parts (Zimbabwe) and/or horn parts (Namibia, Kalahari). The cases in the middle of the series are from Upper Pleistocene dens in coastal Italy; they are also biased toward heads and horn/antler, but values for leg parts approach 50 percent of the leading anatomical regions. The modern Amboseli den from East Africa is placed at the base of the series because the value for lower hind limbs is balanced relative to heads. The Amboseli case actually consists of many prey species, but is dominated by medium ungulates (Hill 1984:117). Spotted hyaenas are known to hunt more in East African habitats, food is more concentrated in space, interference competition at procurement sites is more intense, and more legs consequently may turn up in dens.

The fourth column of Figure 9.10 shows a series of Middle Paleolithic hominid cases (N-cases = 16) from west-central Italy. The series displays much variation, although a substantial gap therein indicates that the variation is discontinuous. As noted earlier, the patterns in the Middle Paleolithic series sort by site, with strictly head-dominated anatomical patterns from Moscerini (M2, M3, M4, and M6) and Guattari (G4–5) at the top of the column, and

roughly balanced proportions of heads to legs in Breuil (Br, B3/4) and Sant'Agostino (S0, S1, S2, and S3) toward the lower part of the column. The lower subset represents situations in which hominids transported most or all anatomical parts of prey to shelters for processing.

A large number of Upper Paleolithic cases from west-central Italy and northern Spain (N-cases = 45) are available for comparison, yet they display a remarkably restricted distribution in the lower part of the fifth column of Figure 9.10. It is generally agreed among archaeologists that hunting was the foremost method by which late Upper Paleolithic humans obtained ungulates (e.g., Clark and Straus 1986), and there is little if any archaeological evidence to contradict this view. The anatomical patterns are analogous only to the lower ends of the Middle Paleolithic and, to a lesser degree, spotted hyaena series.

The final column in Figure 9.10 shows wolf-generated den faunas from modern Alaska and Pleistocene Italy (N-cases = 6). In northern habitats, modern wolves are ecologically dedicated hunters (e.g., Ballard et al. 1987; Bibikov 1982; Mech 1970; Murie 1944; Pimlott et al. 1969). They will scavenge if given the chance, often from old kills (e.g., Haynes 1980, Huggard 1993), but their principal mode of procurement is hunting. The position of the wolf series is most similar to that of the Upper Paleolithic group, but it is slightly lower overall and represents one extreme in the continuum of anatomical patterns generated by predators. The den assemblages display either equivalent proportions of heads and legs or, more commonly, a bias toward legs. The modern Alaskan and Pleistocene Italian cases in the wolf series are relatively invariant in spite of originating from two very different habitats and time periods.

To summarize, the generally diagonal arrangement of cases across the chart suggests that some larger relationship exists between procurement strategies and part transport choices. Experimental situations in which obligate scavengers are provisioned with whole medium-sized ungulate carcasses near their dens (outlier case in lower left corner of Figure 9.10, Skinner et al. 1980) indicate that, at least in this comparative scheme, everybody likes to carry away legs when presented with the choice. However, high levels of food dispersion often characterize natural scavenging contexts (especially nonconfrontational scavenging) and generally prevent such choices from being realized, except when very large prey are concerned. Probability works against scavengers getting most of a carcass most of the time, and cases involving a high dependence on scavenged food will tend to be distributed on the horn/head-dominated end of the continuum. Predators that primarily hunt move relatively more parts, and especially more legs, to shelters.

A surprisingly simple anatomical ratio, called (H + H)/L, describes much of the variation among the cases involving medium-sized ungulates, not only in the kinds of patterns typically produced by each predator, but also in the modes and ranges of variation. It is the relative amounts of leg parts that vary most, because heads and/or horns are well represented in nearly all of the cases considered. (Obviously, the same prey bodies could not have been divided across sites in the Mousterian series, since head parts are present in all.)

Figure 9.11 emulates the most outstanding features of the large anatomical chart for medium-sized ungulates, using the (H + H)/L ratio (data in Table 9.7). Unlike the previous figure, this graph illustrates distinct clustering patterns within series, in addition to the ranges of variation. The late Upper Paleolithic human series is packed tightly together at this scale of comparison, and so is the wolf series; these invariant series converge on anatomically balanced values (expected = .30, Table 9.5) or limb-biased patterns. Predators that do a lot of both hunting and scavenging, such as spotted hyaenas, show good representation throughout the possible range. The same is true for the Italian Middle Paleolithic. The spotted hyaena series and, especially, the Middle Paleolithic series display much more variation and, while weighted toward the lower end of the (H + H)/L axis, they fall short of the modes for the Upper Paleolithic human and wolf series. Striped and brown hyaena den faunas vary greatly, but they clearly gravitate toward the upper end of the (H + H)/L axis.

The (H + H)/L comparison can be extended to small and large ungulates in the study sample, although fewer cases are available for comparison (data in Table 9.8). Figure 9.12 shows the data for small ungulates. The distribution contrasts obligate

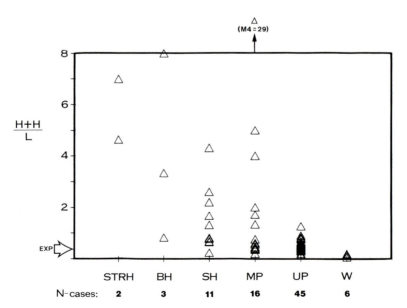

Figure 9.11 Plot of (H + H)/L for medium ungulate remains by predator type. (STRH) striped hyaena, (BH) brown hyaena, (SH) spotted hyaena, (MP) Middle Paleolithic hominid (Italy), (UP) late Upper Paleolithic human (Italy and Spain), (W) wolf; artificial provisioning case for striped hyaenas removed. (From Stiner 1991b)

TABLE 9.7

Anatomical summary data for medium ungulates collected by six types of predators
in Upper Pleistocene and modern shelters

Case name	Predator type	Prey	Horn MNE	Head MNE	All limbs MNE	tMNE	tMNE/ MNI	Horn+ head/ limb	Horn/ limb	Head/ limb
Arad Cave	1	sheep-goat	11	40	11	66	6.6	4.64	1.00	3.64
	1	donkey[a]	0	8	57	79	19.7	.14	.0	.14
	1	dog	0	35	5	50	5.5	7.00	.0	7.01
Kalahari'77	2	CII bovids[b]	16	14	9	70	8.7	3.33	1.78	1.55
	2	CIII bovids[b]	2	7	11	30	15.0	.82	.18	.64
Kalahari'81	2	CII bovids[c]	8	0	0	11	2.7	8.00	8.00	.0
Timbavati	3	all spp.	20	36	13	135	13.5	4.31	1.54	2.77
Kalahari'81	3	CII bovids[b]	7	6	5	26	6.5	2.60	1.40	1.20
	3	CIII bovids[b]	7	4	5	49	12.2	2.20	1.40	.80
Natab	3	CIII bovids[b]	14	2	24	40	5.7	.67	.58	.08
Zimbabwe	3	wildebeest	0	5	3	12	6.0	1.67	.0	1.67
Amboseli	3	all species	0	32	~137	~279	27.9	.23	.0	.23
Buca 1–4	3	red deer	7	2	11	44	14.7	.81	.64	.18
5–6	3	red deer	9	12	16	64	12.8	1.31	.56	.75
Guat G0	3	red/fallow	18	54	93	186	13.3	.77	.19	.58
G1	3	red/fallow	2	24	40	81	13.5	.65	.05	.60
Mosc M5	3	red/fallow	2	28	46	94	13.4	.65	.04	.61
Breuil r	4	red/fallow	1	12	35	101	33.7	.37	.03	.34
3/4	4	red/fallow	1	4	9	17	17.0	.55	.11	.44
3/4	4	ibex	1	3	9	18	18.0	.44	.11	.33
S.Ago S0	4	red/fallow	1	9	22	55	18.3	.45	.04	.41
S0	4	ibex	0	2	5	12	12.0	.40	.0	.40
S1	4	red/fallow	1	15	46	85	21.2	.35	.02	.33
S1	4	ibex	1	4	9	19	19.0	.55	.11	.44
S2	4	red/fallow	0	8	41	61	20.3	.19	.0	.19
S2	4	ibex	1	2	4	12	12.0	.75	.25	.50
S3	4	red/fallow	1	5	10	21	10.5	.60	.10	.50
Gua G2–3[d]	4?	red/fallow	1	11	7	19	6.3	1.71	.14	1.57
G4–5	4	red/fallow	0	4	3	7	7.0	1.33	.0	1.33
Mosc M2	4	red/fallow	0	4	1	7	7.0	4.00	.0	4.00
M3	4	red/fallow	0	60	12	76	5.1	5.00	.0	5.00
M4	4	red/fallow	0	29	1	30	3.7	29.00	.0	29.00
M6	4	red/fallow	1	25	13	41	5.8	2.00	.08	1.92
Pal 33–34	5	red deer	1	29	69	109	13.6	.43	.01	.42
Salvini	5	red deer	1	10	58	199	49.7	.19	.02	.17
Riera 1	5	red deer	0	16	50	129	32.2	.32	.0	.32
2–3	5	red deer	1	4	16	36	36.0	.31	.06	.25
4–6	5	red deer	41	126	334	833	26.0	.50	.12	.38
7	5	red deer	47	222	690	1437	25.7	.39	.07	.32
8	5	red deer	77	143	404	932	23.9	.54	.19	.35
9	5	red deer	29	251	550	1328	21.1	.51	.05	.46
10	5	red deer	13	121	236	713	23.0	.57	.05	.51
11	5	red deer	17	78	201	652	32.6	.47	.08	.39
12	5	red deer	1	27	73	219	31.3	.38	.01	.37

(continued)

TABLE 9.7 (*Continued*)

Case name	Predator type	Prey	Horn MNE	Head MNE	All limbs MNE	tMNE	tMNE/ MNI	Horn+ head/ limb	Horn/ limb	Head/ limb
Riera 13	5	red deer	11	56	159	520	37.1	.42	.07	.35
14	5	red deer	194	220	771	1997	20.6	.54	.25	.28
15	5	red deer	64	89	359	946	29.6	.43	.18	.25
16	5	red deer	57	190	589	1468	29.9	.42	.10	.32
17	5	red deer	26	60	260	584	27.8	.33	.10	.23
18	5	red deer	28	143	541	1286	32.1	.32	.05	.26
19–20	5	red deer	69	347	886	2261	26.0	.47	.08	.39
21–23	5	red deer	16	103	417	765	23.2	.28	.04	.25
24	5	red deer	14	37	178	335	20.9	.29	.08	.21
25	5	red deer	1	4	12	26	13.0	.42	.08	.33
26	5	red deer	0	50	164	310	23.8	.30	.0	.30
27	5	red deer	9	105	383	777	28.8	.30	.02	.27
28	5	red deer	4	10	18	51	17.0	.78	.22	.55
29	5	red deer	0	17	31	90	18.0	.55	.0	.55
30	5	red deer	1	7	13	30	15.0	.61	.08	.54
2–3	5	ibex	0	5	16	42	21.0	.31	.0	.31
4–6	5	ibex	3	163	387	1152	25.6	.42	.01	.42
7	5	ibex	4	50	184	505	29.7	.29	.02	.27
8	5	ibex	3	83	97	450	21.4	.89	.03	.85
9	5	ibex	4	39	88	306	30.6	.49	.04	.44
10	5	ibex	0	22	40	159	26.5	.55	.0	.55
11	5	ibex	0	5	9	60	30.0	.55	.0	.55
12	5	ibex	1	9	8	48	16.0	1.25	.12	1.12
13	5	ibex	1	20	28	150	25.0	.75	.03	.71
14	5	ibex	4	54	119	459	30.6	.49	.03	.45
15	5	ibex	0	12	63	187	37.4	.19	.0	.19
16	5	ibex	2	63	98	394	24.6	.66	.02	.64
17	5	ibex	0	20	31	149	24.8	.64	.0	.64
18	5	ibex	0	28	55	280	40.0	.51	.0	.51
19–20	5	ibex	2	116	143	631	21.7	.82	.01	.81
21–23	5	ibex	1	7	66	128	16.0	.12	.01	.11
24	5	ibex	1	31	90	263	32.9	.35	.01	.34
26	5	ibex	0	13	28	118	29.5	.46	.0	.46
27	5	ibex	1	22	53	151	25.2	.43	.02	.41
WD1	6	caribou	1	2	64	93	15.5	.05	.01	.03
WD2	6	caribou	0	~2	11	~25	25.0	.18	.0	.18
WD3	6	caribou	1	1	12	20	20.0	.17	.08	.08
S.Ago S4	6	red/fallow	0	1	7	9	9.0	.14	.0	.14
S4	6	ibex	0	2	16	25	25.0	.12	.0	.12
SX	6	ibex	2	5	54	128	32.0	.13	.04	.09

[a] Mostly donkey remains, but a few elements of horse also present. Hyaenas were provisioned with whole donkey carcasses by the observers.

[b] Bovid size classes as defined by Brain (1981:275), but may also include a few elements of other taxa of comparable body size.

[c] Zero value for limbs is assigned arbitrary value of 1 to permit ratio calculations.

[d] Guattari G2–3 is listed as an MP hominid case, but actually represents a mixture of hominid and spotted hyaena components with the hominid component being dominant.

Note: Predator types are (1) striped hyaena, (2) brown hyaena, (3) spotted hyaena, (4) Middle Paleolithic hominid, (5) Upper Paleolithic hominid, (6) wolf; (~) approximated value due to minor counting ambiguities.

TABLE 9.8
Anatomical summary data for small ungulates[a] collected by six types of predators
in Upper Pleistocene and modern shelters

Site and case	Predator type	tMNE	MNI	tMNE/MNI	Horn+ head MNE	All limbs MNE	Horn+ head/ limb
Arad Cave[b]	1	5	2	2.50	4	1	4.00
Kalahari' 77	2	43	6	7.17	24	5	4.80
Moscerini M5	3	72	4	18.00	18	26	.69
Guattari G0–1	3	9	2	4.50	2	5	.40
Buca I1–4	3	13	6	2.17	—	8	.01[c]
Buca I1–4	3	11	3	3.67	4	5	.80
Moscerini M2–4 and M6	4	51	9	5.67	20	29	1.00
Breuil Br and B3/4	4	51	3	17.00	7	15	.47
Sant'Agostino S0	4	70	4	17.50	12	18	.67
Sant'Agostino S1	4	59	3	19.67	9	16	.56
Sant'Agostino S2	4	38	3	12.67	5	19	.26
Sant'Agostino S3	4	23	2	11.50	2	8	.25
Palidoro 33–34	5	10	2	5.00	2	5	.40
Salvini 1–10	5	30	1	30.00	2	8	.25
Sant'Agostino S4	6/4	20	2	10.00	3	5	.60
Sant'Agostino SX	6	121	6	20.17	18	48	.37

[a] In the Italian assemblages, small ungulates include roe deer and wild boar, along with rare remains of chamois in IUP assemblages. In modern hyaena dens, small ungulates include Class I bovids (Brain 1981:275) and wart hog.
[b] Case from Arad Cave includes porcupine.
[c] Cell containing zero value is assigned an arbitrary value of .01 to prevent case exclusion. Very small cases are not considered.

Note: Predator types are (1) striped hyaena, (2) brown hyaena, (3) spotted hyaena, (4) Middle Paleolithic hominid, (5) Upper Paleolithic hominid, (6) wolf.

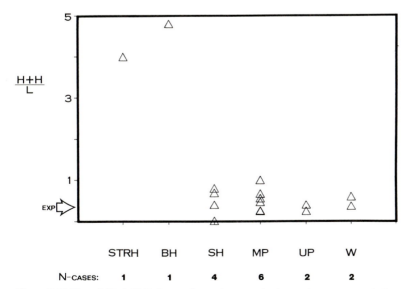

Figure 9.12 Plot of (H + H)/L for small ungulate remains by predator type; symbols as in Figure 9.11.

scavengers (striped and brown hyaenas) with all other predator cases; those collected by spotted hyaenas, hominids, and wolves center around the expected value of anatomical completeness. It may be that only obligate scavengers of medium ungulates also scavenge smaller prey, or that small prey obtained by scavenging normally are not worth transporting for energetic reasons. Whatever the reason, small ungulates are comparatively poor descriptors of the full range of foraging strategies employed by the predators to obtain ungulates more generally.

The relationship between (H + H)/L and modes of procurement appears to deteriorate completely for large ungulates (data in Table 9.9). Figure 9.13 shows that Mousterian hominids created only one head-dominated case (aurochs, in Guattari G4–5), possibly indicating scavenging. All other cases, including one known to have been scavenged by striped hyaenas, hang near the expected value for anatomical completeness, regardless of predator type.

Prey size has an appreciable effect on transport habits, but there is no all-encompassing rule linking anatomical content and procurement tactics across prey body size classes in the study sample. Instead, the relationship between (H + H)/L and foraging strategy is strongest for the medium ungulate size group. The relationship deteriorates for larger and smaller ungulate prey consumed by the same predators. It is clear, then, that the ranges of variation in the (H + H)/L ratio in medium ungulates are especially important for finding niche differences among the predators. This prey size group represented pivotal resources for all six of the predators, based on its relatively great abundance in shelters and dens. This comparison demonstrates that the general tactics—hunting and scavenging—are not unique to any of the species considered and certainly cannot, in and of themselves, distinguish subspecies of *Homo sapiens*. The ranges of variation, on the other hand, can be tied to predominant foraging strategies and niche breadth in modern carnivore control cases, and thus in some way distinguish predatory adaptations more generally. In the case of Mousterian hominids, roughly half of the assemblages point to a strong emphasis on scavenging, the others to hunting.

TABLE 9.9

Anatomical summary data for large ungulates[a] collected by six types of predators
in Upper Pleistocene and modern shelters

Site and case	Predator type	tMNE	MNI	tMNE/MNI	Horn+ head MNE	All limbs MNE	Horn+ head/ limb
Arad Cave	1	114	7	16.28	22	79	.28
Moscerini M5	3	18	12	1.50	—	15	.01[b]
Guattari G0–1	3	113	8	14.12	28	62	.45
Buca I1–4	3	37	6	6.17	2	21	.09
Buca I5–6	3	63	5	12.60	—	32	.01[b]
Guattari G4–7	4	14	3	4.67	7	4	1.75
Breuil Br and B3/4	4	65	5	13.00	12	33	.36
Sant'Agostino S0	4	16	2	8.00	2	5	.40
Sant'Agostino S1	4	25	2	12.50	4	10	.40
Sant'Agostino S2	4	4	1	4.00	—	4	.01[b]
Palidoro 33–34	5	169	7	24.14	22	80	.27
Salvini 1–10	5	67	2	33.50	6	25	.24

[a] In the Italian cases, large ungulates include horse and aurochs. Cases from Buca della Iena also include large ungulate elements that could not be identified to species. In modern hyaena dens, includes Class IV bovids (Brain 1981:275), zebra, and camel.

[b] Cell containing zero value is assigned an arbitrary value of .01 to prevent case exclusion. Very small cases are not considered.

Note: Predator types are (1) striped hyaena, (2) brown hyaena, (3) spotted hyaena, (4) Middle Paleolithic hominid, (5) Upper Paleolithic hominid, (6) wolf.

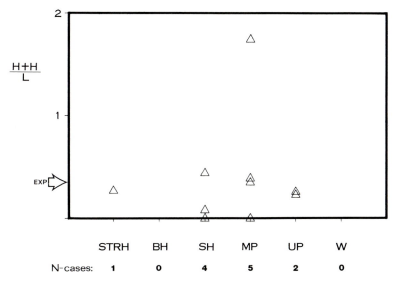

Figure 9.13 Plot of (H + H)/L for large ungulate remains by predator type; symbols as in Figure 9.11.

SAMPLING BIAS AND THE NATURE OF SCAVENGED FAUNAS

Shelter faunas created by scavengers should have lower total MNE (tMNE) values per unit accumulation time than hunted faunas, because scavengers cannot exploit as much of each carcass they encounter on the average. Lower returns should be especially evident if scavenging is limited to nonconfrontational situations, in which leftovers are the most common prizes from partly consumed, starvation depleted or partly decomposed carcasses. This principle is apparent from the three hyaena series in the comparative sample. And, as might be predicted from the previous analysis, all of the suspected scavenging cases from Middle Paleolithic Italy display low tMNE values (see Table 9.7).

The expectation that scavenging could be signaled by low tMNEs is accompanied, however, by a risk that perceptions of anatomical biases are equally explainable in terms of small sample size. In fact, assessing the potential influence of sample size (tMNE) on anatomical content ([H + H]/L) of the head-dominated Middle Paleolithic faunas is a complex and important problem. The lack of analogous examples created by modern humans gives us cause to wonder how much of the perceived pattern

is the product of imagination as opposed to some past reality. But head-dominated archaeofaunas are reported for certain other Upper Pleistocene cave sites, such as at Klasies River Mouth in South Africa (Binford 1984; Klein 1989b; but see review by Turner 1989). If the sampling criteria for accepting these enigmatic cases are very stringent for the wrong reasons, we could, in effect, miss a valuable and informative dimension of variation in ancient, possibly extinct, foraging systems.

The possible effects of sample bias must be addressed, brought into clearer focus if not wholly eliminated. The question is whether the suspected scavenging cases are so small that they prohibit meaningful comparisons of anatomical content to larger (primarily hunted) faunas. The problem of sample size cannot be resolved in its entirety here, but two comparisons, below and in the next section, lend much support to the view that the Italian head-dominated faunas genuinely reflect foraging behaviors of hominids.

While it is axiomatic that scavenged faunas will constitute relatively small samples per unit accumulation time, biases attributable mainly to small

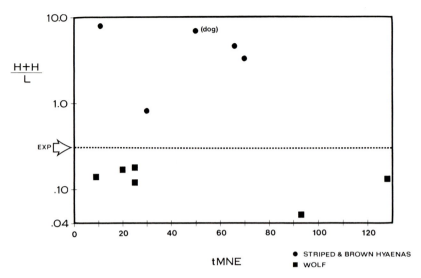

Figure 9.14 Plot of (H + H)/L and tMNE/MNI for medium ungulate remains collected at dens only by obligate scavengers (striped and brown hyaenas) and by obligate hunters (wolves); vertical axis logged. (From Stiner 1991b)

sample size should involve random patterns of anatomical representation—at least after the effects of bone attrition have been excluded. In fact, there are several good reasons to expect that the anatomical patterns associated with scavenged food in shelters will not be random at all. Actualistic studies of carcass consumption sequences *at death sites* (e.g., Haynes 1980; Blumenschine 1986:35–38) show that crania and horn parts are common among the dregs of ravaged carcasses. Wildlife studies cited previously (see also Chapter 8) also relate head and/or horn biases to situations in which predators depend heavily on scavenged sources. Taken together, these contextual data show that each nonhuman predator prefers to transport limbs, but primary feeders (usually hunters) are more likely to actually have access to them. Secondary feeders (scavengers) are more likely to come across heads and/or horns if carcasses already have been fed upon by other predators. Thus, an association between scavenging behavior and a relatively high incidence of horn and/or head parts (high [H + H]/L) in shelters is predicted from modern situations, regardless of the identity of the bone-collecting predator. Biases due exclusively to small sample size, rather than foraging strategies, should not *consistently* result in assemblages dominated by head and/or horn parts

rather than limbs, assuming that preservation issues have already been addressed.

Figure 9.14 tests the effects of sample size bias by contrasting (H + H)/L ratios for small assemblages collected by obligate scavengers (striped and brown hyaenas) and an obligate hunter (wolf). All of the cases have low tMNE values, ranging from 9 to 128 (Table 9.7). The expected, anatomically balanced (H + H)/L value is indicated by a dashed line. Regardless of sample sizes, the proportion of head/horn to limbs effectively separates the two classes of predators in accordance with known foraging behaviors. The results fulfill the predictions of an explanation based on behavior, and contradict the predictions of an explanation based on sample size bias. Turning to the Italian Middle Paleolithic cases, a correlation assay of tMNE to (H + H)/L indicates a nonsignificant relationship (not graphed, $r = -.269$, N = 16, $P >> .10$), meaning that differences in anatomical content do not follow differences in sample size. These comparisons show that the head-dominated pattern of the Middle Paleolithic, and horn/head faunas created by modern predators, are not simply the result of sample size bias. Instead, the head/horn-dominated and meaty patterns appear to have been derived from fundamentally different parent contexts.

Horn- and Head-Dominant Subpatterns in Scavenged Faunas

Most aspects of anatomical variation in the study sample do not distinguish predator species, nor humans from all carnivores. An exception exists, however, with regard to the frequencies of horn/antler to head parts in documented and suspected cases of scavenging. A high (H + H)/L ratio value can arise from elevated proportions of horn/antler *and/or* head parts. While the general circumstances behind the collection of horns and heads may be similar for all predators, tendencies to collect one or the other relate to significant differences in the feeding habits of hominids and hyaenas. Two potentially interesting kinds of information are obscured by the (H + H)/L ratio and merit discussion. The first point concerns the differing processing capabilities of hominids and hyaenas. The second concerns the relative frequencies of cranial versus mandibular elements in head-dominated shelter faunas.

While both horn- and head-dominated faunas suggest a heavy emphasis on scavenging, all species of hyaena tend to focus on horn (and apparently antler when their geographical ranges overlapped with cervids during the Pleistocene), whereas Middle Paleolithic hominids in Italy tended to bring back only heads. Figure 9.15 shows some examples of deer antler collected and gnawed by spotted hyaenas in Guattari G0–1; antler samples from den occupations in this site and in Buca della Iena include substantial quantities of shed and unshed antler (see also Chapter 13). Hyaenas can consume and completely digest virtually any bone tissue (Sutcliffe 1970; Kruuk 1972; Guthrie and Smith 1990), apparently making horns and antlers worth collecting regardless of what else might be attached to them. Horns and antlers are common leftovers at ungulate death sites. Moreover, deer shed their antlers each year and grow new ones. Animals that are able to eat horn and antler therefore may collect them in substantial quantities. Like hyaenas, African porcupines also produce horn biases in their lairs, because they can eat bone, and horns are commonly available in the environment (Brain 1980, 1981). Hominids, on the other hand, are very good at opening bone cavities, but generally avoid ingesting dense bone. It is also significant in the case of the Mousterian that elaborate processing technologies appropriate for grinding trabecular bone or boiling food do not appear to have existed (see Chapter 8).

Differences in the processing capabilities of hominids and hyaenas are clearly expressed in the study sample. Figure 9.16 illustrates the horn (/antler)

Figure 9.15 Unshed red deer antler bases from Guattari G0–1, gnawed by spotted hyaenas.

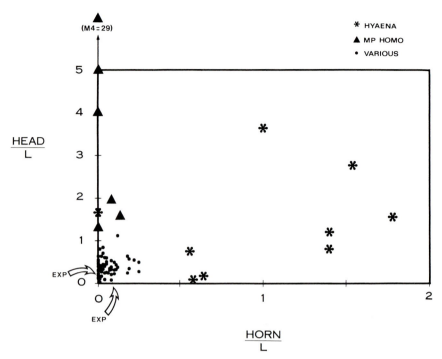

Figure 9.16 Relative frequencies of horn parts (HORN/L) versus head parts (HEAD/L) for medium ungulate remains in assemblages collected by the six predator types; outlier cases marked according to predator type, other cases conform to expected (EXP) values. (From Stiner 1991b)

to head contrast between hyaena- and hominid-collected shelter faunas. When either horn or head parts are overly abundant relative to limbs in shelter assemblages, the hyaena-generated cases tend to be strongly biased toward horn and/or antler elements (high HORN/L, see Table 9.7), whereas hominid-generated cases tend to be strongly biased toward head elements (high HEAD/L). Hominids never produced an overabundance of horn/antler. The tight cluster of points near the graph intercept consists primarily of Upper Paleolithic cases. The fact that, among hominids, only some Middle Paleolithic cases are outliers to the *x-y* intercept further suggests that Mousterian hominids at times engaged in foraging practices quite different from those of all fully modern humans for the same prey in generally comparable ecosystems.

The second point, having to do with the relative abundance of cranial versus mandibular elements within the head region, may have implications for the sources of scavenging opportunities exploited by hominids. Actualistic studies cited above suggest that, if heads are obtained from predator kills, the skull would often have been safely separated away from the mandible, and the latter destroyed by primary feeders. An expectation drawn from the actualistic cases is that the cranium (but not the mandible) is the most common prize available to scavengers from ravaged carnivore kills. However, crania and mandibles are combined to form the head unit (the numerator in [H + H]/L ratio) in this comparison on grounds that they occur in roughly equivalent frequencies, or mandibles are somewhat more abundant, in the Mousterian faunas (see Table 9.3). Equivalent frequencies of crania and mandibles suggest that the hominids' scavenging opportunities arose largely from nonviolent deaths, in which articulated skulls remained intact, rather than from ravaged predator kills.

FORAGING SPECIALIZATION AMONG PREDATORS

The relationships between foraging and transport strategies in predators can be examined further by considering the average amount of food transported from carcass sources (anatomical completeness, tMNE/MNI) relative to anatomical content ([H + H]/L). Dividing tMNE by MNI standardizes the quantity of skeletal parts in shelters relative to the average number of foraging events. Figure 9.17 shows a log-log regression of the two ratios, with predator types distinguished by symbols (data in Table 9.7). The plot indicates a strong negative relationship between anatomical completeness for medium-sized ungulate remains and the proportion of horns and heads to limbs therein ($r = -.689$, $P = < .001$). In other words, the incidence of horn and/or head parts increases as the amount of food carried away per feeding opportunity decreases.

Table 9.10a provides regression statistics by predator type (not graphed) and for all predators combined (graphed). Given the composite uncertainty inherent in the study sample, the fact that the ratio of horn and head parts to limbs explains nearly 50 percent ($r^2 = .475$) of all variation in anatomical patterns is quite significant. The findings indicate a predictable and independent connection between the predominant foraging strategy and anatomical content for medium-sized ungulate prey, regardless of predator species, and confirming visually based observations of the data. When predator types are considered individually, significant relationships are found for the striped hyaena, Middle Paleolithic hominid, and Upper Paleolithic human series. The slopes for the brown hyaena, spotted hyaena, and wolf series, on the other hand, are not significantly different from zero. Wolf cases are the most conspicuous outliers to the regression slope due to wolves' tendency to collect leg elements at shelters more often than any other predator.

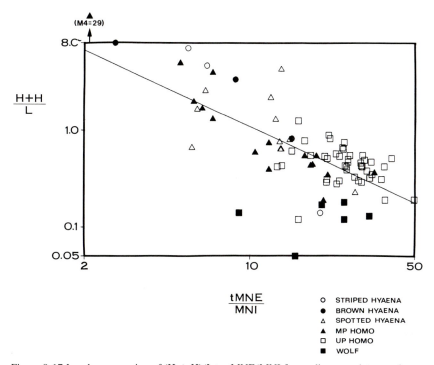

Figure 9.17 Log-log regression of (H + H)/L to tMNE/MNI for medium ungulate remains collected at shelters by the six predator types. (From Stiner 1991b)

TABLE 9.10

Regression statistics for the relationships between (H + H)/L
and tMNE/MNI for medium ungulates

a. By predator, and for all six predators combined

Predator	r *value*	r^2	*N-cases*	P
striped hyaena	−.999	.998	3	.001 < P < .01
brown hyaena	−.942	.887	3	> .1
spotted hyaena	−.471	.222	11	> .1
MP hominid	−.873	.762	16	<.001
UP human	−.316	.100	45	.02 < P < .05
wolf	−.219	.048	6	> .1
all predators[a]	−.689	.475	84	< .001

[a] Plotted in Figure 9.17.

b. For various predator subgroups

Predator groups	r *value*	r^2	*N-cases*	P
all except MP hominids (STRH, BH, SH, UP, W)	−.639	.408	67	< .001
all hominids (MP, UP)	−.707	.500	61	< .001
hominids and hyaenas (STRH, BH, SH, UP, MP)	−.779	.607	77	< .001
hyaenas and wolves (STRH, BH, SH, W)	−.740	.548	22	< .001

Note: (STRH) striped hyaena, (BH) brown hyaena, (SH) spotted hyaena, (W) wolf, (MP) Middle
Paleolithic hominid, (UP) Upper Paleolithic human.

Table 9.10b explores relationships between tMNE/MNI and (H + H)/L further, by comparing regression statistics for a variety of predator subsets. All groupings show significant negative relationships at the .001 level of probability. Assorted recombinations reveal that only the addition of the wolf group visibly affects the r^2 values, but even this set does not reduce the possibility that the relationship among any of the predator sets is highly significant. While the negative relationship between tMNE/MNI and (H + H)/L for medium-sized ungulates across predator cases is strong, no such relationship is apparent for small or large ungulates transported to shelters by the same predators. Table 9.11 lists regression statistics for small and large ungulate cases (ratio values are from Tables 9.8 and 9.9). Even the removal of outlier cases could not improve the statistical appearance of the regressions for the small and large ungulates.

Returning to medium-sized ungulate prey, the differences among predators in Figure 9.17 follow a behavioral grade from scavenging to hunting, with obligate scavengers (striped and brown hyaenas) at the horn- or head-dominated (high) end of the regression line. Obligate hunters (wolves and, appar-

TABLE 9.11

Regression statistics for the relationships between
(H + H)/L and tMNE/MNI for small
and large ungulates

Prey size category	r *value*	r^2	*N-cases*	P
small ungulates	−.535	.286	15[a]	> .1
large ungulates	.190	.036	10[b]	> .1

[a] Spotted hyaena-collected case I1–4 omitted ($y = .01$).

[b] Spotted hyaena-collected case M5 omitted ($x = 1.4$); late Upper
Paleolithic case from Salvini is outlier to the graph ($x = 33.5$).

TABLE 9.12
Results of rank-ordered comparisons of predators based on (H + H)/L
for medium ungulates

	Spotted hyaena	MP hominid	UP human	Wolf
Striped-brown hyaena	$X^2 = 5.94$ $P = .015$	$X^2 = 4.97$ $P = .026$	$X^2 = 12.67$ $P < .001$	$X^2 = 7.50$ $P = .006$
Spotted hyaena	—	$X^2 = 1.07$ $P = .30$[a]	$X^2 = 14.02$ $P < .001$	$X^2 = 11.01$ $P < .001$
MP hominid	—	—	$X^2 = 5.89$ $P = .015$	$X^2 = 12.53$ $P < .001$
UP human	—	—	—	$X^2 = 14.57$ $P < .001$

[a] Nonsignificant value (df = 1).

ently, Upper Paleolithic humans) lie at the meaty end. Predators that do both (spotted hyaenas and, apparently, Mousterian hominids) occupy nearly the entire range. The comparisons indicate that a broader ecological principle is at work, one that effectively cross-cuts phylogenetic boundaries between the species considered. Because the two ends of the regression line can be related to known extremes in the foraging adaptations of modern nonhuman predators, the findings demonstrate predictable and species-independent connections among the predominant foraging strategy, food transport "choices," and anatomical representation in shelters.

Figure 9.17 also shows that some predators are confined to specific segments of the regression line, while others are not. Wolf and late Upper Paleolithic human cases occur only at the low end, while brown and striped hyaena cases are confined to the high end (artificial provisioning case omitted). Spotted hyaenas and Middle Paleolithic hominids appear more versatile, as both series are distributed across most of the regression line. In the case of the Mousterian, however, variation is expressed within one small region of Italy, whereas variation in the spotted hyaena assemblages is expressed across several regions of Africa and Europe. Recall, however, that the regression explains much more of the variation in the Middle Paleolithic series than in the spotted hyaena series (see Table 9.10a).

As compelling as the relationship for medium ungulates appears in Figure 9.17, more precise in-

formation is needed about where significant differences lie among predators on the regression line. Specifically, we need to know just how different is different. These differences are relevant to the degree of foraging specialization exhibited by each kind of predator—at least as evident from patterns of food transport. The distances between nonhuman predators will in turn provide an independent measure of difference for comparing Middle and late Upper Paleolithic hominids.

The (H + H)/L ratio values are rank-ordered in Table 9.12 and subjected to pair-wise comparisons using a Kruskal–Wallis one-way ANOVA test for ranked data. This test makes fewer assumptions about the data than parametric tests, substituting a chi-square approximation for an F statistic and circumventing the problem of nonlinearity in the ratio distributions. The rank-order comparisons reveal significant differences between all predator pairs save one: Middle Paleolithic hominids and spotted hyaenas are essentially indistinguishable. It should be noted again, however, that the spotted hyaena series is compiled across a large geographical cline extending from (modern) South Africa to Mediterranean (Upper Pleistocene) Europe, whereas the Middle Paleolithic series represents only one small region of Italy. Hyaena-collected faunas from Italy vary less, and tend toward the meaty end of the scale.

Mousterian hominids and spotted hyaenas aside, the chances are very slim of confusing predators with one another at this scale of comparison. It is

TABLE 9.13
Highest, lowest, and median values for medium ungulate (H + H)/L
by predator type

Predator type	N-cases	(H + H)/L		
		Lowest	Highest	Median
striped-brown hyaena	5[a]	.82	8.00	4.64
spotted hyaena	11	.23	4.31	.81
MP hominid	16	.19	29.00	.57
UP human	45	.12	1.25	.43
wolf	6	.05	.18	.13

[a] Artificial provisioning case removed.

Note: Expected (H + H)/L value for a complete carcass is 0.3.

impossible, for example, to confuse the Middle Paleolithic series with the Upper Paleolithic one; the range of variation is great for the former and restricted for the latter, even though both series come from generally analogous environments. The data imply that the Middle Paleolithic series is like that of the spotted hyaenas worldwide in that these hominids relied on either scavenging or hunting, depending on local circumstances. In contrast, striped and brown hyaenas were dedicated primarily to scavenging, while Upper Paleolithic humans and wolves were largely dedicated to hunting wherever they took up residence.

Differences in the ranges of variation for medium-sized ungulate cases among the six predator series can be examined further. Table 9.13 presents lowest, highest, and median values for the (H + H)/L ratio by predator type. Striped and brown hyaena cases are combined because so few are available for comparison. Lumping the two species is justified on grounds that both represent obligate scavengers occupying more or less analogous foraging niches in geographically separate regions (compare, for example, Skinner et al. 1980; Mills 1984a, 1984b). Working first with a linear ratio axis in Figure 9.18, it is clear that the (H + H)/L ranges differ markedly among predators and that the relationships are nonlinear. Numbers of cases (N) are listed on the right side of the graph, showing that the ranges of variation are not related to sample size.

Obligate scavengers and species that both hunt and scavenge have much wider ranges of variation than obligate hunters. The scavenging element is largely responsible for this aspect of difference, because scavenging emphasizes opportunism and will, almost by definition, heighten variation among cases. After all, scavenging opportunities can involve anything from a few gristly bits to whole carcasses. Hunters, on the other hand, nearly always get the whole carcass, or, if they lose it, they usually lose it all. The range of variation for the Mousterian series (MP Homo) from Latium is extraordinarily great: some cases are head-biased whereas others are meaty or verge on anatomical completeness. In contrast, Upper Paleolithic cases dating to between 20,500 and 10,000 years ago display only the second aspect of the two potential extremes, and the ranges are very narrow for both Upper Paleolithic humans and wolves. The latter two predators almost certainly scavenged from time to time but, if so, they usually had access to whole carcasses, suggesting they were better prepared to locate and monopolize opportunities.

Figure 9.19 presents the same data using a logged ratio axis. The two extremes of the (H + H)/L ratio correspond to habitual scavenging and habitual hunting, as observed in modern nonhuman predator species. The vertical dotted line on the graph represents the expected value for the natural prey skeleton (see Table 9.5) and provides a baseline for comparison. This graph deemphasizes the higher end of the (H + H)/L range, focusing instead on variation below and just above the expected value. The range occupied by the Latium Mousterian cases effectively spans hunting and scavenging, suggesting that they behaved like effective hunters in some cir-

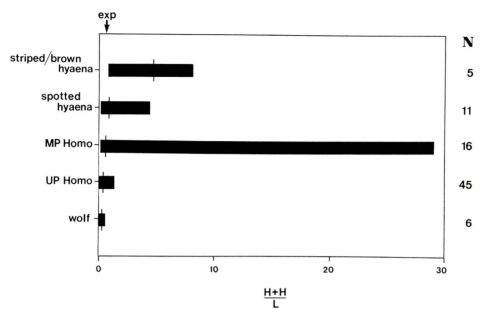

Figure 9.18 Comparison of (H + H)/L medians and ranges for the six predator series, using a linear ratio axis. N refers to number of cases, "exp" refers to the expected value based on the complete prey anatomy, and the vertical line through each bar represents the median for that series. (From Stiner 1993a)

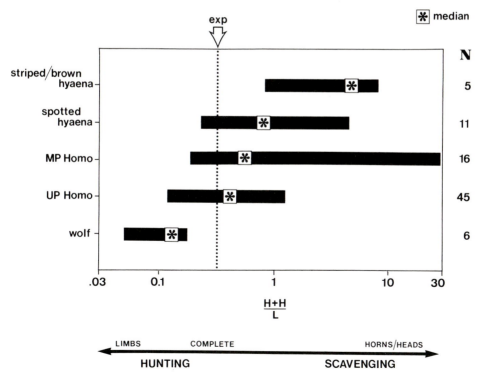

Figure 9.19 Comparison of (H + H)/L medians and ranges for the six predator series, using a logged ratio axis; *median, other symbols as in Figure 9.18. (From Stiner 1993a)

cumstances and like nonconfrontational scavengers in others. Here, the scavenging habits of striped and brown hyaenas serve as the model for nonconfrontational scavenging, in contrast to forceful displacement of other consumers from a relatively complete, fresh carcass. Recent ethnoarchaeological studies of contemporary foragers, such as the Hadza, appear to exemplify scavenging largely in the context of hunting (Bunn et al. 1988; O'Connell et al. 1988a), what I will hereafter refer to as *confrontational* scavenging. The comparative data presented here underline the possibility that such cases represent only one of many contexts in which scavenging may have occurred in the past.

IMPLICATIONS OF HEAD COLLECTING IN THE ITALIAN MOUSTERIAN

To summarize findings thus far, hunting and early access to medium ungulate carcasses correspond to anatomical patterns approaching the natural balance of parts in complete prey in shelters. This pattern is most evident for wolves and late Upper Paleolithic humans, but also emerges in some Middle Paleolithic and spotted hyaena cases. Scavenging and late access are indicated by distinct biases toward horn-antler and/or head parts. Spotted hyaenas produce both patterns according to their environment, whereas Middle Paleolithic hominids produced both patterns within one small geographical area of Italy, sorting by cave site. Closer inspection shows that scavenging hyaenas often collect inordinate quantities of horn or antler in dens, a tendency that clearly separates them from all hominids.

Why should scavenging hominids transport heads —and just about only heads—to shelters? The outstanding proportion of head parts relative to lower limbs and feet (for foot representation, see Figure 9.10) in the Italian cases is not altogether faithful to Speth's (1987) part choice model based on ungulate marrow depletion sequences as a function of season (discussed in Chapter 8). The persistence of crania at death sites has been demonstrated in previous experimental research (e.g., Haynes 1980, 1982; Brain 1981; Blumenschine 1986) and could partly explain the attraction of head parts for bone-collecting predators, especially scavengers. However, there is a nutritional element as well, and this is where environmental setting becomes an important consideration.

In biomes ruled by freeze-thaw cycles and where large predator guilds have not been destroyed by human intervention, nonviolent deaths rather than carnivore kills often form the principal sources of scavenging opportunities (see Chapter 10). The generally equivalent frequencies of crania and mandibles in the head-dominated Mousterian faunas of Italy are consistent with this interpretation. Nonviolent deaths in turn show a very strong link to starvation and tend to be concentrated in certain seasons, particularly late winter through late spring. Thus, scavenging opportunities in cooler parts of the world may involve primarily animals in poor nutritional condition.[7]

It was shown in Chapter 8 that soft cranial and upper neck tissues, such as the brain, thymus, and to some extent the tongue, have two unusual nutritional properties from the perspective of a carnivorous forager: (1) soft head and some upper neck tissues contain relatively high fat levels because, among other things, they are the locus of myelinated nerve fibers (proteinaceous cells sheathed in fat, often called white matter, e.g., Kimber et al. 1961); and (2) unlike muscle fat and yellow marrow, most fat in the head organs is quite stable relative to changes in prey health, because neurological function is essential for sustaining life in all circumstances. The mandible meanwhile is among the last parts to be depleted of yellow marrow in situations of poor nutrition (Speth 1987, 1989). The total fat value of head parts is relatively unaffected by starvation for these reasons.

Three inter-related reasons for preferential transport of heads of medium ungulates are proposed,

[7] Just as pneumonia is the foremost proximate cause of modern human deaths in hospitals, starvation is the foremost proximate cause of nonviolent (and many predator-caused) deaths in wild mammals. Any congenital or infectious disease, for example, will reduce an animal's ability to forage. This means that a significant proportion of potential scavenging opportunities in temperate and cooler environments will involve fat-depleted prey.

based on information presented above and in Chapter 8. First, heads require considerable processing and taking them to a secure place is often worthwhile. Second, the main procurement tactic represented by head collecting appears to have been scavenging, the opportunities for which may have been regulated by seasonal shifts in food supply. Third, the nutritional value of head parts (and the thymus in the upper neck) is unique relative to the rest of the prey anatomy. Head parts represent the final bastion of fat tissue in prey suffering from seasonal or other causes of malnutrition.

While more information on seasonality is needed for the head-dominated cases of Middle Paleolithic Italy, the apparently strict choice of parts suggests that other skeletal elements of medium ungulates were either not available or not worthy of transport for intensive processing. The latter possibility would point to months of procurement other than those associated with peak fat yield in prey. The possibility that Mousterian hominids scavenged carcasses of animals perishing from nonviolent causes during lean seasons could explain the generally equivalent proportions of crania and mandibles in these enigmatic faunas.

Consideration of the nutritional value of head parts is directly relevant to questions about hominids' responses to variations in food supply. The absolute volume of soft head tissue is small, but consistent richness in fats sets heads apart from other prey body tissues. In lean periods of the year, when scavenging opportunities are more abundant and fat is most prized by predators, the relative availability and value of head parts will be inflated. We can also expect hunters to respond to the unique nutritional qualities of head parts. Interest in head parts is seasonal in colder habitats (e.g., Binford 1978) and more or less continuous in lower latitudes where fat is chronically scarce (see Chapter 8). In situations of hunting and access to complete carcasses, however, preferential treatment of head parts may be more apparent in processing decisions at the final destination than in transport decisions.

CONCLUSIONS

Holding preservation and recovery practices constant, the general framework provided by the (H + H)/L ratio may diagnose the relative emphasis on hunting and scavenging in predatory adaptations, as expressed by the cumulative products of food transport. This contrast is reflected primarily as variation in the amount of limb bones relative to head and/or horn parts, since the latter are a nearly universal feature of the shelter faunas examined.

The relationships between procurement and transport habits documented here emerge only at relatively broad scales of comparison, and it is only at this level that they are relevant to the problem of distinguishing predator niches. Of greatest interest are the central tendency and the range of variation in an array of cases produced by a predator species, reflecting the plasticity with which that predator responds to prevailing foraging conditions. Taken to the level of interspecific comparisons, these data reflect the ecological (and sometimes evolutionary) distances between foraging adaptations of one predator and those of another. While the (H + H)/L ratio for medium ungulates potentially tells a great deal about foraging systems of extinct hominids, it cannot provide a fully inclusive diagnosis of scavenging for every (isolated) circumstance; the findings may not apply, for example, to the treatment of suids in the Italian study sample (see also O'Connell et al. 1988a). While informative about predator niches, moreover, these data disconfirm the widespread notion that anatomical representation of prey in cave faunas identifies the predator to species or genus (cf., for example, Klein 1975).

The major differences described among the predators considered here, and between the Middle and Upper Paleolithic specifically, are really about the *scale* at which variation in foraging strategies is expressed in time and space. We can expect that every one of these predators scavenged, and that most of them hunted, too. Mousterian hominids were, in some situations, capable hunters by late Upper Paleolithic standards, even if they did not always choose to do so. The Mousterian scavenging pattern stands apart because the strategy was somehow spatially and temporally separated from hunting, a striking contrast to modern human situations in which the products of both strategies are pooled at the same residential places (e.g., Binford 1978; O'Connell et al. 1988a, 1988b; Bunn et al. 1988). Limited evidence indicates that late Upper Paleolithic foragers in Italy also scavenged from time to time (e.g., evident for rarer species, such as horse at Grotta Polesini, Stiner 1990a), but the visible fallout of this behavior was either swamped by the more consistent and pervasive products of hunting at each shelter they used, or scavenging was undertaken only for relatively whole carcasses that were both fresh and fat.

In niche theory, the trophic relationships among species in communities are defined not only by the resources that the animals depend upon, but also by how and when they use them (Chapter 2). Ungulates are one set of resources many predators share an interest in, but may use differently. As discussed in Chapter 8, we can expect that head parts will represent something special to all carnivorous foragers whenever and wherever fat is scarce. We can also expect that ancient hominids needed a good bit of fat in their diets just as we do now, because fat is critical for neurological development in children, as well as for meeting caloric needs in humans of all age groups. The need has not changed, but the archaeological data suggest significant differences in how hominids went about getting fat during various periods of the Upper Pleistocene and how ungulate exploitation may have offset the use of other (perhaps now invisible) resources (see Chapters 14 and 15). This contrast is greatly reinforced by other lines of archaeological evidence in west-central Italy, including prey age selection patterns (Chapter 11), small animal exploitation (Chapter 6), and seasons of shelter use (Chapters 12 and 13), as well as aspects of tool manufacture, reuse, and transport pertaining to hominid mobility (Chapter 14).

Treatment of head parts, and the extent to which they dominate transport trajectories, may provide valuable clues about foragers' responses to seasonal or chronic scarcity of fats, regardless of whether they were hunters, scavengers, or both. However, the two contingencies—procurement strategy and nutritional considerations—are difficult to separate in these comparative data. Indeed, the strong asso-

ciation of the two contingencies in the control cases suggests that foraging strategy and fat scarcity are inextricably linked in natural foraging situations, possibly because hunters have more choices both at the level of transport decisions and in selecting live prey. As for head collecting in the Italian Mousterian specifically, ungulate age structures in these enigmatic faunas point independently to scavenging (Chapter 11).

Modern reference cases also suggest that Mousterian scavenging was of a nonconfrontational nature, making these cases more akin to gathering than hunting. Any human being is capable of gathering food, but some members of modern human social groups are confined to such practices while other individuals are not; often the patterns of movement necessary for hunting and for gathering are incompatible (e.g., Blurton Jones et al. 1989; Hurtado et al. 1985). Social factors therefore impinge upon the rate and spatial patterns of the search process and even the kinds of food likely to be procured. For these reasons, scavenging in the context of hunting may not be strategically equivalent to scavenging in the context of gathering. The Mousterian evidence points to a fundamental difference in how foraging systems were organized between the two periods (acknowledging the rather arbitrary chronological boundary between them).

Placing the comparisons of hominid foraging habits within the larger world of predators provides independent insights on the changing place of hominids in animal communities, something that an exclusive focus on humans beings simply cannot give. An interspecific perspective alters, for example, conceptions of how shifts in hominid predatory niche should be modeled. Mousterian hominids were at times capable hunters, but at other times turned to alternative foraging modes (such as persistent scavenging) not characteristic of fully modern humans in the same region. One can find some Middle Paleolithic cases that fall within the Upper Paleolithic range of variation, but it is not possible to squash the entire Middle Paleolithic complex into that of the Upper Paleolithic. The comparisons show that the Middle Paleolithic hominid series is neighbor to both spotted hyaenas and fully modern (late Upper Paleolithic) humans, but all are quite distinct from the obligate scavengers (striped and brown hyaenas). The comparisons also show that there is a world of difference between a predator that cannot hunt and one that does not always hunt.

The simple heuristic dichotomy often made between hunting and scavenging is probably a false one. At best, it only narrowly describes one aspect of the resource base used by omnivorous hominids. This artificial dichotomy has served its intended purpose, however, by improving our understanding of what hominids are and were as foragers, meanwhile discouraging unqualified and fanciful presumptions about ancient hunters. However, we no longer should be dealing with questions of whether Mousterian hominids were hunters or scavengers. It is the rules of strategic combination that distinguish large predator adaptations, and perhaps also those of two subspecies of *Homo sapiens*. I would argue that a major difference between hominid forms involved how the two general procurement strategies—hunting and scavenging—were integrated within foraging systems, geographical scales of movement, and the degree to which their application was sensitive to the choice and timing of shelter use.

Four methodological issues also deserve review in closing: (1) modeling hominid transport choices on the basis of fat content; (2) reemphasis of the fact that anatomical representation, in itself, cannot diagnose predator species; (3) ways of seeing behavioral tendencies in archaeological records; and, finally, (4) the possibilities that variation within the Mousterian follows a trend or is representative of a single, more or less stable foraging niche.

It is clear that marrow indexes alone are insufficient for ranking nutritional returns of prey body parts or predicting choices, especially in situations in which scavenging and/or stress are suspected. Models are developed and improved through periodic visits to the real world. In this study, interspecific comparisons of transport choices by living carnivores alongside nutritional analyses of head tissues place rather different values on skeletal body parts of medium-sized ungulate prey. These reference data in turn make enigmatic faunas of the Italian Middle Paleolithic easier to comprehend.

The analyses presented in this chapter demonstrate that the full range of variation in anatomical content produced by two species can overlap com-

pletely (see also Hill 1984; Turner 1984). No single anatomical pattern in shelter faunas can diagnose predator species; the only significant exception to this general rule may be the excessive proportions of horn or antler that often mark hyaena den occupations. By the same token, no single case can serve as a general model for the bone-collecting habits of a particular predator, hominid or otherwise. This is especially important with respect to adaptations that emphasize variable response, as exemplified by both spotted hyaenas and Middle Paleolithic hominids.

In considering the results of the anatomical analyses, it must be appreciated that the variation in the Italian Mousterian is only perceptible when many assemblages from several sites are compared. The comparative approach adopted here completely over-rides possible variation at the intra-assemblage level. The data register the degree to which foraging strategies varied in the context of bone accumulations forming over a relatively long time and in a particular place. In this way, the data reflect the behavioral *tendencies* of predators, not what they will do in every situation. The study meanwhile ignores finer variation known to exist in modern human systems and, from this perspective, the Upper Paleolithic cases discussed are remarkably uniform. Yet ethnoarchaeological studies document considerable variation in modern human situations, depending on site function, season, kinship, and so on (e.g., Binford 1978; O'Connell et al. 1988a, 1988b; Yellen 1977, 1991a). The data presented here do not contradict more detailed observations about modern humans; my data simply embody broader scales of variation.

Finally, the two Paleolithic hominid series here are treated as temporally homogeneous. Possibilities of linear trends in the data are ignored, and each series, hominid or carnivore, is assumed to describe the boundaries of a single, unchanging adaptation. This is fair enough for the carnivores, whose adaptations have not changed so much over the past 110,000 years. It is also appears to be valid for the late Upper Paleolithic series, at least from an interspecific perspective, because the range of variation for this series is very narrow. The assumptions of temporal homogeneity for the Latium Mousterian series may be valid, but aspects of the Italian sample also pose some contradictions. Statistically significant trends are apparent through time for assemblages from the four coastal sites, in terms of both food transport patterns and prey age selection (addressed in Chapter 14). It is essential to bear in mind, however, that the study area is small and aspects of its geography may account for the variation in Mousterian foraging strategies. All available information considered, the most proximate explanation for the variation is the gradual lowering of the Mediterranean Sea between 110,000 and 35,000 years ago and corresponding changes in local forging opportunities in the vicinities of the four caves. A seasonal factor may also have contributed to the variation (Chapter 13), but a full assessment of these issues is postponed until Chapters 14 and 15, where the many sources of information are gathered together and synthesized.

On the Meaning of Mortality Patterns
in Archaeofaunas

IF TAPHONOMY is a mean dog (see Chapter 5), then mortality studies are like the New York subway system: having traveled widely, I am sure that they can get you almost anywhere, providing you board the right train. Assuming as little as possible is, in my view, the place to begin when researching mortality patterns in fossil faunas. Latching on to something that can be established independently of the archaeological problem, something about modern mammalian populations or predator-prey dynamics, provides the firmest footing for interpretations of prehistoric cases.

Mortality patterns do not do a very good job of distinguishing among the various species of predators, nor between predators and other death phenomena. Age structures, or mortality patterns, in mammalian archaeofaunas instead may reflect some very basic ecological relationships between predators and their prey. With the support of taphonomic data, they have considerable potential for learning about human land use, food search practices, labor organization, and the very nature of the human foraging niche itself, providing the expectations and test implications are sound. Because certain predictable links exist between the age structures of prey death assemblages and general ecological principles of predator-prey dynamics, mortality patterns present an opportunity in this study to map changes in humans' position in animal communities through time.

A number of theoretical and methodological issues are relevant to how mortality data may be analyzed and interpreted with regard to prehistoric human behavior. One set of issues concerns the place of large predators in the food web, and, by extension, how their foraging niches evolve. Another group of issues concerns idealized models of population structure, normal variation therein, and methods for analyzing death assemblages. Finally, there is the matter of spatial and temporal scales of observation, which can enhance, bias, or completely obscure the heuristic potential of age structure data, depending on the problem being addressed. The scale issue is one of the most troublesome aspects of mortality analyses in zooarchaeology.

Here, I describe the common age structure models, their underlying assumptions, and some demonstrable relationships between pattern and cause. The review illuminates the numerous potential applications of mortality data for archaeological research, and for this study in particular. Questions about predatory niche shape most analyses of mortality in this research (Chapter 11), but age data in other forms serve for investigating seasonality (Chapters 12 and 13). I therefore turn, at the end of this chapter, to mortality in ungulates and in carnivores relative to the annual cycle.

PREDATOR-PREY DYNAMICS AND PREDATOR EVOLUTION

Although the long-term dynamics are not fully understood, predators evolve at least partly in response to the availability of prey. Understanding the demographics of prey populations therefore is integral to interpretations of what prey age groups predators normally consume and the evolution of predator niches in ecosystems. The processes by which mammalian populations grow, stabilize, and are limited have as much to do with where infants come from as how and when they die (e.g., Caughley 1966, 1977; Sattenspiel and Harpending 1983)—this fact is fundamental and essential to mortality studies. The content, structure, and size of populations at any given time are products of two processes that operate at the opposing ends of the lifetime: recruitment via live births and loss through deaths. New members are born to the population by healthy fit adults. Apart from the husbandry practices of some human cultures, predators exert little if any control over birth rates. Predators certainly can take fertile females from the reproductive core of a prey population, but their potential impact in this regard is greatly diluted by a variety of factors; many large predators tend to harvest age groups other than those comprising the reproductive core, or they take only a random toll. Death waits at the other end of the lifetime, and here predators may play a greater role, but always in conjunction with other factors such as starvation and disease. If the processes of recruitment and loss are considered together, it is difficult to conclude that predators are in the driver's seat when it comes to limiting prey populations.

Predators, like parasites, extract food from populations without significant reinvestment, and they may do so at surprisingly similar harvest rates (see Davies et al. 1989). The survival of predator-prey relationships over the long term requires that exploitation not destroy the food base, and the predator along with it. And like parasites (Davies et al. 1989), predators always interact with the prey items they take as a matter of definition, but not all prey come in contact with predators. So predators and parasites must be the dependent ones to a significant degree, sensitive to the amount of harvesting that prey populations can sustain across generations of exploitation.

Many field studies of carnivore ecology in temperate and arctic environments show that predators are not the foremost cause of death in prey populations (Bartmann et al. 1992; Bertram 1979:229; Bibikov 1982:26; Hauge and Keith 1981:585; Peterson and Page 1988; Thompson and Peterson 1988;

cf. Bergerud and Snider 1988). It now appears that predator populations are limited by food supply, at least in situations of high prey densities (Gasaway et al. 1992:26–41). The only compelling exceptions are situations in which prey densities are low (Gasaway et al. 1992), but the factors often are left unexplained in these studies (Boutin 1992) and inferences about ultimate cause at times appear unscaled with respect to the theoretical predictions (Gavin 1991; Sinclair 1991). Long-term studies (Ballard et al 1987:41–42; Peterson and Page 1988; Thompson and Peterson 1988; White et al. 1987) and cross-regional comparisons (Kruuk 1972:293–296) suggest that a compensatory relationship exists between predator effects and other causes of ungulate death in many situations (Sinclair 1991; but also see Nudds and Morrison 1991).

The question of whether predators limit prey populations or, conversely, are limited by them, is an important theoretical premise for any study of predator ecology, because it affects how we model the evolutionary constraints operant on predators—humans or otherwise—and hence our decisions about research design. Why should mobile foragers adjust their strategies from time to time, if the net productivity of the lands they occupy is guaranteed? There is, as yet, no perfectly clear or all-encompassing answer to the question of who limits whom, but scale is at the root of most disagreements, and food supply remains the most compelling force across study areas and across time. Special, and very interesting, exceptions may arise where prey densities are low. The former view nonetheless sets a founding premise for this study.

Larger than a lifetime

Harvesting by predators is best modeled in terms of many procurement events, spanning appreciable increments of time and space. The debate that has recently surfaced in the wildlife literature, provoked by new cases contentious to the view that predator populations are limited by food supply (e.g., Bergerud and Snider 1988), is a contest between theoretically and empirically driven approaches to population research and game management (Boutin 1992; Gavin 1991; Sinclair 1991). The data and the issues claimed to be at stake are not always well matched; there are the conceptual and practical problems of how one can weigh predator effects against natural, inevitable attrition (Nudds and Morrison 1991). Because mortality concerns the rates at which individuals die in species that can live a long time, mortality phenomena in large mammals operate at a level larger than we are biologically designed to witness. With the aid of demographic theories, we can see small fragments of the process, like watching a baseball game through a small hole in a big fence, but without a view of the dugouts and having to go home before the game is over.

Population dynamics is a continuous process, wherein births and deaths go on everywhere at once and death factors may act in compensatory ways. We see only episodes, such as death in action. This is because an observer can be in only one place at a time. Given the limits of human perception, the question of who limits whom in predator-prey relationships is not simply an empirical issue. As regards this study, it is assumed that large predators exist more or less at the top of the trophic pyramid. It also is assumed that, short of domestication practices, hunter-gatherers did not limit prey birth rates in the past, and that they only partly contributed to prey death rates. In other words, humans' evolutionary history was to some extent constrained by prey demography; prey populations oscillated independently of human resource interests for the most

part and, by extension, affected humans' coexistence with other predators that depended on the same prey populations.

Animal husbandry may pose a fascinating exception. Modern animal husbandry involves deliberate management or concerted redirection of energy by human consumers back into a prey population of choice, usually at the expense of other coexisting species. Humans in hunter-gatherer economies, in contrast, merely intercept energy flow through the food web, in the packages that nature presents and when nature presents them. Human foragers may deliberately burn large areas of habitat to enhance local forage and thereby encourage population growth in prey species, but even in this situation humans are merely simulating natural conditions in which populations may expand. Such practices in no way restrict population growth. Predators undoubtedly have evolved and continue to evolve relative to the challenges imposed by certain characteristics of prey populations and vice versa, but this concept is logically separate from generalizations that predators are necessarily the primary limiters of prey population growth in the big picture. By recognizing that food sources constrain predators in ways that are insensitive to their needs, we have something to work with in evolutionary studies of humans as predators.

Zooarchaeological Applications of Mortality Data: Back to 1972

The presence of tool marks on fossil bones up to 1.5 to 2 million years old suggests that ungulates were a significant food resource for early hominids (e.g., Bunn 1981; Potts 1982, 1988). The increasing importance of such foods in later segments of prehistory eventually set *Homo* adaptations apart from those of all other primates (Chapters 1 and 2). The highly dedicated hunting adaptations of modern Eskimo and other hunter-gatherer cultures represent some of the most recent and spectacular expressions of this trophic characteristic. Equally extraordinary is the ability of modern humans to occupy almost any environment without undergoing major physiological changes (Foley 1987). In a word, meat eating allows humans to cope with seasonal hiatuses in

plant food availability, a problem that other great omnivores solve through metabolic torpor. The fact that archaic hominids were carnivorous does not mean, however, that they were the same kind of predator as modern humans. The ways that hominids obtained ungulates may have undergone radical changes since the Middle Pleistocene. Because the cumulative products of prey age selection, known as mortality (age-frequency) patterns, are functionally related to how modern carnivores search for food and their *habitual* techniques of procurement, mortality data should also be suitable for tracing the evolution of hominid predatory adaptations.

Archaeologists and biologists have been aware of

the potential of mortality data for studying predator-prey relationships for some time. As for archaeological applications, some especially insightful work emerged in the British literature in the early 1970s. I refer, in particular, to Jarman and Wilkinson's (1972; also Higgs and Jarman 1982) essay on how best to investigate problems of human exploitation (specifically, animal domestication) from the perspective of mortality data. These authors recognized that alterations in prey skeletal morphology could only provide signatures of the later phases of certain kinds of domestication. Mortality patterns were seen as a potentially powerful alternative for investigating earlier stages of the same processes, but with the recognition that their analytical utility was contingent upon knowledge of causality and natural variation in population composition outside of the human sphere. Jarman, Wilkinson, and Higgs were among the first to outline just how and where archaeologists must push the boundaries of knowledge about mortality phenomena in order to realize their full potential for behavioral research of any kind. Their recommendations pointed to the areas of prey behavior and physiology and to predator-prey relationships in other species.

Klein has been a pioneer in describing some types of mortality patterns in Pleistocene faunas, particularly those associated with archaic *Homo sapiens*. Klein and co-workers have chosen, however, to interpret those patterns solely in terms of other archaeological cases (e.g., Klein and Cruz-Uribe 1984; Klein 1978, 1987), and they have made inferences about foraging behaviors without the benefit of systematic consideration of independent, real-life phenomena. Klein reasoned at one time that attritional mortality patterns in archaeological cases should be evidence for hominid hunting (1979, 1982a), later claimed that catastrophic profiles should be evidence of hunting, and most recently stated that evidence of scavenging should be confined to attritional (U-shaped) patterns (1987, 1989a).

Archaeological data from different regions and/or time periods may provide useful points of contrast in comparative studies of ungulate mortality, but these sources are not sufficient, by themselves, for interpreting still other archaeological cases (also see Turner 1989:3). Archaeology is, by definition, about the past, and interpretations of archaeofaunas are strengthened by information on how things more basic to life operate in the present. Both modern control and archaeological data are needed for setting observed mortality patterns into a rigorous interpretive framework and a reasonable temporal framework as well. The modern control data delimit the relevant domains of causality that can shape mortality patterns in death assemblages, thereby allowing one to know the degree to which any pattern conforms with specific kinds of predatory behaviors. A multisite archaeological perspective, in turn, allows analysts to evaluate the relative importance and context of any particular case in ancient behavioral patterns overall.

Given the possibility that Pleistocene hominids might have scavenged as well as hunted, how do we distinguish modes of procurement from the choices available? The answer lies in two nonarchaeological classes of information: (1) the full range of modern circumstances in which the identified mortality patterns can occur; and (2) how mortality patterns vary with the ecology of both predator and prey. The observed range of variation in control sources is particularly important for linking prey mortality patterns to behavioral adaptations. The most interesting behaviors from ecological and evolutionary perspectives are those that are repeated—the behaviors that make a difference in foraging adaptations and, therefore, the faunal record. In the discussions that follow, I present a variety of modern situations in which the causes of death are known. Not every example is immediately germane to my research in Latium, but the survey of modern cases outlines and qualifies the baselines for comparisons undertaken in Chapters 11, 12, and 13.

BASIC AGE STRUCTURE MODELS OF LIFE AND DEATH

Two mortality models are fundamental to archaeological and paleontological studies of death assem-

blages, and these models are based on simple, well-documented age structure patterns in a wide variety of animal species (Caughley 1966, 1977). The models have nearly universal applicability for mammals, because they are the direct products of recruitment (live births), development rates, and survivorship. The first of these models is simply the age structure of living populations at any given moment, basically the "parent structure". The second model is the most standard product of attritional deaths, although the causes of death are many. When modeled in idealized form, the models correspond to the parent (living-structure) pattern and the first most common derivative death pattern (U-shaped), respectively. Not all mortality patterns created by predators will ultimately conform to these basic models, but, just as Mendelian inheritance is fundamental to our understanding of genetics, these are the building blocks of more complex mortality models; the first or both models precondition all subsequent selection biases by predators and other bone-collecting agencies.

Age structure models used in archaeology are based on the frequencies of individuals in a series of consecutive age cohorts, usually of equal duration. In contrast, two alternative measures of age composition are used in demographic studies of modern living populations: age frequency-counts and mortality rates (a probabilistic expression of survivorship). Archaeological studies are largely confined to the former, because the absolute live composition of ancient prey populations is unknown. We can only approximate what the age structure of the living population was like by extrapolating from the average condition in modern unmanaged populations, and by working from an abstract or empirically defined range of variation for each class of mortality pattern (e.g., Cribb 1987; Lyman 1987b; Stiner 1990b).

When the frequencies of individuals in successive age cohorts are plotted two-dimensionally, the instantaneous structure of a living population displays a half-pyramidal or staircase form (Figure 10.1). Some variation should be expected in the slope of the half-pyramid, depending on whether the living population is in a stable, growing, or declining state (e.g., Caughley 1977:121; Sattenspiel and Harpending 1983). The slope varies within predictable limits, however, and this variation can be incorporated with idealized static

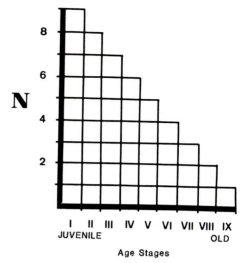

Figure 10.1 Idealized stable structure for a living population divided into nine age cohorts. (From Stiner 1990b)

models for analytical purposes. The fact that some mammals give birth to several young at once, others to only one, may alter the slope of age pyramid but does not change the overall structure.

Attritional death in mammals results in a second kind of mortality profile, here termed a *U-shaped pattern* (Figure 10.2B). It differs significantly from the age structure of the parent living population, because the probability of dying is significantly lower during the prime years of life (e.g., Caughley 1977:99; Lyman 1987b:126). As a consequence, old animals and especially juveniles are superabundant in attritional death assemblages. The U-shaped mortality pattern reflects age-specific vulnerability to any number of death factors such as disease, accidents, malnutrition, and many (but not all) types of predators. Where one agent of attritional death (e.g., wolves) is rare or absent, other factors take over and may produce essentially the same result.

The living-structure and U-shaped models were developed by population biologists interested in modern demographic phenomena (e.g., Caughley 1966, 1977). The models have subsequently been borrowed in archaeological studies of ungulate exploitation by humans (e.g., Klein 1978, 1982a, 1982b) and for paleontological studies of how fossil

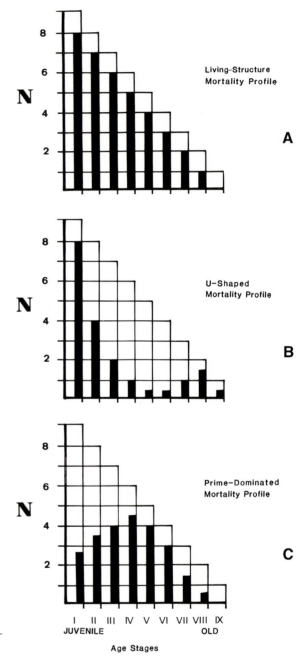

Figure 10.2 Three idealized mortality structure profiles superimposed on an idealized stable living population model.

faunas were formed (e.g., Voorhies 1969). In the process, the models have also received new names, "catastrophic" in the place of living-structure, and "attritional" in the place of U-shaped. Unfortunately, the newer labels imply causes of death rather than simply describing the age structure

patterns—fewer causes, in fact, than actually may account for the patterns. Hence, I prefer the purely descriptive nomenclature used in population biology, although corresponding archaeologists' terms are also provided as appropriate.

Some studies, such as Haynes' (e.g., 1987,

1988) work on proboscideans, indicate that the above models may require some qualification for certain higher mammals. The general principles of recruitment and death are the same, but unusual life history and developmental characteristics of some long-lived species introduce potentially confusing variation in mortality patterns. As is true for humans, elephants and whales (Savelle and McCartney 1991) mature relatively slowly, and individuals reach maturity at roughly one-third of their maximum potential lifetime. Here, maturity refers strictly to the level of physiological development,

the point when an animal is biologically *capable* of reproducing. This developmental threshold may or may not correspond to the age at which most individuals *actually* begin reproducing. Prolonged development and high levels of parental investment relative to the overall life course bias mortality patterns in relatively unique ways from the perspective of research on predation, although its significance varies with the type of problem studied. The basic age structure models are quite appropriate, however, for all of the ungulate species to be discussed in the next three chapters.

Derivative Mortality Models

So far I have described age structures of living populations and death patterns more or less independently of what predators do. From the perspective of modeling human predation, mortality patterns in prey death assemblages represent the final expressions of what live populations have to offer, and how humans responded to resources whose existence did not depend much on their own. Predators extract some portion of a living population according to the general search and procurement strategies employed and, in the process, unwittingly create mortality patterns wherever they collect the bones of their prey. However, the relationships between predators and food species are not always directly or simply inferable from the mortality patterns in archaeofaunas. Whatever sorts of mortality patterns predators may produce, all may be considered derivative, including those that simply mimic the age structure of the living prey population. Significant departures from the living age structure may arise from predation, biased because live or dead prey animals are distributed unevenly in space, or because the predator's procurement strategy for some reason focuses on certain age groups independently of live age group abundances. Some examples of derivative mortality patterns that are biased with respect to prey age include those weighted toward juveniles, old adults, or prime adults.

Prey animals may group themselves in a habitat according to sex and age classes, creating resource patches that are locally anomalous relative to the prey population as a whole. This is one reason why studies of predators' adaptations require samples

that span multiple search and procurement events. The structures of death assemblages can also be affected by whether the predator took live or dead prey within a given period. Nearly all species of predator will scavenge (including modern humans, e.g., Gusinde 1961; Bunn et al. 1988; O'Connell et al. 1988b), drawing, in these circumstances, on sources created by independent agents of death (e.g., other predators or nonviolent causes). The problem of learning how mortality patterns are derived in archaeological cases is therefore compounded by the fact that predator-generated patterns can mimic those occurring in other contexts (Stiner 1990b).

These basic facts about mortality in mammals pose some interpretive challenges to archaeologists interested in human predatory behavior. The first step toward a solution is to establish the identity of the bone collectors in fossil assemblages. Because most mortality patterns are not exclusively diagnostic of cause, taphonomic data rather than age structure are needed to attribute a faunal accumulation to a specific bone collector and to identify preservation biases that might affect the apparent age structure of species therein. The fact that multiple factors can produce analogous mortality signatures is important and merits illustration with real-life examples below.

Causes of death that do not select for age

A living structure mortality pattern (Figure 10.2A) can result from a variety of causes, includ-

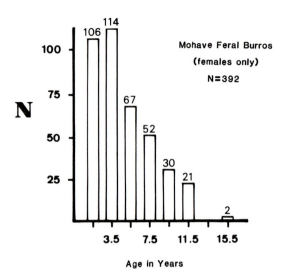

Figure 10.3 "Living-structure" mortality profile for female feral burros created by a mass removal program. (Data from Johnson et al. 1987; figure from Stiner 1990b)

ing the cumulative effects of predation. If the predator takes prey on the basis of chance encounter, individuals will be killed more or less in proportion to their natural abundance. Sudden disasters, such as large-scale floods, fire, volcanic eruptions, and some highly virulent diseases, also may create living-structure mortality patterns. In each of these circumstances, all animals in a population have an equal probability of dying irrespective of age and thus are represented in proportions reflecting their natural abundance. The living-structure pattern *appears* nonselective, and sometimes is called catastrophic by archaeologists (e.g., Klein 1982a) and paleontologists (Voorhies 1969).

Figure 10.3 illustrates a modern example of living-structure (or catastrophic) mortality. The histogram shows the relative frequencies of female burros (N = 392) by two-year age increments. The data are from a demographic study of a modern feral population following its complete eradication from a military reservation in the Mohave Desert (Johnson et al. 1987:917). The population had not been hunted or managed for almost thirty years prior to removal in 1981, and the death assemblage closely resembles the ideal living-structure model in Figure 10.2A. Lyman (1987b) documents similar mortality patterns for cervids killed by the 1980 Mount St.

Helens volcanic eruption in Washington state, although this case is slightly deficient in old adults relative to the stable version of the living-structure model. Other examples of the age composition of *living* mammalian populations are available in the vast literature on controlled census research (e.g., Bunnell and Tait 1981; McCullough 1981; Rogers 1987; Boer 1988).

Causes of death that are age-dependent

U-shaped mortality is the most common death pattern in nature. The U-shaped pattern can result from predatory strategies that focus on age-specific vulnerability, so that old, very young, and sick individuals are most often killed. The U-shaped pattern also typically results from other age-dependent causes such as most kinds of disease, accidents, parasites, and malnutrition (e.g., Chapman and Chapman 1975:197; Clutton-Brock et al. 1982:273; White et al. 1987).

Figure 10.4 compares U-shaped mortality patterns occurring in nonpredated and predated contexts. Figure 10.4A shows the natural mortality pattern for fallow deer in an environment lacking predators (Chapman and Chapman 1975:196–197), where accidents and malnutrition were identified as the principal causes of death in yearlings and adults. The investigators report that the fawn age group is the largest in the death assemblage, although absolute counts are not available. The second histogram in Figure 10.4B shows a U-shaped profile for wolf-killed moose in south-central Alaska (Ballard et al. 1987). As is true for the first histogram, the absence of juvenile cohorts is an artifact of the field methods, but the 0–2 year cohort contains approximately twenty eight individuals, based on the illustrations in the report.

The nonpredated fallow deer case and the wolf-killed moose case exemplify some of the variation that one can expect within the U-shaped mortality pattern type. They also demonstrate that essentially similar death patterns may arise from distinct causes. While both cases display U-shaped mortality profiles, however, the wolf-generated case is somewhat richer in old moose and, to a lesser degree, moose late in their prime. The pattern created by wolves may reflect short-term or local imbal-

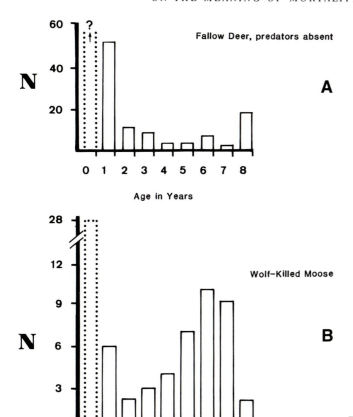

Figure 10.4 U-shaped mortality profiles for (A) fallow deer in the absence of predators (data from Chapman and Chapman 1975), and for (B) wolf-killed moose. (Data from Ballard et al. 1987; figure from Stiner 1990b)

ances in predator-prey densities in the study area (Peterson and Page 1988) and temporarily intensified predation. Figure 10.5 shows that, while wolf-generated cases generally display U-shaped profiles, the details of these profiles vary between studies (Peterson et al. 1984); the central gap expands and contracts (apparently) in concert with cyclical shifts in prey abundance. Obviously, no single short-term assemblage of wolf kills can adequately characterize the wolf's dynamic relationship with prey populations.

The prime-dominated mortality pattern (Figure 10.2C) is uncommon in nature overall, but it is typical of cervid and bovid remains in some archaeological records. Humans appear to be the only agencies that *regularly* produce prime-based mortality in prey, making this pattern somewhat more

specific to cause than the other types of death patterns. Ethnographic and historic accounts (e.g., Benedict 1975; Egan 1917; Regan 1934; Steward 1938; Tatum 1980), ethnoarchaeological studies (Binford 1978), and some archaeological evidence (e.g., Frison 1984; Todd 1983; Todd and Hofman 1987) associate the pattern with selective ambush hunting, regardless of hunting party size. In modern contexts, the prime-dominated pattern is also produced by trophy hunters using firearms (e.g., Sowls 1984; Woolf and Harder 1979), associations documented in Chapter 11.

A focus on prime adult prey runs counter to natural age-specific abundance and the usual pattern of age-specific vulnerability in living populations. Prime-dominated mortality certainly diverges from natural recruitment and survivorship in nature and,

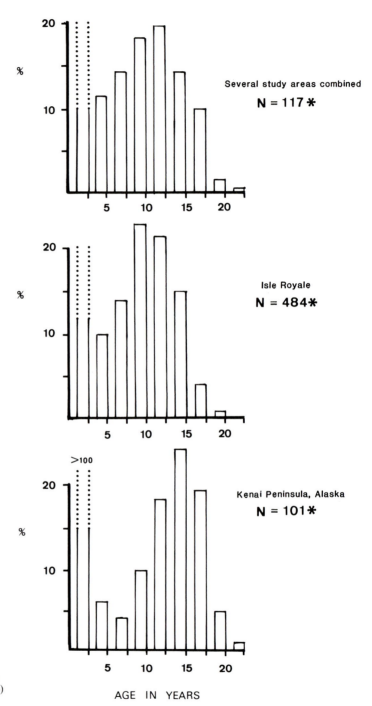

Figure 10.5 Mortality profiles for wolf-killed moose from various study areas in Canada and Alaska. (Data from Peterson et al. 1984:16)

perhaps more significant, from the typical prey se-lection patterns of nonhuman predators. Because prime-dominated procurement focuses on the age group with the highest reproductive potential, it may also suggest a more delicate ecological balance between harvesting and the population's ability to replenish itself and/or a hidden spatial element re-lating to how intensely one ungulate resource "patch" is used before moving on to another (see Chapter 11). Prime-dominated harvesting nonethe-less appears to track a population's intrinsic rate of increase (*r*) more closely than any other procure-ment strategy, possibly mediated by focusing on one sex, in addition to the prime adult age category. But this could be practiced at more than one spatial

level by shifting the size of a predator's territory. For all of these reasons, the timing of its appearance and growing importance in human evolutionary his-tory are of great interest.

U-shaped, living-structure, and prime-dominant mortality describe the vast majority of cases pro-duced by nonviolent and predator-caused deaths. Two rarer types of mortality patterns, the old-dominated and the juvenile-dominated profiles, are also of interest for hominid subsistence research. Discussion of these two patterns is postponed until Chapter 11, because the context of their occurrence is an important part of their definition, and more study of how they may arise in modern situations is needed.

NUMBERS OF AGE COHORTS AND MORTALITY PROFILE CONTOURS

Mortality patterns for mammalian death assem-blages are usually constructed from age-frequency data based on dental remains. Mammal teeth are among the most persistent materials in archaeo-faunas and are the best descriptors of individual age. Dentitions undergo progressive, measurable changes over the entire lifetime, first through growth and later through occlusal wear and the for-mation of cementum layers. Living bone also un-dergoes alterations as a function of individual age, but easily perceived changes in these tissues gener-ally cease with skeletal maturity and bones gener-ally do not preserve as well as teeth in most geologi-cal deposits.

On the other hand, each tooth in the large mam-malian skull has a somewhat different development and wear history throughout the life course, making some teeth more suitable for analysis than others. This fact is most obvious from comparisons of pro-files constructed on the basis of M1 and M3 molars for the same death assemblage (Severinghaus 1949 on white-tailed deer; Gifford-Gonzalez 1991 on bovids). Moreover, some teeth, especially molars, have no counterpart during the juvenile phase of life, and hence cannot directly inform us about indi-viduals perishing before the permanent teeth de-velop. There is not a great deal of agreement on which tooth element is best for eruption-wear studies; the choice depends in part on what is being

asked of teeth, how many age stages are needed for an analysis, and whether nonlinear rates of wear is a significant issue. Once a tooth element or set of elements has been selected for study, however, it is best to stick with it as much as possible; shifting across tooth elements to construct mortality profiles is bound to undermine efforts to compare mortality patterns. It is also significant that M1 and P4 teeth lie at the fulcrum of wear in the dental apparatus, whereas other teeth erupt later and are farther from the fulcrum of wear.

In constructing age structure histograms, re-searchers can scale the age cohort axis in mortality profiles in different ways. For the standard profile representing all age groups in a population, the hori-zontal axis typically begins at birth and ends around the maximum potential lifetime (MPL; AGEpel in Klein and Cruz-Uribe 1984). We all have a pretty good idea when the lifetime begins, but this is no guarantee that we know when it should end (Caugh-ley 1977). MPL is a tenuous parameter by popula-tion biologists' standards, yet some marker of the end of the fullest potential lifetime is necessary for constructing and calibrating age structure profiles for death assemblages. The problem is that long-evity in a given species can vary extensively be-tween populations as the result of environmental factors, genetics, chance in small samples, and so on. Record lifetimes for one or a few individuals are an especially poor source for this parameter, because they usually involve extraordinary individuals, often living in a protected or captive situation (e.g., zoos). These sources in no way typify maximum longevity in free-ranging populations of the same species. Archaeologists have attempted to cope with the ambiguities inherent in the MPL parameter by using sources for wild populations only and/or by excluding suspiciously long-lived individuals from the control set (e.g., Gifford-Gonzalez 1991; Klein 1982a). Clearly, the less analyses depend on a precise estimate of MPL in real years, the better, because adjusting MPL (or AGEpel) also adjusts one's results. One solution is substituting the maximum wear state of the tooth, corresponding to total destruction of the crown, a parameter that can be defined in larger archaeofaunas. It usually is not necessary to know exactly how every age category corresponds to real years; rather, the issue is to know the overall shape of the age distribution *between* definable limits, such as birth, the age at which the deciduous tooth is shed, and when mastication is no longer possible.

Analysts normally subdivide the age axis into cohorts of roughly equal duration. This way, the data are easily collapsed into grosser age units so that the results of diverse studies can be compared. There is much freedom in choosing how many cohorts to work with—it depends on what you want to know, as well as the sample sizes available for study. However, altering the *x*-axis scale can have major consequences for the overall shape of the mortality profile (as can the tooth element selected for study), and, for this reason, subjective comparison of mortality profile shapes (contour) is not a rigorous procedure. In fact, playing with the *x*-axis

by changing the number of age cohorts is not unlike playing a small accordion; its outline changes from smooth to bumpy as the instrument is stretched. More stretching eventually will reveal empty cohorts and, oftentimes, an entirely new contour; packing it up leads to still greater alterations of form. If prey were born and killed in seasonally restricted periods, one might observe waves of similar periodicity as the age axis of plotted mortality data is stretched; otherwise the profile may just seem irregular. The nomenclature for mortality profiles discussed above applies to systems using anywhere between seven and fifteen cohorts, for which the overall contours remain pretty much the same for each profile type (see Lyman 1987b for a related discussion on sample size). Still other sources of variation in mortality profile contours are introduced via classifications that assume linear rather than curvilinear tooth wear progressions based on crown height (reviewed by Gifford-Gonzalez 1991; first demonstrated by Severinghaus 1949) or, deliberately, by dividing MPL (defined from complete tooth crown destruction) into age stages of unequal duration but keyed to life history phases, as in this study (Chapter 11).

Finally, it should be clear that mismatching significant age junctures in the life course in cross-study comparisons will guarantee specious results (e.g., inconsistent demarcation of the juvenile-adult juncture). Likewise, using only permanent teeth to construct mortality profiles tells us nothing about the juvenile age groups, and without data on the juvenile cohorts, it is impossible to establish whether the age structure is or is not biased toward any other age group.

SCALES OF OBSERVATION AND CLASSES OF INFORMATION

Observing a phenomenon such as prey mortality at differing scales can reveal qualitatively distinct kinds of information about human life in the past. Because the temporal and spatial scales chosen for analysis determine what can be learned from mortality data in archaeofaunas, these scales can and should be adjusted in response to the precise nature of the problem to be addressed. At the finest level,

mortality data inform us about seasons of resource use with respect to specific places on a landscape. Examining death patterns at the level of seasons and expanding the geographical scale considered make it possible to address questions about human territory use (e.g., Todd 1991; Todd et al. 1990). This scale of observation is especially promising for investigating variation *within* particular subsistence systems and, ultimately, how the internal structure of one culture might have differed from that of another, if aspects of food supply can be held constant.

In contrast, mortality profiles representing multiple procurement events over many years are more informative about the predominant food search and procurement strategies of human groups. The averaging effect of this intermediate scale has its own distinct analytical value, as it summarizes longer-term interactions between human predators and prey populations by over-riding transitory growth or

decline phases of populations and the adjustments that humans normally make to them.

At the grossest level of observation, simultaneous consideration of prey death assemblages scattered in time and space provides a measure of human niche and, when compared to data for non-human predators, can be used to monitor the degree and direction of change in prehistoric human foraging adaptations through time. This study concentrates primarily on the largest and the finest (season) scales of observation in Chapters 11 and 12 and Chapter 13 respectively.

Seasonal Mortality in Ungulates and Its Ecological Ramifications for Predators

Demographic studies of ungulate populations in temperate and colder environments register natural peaks in mortality by season. These peaks occur regardless of whether predators are present, because seasonal mortality is ultimately linked to vulnerable phases in the life history strategies of species, periodic environmental stress (e.g., food supply, winter cold, examples to follow), competition for mates, and late summer parasites (e.g., Sattenspiel 1986). While seasonal mortality has at times been correlated with elevated predation intensity, predators generally do not create the cycles as much as slightly modify them. This fact underlines a fundamental causal relationship between seasonal death peaks and U-shaped mortality in general, and it is important for understanding the foundations of specialized predation and scavenging opportunities in a variety of foraging circumstances.

In the juvenile age groups of ungulate populations, bimodal mortality patterns within years appear to be the rule in temperate and arctic regions. Juvenile mortality is high during and just after the birthing period, and again at the end of winter-early spring. Bimodal juvenile mortality cycles have been documented for a variety of ungulate species, including moose (Ballard and Whitman 1987:67–68; Ballard et al. 1987:30, 40; Hauge and Keith 1981:583; Peterson et al. 1984:15, 38), mountain sheep (Geist 1971:284–293), mule deer (White et al. 1987), white-tailed deer (Nelson and Woolf 1987), fallow deer (Chapman and Chapman

1975:198), feral horses (Berger 1986:81–89), and peccaries (Sowls 1984:94).

While adult ungulates also experience seasonal peaks in mortality, the timing differs slightly from that for juveniles, as illustrated for fallow deer in Figure 10.6 (data from Chapman and Chapman 1975:198–199). Only the first peak is asynchronous between the two age groups, however; many fallow deer fawns die in mid- to late spring, whereas the probability of adult death rises sharply in the fall, when rutting males are more subject to distraction, injury, accidents, and rapid depletion of nutritional stores. The second seasonal peak in mortality affects both adults and juveniles at about the same time; this is known as winter-kill, although many of the deaths actually occur in the spring. Broadly, analogous differences between the adult and juvenile cohorts are reported for red deer (Clutton-Brock et al. 1982:269–272) and feral horses (Berger 1986).

Predators and other agencies of death may operate similarly with regard to season. Figure 10.7 illustrates two cases of bimodal mortality in mule deer populations in Colorado (data from White et al. 1987:854) between 1981 and 1985. One population experienced considerable predation on fawns by coyotes (Figure 10.7B). The other population was free from predators, and starvation was the foremost cause of fawn deaths (Figure 10.7A). Despite somewhat different death factors, the timing of fawn mortality was about the same for both study

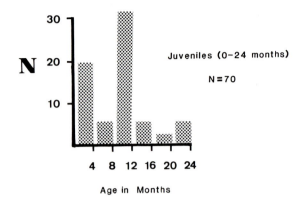

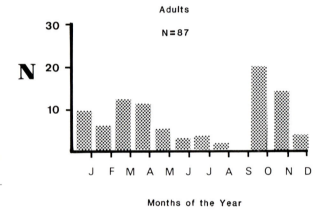

Figure 10.6 Seasonal mortality in juvenile and
adult fallow deer in the absence of predators.
(Data from Chapman and Chapman 1975:198–
199)

areas. Fawn deaths peaked first in May and again
around December–January, whereas only one fawn
died in each study area in summer (not illustrated).
White et al.'s study shows that coyote predation on
mule deer fawns was highly opportunistic and paralleled the effects of winter-kill and high mortality
normally associated with the birthing season. Coyotes are seldom able to kill adult deer, but, by
spooking or outmaneuvering mothers, often steal
their infants (e.g., Paquet 1992). This is a case of a
predator harvesting prey at the upward limit of its
typical size range, a seasonal harvesting tactic
which in turn results in a distinctive age bias toward
neonates. Most important for the purposes of this
discussion is the fact that the opportunities and high
payoffs of a particular kind of predatory tactic were
directly controlled by season.

Modern examples of season-mediated scavenging can be found among bears. That for the Cantabrian brown bear is especially relevant to this research because it involves a classic omnivore
scavenging in a Mediterranean-type environment
(Clevenger 1990, 1991; Clevenger and Purroy
1991; Clevenger et al. 1987, 1990). The overall diet
of this animal, based on 929 scat samples collected
across seasons, centers on plants and insects, but
includes a small but seasonally important ungulate
component, nearly always obtained through scavenging. The Cantabrian brown bear is not a great
hunter of ungulates (wild or domesticated), but is,
instead, a clever and determined locator of scav-
engeable carcasses. The bears will consume meat
almost any time, but scavenging is most important
to their survival during the spring. Soon after

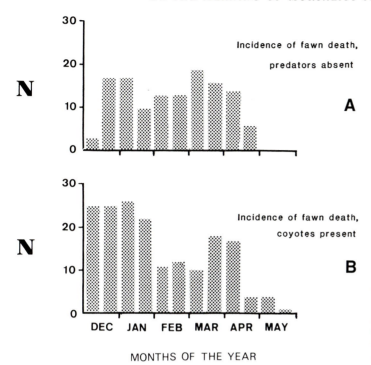

Figure 10.7 Seasonal mortality in mule deer fawns from (A) nonpredated and (B) predated populations in Colorado. Note that only one fawn died in each area after May 31 over the period of study. (Data from White et al. 1987:854)

emerging from the winter den, one bear routinely dug winter- or wolf-killed carcasses out from under the snow and consumed them along with emerging grasses in the area (Clevenger 1991:42–43). It is clear from the Cantabrian bear case that the availability of scavenging opportunities is structured by both natural mortality cycles in ungulates, which peak in winter-spring, and snow cover. Carcasses accumulated throughout the winter, refrigerated naturally in the snow until the spring thaw. This process made carcasses especially abundant by spring in Cantabria, when bears became active and needed them most to supplement scarce plant resources. Clevenger and Purroy (1991:34, 45) report that the proportion of wild ungulates consumed by brown bears in spring across years is positively correlated with the amount of accumulated snow during the previous winter, clarifying the link between scavenging opportunities and cyclical mortality. Also important, the distribution of carcasses in spring coincides to a large degree with that of emerging grasses at the edge of the snow melt. In other words, scavenging in the style of the brown bear employs the same spatial search pattern as that for finding emerging grass shoots along the snow melt line, making the practice economical and foraging more certain. The link between carcass densities and ranging patterns as a function of snow depth is also apparent for wolves in Alberta (Huggard 1993), as discussed in Chapter 8.

To summarize, combined data on prey age selection and season of death can contribute to paleoanthropologists' understanding of how hominids obtained ungulate foods, and whether land use was dependent on ungulate procurement (see Chapters 14 and 15). When framed within broader demographic phenomena, research on prey death patterns can also help resolve whether hominid hunters were in any way limited by prey size or predator defense mechanisms (e.g., Klein 1989b), or merely adjusting their tactics to spatial and temporal patterns of opportunity. Sympatric predator species do not, for example, have equivalent territory sizes in a given ecosystem, and the normal territory size of any one predator species could also change in evolutionary time (for a generally related discussion, see Grayson 1991). The seasonal correlates of ungulate death may be especially helpful for investigating the degree of ecological dedication to ungulate procurement and the importance of scavenging in hominid diets. These investigations must be conducted across sites, however, to exclude the possibility of special use situations. Not all evidence of scavenging necessarily signals limits in predatory capacities or primitiveness from an evolutionary standpoint. While adult ungulates are usually out of the reach of bears (but see Ballard 1982) and coyotes (see also Ozoga et al. 1982 on foxes), many other large predators shift to scavenging only because the immediate gain is high, not because they are incapable of hunting the animals.

As is true of mortality patterns more generally, seasonal death patterns are deeply rooted in the workings of prey demography. Predators often capitalize on these cycles, sometimes tracking them closely and other times switching to alternative food sources. The value of one foraging strategy over another in a foraging system changes with season, and we can expect complex predators to respond accordingly. Communal or solitary ambush hunting, for example, may be best suited to environments where and seasons when live prey naturally aggregate, such as during the rutting or birthing periods. Scavenging opportunities, which theoretically can occur at any time of year, also wax and wane with the seasons. The relative emphasis on scavenging tactics may be further conditioned by what other resource opportunities the same search pattern affords, therefore implying something about patterns and scale of territory use. Scavenging opportunities vary most conspicuously according to cyclical dieoffs in prey populations and, in most situations, tend to be spatially dispersed so that locating only these kinds of feeding opportunities is costly. We can expect scavenging opportunities to be especially high in spring in temperate and colder regions.

Seasonality and resource specialization

Archaeological data on the seasons of resource use not only are place-specific, but usually are limited to a particular class of food. Because any single archaeological case yields information only on what was eaten there, it does not account for the possibility of resource switching elsewhere. The site of interest represents one of many places that a predator might use within the annual cycle, and hence it may reflect a seasonally unique behavior by the occupants, and thus only a narrow, biased glimpse of a larger and more complicated foraging system. Sedentism is untenable for most or all of the Paleolithic, and thus our questions about seasonality should address range size, rates of movement through territory, and occupation schedules of multiple sites therein.

Demonstrations of seasonal use of a site by hominids may or may not bear on whether use of a place was strategically specialized (see also discussion in Chapter 7). Such interpretations would require knowing the living abundances of various kinds of prey and having excellent temporal control on season and the number of years an accumulation represents—facts not within the easy grasp of archaeologists. Given the limitations normally set by archaeological records, species and season of death biases are not particularly meaningful until they advance upon the intersite level of comparison. This can be done by tracing the degree of heterogeneity in seasons represented among cases on either a predetermined or expanding geographical scale. When the degree of heterogeneity in seasons of occupations differs in a predetermined area (as attempted in this research) or levels off as the geographic scale increases, one may learn something about changes in the scale of human land use over time.

Carnivore denning seasons

Yet another analytical dimension of mortality data, concerning carnivore remains, is relevant to questions about seasonality in this study. Hominid occupations at coastal Italian caves alternated with carnivores during the Upper Pleistocene. Data on the seasons of shelter use by carnivores are useful for addressing some general questions about hominid mobility and patterns of coexistence with other predators (sensu Gamble 1983, 1986). The data do not inform about carnivore denning on a year-to-year basis, but rather in a more general way. Carnivore occupation schedules can be estimated from wildlife accounts provided that denning behavior is demonstrated in the paleontological cases. One important line of evidence for carnivore denning comes from the age structures of the carnivores themselves (addressed in Chapter 12). A strong juvenile bias is consistent with the long-term expectations for denning in caves. Shelter deaths are common in carnivores, due to juvenile mortality and interspecific aggression associated with den defense (Brain 1981; Fox 1984:71; Kurtén 1976; Major and Sherburne 1987:606; Miller 1985; Peterson et al. 1984:38; Rogers 1987:53–55). Of foremost importance in the analysis of carnivore mortality from an archaeological perspective is the question of why

the carnivore remains occur in cave sites. If denning behavior is indicated, then knowing the season(s) when carnivores used dens could help elucidate the context of alternations between hominids and nonhuman predators across years. In considering this kind of information, I assume that repeated alternations of hominid and carnivore tenants in caves reflect a generally low chance of schedule interference, since avoidance is less costly than open conflict.

SUMMARY

Certain types of mortality patterns in ungulate remains have been cited as proof of hominid hunting behavior (e.g., Callow 1986a:390; 1986b; Klein 1978, 1982a; Levine 1983:38–39; Scott 1986a:129–137; 1986b:182–183). The weakest links in these investigations are between the theoretical constructs of how mortality patterns are created in nature and how they could serve to identify specific predatory behaviors in the past. It is a fact that most mortality patterns are not absolutely diagnostic of the cause of death per se. Yet when age patterns are tied to particular agents through independent (taphonomic) evidence, they may take on greater meaning with respect to predatory behaviors and resource niche. Mortality data are most informative at the multisite level of comparison. More than distinguishing hunting from scavenging in archaeological records, the information sets predators' foraging tactics into broader ecological perspective; the value of any given predatory tactic is seated within a larger demographic domain, and it is the relationship between prevailing acquisition methods and the structure of opportunity that matters in the coevolution of predators. The next three chapters address questions about prey age selection by hominids relative to other large carnivores and the seasons of carnivore and ungulate deaths in the context of this philosophy.

11

Mapping Predator Niches from Prey Mortality Patterns

THE MODELS and principles of mortality analyses outlined in the previous chapter provide an arena in which to compare the prey age selection habits of modern and Upper Pleistocene predators. Here, the relative frequencies of various prey age groups are used to map the niche spaces of hominids and carnivores and to evaluate the predators' respective impacts on prey populations (Stiner 1990b). Supported by taphonomic and other information (Chapters 4 and 5), the mortality data effectively diagnose important aspects of hominid and carnivore foraging habits relative to place. The comparisons employ a simple three-age system consisting of juvenile, prime adult, and old adult cohorts. These cohorts efficiently describe the classes of mortality patterns found in nature, because they correspond to major life history phases in most small, medium, and large ungulate species. Consistent with my approach to investigating food transport patterns, the mortality analysis employs independent measures of ecological distance among predators, measures that might also translate to evolution-

ary distances through time. I begin by examining prey age selection habits of nonhuman predators and mortality patterns occurring independently of predator effects, followed by comparisons of modern humans from the historic through late Upper Paleolithic periods, and, finally, Mousterian hominids from west-central Italy.

Ungulate mortality patterns in the Italian Paleolithic show that the procurement techniques of Mousterian hominids were considerably more diverse than those of late Upper Paleolithic humans in the study area, and than modern humans more generally. The Mousterian cases indicate heavy emphases on hunting or scavenging, varying by site, whereas late Upper Paleolithic and modern human cases consistently point to hunting as the dominant mode of procurement. The possibility of a trend toward increasing predatory specialization in the Italian Upper Pleistocene is also raised by the mortality data. The shift appears to have taken place within the Mousterian, but its exact timing is unclear.

CONSTRUCTING MORTALITY PATTERNS FROM TOOTH ERUPTION AND WEAR DATA

The analyses of mortality patterns in ungulates are performed on cases. A case consists of the dental remains of one animal species from a specified living or death assemblage. The modern cases represent samples from known populations, derived

from demographic and ethological studies published in the wildlife literature. Modern cases arising from predation are cumulative, the compilations of deceased individuals over time. Cases from fossil fauna assemblages represent palimpsests of multi-

Portions of this chapter first appeared in a different form in the 1990 article entitled "The Use of Mortality Patterns in Archae-

ological Studies of Hominid Predatory Adaptations," *Journal of Anthropological Archaeology* 9.

ple procurement and transport events as well, but may have formed over many more years.

The number of individual animals (tooth-based MNI) in each fossil case is calculated from tooth data according to two slightly different criteria: only nearly or fully complete tooth elements were used for cervids; and only complete teeth are used for bovids and equids because wear stage was based on combined consideration of occlusal wear and crown height. Many ageable teeth in the Italian assemblages are still seated in bone, but tooth rows are almost always broken into segments containing one to four teeth, or the teeth are isolated from bone altogether (see Chapters 4 and 5). Maximizing sample size in the Italian cases therefore necessitates an aging method that treats all teeth as if they were isolated. Tooth-based MNI was determined by adding the number of right and left sides for the tooth element and dividing the sum by two. Unless otherwise stated, this MNI value is used instead of the more common side for constructing the triangular plots. The procedure guards against the worst effects of sampling error in smaller samples; averaging the two sides tends to eliminate empty cohorts in the small cases, thereby facilitating comparisons to larger cases.

The number of age stages used for any mortality study is the choice of the analyst, and the minimum sample sizes required vary according to the number of cohorts selected (e.g., Lyman 1987b). Although my working definitions and data collection procedures initially employed the traditional histogram format with multiple age cohorts, I use a three-age system for the comparisons presented below, because some of the Middle Paleolithic samples I ultimately wish to interpret are small. The three age groups are *juveniles* (birth to the age at which a particular deciduous tooth is normally shed), *prime adults*, and *old adults*. No attempt is made to estimate the real age of individual animals, except at the deciduous-permanent tooth replacement boundary. The three age divisions are illustrated in the

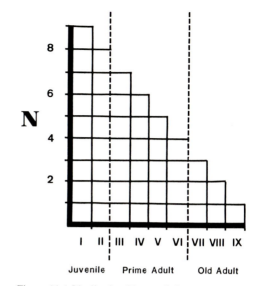

Figure 11.1 Idealized stable population structure compressed into three age stages: juvenile, prime adult, and old adult. (From Stiner 1990b)

context of a stable population structure model in Figure 11.1.

The comparisons of mortality patterns below include samples from a variety of published wildlife and zooarchaeological studies, in addition to the data on Paleolithic faunas from Italy. Occlusal tooth eruption and wear sequences for the lower fourth premolar (second premolars in equids) are the bases of age categories in the archaeological and paleontological cases, constructed for cervids and bovids from deciduous and permanent lower fourth premolars unless specified otherwise. The wear stage criteria correspond to collapsed versions of systems developed by Payne (1973), Grant (1982), and Lowe (1967),[8] illustrated in Figure 11.2. With the exception of equid teeth, I favor the P4 sequence for several reasons: (1) the tooth is easily distinguished from the other cheek teeth in cervids and bovids; (2) it is located at or very near the fulcrum of wear (as is the M1, Gifford-Gonzalez 1991) and will be completely worn away with advanced age; (3) it effec-

---

[8] The occlusal wear methods for relative aging of ungulate teeth developed by Payne (1973) and associates (e.g., Grant 1982) and by Lowe (1967) remain among the best for cervids and bovids. The data are easy to collect (even under adverse research conditions), the methods are precise and nondestructive, and, in my comparisons, produce results comparable to those obtained

from crown height measurements (corrected for variation in individual size) of ibex and aurochs teeth. Note that a combination of crown height data and occlusal wear for the deciduous through permanent sequence of upper and lower second premolars (rather than P_4) was used to determine relative age in equids.

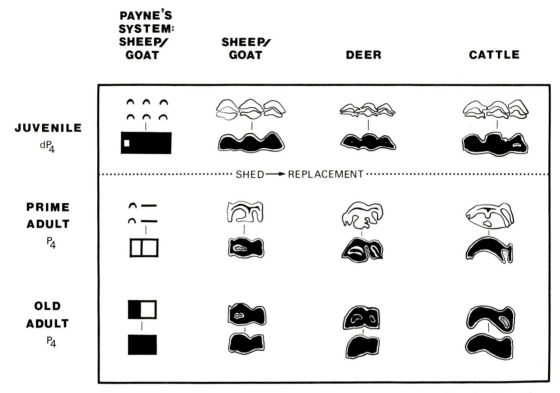

Figure 11.2 Occlusal wear stages according to the three-age system for deciduous and permanent lower fourth premolars of sheep/goat, cattle, and deer (from Stiner 1990b). Drawings of domestic sheep/goat and cattle teeth are adapted from Grant (1982); deer teeth are based on Lowe (1967) and on Stiner's comparative drawings for red, fallow, white-tailed, and mule deer.

tively represents the complete lifetime of individuals at a single anatomical locus if data for deciduous and permanent counterparts are combined, so error-prone corrections across elements in the tooth row are avoided; and (4) the deciduous counterpart is not much more fragile than the permanent tooth that supplants it, so preservation should not favor adult teeth significantly more than those of juveniles in a given deposit.

The three age cohorts—juvenile, prime adult, and old adult—do not represent equal fractions of the maximum potential lifetime, but instead are based on major life history transitions typical of most ungulates.[9] The three age stages correspond to

differing susceptibilities to attritional death, as well as to significant differences in body composition. Particularly important from a predator's perspective is the fact that adult cohorts offer substantially higher fat returns on the average than do juveniles in wild populations. Fat content in adults may vary radically with season, but the generalization holds for assemblages representing many procurement events. Because only three age stages are considered, the age-frequency data can be converted to percentages and plotted as single coordinates on a triangular graph.

The transition between juvenile and prime adult age groups is very clear, since it corresponds to the

[9] The discussion that follows applies to small, medium, and large ungulates (e.g., roe deer, ibex, red deer, aurochs, and horse). The same generalization cannot be applied to all mammals. Those species that are both long-lived and invest in extensive parental care exhibit relatively long juvenile dependency periods. Reproductive maturity is correspondingly delayed so that the three age group increments are nearly equal in length. This pattern is documented, for example, among elephants (Haynes 1985, 1987, 1988).

time when the milk tooth is replaced by a new, permanent one. Because the permanent tooth supplants the deciduous counterpart by pushing it up and out of the jaw, a permanent tooth must show some evidence of occlusal wear, however slight, in order to be counted; wear on the occlusal surface is the only reliable indication that the permanent tooth was truly exposed at the time of death. The prime-old age boundary is based on how much of the tooth is left relative to the complete form and the appearance of the occlusal surface. The old age category begins when more than half of the tooth crown is worn away, and it theoretically ends when animals run out of tooth (see Figure 11.2). That the fourth premolar in animals can actually reach such an advanced state of wear is confirmed by a few individuals in several of the Italian archaeological assemblages used for this study.

Borrowing and transposing age data from other studies, which employ diverse methods and styles of presentation, is more difficult. However, wildlife data usually supply the transition points corresponding to the three age groups described above, either as increments in real years or based on reproductive state and appearance. In these cases, data transformation is fairly straightforward. The juvenile group can be separated from adults using both the age at which the deciduous tooth is normally shed and associated changes in physiological development. The two adult age groups—prime and old—are split more or less equally, with the prime age span being slightly longer. The prime-old adult boundary can be ascertained as long as at least one very old animal is present in the sample; hence estimates of maximum age in real years is unnecessary for this analysis.

Transposing mortality data for published fossil faunas is complicated by the fact that any of several different tooth elements may be chosen for analysis, some of which may show distinctly nonlinear patterns of wear throughout the lifetime (Gifford-Gonzalez 1991; Severinghaus 1949). While the use of only three age groups for cross-taxa and cross-cultural comparisons of mortality minimizes the sources of potential errors, I acknowledge a minor degree of ambiguity in my transformations of others' data into the three-age format. Separations at the prime-old adult boundary are more prone to

error than at the boundary separating juveniles and prime adults, because maximum potential longevity varies more among wild populations as a rule than does the age at which a deciduous tooth element is shed.

The physiological correlates of the three age categories are of considerable interest, because they relate to changes in the potential nutritional yield of prey. Hemopoietic zones in the ungulate skeleton are loci of red blood cell and granular leukocyte formation. In juveniles, the process occurs in medullae and trabeculae throughout the skeleton, whereas hemopoiesis becomes localized in the axial elements and proximal upper limb elements of adults (e.g., Crouch 1972 on humans; but the process applies to mammals more generally, B. Snyder D.V.M., Rio Grande Zoo). Zones of active hemopoiesis are associated with red marrow tissues. The nutritional value of these tissues is largely in the form of proteins and minerals, assuming the prey animal is in fairly good physical condition at the time of death. Adults of many ungulate species (particularly cervids and certain other artiodactyls) are capable of storing substantial quantities of renderable fat (yellow marrow) in the medullary cavities of the limbs and the mandible (reviewed in Chapter 8). The quality and quantity of fat vary with season, peaking in early fall and diminishing by spring, or according to wet-dry cycles in tropical environments. In the juvenile age group, defined here by the presence of deciduous dentition and/or emerging but unworn permanent teeth, the zones of hemopoiesis (red marrow) are not yet restricted to the cancellous (trabecular) tissues of the axial skeleton and proximal upper limbs. Relatively little fat (yellow marrow) is stored in the medullary cavities of the long bones of juveniles as a consequence. The social and neurological immaturity of juveniles also makes them more vulnerable to harsh environmental conditions, disease, and predators. These facts, along with the naturally great abundance of juveniles in living populations, are responsible for their great abundance in both living-structure and U-shaped (a.k.a. attritional) mortality patterns.

The prime adult age group consists of sexually mature individuals in which the permanent tooth is in place and in use. This stage represents the peak reproductive years in ungulates, although the beginning and end of this phase may vary according to gender. It is important to note that the juvenile to prime adult transition is based on the physiological capability to reproduce, not on realized productivity (e.g., Festa-Bianchet 1988; Seal and Plotka 1983); the former better reflects changes in an individual's ability to store fat. Separation of the juvenile and prime age groups in this study best corresponds to *females'* entry into reproductive phase, because males' mating opportunities are more heavily affected by social status and male-male competition. In temperate and colder environments, healthy prime-aged adults develop substantial fat stores in the limb bones in advance of the cold season and, in the case of dominant males, in preparation for the fall rut.

The old age stage begins at roughly 61 to 65 percent of the maximum potential lifetime. Variation in longevity among populations introduces some confusion if this criterion is used alone, so tooth wear information was given priority whenever possible. An average (population level) decrease in productivity is associated with the old age group in modern ungulates, although this does not affect every individual equally (e.g., Berger 1986 on feral horses; Clutton-Brock et al. 1982 on red deer; Geist 1971:284 on wild sheep and reindeer; Leslie and Douglas 1979:23 on desert bighorn; Sinclair 1977:226–228 on African buffalo). Lasting from late prime to senscence, the old age category differs from the prime age category because of a generally higher probability of mortality and a lower average

productivity; in essence, the beginning of the old age stage corresponds to a general reproductive decline for the age group as a whole. In many ungulate species, female productivity stabilizes with maturity and remains at that level until the final year of life. A lag time of up to twelve months between the end of the reproductive lifespan and female death, combined with generally higher mortality rates, is the basis of the reproductive decline for the old age group. The probability that old animals will build up nutritional stores is also correspondingly lower than in prime adults.

Scale of consideration

The analysis may obscure short-term, idiosyncratic variation in the age structures of living populations and in death assemblages (e.g., episodes of juvenile procurement for soft hides), because it seeks the long-term average in mortality patterns. This is not a shortcoming of the three-age method, but instead depends on the nature of the archaeological samples considered and the availability of detailed provenience data. Neither demographic oscillations (waves in an instantaneous population structure), nor variation in procurement tactics at a finer temporal scale, contradict the overall patterns of prey age selection to be discussed: variation is to be expected and augments rather than falsifies a general model based on both an average condition and the normal variation surrounding that ideal.

LIVING POPULATION STRUCTURE AND BACKGROUND (NONVIOLENT) MORTALITY

To facilitate the case comparisons, the frequencies of individuals in each of the three age groups are converted to percentage values and plotted on triangular graphs. Because mortality patterns are most often considered in a two-dimensional format in the archaeological literature, some explanation of pattern type correspondences in the three-dimensional graphs used in this presentation is needed. Figure 11.3A defines the three age axes and relates areas of the graph to general classes of mortality patterns, as

defined in Chapter 10. Each of the three axes *bisects* the triangle and ranges from 0 to 100 percent. Figure 11.3B schematically relates areas of the graph to the observed range of variation within each class of mortality pattern. The distribution of the two most common mortality patterns, U-shaped and living-structure, occupy the lower central areas of the graph. The corners of the graph correspond to strong biases toward each of the three designated age groups. Old individuals are naturally rare in

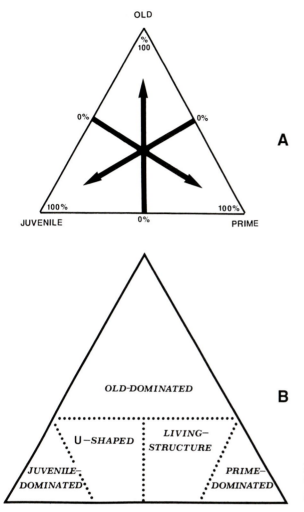

Figure 11.3 Triangular diagrams (A) defining the three age axes and (B) relating areas of the graph to general classes or "families" of mortality patterns.

living populations, so that any case falling in the upper half of the triangle (above the level where the three axes intersect) is significantly biased toward the old age cohort.

Though integral to this analysis, variation associated with any type of mortality pattern is seldom addressed in archaeological studies (but see Cribb 1987; Lyman 1987b), which instead rely only on the idealized patterns. In fact, idealized models approximate only the mean condition for a family of profile patterns. Knowing the typical range of variation associated with each ideal model is critical for assessing differences among real cases, especially when working with static models. The range of variation is likely to be of greatest ecological or evolutionary significance in the study of predators, human or otherwise. For these reasons, I have constructed expected variation ranges (corresponding to areas in Figure 11.3B), based on empirical observations and with a generous margin subsequently added (from Stiner 1990b:319–323). The analyses to follow emphasize distributions in the data set rather than pattern matching.

Figure 11.4 summarizes the empirically documented and modeled differences in age composition of living-structure and U-shaped patterns arising

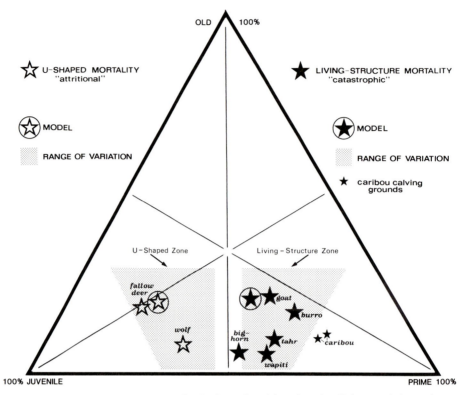

Figure 11.4 Triangular plot showing the distributions of models and modern living population and death census cases that display living-structure or U-shaped age structures. (From Stiner 1990b)

from causes *other than* predators. The data are from wildlife census[10] studies (Tables 11.1 and 11.2 respectively). The shaded zones demarcate the expected range of variation within the U-shaped (shaded area on left) and living-structure (shaded area on right) domains. These domains are repeated on all succeeding triangular diagrams as aids for characterizing the distributions of cases created by predators. The U-shaped mortality model and the real-life cases of mortality resulting from disease, malnutrition, and accidents occur in the lower left-central region of the graph (open stars). The living-structure model, live census data, and cases of mass

unselective (catastrophic) death are distributed in the lower right-central region of the graph (filled stars).

With the exception of the New Zealand wild goats and Mohave burros (an unmanaged population), all of the census cases occur below and to the right of Lyman's (1987b) theoretical stable living-structure model. There is no reason to doubt the accuracy of Lyman's and others' predictions of the ideal condition. The relatively extreme position of the two caribou live census cases is explained by the fact that they were undertaken at calving grounds (Miller 1975), where most pregnant adult females

---

[10] I reviewed the census methods for each "live" population case before accepting it for this comparative study. Many potential cases were rejected on grounds that the census methods could not extract a random sample from the population. As archaeologists are aware, so-called random samples often are not random at all, and the problems that archaeologists face in collecting cultural materials are equally critical in demographic studies of animal populations. For example, helicopter surveys or harvesting (e.g., Wilkinson 1976) are excluded from consideration,

because the tendency to hide varies with age and sex in many species, and these individuals are less likely to be visible from the air. As a related point, short-term sampling and/or small samples often do not fit the idealized model of a living population structure, nor should this be expected. Census data that do not cross-cut the effects of "demographic waves" and the social habits of a species will always show greater variation around the norm, and sampling schemes do not always reckon with this problem.

TABLE 11.1
Living population structure cases divided into three age cohorts

Species	Location	Context and method[a]	N[b]	Percentages of N			Source
				JUV	*PRIME*	*OLD*	
model	anywhere	perfect	55	.34	.45	.21	Lyman 1987b
wapiti[c]	Washington	mass death	86	.38	.57	.05	Lyman 1987b
feral burro	Mohave Desert	mass removal	392	.27	.59	.13	Johnson et al. 1987
tahr	New Zealand	live census (sightings), females only	—	.34	.57	.09	Schaller 1977:135
wild goat	New Zealand	live census (sightings), females only	—	.29	.50	.21	Schaller 1977:135
desert bighorn	Nevada	live census (telemetry and sightings), males only	654	.52	.44	.04	Leslie and Douglas 1979:23
caribou	Saskatchewan	live census at calving grounds, mostly reproducing females					Miller 1975:217
winter 1967 (Nov 28–Dec 12)			105	.24	.67	.09	
spring 1968 (Apr 12–May 2)			103	.22	.69	.09	

[a] Context of data collection and field methods used.

[b] N refers to the number of individuals in a living population or death assemblage.

[c] Deaths were caused by the volcanic eruption of Mount St. Helen's. Lyman's data here are collapsed into three age categories: Lyman's ages F and 1 are subsumed into the juvenile category, ages 2 through 7 into the prime adult category, and ages 8 through 12 into the old adult category.

and some yearlings gather in spring. The presence of fewer old animals than expected in all other cases may be due to management and heavy hunting of populations in modern game reserves. Controlled harvesting and poaching often prevent managed populations living near developed areas from ever reaching a declining state. The same logic would apply to any prehistoric ungulate population that was periodically subjected to heavy predation by humans across years.

TABLE 11.2
U-shaped mortality cases arising from causes other than predation, divided into three age cohorts

Species	Location	Context and method[a]	N[b]	Percentages of N			Source
				JUV	*PRIME*	*OLD*	
model	anywhere	perfect	—	.59	.22	.19	see Chapter 10
wolf	Israel	skull pickup	41	.58	.34	.07	Mendelssohn 1982:191
fallow deer	Britain	death census	170	.68	.15	.18	Chapman and Chapman 1975

[a] Context of data collection and field methods used.

[b] N refers to the number of deceased individuals.

HARVESTING BY CARNIVORES IN THE CONTEXT OF BROADER
DEMOGRAPHIC PHENOMENA

Predator is a general term that embodies a diverse array of adaptations. Here, the word refers to species that are carnivorous and acknowledges that, among higher mammals, methods of prey procurement vary. Humans, for example, may hunt, trap, scavenge, gather small animals, and, in later cultural periods, practice animal husbandry. Tigers hunt, scavenge, or may inadvertently cause deadly infections in prey from scratching during failed hunting attempts (Schaller 1967).

The factors that motivate and limit a predator's choice of prey age groups cannot be defined precisely. Choices certainly are influenced both by the predator's anatomical and behavioral characteristics and by demographic characteristics of the prey population (as discussed in Chapter 10). There is a general consensus among wildlife biologists that the large carnivores fall into two broad strategy types, based on the ways that they normally capture prey. Individual predators may not always fulfill the generalization assigned to their species, but the point is that they do most of the time. The two strategy types are *cursorial* and *ambush/short-chase* (Bertram 1979:228; Ewer 1973; Kruuk 1972:274–283; Schaller 1972:392), a dichotomy clearly reflected by differences in carnivore anatomy and disposition. Each type of predator produces relatively distinct prey mortality patterns. The dichotomy between predators on the basis of their foraging strategies is a very general one and acknowledges considerable variation in predator response to local environmental conditions. The contrast is sufficiently strong, however, to be useful for examining human patterns of prey selection at the community level.

Cursorial predators, most of which are social, normally engage in long chases of their quarry. Species falling within this classification are wolves, African wild dogs, spotted hyaenas, and the cheetah (a relatively nonsocial species). The cursorial strategy is especially suited to open habitats. Procurement techniques appear to select for endurance in both predator and prey, such that weak, young, and old individuals are most often singled out (Ballard et al. 1987:35; Bertram 1979; Burton 1979; Estes

and Goddard 1967; Fuller and Keith 1980:591; Kruuk 1972:101; Peterson et al. 1984:15, 38; Schaller 1972:392, 442; 1977:140; C. A. Smith 1986:744). The resulting death assemblages tend to be deficient in prime adults and correspond to U-shaped mortality profiles (see Figures 10.2B and 10.4B). Some cursorial hunters, such as spotted hyaenas and wolves, are also avid bone collectors and often transport carcass parts to dens or resting sites (e.g., Fentress and Ryon 1982; Haynes 1980; Kruuk 1972; Sutcliffe 1970). Substantial faunal accumulations exhibiting the U-shaped mortality pattern consequently may form in the context of denning by wolves and spotted hyaenas.

The second predator strategy class is the true ambush hunter, animals that programmatically engage in hide and wait and/or short chase tactics. Ambush predators tend to be specialists, at least in terms of the behaviors associated with prey capture (Burton 1979:143). Most ambush predators are solitary hunters, although important exceptions exist. The best-known ambush hunters are found among the felids (Leyhausen 1979), including the European wild cat, leopard, tiger, jaguar, and mountain lion (a.k.a. cougar or puma). Ambush strategies depend on the elements of surprise and escape prevention; an ambush predator typically seeks good spots for interception, waiting or searching along dry or active stream channels, in marshes or ravines, and along well-traveled game trails (Schaller 1967, 1972 on the large cats; also see Fox 1984 on Asiatic dholes). Most ambush predators depend on landscape surrounds or vegetation features as facilities for capturing prey, and these places may form critical parts of their territory. African lions are unusual among ambush carnivores because they may cooperate with one another to check prey escape, thereby entrapping ungulates without the benefit of landscape features.

Predators that normally operate in the cursorial mode also may occasionally generate living-structure (nonselective) mortality patterns, matching those produced by ambush predators. Modern wildlife data indicate that cursorial predators, as defined by anatomy, take prey age groups in a more random fashion in situations in which topographical features can be used to slow or prevent prey escape. Ambush behavior is documented for the Indian dhole, for example, when packs use standing water and stream channels as traps (Fox 1984:54–74). Bibikov (1982:128–129) cites several instances in which wolves cornered prey in natural corrals, on frozen lakes (also see Miller 1975:218), or in snow-filled ravines.

Because prey selection by ambush hunters is determined principally by encounter, ambush strategies tend to result in living-structure mortality patterns (Schaller 1972:392; Fox 1984:61). The age structure of the death assemblage is more or less equivalent to the age structure of the living population from which prey were extracted. Ambush-caused death patterns are also analogous to those caused by natural disasters (e.g., Lyman 1987b), because the ability of prey to avoid death is uniform with regard to age. Where ambush predators reuse trap and/or protected feeding localities again and again, substantial paleontological bone deposits may accumulate.

To summarize thus far, a predator's feeding choices are conditioned by what living prey populations have to offer and, only in some cases, by age-specific susceptibility of individual prey to a predator's procurement techniques. It is for these reasons that mortality patterns generated by most predators either mimic those arising from attritional factors such as disease, malnutrition, and accidents or represent a fairly random sample of the living population.

The differences in mortality patterns generated by cursorial versus ambush strategies, and the ranges of variation typifying each strategy group, can be compared using the three-age system. Contemporary cases of predation on bovids, cervids, and equids come from wildlife studies conducted in North America, India, and East Africa (Table 11.3). The cursorial carnivore species considered include wolf, African wild dog, cheetah, and spotted hyaena. The ambush/short-chase species include African lion, leopard, and tiger. One Pleistocene case of spotted hyaena predation on red deer (Buca della Iena 11–6) in Italy is also presented. The distribution of predator cases in Figure 11.5 illustrates the behavioral and niche differences between cursorial

and ambush carnivores. Most cases produced by cursorial carnivores—species that run down their prey—fall in the lower left half of the graph, in the U-shaped mortality domain. The Upper Pleistocene spotted hyaena case from Italy (Buca della Iena) is consistent with the modern hyaena cases, although slightly more biased toward juvenile prey. The classic ambush or stalking predators are represented in the lower right half of the graph, corresponding to the living-structure domain. The distribution of cases is generally consistent with observed behavioral and niche differences between cursorial and ambush carnivores described by Bertram (1979:228), Ewer (1973), Kruuk (1972:274–283), and Schaller (1972:392).

There are two interesting exceptions to these generalizations, however. The first, noted earlier from behavioral accounts, is that cursorial species sometimes behave like ambush predators by using natural corrals, lake ice, thick vegetation, and other landscape features to disadvantage prey. These conditions are documented for three of the four aberrant cursorial predator cases occurring in the lower right half of Figure 11.5. The spotted hyaena case (Table 11.3) involved over one hundred Thompson's gazelles bedded down for the night; it represents a highly unusual situation in which the prey were massacred within the space of a few hours (Kruuk 1972:99). The two Saskatchewan wolf cases in the aberrant cursorial group involved forcing caribou onto a frozen lake and setting them at a disadvantage. The age structure of one of these cases is further biased by the fact that hunting took place at caribou calving grounds (before and after the birthing peak), resulting in a slight bias toward prime adult females (Miller 1975). It is significant, however, that the death patterns created by the wolves are less biased toward adults than live census data for the same prey population, shown in Figure 11.4. The circumstances of the fourth aberrant case (wild dogs) are not known. Ambush behavior may not be particularly common in any cursorial species, but it is occasionally documented in nearly all of them; the most vivid accounts are for Asiatic dholes (Fox 1984), wolves (Bibikov 1982; Miller 1975), and spotted hyaenas (Kruuk 1972). Cursorial species behave like ambush hunters (producing living-structure mortality patterns) only with the aid of

TABLE 11.3
Modern cases of ungulate predation by humans and carnivores, divided into three age cohorts

Prey	Predator	Location	Time frame	N^a	JUV	PRIME	OLD	Source
collared peccary	trophy[b] (human)	Arizona	1957–73	2662	.18	.61	.21	Sowls 1984:79
white-tailed deer[c]	"	Pennsylvania	1961	74	.00	.74	.26	Woolf and Harder 1979:19
	"		1964	74	.13	.78	.08	
	"		1967	109	.17	.64	.18	
	"		1970	103	.09	.79	.12	
	"		1973	149	.21	.70	.08	
	"		1976	201	.36	.59	.05	
zebra	"	Serengeti	—	313	.19	.70	.11	Schaller 1972:440
caribou	wolf	Saskatchewan	1968 (Feb 27–Apr 18)	94	.28	.69	.03	Miller 1975:217
	"		1968 (Apr 19–May 17)	53	.32	.57	.11	
moose	"	Alberta	1976–78 (Aug–May)	48	.53	.30	.17	Fuller and Keith 1980:591
moose	"	Alaska	—	198	.56	.22	.22	Peterson et al. 1984:15–16
white-tailed deer	"	Ontario	—	331	.22	.32	.46	Pimlott et al. 1969
chital	tiger[d]	India	—	98	.18	.45	.36	Schaller 1967:320
barasingha	"			39	.23	.55	.22	
sambar	"			56	.13	.38	.48	
gaur	"			14	.54	.36	.11	
wildebeest	lion	Serengeti	—	262	.27	.48	.24	Schaller 1972:439–441
zebra	"		—	174	.21	.48	.32	
Af. buffalo	"		—	50	.16	.62	.22	
Thompson's gazelle	"		—	204	.39	.46	.16	
Thompson's gazelle	leopard	Serengeti	—	28	.39	.54	.07	Schaller 1972:448
Thompson's gazelle	cheetah	Serengeti	—	163	.59	.27	.13	1972:442
Thompson's gazelle	wild dog	Serengeti	—	61	.52	.34	.13	Schaller 1972:449
	"			74	.97	.03	.00	
wildebeest								
Thompson's gazelle	"	Serengeti	—	60	.18	.66	.16	Kruuk 1972:99
zebra	hyaena[e]	Serengeti	—	17	.47	.41	.12	1972:98
zebra	"	Ngorongoro	—	29	.48	.31	.21	
wildebeest	"	Serengeti	—	86	.53	.18	.29	1972:95
wildebeest	"	Ngorongoro	—	191	.68	.27	.05	

TABLE 11.3   (Continued)

Prey	Predator	Location	Time frame	N[a]	Percentages of N			Source
					JUV	PRIME	OLD	
Thompson's gazelle	"	Serengeti	—	98	.44	.35	.21	1972:99
Thompson's gazelle	"[f]		hours	> 100	.26	.57	.17	
red deer	"[g]	Italy (Pleistocene)	—	6	.75	.08	.17	Stiner 1990b
gemsbok	hyaena	Namib	—	29	.10	.10	.79	Tilson et al. 1980:47–49
mountain zebra	"[h]		—	26	.19	.40	.40	

[a] N refers to the number of deceased individuals.

[b] Trophy refers to managed ungulate populations wherein prime-aged adults were hunted recreationally by humans using firearms.

[c] The Pennsylvania sample is for females only, but follows the trophy model.

[d] The tiger predation cases represent some combination of hunted and scavenged prey.

[e] The sample includes only those situations in which prey were actually killed by spotted hyaenas.

[f] Over one hundred Thompson's gazelles were massacred by hyaenas; Kruuk (1972) describes the incident as very unusual in his study area.

[g] The data are for all levels of Buca della Iena (I1–6) combined, a Pleistocene spotted hyaena den complex from west-central Italy.

[h] Because Tilson et al.'s (1980) 8–12 year age group straddles the boundary between my prime and old classifications, mountain zebra of this age category were equally divided between the prime and old categories.

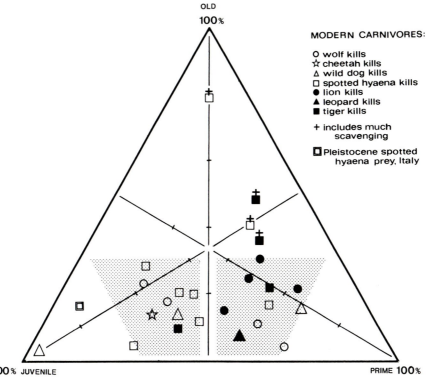

Figure 11.5 Triangular plot of ungulate mortality cases created by modern cursorial and ambush carnivores. Prey species not designated; instead see Table 11.3 (From Stiner 1990b)

natural surround features or slippery substrates, however. This fact shows that prey age choice is not intentional on the part of individual predators, but rather is an artifact of the way in which a strategy allows the predator to get close enough to prey animals to take hold of them.

The second set of exceptions apparent in Figure 11.5 includes two tiger and two spotted hyaena cases. All display old-age biased mortality patterns and are distributed above the level where the three age axes intersect. Each example involved a relatively high dependence on scavenging, as indicated by Schaller's (1967) discussion of his sample and field methods in the Indian tiger study, and by Tilson et al. (1980:49) in their study of Namibian spotted hyaenas. In both situations, the predators existed at or near the top of the local carnivore hierarchy and scavenged ungulates perishing primarily from nonviolent causes, including eventual infections from predator-caused injuries. The patterns, associated with what is normally a cursorial predator (spotted hyaena) on the one hand and an ambush predator (tiger) on the other, converge on the same area of the graph as the importance of scavenged food in the diet increases.

The fact that attritional death is the most common mortality pattern in nature (see Chapter 10) may explain the relationship between the old bias and scavenging behavior. Prime-age animals are much less likely than young and old animals to succumb to attritional causes of death, and more juveniles die than old adults because there are more young animals in the living population. However, the destruction of juvenile carcasses by primary feeders is quite thorough (e.g., Schaller 1967, 1972; Haynes 1980, 1982; Blumenschine 1986, 1987), and the difficulty of locating small carcasses and faster rates of biochemical deterioration due to low volume relative to surface area (e.g., Lyman 1984a) often prevent scavengers from benefiting much from juvenile deaths. As a result, old adult carcasses, which are more persistent due to larger size and tougher tissues, may become available to scavengers more often, even though not as many old animals die within a given period. Tilson et al. (1980:47, 49; also Mills 1984b) make explicit links between scavenging and the old-age bias in their study of spotted hyaenas in the Namib Desert, and Schaller (1967) implies a similar explanation in his study of Indian tigers.

Mills (1984b) reports a generally analogous situation for spotted hyaenas and lions in the southern Kalahari. Of the various contexts in which scavenging might take place, old-biased mortality is most likely in nonconfrontational situations, because procurement does not depend on taking over fresh kills made by another predator (but see Blumenschine's [1991] actualistic case, which is only slightly biased toward old adults by my calculations).

Behavioral and environmental data for modern predator cases also relate some procurement strategies to spatial properties of food supply and to significant differences in levels of mobility and search time required for hunting as opposed to scavenging (see also Houston 1979). Links between highly scattered food supplies and old-biased prey selection among spotted hyaenas and lions in arid southern African environments, in particular, suggest that environmental stress and food dispersion, whether acute or chronic, can exert a strong influence on foraging responses of species that both hunt and scavenge (as is also true for food transport; see Chapters 8 and 9). The documented association of the old-age bias and scavenging in cursorial and ambush nonhuman predators suggests a more general mortality model that could be helpful for identifying nonconfrontational scavenging by hominids.

The associations between carnivore behavior and the mortality patterns that carnivores create in prey are provocative, but it is important not to lose sight of the larger demographic domains in which these predators operate. Figures 11.4 and 11.5 show that, with the exception of situations involving a heavy emphasis on scavenging, the total distribution of predator cases is the same as that for nonpredated death assemblages and live population structures combined. The nearly complete overlap between death assemblages created by predators and those arising from other causes of death demonstrates that U-shaped and living-structure mortality patterns are not, in themselves, diagnostic of how deaths occurred. The analytical value of mortality patterns in fossil faunas is contingent upon whether a clear connection can be made between predator activities and a death assemblage via taphonomic methods. Then, and only then, are patterns of prey age selection powerful analytical tools for distinguishing predator habits and predatory niches.

Human Beings, a Type of Social Ambush Predator

Few social ambush predators exist in nature, and it may be that this kind of strategy is a relatively recent development in animal communities. The African lion is one example of a social ambush predator (Schaller 1972), and modern humans represent a second. The hunting techniques of humans are widely documented by ethnohistoric and ethnoarchaeologic studies (e.g., Binford 1978; O'Connell et al. 1988a; Steward 1938; Tatum 1980:156). Human practices often feature sophisticated traps, prey interception on migration routes, and/or cooperation of many people to corner animals in natural or man-made enclosures. However, other peoples tend to hunt solo, either from blinds or on foot. Large-scale ambush practices on the High Plains of North America have also been documented archaeologically (e.g., Frison 1978, 1984; Reher 1970, 1973, 1974; Todd 1983). Given that human hunting techniques vary greatly, the mortality patterns that humans create in ungulate prey are remarkably uniform—at least from the late Upper Pleistocene onward. Tables 11.4 and 11.5 present mortality data for various cases of hominid predation on ungulates. The cases span a time range beginning circa 120,000 B.P. and continuing right through the historic period. The cases represent a limited array of prey species in order to minimize the influence of family-specific behaviors and natural abundance on procurement practices. Of these, only data for cervids and bovids are graphed below, because these

TABLE 11.4
Three age group mortality data for ungulate remains
in Holocene archaeological sites, North America

Site	Tooth element used	N[a]	Percentages of N		
			JUV	PRIME	OLD
Historic Nunamiut Eskimo caribou assemblages, Alaska:[b]					
Net	dP_4-P_4	9.5	.26	.68	.05
Kakinya	dP_4-P_4	6.5	.69	.31	.00
Tulekana	dP_4-P_4	8.0	1.00	.00	.00
Akp Dogyard	dP_4-P_4	15.5	.03	.81	.16
Palingana	dP_4-P_4	77.5	.16	.72	.12
Paleoindian/Archaic bison assemblages, Great Plains:[c]					
Hawkin	—	96.0	.15	.65	.20
Casper	—	71.0	.24	.52	.24
Agate Basin	—	69.0	.16	.77	.07
Carter/Kern-McGee	—	32.0	.41	.50	.09
Late Prehistoric bison assemblage, Pecos River Valley:[d]					
Garnsey	—	30.0	.08	.68	.23
Middle Mississippian village white-tailed deer assemblages:[e]					
Chucalissa	—	55.0	.27	.62	.11
Banks Village	—	81.0	.38	.53	.09
Lilbourn	—	10.0	.30	.60	.10
Turner	—	20.0	.15	.80	.05
Snodgrass	—	130.0	.31	.59	.09
Gooseneck	—	8.0	.25	.62	.12

[a] N is calculated for the Nunamiut caribou cases by dividing the total MNE for the lower fourth premolar by 2; N otherwise refers to MNI values provided by other authors.
[b] Stiner's data (1990b) on Binford's collection.
[c] Frison (1984).
[d] Speth (1983:71).
[e] B. D. Smith (1975:28).

TABLE 11.5
Three age cohort mortality data for ungulates procured by Paleolithic hominids in Italy

Site and assemblage	Prey	Tooth element used	N^a	Percentages of N		
				JUV	PRIME	OLD
Late Upper Paleolithic cases:						
Polesini (1–12)	red deer	dP_4-P_4	392.0^b	.33	.51	.16
	aurochs[c]	M_3	9.5	—	.95	.05
Palidoro (33–34)	red deer	dP_4-P_4	5.0	.20	.70	.10
	aurochs	dP_4-P_4	3.5	.29	.71	.00
Middle Paleolithic cases:						
S. Agostino (S0–3)	red deer	dP_4-P_4	23.0	.41	.43	.15
Breuil (Br)	aurochs	dP_4-P_4	24.0	.00	.87	.12
"	red deer	dP_4-P_4	21.0	.00	.71	.29
(B3/4)	"	dP_3-P_3	9.0	.55	.44	.00
Moscerini (M2)	red deer[d]	dP^4-P^4	3.5	.00	.43	.57
(M3)	"	dP^4-P^4	4.5	.00	.55	.44
(M4)	"	dP^4-P^4	4.5	.22	.22	.55
(M6)	"	dP^4-P^4	7.0	.14	.36	.50
(all)	"	dP^4-P^4	19.5	.10	.38	.51
Guattari (G4–5)	red deer	dP_4-P_4	12.5	.24	.44	.32
"	aurochs	dP_4-P_4	6.5	.15	.61	.23

[a] N is calculated for the Paleolithic cases by dividing the tooth-based MNE value for the designated element by 2.

[b] In this case, N is calculated using the total number of right-side specimens.

[c] Data are adjusted to compensate for use of the M_3 here. Individuals with the permanent tooth in the process of erupting represent the youngest age stage that can be known from this element; no milk teeth present.

[d] The dP^4-P^4 tooth sequence is more consistently represented than the dP_4-P_4 sequence in Moscerini and hence is used to construct the mortality patterns here. The upper tooth wears slightly faster than the lower, based on my comparisons of upper and lower premolars in reference faunas, and the data have been adjusted to compensate for this effect.

taxa are especially common in archaeological assemblages worldwide (but see Table 11.6 for other species in the Italian sites).

Figure 11.6 shows the distribution of deer and bison cases from Holocene human sites in North America, dating from about 12,000 B.P. to the present. The North American sample includes five cases of caribou hunting by historic Alaskan Nunamiut Eskimo using firearms or bow and arrow (my data on Binford's collections; also see Binford 1978), along with four Paleoindian/Early Archaic bison (*Bison bison*) hunting cases from the High Plains (Frison 1984), one case of bison hunting from a late prehistoric Southern Plains site in New Mexico (Speth 1983), and six cases of white-tailed deer (*Odocoileus virginianus*) hunting by Middle Mississippian villagers (B. D. Smith 1975). Eight cases of recreational trophy hunting of white-tailed

deer (Woolf and Harder 1979), peccary (*Tayassu tajacu*, Sowls 1984), and zebra (*Equus burchelli*, Schaller 1972) are also considered (from Table 11.3). The trophy cases consist of legal kills that were registered by park officials during one or more hunting seasons; obviously, they do not include poached game. In spite of the diverse time periods, cultures, environments, and technologies represented, nearly all of the human-generated cases cluster in the lower right-half of Figure 11.6. The Holocene cases form a continuum between living-structure mortality and prime-dominated mortality.

The distribution of cases in Figure 11.6 illustrates two things about humans as predators. The first is a propensity for ambush-style hunting in general. The second is a tendency for many human cultures to harvest prime adult prey. Humans appear to be the only predatory agencies that *regularly* produce

TABLE 11.6
Three age cohort mortality data for "other" ungulates procured
by Paleolithic hominids in Italy

Site and assemblage	Prey	Tooth element used	N[a]	Percentages of N		
				JUV	PRIME	OLD
Late Upper Paleolithic cases:						
Polesini 1–12	wild ass	dP^2-P_2	55.5	.25	.58	.16
	horse	dP^2-P_2	60.0	.22	.36	.42
	roe deer	dP_4-P_4	101.0	.21	.66	.13
	chamois	dP_4-P_4	39.5	.48	.27	.25
	ibex	dP_4-P_4	6.5	.00	.85	.15
Palidoro 33–34	wild ass	dP_2-P_2	1.5	.33	.67	.00
Middle Paleolithic cases:						
S. Agostino	fallow deer	dP_4-P_4	13.0	.35	.50	.15
S0–3	roe deer	dP_4-P_4	9.0	.44	.39	.17
Breuil Br	ibex	dP_4-P_4	8.0	.37	.25	.37
B3/4	ibex	dP_4-P_4	15.0	.00	.87	.13

[a] N refers to the estimated number of individual animals; the value is calculated for the archaeological cases by dividing the tooth-based MNE value for the designated element by 2, unless specified otherwise.

prime-biased mortality patterns in prey death assemblages, making this kind of pattern more specific to cause than the other mortality patterns described previously (see also Stiner 1990b). Ethnographic and historic accounts (e.g., Benedict 1975; Egan 1917; Regan 1934; Steward 1938; Tatum 1980), ethnoarchaeological studies (Binford 1978) and some archaeological evidence (e.g., Frison 1984; Todd 1983; Todd and Hofman 1987) generally associate prime-dominant harvesting with selective ambush hunting. In modern contexts, the prime-dominated mortality pattern occurs when trophy hunters use firearms (e.g., Sowls 1984; Woolf and Harder 1979), and the law genuinely predisposes hunters to focus on adult animals.

Like the age structures of modern managed ungulate populations, the Holocene case distributions are slightly compressed toward the low end of the old-age axis, if compared to the model shown in Figure 11.4. The Holocene human distribution also differs from the total distribution for nonhuman ambush predators (Figure 11.5) in this respect. Because none of the Holocene cases occur above the intersection of the three age axes, their distribution may also indicate that these hunters seldom resorted to nonconfrontational scavenging. The larger implications of these points will be discussed in due course below.

Two Nunamiut Eskimo cases (Tulekana and Kakinya) display exceptional biases toward juveniles, because the hunters deliberately focused on caribou calves to obtain soft hides for clothing (Binford 1978 and field notes). The other Nunamiut cases demonstrate that the hunters could take individuals of any age group they desired and usually did so, but that they at times deliberately sought out young prey. The juvenile-biased cases are homogeneous with respect to prey age and represent short-term episodes (subsets) within a more general system focusing on adult prey; the number of juveniles taken over the course of a year nonetheless was many fewer than adults. Assuming that analogous situations existed in the past, episodes of juvenile hunting would be archaeologically visible only in contexts were fine-grained provenience information is available. Juvenile-biased procurement subsets may exist, for example, within generally prime-dominated patterns in some late Middle Paleolithic and Upper Paleolithic sites, but provenience data for older collections seldom are fine enough to per-

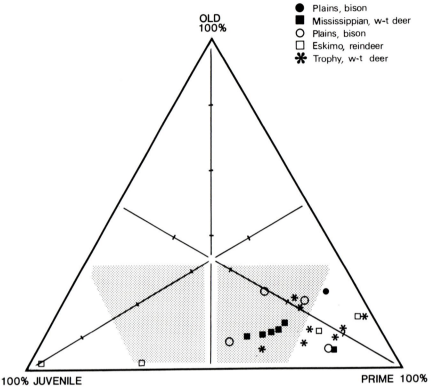

Figure 11.6 Triangular plot of mortality patterns for cervid and bovid remains in North American Holocene archaeofaunas and patterns generated by modern human trophy hunters. (From Stiner 1990b)

mit their recognition. (Ungulate remains from a late Mousterian stratum B3/4 of Grotta Breuil do show a slight juvenile bias, however, as do chamois from the late Upper Paleolithic site of Grotta Polesini [not plotted; see Table 11.6].)

Figure 11.7 shows variation in red/fallow deer and aurochs cases from Mousterian and late Upper Paleolithic caves of west-central Italy. The distribution of the late Upper Paleolithic cases (designated by open circles) is entirely consistent with the Holocene human pattern. The Middle Paleolithic cases, on the other hand, are distributed over a much larger area of the ambush (right portion) of the graph, encompassing the zones associated with both scavenging and hunting in nonhuman predators. Only the late Mousterian cases (Br, aurochs and red deer; B3/4, ibex) from Breuil (ca. 40–35,000 B.P.) display a strong bias toward prime adult prey.

Variation among the Mousterian cases (120,000–35,000 B.P.) is far in excess of that for all Upper Paleolithic and Holocene cases combined (compare Figures 11.6 and 11.7). Mortality patterns segregate according to site; essentially the same procurement practices were repeated throughout each stratigraphic sequence. Some Mousterian cases fall within the modern human scatter (Breuil Br, B3/4, Sant'Agostino S0–3), but the old-biased mortality cases from the two other Mousterian sites (Moscerini M2, M3, M4, and M6, Guattari G4–5) greatly expand the overall spread of points. The old-biased cases are distributed in the upper right part of the graph, occurring in the same area as the nonhuman predator cases associated with high levels of scavenging (see Figure 11.5). The old-age bias consistently associates with the head-dominated Mousterian faunas documented in Chapter 9, whereas the living-structure pattern and prime-age biased pattern associate with meaty faunas. The mortality data

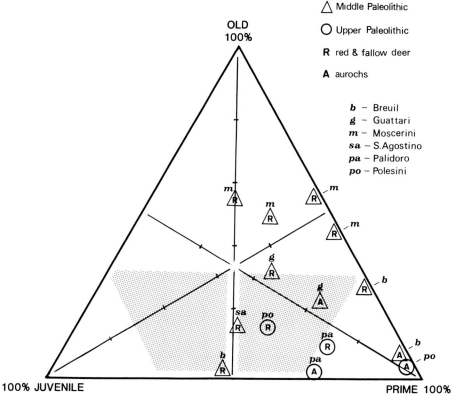

Figure 11.7 Triangular plot of mortality patterns in cervid and bovid remains in Middle and late Upper Paleolithic Italian shelters. (From Stiner 1990b)

therefore concur with evidence of body part transport patterns in showing that two distinct ungulate procurement strategies—hunting and scavenging —were important during Mousterian occupations at the four Latium caves. Only evidence of hunting dominates in the late Upper Paleolithic cases from Latium and in the Holocene cases more generally.

The fact that some late Mousterian cases display prime-dominant mortality patterns may be of ecological and evolutionary significance. Because prime-dominant mortality patterns appear nearly exclusive to human predation, the next question is when prime-dominant harvesting first emerged in prehistory and, more important, when it became an outstanding feature of human predatory practices. Consistent with observations of what many modern humans do, prime-dominant mortality patterns are evident in a variety of archaeological records and across many geological settings—more, in fact,

than are presented here. Though observed elsewhere, such patterns were seldom recognized for what they are (or, at least, could be). Some researchers argue that what appears as prime-dominance is really living-structure (catastrophic) mortality, distorted postdepositionally by preservation biases against juvenile teeth (e.g., Levine 1983; Klein and Cruz-Uribe 1984). The tacit assumption is that the mortality patterns of interest are directly reducible to two basic forms, living-structure or U-shaped (attritional). Other researchers simply did not consider the juvenile cohorts (represented by milk teeth), thereby making prime-dominant mortality inconceivable. Differential preservation can be a genuine issue in some archaeological records (e.g., Hoffecker et al. 1991), but it need not be overgeneralized; the assumption that juvenile (deciduous and incompletely formed permanent) teeth are lost to in situ destruction much faster than adult teeth has not been taphonomically addressed in most cases nor has it been evaluated experimentally. Using an example from the Italian caves, we see that hyaena-collected faunas of Buca della Iena display a strong predominance of juvenile teeth (see Figure 11.5). Modern hyaenas are known to consume bone, sometimes in large quantities, and they can be especially hard on juvenile bones, yet juvenile ungulate teeth greatly exceed adult teeth throughout the Upper Pleistocene hyaena den levels of Buca della Iena. In analogous geological settings of the same region of Italy, people often produced prime-dominant mortality patterns and, in other cases, old-dominant patterns.

Prime-dominant mortality is a real behavioral phenomenon, crucial to understanding human ecology and human evolution. What makes prime-dominated harvesting by humans so interesting is that it departs from all common predatory patterns in animal communities. In west-central Italy, the shift occurred before the end of the Middle Paleolithic and thus may not be chronologically associated with the appearance of modern humans in that region (see next section). The old-biased mortality pattern meanwhile decreases in frequency, although it never disappears completely. For example, horse remains from the late Upper Paleolithic site of Polesini exhibit an old-dominated mortality pattern (not plotted; but see Table 11.6). At Polesini, however, old-dominant mortality occurs only for a relatively rare species in the overall assemblage and constitutes a very minor fraction of the meat transported to and processed at that site. All other ungulate species in the assemblages show living-structure or prime-dominant mortality patterns. In contrast to the situation in the late Upper Paleolithic, old-dominated mortality and head-dominated anatomical patterns occur for the most common prey species in the Mousterian hominid-collected faunas from Moscerini and Guattari. There is little if any evidence of hunting of any ungulate species by hominids at the latter two sites.

The variation in prey selection habits is not accompanied by changes in extractive technologies in the Italian Mousterian. Moreover, pointed tools are less common in Mousterian sites yielding clear evidence of ungulate hunting (see Chapter 14). While many aspects of human social organization and technology vary, the human predatory niche apparently stabilized sometime in the Pleistocene and remained an important adaptation in a wide variety of human contexts into historic times, even if it is not altogether clear when this shift in predator-prey relationships occurred.

Catastrophic (living-structure) mortality is often associated with ambush-hunting practices of humans, but the pattern does not demonstrate communal hunting behavior nor, specifically, driving prey off cliffs. The known causes of living-structure death patterns are more varied, and certainly include solo hunting. Prime-adult harvesting is common in the archaeological record of later Pleistocene and Holocene humans. Though not the only mortality pattern apparent in ungulate faunas, its implications about humans' niche relationships with other large predators are very significant. The data presented do not support the idea that hunting by hominids would ever result in U-shaped mortality patterns in ungulates (cf. Klein 1978, 1981a, 1981b, 1982a, 1982b; but see 1987, 1989a for some revision in view). It is conceivable that hominids could produce U-shaped mortality patterns in sites by scavenging (Klein 1987, 1989a). This would require, however, that scavenging opportunities were obtained from cursorial predator kills and/or nonviolent deaths, and that the carcasses of juveniles were sufficiently large to persist on a landscape and so could be found. Nonhuman predator cases from modern contexts instead generally associate old-dominant mortality in medium-sized ungulates with a heavy emphasis on scavenging. Catastrophic (living-structure) mortality need not strongly contradict the possibility of scavenging (compare Klein 1989a:541 with Blumenschine's 1991 actualistic example); it is only less likely.

Two observations from the mortality comparisons are especially important to this study. One is the relatively greater variation in prey age selection apparent in the Middle Paleolithic. The second concerns the behavioral and ecological implications of prime-dominant mortality patterns characterizing modern human hunting practices. The implications of these observations with regard to the emergence of the modern human predatory niche are explored further in two sections to follow.

The Behavioral Significance of Prime-Dominated Mortality Patterns

The concept of cooperative ambush by humans is very attractive to archaeologists, and scenarios of game drives have been used to explain large accumulations of ungulate bones in Pleistocene sites. The most sensational interpretations incorporate some version of the fatal leap en masse over a steep precipice. Driving ungulates over a *jump* may well have occurred in the past, but the method was probably highly specialized and only suitable for certain prey species, such as bison. Indeed, only a small fraction of the many mass kill sites on the Great Plains merit the jump classification, and the method appears to have been a relatively late development in that region and by no means the only hunting tactic in use by those cultures (Frison 1978:229–231). Most of the rich bison bone beds of the prehistoric period are actually sites in which live prey are cornered; Frison and others argue that hunters harvested smaller groups of bison with the aid of geomorphic features, such as parabolic dunes and box canyons (also see Speth 1983; Todd 1983), and that the trap method actually dominated the bison-hunting scene in Wyoming until the Late Prehistoric period (Frison 1978:247).

Broad comparisons of Holocene archaeological and ethnoarchaeological data provide useful expectations of what mortality patterns resulting from group harvesting practices might look like in the archaeological records of earlier periods. While it is impossible to know exactly what took place in every case, the data appear to stress prey entrapment in ambush hunting and to deemphasize the influence of specific technological elements; if a group of prey animals is cornered simultaneously, animals can be killed selectively with a variety of weapons. Because the members of prey populations may naturally divide into small, relatively homogeneous age and sex groups, hunters could target prey primarily at the level of these groups and secondarily at the level of individual animals. The existence of prime-dominant mortality patterns in the late Mousterian is especially striking because it suggests that stone-tipped projectiles were not prerequisites for success.

In Holocene cases other than those involving modern trophy hunters using firearms, the prime-dominated focus may have been facilitated by planned use of space, such as interception of prey at predetermined locations, and cooperative labor during procurement and carcass processing. Nunamiut Eskimo set up hunting camps at narrow passes in the caribou migration routes and killed animals with bows and arrows or rifles (Binford 1978). Technological associations for the earlier portions of the High Plains sequence include both spears (possibly used with atl-atls in Paleoindian and Archaic periods) and bows and arrows for the Protohistoric period. Middle Mississippian hunters, on the other hand, may have relied more heavily on solo encounter hunting, using a generally similar range of projectile weaponry, based on historic accounts of later peoples in this region (B. D. Smith 1975:37).

It is interesting that an association between a prime adult bias in prey and the use of trap features commonly arises in human cases. When topography is used by some nonhuman cursorial predators, prime-biased patterns seldom arise. Human sociality and cognitive capabilities may have permitted them to take a more active role in prey selection and, in much later cultural periods, management of wild prey populations (also see Hecker 1982). Topographic features suitable for ambushing groups of ungulates occur in the vicinity of the Paleolithic sites in west-central Italy. Similar features are common in the Dordogne region of France (e.g., White 1982). The Middle Paleolithic coastal cave sites of Sant'Agostino and Breuil, and the late Upper Paleolithic rockshelters of Salvini and Polesini, are associated with natural bottlenecks or small amphitheater-like canyons. These narrow shoreline passages alternate with broad expanses of rich coastal plain. The constricted passages, bordered on one side by the Mediterranean Sea (adjusting for sea level) and steep cliffs on the other, might have enabled small groups of hunters to surround game animals. The Breuil faunas contain a nearly complete range of anatomical parts, indicating few constraints on carcass transport—possibly because the kill sites were near the shelters (Chapter 9). Not all of the sites show evidence of selective hunting, however. Such hunting behavior was not conditioned simply by the presence of suitable landscape features.

Hunting favoring prime adult prey[11] implies controlled, perhaps selective, procurement. It is not altogether clear whether prime adult biases represent deliberate or inadvertent products of a hunting method. Juveniles are the most abundant age group in living populations and the most vulnerable to predators in general, yet some human hunters more frequently obtained adult prey, especially prime adults. Selectivity toward adult prey may have been exercised by Paleolithic hunters at the level of choosing individual animals or by seeking out self-segregated age and sex groups that many ungulate species naturally form as the result of their social adaptations (e.g., Clutton-Brock et al. 1982). Either way, wide recurrence of prime-dominant mortality patterns in human-collected faunas is an extraordinary development in the human evolutionary sequence, especially in light of the near absence of this kind of mortality pattern in ungulates procured by nonhuman predators. It may imply, among other things, changes in the scale of human territory use and, perhaps, social interaction.

The observations cited above may be helpful for understanding *how* hunters exercised options for prey choice in some circumstances. But they do not explain *why* hunters focused more on prime adult prey over time. Hunters' choices presumably relate to processing and nutritional needs of the human social group. Although more data are needed, the shift toward a preference for prime adult prey in west-central Italy generally corresponds to the increasing cold of the Last Glacial. An emphasis on prime adult ungulates would make access to animal fat more reliable. Humans' need for fat increases beyond the normal nutritional baseline in colder environments (Binford 1978), because animal fat represents a major energy source in the absence of carbohydrates (i.e., stored plant products). While all of the Italian Mousterian assemblages indicate thorough marrow processing of the skeletal parts carried to shelters (e.g., limb shafts, mandibles, and cranial tissues; see Chapters 5 and 9), proportions of the fat-storing age groups in prey death assemblages vary. None of the mortality patterns in the Italian Mousterian contain many juveniles, but, by the late Mousterian in this sample, there is a rise in the proportion of prime adults harvested, indicating access to adult prey via hunting rather than scavenging. The broader significance of a focus on prime adult harvesting in Latium is difficult to evaluate in precise chronological terms (but see Chapter 14), but it can be evaluated relative to the niches of other ungulate predators in animal communities.

DIVERGING PATTERNS OF PREY AGE SELECTION BY SYMPATRIC PREDATORS

The mortality patterns generated by predators describe an important dimension of the niche relationships among them. Sympatric predators that depend on the same prey populations are bound to impinge upon one another from time to time, and, according to the tenets of niche theory, natural selection should favor ways of reducing competition over the course of their evolutionary histories. The prey age selection habits of cursorial and ambush carnivores and sympatric hominids appear to have diverged with time. The dominant patterns of age harvesting by these three predator groups became more complementary in the process, with each class of predator extracting rather different age groups from ungulate populations.

The niche relationships among predator types take on evolutionary significance in that they may illustrate potential directions for adaptational change

---

[11] An occasional, selective focus on juvenile prey is observed, for example, among the Nunamiut Eskimo (Binford 1978). This behavior should not be confused with opportunistic hunting of very young prey by physiologically limited predators, such as brown bears and coyotes; even grizzlies do not often capture adult ungulates. Bears and coyotes programmatically rob mothers of their infants in the spring, however (e.g., Ballard and Whitman 1987:67–68; Ballard et al. 1987:40; Hauge and Keith 1981:583; Nelson and Woolf 1987; Sowls 1984:94). Such a situation is conceivable for early periods of hominid prehistory, but should not co-occur with prime-dominated or nonselective hunting in a given culture.

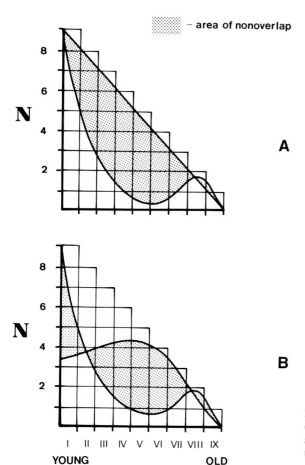

Figure 11.8 Superimposed mortality profiles comparing (A) idealized living-structure and U-shaped patterns, and (B) idealized prime-dominant and U-shaped patterns. (From Stiner 1990b)

in the case of humans, a late arrival to predatory guilds that may have been established as early as the Miocene (Chapter 2). Pairs of idealized mortality profiles are superimposed on a pristine, stable population model in Figures 11.8A and 11.8B. The diagrams illustrate how predators with fundamentally different procurement strategies theoretically can exploit the same prey population while minimizing food competition. Both the living-structure and the prime-dominated mortality profiles are partially complementary to the U-shaped profile; the areas of nonoverlap within profile pairs are roughly equal to the areas of overlap. The U-shaped and prime-dominated mortality patterns (Figure 11.8B) may be slightly more complementary than the living-structure and U-shaped patterns (Figure 11.8A), because there is less overlap in the area of the juvenile cohorts.

The concept of limiting similarity for coexisting species, discussed in Chapter 2, states that species dependent on similar resources should reduce the effects of interspecific competition, or risk of interference, by emphasizing different ways to exploit those resources. Such a process may be manifest in the Paleolithic culture sequence. Specifically, ecological relations with sympatric cursorial and ambush carnivores appear to have influenced the direction of hominids' shift in predatory focus during the later part of the Pleistocene. The relatively more specialized mode emphasizing prime adult ungulate prey was an unrealized niche until this time. Interspecific relations with the carnivores may not have been the cause of the shift; after all, hominids and carnivores existed alongside one another prior to that period in Africa, Asia, and Europe. The influence of sympatric carnivores on the direction of change is another story, because adaptational shifts, like colonization, should move into areas posing the least resistance.

These generalizations can also be explored using the three-age mortality format. So that the habitual behaviors of predators may emerge more clearly, only median values for each carnivore species and for various human cultures are considered (Table 11.7). Three clusters are apparent when the median patterns are plotted in Figure 11.9A, and the clusters lie roughly equidistant from one another. Variation associated with each set is not plotted; suffice it to say there is some overlap between the ranges associated with each cluster, as evident from previous triangular graphs.

The first cluster, on the lower left portion of Figure 11.9A, consists of medians for cursorial carnivores, including wolves (N-cases = 3), spotted

hyaenas (N-cases = 8), and African wild dogs (N-cases = 3). The second cluster, high on the right, contains medians for two classic ambush predators, lions (N-cases = 4) and tigers (N-cases = 4). Leopards are not considered because only one case was available. The third cluster, on the lower right, consists of medians for various Holocene human cultures, as well as the median for the two special cases in which wolves used lake ice to entrap caribou at their calving grounds. As is true for the big cat group, this third cluster generally represents ambush predatory behaviors, but of a different, more biased character.

The second wolf median exists only because it took place at calving grounds and is atypical for wolves overall. The bias in the Holocene human medians, on the other hand, is consistent across many cultures, time periods, technological sys-

TABLE 11.7
Median percentages for the ungulate mortality data by case group

Case group	N-cases	JUV	PRIME	OLD
nonhuman predators:				
Indian tiger (A)	4	.15	.41	.29
African lion (A)	4	.24	.47	.23
African wild dog (C)	3	.52	.34	.13
spotted hyaena (C)	8	.47	.29	.21
wolf, long chase (C)	3	.53	.30	.22
wolf, "ambush" behavior[b]	2	.30	.63	.15
Paleolithic hominids, Italy:				
late UP human	10	.23	.66	.15
MP hominid	19	.26	.54	.20
Holocene humans, North America:				
modern trophy hunters	8	.17	.70	.11
historic Nunamiut hunters	5	.26	.68	.05
(without "skin hunting")	3[c]	.16	.72	.12
Mississippian hunters	6	.28	.61	.09
Paleoindian/Archaic hunters	4	.20	.58	.14

[a] The median values for percentages in the three age stages do not always equal 100, because the medians are for multiple cases and the value for each age stage was calculated independently.
[b] Two prey age selection behaviors are documented for North American and Eurasian wolves; wolves usually produce U-shaped mortality patterns in prey through the cumulative effects of hunting, but some environments contain vegetational or geomorphological features that allow the packs to ambush or "corral" prey, as in the cases noted.
[c] Those situations in which Nunamiut hunters sought juvenile reindeer skins for clothing are omitted from the calculations.

Note: (A) generally classified by wildlife biologists as an ambush predator or (C) cursorial predator.

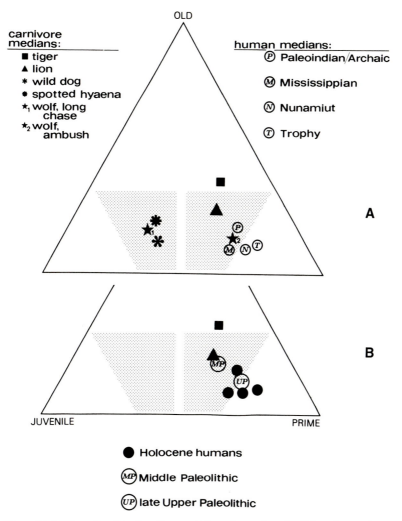

Figure 11.9 Triangular plot of median mortality pattern values for (A) modern predators grouped by strategy class or (in human cases) environment and culture, and (B) late Upper Paleolithic and Middle Paleolithic hominid groupings.

tems, and geographical origins. The median values represent Paleoindian, Archaic, and Protohistoric bison hunters of the North American Plains (N-cases = 4), Nunamiut caribou hunters (N-cases = 5), Middle Mississippian deer hunters (N-cases = 6), and modern trophy hunters using firearms (N-cases = 8). The medians are remarkably similar to one another in spite of the diverse origins, all showing some bias toward prime adult prey.

Figure 11.9B repeats elements from the ambush half of the upper graph—large cats and Holocene peoples—but with Italian Paleolithic medians added to the comparison (various prey species). The dark symbols denote big cats and various Holocene humans, whereas the open symbols denote Mousterian (MP) and late Upper Paleolithic (UP) medians. As we might expect, the median for the late Upper Paleolithic (N-cases = 10) is nested in the center of the Holocene human cluster. The Mousterian median instead falls closer to the big cat cluster, just below the African lion median. (Late Mousterian cases therein diverge most from the mean, however.) The difference between the Mousterian median and those of all other humans in the study sample is quite significant and suggests a shift in hominid foraging niche in the study area during the Upper Pleistocene. Returning to the two-dimensional format used to compare harvesting patterns by modern carnivores above (as in Figure 11.8A), superimposing the pattern typical of the big cats and Mousterian cluster over a prime-dominant (representing all other human cases) profile in Figure 11.10 reveals a substantial area of nonoverlap. Considerable competition avoidance is possible between late Upper Paleolithic and Holocene peoples and the big cats, less between Mousterian hominids and big cats from this perspective—except, perhaps, toward the end of the Middle Paleolithic in the study area.

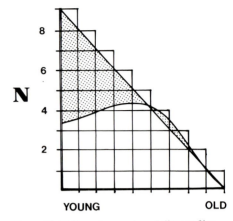

Figure 11.10 Superimposed mortality profiles comparing idealized living-structure and prime-dominant patterns; shading as in Figure 11.8.

CONCLUDING DISCUSSION

The three-age approach to mortality analysis highlights some of the boundaries of hominid foraging niches by comparing human harvesting patterns to those of other Old World predator species. Inferences are grounded in what predators really do and the consequences of their behaviors for mortality patterns in prey. Consistent with the situation presented by archaeological records, the control sets represent cumulative records of predatory events. These cases are compared across time and across places, scales at which the potential contradiction or support posed by any one case weighs only lightly. When applied to Upper Pleistocene cave faunas in one small region of Italy, the approach indicates significant niche separation between Middle and late Upper Paleolithic hominids, with the earlier period displaying more diverse harvesting practices across sites. The differences reflect how hominids obtained animal prey, the extent and character of variation in their subsistence practices, and, probably, the relative scales of mobility. These results are discussed below, first in terms of levels of strategic variation between cultural periods as traditionally defined, followed by consideration of increasing predatory specialization independently of the Middle-Upper Paleolithic chronological boundary.

Strategic variation: Hunting and scavenging

The mortality data, like the anatomical data presented in Chapter 9, provide a means for documenting hunting versus scavenging strategies at the assemblage level. Of the mortality patterns discussed, the prime-dominated and old-biased patterns are of special interest for comparative studies of hominid predatory strategies, because these patterns are more specific to cause than most.

One of the outstanding findings on ungulate mortality concerns the total ranges of variation in hominid foraging strategies within and after the Middle Paleolithic period. Late Upper Paleolithic and all Holocene human cases are surprisingly similar to one another, whereas Mousterian cases vary greatly, essentially dividing into two very different kinds of faunal assemblages. All variants of *Homo sapiens* studied, from roughly 120,000 years ago to the present, appear to have been ambush predators, but the predatory tactics of Middle Paleolithic foragers varied more between shelter sites than did those of Upper Paleolithic peoples in Italy and Holocene peoples elsewhere in the world. Middle Paleolithic hominids either hunted or scavenged the same ungulate species (usually red deer and aurochs), whereas late Upper Paleolithic humans almost exclusively hunted them. Strong parallels are found between the mortality patterns and anatomical representation in the Mousterian sample (summarized in Chapter 14), both of which point to hunting in Sant'Agostino (S0–3) and Breuil (Br, B3/4) and scavenging in Moscerini (M2, M3, M4, and M6) and Guattari (G4–5). Unfortunately, no information is yet available on the early Upper Paleolithic in Latium (see Chapter 3).

It is unlikely that any of the foraging tactics outlined above were unique to either Mousterian or later hominids. However, the rules by which alternative procurement techniques were combined or emphasized appear to have been different. Mousterian hominids were capable hunters of ungulates, but they did not hunt them as consistently as Upper Paleolithic forgers while occupying the coastal shelters. Both varieties of hominid certainly were mobile, but Mousterian foraging responses may have been governed more by local, immediate exigencies than was true for Upper Paleolithic peoples, making the most of every conceivable foraging opportunity in a small area by combing it thoroughly. It is not clear if the level of strategic variation in food procurement within the Italian Mousterian, the character of that variation, and the geographical scale at which it occurred would be equivalent for the Middle Paleolithic of other regions of Eurasia. In the long run, the *range* of variation may more accurately characterize Mousterian foraging patterns than the specific array of tactics used in any given region.

Increasing predatory specialization

Comparisons to nonhuman predators reveal that modern people are a rather specialized variety of ambush predator, at least with regard to ungulate prey. From the perspective of prey age selection, the genus *Homo* appears to have evolved away from an ecologically common predatory pattern or niche that overlapped most with the big cats (but also with the cursorial carnivores) to a relatively unique one sometime in the Upper Pleistocene. Comparisons of food transport habits in Chapter 9 also suggest decreasing variation across the same time range, although the transport data expose no ecologically unique qualities of human foraging adaptations. Whatever the reason for its existence, the apparent trend in the Italian study area toward increasing predatory specialization can be considered at two separate but related levels. Cases attributed to scavenging (Moscerini, and probably Guattari G4–5) comprise the earlier part of the sequence, whereas evidence of hunting is identified primarily in the later part (Sant'Agostino and Breuil). It is conceivable at this stage in the research that the observed variation in hunting and scavenging in the Mousterian record represents *either* an evolutionary change in lifeways or just seasonal or extra-annual adjustments in site use within a single, stable adaptation. In either case, the contrast between the Middle and Upper Paleolithic periods overall is striking.

A general trend in hunting practices toward prime-dominated prey selection by at least the late Mousterian (Breuil) is difficult to deny, particularly since noticeably reduced variation persists in late Upper Paleolithic through Holocene times. The Italian evidence suggests that hunting practices had become significantly more specialized by forty thousand years ago, perhaps earlier, but within the temporal range of Mousterian technologies. The increasing focus on prime adult prey corresponds to a growing separation between hominid predatory niche and the niches of sympatric carnivores. Here, the term *specialization* is warranted only by the facts that a prime adult focus is ecologically unprecedented relative to other well-established predator species in the same ecosystems and that the range of tactical variation across sites narrows.

Habitual prime-dominant prey age selection appears to be unique to humans. This class of mortality pattern diverges from natural processes of recruitment and survivorship in mammalian populations and from the typical prey selection patterns of nonhuman predators. It is the only harvesting pattern that operates *directly* upon the most reproductively active age groups at any given time, since most wild ungulate species do not begin reproducing until at least their second year of life. Prime adults also are the richest sources of stored metabolizable fats and can be the most difficult (or at least the bulkiest) individuals in prey populations to kill.

As noted earlier, recurrent prime-dominant mortality patterns imply selective or controlled harvesting on the part of human hunters, either as the deliberate or inadvertent product of the strategies employed. Individual prey may have been targeted, or hunters may have deliberately sought self-segregated sex and age groups that social ungulates often form, meanwhile ignoring other age and sex groups. Isolated contradictions may be found among modern humans (e.g., Hudson 1991), but these do not refute the broader pattern: prime-dominant harvesting cannot simply be a random product of encounter, because the archaeological and modern human records are consistently poor in juveniles across assemblages, prey species, cultures, and environments. No carnivore consistently produces prime-dominant patterns, although they rely on the same ungulate species for their survival. The evidence points to something that human hunters were doing consistently across time and space, independently of the details of prey behavior—something that nonhuman predators almost never did.

Choice is a sticky concept in research on foraging, because the consequences of a behavior may easily be confused with assumptions about intention or premeditation. No doubt, the inference that hunters made deliberate age-biased choices merits further testing. It is clear, on the other hand, that human harvesting has impacted prey populations in distinct and selective ways well into prehistory, if viewed from the perspective of mammalian demography.

Preferential acquisition of prime-aged prey may be facilitated by technology (particularly long-range weapons), cooperative ambush strategies, and/or by monitoring and targeting particular sex- or age-segregated prey groups in the area. Any of these aspects of human behavior—technology, cooperation, or monitoring prey groups—can result in mortality patterns that appear "selective" with regard to prey age. The apparently great importance of cooperation among hunters in some historic situations, for example, shows that prime-dominant prey selection is not necessarily technology-bound (e.g., see review in Frison 1978, 1984). A focus on prime adult prey also occurs within the Mousterian

of Italy, where we find no convincing evidence that stone-tipped projectiles were in regular use. Even the very pronounced prime-dominant pattern of the late Mousterian is not accompanied by changes in or elaboration of extractive technologies (Kuhn 1989a, 1990a). In the absence of such technology, prime-dominant procurement by the Mousterian occupants of Grotta Breuil may indicate that relatively larger pools of human labor were sometimes available for capturing, transporting, and processing ungulate prey. Prime-dominant mortality in ungulate prey may also indicate locally intense harvesting for short periods in a larger territory.

Prime-dominant harvesting: Stable or unstable?

Short of extermination, the potential relationships between predators and prey populations are determined partly by how many deaths predators cause in a given year relative to other agencies and partly by which age groups they commonly take. With the advent of selective ambush hunting, humans entered a new ecological relationship with ungulate prey, and humans' impact on ungulate demography may have changed in significant and unprecedented ways. Nonhuman predators, by contrast, inadvertently leave the most productive age cohorts free to generate more prey—the main source of new infants in the coming year. Cursorial carnivores, for example, are most likely to take young and old animals, but even ambush carnivores do not take an especially heavy toll on the prime age cohort. The low potential for affecting prey population growth by either class of nonhuman predator is not surprising given the long evolutionary history of predator-prey relationships between the carnivores and the ungulates (see Chapter 1).

Humans are therefore unusual among predators in that they concentrate on prime adult prey in many situations. Such practices certainly have altered (if only slightly) the structures of living populations in historic times (e.g., McCullough et al. 1990) and may have done so in the past as well (e.g., Koike and Ohtaishi 1985, 1987). That this kind of harvesting necessarily leads to situations of overexploitation is unlikely, however (see also Lyman 1987b:138–140). The success of many game management programs today demonstrates that balanced predator-prey relationships are achievable using the prime-dominant exploitation scheme (e.g., McCullough et al. 1990). Heavy levels of managed trophy hunting nonetheless leave characteristic traces on the age structure of living populations in game parks (for a related discussion, see Schultz and Johnson 1992). This phenomenon probably explains why census data for many modern ungulate populations indicate some deficiency in late-prime and especially elderly adults relative to an idealized living-structure model. Graphically, these cases appear to be compressed toward the low end of the old-age axis in the triangular plot in Figure 11.4. Such populations appear to be viable, but exhibit a decreased mean lifespan (sensu Caughley 1977), and in some cases, a lower mean age of first reproduction (especially in males). These populations may simply remain in a growth phase rather than achieving the classic stable structure of populations that are unaffected by humans. Modern examples of the latter are in fact quite rare, but may still be found in situations in which hunting by humans is either not allowed or not feasible (e.g., Mohave feral burros, Johnson et al. 1987).

Like modern trophy-hunted death assemblages, the archaeological cases dating to after roughly 40,000 B.P. are compressed toward the low end of the old-age axis (see Figure 11.6). The archaeological cases fit within the expected range of variation in the continuum between living-structure and prime-dominant mortality pattern domains, but they often are deficient in late prime and old prey, a situation seldom observed in death assemblages generated by the nonhuman predators. It is impossible to know the real composition of ancient prey populations, but it is significant that procurement practices of late Mousterian, late Upper Paleolithic, Paleoindian, historic Nunamiut Eskimo, and other traditional human cultures resulted in mortality patterns equivalent to those arising from managed trophy hunting in modern game parks. The mechanisms preventing overexploitation in the past certainly differed from those of the modern era, but the net effect on prey population structure appears much the same.

What do compressed age structures in ungulate death assemblages associated with prehistoric human activities really mean with regard to humans' long-term ecological relationships with prey? We know that humans have hunted some species to extinction, especially in the past few centuries (e.g., Diamond 1989). However, it is essential to guard against equating recent or impending extinctions of persecuted species with what may be basic characteristics of the human predatory niche. Compression of living ungulate age structures may be the result of intense short-term exploitation of a natural resource at the local level. People may move on to other resource patches (or areas) when the current one is depleted—without overstepping the dynamic balance at a larger community level. This kind of practice requires, however, extensive travel from time to time and relatively large territories.

The repetition of compressed age structures in archaeological records may simply reflect a basic and potentially stable property of the human predatory niche that has been around at last as long as anatomically modern humans in Europe, and probably longer. Its appearance in Paleolithic faunas may signal important changes in humans' game search and monitoring practices, a question of territory use. The great antiquity of these practices (40,000+ years) shows that there is no a priori reason to assume that this unique predator-prey relationship was unstable. The balance required for prime-focused exploitation may have been more delicate and the rules of regulation somewhat different than those typical of nonhuman predators, but it should be more practical for an omnivore than for a strict carnivore. It may be no coincidence that omnivorous humans were the only large predators to evolve this kind of predator-prey relationship with ungulates; bears, the only other large omnivores of note, solve their problems by sleeping through winter.

12

Carnivore Mortality and the Denning Hypothesis

MOST DISCUSSIONS of resource use in this book are about food. However, shelters were another class of resource important to Pleistocene humans and large carnivores in Italy. Carnivores' needs for shelter do not limit them to natural caves and fissures; those species that rely on dens are wholly capable of excavating their own. However, a clean, dry natural cave is bound to be attractive, if available in the right time and place. The role of dens in carnivore life histories varies by species, but a few aspects of denning behavior and its paleontological consequences are nearly universal. The den may represent a safe place to raise young for a short time or, in the case of bears (genus *Ursus*), a hiding place where the animal may sleep through the winter and, if female, harbor her infants. More than anything, dens are safe places, small enough to be defended or at least to bar the entry of larger intruders. Dens also afford protection from the elements, either by trapping the animal's body heat in cold climates or keeping the animal cool in arid ones. Because of the role of shelter in their life history strategies, carnivores that use dens frequently die in them. As carnivore remains accumulate, the resultant age patterns take on distinctive signatures.

This chapter considers the hypotheses that spotted hyaenas, wolves, foxes, and bears denned in some of the Italian caves from the standpoint of carnivore mortality patterns. The denning hypothesis was examined from a taphonomic point of view in Chapters 5 and 6, where the general results of this presentation were first noted. Carnivore mortality patterns are not widely used for identifying den faunas, although their potential for this purpose is great. Here, I conduct mortality analyses of Pleistocene hyaenas, wolves, foxes, and bears, exploring both the assumptions behind the age patterns and the implications of the results. The analyses examine carnivore age structures across the maximum potential lifespan. Wildlife studies supply the expectations for carnivore mortality in denning contexts, as well as the seasonal timing and duration of denning periods as a function of latitude. Because few comprehensive guidelines are available for constructing carnivore age profiles across the full potential lifetime, detailed tooth eruption and wear schemes for canids, hyaenids, and ursids are presented.

AGE STRUCTURE MODELS AND DENNING BEHAVIOR

The remains of large and small carnivores are common in some levels of the Latium (and Tuscan) caves, especially in the time range encompassed by the Middle Paleolithic. The situation is different in

late Upper Paleolithic assemblages, wherein large carnivore remains are rare or absent from human sites, but small carnivores continue to be common. This contrast in large versus small carnivore representation through time is consistent with that shown by Gamble (1983, 1986) for the Mediterranean rim more generally. Differing patterns of carnivore representation in shelters between the Middle and late Upper Paleolithic cultural periods suggest that the causes and circumstances of accumulation also differed.

Patterns of bone damage and coprolites may effectively diagnose carnivore activities in sites. Although the taphonomic data supply clear indications of carnivore "presence," they are not always so clear about why the carnivores were there. Carnivore mortality patterns represent an independent line of evidence about the possibility of denning that, sample size allowing, provide fairly definitive results. If carnivores used the Italian caves as dens, then the seasonal correlates of denning in modern control populations may also imply the seasons of occupations by wolves, foxes, and bears, but not hyaenas (see below). If denning behavior is indicated by the mortality data, we should probably assume that hominids and carnivores did not reside in the same caves in the same years. Modern carnivores typically avoid placing their dens where recent disruptions are evident (e.g., Clevenger 1991; Mattson et al. 1992; Rogers 1987). The way that hyaenas use maternity (as opposed to birthing) dens altogether precludes the possibility of alternation with humans or other predators within years, because of hyaenas' tendency to use a shelter for a long time, not to mention the dismal condition of the shelter upon abandonment (prodigious latrines, fleas, etc.).

Carnivore mortality data likewise are useful for evaluating possible hunting of carnivores by hominids. Evidence that late Upper Paleolithic humans hunted small carnivores for furs, ornaments, and food is fairly secure (e.g., Soffer 1985). That Middle Paleolithic hominids were significant predators of large carnivores, on the other hand, has often been assumed (e.g., Bächler 1921, 1940) and is highly questionable. Bones of leopards, wolves, bears, and hyaenas are prevalent in so-called Mousterian cave faunas throughout Eurasia. The question is whether these cases represent alternating and independent occupations of the caves by people and carnivores, or humans hunting large carnivores as prey, or large carnivores hunting or scavenging hu-

mans and carrying parts of their bodies, along with other foods, into caves (e.g., Guattari G0; see also Brain 1981). All of these situations have come about in the past, but we need to know which were common, when, and where in a given cultural period. The three interpretations of carnivore remains in sites posed above have very different ecological implications for human life in the Pleistocene. Because carnivore remains are so prevalent in Paleolithic caves, moreover, we need to develop straightforward ways of addressing hypotheses of carnivore denning. Working primarily from Kurtén's (1958, 1976) insights on this problem, carnivore mortality analyses here offer such an advantage.

There are two reasons to expect elevated juvenile mortality in carnivores in denning contexts. First, the incidence of death is highest in the early years of life (e.g., Van Ballenberghe and Mech 1975). This is true for virtually all mammalian species (Caughley 1977; see Chapter 10), a fact that accounts in large part for the form of U-shaped (attritional) mortality patterns in death assemblages. Second, the young of carnivores tend to be concentrated in dens for months at a time; juveniles stay in these places day-in and day-out, whereas most adults in the population (including those attending to infants) move about. The combined effects of high juvenile mortality and the fact that many carnivore species harbor their young in dens produce a juvenile-biased mortality pattern in excess of that predicted by a classic model of attritional death (e.g., Kruuk 1972:35–36). The bias toward the juvenile age group may be amplified further in species that use communal dens (e.g., spotted hyaenas, Kruuk 1972:243–247; and red foxes, Macdonald 1979), where sibling cannibalism is common (spotted hyaenas), or by the presence of subadult helpers (wolves and jackals, e.g., Fentress and Ryon 1982:256–257; Macdonald 1979). Human hunting of carnivores for fur is unlikely to result in a strong juvenile bias; it should produce a bias toward adults. Some real-life contradictions to this expectation may exist, but ethnographic accounts of fur hunting generally indicate that humans are interested in fur quality (as opposed to hide thickness and pliability), which is only fully realized in carnivores upon maturity (e.g., Binford 1978).

The expectations for mortality in bears (genus *Ursus*) may differ from those for other den-dependent species by simply fulfilling the classic pattern of attritional death. Bears of both sexes may hibernate (e.g., Clevenger and Purroy 1991; Wooding and Hardisky 1992), whereas only some adult females give birth during that time. The extent to which adult males of the population hibernate is explained by their relative reliance on plants and small animals in a given ecosystem, because access to these foods is directly affected by winter temperatures and snow cover. Adult males and barren females will hibernate for shorter periods, if food is available. Pregnant females den longest (minimally three to four months), a period that appears to be intrinsic to bears' reproductive biology (Wooding and Hardisky 1992). The denning period of bears usually lasts much longer than that of canids or felids. Hibernation is at once an adaptive response to reproductive concerns and winter scarcity of plants and small animals, the dietary mainstays of bears inhabiting the temperate zone (e.g., Clevenger et al. 1992). Delayed implantation of fertilized zygotes in the uterus of the female bear (Ewer 1973) underlines the convergence of the two concerns in the hibernation process (Johnson and Pelton 1980; Wooding and Hardisky 1992). Bears are especially prone to starvation during the cold season (Watts et al. 1987; Watts and Jonkel 1988), wherein the end of this phase is most difficult (e.g., Rogers 1987). The risk of starvation in particular warrants the expectation of U-shaped mortality (Kurtén 1976:97). Because many or all adults from the population will hibernate each year, the mortality pattern resulting from hibernation deaths may not be overly biased toward juveniles. Inter- and intraspecific violence, provoked by winter food stress (e.g., Mattson et al. 1992), should also produce U-shaped mortality in den assemblages over the long run.

If denning activities are confirmed in the Italian Pleistocene cases by carnivore age structures, the maximum potential denning period can be estimated using modern ethological data from analogous climatic provinces. The reproductive seasons of canids and most cats are tightly restricted in temperate and arctic environments, although some lati-tudinal variation in denning schedules is to be expected; data and sources are presented in Table 12.1. The hibernation period of brown bears is also predictable in relation to latitude and the duration of winter snow cover. Populations living closer to the equator will display more variation in the timing of den entry and exit, and shorter hibernation periods overall. In this study, data on modern carnivore populations from Mediterranean environments are used as much as possible to reconstruct denning schedules in Pleistocene coastal Italy.

Contra the situation for canids, ursids, and felids, no assessment of denning season is possible for the Italian spotted hyaenas, because modern hyaenas display aseasonal birthing patterns in tropical and subtropical environments. African spotted hyaenas, for example, may give birth in any month of the year, although a birthing peak is apparent in some regions (Ewer 1973; Kruuk 1972). Of course, modern spotted hyaenas occupy only a fraction of their former Upper Pleistocene range, and these populations currently are restricted to relatively warm regions. Spotted hyaenas once also thrived in temperate Pleistocene Europe; the collective range of this species has contracted since. It is possible that there was greater seasonal restriction in their birthing schedules in southern Europe, consistent with clinal variation in denning seasons among virtually all of the modern carnivores. However, spotted hyaena denning seasons would never have been as short as those of canids or felids. Hyaena dens serve as refuges for young animals until they are ready to travel extensively and to cope with the intense feeding competition posed by adults of the same clan at procurement sites (e.g., Mills 1985; Tilson and Hamilton 1984). The safety of dens is required well into the second year of life in modern spotted hyaenas, sometimes longer (Kruuk 1972).

Inferences about the seasons of denning in carnivores other than hyaenas depend on control data for modern populations of the same or similar species. It is not always possible to find good ecological analogs, because some taxa have not received much study and others are extinct, or the characteristics of the wild progenitors have been masked by domestication. To compensate for these problems, a wide array of modern sources are considered in Table

TABLE 12.1
Characteristics of carnivore reproductive schedules

Species	Geographic location	Denning season[a]	Source
brown bear	Leipzig Zoo	Dec–*Jan*–March	Ewer 1973:306
	Alaska	Dec–*Jan*–March	Burton 1979:64
	Spain	Jan—March	Clevenger and Purroy 1991:116–117
black bear	Minnesota	—*Jan*—	Rogers 1981; 1987:5
	Florida	Dec–*Jan*–April	Wooding and Hardisky 1992
badger	Britain	Jan–*Feb*–March	Ewer 1973:306
wolf	Alaska	*May*–July[b]	Ballard et al. 1987
	Alaska	late May–June	Ewer 1973:308–309
	New Zealand[c]	Feb–*March*–May	Burton 1979:54
	Israel	*May*	Mendelssohn 1982:192
	Jaipur Zoo[c]	Nov–Jan	Burton 1979:54
	London Zoo	March–May	Burton 1979:54
red fox	Scotland	April	Ewer 1973:308–309
	England/Ireland	March	Burton 1979:40
	England	March–April	Burton 1979:40
lynx	New Zealand[c]	late May–June	Ewer 1973:312–313
wild cat	captive (Europe)	April–May	Ewer 1973:312–313
bobcat	Idaho	April–May	Knick 1990
spotted hyaena	Tanzania	aseasonal[d]	Ewer 1973:305
	Zululand	aseasonal[d] (but peak = *June–Aug*)	Ewer 1973:305
	Serengeti and Ngorongoro	aseasonal[d] (but lowest in Sept–Dec)	Kruuk 1972:28, 306

[a] Italicized month indicates birthing peak, whereas the range refers to the full potential denning period. Wolf, fox, and wild cat denning seasons extend roughly six–eight weeks beyond the birthing peak; bear and hyaena denning seasons last longer.

[b] Authors report heavy use of rendezvous sites by wolf packs with young juveniles from July through mid-September.

[c] Case is from the southern hemisphere; reversal of the reproductive season relative to calender months occurs in this species.

[d] Modern spotted hyaenas display aseasonal reproductive schedules in modern equatorial and subequatorial environments. Because the timing and the range of the reproductive period in mammals normally vary with climatic severity, and hyaenas today occupy only a fraction of their Pleitocene range, it is possible that hyaenas in Italy had a somewhat more restricted reproductive season than is true of this species today. Even hyaenas in Europe would have displayed less seasonal demarcation in den use than canids, small cats, and mustelids, however, because juveniles' dependence on dens for protection and on mothers for milk would not be significantly reduced.

12.1. Modern populations from southern Europe are preferred analogs, but Britain represents another important source of information. Although the British Isles lie farther to the north, Britain's climate is regulated by maritime winds, as is that of coastal west-central Italy and the northern skirt of the Cantabrian Mountains in Spain. In estimating denning seasons, I only attempt to define the space of months in which the possibility of carnivore occupation cannot be excluded.

Tooth Eruption and Wear Classifications for Canids, Hyaenids, and Ursids

This analysis of carnivore mortality patterns only uses teeth. Ideally, juvenile and adult individuals can also be distinguished on the basis of bone fusion, but the probable behavioral context of cave faunas rich in carnivore remains prohibits this approach. Many of the Italian faunas have been extensively modified by carnivores. Immature bones may fare worse than mature bones in the face of most decomposition factors, carnivore chewing in particular. The situation is different in the case of teeth, which resist destruction significantly better. Emerging permanent mammalian teeth are not fully ossified, and they are somewhat more fragile than fully formed teeth. But the relative fragility of milk teeth and developing permanent teeth was not enough to erase, for example, a strong juvenile bias in red deer in the hyaena-rich levels of Buca della Iena (see Figure 11.5), nor in the Pleistocene hyaena and wolf tooth remains discussed below. Juvenile carnivore bones in the same proveniences clearly did not fare as well. To set this observation in broader perspective, the Italian cases are relatively well preserved assemblages, but, even here, in situ decomposition factors favored (albeit slightly) the preservation of teeth over bone wherever any discrepancy was found between bone-based and tooth-based MNI (Chapter 5). Teeth are therefore the appropriate material for the mortality pattern comparisons; bone fusion data only confuse efforts to learn about carnivore age structures in cave faunas.

Deciduous carnivore teeth are rare in the study sample, but erupting permanent teeth are common (e.g., Figure 12.1). The method for analyzing tooth eruption-wear patterns in the carnivores is similar to that described for ungulates in Chapter 11. Dental elements from the middle area of the cheek tooth row of mandibles and maxillae are preferred for analysis because this zone represents the fulcrum of occlusal wear, where friction is most continuous and profound throughout the life course. Moreover, midrow tooth elements tend to be large and easy to identify, and the occlusal wear patterns are highly readable. Most anterior premolars and last molars, in contrast, are small or nominally used during life and therefore are not as appropriate for constructing

age structures of carnivore death populations (but see the discussion on bears below).

Although the carnivore age stages are essentially the same as those employed for ungulates, the divisions of the carnivore lifetime are adjusted to compensate for relatively precocious tooth development (data and sources in Table 12.2), so that erupting and very slightly worn permanent carnivore teeth fall within the *juvenile* category. Foxes, for example, shed their deciduous (milk) premolars at about 4.5 months of age, and wolves may lose them at around 5.5 months. Spotted hyaenas shed deciduous premolars at around 9 months of age, well within the period that they require dens for protection. The red deer, for example, loses its fourth milk

Figure 12.1 Juvenile spotted hyaena (top) mandible and (bottom) maxilla fragments showing emerging permanent teeth. Development of the permanent dentition is precocious in carnivores, necessitating some minor adjustments in age structure calculations relative to those used for ungulates.

TABLE 12.2

Deciduous and permanent tooth eruption and shed schedules for carnivore species

Species	Tooth element sequence	Age in months				Source
		Deciduous tooth in place	Permanent tooth:			
			begins to erupt	in place		
domestic cat	dP-P	1	3.5–5.5	6		Hillson 1986:216
	↑ M		4.5–5	5.5–6		
bobcat	dP-P	0.5	3–4	6		Jackson et al. 1988
domestic dog	dP-P2,P3	1–2	5–6	6		Hillson 1986:217
	↑ M1		3–5	5		
red fox	dP-P	1–2.5	4–4.5	5		Hillson 1986:217
	↑ M1		4–5.5	6		
spotted hyaena	dC-C	0	—9.5–10—			Kruuk 1972:249
	dP-P[a]	2	—9.5–10—			

[a] The P₃ does not come into wear until at least one year of age, and it may not be noticeably worn until up to three years of age (Kruuk 1972).

Note: (↑) indicates permanent tooth in the process of eruption.

premolars only by 24 months of age (Chapter 13), but its maximum potential lifetime is not proportionally that much greater than those of the larger carnivores (compare, for example, Clutton-Brock et al. 1982; Mech 1988).

Whereas some good tooth eruption and wear schemes are available for ungulates (e.g., Grant 1982; Lowe 1967; Payne 1973), diagrams suitably detailed for aging isolated teeth of the carnivores are either difficult to find or do not exist. Kruuk (1972) provides a general guide for aging spotted hyaenas based on his study of a modern population in East Africa. Paleontological studies of bears by Andrews and Turner (1992), Dittrich (1960), Kurtén (1958, 1976), Torres (1988), and Wiszniowska (1982) also describe milk tooth replacement or gross wear patterns for permanent cheek teeth. Though valuable contributions in their own rights, none of these sources provides a fully illustrated reference set for the total potential lifetime. I therefore elaborate on the carnivore deciduous tooth eruption-wear sequences developed for this study, acknowledging that my drawings and calibrations of the sequences merely build upon what is already known about carnivore teeth. Illustrations are presented for selected tooth elements of canids, spotted hyaenas, and bears, formulated from real paleon-

tological specimens from Pleistocene localities in Italy and Turkey. The observed tooth eruption and wear sequences are keyed whenever possible to modern demographic data on the same or similar species.

Phrased in terms of nine age stages, the eruption-wear diagrams include guidelines for collapsing the data into three age stages: juvenile, prime adult, and old adult. The three-age system is especially important for evaluating small samples and is more effective than more elaborate two-dimensional age profiles for distinguishing the major classes of mortality patterns described in Chapter 10 (see also Figure 11.3B). The eruption-wear schemes commence with the deciduous tooth, followed by development, replacement, and occlusal wear of the permanent counterpart. The scheme ends with complete or nearly complete destruction of the permanent tooth; it does not rely on modern estimates of maximum potential lifetime (MPL). The age categories are keyed to the life history characteristics of females—a premise discussed in Chapter 11. Because the carnivore tooth eruption-wear schemes are developed from real specimens, some variation between individuals and between death populations is to be expected, both in the patches of dentin exposed on the occlusal surface and in the absolute correspondences between the onset of wear and completion of root development in young individuals (see also Dittrich 1960:133–135 on bears). These are relatively minor sources of ambiguity in the nine-stage scheme and probably are completely irrelevant in the simpler three-age scheme.

Figure 12.2 contrasts wolf milk teeth and adult fox teeth that are suitable for aging and counting individuals but are also easy to confuse in the absence of good comparative material. Figure 12.3 presents the complete (lifelong) eruption and wear sequence that I prefer for canids; after the deciduous tooth stage (I), this scheme uses the M_1, a large tooth possessing structures for both shearing and grinding. Positioned at the fulcrum of wear in the canid mandible, the M_1 undergoes fairly continuous and heavy wear throughout the adult lifetime. The system is appropriate for aging virtually any canid species, from large wolves to small foxes.

The juvenile age cohorts (stages I, II, and III)

require additional explanation. Because the permanent tooth supplants the deciduous counterpart, there is some risk of recording young individuals twice in fossil assemblages consisting of isolated teeth. The degree of root development in the emerging permanent tooth can be used to correct for this problem by referring to intertooth development rates in intact hemimandibles and hemimaxillae in modern or paleontological specimens. Stage I is represented by the deciduous tooth (the dP_4, dP^3, or dP^4 will suffice) in any phase of development or wear. I assume that deciduous teeth in the assemblage represent individuals that died at that age stage rather than simply shedding the tooth on site; this may not have always been true, but it is not a great problem in the Italian cases because so few milk teeth are present. Stage II is represented by the permanent tooth in the later phases of eruption; root development must fall between 10 and 50 percent and there must be no evidence of enamel wear on

WOLF,

DECIDUOUS

RED FOX,

PERMANENT

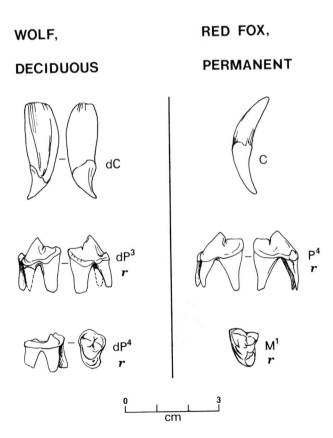

Figure 12.2 Morphological and size comparisons of wolf deciduous (milk) teeth and fox permanent teeth suitable for aging and counting individuals but easily confused. Similarities in the sizes and forms of the premolars can lead to confusion of these elements; one set represents a large immature wolf and the other a small adult fox. The differences between the wolf dP^3 and the fox P^4 are especially subtle; the position of the lingual cusp, root form, and lengthwise (anterior-posterior) contour of the main (buccal) cusps all should be considered in the identification process if possible. The wolf dP^4 and the fox M^1 also resemble one another, but the occlusal aspects of the outer rims of the crowns differ: that of the adult fox is angular, whereas the wolf milk tooth is more rounded and the cusps less convoluted.

M₁   CANID ERUPTION AND
     WEAR SEQUENCE

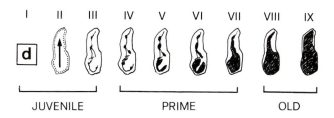

I   II   III   IV   V   VI   VII   VIII   IX

JUVENILE   PRIME   OLD

| d | deciduous tooth |

erupting, unworn permanent tooth, root 10-50% formed

erupted permanent tooth, slightly worn, root >50% formed

Figure 12.3 The canid tooth eruption-wear sequence based on the M_1, illustrated here for the red fox (*V. vulpes,* left side). The age stages are divided into nine cohorts, collapsible to three. The sequence begins with development of the deciduous tooth, followed by development and emergence of the permanent counterpart. The sequence ends with nearly complete destruction of the permanent tooth by occlusal wear. The scheme is compiled from wolf and fox mandibles and maxillae from Grotta di Sant'Agostino, Grotto Breuil, Grotta Polesini, and modern specimens. Note that this system makes no attempt to estimate real age for any cohort, nor does it assume that the cohorts are equal in duration; neither assumption is necessary for the age structure comparisons.

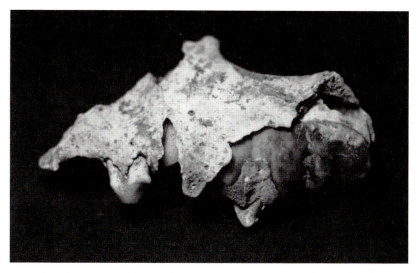

Figure 12.4 An example of the deciduous upper fourth premolar (dP⁴) straddling the erupting permanent fourth premolar (P⁴) in the maxilla of a young spotted hyaena. Double counting of juveniles can occur in this circumstance, if tooth elements have become isolated from the bone in fossil assemblages. The specimen shown is from Grotta del Fossellone (Monte Circeo).

the occlusal surface. Intact hemimandibles and hemimaxillae from reference collections indicate that a permanent tooth germ with less than 10 percent root development may still be capped by its deciduous precursor, as exemplified by the juvenile hyaena specimen in Figure 12.4. Thus, permanent teeth with less than 10 percent root development must be ignored to avoid counting the same individual twice. Stage III is represented by the fully (or nearly) erupted permanent tooth just coming into wear; root development in stage III must exceed 50 percent and pin-points of enamel wear or even minute dentin exposure may be apparent on the occlusal surface (see Figure 12.3). The three stages comprising the juvenile age group represent fine divisions of the lifetime on the order of weeks or months, whereas later age stages may encompass years. This system for aging canids and hyaenids (below) does not attempt to estimate real age nor does it assume that the cohorts represent equivalent spans of time; neither assumption is necessary, provided the methods described here are applied consistently.

Figure 12.5 shows the largest deciduous teeth of spotted hyaenas. The dP^3 and dP_4 are most appropriate for counting MNI in stage I, owing to their distinctive forms, relatively large sizes, and central positions in the cheek tooth rows of infants. Figure 12.6 presents the eruption and occlusal wear sequence for spotted hyaenas over the course of the maximum potential lifetime. The scheme is serviceable for other species of hyaena as well, requiring only minor adjustments for differing tooth forms. In keeping with Kruuk's (1972:33ff.) more general aging system, my scheme emphasizes the P_3 among permanent teeth, although the P^3 of P_4 appear to be equally suitable. The procedures for counting the youngest cohorts (stages I, II, and III) are the same as for canids.

The eruption-wear sequence for bears (*Ursus*) differs from those for canids and hyaenas because of the unusual morphologies and development schedules of bear teeth. The scheme is based on Pleistocene brown and cave bear (*U. arctos* and *U. spelaeus*) mandibles and maxillae from Buca della Iena, Grotta del Fossellone, Grotta dei Moscerini, and Grotta di Sant'Agostino in Italy and on cave bears (*U. deningeri*) from Yarimburgaz Cave in eastern Turkey (for background information on this

SPOTTED HYAENA (CROCUTA CROCUTA)
DECIDUOUS PREMOLARS

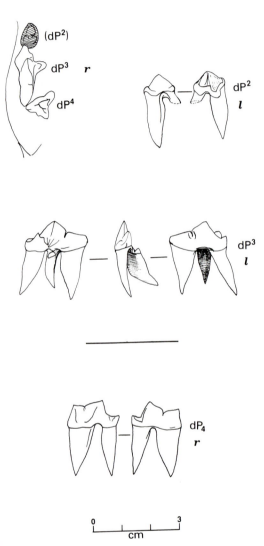

Figure 12.5 The larger deciduous teeth of the spotted hyaena (*C. crocuta*) suitable for aging and counting juvenile individuals, and the positions of the three upper deciduous premolars in the infant maxilla (right side). Note the fragile, attenuated roots of the milk teeth: the dP^2 and the dP^4 have two roots; the dP^3 has three roots and a small, isolated lingual cusp.

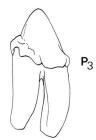

P₃ **SPOTTED HYAENA** (CROCUTA CROCUTA)

ERUPTION AND WEAR SEQUENCE

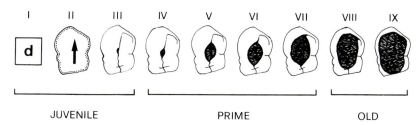

JUVENILE   PRIME   OLD

Figure 12.6 The spotted hyaena tooth eruption-wear sequence based on the dP-P₃ (left side). The age stages are divided into nine cohorts, collapsible to three. The sequence begins with development of the deciduous tooth, followed by development and emergence of the permanent counterpart (symbols as in Figure 12.3). The sequence ends with nearly complete destruction of the permanent tooth by occlusal wear. Suitable with some minor modifications for the upper third premolar, this scheme is compiled from hyaena mandibles and maxillae from Buca della Iena and Grotta del Fossellone. Note that this system does not attempt to estimate real age for any cohort, nor does it assume that the cohorts are equal in duration; neither assumption is necessary for the age structure comparisons.

site, see Arsebük et al. 1990, 1991; Howell and Arsebük 1989, 1990; Özdoğan and Koyunlu 1986). Figure 12.7 shows the eruption-wear sequence for the M₁ and the M₂ of bears over the course of the full potential lifetime of these teeth. Although the illustration emphasizes the lower central molars, similar patterns of wear occur on the M¹ (my current research). The anterior molars come into wear early in life and are completely worn away in very old animals. Bears of the genus *Ursus* are thoroughly omnivorous and, like unrelated taxa such as pigs and humans, their molars have multiple cusps adapted to grinding foods. Other things being equal, the deciduous dentition of bears is less elaborate or robust than that of canids or hyaenids. Milk teeth are unimpressive in black bears, brown bears, and cave bears; infant bears are especially altricial among carnivores. The morphologies of bear teeth are therefore atypical among Quaternary carni-

vores, and some modifications of the eruption-wear scheme outlined above are needed, especially with respect to the youngest and oldest age stages.

Stage I for bears (Figure 12.7) combines data on deciduous incisors or canines with those for emerging but unworn permanent teeth. The procedure for counting deciduous teeth is practically irrelevant to the Italian cases, but was useful for the reference assemblages from Turkey and is included here for the sake of completeness. Dittrich (1960) provides an excellent account of the deciduous-permanent tooth replacement process for modern brown bears, points of which are summarized briefly here. Born toothless, brown bears develop the full deciduous dentition only by the third month of life. Of the permanent molars, the M1 is the first to emerge, usually within the fifth month, and young bears may begin to eat solids around this time. The presence of milk teeth and their permanent counterparts can

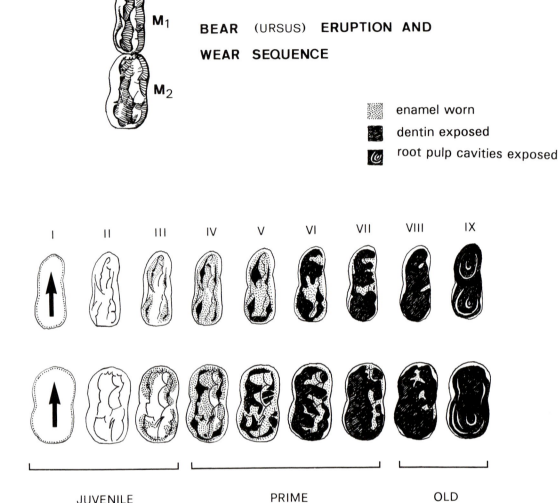

Figure 12.7 The tooth eruption-wear sequence for cave and brown bears (genus *Ursus*), based on the M_1 and M_2 (left side). The age stages are divided into nine cohorts, collapsible to three. The sequence begins with development of the deciduous tooth and development of the permanent counterpart (both incorporated into stage I), followed by successive categories of occlusal wear (symbols as in Figure 12.3). The sequence ends (stage IX) with complete destruction of the tooth crown and exposure of the root pulp cavity. Suitable with minor modifications for the M^1, this scheme is compiled from brown and cave bear mandibles and maxillae from Buca della Iena, Grotta dei Moscerini, and Grotta di Sant'Agostino in Italy (*U. arctos* and *U. spelaeus*), and from Yarimburgaz Cave in eastern Turkey (*U. deningeri*). Note that this system does not attempt to estimate real age for any cohort, nor does it assume that the cohorts are of equal duration; neither assumption is necessary for the age structure comparisons.

overlap for considerable spans of time in young bears, but all permanent teeth with the exception of the canines will have pushed through the gums by the end of the first year. The final phases of permanent tooth development, including emergence of the canines and completion of all tooth root development, takes place during the second year of life.

Because deciduous teeth may straddle emerging permanent ones in a young bear, it is best to count all permanent teeth from the germ stage onward, but only count those deciduous teeth that have inter-mediate occlusal wear or less. This procedure may underestimate the total number of individual animals (MNI) for the assemblage, but effectively avoids the more serious problem of double counting juveniles. In addition to deciduous tooth counts, stage I for bears includes all phases of permanent tooth development up to the halfway point (0 to 50 percent) of root formation. Stage II is represented by a fully (or nearly) emerged permanent tooth with root development in excess of 50 percent but lacking visible wear of the occlusal surface (or, at most, small pin-points of wear). By stage III, root development is complete and some wear of the occlusal enamel is readily evident, but little or no dentin is exposed. A bear that dies during stage II or III would still be quite young, probably hibernating

alongside its mother through a second winter (see also Andrews and Turner 1992:142).

The reference assemblages used to construct this scheme for bears reveal that the M_1, M_2, and M^1 will be worn down to the roots and the top of the pulp cavities exposed in very long-lived individuals. Stage IX therefore represents complete destruction of the molar crown and generally signals the end of the maximum potential lifetime. Because the posterior molars (M_3, M^2) in the reference assemblages never reach this stage, they should not be used for aging bears without also compensating for their naturally "younger" appearance. It is important to understand that this system for constructing mortality patterns in bears does not attempt to estimate real age, nor does it assume that the cohorts represent equivalent spaces of time.

CARNIVORE MORTALITY PATTERNS IN THE ITALIAN CAVES

Table 12.3 presents age frequency data for various carnivore species in the Italian caves, using the nine age categories. The eruption-wear frequency data for larger cases are then collapsed into three age stages—juvenile, prime, and old adults—in Table 12.4. Deciduous teeth are not present in these cases, but newly emerging permanent teeth are common in many of them. Because the samples tend to be quite small, more than one kind of tooth element is considered for each species wherever possible.

Figure 12.8 is a triangular plot of the three age mortality data for bears, foxes, spotted hyaenas, and wolves in the Italian shelters. Two tooth elements per provenience are plotted per case to see if the mortality pattern observed for one element is consistent with that for another from the same kind of animal; midrow tooth elements include third and fourth premolars and first and, rarely, second molars. The juvenile bias for spotted hyaenas and wolves is great, despite the near absence of deciduous teeth. These cases fall beyond the "young" edge of the U-shaped mortality domain; they are devoid of old adults and very poor in prime adults. The hyaena and wolf remains and associated herbivore bones were inferred to represent denning situations previously on the basis of taphonomic evidence (Chapter 5), and the mortality data clearly

support these interpretations. Three of the largest tooth samples cluster at the same place on the graph (marked by arrows); they include the only significant data point for Grotta di Sant'Agostino wolves (based on M_1) from layer SX and those for spotted hyaenas (based on P_3) from Grotta Guattari (G0–1) and Buca della Iena (I1–6). As an additional point for comparison, a nearly identical mortality pattern is observed from spotted hyaena premolars found in Grotta del Fossellone, another Upper Pleistocene cave site on Monte Circeo (Table 12.4, not plotted). Repetition of the same mortality pattern across sites shows that it is not explained by chance, despite the small sizes of the samples.

It is significant that all of the hyaena and wolf values gravitate toward the young-biased corner of the triangular graph, and not in any of the other mortality domains. The consistent weighting of data points toward one of five possible mortality patterns is important for this kind of analysis. Though the total MNIs for the cases are low, the results consistently fulfill the expectation of a strong juvenile bias in the age structures of the wolves and hyaenas, but not for the smaller red fox.

Confirmation of denning for wolves in Sant' Agostino SX suggests they occupied the cave sometime between spring and midsummer. Data on mod-

TABLE 12.3
Tooth wear frequency data for carnivores in the Italian shelters

Site, species, and tooth[b]	Age Stages[a]									(MNI)[c]
	Juvenile			Prime adult				Old adult		
	I	*II*	*III*	*IV*	*V*	*VI*	*VII*	*VIII*	*IX*	
SANT'AGOSTINO (all layers):										
wolf (P⁴)	—	0.5	1.0	—	0.5	—	—	—	—	(2.0)
(M₁)		0.5	3.5	—	1.0	0.5	—	—	—	(5.5)[d]
red fox (P⁴)	—	1.0	1.0	1.0	1.0	1.0	—	—	—	(5.0)[d]
(M₁)		1.0	1.0	1.5	—	1.5	—	0.5	—	(5.5)[d]
wild cat (P⁴)	—	0.5	0.5	—	—	—	—	—	—	(1.0)
(M₁)		1.0	—	—	—	—	—	—	—	(1.0)
brown bear (M¹)	—	1.0	1.0	—	0.5	—	—	0.5	—	(3.0)[d]
MOSCERINI (M5, also M4 and M6 for bears):										
red fox (P₄)	—	—	—	—	—	0.5	—	—	—	(0.5)
(M₂)			—	0.5	0.5	1.0	—	—	—	(2.0)
wild cat (P⁴)	—	—	—	0.5	—	—	—	—	—	(0.5)
monk seal (P)	—	—	0.5	—	—	—	—	—	—	(0.5)
hyaena (P³)	—	—	—	—	—	1.0	1.0	—	—	(2.0)
(M₁)	—	—	0.5	—	—	1.0	—	—	—	(1.5)
brown bear (M¹)	—	0.5	0.5	—	—	—	—	—	—	(1.0)
(M₃)	—	0.5	—	—	—	—	0.5	0.5	—	(1.5)
cave bear (M¹)	—	—	—	—	—	—	0.5	—	—	(0.5)
(M₃)	—	—	—	0.5	—	—	—	—	—	(0.5)
GUATTARI (G0–2):										
bear sp. (M₁)	—	—	—	0.5	—	—	—	—	—	(0.5)
(M₂)	—	—	—	—	—	0.5	—	—	—	(0.5)
hyaena (P₃)	—	3.0	1.0	0.5	—	0.5	0.5	—	—	(5.5)[d]
(P⁴)	—	0.5	3.0	0.5	1.0	1.0	—	—	—	(6.0)[d]
BUCA DELLA IENA (I1–6):										
brown bear (M₁)	—	0.5	0.5	0.5	—	—	1.0	0.5	—	(3.0)[d]
(M₂)	—	0.5	1.5	—	—	0.5	1.0	—	—	(3.5)[d]
hyaena (P₃)	—	5.5	3.0	0.5	1.5	1.5	—	—	—	(12.0)[d]

[a] All stages are for permanent teeth. Few deciduous teeth occur in the deposits, possibly because the caves served as maternity dens rather than birthing dens or the infants that died were consumed by other carnivores. Age stages I–III represent juveniles because permanent tooth eruption is precocious in carnivores; prime adults are represented by permanent tooth stages IV–VII; old adults are represented by permanent tooth stages VIII–IX.

[b] More than one tooth element is considered when possible to check sampling biases. Tooth eruption and wear sequences are not wholly equivalent between elements, however. The P₃ is preferred for hyaenas; the M₁, for wolves and foxes.

[c] MNI is calculated by dividing total MNE for the permanent tooth element by 2.

[d] Plotted.

TABLE 12.4
Mortality data for carnivores in the Italian shelters divided into three age stages

Site[a]	Species	Tooth element used	MNI	Percentages of MNI		
				JUV	PRIME	OLD
Sant'Agostino	wolf	M$_1$	5.5	.73	.27	.00
	red fox	dP^4-P^4	5.0	.40	.60	.00
	"	M$_1$	5.5	.36	.54	.09
	brown bear	M^1	3.0	.67	.17	.17
Guattari	hyaena	dP$_3$-P$_3$	5.5	.73	.27	.00
	"	dP^4-P^4	6.0	.58	.42	.00
Buca della	brown bear	M$_1$	3.0	.33	.50	.17
Iena	"	M$_2$	3.5	.57	.43	.00
	hyaena	dP$_3$-P$_3$	12.0	.71	.29	.00
Fossellone[b]	hyaena	dP^3-P^3	7.0	.71	.29	.00
	"	dP$_3$-P$_3$	11.0	.72	.27	.00
	"	dP$_4$-P$_4$	10.0	.70	.30	.00

[a] Carnivore data for Moscerini are omitted because MNIs are 2.0 or less.

[b] Spotted hyaena remains from Grotta del Fossellone (Monte Circeo) were studied using the same methods described in the text. The hyaena teeth come from Upper Pleistocene sediments of the cave and are listed here for comparison; the results for third premolars are nearly identical to those for the Guattari and Buca della Iena hyaenas, suggesting that the mortality patterns are not due to chance despite the small sizes of the samples.

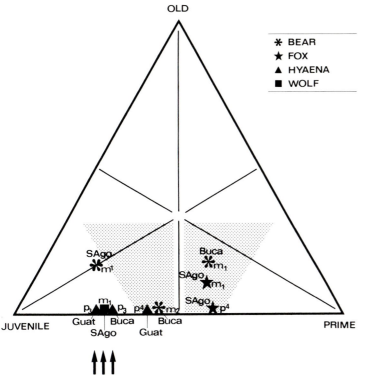

Figure 12.8 Triangular plot of carnivore mortality patterns in Middle Paleolithic shelters in Italy. The hyaena and wolf cases fall within the juvenile-dominated domain on the lower left corner of the graph (see Chapter 11) and indicate denning situations. The three cases marked by arrows represent the largest samples of the most appropriate tooth elements; the results for these cases are very consistent.

ern wolves in Britain and Israel (see Table 12.1) suggest a parturition date in March and an average denning period lasting about two months thereafter (Ballard et al. 1987). Because den use by modern hyaenas is a seasonal, confirmation of denning for the Italian Pleistocene hyaenas merely indicates that they could have used the shelters at any time and for many months.

The distribution of bear mortality cases is more variable; two lie at the edges of the U-shaped mortality domain, but another falls in the center of the living-structure domain. All of these samples are very small, making the distributions difficult if not impossible to evaluate. When all bear data from all sites are combined, however, they display a generally attritional pattern (not plotted). By way of com-

parison, U-shaped mortality patterns are found in larger paleontological assemblages from Bacho Kiro in Bulgaria (Wiszniowska 1982) and Yarimburgaz Cave in Turkey (MNI = 45, my current research).

The mortality results for red fox from Sant' Agostino show a distinctly different pattern and contradict the expectation for denning animals. Nearly all of the fox remains from this site are from layers S0–4 (see Chapter 4), where they are associated with stone tools, yet are heavily gnawed and lack cut marks (Chapter 5). Eruption-wear data for two midrow tooth elements (M_1 and P^4) indicate a living-structure mortality pattern. The results suggest that foxes fell prey to other predators, possibly including hominids.

CONCLUSIONS

Mortality patterns in carnivores represent a compelling alternative for testing hypotheses of denning in Pleistocene caves. The analyses here are limited by small sample sizes, yet these data add a different and valuable dimension to research on the causes of carnivore skeletal representation in shelter deposits. The age structures of carnivore remains from the Italian Mousterian caves indicate that spotted hyaenas and wolves used these places as dens, but that foxes may have been introduced into Sant'Agostino as prey of other predators, perhaps both by wolves and Mousterian people.

Because the wolf mortality data show that Sant'Agostino SX is a wolf den, the data specify use in spring and early summer only. The findings are entirely consistent with taxonomic and bone damage data presented in Chapters 4, 5, and 6. Although the denning schedule of wolves would not be canceled out by the hypothesized fall-winter schedule suggested for hominids at Sant'Agostino (Chapter 13), it is unlikely that wolf and hominid occupations took place there in the same years.

The spotted hyaena mortality data show that, like Buca della Iena (I1–6), Guattari G0–1 was a hyaena den. Taphonomic (Chapter 5) and mortality results together suggest that hyaenas occupied the dens for extended periods in the annual cycle, probably across all seasons. Spotted hyaena remains also oc-

cur in one level group of Moscerini (M5), where denning is suggested by other kinds of evidence, but hyaena teeth are too few in number to construct mortality patterns. Year-round den occupations by hyaenas would certainly have affected the potential utility of a shelter for hominids in the past. Den sites often become traditional parts of clan territories across generations, and this would greatly diminish the potential utility of a cave for hominids for long periods of time. In the Italian study area, there is no indication of alternations *within* years between hyaenas and hominids, nor, perhaps, within decades. Mousterian hominids visited Guattari (G1, G2, G4, and G5), Moscerini (M2, M3, M4, and M6), and even Buca della Iena in the later phases of deposit formation (I1–4), but each site eventually fell out of use by carnivore or hominid tenants and was subsequently taken over by the other (for greater discussion, see Chapters 4 and 5).

The taphonomic data reviewed in Chapter 5 showed that bear bones in the cave deposits were primarily the results of hibernation deaths. Though suggestive, the mortality data on bears are unclear because the samples are very small, but they generally appear to fit the expectation of a simple U-shaped mortality model for hibernation deaths. On the strength of the taphonomic evidence alone, we may conclude that brown and cave bears sometimes used most of the Italian caves as hibernation dens. Among modern members of the genus *Ursus,* black bears are not known to use natural shelters much (Garshelis and Pelton 1980; Johnson and Pelton 1980; Rogers 1981, 1987). This fact is at least partly explained by the near absence of suitable caves in the areas where most studies of black bears have been conducted; tree cover is thick and fallen logs are common, and the bears usually excavate below live or dead trees. The situation is different, however, for modern brown bears in the Cantabrian Mountains of Spain, populations that closely resemble the modern and Pleistocene Italian brown bears. Caves and fissures are abundant in the Cantabrian Mountains and are routinely used as hibernation dens by the bears (Clevenger and Purroy 1991:115–123). Some of these caves are reused year after year (Clevenger 1991:42). Den fidelity cannot be evaluated at the level of individual behaviors in the Pleistocene cases, but it is clear that the more any cave is used by bears, the more bears that will eventually perish there over the long term. Italian Upper Pleistocene bear populations appeared to favor certain caves over others in the vicinity, consistent with information on the habits of modern Mediterranean populations.

It is interesting that bears denned at some time or another in all of the Middle Paleolithic caves. Bears are especially common in the stratigraphic sequences of Moscerini, also in Buca della Iena (Chapter 4). Though relatively less abundant, bears also are represented in some proveniences of Guattari, Sant'Agostino, and Breuil. There seems to have been less exclusion in cave strata sequences between bears and humans overall than between humans and spotted hyaenas. Yet modern black bears are furtive in their choice of den sites (Garshelis and Pelton 1980; Johnson and Pelton 1980; Rogers 1981, 1987), presumably because of the high potential for persecution by humans, dogs, and wild predators emboldened by winter food shortages (e.g., Mattson et al. 1992; Ross et al. 1988). Modern brown bears, though larger and more aggressive as a rule, are also secretive about the placement of winter dens (Clevenger 1991:42; Miller 1985; Peterson et al. 1984:38; Rogers 1987:53–55). Any sign of major disruption may be enough to dissuade a den-seeking bear. The nearly universal presence of bear remains in the Latium and Tuscan caves therefore may suggest fairly long windows of safe use for bears, possibly reflecting the tempo of alterations by all tenants. In the case of Grotta dei Moscerini and Buca della Iena, the tempo of revolving use by bears and hominids, or bears and hyaenas, may have been on the order of hundreds of years, significantly less in the other caves (Breuil and Sant'Agostino).

Seasons of Ungulate Procurement

SCHEDULES OF resource use represent an important dimension of predator niches. Behaviorally complex species frequently shift their foraging regimens in response to seasonal changes in the availability and quality of food. The data presented in earlier chapters hint that seasons of food procurement and site occupations contributed to the variation in the Mousterian cave faunas. Dichotomous anatomical patterns and ungulate age structures indicative of hunting and scavenging, in particular, suggest that hominid foragers were responding to variation in prey (primarily ungulate) fat yields.

This chapter investigates the seasonal correlates of resource use by Mousterian hominids, late Upper Paleolithic humans, and, to a lesser extent, wolves and spotted hyaenas in the Latium caves. Questions about seasonality are examined from three perspectives. The first analysis focuses on death patterns in juvenile ungulates based on eruption-wear data for deciduous premolars. The second analysis examines the presence and developmental states of deer antlers for information on the timing of shelter occupations by hominids and other predators, based on growth-shed cycles in modern red, fallow, and roe deer. This analysis is pertinent to both a general assessment of seasonality and prey sex ratios. The third analysis considers possible adult sex ratios for red deer based on the frequencies of upper canines (pearl teeth), a tooth that normally develops fully only in adult males. The use of red deer canines to

check for sex biases would be problematic in the case of Upper Paleolithic faunas, because people clearly valued these teeth as ornaments. Even those canine specimens that lack clear signs of modification (perforation, abrasion, incised grooves) could have been intentionally separated from prey skulls by humans and set aside for future use. This is not a problem in the Middle Paleolithic, because there is no evidence of ornament use of any sort during this (or earlier) cultural periods.

Although limited in scope, the seasonality results supplement data from other chapters in interesting ways. The full cycle of seasons is represented in the Mousterian sample as a whole, but the seasons of occupation vary by site. Data on juvenile ungulate mortality, adult deer antlers, and red deer pearl teeth suggest that some Mousterian occupations could have occurred during spring and summer, whereas other caves were almost certainly occupied during fall and winter. Seasonality data for the late Upper Paleolithic sample from west-central Italy indicate only fall-winter and early spring occupations at the shelters examined. The seasonality results are less than definitive, however, and only some very general interpretations are attempted here. The value of the seasonality data at this stage is for elucidating general contrasts in the seasons of cave use and prey sex ratios between the Middle and late Upper Paleolithic in the study area and for refining hypotheses for future research.

METHODS FOR DETERMINING SEASONS OF DEATH FROM DECIDUOUS UNGULATE TEETH

Eruption and wear patterns in deciduous ungulate teeth, especially for deciduous fourth premolars, can be calibrated to real age in a manner that is not possible for most permanent teeth, except possibly the M1. This is because the error in the estimated age at death generally increases geometrically over the life course; deciduous teeth are present only during the earliest stages of life, when growth and development take place. The use-life of a deciduous tooth is bracketed by two developmental transitions corresponding to the birth of the individual (or soon thereafter) and its sexual maturation (in females, see Chapter 11). In high-latitude environments, these developmental transitions in juveniles are strictly synchronized to season (Table 13.1). The relationship between juvenile development and sea-

TABLE 13.1
Characteristics of female ungulate reproductive schedules

Species	Geographic location	Birthing months: [peak] or range	Maternal[a] age at first parturition	Source
roe deer	England France	April–June [May]	2 y	Prior 1968:95–98 Gaillard et al. 1993
red deer	Scotland	[June]	3 y	Clutton-Brock et al. 1982:183
wapiti	Washington	[late May– early June]	3 y	Lyman 1987b:130; Taber et al. 1982
fallow deer	England	[June]	2 y	Chapman and Chapman 1975:140–144
	Spain	[late May– early June]	—	Braza et al. 1988
chamois	Switzerland southern France	July[b] May–June	3 y —	Schaller 1977:364–365 Spiess 1979:263–264
alpine ibex	Switzerland southern France	July[b,c] June	3 y —	Schaller 1977:364–365 Spiess 1979:262
Spanish ibex	southeast Spain	May	—	Alados and Escos 1988
Nubian ibex	Egypt	Feb–March[b,c] (nearly asseasonal)	3 y	Schaller 1977:364–365
horse (feral)	Great Basin	March–June [May]	2–3 y	Berger 1986:79, 104–105
Prezwalski's horse	Mongolia and captive	April–June [May]	3–4 y	Groves 1974:62–64
burro (feral)	Mohave Desert	—	2.5 y	Johnson et al. 1987:917
wild ass (Asian)	Mongolia, Iran, Pakistan, Turkmenia	April–May (kulan) June–July (ghor-khar)	3 y	Groves 1974

[a] Maternal age at first parturition does not correspond to the peak reproductive years of an animal's life; it demarcates onset of physiological maturity, including appearance of most secondary sexual characteristics and the permanent dentition.

[b] The birthing season is calculated in this case by adding the gestation time to the peak time of the rutting season.

[c] The birthing schedules of alpine and southern ibex are very different; the birthing period of the Nubian ibex is both longer and more variable, and it peaks earlier in the year (Schaller 1977). I use the modern cases from southern France (Spiess 1979) and Spain (Alados and Escos 1988) as models for the Upper Pleistocene populations of west-central Italy. Because modern chamois and ibex in alpine Switzerland have the same birthing periods, I assume that their birthing seasons also were synchronous in Pleistocene west-central Italy.

son breaks down somewhat in populations of the temperate zone, and may be absent in the same or similar species of the equatorial zone (e.g., Schaller 1977:121). Female alpine ibex in Switzerland and France, for example, display restricted seasonal birthing patterns (Schaller 1977:364–365; Spiess 1979:262); birthing is nearly aseasonal, however, in the Nubian ibex of North Africa (Nievergelt 1981).

The severity of seasonal cycles in an environment, whether in terms of temperature or moisture, affects the potential precision of any kind of seasonality analysis based on juvenile development or the accumulation of cementum layers on adult teeth. The climate of west-central Italy during the Upper Pleistocene ranged from warm-temperate to cool-temperate (Chapters 3 and 4). In contrast to the situation for ungulate populations inhabiting cold deciduous forests, boreal forests, or tundra habitats, somewhat more developmental variation with respect to the annual cycle can be expected in ungulate populations inhabiting the coastal zone of Upper Pleistocene Italy. This level of inherent error could make it difficult, for example, to distinguish prey deaths occurring year-round from those occurring over a period of only nine or ten months on the basis of deciduous tooth wear or cementum annuli. Some information certainly can be gained from seasonality analyses of teeth, but overly confident or stringent interpretations are to be avoided. The purpose here is merely to link ungulate death patterns to warm or cold segments of the annual cycle if possible.

Before applying the eruption-wear method for fourth deciduous premolars to the Italian cases, trials were conducted on the juvenile subset of a modern death population of Alaskan caribou (Palingana, dMNI = 27), killed by Nunamiut Eskimo hunters. Ungulate species in Italy do not include caribou, nor does Italy represent a high-latitude setting, but the trials are important for evaluating how effective the methods could be under ideal conditions; Palingana represents a fairly large sample of known history from an arctic environment and involves a prey species with a birthing season of only two weeks (Miller et al. 1975). The method reliably identifies the *peak* time of seasonal harvesting as independently documented for this test case (Binford 1978, and notes), but the tooth-determined

range is about twice as great as the real harvesting time recalled by Nunamiut people. Of course, the error could originate from the frailties of human recollection, but, in this instance, we are probably justified in pinning blame on the method instead. The trials indicate that, while the method is fairly reliable for identifying peaks in seasonal harvesting, it is more difficult to distinguish between an absolutely empty category(s) in the age stage sequence and a low point, especially if the trough is narrow (for a related discussion, see Grayson 1984:174–177). Large samples do not necessarily eliminate this problem, because the margin of error is inherent to all current methods for determining seasons of death, and large samples are more likely to be palimpsest accumulations, possibly representing more diverse foraging agendas, anyway. While sometimes construed as a matter of counting how many deaths in each phase of an idealized annual cycle, thereby knowing when people were at the place and when they were not, the signatures used to gauge the seasons of deaths from skeletal tissues are fuzzy at best and embody considerable error due to the biology and ecology of the subject species.

The inferential limits of the eruption-wear method employed can be explored in the Italian cases by plotting dMNI against the number of age stages filled across the seven-stage wear sequence. Spearman's rank order correlations for small (SU) and medium ungulate (MU) cases indicate strong positive relationships (SU: r_s = .743, N = 22, P < .01; MU: r_s = .706, N = 16, P < .01). This means that increasing sample size could conceivably expand the ranges. Additional ambiguities for the Italian cases stem from the likelihood that faunas represent palimpsest accumulations from many foraging events, especially if visits to a shelter did not take place in exactly the same month each year (e.g., Polesini below).

Having acknowledged the shortcomings of the eruption-wear method, it nonetheless is apparent that a conspicuous peak in the data may be regarded as meaningful particularly if all other age/season categories are empty. The analysis naturally assumes that juvenile death periods are representative of humans' procurement schedule for all age groups of the subject species. Late Upper Paleolithic archaeological cases from Grotta Polesini and Grotta

Palidoro are included in the study sample for comparison. Eruption-wear data for the dP_4 (deciduous lower fourth premolar) of cervids and chamois are considered. This premolar is difficult to distinguish in equids, however, so the second deciduous premolar is used for wild ass and horse. The deciduous teeth from the Italian caves tend to be in very good condition, suggesting little if any loss via postdepositional destruction. Differing rates of development make some ungulate species better candidates than others for investigating seasons of death. Deer and chamois teeth will tend to provide clearer results than those of equids and aurochs, because maturation and tooth replacement in the former occur within one or two years, and as late as the third or

fourth year of life in the latter pair (Table 13.1). An ideal species for this kind of analysis is roe deer, because of its tightly synchronized birthing season (e.g., Gaillard et al. 1993).

The data are presented as frequencies of individuals (dMNI) in seven deciduous tooth wear categories (wear stages 0–6), hypothetically of equal duration. The wear increments are scaled to the number of months that the deciduous tooth is present in the tooth row: the space of time between birth and tooth shedding. The data are also scaled to the annual cycle. Both scales are calibrated to the estimated birthing schedule for each species (Table 13.1) and to the age at which the deciduous tooth is normally replaced (Table 13.2). The calibrations take clinal

TABLE 13.2
Deciduous and permanent tooth eruption and shed schedules for ungulate species

| Species | Tooth element sequence | Peak birthing month | Age in months | | | Source |
			Deciduous tooth in place[a]	Permanent tooth: begins to erupt	in place	
red deer	dP3-P3	June	1–2	23–27	27	Hillson 1986:210
	dP4-P4		1–2	23–27	27	
	dP3-P3			25–26	27	Lowe 1967:138
	dP4-P4			25–26	27	
fallow deer	dP3-P3	June	0	19–22		Chapman and Chapman
	dP4-P4		0	19–22		1975
	dP3-P3		0	17–20		Hillson 1986:211
	dP4-P4		0	17–20		
roe deer	dP3-P3	May	0	7	8	Prior 1968:135;
	dP4-P4		0	7	8	Gaillard et al. 1993
caribou	dP3-P3	June	0	22–29	29	Hillson 1986:211
	dP4-P4		0	22–29	29	
horse[b] and	dP2-P2	May	0–1	?		Groves 1974:23
other	dP3-P3		0–1	36		
equids	dP2-P2		0–1	?		Hillson 1986:215
	dP3-P3		0–1	30–42		
cattle[c]	dP3-P3	?	0–1	18–30		Hillson 1986:206
(domest)	dP4-P4		0–1	30–36		
feral goat	dP4-P4	?	—	24	35	Bullock and Rackham 1982

[a] Zero months indicates that the tooth is emerged by the time of birth.
[b] Prezwalski's horse supplies tooth eruption parameters for this study (Groves 1974); wild equid stock show a tighter seasonal pattern in birthing, tooth eruption, and deciduous tooth shed schedules than do domesticated populations of *Equus caballus* (also see Berger 1986:228).
[c] Because wild aurochs is extinct, data on domesticated cattle are used here; birthing season is both more variable and more prolonged in domesticated cattle as a rule (e.g., Levine 1982:224–225).

variation in modern populations into account, or, in lieu of comprehensive reference data, use geographical cases best resembling the probable climatic conditions of coastal Upper Pleistocene Italy. In calibrating eruption-wear sequences to birth month in modern counterparts, I assume that the deciduous tooth is fully erupted at birth unless stated otherwise, the tooth is always shed by a certain age, and the wear rate is roughly continuous. The assumption of continuous wear is somewhat problematic, since wear patterns for the deciduous

premolars probably are no more continuous than those of permanent premolars and molars (Severinghaus 1949). The fact that juveniles use their teeth more and more in the later stages of weaning would suggest that the wear process begins slowly and accelerates as the time of shedding approaches. Of the premolar elements, however, the last deciduous and permanent premolar are the most suitable by far (Severinghaus 1949:204–205), the same character of difference noted for the molar row.

RESULTS ON SEASONAL DEATHS IN JUVENILE UNGULATES

Table 13.3 presents juvenile age frequency data for roe deer and chamois from late Upper Paleolithic Polesini (all cuts combined), late Middle Paleolithic Grotta di Sant'Agostino (S0–3), and Middle Paleolithic Grotta dei Moscerini (M2–4). Only Polesini yields substantial samples for roe deer and chamois, as shown in Figure 13.1 (see dMNI). Although the range of months in which juvenile roe deer and chamois died is nearly as great as the use life of the deciduous P_4, both species show death peaks in fall. Infants born the previous spring are absent from the samples. The roe deer samples from Middle Paleolithic Sant'Agostino and Moscerini are very small, but the few data points available do not contradict the human-generated pattern documented for late Upper Paleolithic Polesini (Figure 13.1). The wolf

den fauna from Sant'Agostino, though rich in roe deer bones, is poor in head parts and hence does not provide an adequate deciduous tooth sample for seasonality comparisons.

Table 13.4 presents seasonal death patterns for two larger cervids, red deer (Pleistocene Italy) and caribou (modern Alaska); both species shed the dP_4 at about two years of age (see Table 13.2). The Italian cases to be examined are from late Upper Paleolithic Polesini and Palidoro, the four Latium Mousterian caves, and the spotted hyaena den complex of Buca della Iena. Sample sizes vary greatly and the Middle Paleolithic samples are very small.

The Nunamiut caribou data, plotted in Figure 13.2, are a useful reference point, because they represent seasonally restricted exploitation across a

TABLE 13.3

Deciduous tooth wear frequency data for roe deer and chamois from the Italian sites

Site, (agency), and species	Deciduous tooth wear stages[a]							(dMNI)[b]
	0	*1*	*2*	*3*	*4*	*5*	*6*	
Polesini 1–12 (lUP):								
roe deer	—	0.5	2.0	2.0	13.5	1.0	—	(19.0)
chamois	—	—	2.5	2.5	7.0	5.5	1.0	(18.5)
Sant'Agostino S0–3 (MP):								
roe deer	—	—	0.5	—	2.0	1.0	0.5	(4.0)
Moscerini M2–4 (MP):								
roe deer	—	—	0.5	—	0.5	—	—	(1.0)

[a] Data are for dP_4.
[b] dMNI is calculated by dividing total MNE for the deciduous tooth element by 2.

Note: (lUP) late Upper Paleolithic, (MP) Middle Paleolithic.

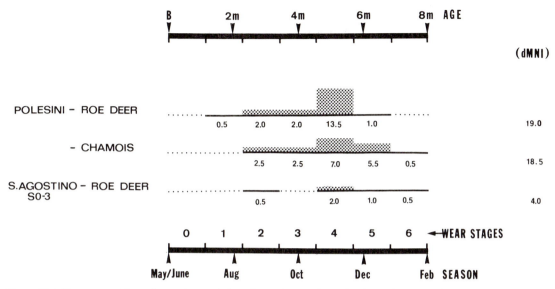

Figure 13.1 Histograms of juvenile roe deer and chamois age frequencies and estimated seasons of death, based on deciduous tooth eruption-wear stages.

two-year age axis. Consistent with ethnographic accounts (e.g., Binford 1978, and notes), the eruption-wear data indicate an autumn death peak at Palingana. Concerted hunting of juveniles for skins in spring is known for the Nunamiut in other situations (see Chapter 11) and could be responsible for the attenuation to the right side of each yearly peak, or it could be method-caused error. No isolated peaks occur in the data for red deer from late Upper Paleolithic Polesini (Table 13.4). However, lumping the twelve arbitrary cuts for this site fosters the impression that deaths occurred throughout the year; hence Barker's (1974) conclusion about human occupations there. When the data are partitioned by arbitrary level, as in Table 13.5, the death periods for red deer span roughly six to eight months instead. Data from some layers may even indicate a bimodal pattern across the two-year span, further suggesting that exploitation occurred on a seasonal rather than year-round basis.

Most of the Polesini roe deer died in late autumn, and most of the chamois died in early autumn through early winter (Table 13.5). The positions of the roe deer and chamois death periods in the annual cycle also appear to vary across layers. Because roe deer and chamois possess the highest potentials for seasonal resolution as a rule, these data would seem most important to evaluations of humans' seasonal use of the Polesini shelter. The data for other ungulate taxa suggest, however, that hunters switched among prey species in response to local availability. This took place within a time window of approximately eight to nine months. The results do not support claims of year-round use of the Polesini shelter; a summer vacancy is consistently evident in the ungulate death patterns. Moreover, the hunters that occupied Polesini seldom killed very young animals. The juvenile deciduous tooth stages 0 and 1 are usually empty, although a few yearling red deer just one year older are represented. Hunting appears to have taken place during the time when neonates might have been present in the living population, but, if so, hunters avoided taking females with new fawns (see Chapter 11). The ungulate death peak centering on late winter or early spring persists in the Polesini data when the counts are partitioned by layer, but the timing of deaths appears to differ somewhat across layers. This variation, both across layers and among prey species, may indicate that occupations of Polesini did not always occur in the same time of year and/or people were switching among prey species across months.

The late Upper Paleolithic case of Riparo Salvini (data not listed; see Bietti and Stiner 1992) provides

TABLE 13.4
Deciduous tooth wear frequency data for caribou from historic Nunamiut sites
and red and fallow deer from Italian sites

Site, (agency), and species	Deciduous tooth wear stages[a]							(dMNI)[b]
	0	1	2	3	4	5	6	
Nunamiut Eskimo sites, caribou:								
Net Site	—	1.5	—	—	—	0.5	—	(2.0)
Kakinya	—	2.5	1.0	—	1.0	—	—	(4.5)
Tulekana	—	4.0	1.0	—	0.5	1.5	1.0	(8.0)
Akp Dogyard	—	—	—	—	0.5	—	—	(0.5)
Palangana	—	1.5	2.0	—	5.5	3.0	—	(12.0)
ALL SITES	—	9.5	4.0	—	7.5	5.0	1.0	(27.0)
Polesini 1–12 (lUP):								
red deer	1.0	1.0	38.0	24.0	19.0	14.0	5.0	(102.0)
Palidoro 33–34 (lUP):								
red deer	—	—	—	0.5	0.5	—	—	(1.0)
Sant'Agostino S0–3 (MP):								
red deer	—	—	—	—	3.5	1.5	1.5	(6.5)
fallow deer	—	—	1.0	—	1.0	—	0.5	(2.5)
Sant'Agostino SX (w):								
red deer	—	—	—	0.5	0.5	—	—	(1.0)
Breuil Br (MP):								
red deer	—	—	—	—	2.0	0.5	0.5	(3.0)
Moscerini M2–4 (MP):								
red deer	—	—	1.0	1.0	0.5	—	—	(2.5)
Moscerini M5 (sh):								
red deer	0.5	0.5	0.5	—	1.0	1.0	—	(3.5)
Guattari G0–1 (sh):								
red deer	—	—	2.5	—	0.5	1.0	—	(4.0)
Buca della Iena I1–6 (sh):								
red deer	—	—	1.0	1.5	2.0	—	—	(4.5)

[a] Data are for dP_4.
[b] dMNI is calculated by dividing total MNE for the deciduous tooth element by 2.

Note: (lUP) late Upper Paleolithic, (MP) Middle Paleolithic, (w) wolf, (sh) spotted hyaena.

limited information on seasons of occupation by anatomically modern humans on the coast. The small number of individual animals eclipses the possibility of a rigorous analysis, but it is worth noting that, of the five red deer represented in the 1988 sample, two were juveniles one year apart in age; the younger individual was roughly six to seven months old at death and the yearling roughly eighteen to nineteen months. Both animals died sometime between December and late February,

and one juvenile roe deer specimen also indicates death in winter. These findings, as well as the presence of two fetal individuals, support the interpretation that this site was a cold season residential camp.

The death pattern for ungulates in the Mousterian faunas from Sant'Agostino and Breuil (Table 13.4) suggests that deaths peaked in fall-winter (see S0–3, Figure 13.2), although sample sizes are not sufficient to demonstrate that hominids vacated the sites during other seasons of the year. As is true at Riparo

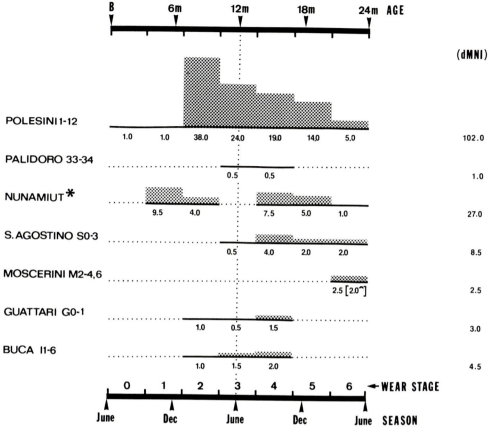

Figure 13.2 Histograms of juvenile red deer (or caribou*) age frequencies and estimated seasons of death, based on deciduous tooth eruption-wear stages.

Salvini, the presence of some fetal ungulate remains in Breuil (Br), further supports a cold-season interpretation. The Mousterian assemblages from Moscerini contain very few juveniles; in fact, the mortality patterns are strongly biased toward old adults (Chapter 11). What few data points exist from level groups M2–4 suggest warm-season deaths, probably in late spring; the possibility that the cave was also used during other times of year cannot be excluded, however.

The few juvenile specimens from the wolf den in Sant'Agostino (SX) center on the warmer part of the year (Table 13.4, keyed to plotted cases in Figure 13.2), although slightly later than expected based on the denning seasons of modern Mediterranean wolves. In fact, wolves may continue to use dens intermittently until late summer (e.g., Ballard et al.

1987). The sample from the spotted hyaena den in Moscerini M5 is relatively small yet is spread fairly evenly across the two years in which young red deer retain their deciduous teeth. As a group, the spotted hyaena components in Moscerini (M5, see Table 13.4), Grotta Guattari (G0–1), and Buca della Iena (I1–6) show no clear peaks, spreading instead over most of the year, although bone collection activities may have centered on the warmer half of the year (Figure 13.2). These results fit the expectation that hyaena den use was prolonged and generally aseasonal in Upper Pleistocene Italy.

Table 13.6 presents juvenile tooth eruption-wear data for wild ass, horse, and aurochs. Birthing schedules in wild equid populations are more restricted in the annual cycle than is true for domesticated populations (Table 13.1). These species retain

TABLE 13.5
Deciduous tooth wear frequency data for roe deer, chamois,
and red deer from Grotta Polesini

Species and layer	Deciduous tooth wear stages[a]							(dMNI)[b]
	0	1	2	3	4	5	6	
roe deer:								
1	—	—	—	1	2	1	—	(4.0)
2	—	—	—	—	2	—	—	(2.0)
3	—	—	—	1	1	—	—	(2.0)
4	—	—	—	1	3	—	—	(4.0)
5	—	—	2	—	4	—	—	(6.0)
6	—	—	—	—	1	—	—	(1.0)
7	—	—	—	—	—	—	—	(0.0)
8	—	—	—	—	2	—	—	(2.0)
9	—	—	—	—	1	—	—	(1.0)
10	—	—	1	—	—	—	—	(1.0)
11	—	—	—	—	—	—	—	(0.0)
12	—	—	—	—	—	—	—	(0.0)
chamois:[c]								
1	—	—	2	—	—	2	—	(4.0)
2	—	—	—	1	1	—	1	(3.0)
3	—	—	—	—	—	—	—	(0.0)
4	—	—	—	—	1	1	—	(2.0)
5	—	—	1	1	1	—	—	(3.0)
6	—	—	—	1	—	3	—	(4.0)
7	—	—	—	—	—	—	—	(0.0)
8	—	—	—	—	2	2	—	(4.0)
9	—	—	—	—	2	—	—	(2.0)
10	—	—	1	1	—	—	—	(2.0)
11	—	—	—	—	1	—	—	(1.0)
12	—	—	1	2	—	—	—	(3.0)
red deer:								
1	—	1	8	1	3	—	1	(14.0)
2	—	—	3	2	2	—	—	(7.0)
3	—	—	4	2	—	—	—	(6.0)
4	—	—	5	—	—	2	1	(8.0)
5	—	—	3	3	3	3	—	(12.0)
6	—	—	2	—	2	—	—	(4.0)
7	—	—	3	1	—	—	—	(4.0)
8	—	—	4	2	4	1	2	(13.0)
9	—	—	1	3	2	4	—	(10.0)
10	—	—	—	3	1	2	1	(7.0)
11	—	—	—	1	—	—	—	(1.0)
12	—	—	2	2	2	—	—	(6.0)

[a] Data are for dP$_4$ and exclude specimens lacking vertical provenience designations; counts by layer may be less than the combined counts for all layers (1–12) presented in Table 13.4.
[b] dMNI is calculated by dividing total MNE for the deciduous tooth element by 2.
[c] Birthing season in Pleistocene Italy is estimated to be May–June (see Table 13.1).

TABLE 13.6
Deciduous tooth wear frequency data for equids and aurochs from Italian sites

Site, (agency), and species	Deciduous tooth wear stages[a]							(dMNI)[b]
	0	1	2	3	4	5	6	
Polesini 1–12 (lUP):								
wild ass	—	1.0	1.0	4.0	6.0	2.0	—	(14.0)
horse	—	—	—	—	2.0	6.0	5.0	(13.0)
Palidoro 33–34 (lUP):								
wild ass	—	—	—	—	0.5	—	—	(0.5)
aurochs	—	—	—	—	1.0	—	—	(1.0)
Guattari G0–1 (sh):								
aurochs	—	—	0.5	—	—	—	0.5	(1.0)

[a] Data are for dP$_4$ for aurochs, dP^2 for equids.
dMNI is calculated by dividing total MNE for the deciduous tooth element by 2.

Note: (lUP) late Upper Paleolithic, (sh) spotted hyaenas.

their deciduous premolars until about three years of age (Table 13.2). Wild ass deaths appear to peak sometime between fall and early spring at Polesini and sometime in late summer-fall for horses (Figure 13.3). The Polesini horses are interesting because their overall death patterns diverge from those of all other ungulates in this late Upper Paleolithic shelter; of course, the data for equids are also more prone to error. The overall mortality pattern for horse, a minority species among what otherwise repre-

sent hunted ungulate prey, is distinctly old-biased (Chapter 11), suggestive of procurement by scavenging. The possibility that juvenile horses died primarily in spring and perhaps late summer coincides with natural peaks in attritional deaths among modern feral horses in North America (Berger 1986). It is possible that many of the horses at Polesini were scavenged by people. Unlike the Mousterian faunas of Moscerini and Guattari G4–5, however, horses are relatively uncommon in Polesini

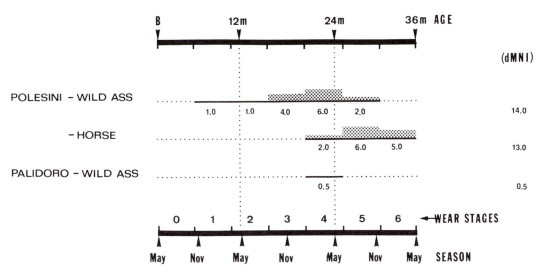

Figure 13.3 Histograms of juvenile wild ass and horse age frequencies and estimated seasons of death, based on deciduous tooth eruption-wear stages.

and co-occur with a pervasively meaty, prime adult focus for other prey. The equid and aurochs samples from late Upper Paleolithic Palidoro and the spotted hyaena component of Guattari (G0–1) are too small to evaluate, but it is interesting that the human-generated cases generally tend to align with the peak for wild ass from Polesini, whereas data points from the hyaena den fall at opposing extremes.

To summarize, the Mousterian hominid-collected ungulate faunas from Sant'Agostino (S0–3) and Breuil (Br) seem to point to fall-winter occupations, as may the coastal late Upper Paleolithic case from Riparo Salvini; these faunas also display "meaty" anatomical patterns (see Chapter 9). Seasons of site use at late Upper Paleolithic Polesini are more difficult to understand, because the site clearly represents many occupations and the seasonal timing of visits by humans may have varied across years. Humans' use of the Polesini shelter apparently cen-

tered on the colder half of the annual cycle, however. Too few data points are available for the head-dominated, old-age biased ungulate assemblages collected by hominids in Moscerini (M2–4) and Guattari (G4–5) to assess them with confidence; the Moscerini case at least suggests deaths in spring-early summer, which is generally consistent with a natural rise in scavenging opportunities that occurs in modern northern ecosystems each spring (Chapter 10).

Figure 13.4 presents a general synopsis of the seasonality results obtained from milk teeth. The summary is provisional, but nonetheless illustrates a few general patterns in the data. It is likely, for example, that late Upper Paleolithic peoples switched among prey species while staying at Polesini in any given year. Cross-taxa samples from the Mousterian caves are not adequate for comparison on this particular question, but the possibility of

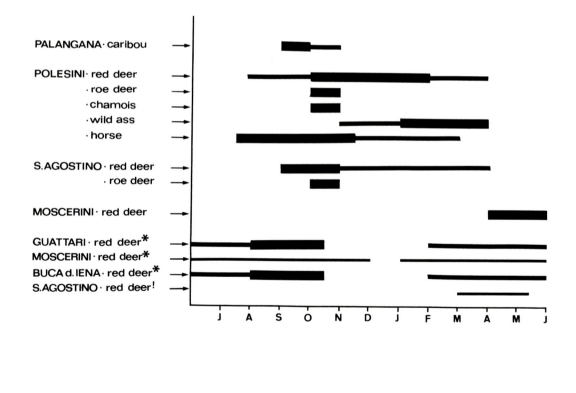

Figure 13.4 General synopsis of seasonality results based on juvenile ungulate eruption-wear data; (*) hyaena-collected, (!) wolf-collected.

food switching certainly exists for the earlier periods as well; shellfish and tortoise exploitation is evident at Moscerini, and the rates of shellfish accumulation do not precisely match those for ungulate bones across fine layers (Chapter 6). Hominid-procured red deer at Sant'Agostino (S0–3) pose an interesting contrast to the pattern at Polesini by displaying similar ranges but different peaks. At Sant'Agostino, most red and roe deer died during the fall, whereas the heaviest use of red deer at Polesini apparently began in fall, but continued through winter-spring (based on cut by cut information in Table 13.5). Many more animals and episodes of human occupation are represented at Polesini, facts that account for erroneous impressions of year-round use of this site. Red deer collected by Mousterian hominids at Moscerini form an outlier to all other human-collected cases in the study

sample, because deaths appear to have occurred in spring and, perhaps, early summer. The Mousterian case of Moscerini falls beyond the range of hominid components at Polesini and Sant'Agostino (S0–3), but matches the wolf den occupation at Sant'Agostino (SX, Figure 13.4); wolves den in spring in the northern hemisphere. Three hyaena-collected red deer cases from Guattari, Moscerini, and Buca della Iena are shown at the bottom of Figure 13.4. Taken together, they may suggest year-round use of dens, but appear to emphasize the half-year when human use was least intense in the coastal caves during the Middle Paleolithic. The gross contrast between hominid and hyaena use of caves most probably was not the result of direct contests or alternations within years, but instead may reflect different resource and land use agendas of these species.

METHODS FOR DETERMINING SEASONS AND ADULT SEX RATIOS FROM DEER ANTLER AND PEARL TEETH

The yearly cycle of antler development and casting is restricted to males in most deer genera other than *Rangifer,* and the process is regulated principally by day length and secondarily by individual age and food supply (e.g., Ozoga 1988). The cycle shifts slightly and may vary more as latitude decreases (Chapman 1975; Stuart 1982:95–97). Only the males in red, fallow, and roe deer populations develop antlers, and, within populations, younger males retain antlers somewhat longer than fully adult males. These facts about antler development and shedding in modern deer expose three competing concerns for archaeological studies of antler condition and abundance: antler growth is at once sex-limited, age-limited, and season-limited in living deer populations. The question to be addressed in this section is mainly about season-limited antler frequencies, but the analysis must control for the two other factors as much as possible.

Two kinds of antler comparisons are undertaken for the Pleistocene cave faunas: (1) the abundance of antler (antler base MNE/2 = MNI) relative to heads (cranial *bone* MNI); and (2) the proportion of shed versus unshed antler (a.k.a. *antler state*). Cranial bone MNI is calculated from bony portions of

the skull only (not teeth, see Chapter 9) and is independent of antler counts. The proportions of shed to unshed antler are determined from the condition of antler bases, the area of tissue where antler conjoins to the skull. The relationship between antler MNI and cranial bone MNI frequencies should expose any biases in human procurement practices as a function of one or more of the three factors noted above. The second comparison of antler state (shed versus unshed) is limited to faunas in which antler material is present; antler is especially abundant in spotted hyaena dens in Italy, and it is relatively uncommon in hominid-generated shelter faunas (Breuil Br, B3/4, Sant'Agostino S0–3, Moscerini M6) and virtually absent from others (Moscerini M2–4).

Because the relative abundance of antlered individuals in living deer populations is a function of (a) sex, (b) season of the year, and (c) individual age, each value can only be a fraction of the whole living population at any given time (1), warranting the rudiment of an equation:

$$1 \times [a] \times [b] \times [c]$$

By assigning year-round averages for a, b, and c, the product of this equation provides a rough base-

TABLE 13.7
Seasons of antler casting in modern European cervids

Species	Geographic location	Shedding months	Source
roe deer	Sweden	Nov–Dec	During 1986
	England	Oct–Nov	Prior 1968:88, 107
red deer	Sweden	March–May	During 1986
	Scotland	April (?)	Clutton-Brock et al. 1982:133, 183, 206
fallow deer	England	late spring	Chapman and Chapman 1975: 110–111, 126–127

line expectation for the ratio of antler MNI to cranial MNI in an assemblage. The baseline represents a situation in which predators were not choosy with regard to sex, age, and season. The population sex ratio is assumed to average around 33 percent for adults and juveniles combined (a = .33). A bias toward females is common in cervid populations because of relatively higher mortality in males (e.g., Clutton-Brock et al. 1982). Adult male cervids possess hardened antlers for about nine months of each year (b = .75), based on information in Tables 13.7 and 13.8. Adults normally comprise about 65 percent of a stable living population on the average (c = .65), using the age boundary defined in Chapter 11. The number of adult prey actually obtained by hominids in the Italian Paleolithic cases relative to the living population is known to vary,

however; most of the cases display a bias toward adult prey, such that two predictions, the baseline and subsequent adjustments in the value of [c] to account for observed biases toward adults or juveniles, must be entertained simultaneously:

Baseline: If deer were obtained by a predator without regard to sex, season, and individual age ($1 \times [.33] \times [.75] \times [.65]$), then antler MNI will average around 16 percent of cranial MNI. Note that the prediction for archaeological assemblages can vary between values of 1 and 0, provided hominids did not collect cast (shed) antler. A ratio significantly greater or less than 16 percent instead suggests seasonal procurement and/or a selective bias toward one sex when procuring individual prey. The baseline expectation may be suitable, for example, for cervids procured by

TABLE 13.8
Antler development and casting schedules for red deer,
fallow deer, and roe deer in Great Britain

fallow deer:
        shedding − mid-April to mid-June
    new growth completed by − mid-August
    without hardened antler − 2.5 months

red deer:
        shedding − mid-March to mid-April
    new growth completed by − mid-August to early September
    without hardened antler − 3 months

roe deer:
        shedding − mid-October to mid-December
    new growth completed by − early April
    without hardened antler − 3 months

Source: Stuart (1982:97).

hominids at Sant'Agostino because the mortality patterns resemble the living age structure of the same species (S0–3, see Chapter 11).

Adjustments in the adult:juvenile ratio, [c]: If deer were obtained by the predator without regard to sex and season, but with a strong bias toward adult (prime and/or old) or juvenile prey, then the antler MNI should be biased too. Adult-juvenile age ratios [c] can be recalculated from age biases already observed for a given assemblage, such as those documented in Chapter 11. Assuming that the circumstances of antler preservation in geological deposits are good, adjustments for selected Italian cases are as follows:

Prime-dominant ungulate mortality (Breuil B3 and B4)

$$(1 \times [.33] \times [.75] \times [.80]) = \text{antlers } 20\% \text{ of cranial MNI}$$

Old-dominant ungulate mortality (Moscerini M2–4, 6, Guattari G4–5)

$$(1 \times [.33] \times [.75] \times [.90]) = \text{antlers } 22\% \text{ of cranial MNI}$$

Juvenile-dominant ungulate mortality (spotted hyaena dens in Buca dell Iena I1–6)

$$(1 \times [.33] \times [.75] \times [.25]) = \text{antlers } 6\% \text{ of cranial MNI}$$

Both the baseline and adjusted predictions anticipate antler values significantly lower than 1, usually rather close to one another, so that divergence from the baseline value on the order of more than 5 percent could be significant. The expectations are for living cervid populations over the entire year, however, and, hence, they only partly address the question of seasonal death; divergence from the baseline prediction cannot, in fact, distinguish a sex bias from a season-caused bias in a death assemblage.

While the kinds of osteometric data normally used for sex ratio analyses were recorded for the subject assemblages, none of the samples is sufficiently large to warrant the osteometric approach. However, data on the frequencies of adult male red deer upper canines (pearl teeth) are useful for studying adult sex ratios and can be compared to antler data. The canine samples from the Italian caves are small, but the data are quite interesting.

The second comparison of antler focuses on the relative abundances of shed and unshed specimens. This aspect of the antler data distinguishes the transport habits of Mousterian hominids and hyaenas to a large degree (Chapter 9), only the latter of whom showed much interest in shed antler. (A different response may have been true in the Upper Paleolithic, when antler became an important raw material for making tools.) Because partly developed antler is very fragile, it is less likely than hardened antler to be preserved in geological deposits, and an analytical blind spot of roughly two months of the annual cycle must be acknowledged for this reason. Table 13.8 summarizes the relative duration of antler growth and casting phases in fallow deer, red deer, and roe deer in Great Britain (Chapman 1975; Banfield 1974 cited in Stuart 1982:97). Because antler growth proceeds at a phenomenal pace each year, the amount of time that antler is available to become part of an archaeological or paleontological deposit in any given year is reduced to about nine to eleven months. Cast antler is comprised of fully hardened tissue and certainly can last more than one month after it is shed by the deer, even in environments where antler may provide an important food supplement for rodents, deer, wolves, and hyaenas (see also discussion in Chapter 9).

RESULTS ON DEER ANTLER AND PEARL TEETH

MNE counts for shed and unshed antlers of roe, red, and fallow deer are presented in Tables 13.9 and 13.10, respectively; the principal agency of accumulation, as determined from taphonomic and carnivore mortality data, is noted for each case. While red and fallow deer data are grouped together, the great majority represent red deer. Total antler MNI and bone-based cranial MNI are compared in each table; male canine MNI (i.e., canine MNE/2) is also listed in Table 13.10. It is immediately apparent from Table 13.10 that hyaena dens in Italy contain a great deal of red (and fallow) deer antler, roughly half of which was shed prior to being collected by the hyaenas. Canine-based adult male red

TABLE 13.9
Antler and crania counts for roe deer in the Italian shelters

Agency and assemblage	Shed antler MNE	Unshed antler MNE	Total antler MNI	Cranial[a] bone MNI
collected by hyaenas:				
Buca d.Iena I1	—	—	—	—
I2	—	—	—	—
I3	—	—	—	—
I4	—	—	—	0.25
I5	—	—	—	0.25
I6	—	—	—	0.25
Moscerini M5	—	2	1.0	4.0
collected by Mousterian hominids:				
Moscerini M2	—	—	—	—
M3	—	—	—	3.25
M4	—	—	—	1.25
M6	—	—	—	0.25
S.Agostino S0	—	?	0.5	2.25
S1	—	—	—	1.5
S2	—	—	—	0.75
S3	—	—	—	0.25
Breuil Br	—	—	—	1.0
collected by wolves:				
S.Agostino SX	—	1	0.5	4.25
collected by late Upper Paleolithic humans:				
R.Salvini 10–15	—	—	—	0.5

[a] MNI is calculated by dividing antler base MNE by 2. Bone-based cranial MNI is listed for comparison; cranial and antler MNIs are calculated independently of one another.

Note: (?) probably unshed antler, not certain.

deer MNI is zero or relatively low, supporting the idea that prey heads and antlers parted ways before many of the antlers were collected by predators. Hyaenas' tendency to collect antlers at Upper Pleistocene dens (Guattari G0–1, Buca della Iena, and Moscerini M5) is generally consistent with their tendency to accumulate bovid horns in modern dens. Bovids never shed their horn cores; horn cores are separated from skulls at kill sites, or hyaenas are more likely to destroy skulls than horn on complete heads carried to dens. Either way, the resultant pattern in den faunas often is marked by an overabundance of horn. The geographic distributions of deer and hyaenas no longer overlap as they once did in Pleistocene, and so a direct analog for antler collecting probably cannot be found among modern hyaenas. The absence of analog cases therefore is

explained by changes in hyaena biogeography, not changes in their food-collecting habits. The prevalence of horns in modern dens, illustrated in Table 13.11, leaves little reason to doubt that the behavior observed with regard to horns would not also apply to antler if it were available in the hyaenas' environment (see also Chapter 9).

On the Guattari surface (G0), the frequencies of shed and unshed red deer antler are equivalent (Table 13.10), and antler MNI is 67 percent of the cranial bone MNI (fallow deer is always rare). The proportion of antler is high, especially in light of the strong bias toward juvenile prey noted for hyaena-collected assemblages in Buca della Iena. Taking the juvenile bias into account pulls the expected value for antler down to about 6 percent (see above). Clearly, antler collecting and head collect-

TABLE 13.10
Antler and crania counts for red/fallow deer in the Italian shelters

Agency and assemblage	Shed antler MNE	Unshed antler MNE	Total antler MNI	Male canine MNI	Cranial[a] bone MNI
collected by hyaenas:					
Guattari G0	9	9	9.0	—	13.5
G1	—	2	1.0	0.5	6.0
G2	—	1	0.5	—	2.75
Buca d.Iena I1	2	1	1.5	—	0.5
I2	—	—	—	—	—
I3	—	—	—	—	—
I4	3	1	2.0	—	—
I5	—	—	—	—	—
I6	7	2	4.5	—	3.0
Moscerini M5	1	1	1.0	—	7.0
collected by Mousterian hominids (head-dominated faunas):					
Moscerini M2	—	—	—	—	1.0
M3	—	—	—	—	15.0
M4	—	—	—	—	7.25
M6	—	1	0.5	—	6.25
Guattari G4–5	—	—	—	—	1.0
collected by Mousterian hominids (meaty faunas):					
Breuil Br	—	1	0.5	0.5	3.0
B3/4	—	1	0.5	—	1.0
S.Agostino S0	—	?	0.5	1.0	2.25
S1	—	1	0.5	1.0	3.75
S2	—	—	—	1.0	2.0
S3	—	?	0.5	0.5	1.25
collected by wolves:					
S.Agostino SX	—	—	—	—	—
collected by late Upper Paleolithic humans:					
Palidoro 33–34	—	1	0.5	—	7.25
R.Salvini 10–15	—	?	0.5	2.0	2.50

[a]MNI is calculated by dividing antler base MNE by 2. Bone-based cranial MNI is listed for comparison; cranial and antler MNIs are calculated independently of one another.

Note: (?) probably unshed antler, not certain.

ing by hyaenas were not linked in a straightforward anatomical way. The co-occurrence of both shed and unshed antler in hyaena lairs of Guattari, Buca della Iena, and Moscerini is consistent with the prolonged den use typical of modern spotted hyaenas in Africa, spanning many seasons (e.g., Kruuk 1972; Schaller 1972). The Italian cases (especially Guattari G0–1 and Buca I6) indicate that antlers need not be attached to the skulls of prey to attract hyaenas.

Faunas collected by Mousterian hominids at Breuil and Sant'Agostino and by late Upper Paleolithic humans at Salvini also contain antler, but these specimens are attached to skulls (i.e., unshed), and antler MNI is more or less consistent with male canine MNI. At Sant'Agostino, where red and roe deer remains display living-structure mortality patterns, the expected ratio for antler at 16 percent of cranial MNI is matched by the observed value. However, male canines occur at 38 percent of cranial MNI, possibly indicating that some male

TABLE 13.11

Antler and horn bases and crania counts for ungulates in modern wolf, brown
hyaena, and spotted hyaena dens

Agency and case	Shed antler MNE	Unshed antler MNE	Total antler/horn MNI	Cranial[a] bone MNI
caribou in Alaskan wolf dens:[b]				
WD1	—	1	0.5	0.5
WD2	—	—	—	0.5
WD3	—	1	0.5	0.25
ungulates in spotted hyaena dens:				
Kalahari[b]			7.0	2.5
Zimbabwe[c]			—	1.25
Timbatavi[d]			10.0	9.0
Natab[e]			6.5	0.5
ungulates in brown hyaena dens:				
Kalahari[b]			5.0	—
Kalahari[f]			10.0	10.75
ungulates in striped hyaena dens:				
Arad Cave[g]			6.0	10.0

[a] MNI is calculated by dividing antler base MNE by 2. Bone-based cranial MNI is listed for
comparison; cranial and antler/horn MNIs are calculated independently of one another.
[b] Binford's unpublished data.
[c] Haynes' collection, unpublished.
[d] Bearder (1977), Brain (1981).
[e] Henschel et al. (1979).
[f] Mills and Mills (1977).
[g] Skinner et al. (1980).

deaths occurred during the late winter-spring "blindspot" described above (see also Figure 13.2). Antler values are around 25 percent at Breuil, roughly 5 percent higher than expected values for antler, even though the data are adjusted to account for a prime adult harvesting pattern there. A minor bias favoring the harvesting of adult males may be indicated at Breuil, but it is not very pronounced; the data corroborate the pattern of fall-winter harvesting noted earlier, with no strong sex bias. Late Upper Paleolithic Palidoro contains one antler base and no male canines, despite a cranial MNI of 7.25, perhaps suggesting late spring and/or female-biased procurement.

A very different situation is apparent for the Mousterian faunas in Moscerini, where deer heads are abundant but antler is absent or rare, and there are no adult male red deer canines (Table 13.10). While hominid-collected samples at Moscerini are smaller for roe deer (Table 13.9), these remains also

lack antler. The cases collected by hominids at Moscerini are strongly biased toward old adult prey, yet evidence of male individuals is virtually nonexistent. There are three potential explanations for the absence of antlers in these cases: one is that deaths occurred in spring when no living deer possessed antlers; the second is that only females were procured by the hominids; or, finally, both conditions were true (most likely). None of these data contradict information from the previous section indicating (juvenile) deaths in spring, because relatively higher food returns from female carcasses and males lacking hardened antlers often coincide in this season (see Chapter 8; also Binford 1978). In contrast to the hominid-collected faunas, the carnivore den component (primarily spotted hyaena) in Moscerini M5 does contain antler.

The wolf den fauna of SX in Sant'Agostino contains some roe deer crania (Table 13.9), and the proportion of antler is around 11 percent. The relative paucity of antler in this case is consistent with the estimated denning season of wolves (e.g., March; see Table 13.8). The complete absence of red deer antler is explained by the facts that wolves tend to emphasize juvenile prey in general (Chapter 11) and cranial bones of red and fallow deer are also absent (Chapter 9). Like the modern Alaskan wolf den cases presented in Table 13.11, wolves apparently collected antler only if it was attached to skulls. It remains to be seen whether shed antler interests them much in other modern situations.

The results on deer antler abundance and state appear to be consistent with the seasonality results presented above. At this point, the methods of analysis may be more interesting than the results, be-cause most of the samples are small and cannot provide clear answers. The antler data nonetheless suggest that ungulate procurement by Mousterian hominids at Sant'Agostino, Breuil, and by late Upper Paleolithic humans at Salvini, occurred during the colder half of the year. The lack of antlered individuals in the Mousterian faunas of Moscerini (M2–4, M6) is striking in light of the abundance of cranial material and suggests that procurement of adult ungulates took place in spring-early summer and/or hominids focused exclusively on adult females. The antler data for the hyaena dens at Moscerini (M5) and Buca della Iena (I1–6) support prior inferences of prolonged den occupations in this region of Italy, probably year-round.

Conclusions

While partly corrected for clinal variation in mammalian growth and development patterns, the seasonality results for the Italian cases are often unclear, confounded by small sample sizes or, in other cases, palimpsest accumulations formed over many years and many human occupations. Some general contrasts in seasonal exploitation of ungulates nonetheless emerge from the eruption-wear, antler, and pearl tooth data; these results are summarized in Table 13.12.

Considered as a whole, the Mousterian cases cover more of the annual cycle than is true for the late Upper Paleolithic cases from coastal Latium. The seasons of Mousterian occupations divide according to patterns of ungulate procurement inferred from small animal exploitation, ungulate body part representation, and mortality patterns in earlier chapters. The head-dominated, old age-biased faunas of Moscerini may have been collected by people primarily in spring-early summer. The

TABLE 13.12
Provisional seasonality results for the Italian shelter faunas

Agency	Site	Vertical provenience	Seasons
Mousterian hominids	Moscerini	M2–4,6	spring-summer
	Guattari	G4–5	?
	Sant'Agostino	S0–3	fall-early spring
	Breuil	Br	fall-early spring
late Upper Paleolithic humans	Salvini	10–15	fall-early spring
	Polesini	1–12	fall-spring
	Palidoro	33–34	?
denning spotted hyaenas	Moscerini	M5	all seasons
	Guattari	G0–1	all seasons
	Buca d. Iena	I1–6	all seasons
denning wolves	Sant'Agostino	SX	late spring-early summer

meaty, living-age-structure faunas of Sant'Agostino and the prime-age-dominant faunas of Breuil correspond to ungulate deaths in fall, winter, and probably early spring. Only the second group of Mousterian faunas in any way resembles the late Upper Paleolithic sample from this region.

Zooarchaeological evidence indicates that hunting was an important activity of the hominids that occupied Breuil and Sant'Agostino. Because most ungulates died in fall-winter, the timing of humans' visits may have been keyed to ungulates' heavier use of lowland pastures during the cold season, where they may capitalize on both terrestrial plant foods and seaweed (Clutton-Brock et al. 1982:230, 240–241). There are no clear-cut rules governing pasture movements by modern ungulates; some individuals or subgroups of a population move more than others. Yet ungulates may generally gravitate toward lowland areas to avoid exposure from severe cold and, more important, to take advantage of the longer growing seasons there (e.g., Berger 1986:86; Chapman and Chapman 1975:160–161; Clutton-Brock et al. 1982:228; Garrott et al. 1987; Schaller 1977:179–180). Ungulates may disperse upland with the return of warm weather to avoid parasites and the summer heat, and to feed on pastures that have been less intensively browsed. If people depended upon ungulate resources throughout the year, they too might move. This principle guided land use practices of local herders in the Pontine Marshes (Latium) of coastal Italy, before the area was successfully drained in 1930.[12] It is likely to have characterized seasonal movements of wild ungulates in prehistoric times as well—even if drainage patterns of the area changed somewhat with global climate.

No seasonality data are available for Mousterian occupations at Guattari (G4–5), and, although those for Moscerini (M2–4, M6) are interesting, they are less than clear. Head parts dominate among the ungulate remains collected by hominids at Moscerini and spring occupations are suggested by the data, but juvenile individuals are rare in these assemblages (because old adults are common) and thus the deciduous tooth samples are too small to

yield substantive results. Spring occupations at Moscerini may be supported by the virtual absence of deer antler there, but the lack of male canines also indicates that most or all of the deer were adult females and therefore would lack antlers in any season.

The sex bias toward female deer at Moscerini could also be linked to season-governed food choices; adult females, especially those that were not pregnant, might retain somewhat more fat in spring than males. The ungulates in Moscerini appear to have been obtained primarily by scavenging (Chapters 9 and 11), and gathering of small animals, such as clams, mussels, and tortoises, was also important to hominids at this cave. Preliminary isotopic assays of a few mollusk shells from Moscerini (M2–4, M6) also suggest deaths in spring or early summer (see Chapter 6). It is interesting that the frequencies of ungulate remains do not rise and fall in tandem with those for mollusk shells in the thick exterior strata sequence of Moscerini. Differing frequencies of food types across the thirty fine levels of this site raise the possibility of resource switching by the hominid residents, suggesting that people's use of the shelter was not wholly conditioned by any one kind of food. Plant procurement could have been an important focus during some or all of the occupations, perhaps including seaweed (sensu Speth 1990:157 and references cited therein), which today is an important alternative food for European red deer and (North American) bears in winter and spring.

The ungulate body parts that Mousterian hominids carried to shelters also suggest differing seasons of procurement. Modern humans respond to the availability of animal fat when choosing parts for transport or intensive processing (e.g., Binford 1978; O'Connell et al. 1988a; O'Connell and Marshall 1989; Speth 1990; Speth and Spielmann 1983; Yellen 1977). It is reasonable to assume that fats were equally important to archaic *Homo*. The physiological rules of fat storage and metabolism in the appendicular skeleton of mammalian prey and the uniquely fat-rich nerve tissues in the cranium can be tied to humans' transport and processing decisions,

[12] This information comes from my interview with A. G. Segre, who, as a boy, accompanied his father on surveys of the

Pontine Marshes prior to their being drained during Mussolini's 1930 "Bonificazione" and resettlement campaign.

especially in response to seasonal narrowing in the sources from which these nutrients can be obtained (see also Speth 1990). In the Italian cases, hominids processed every ungulate part that reached each Paleolithic shelter: long bones were opened for marrow, brains were removed from skulls, and mandibles were separated from skulls (presumably to remove the tongue) and opened to extract their marrow. Humans were less consistent with regard to transport tactics; indeed, this is where most decisions regarding food value are expressed in the Italian caves.

The limb- and head-rich faunas from Breuil and Sant'Agostino indicate hunting by hominids, whereas the head-dominant faunas from Moscerini and Guattari strongly suggest scavenging. In Chapter 10, I discussed seasonal mortality cycles in prey populations that exist independently of predator effects. Malnutrition is expressed primarily as fat depletion in mammals, and disease has a similar impact, because it inhibits foraging. The study sample cannot reveal what Middle Paleolithic hominids ate outside of rockshelters in coastal Italy. It is clear, however, that hominids' decisions about what parts of ungulates to transport to shelters varied greatly across sites, at least partly in response to season. And the age structures of the prey death assemblages differ in corresponding ways. The head-dominated, old-age biased faunas from Guattari G4–5 and Moscerini M2, M3, M4, and M6 reflect situations in which fat was scarce and valuable. If ungulates were in poor condition at the time of death, then limb elements may not have been worth carrying to shelters for intensive processing (see Chapter 8), a situation most typical during late winter through spring. Animals would be much fatter on the average in early autumn through early winter, thereby changing the relative value of their constitu-

ent parts in humans' transport decision hierarchies.

The late Upper Paleolithic faunas of Polesini show that, even if one can narrow the seasons of occupation to one half of the year or the other, many questions about how people coped with shortages are left unanswered. Archaeologists' perceptions of the seasons of human occupations are contingent in large part on which species and how many species are used to determine seasons of prey deaths at a given site. More often than not, sample sizes are uneven across taxa within assemblages, so seasonality analyses can be performed only for one or two species. Yet it is clear that modern humans and their more recent predecessors were both complex strategists and thoroughly omnivorous in most of the environments that they inhabited. Modern humans living in mobile societies typically switch among resource categories in response to seasonal and other changes in food supply. This appears to have occurred at Polesini, for example, where samples are large enough for several ungulate species to be examined. Switching tactics could also have been employed during the Middle Paleolithic. Certainly, there is no case for sedentism at any Mousterian cave in Italy, nor elsewhere in Eurasia, but more than one pattern of mobility may be viable in most kinds of environments. Perhaps this is what is evidenced by the Middle and late Upper Paleolithic records of coastal Italy. With such differences, we could also expect to see contrasts in lithic raw material transport and territoriality (one of the topics of the next chapter), and possibly new scales of social interaction as well. By recognizing the analytical problems inherent to seasonality analyses, we may also learn much more about their scientific value. Suffice it to say there is considerable potential to learn about Mousterian land use at the regional (multisite) level in the future.

14

Covariation in Mousterian Technology and Game Use

(CO-WRITTEN WITH STEVEN L. KUHN)

THIS CHAPTER undertakes two problems simultaneously: documenting the parallels between Mousterian technology and game use within the Middle Paleolithic period and examining the possibility that variation in both forms a trend within the Latium sequence (Stiner and Kuhn 1992). The faunal analyses presented in earlier chapters of this book generally assume that variation in the Latium Mousterian assemblages represents one stable adaptation or niche. Yet trends in this region are suggested by the data on food transport (Chapter 9) and prey age selection (Chapter 11), indicating either adaptive change through time or adjustments by hominids to local foraging conditions as the Mediterranean sea retreated between 120,000 and 35,000 years ago. Before the causes of the variation can be interpreted from an evolutionary perspective, the nature and scope of these local trends must be documented and qualified.

My research on Italian cave faunas has benefited greatly from collaborations with Steven Kuhn, who studied technological variation in the associated Mousterian stone industries of Latium. The first problem undertaken in this chapter, concerning parallels between Mousterian technology and game use, is very interesting from a broader perspective, and the Latium case contributes some unprecedented insights. The relationships between technology and subsistence are critical for gaining a fuller understanding of behavioral variation and niche boundaries of Middle Paleolithic and other hominids. Here, we present a series of comparisons that demonstrate strong covariation between Mousterian subsistence practices and the economics of stone technology. The data imply changes in human land use over the long term.

This chapter differs from all others in that it focuses on the Mousterian almost exclusively. The rationale and bases of interpretation for the faunal patterns are briefly encapsulated here, having been covered at length in earlier chapters, whereas Kuhn's methods for analyzing the technologies receive fuller explanation. The technological analyses emphasize those lithic variables expected to have been heavily influenced by food search (land use) and procurement strategies, especially core reduction tactics and tool life histories. Although the arrays of formal tool types and mammalian prey species consumed stayed much the same throughout the Middle Paleolithic period in the study area, evidence suggests that the techniques of flake production and raw material economy varied in concert with important aspects of animal exploitation, both by site and with time.

The relationships between variation in Mousterian technology and subsistence are strong and intriguing. Together, they document a striking array of hominid responses to resource opportunities during the Middle Paleolithic as a whole. The causes of this variation in coastal Latium are less clear, pri-

This chapter is reworked from the 1992 article co-authored by Stiner and Kuhn, entitled "Subsistence, Technology, and Adaptive Variation in Middle Paleolithic Italy," *American Anthropologist* 94.

marily because of the small geographic size of the study area. Two competing explanations—normal variation within a single, complex adaptive pattern as opposed to vectored evolutionary change—here are illuminated in concrete and ultimately testable terms. Parallel trends identified in the faunal and lithic data may reflect responses to changes in local coastal habitats and foraging opportunities due to lowering sea levels during the early part of the Würm. We know that the sea went down during the Upper Pleistocene, and we know that it came back up during the Holocene. The caves stayed where they were, while the character of their settings varied from littoral to inland habitats over time. It is at least conceivable, however, that the trends in the Italian Mousterian represent the appearance of genuinely new strategies of foraging and tool making,

fostering the notion that changes in human adaptations proceeded quite gradually and that the modern version originated somewhere within the heart of the Mousterian. While alternative explanations cannot be summarily addressed with this data set alone, our observations challenge previous assertions that Mousterian behavioral patterns were monotonous. Much of the behavioral raw material evident in modern human adaptations existed in earlier populations, but the emphases and scale at which these behaviors were expressed changed. The case from west-central Italy offers key insights about the importance of the ranges of variation in hominid behavioral responses across places, rather than single-site analyses, as descriptors of hominid adaptations and resource niche.

ANALYTICAL APPROACH

A number of local trends in the Mousterian faunal data were suggested in earlier chapters. The relationships drawn between the faunal patterns and hominid foraging behaviors, especially between food choices and procurement strategies, are based on what other predators habitually do. Of greatest interest are the differing ways that Mousterian hominids obtained and used the very same food species, as manifest in search patterns, the prey age groups most commonly targeted, processing and transport strategies, and, to the extent that the data allow, schedules of resource use and thresholds for switching among resources.

Alternatively, technologies can be seen as adaptations both to external factors and to the requirements and limitations imposed by human subsistence systems (following Kuhn 1990a, 1992, n.d.). What hominids did with tools and the forms that tools took were heavily constrained by both the physical properties of the human organism and the mechanics of stone fracture. For this reason, major evolution-related changes in human technologies are most likely to have involved their role within a larger economic system, not simple alternations in tool forms and functions. This would have been

particularly true for Mousterian and earlier technologies, since stone tools specially designed for procuring ungulates were either rare or nonexistent (Kuhn 1989a, 1993; Holdaway 1989; cf. Shea 1989). The relationship between technology and subsistence is here considered central to understanding adaptive variation in tool-making behavior during the Upper Pleistocene. The lithic analyses emphasize those variables expected to have been heavily influenced by resource search and procurement strategies. Patterns of association between lithic and faunal evidence are ultimately used to assess ideas about Mousterian land use relative to that of later peoples in the study area.

Faunas: Review of the interpretive bases and variables

The faunal presentation here concentrates mainly on variables that reflect two kinds of foraging procedures: anatomical part transport evident from patterns of skeletal representation (from Chapter 9), and prey age selection evident from mortality patterns (from Chapter 11). The comparisons are confined to red and fallow deer,[13] the most common prey exploited

[13] Red deer are much more common than fallow deer in all of the faunal assemblages. The two taxa are combined into one prey

category because many skeletal element fragments of these deer cannot be distinguished to the species level (see Chapter 4).

by Upper Pleistocene hominids in west-central Italy. Findings on species consumed by Middle Paleolithic hominids, and seasonality for the same array of faunas, are also summarized from Chapters 7 and 13 where pertinent to the discussion below.

Because the faunal assemblages were deposited inside shelters, they represent cumulative outcomes of transport, rather than items discarded where food was obtained. The animal remains therefore are subsets drawn from larger resource pools, the general composition of which can be modeled from modern analogs. In the case of body part transport choices, the pool is simply the ungulate body; foragers took certain parts from the carcasses of prey to new locations for processing and consumption, often leaving other parts behind. Because scavenging could have been involved, carcass completeness at the procurement site is not taken for granted. Instead, the analyses assume only that the number of parts taken away must have equaled or been less than what was present on carcasses when encountered by the hominids. Prey age selection occurs in the context of much larger resource pools, the age structures of living animal populations if hunted, or any subset thereof if scavenged. In the case of scavenging, processes affecting carcass destruction and predators' abilities to locate carcasses can be as important in determining age structure as the agencies of death (see Chapter 10).

Both transport patterns (anatomical representation) and prey age selection (mortality patterns) are closely tied to search and procurement strategies in nonhuman predators. From this perspective, hunting and scavenging are most interesting for their correspondences to fundamentally different ways of searching for food, even though each foraging mode can involve exactly the same prey species. Ungulate hunting involves capturing large, whole prey that often move about in groups while alive. In contrast, scavenging in its more passive forms requires finding animals already dead, perhaps nutritionally depleted or ravaged, and oftentimes more dispersed on a landscape (e.g., Houston 1979; Huggard 1993). Picking up items that are scattered and

immobile makes nonconfrontational scavenging more like gathering than hunting, both in the spatial characteristics of these food sources and the potential average returns gained from them.

Efforts to distinguish the zooarchaeological products of scavenging and hunting are potentially subject to several sources of ambiguity, however. This point merits discussion, since a great deal hinges on how the faunas in this comparison have already been interpreted. Generally speaking, both classes of foraging behavior can take more than one form, depending on the nature of opportunity and details of the subsistence system in use. Moreover, some patterns that hunting and scavenging behaviors impose upon faunal assemblages overlap (compare, for example, results obtained by Blumenschine 1986, 1991; Bunn et al. 1988; Haynes 1980; O'Connell et al. 1988a, 1988b; Stiner 1990b, 1991b, 1991d). These issues are briefly reviewed in terms of the variables outlined below.

Measures of anatomical representation are based on minimum number of skeletal element (MNE) counts for *bone*, as defined in Chapter 9. MNE is determined from the most common portion or landmark of each skeletal element and, in this study, represents the sum of right and left sides for elements that naturally occur in pairs. Teeth are not used for the MNE determinations, because they can distort head counts *relative to* postcrania wherever preservation conditions are less than ideal. My use of strictly bone-based MNE counts ensures numerical comparability between head and limb parts. Mortality patterns, in contrast, are based exclusively on teeth—specifically tooth eruption and wear data for the fourth premolar sequence, as described in Chapter 11. Only two adult age categories are considered here, however: prime adults and old adults.

Faunal assemblages attributable entirely or largely to the actions of nonhuman carnivores are excluded from consideration; the comparison here focuses on assemblages from Grotta Breuil B3/4 and Br; Grotta Guattari G2, G4, and G5; Grotta dei Moscerini M2, M3, M4, and M6; and Grotta di Sant'Agostino S0, S1, S2, and S3.[14] While some

[14] The faunal assemblage from G2 of Grotta Guattari represents some mixture of hominid and spotted hyaena components (see Chapters 4 and 5; also Stiner 1991a), and thus is not an ideal case for this comparison. G2 exhibits a number of qualities that more closely resemble hominid-associated patterns of faunal exploitation in neighboring sites than those patterns typically associated with spotted hyaenas. For these reasons, G2 is included in a sample of otherwise more definitely hominid-associated cases. Acceptance or deletion of this case does not undermine the overall results.

postdepositional bone destruction is inevitable in archaeofaunas, particularly for skeletal elements composed mainly of trabecular (spongy) tissue (e.g., Lyman 1985; 1991b), in situ bone attrition does not explain most of the variation in anatomical part representation among the subject assemblages (Chapters 5 and 9). Potential biases due to differential bone decomposition are further circumvented by considering only head and limb elements, the more durable parts of the bony skeleton.

To simplify the presentation and move toward a more ambitious level of synthesis, patterns of variation in the archaeofaunas are summarized in terms of only three derived variables. Each is an index suitable for the interpretation of series of assemblages, but probably not for isolated archaeological cases. The first variable is the ratio tMNE/MNI from Chapter 9, which serves as a rough index of anatomical completeness for ungulate prey (deer, in this presentation). The ratio is obtained by dividing the *total* number of skeletal elements (tMNE, including carpals, ribs, etc.) by the minimum number of individual animals (MNI). The ratio represents the average quantity of bony parts transported to shelters per carcass source. Variation in this index loosely corresponds to differences in transported returns from hunting (high values) as opposed to scavenging (low values) in a variety of modern carnivore and human situations.

The second anatomical variable, called (H + H)/L in Chapter 9, is calculated by dividing the total minimum number of head parts by the total minimum number of limbs for red and fallow deer in each assemblage. Limb MNE includes all substantial leg elements except phalanges, carpals, and tarsals other than the calcaneum and astragalus. Head MNE here includes antler as well as cranium and mandible elements, although antler is rare in the hominid-collected faunas; crania and mandibles occur in roughly equal proportions. In effect, (H + H)/L concerns only relatively large bones, those which in principle could represent attractively sized, transportable parcels. The (H + H)/L ratio accounts for much of the variation in anatomical representation in the Mousterian shelter faunas. In controlled comparisons of other predators, the ratio is a strong predictor of the general way that prey are most commonly obtained: hunting results in a more or less balanced anatomical ratio relative to the

complete living anatomy, while nonconfrontational scavenging tends to lead to head- and/or horn-dominated assemblages. The interpretation that head-dominated faunas represent mainly scavenged sources is based on evidence from modern nonhuman predators rather than contemporary humans. While no analogous situations for head collecting are documented in the ethnographic or ethnoarchaeological literature on modern humans to my knowledge, three species of scavenging carnivores (striped, brown, and spotted hyaenas) frequently create head- and/or horn-dominated anatomical biases for medium-sized ungulate prey in modern dens. The head-dominated pattern produced by nonhuman predators in the context of scavenging is best explained by properties of ungulate hard and soft tissue anatomy (see Chapter 8).

The third ratio, called PRIME/OLD, refers to mortality patterns in the deer, specifically the relative frequencies of prime and old adults. These adult age categories are defined on the basis of life history characteristics and associated physiological changes in deer and other ungulates. The ratio effectively registers two potential directions that age biases often take in predated faunas. Comparative research indicates that this ratio is very responsive to the relative emphasis on ambush hunting as opposed to scavenging (Chapter 11). Ambush hunting by modern humans frequently results in a prime-dominant mortality patterns, while scavenging by carnivores (or any kind of predator) can result in a bias toward old-aged animals.

Not all foraging tactics leave strong or mutually exclusive signatures on mortality patterns in prey death assemblages, a fact unequivocally demonstrated in Chapter 11. This study is fortunate because the old-biased age pattern observed in some Italian Mousterian cases matches an outstanding signature of scavenging in modern ecosystems, probably nonconfrontational scavenging at that. Alternatively, attributions of deer mortality patterns to hominid hunting behaviors are greatly aided by the fact that the patterns often take a relatively distinct, prime-dominant form. Though not entirely unique to the human species, the tendency to focus on prime adults of ungulate populations is far more pronounced in humans than it is in any nonhuman predator; prime-dominant mortality is regularly associated with modern human hunting practices. The pattern varies from a slight to great overabundance of prime-aged animals in relation to their live abundance. On the whole, then, prime-dominant harvesting represents a long-established tendency in humans, generally setting them apart from other large predators that depend on ungulate prey.

Even with the benefit of controlled associations between transport patterns, mortality patterns, and foraging behaviors of modern predators, it would not be appropriate to assume that each and every whole animal procured by Mousterian hominids had to have been hunted, nor every head from an old animal scavenged. The interpretations are probabilistic assessments about what Mousterian people usually did when presented with a general set of circumstances. The comparisons are about foraging practices at the level of interactions between predator and prey populations, in which only the cumulative patterns, representing repeated behaviors, are meaningful.

Lithics: Methods and bases of interpretations

The lithic assemblages to be discussed occur in direct association with the faunal remains. Indeed, the industries are partial basis, along with taphonomic evidence, for assigning the faunas to Mousterian hominids in particular. As explained in Chapter 3, the lithic assemblages belong to a regional facies of the Mousterian, called the Pontinian (Blanc 1937b; Taschini 1972), which is relatively invariant from the perspective of Bordes's (1961b) Middle Paleolithic stone tool typology. All of the industries exhibit a strong predominance of sidescrapers and generally low Levallois indexes (Bietti 1980, 1982; Taschini 1972, 1979). Recent U-series dating indicates that the Guattari I cranium was deposited no later than $51,000 \pm 3000$ years ago (Schwarcz et al. 1991), suggesting that all chipped stone deposited before this date is attributable to Neandertals exclusively; no anatomically modern human fossils have ever been found in stratigraphic association with Mousterian tools in west-central Italy. However, human fossil associations for later Mousterian assemblages are not known, and we remain open to surprise.

The analyses of the Mousterian industries address some of the potential links between technol-

ogy and subsistence, particularly those connections involving the shared time and energy budget. Among modern hunter-gatherers, the timing of subsistence activities and movement from one place to another determine the scheduling of both humans' needs for tools and the opportunities to make them. Any number of technological strategies may be employed to manipulate the utility of artifacts or raw materials, thereby bridging the spatial and temporal discontinuities between need and opportunity (e.g., Binford 1977, 1979; Bleed 1986; Kuhn 1989b, 1992; Nelson 1991; Shott 1986; Torrence 1983, 1989). Tactics for producing flakes and blanks from cores, the resharpening or renewal of stone tools, and the transport of tools and raw material all play a role in determining how long stone tools and raw materials will last. Studies of these variables should therefore provide information about the contingencies faced by hominids in making stone tools available when and where they were needed.

It is significant that, in coastal Latium, the only workable stone found within at least 40 to 50 km of the coastal caves is in the form of small flint pebbles, normally much less than 10 cm in maximum dimension. The pebbles occur in scattered active and fossil beach deposits on the coastal plains. Such small and dispersed raw materials would have placed a special premium on tactics for stretching raw materials and maximizing tool size. Hence, the lithic analyses focus on two dimensions of the technological record: (1) the intensity or duration of tool use and renewal; and (2) core reduction techniques, or the tactics used for manufacturing flakes and tool blanks. Very different analytical approaches are required to monitor these disparate phenomena (see also Kuhn 1990a, 1990b, 1991). The intensities of tool use and reduction are measured using two variables. One is the frequency of retouched tools relative to unmodified but potentially usable flakes (> 2.0 cm in length), a measure that has been employed in other studies (e.g., Rolland 1981; Rolland and Dibble 1990). The other is an experimentally derived index of scraper reduction developed by Kuhn (1990b). This index monitors how much of a tool blank has been removed by previous retouch, based on the angle of the retouched edge and the extension of retouch scars relative to the medial thickness of the blank.

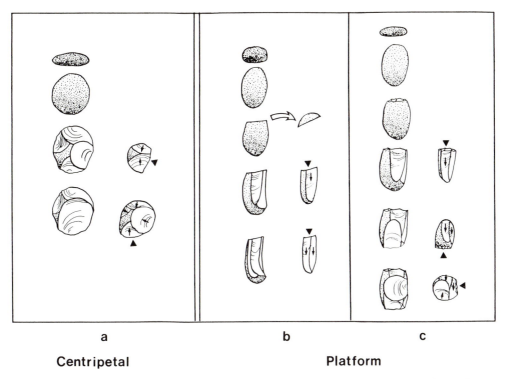

a   b   c

Centripetal   **Platform**

Figure 14.1 Schematized (a) centripetal and (b, c) platform core reduction techniques. (From Stiner and Kuhn 1992)

The analyses of core reduction techniques use a different approach and require more detailed explanation. Two techniques for making flakes and tool blanks, here termed *centripetal* and *platform* core reduction (Figure 14.1), were very important in the Pontinian Mousterian. There are, of course, numerous variations on the two basic ways of producing flakes from pebble cores, and they may sometimes overlap (e.g., Bietti et al. 1989; Kuhn 1990a; Laj-Pannocchia 1950). Nonetheless, there is ample reason to believe that these are distinct ways of exploiting raw material, as discussed below.

The centripetal technique, schematized in Figure 14.1a, is typical of the Mousterian in general (Bordes 1961b:26–27; Tixier et al. 1980:43), although many variants exist (e.g., Boëda 1986, 1988; Crew 1975; Geneste 1985). Centripetal core reduction in west-central Italy involved striking flakes from around the perimeter of a flat round pebble, gradually spiraling toward the center by rotating the core with each new blow. For the purpose of this study, evidence of Levallois technique with centripetal core preparation (represented largely by atypical products) is combined with more generalized centripetal reduction.

Platform core reduction techniques (schematized in Figure 14.1b,c) differed from centripetal techniques in that flakes were removed parallel to the long axis of a core from a striking platform, or from two opposing platforms located at the end(s) of the piece. Occasionally one or two flakes were also struck from the side of a core as it neared the end of its useful life (Figure 14.1c). These platform core techniques are similar but not identical to classic prismatic blade core techniques of the Upper Paleolithic. However, the Mousterian versions are decidedly less complex, beginning only with platform preparation at one or both ends of a pebble. The crested blade technique, in which a ridge is created along the length of the core to guide the initial removals, was not employed in the Pontinian Mousterian. Moreover, flakes detached from Pontinian platform cores rarely can be classified as blades, primarily because small pebbles make it very diffi-

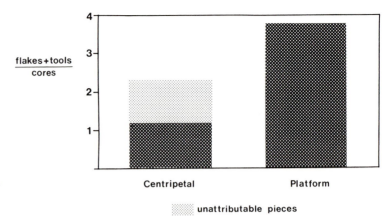

Figure 14.2 Comparison of the relative efficiencies (flakes + tools/cores) of centripetal and platform reduction techniques in Mousterian lithic assemblages. (From Stiner and Kuhn 1992)

cult to manufacture usable flakes that are twice as long as they are wide.

Hominids' use of different core reduction techniques is inferred from the orientations of flake scars both on cores and on the dorsal faces of many flakes and tools. Flakes produced from centripetal cores tend to exhibit dorsal scars originating from several directions, often orthogonal to one another (Figure 14.1a). In contrast, flakes detached from platform cores generally have dorsal scars running parallel to one another along the long axis of the flake (Figure 14.1b,c): when pebbles are used, flakes often retain remnant cortex along one edge.[15]

The two basic core reduction techniques, platform and centripetal, have somewhat different economic properties. Platform core reduction appears to maximize the *number* of flakes produced per pebble core, while centripetal techniques maximize the *sizes* of flakes and tool blanks. To illustrate this difference, Figure 14.2 compares the number of large flakes and tools attributable to each technique relative to the number of cores in the total Mousterian sample. The ratio of flakes and tools to cores is much higher for the platform reduction technique; even when all of the unattributed pieces (specimens that cannot be assigned to any mode of manufacture) are added to the identifiable products of centripetal reduction, the ratio of flakes and tools per core is still much lower than that for platform cores. On the other hand, the flakes produced via centripetal core reduction techniques tend to be larger in the Italian study sample, with more sharp edge per piece than those made from platform cores. The flakes and blanks attributed to centripetal reduction are approximately 25 percent longer in maximum dimension and roughly 1.5 to 2 times larger in plan view area than those attributed to platform cores (Kuhn 1990a:226). It should be noted that the proportions of total products that can be reliably attributed to either basic technique may vary, so that the actual contrasts in productivity may have been somewhat less marked (Kuhn 1990a:232).

VARIATION IN THE FAUNAS

In the following discussion, twelve hominid-generated faunal assemblages are arranged in chronological order to illustrate patterns of change over time. Assemblages at the early (M4, M3, G2, and

[15] The core reduction schemes represent idealized models of two basic tactics for taking apart a piece of stone. In reality, a single core can change form in the course of its useful life, although the small raw materials available to hominids in the study area probably limited the overall extent of these transformations. It is clear in some cases that platform cores were modified into something like centripetal cores near the end of the reduction sequence (Bietti et al. 1989), as observed in Mousterian industries from other regions (e.g., Baumler 1988). However, by examining variation in the frequencies of both cores and the flakes or tools made from them, it is possible to control for the kinds of flake production techniques used before cores reached a state of exhaustion and were discarded.

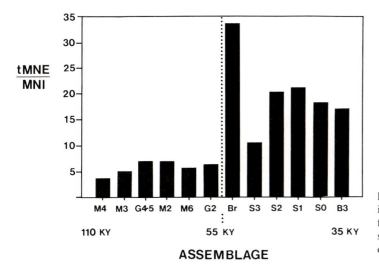

Figure 14.3 Anatomical completeness index values (tMNE/MNI) for red and fallow deer in Mousterian faunal assemblages, arranged in chronological order. (From Stiner and Kuhn 1992)

G5–4) and late (S1–3, B3/4) ends of the sequence are dated by ESR and U-series methods, whereas four assemblages in the middle (M2, M6, S0, and Br) are ranked on the basis of stratigraphic criteria only. Because we want to consider both radio-metrically dated and stratigraphically ordered assemblages, and because the ESR dating technique remains somewhat experimental (Grün 1988), the chronological sequence is treated as a simple rank ordering. For ease of discussion, the assemblages are often referred to as dating before or after 55,000 B.P., the boundary of which is marked on the bar graphs.

Figure 14.3 shows a trend in the average amount of transported food returns per red and fallow deer carcass, using the bone-based ratio of anatomical completeness (tMNE/MNI). In the earlier half of the chronological scale, the quantity of bony parts carried to shelters by hominids per procurement event is relatively low. The values increase significantly toward the more recent end of the scale. The changes appear gradual overall, although a sharp increase may be indicated around the 55,000-year boundary.

The second trend, shown in Figure 14.4, traces changes in the proportion of deer head parts to limb

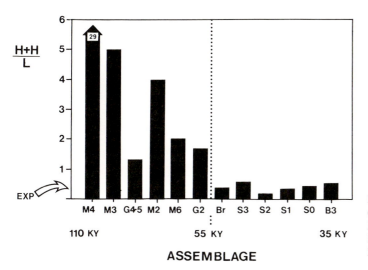

Figure 14.4 Ratios of head to limb parts ([H + H]/L) for red and fallow deer in Mousterian faunal assemblages arranged in chronological order. (From Stiner and Kuhn 1992)

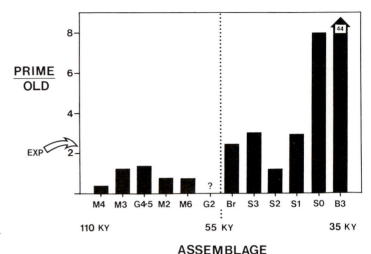

Figure 14.5 Ratios of prime-aged to old-aged adult (PRIME/OLD) red and fallow deer in Mousterian faunal assemblages arranged in chronological order. (From Stiner and Kuhn 1992)

parts transported to the caves by hominids, using the (H + H)/L ratio based on bone. The expected balanced value for the complete deer skeleton (0.30) is indicated on the vertical axis. Head parts are extraordinarily abundant relative to limbs in assemblages dating to before 55,000 years ago. The ratio declines gradually early on and then stabilizes around the expected value for relatively complete prey.

A third trend (Figure 14.5) in the study area is found in the mortality patterns for deer, based on tooth eruption and wear. The expected value shown on the y-axis (PRIME/OLD = 2.14) refers to the ratio of prime-aged to old-aged adults in an idealized, stable live prey population (from Chapter 11). The expected value on the graph would represent nonselective harvesting by hominids, regardless of just how the animals were obtained. Deer mortality patterns are significantly biased toward old-aged prey in all cases dating to before 55,000 B.P., and the bias lies well outside the range of normal variation displayed by living populations. The cases dating to just after 55,000 show essentially nonselective procurement, while values for the most recent Mousterian assemblages (about 40,000–35,000 B.P.) are strongly biased toward prime adult prey. The prime-dominant cases exceed the range encompassed by normal variation in the structures of natural living populations, even when phases of growth and decline are taken into account.

Rank order correlations (Spearman's r_s) of the three ratios against chronological rankings evaluate the statistical significance of the trends within the confines of this study sample. Two alternative chronological rankings are used. Table 14.1a lists correlation coefficients for all dated and undated assemblages. Variation in each of the three faunal ratios is highly correlated with assemblage age at the .01 level of probability. Not all assemblages could be dated by radiometric techniques, however, and proper chronological ordering is important to any conclusion regarding trends in the data. In order to check this problem, Table 14.1b lists correlation

TABLE 14.1

Spearman rank order correlation (r_s) of faunal variables against increasing assemblage age

a. All assemblages

Faunal variable	N	r_s	P
tMNE/MNI	12	−0.744	< .01
(H + H)/L	12	0.818	< .01
PRIME/OLD	11	−0.773	< .01

b. Radiometrically dated assemblages only (excludes M2, M6, S0, and Br)

Faunal variable	N	r_s	P
tMNE/MNI	8	−0.714	= .05
(H + H)/L	8	0.881	< .01
PRIME/OLD	7	−0.905	< .01

Note: Values of r_s indicate correlations with increasing age.

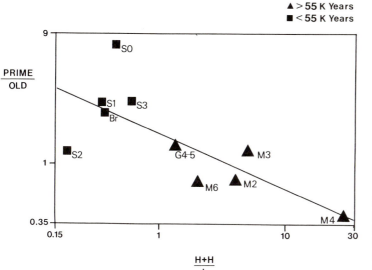

▲ > 55 K Years
■ < 55 K Years

Figure 14.6 Log-log regression of (H + H)/L based on bone data, and PRIME/OLD mortality based on tooth data for red and fallow deer in Mousterian faunal assemblages. (From Stiner and Kuhn 1992)

coefficients for radiometrically dated assemblages only, therefore excluding M2, M6, S0, and Br. Correlations remain significant for this subset, although the value for tMNE/MNI drops to the .05 level of probability.

The relationship between two of the faunal ratios, (H + H)/L and PRIME/OLD, is evaluated another way in Figure 14.6. A log-log regression of the ratios documents a strong negative relationship between the occurrence of head biases and prime-aged prey ($r = -.733, r^2 = .54, .02 < P < .01, N = 10$). Because the first variable is based exclusively on bone material, whereas the second is based exclusively on more resistant tooth material, the comparison serves as a partial check against possible biases created by differential preservation among skeletal tissue classes. Bones and teeth tell similar stories about the context in which food was obtained. The B3[/4] assemblage from Breuil is an outlier to the graph and, while not included in the regression calculation, falls at the appropriate extreme of the differences as described. The case from G2 of Guattari is excluded from consideration because of insufficient age data and because its taphonomic origin is more ambiguous than all of the other cases (see Chapters 4 and 5). The assemblages align in a manner consistent with the general chronological order defined previously, although cases dating after 55,000 display less variation on the anatomical axis

([H + H]/L); in fact, one might simply divide them into two categories on the basis of this graph.

To summarize, low returns for transported food (low tMNE/MNI values) and head-dominated anatomical patterns (high [H + H]/L values) in the earlier Mousterian faunas from Moscerini and Guattari indicate a heavy reliance on nonconfrontational scavenging of deer carcasses. Conversely, higher transported returns and higher (balanced) frequencies of limb to head elements in the later Mousterian faunas from Sant'Agostino and Breuil indicate a strong emphasis on hunting of the same prey species. Variation in the PRIME/OLD mortality ratio likewise points to differing reliance on scavenging (old-biased) and hunting (prime-dominant patterns) by hominids at the respective pairs of cave sites.

Some additional features of the Mousterian faunas are of interest with regard to the local trends illustrated here, as well as to the discussions that follow. Data on juvenile tooth eruption and wear and the absence of antler suggest that Mousterian occupations dating before 55,000 years ago may have centered on spring and/or early summer, although they probably were not restricted to these seasons (Chapter 13). Later assemblages from Sant'Agostino and Breuil more clearly represent fall through late winter occupations. The seasonality data are subject to considerable error, for reasons of sampling, latitude, and environment.

These results nonetheless introduce the strong possibility that seasonal factors (as opposed to diachronic changes) explain some of the differences among the faunas, although it must also be recognized that each site represents thousands of years of debris accumulation.

In marked contrast to other properties of the Mousterian faunas, the arrays and relative frequencies of mammalian species consumed by hominids did not differ significantly among sites or within the overall sequence (Chapter 7). Moreover, a variety of statistical analyses reveal no significant differences in the relative dietary emphases on mammalian species consumed at caves by Middle Paleolithic hominids, spotted hyaenas, and late Upper Paleolithic humans in this region of Italy. Small-scale exploitation of marine shellfish and aquatic tortoises by hominids is evidenced in the pre-55,000 B.P. assemblages of Moscerini, but not at the other three caves (Chapter 6). Shellfish and tortoise remains occur in general association with (inferred) scavenging of ungulates, but the relative frequencies of shells and mammal bones do not predict one another very well within the thirty fine layers of this cave.

VARIATION IN TECHNOLOGY

The strongest patterns of technological variation among the Mousterian lithic assemblages involve the use of different core reduction techniques. Figure 14.7A compares the ratios of platform cores to centripetal cores in the subject assemblages; Figure 14.7B shows the ratios of the tools and flakes attributable to these two different reduction tactics. It is clear that the use of platform core techniques increased over time in the Pontinian sites at the expense of centripetal core reduction. It is less certain whether the trend observed in the study area represents a gradual versus sudden increase in the use of platform core techniques after 55,000 B.P.

Figure 14.7 also shows that core reduction techniques varied from site to site, as well as through time. Since the two basic techniques would be more conveniently practiced using different pebble shapes (see Figure 14.1), it could be suggested that the observed variation might simply represent a highly expedient response by hominids to the shapes of pebbles available in the immediate vicinity of each shelter. Alternatively, because platform cores appear to yield more flakes per core, it is conceivable that this technique could have been used preferentially at sites where pebbles were relatively scarce. Neither of these explanations holds, however. Raw material qualities certainly influenced many of the general characteristics of the Pontinian assemblages, particularly tool sizes (Bordes 1968:119; Taschini 1970:70–74). The proximity of raw material sources also seems to have determined the extent to which cores were used up, regardless of which technique was more common (Kuhn 1991). However, studies of interassemblage variation in the frequencies of different kinds of flakes and cores indicate that local variation in the shapes and/or abundances of raw materials *does not* account for variation in the frequencies of the alternative core reduction techniques independently of the time element (Kuhn 1990a:436–439).

Changes over time in tactics of flake and tool manufacture in coastal west-central Italy were accompanied by declines in both the overall intensity of raw material exploitation and the extent to which individual tools were used up. There is a marked decrease through time in the frequencies of retouch on flakes and blanks larger than 2 cm in maximum dimension (Figure 14.8). The median reduction index values for single-edged tools also decrease with time (Figure 14.9), indicating that tools were resharpened less often in the later assemblages. Since sediments were screened even in the first major excavations undertaken at these sites, variation in the frequencies of unretouched flakes (all larger than 2 cm) is not due to differential recovery. Nor can this pattern be attributed to differences in the availability of lithic raw materials from one cave to the next; assemblages from the site located closest to a source of pebbles (Guattari) exhibit relatively high frequencies of retouch and high levels of scraper reduction. Hominids' technological responses clearly were keyed to something else in their economies.

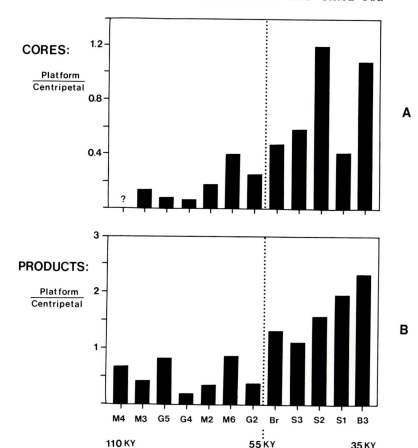

CORES:

$\dfrac{\text{Platform}}{\text{Centripetal}}$

A

PRODUCTS:

$\dfrac{\text{Platform}}{\text{Centripetal}}$

B

M4 M3 G5 G4 M2 M6 G2   Br S3 S2 S1 B3

110 KY   **55 KY**   **35 KY**

ASSEMBLAGE

Figure 14.7 Changing emphases on centripetal and platform reduction techniques in the Mousterian lithic assemblages, as measured by (A) core ratios and (B) ratios of core products; assemblages are arranged in chronological order. (From Stiner and Kuhn 1992)

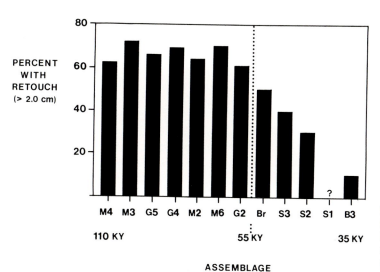

PERCENT WITH RETOUCH (> 2.0 cm)

M4 M3 G5 G4 M2 M6 G2   Br S3 S2 S1 B3

110 KY   **55 KY**   **35 KY**

ASSEMBLAGE

Figure 14.8 Frequencies of retouch on flakes and blanks larger than 2.0 cm in Mousterian lithic assemblages arranged in chronological order. (From Stiner and Kuhn 1992)

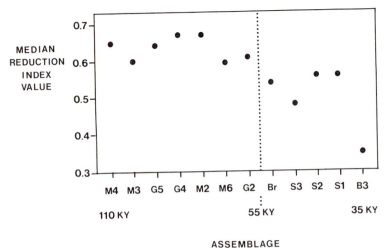

Figure 14.9 Median reduction index values for single-edged tools in Mousterian lithic assemblages arranged in chronological order. (From Stiner and Kuhn 1992)

Rank order correlations (Spearman's r_s) between each of the technological variables and assemblage age confirm the statistical significance of local trends in the lithic data. Table 14.2a lists correlation coefficients for dated and undated lithic assemblages, showing that four of the variables are highly correlated with time at the .01 level of probability. The coefficient for a fifth variable (percent without pebble cortex) is weaker, but still significant. Table 14.2b lists correlation coefficients for the dated assemblages only (excludes M2, M6, S0, and Br). The relationships of the five variables to time remain significant in spite of the smaller array of assemblages considered, although the probabilities drop to the .05 level for most.

Another, less clearly defined pattern in the lithic data deserves mention. The pebble raw materials used in the subject assemblages were transported by fluvial processes from a number of distant primary geological sources. Moreover, there is little indication at present that raw material characteristics or pebble forms vary predictably within the study area. This makes it difficult to obtain direct or exact measures of the distances artifacts were moved around the landscape. However, alternative analyses of variation in artifact sizes, raw material qualities, and the relative frequencies of flakes, tools, and cores suggest that the frequencies of artifacts transported from sources of larger raw materials (either outside or within the coastal zone) decrease with time (Kuhn 1990a:325–330; 1991). Large sharp-

edged tools made on blanks from centripetal or Levallois cores appear to have been the items most frequently moved around the Pontinian area, as has been noted for some Mousterian cases elsewhere in Europe (e.g., Geneste 1989; Otte 1991).

In sum, changes through time in the use of centripetal versus platform core reduction techniques correspond to different artifact life histories in the Pontinian Mousterian. An emphasis on the produc-

TABLE 14.2

Spearman rank order correlation (r_s) of lithic technology variables against increasing assemblage age

a. All assemblages

Lithic variable	N	r_s	P
platform/centripetal cores	12	−0.769	< .01
platform/centripetal products	11	−0.882	< .01
% retouched pieces	11	0.800	< .01
% without pebble cortex	12	0.634	< .05
median reduction index	12	0.786	< .01

b. Radiometrically dated assemblages only (excludes M2, M6, S0, and Br)

Lithic variable	N	r_s	P
platform/centripetal cores	9	−0.733	< .05
platform/centripetal products	8	−0.786	< .05
% retouched pieces	8	0.833	< .01
% without pebble cortex	9	0.650	< .05
median reduction index	9	0.778	< .05

Note: Values of r_s indicate correlations with increasing age.

tion of relatively large flakes through centripetal core reduction in the earlier assemblages is associated with frequent retouch and fairly extensive use and renewal of tools. The emphasis on large flake production appears to associate with somewhat higher frequencies of transported artifacts as well.

The increasing use of more economical platform core techniques with time in west-central Italy is actually accompanied by less intensive exploitation of tools and flakes, and by declining frequencies of transported or exotic artifacts (Kuhn 1990a:325–330).

THE CONNECTIONS BETWEEN SUBSISTENCE AND TECHNOLOGY

The ways that Mousterian hominids made and used stone tools at the four caves covaried with marked differences in animal exploitation, and significant time-trends are documented for both data sets within the confines of the Latium study area. Shifts in animal procurement and use are somewhat more striking and appear more continuous than the technological shifts. The parallel trends and their behavioral implications are best summarized by comparing assemblages deposited before and after the 55,000-year juncture.

The older group of assemblages suggests procurement of ungulates largely by nonconfrontational scavenging, as suggested by old-biased mortality patterns and selective transport of head parts to shelters. All cavities of the head bone elements had been opened while fresh to extract their contents. Ungulate procurement activities appear to have centered on spring, although they probably were not entirely confined to that season. Head collecting is also associated with evidence of low-level but persistent exploitation of marine shellfish and aquatic tortoises at Moscerini. Relatively large tools and flakes produced via centripetal core reduction techniques are more common in the associated industries, and lithic artifacts exhibit evidence of more intense, prolonged use and greater frequencies of transport. The overall picture is one of frequent movement and relatively ephemeral occupations by the hominids.

The faunas dating after 55,000 years ago are very different from the older ones. Ungulate mortality patterns resemble either the structure of living prey populations or, more commonly, are biased in favor of prime-aged adults. Substantial quantities of food were transported to shelters from each carcass obtained, and the ungulate remains represent meaty or nearly complete arrays of body parts. All of the limb

bones were thoroughly processed for marrow, and soft tissues encased in the head bones were extracted as well. The characteristics of these faunas are entirely consistent with the expectations for procurement by hunting, as determined from the control studies; they resemble faunas from late Upper Paleolithic shelters of Latium. Harvesting began in fall and continued through winter. The associated lithic assemblages are dominated by platform core reduction techniques that yielded relatively large numbers of small flakes per core. The tools produced in these contexts were not modified or resharpened intensively, and there is comparatively little evidence that they were transported over long distances.

In contrast to our results on *technological* features of the Pontinian industries, there are no direct or obvious functional links between tool *types* or forms and subsistence in these Mousterian data. The vast majority of retouched tools in all assemblages are sidescrapers (primarily simple and transverse varieties)—unlikely candidates for food procurement implements. There are no statistically significant changes in the frequencies of putative points, in spite of the apparently different emphases on hunting among the assemblages: if anything, the frequencies of pointed retouched and unretouched objects actually decline over time. Instead, we find strong correspondences between foraging strategies and the life histories of artifacts. We would argue that the patterns of covariation express the influence of differing patterns or scales of mobility and land use, revolving around how hominids searched for resources in space within and across years. Shifts in the frequency of residential movement and duration of particular occupations would have resulted in changing constraints over where and when lithic raw materials could be gathered and where tools could be made and maintained. The advantages of alternative tactics of tool manufacture and renewal would vary accordingly.

Nonconfrontational scavenging, evident in the earlier Mousterian faunas, is normally a strategy that targets relatively dispersed resources and tends to yield lower transportable returns on the average (see discussion in Chapter 8). It is more like gathering than hunting, in both energetic returns and the ranging patterns that may be required; such scavenging implies more frequent movement and perhaps wide-ranging search patterns on the part of hominids, regardless of whether scavenging opportunities were actively sought or (more likely) merely taken advantage of when encountered. It seems no coincidence that nonconfrontational scavenging of ungulate parts occurs alongside collection of small, more or less sessile animals in at least one coastal Mousterian cave. An interest in scavenging probably did not drive hominids to expand their foraging radii, but because they were already ranging widely for some other energetic reason(s), this kind of scavenging was both feasible and rewarding. Centripetal core reduction would have been advantageous in the context of relatively extensive foraging, because it produces larger flakes and tool blanks suitable for prolonged use in a raw material-poor environment, as evidence of tool reduction and transport indeed suggest. Prolonging the potential use life of tools through persistent reduction or re-sharpening is, in turn, a way of coping with uncertainties about just when the tools will be needed as opposed to when and where the next chance to make new tools will arise.

Evidence for hunting in the later Mousterian assemblages includes far richer transported returns per procurement event and may imply targeting relatively concentrated food patches. After all, deer and most other ungulate species tend to congregate while alive, especially in fall and early winter, whereas carcasses generally do not do so of their own accord. Moreover, the nearly complete arrays of anatomical elements indicate minimal levels of selective discard of less economic body parts prior to reaching the shelters. More restricted ranging for food and longer occupations provisioned with hunted meat would have made it less important to produce the largest, most durable flakes from pebble cores. Hominids instead made greater numbers of relatively small tools destined for light use and little transport. Processing of hunted game, which certainly took place at the later Mousterian shelters, may also have set a premium on unmodified or lightly retouched edges suitable for cutting animal tissues. Thus, in the Pontinian Mousterian, bigger tools and tool blanks were selected only when people needed things to last, such as when they had to carry tools around for extended periods and the actual moments of need were unpredictable.

ACCUMULATION RATES OF BONES VERSUS STONES

Information on the varying rates at which bones and stones accumulated in strata of the four caves lends additional perspective on the relationship between animal exploitation and technology. We assume that the *total* frequencies of both kinds of materials in the cultural deposits are largely a consequence of two conditions: (1) the frequency or intensity of hominid use of the cave sites; and (2) the volume of sediment excavated. The relative amounts of bones and stones among strata should, on the other hand, relate in some way to the economic relationship between them independently of sedimentation rates. Recall that the confounding influences of bone preservation were considered in advance and were not found to be sufficiently great to prohibit this kind of comparison (Chapters 5 and 9).

If the main differences between accumulation rates of bones and stones before and after 55,000 B.P were tied to the relative incidence of hunting versus scavenging, we would expect their relative frequencies to show positive correlations but different slopes, in accordance with time period. This is because scavenging of ungulates by itself (i.e., without plant and/or small animal supplements) should not operate at a loss, but would tend to offer fewer transportable parts than hunted sources.

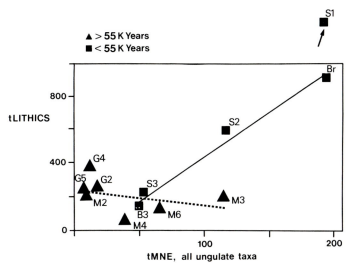

Figure 14.10 Scatter plot and regressions for combined ungulate tMNE (cervids, bovids, and equids) and the frequency of lithic artifacts (tLITHICS = tools + flakes + cores) for Mousterian assemblages before (dashed line) and after (solid line) 55,000 years ago. (From Stiner and Kuhn 1992)

Figure 14.10 plots the total frequencies of Mousterian stone tools, flakes, and cores (tLITHICS) against the total number of bones (tMNE) for all ungulate species (bovids, equids, and cervids) in each assemblage. Triangles represent the earlier Mousterian cases from Moscerini (level groups M2, M3, M4, and M6) and Guattari (G2, G4, and G5), dating between 110,000 and 55,000 years ago. Squares represent later cases from Breuil (Br and B3/4) and Sant'Agostino (S1, S2, and S3), dating between 55,000 and 35,000 years ago. It is immediately clear from the graph that the relationship between faunal and lithic abundances is not the same for the two groups of assemblages. The correlation between tMNE and tLITHICS for the earlier group is not statistically significant ($r^2 = 0.084$, $P = .577$, N = 7), indicating that the quantities of stones and ungulate bones vary more or less independently of one another. In other words, hominids' use of stone at these caves is not directly explained or predicted by their use of ungulate resources. To the extent that there is any relationship, however, it appears to be negative (dashed regression line), hinting at the existence of some component of subsistence not directly monitored by the data on large mammal remains.

In contrast to the earlier group, bones and stones occur in roughly equal proportions in the younger Mousterian assemblages. These cases display a strong positive relationship (solid regression line) between tMNE and tLITHICS ($r^2 = .986$, $P = .007$, N = 5). The S1 assemblage is much larger than the others, representing an outlier to the graph, but it is consistent with the general relationship as described. The strong positive relationship for this later group of assemblages suggests that lithic material cycled through the system more or less in tandem with the number of ungulate body parts brought to the shelters by the hominids.

The frequencies of faunal and lithic debris suggest that, prior to 55,000 B.P., the amount of tool making that went on in the Italian caves did not depend on success in obtaining scavenged ungulate parts. While conspicuous from an archaeological perspective, scavenging may have in fact been ancillary to subsistence activities at Moscerini and Guattari. It more likely was integrated within a wide-ranging foraging pattern that actually focused on a variety of dispersed sessile resources, including small quantities of marine shellfish, tortoises, and probably vegetable foods. In contrast, the amount of technological activity represented in the later assemblages *was* responsive to the quantities of ungulate parts procured and subsequently carried to the shelters. Hunted game may actually have been central to subsistence during occupations at Sant'Agostino and Breuil, and the duration of occupations may well have been determined directly by the amount of meat procured.

What Do Hunters Need in Order to Succeed?

The range of formal tool types (as opposed to reduction techniques) in the Mousterian sample stays about the same across the 55,000-year boundary, while subsistence strategies appear to change radically. Why is there not an equally drastic change in the kinds of tools being produced, either in the weapons for dispatching animals or in the implements used to make weapons? We are not in a position to completely answer this question, but recent work shows that increasing sophistication of formal weapons used by modern human hunters and hunting success (as measured by prey nutritional returns, age classes taken, etc.) vary somewhat independently of one another. Human hunters are not entirely weapon-dependent; they are only partly so. There is no question that weapons can facilitate the food quest, but there is more than one solution for maintaining regular access to high-quality live prey. Prey selection and getting enough to eat are products of a complex interplay between the technological system in use, demography-mediated possibilities for human cooperation during procurement and subsequent tasks, and species- and seasonal-specific behaviors of the animals pursued (see Chapter 11; also Binford 1978; Frison 1991; Hudson 1991; Lyman 1991a).

In the survey of ethnohistorical and archaeological cases presented in Chapter 11, I document analogous patterns of ungulate prey age selection by anatomically modern humans across a diverse array of technological systems and environments. Prey age selection is an important diagnostic of predator-prey relationships, implying hunting success only in broad ecological terms. Alvard and Kaplan (1991) compare prey age and sex selection of terrestrial and arboreal species by modern native hunters in a Peruvian rain forest, finding that greater levels of cooperation among bow-hunters can effectively substitute for the advantages conferred by long-range weapons, such as shotguns. Of course, neither bows nor shotguns would have existed in Middle Paleolithic times. But if cooperation can in any way substitute for the advantages that sophisticated modern weapons offer, then we are obliged to allow for the possibility that cooperation among Mousterian foragers (who created modern-looking prey mortality patterns in some sites without the benefit of stone-tipped weapons) worked in basically the same way.

Finding evidence of increasing emphases on hunted prey in the Mousterian, including prime adult harvesting, need not demand a corresponding increase in the quantity of stone weapon heads produced nor an increasing sophistication in the types of weapons used. It could happen, but it does not have to happen, because many potential advantages provided by technology in the capture of game overlap with those afforded by social cooperation. More than any other period in prehistory, the Middle Paleolithic (and Middle Stone Age) seems to illuminate a substantial blind spot in archaeology, lying just between the specialties of zooarchaeology and technology research as currently practiced.

Conclusion

The faunal and technological patterns described above involve a set of variables that are demonstrably relevant to how hominids used resources. The faunal variables were chosen based on cross-species surveys of modern (human and nonhuman) predators, and the technological variables were selected based on expectations about how technology should relate to human foraging practices. The approach reveals considerable variation in the manufacture and use of stone tools in Pontinian Mousterian assemblages, primarily concerning raw material economy, which closely paralleled shifts in game use, especially patterns of prey age selection and body part transport. Such variation exists within an archaeological record that, from the classical perspectives of tool typologies and species representation, is quite monotonous.

It is clear that some facts about the Middle Paleolithic can only be understood through simultaneous consideration of zooarchaeological and technological evidence at the intersite level of comparison. In research on the Italian Middle Paleolithic, collaboration reveals several important things about the relation between Mousterian technology and subsistence practices that may be summarized as follows:

1. Strong covariation exists between artifact (core and tool) life histories and basic classes of hominid foraging strategies (hunting and nonconfrontational scavenging).
2. In situations that apparently involved scavenging, Mousterian hominids preferred to transport heads (but not many other ungulate parts) back to shelters. This relatively strict choice was responsive to the unique nutritional assets offered by cranial soft tissues in times of fat/carbohydrate scarcity and, perhaps, the limitations set by extant processing technology during that cultural period.
3. There are no complete or absolutely necessary connections between many of the most obvious (i.e., visually striking) aspects of stone weapons technology and the relative dependence on hunted large prey, either in the Mousterian or in modern human situations.
4. Patterns in lithic technology and animal exploitation converge most clearly at the level of mobility and land use. More significant than any finding about hunters and scavengers is the spatial element implied by these data. Covariation observed between the lithic and faunal data sets appears to reflect how foragers used territory, the distribution of opportunities to collect or hunt various classes of resources, and ways of offsetting needs for key but sometimes scarce resources such as protein, animal fat, and workable stone.

All of the trends observed in the Middle Paleolithic of Latium represent shifts over time in the frequencies of various aspects of technology and foraging, not the appearance of entirely new components of behavior. For example, evidence of both centripetal core reduction and platform core reduction are present throughout the Pontinian sequence; platform core reduction simply overtakes centripetal techniques with time. This is argued to be an adjustment of tool manufacture to the requirements and limitations of foraging and land use, an adaptive frequency shift within an extant range of alternatives. The same must be said for scavenging and hunting. Mousterian scavenging practices appear

odd in light of what modern humans do, but there is no reason to assume that Mousterians never scavenged after 55,000 years ago, or never hunted before this time.

Within the geographical limits imposed by the study sample, the observed trends in foraging and technology nonetheless appear somewhat "progressive." Scavenging appears to be replaced by hunting, and classic Mousterian centripetal reduction techniques are superseded by single- and double-platform approaches reminiscent of Upper Paleolithic blade core reduction techniques. However, two more general issues must now be considered in order to properly qualify these observations: the overall pace of the local trends, and the risk of accepting what is in fact a teleological rather than evolutionary explanation of change.

First, is the variation really continuous through time, or is the shift very abrupt? Figure 14.6, which combines two important dimensions of the faunal variation, separates the Mousterian assemblages into two more or less discrete sets, thereby undermining the possibility of a smooth or simple trend. That the faunal patterns and the technological patterns closely parallel one another (and both appear to change fairly abruptly across the 55,000-year boundary) is actually more suggestive of two distinct sets of behaviors or foraging modes, not necessarily evolution within the Mousterian per se. Discrete foraging or searching modes might be the very thing to expect within one subsistence system of any complex predator. The only substantive contradiction to wholesale acceptance of the latter explanation is to be found in the mortality data.

Second, the fact that the observed changes within the Italian Mousterian appear to point to a stereotypically modern pattern does not in itself constitute an explanation. The technological changes may indeed represent responses to alterations in foraging patterns, but the ultimate causes of long-term variation in subsistence remain unclear. If variation is the medium upon which natural selection operates—as, indeed, we think it is—then we can expect to see numerous glimmerings of "modern" behavior in the Middle Paleolithic without all of them being directly ancestral to the modern behavioral package. Nor, if evolution could start over again, should the outcome of this process be exactly the same every time. The local trends in the Mousterian might represent a permanent (evolutionary) shift in hominid foraging niche *within* the Mousterian, or they might simply reflect changes in how these particular cave sites were used and some of the behavioral raw material already in existence in archaic humans more generally. Oscillations in sea level between 120,000 and 35,000 years ago certainly altered the setting of each shelter and probably its utility to hominid foragers. During warm climate phases, all of the caves would have been situated quite close to the beach just as they are now, whereas in colder periods they would have been separated from the sea by ribbons of dunes, coastal plains, and/or small marshy lagoons. These questions are considered in the final chapter of this book.

15

Neandertal Niche

I WAS TRAINED to think of Neandertals as strikingly different from anatomically modern humans, in both their anatomy and their behavior. The design of this research consequently is antithetical to that view of Neandertal behavioral ecology in that it works from null hypotheses stating that there was no difference. Because the background for the comparisons of human subspecies is based on *interspecific* differences between nonhuman predators, the *no difference* position is especially tough to refute. A wide variety of analyses have been brought to bear on questions like "Were Neandertals people like us?" and "Did Mousterians occupy an ecological niche analogous to those of modern hunter-gatherers?" The answers are largely negative: the order of difference between Middle Paleolithic hominids and all humans from the late Upper Paleolithic onward is significant when measured against the differences that normally separate sympatric nonhuman predators, probably indicating greater specialization within hunting practices over time. The range of resource and land use tactics used by Mousterians overlaps and surpasses that of anatomically modern humans living in generally similar ecosystems. Of course, the time frame of the Mousterian sample (120,000–35,000) is much longer than that of the late Upper Paleolithic (20,000–10,000), leaving more time for inevitable restructuring of local habitats and foragers' adjustments to them, but there is more to the discrepancies observed between the two cultural periods in west-central Italy.

Neandertals have often been depicted as the one-trick ponies among *Homo sapiens,* sometimes by researchers who agree on little else. Contra the stereotype, this study shows that Mousterian foraging practices, technology, and use of places were quite flexible, varying greatly from shelter to shelter and across large spans of time. But how does this variation contrast with Upper Paleolithic and modern hunter-gatherers from a cross-cultural perspective? The final chapter of this book is about what I think the Italian data in Neandertal niche mean with regard to human evolution. I have been cautious in analyzing the Middle Paleolithic cases, and I remain cautious about what the data imply about the evolutionary status of the Neandertals. However, such a stance contributes little if held strictly for its own sake, and, after several hundred pages of analyses, a synthetic interpretation fit for another generation of testing is in order.

The zooarchaeological data indicate that Mousterian foraging practices in west-central Italy were structured differently from those of fully modern humans—at least from those populations living after about 20,000 B.P. Some overlap is apparent between Mousterian and later human foraging practices, but the patterns and the scales of their responses to resource availability were not wholly equivalent. Mousterian people were competent hunters of small, medium, and large ungulates but at times turned to very different foraging agendas while using coastal caves in Latium, scavenging the very same kinds of ungulates they hunted elsewhere in addition to collecting shellfish and tortoises. If Mousterian foraging practices were to be considered in isolation, or, worse, on the basis of one or a few assemblages, there would be either no case for ecological difference from Upper Paleolithic humans or, by chance of the draw, evidence for a complete lack of overlap. There can be little doubt that both varieties of hominid hunted, gathered, and sometimes scavenged for food. Both kinds of hominid focused on prey species that were common in the environment, and they used many of the same basic techniques for making tools and cutting edges from stone. There is nothing ecologically or economically extraordinary about these simple resemblances, however. Setting Mousterian and late Upper Paleolithic (and more recent) peoples apart were the ways that resource use tactics were employed and recombined *across* their territories, and also the geographical scale at which these differences were played out.

The contrasts between Mousterian resource niche and that of later humans are evident from several dimensions of behavior, including the methods for searching for food, the ungulate age groups procured and body parts transported, small animal exploitation, seasonal responses to food supply, and technology. Some remarkably strong economic parallels existed between Mousterian technology and foraging in Latium. The technological correspondences are not apparent in the use of formal tools, but instead are seen in the strategies of tool and blank production and artifact "life histories." The lithic data demonstrate that Mousterian strategies were practiced on a different geographic scale in the study area than were those of the late Upper Paleolithic. Both variants of *H. sapiens* certainly lived in mobile groups, but Mousterian responses to resource opportunities appear to have been governed more by local, or otherwise immediate, exigencies.

Much of the variation in the Italian Middle Paleolithic (here synonymous with Mousterian) may be about opportunism tuned to a finer spatial scale than was true of late Upper Paleolithic foragers. The Mousterian differs from the Upper Paleolithic in Italy, but the Mousterian itself incorporates many differences from cave site to cave site. Much of the latter appears to represent tactical variation describing the behavioral repertoire of one adaptive system; the variation in Mousterian behavior is manifest as responses to the restructuring of coastal habitats and foraging opportunities in this area over a long time—some 80,000 years. Although the trends in technology and game use in the Latium Mousterian are verified statistically (Chapter 14), they are local phenomena with the notable exception of the prime adult harvesting focus in ungulate

hunting. Most dimensions of the faunal and technological data divide into two relatively distinct groups of cases, corresponding to hunting and scavenging activities in the coastal area. They are most easily explained by deteriorating climate, especially after 55,000 years ago, based on more open-land floras in local pollen records (Follieri et al. 1988; Frank 1969) and an overall decline in sea level that left the caves more inland than before.

Not every aspect of the variation observed in the Italian Mousterian can be explained by local changes in foraging opportunities, however. When the Italian data are compared to a wider array of modern human and carnivore cases, a trend toward increasing foraging specialization in the hominid niche is also suggested. This trend concerns only changes in ambush hunting of ungulate prey, and is *not* apparent from the prey species consumed (Chapter 7) nor directly from the seasonality data (Chapter 13). With time, humans increasingly emphasized prime adult prey in the context of ambush hunting and their long-term impact on prey populations diverged from all other predators as a result (Chapter 11). Greater specialization in humans may also be evident from ungulate body part transport patterns (Chapter 9), but the anatomical data are less clear on this point. The emphasis on prime adult ungulate prey was an ecologically unique, *species-wide* development in the human predatory niche, and there appears to have been a rapid shift in this direction within the late Middle Paleolithic in west-central Italy. Niche theory predicts that a late-coming species to an established predator guild will tend to shape its habits around the niches already present and, for this reason, may tend to become relatively specialized in one dimension or another. The archaeological data appear to uphold this prediction, with the unexpected result that the shift begins *within* the Mousterian (see below), not with its conclusion. Specialization is, of course, a phenomenon of many potential dimensions, and the trend noted here is merely confined to one or two dimensions of predatory behavior in the context of ungulate hunting.

A plain yet compelling fact rises from this research about scales of observation in zooarchaeology and their relationships to questions about human behavior, human niche, and human evolution.

The differences between subspecies of *Homo sapiens* perceived in this study clearly hinge upon the scale at which the data are viewed: the contrasts move in and out of focus according to, for example, the geographic level of consideration and how the data are partitioned in time. I would never have seen the variation in the Latium Mousterian had I not looked at several cave sites at once. The point about scale also applies to archaeologists perceptions of behavioral tactics: Mousterians appear as hunters at some places and as scavengers and gatherers at others. If these things are true in Italy, then they could be equally true elsewhere in the range of the Neandertals and other archaic *H. sapiens*. One simply cannot expect to arrive at ecological or evolutionary conclusions about humans by studying one archaeological site, much less one or a few strata therein.

The results on Mousterian game use and technology beg a deeper understanding of space-dependent and time-dependent phenomena in human adaptations. No finished answers on this issue yet emerge, but the Latium case clearly points to patterns of territory use as central organizational differences between the two Paleolithic periods. This realization comes by virtue of working in a geographically delimited area, the dimensions of which were defined not least by good luck. Time is more difficult to deal with in archaeology as a rule, and preordained chronologies do not necessarily make the job easier. When the culture periods are compared as bulk temporal units within the traditional chronology, differences are bound to emerge because the conditions of life have shifted and/or evolutionary change has occurred. Such observations say nothing about the possible existence and character of variation therein, because the data are not partitioned in a way that could reveal these kinds of facts.

That the Mousterian as a whole differs from later human patterns is clear and represents one of the foremost conclusions of this research, but a shift toward the "modern" pattern before 35,000 years ago, before the end of the Middle Paleolithic as currently defined, naturally raises the question of whether any trend in the data represents evolutionary change or simply bipartite (or continuous) variation within a single system. It is fascinating that, in the current milieu of argumentation, one could come close to playing most published data on the Paleolithic either way. Few independent footings exist for measuring or interpreting change, because archaeology takes its name strictly from the study of ancient human cultures. If it is possible to argue two very different points of view from the same bodies of information and thereby gain a sizable and loyal audience, then chances are that the measures of difference lack a firm footing in reality, or, at the very least, focus too much upon what is unique to humans; either way, something is wrong with the questions being asked of the data. For these reasons, some of the most important controls for interpreting zooarchaeological patterns come from outside the traditional boundaries of archaeology. As we focus more on problems of behavioral ecology of premodern hominids, so we come to depend on general ecological principles based on studies of other animals. Like every species on earth, humans are unique and, like every species, they resemble a variety of other taxa in at least a few important ways.

It is the interspecific perspective in this research, relating characteristics of faunal accumulations to basic and more pervasive categories of behavior in the animal kingdom, that makes the approach effective for addressing questions about evolutionary changes in the human predatory niche. Moreover, the investigations of bone and lithic raw material use emphasize economic variables whose ecological and evolutionary implications can be evaluated independently of the human situation. This research on the faunas breaks with zooarchaeologic tradition by considering nonhuman predators alongside humans, analyzed by the same methods and attention to detail, both in Pleistocene Italy and in modern ecosystems worldwide. The paleontological reality in Italy and elsewhere is that sympatric predators used many of the same caves as did Paleolithic hominids. The presence of carnivore records within archaeological sites is ordinarily treated as a source of disturbance to be isolated and eliminated. Yet coexistence was an essential part of hominid life, and to study hominids apart from the world that defined them closes many doors on ecological research on premodern *Homo*. While it is important to separate the effects of one agency from another in depositional sequences, these alternating records of human and carnivore occupants teach by virtue of the checkered histories they embody.

The sections below summarize the main results of this work, then unfold into a series of discussions on land use, technology and resource specialization, and the case for natural selection operating on a range of behavioral alternatives in hominid adaptations. The discussion ultimately turns to the much debated Middle-Upper Paleolithic transition in Eurasia. Granted, my study sample does not include the early Upper Paleolithic (circa 30,000–20,000). But the Latium data spring some surprises on the

transition problem anyway. There is evidence of greater resource specialization over time, for example, but not in the kinds of data (species profiles, seasonality) where it is commonly sought, nor in the period expected. While this study permits an evaluation of Neandertal resource niche in terms of human evolutionary history, it argues against concentrating on the Middle-Upper Paleolithic transition in particular, except to show that significant changes in human predatory behavior did not occur in concert with changes in human skeletal anatomy, material expressions of art and symbols, nor the most formalized elements of stone (or bone) technology.

FAUNAL RESULTS IN FIVE DIMENSIONS

The main results of the zooarchaeological analyses are summarized in five major dimensions as an initial step toward synthesis: (1) species data, (2) ungulate mortality patterns, (3) ungulate body part representation, (4) seasonality, and (5) small game use. Variation in these dimensions is considered primarily in terms of their extremes in Table 15.1.

Predator diets and predator guilds

Species abundance data provide two very important observations for this research on hominids and coexisting social predators. The first is that living species diversity in the west-central Italian ecosystem was relatively stable throughout the Upper Pleistocene (Chapter 4). The second is strong evidence that nearly all of the predators compared—Middle and late Upper Paleolithic hominids and spotted hyaenas —responded in the same way to standing species abundance in their choice of prey. The species data therefore reveal the general themes of coexistence and coevolution among humans and other predatory mammals. When it comes to diets, however, species consumed to not effectively distinguish predator adaptations across genera, and certainly not between subspecies of *Homo sapiens* (Chapter 7). The Italian wolves differed from the hominids and hyaenas because the data come strictly from denning contexts; wolves roaming at large would certainly show greater similarity to the other predators, just as they do today. Because hominids and hyaenas

(and probably wolves) in Latium consumed the same prey taxa in similar proportions, they were bound into a single resource guild centering on ungulate prey. Mousterian and late Upper Paleolithic peoples were thus subject to many of the same ecological constraints as other large predators in the study area.

Hominids' membership in this ungulate predator guild provides the all-important arena for comparisons of predatory niches. Trophically linked predators often share an interest in the same food species, but may reduce the risk of interspecific competition by exploiting them differently. Changes in Paleolithic hominid niche and subsistence adaptations must therefore be addressed at some finer level than species in the diet. Indeed, the most definitive results on predator niches, and differences between variants of *Homo sapiens* in the study area, concern the methods of food procurement, transport and processing strategies, and the temporal and spatial contexts of provisioning shelters with food.

Ungulate mortality patterns

Among modern predators, the prey age groups most commonly eaten show some consistent relationships to procurement tactics. These relationships correspond best to how predators search for food and to their relative emphases on hunting and scavenging. Mortality patterns in cervids and bovids reveal two things about modern *Homo sapiens* as

TABLE 15.1
Contrasting patterns of animal exploitation in the Italian Mousterian and inferences
about the context of procurement

a. Observed points of contrast

	Set 1	Set 2
gross anatomical pattern	HEADS	MEATY-COMPLETE
ungulate age structure	OLD-DOMINATED	PRIME-DOMINANT OR LIVING-STRUCTURE
# parts transported per carcass	LOW	HIGH
probable seasons of procurement	SPRING-SUMMER	FALL-WINTER-(e)SPRING
animals exploited[a]	UNGULATES AND AQUATIC TAXA	UNGULATES
relationship between rates of bone and stone accumulation	NO RELATIONSHIP	STRONG POSITIVE RELATIONSHIP

b. Inferred points of contrast

	Set 1	Set 2
main procurement mode	SCAVENGING AND GATHERING	HUNTING
search mode	EXTENSIVE, FREQUENT CHANGE OF FORAGING HUB	INTENSIVE, LESS FREQUENT CHANGE OF FORAGING HUB

[a] Ungulates were used by hominids at all of the cave sites, but with the addition of small (gatherable) aquatic taxa in the Set 1 cases from Grotta dei Moscerini.

Note: Set 1 refers to hominid-collected assemblages from Moscerini and Guattari; Set 2, to assemblages from Sant'Agostino and Breuil.

a predatory species: (1) their propensity toward ambush-style hunting regardless of culture; and (2) from perhaps the late Mousterian onward, a tendency to harvest prime adult prey in many ecosystems, using a wide variety of technologies (Chapter 11).

Like modern people, Mousterian hominids were ambush predators, but their tactics for obtaining ungulates were more diverse across sites than for all of the modern human cases (15,000 to present) considered together. The Mousterian faunas from Latium indicate the existence of at least two distinct foraging modes. The assemblages from Grotta Breuil and Grotta di Sant'Agostino represent primarily the products of ambush *hunting,* and, in this study sample, all such cases formed after around 55,000 years ago. In contrast, faunal assemblages from Grotta Guattari and Grotta dei Moscerini appear to represent *nonconfrontational scavenging* of

ungulates, based on documented associations of this behavior with the old-age bias (and head bias, see below) in shelters where modern predators gather bones. All of the scavenging cases date to before 55,000 years ago, and some of them associate with the use of gatherable aquatic prey (shellfish and tortoises). Variation in Mousterian game use at this level of comparison probably reflects hominids' adjustments to local foraging conditions (based on pollen and geological evidence), and no evolutionary change is necessarily indicated.

A second observation about prey mortality patterns in the Italian Mousterian concerns humans' overall tendency to emphasize prime adult ungulate prey in the context of ambush hunting. This may indicate an evolutionary trend toward increasing predatory specialization. Some ethnographic and historic accounts relate prime adult harvesting by humans to the degree of cooperation involved and, additionally, the use of topography to entrap groups of animals. But prime-dominant mortality patterns can also arise from solo hunting. The common denominator in these patterns is simply humans' focus on the richest prey age group, contra the natural abundance of that age group in living prey populations. Such harvesting can be achieved by targeting individuals or seeking out self-sorted sex or age herds in a given region, implying that humans' search (land use) strategies contribute to the pattern.

A focus on prime adult ungulates can eventually affect the age structure of the living prey population. A variety of wildlife studies show that individuals are physically capable of reproducing at a younger age than what normally occurs in a classic age-pyramid situation (e.g., Festa-Bianchet 1988; Seal and Plotka 1983; see also Ozoga 1988), yet they usually do not unless pressure from intraspecific competition for food and mates is relaxed (somewhat older adults often compete better for both). Preferential culling of prime-aged adults creates more breeding opportunities for younger adults in the same population. Though the signature of this process is distinctive (basically, a strong foreshortening of the age pyramid), its ecological impact can be relatively benign, provided that hunters withdraw once the encounter rates decline below some threshold. Neither wildlife biologists nor zooarchaeologists fully understand how this works, but the patterns documented in Chapter 11 are robust. Wildlife management studies seem to point to the harvesting intervals (schedule) and, to a lesser extent, the sex most often targeted by hunters in relation to the amount of time a prey population needs to produce the next generation; more young adults may have the opportunity to breed and thereby contribute proportionately more individuals to the next crop of offspring. Perhaps substantial increases in the scale of human territory use (and social interaction) made prime-dominant harvesting more feasible over the course of the Upper Pleistocene.

There is some evidence for a trend toward biased procurement of prime adult ungulates in the youngest Mousterian cases, those from Grotta Breuil dating to around 40,000–35,000 B.P. These most recent Mousterian assemblages show virtually identical mortality patterns to those commonly generated by late Upper Paleolithic and modern hunter-gatherers, whereas the earlier Mousterian cases are very different. It is not clear just when in the Italian chronological sequence this tendency became a stable feature of the human predatory niche, but it definitely antedates the Middle-Upper Paleolithic cultural boundary and, hence, becomes important before the appearance of Upper Paleolithic technologies.

The prime-dominant hunting focus by humans is very significant from an evolutionary point of view, because it distinguishes the modern human niche from that of all other predators. The emergence of a prime-age focus in ungulate hunting was a species-wide phenomenon in human beings, evident well beyond the reaches of Latium and different from the predator-prey relationships of the carnivores. Most faunal patterns construed as the products of hunters' choices in the archaeological literature are really the products of search strategies and are not deliberate or premeditated. The prime-age focus on the part of humans may be a significant exception. Moreover, of the many dimensions of the faunal evidence, only this one—the appearance of a prime-age focus in ambush hunting by humans—provides a compelling argument for specialization by humans over the course of the (Middle and?) Upper Pleistocene.

Harvesting biases with regard to prey age, whether in the context of hunting or scavenging, imply deliberate responses to food quality. For the most part, hominids of all of the periods considered harvested mostly adult animals. In the context of scavenging, the bias toward old adults is mainly the result of factors beyond the control of foragers, but it is significant that some adult ungulates naturally harbor more fat in their bodies at any time than juveniles for developmental reasons (see below). In hunting situations, the age groups taken can also be determined directly by the rates at which hunters encounter them in the environment. Humans somehow go a step beyond this in the case of prime adult harvesting. Prime adult harvesting implies something interesting about hunters' uses of territories and the scales at which they monitored prey movements. Equally intriguing is the fact that this tendency emerges only in humans, the only regular consumers of ungulates that are also highly omnivorous. In principle, omnivory presents greater options for periodically releasing prey populations from hunting pressure on a yearly basis.

Given the natural differences in potential fat yields of juvenile versus adult animals, especially when they are subjected to food stress, it may be no coincidence that hominids preferred adult prey. However, *prime* adults embody more of it. Prime-dominant hunting emphasizes the strongest—or at least the bulkiest—individuals in a living population, and it implies some degree of controlled targeting of prey. In Latium at least, the prime adult hunting focus emerges in the Paleolithic record during or soon after 55,000 years ago, when the climate deteriorated fairly rapidly and the overall content of local plant communities shifted. The prime-age focus could represent a more reliable mode for gaining access to animal fat (as a complement to protein in prey) under these conditions and, meanwhile, make for less overlap with carnivore harvesting patterns, especially those of wolves, spotted hyaenas, and (perhaps) some of the big cats.

Food transport

Anatomical representation varies greatly among the Mousterian cave assemblages in Latium and is closely correlated with the ungulate mortality patterns noted above. Ungulate body part profiles in shelter contexts do not distinguish one predator species from another, but instead relate to their habitual foraging tactics in response to spatial and nutritional aspects of food supply (Chapters 8 and 9). The basic principles governing transport of prey body parts apply equally well to humans, hyaenas, and wolves, even if *Homo sapiens* transported larger quantities of food to shelters overall. Controlling for problems of in situ bone attrition and archaeologists' recovery biases (Chapter 5), horn- and head-dominated assemblages generally correlate with a heavy emphasis on scavenging among predators (at least for medium-sized ungulates). Assemblages rich in both head and limb parts, on the other hand, are more likely to result from immediate access to prey via hunting.

Interspecific comparisons of the foraging and food transport habits of modern predators indicate

that the variation in ungulate body part representation in the Mousterian faunas corresponds to differing emphases on hunting and scavenging across sites. These Mousterian cases occur within a restricted region of coastal Italy, yet display a range of patterns analogous to those observed for modern hyaena cases across Africa and western Asia. Although the spotted hyaena den cases vary across environments, temporal variation in food dispersion within environments can exercise a similar effect on foragers at a smaller geographic scale. In the latter situation, the variation may be a function of seasonal or otherwise local changes in prey movement patterns and prey nutrition, as it appears to have been in the Latium Mousterian.

The range of variation in the Mousterian cases is far in excess of that observed in shelter faunas created by late Upper Paleolithic peoples in Latium and in a generally similar environment of Spain. While the Mousterian range of variation is best matched by the spotted hyaena sample, the hyaena series is explained by clinal differences across regions, whereas the Mousterian involves only four caves lying at similar elevations along a 50 km stretch of Latium coast—formed over a very long time. Moreover, the variation in the Mousterian series is discontinuous; assemblages are either dominated by head parts, or they contain more or less balanced frequencies of head and limb bones. It is very significant that the dichotomous anatomical patterns in the Mousterian faunas sort by site and display consistent associations with the different mortality patterns described above. Head-dominated ungulate faunas from Moscerini (M2, M3, M4, and M6) and the lower levels of Guattari (G4–5) are biased toward old-aged prey. The meaty or nearly complete anatomical patterns from Breuil (Br, B3/4) and Sant'Agostino (S0–3) associate either with living-structure or prime-dominated mortality patterns.

That these differences reflect distinct foraging modes by the Mousterian hominids appears impossible to refute. The dichotomous anatomical patterns cannot be explained by circumstances of preservation, details of horizontal site structure, or sample size. The associations between anatomical representation and age structure in ungulate prey specifically argue against citing intrasite activity areas as an explanation, or hominids having carried off some parts (except the head) to yet a third location. It is often difficult in archaeological research to sort out the influences of postdepositional bone destruction and the anatomical biases produced by human economic practices. It is only through a wide array of cross-referenced taphonomic analyses that much separation has been achieved in this study, and because of this, the kinds of differences recorded in the Latium area are not readily compared to other regional data sets, if only because few such studies currently are supported by taphonomic investigations or considerations of biases from bone recovery procedures. For example, a seemingly head-dominated pattern, evident because preservation favored teeth over bone, is a common product of advanced in situ bone decomposition. This is not so in the Italian data set, because head parts were not counted on the basis of teeth in the body part comparisons (see Chapters 5 and 9); indeed, it is my strong view that no anatomical comparisons should cross major classes of skeletal tissue (e.g., bones versus teeth) without accounting for the potential effects of bone attrition. I look forward to a time when comparisons of other regional data bases to the variation documented in Latium will become possible; they will also require, however, parallel demonstrations of the kinds of mortality patterns and anatomical profiles specified here.

Seasons of ungulate procurement

The hunted faunas from Sant'Agostino (S0–3) and Breuil (Br, B3/4) indicate occupations of the caves by Mousterian hominids during fall-winter (Chapter 13). Fused antler bases are represented in the cervid remains in the frequencies expected for a fall-winter population. The scavenged faunas from Moscerini (M2, M3, M4, and M6) and Guattari (G4–5) may represent spring and, perhaps, early summer occupations by contrast. In Moscerini, the absence of both antler bases and male red deer canines suggest, however, that most of the deer were females. Because adult females may be preferred eating in spring among the modern Eskimo (Binford 1978; see also discussions in Chapter 8), the bias toward females does not necessarily contradict the

interpretation that occupations took place in spring. Seasonality data for the scavenged ungulate cases are meager, and the possibility that hominids used these two sites during other seasons is difficult to exclude. It is significant nonetheless that the spring-early summer period is not represented at the other two caves (Breuil and Sant'Agostino) in the study area. The samples are fairly large, yet no individuals occur in the warm-season categories.

Small animal exploitation

Ungulate remains comprise the bulk of the animal products transported to the Mousterian shelters, but small aquatic taxa and land tortoises were also consumed by hominids at Moscerini (Chapter 6). Moscerini is the first systematically documented case of mollusk harvesting in the Mousterian of Eurasia of which I am aware; it certainly is the first to receive a concerted taphonomic investigation. Shellfish have been reported in Middle Paleolithic sites in Italy and elsewhere previously, but their association with human activities are unclear. Other unequivocal cases of aquatic resource use in the Mousterian are bound to emerge from future investigations on this topic; new work on faunas from the Middle-Upper Paleolithic site of Riparo Mochi, for example, provides ample evidence of shellfish exploitation throughout these cultural periods (my current research).

It is interesting that evidence of small animal exploitation at the Latium caves is nearly restricted to aquatic species. Rodent and lagomorph remains are preserved in two of the caves, Moscerini and Sant'Agostino, but taphonomic evidence shows that these small terrestrial mammals were consumed by other predators, not hominids. The absence of small terrestrial prey in hominid-collected cases does not mean that Mousterians never ate these kinds of animals. Rather, the data show only that hominids did not carry small terrestrial prey to shelters before consuming them. Assuming that the economic principles guiding food transport were the same for terrestrial and aquatic prey, aquatic species may have been brought into Moscerini only because they were available very near the shelter entrance at the time. Shellfish of the types consumed by Paleolithic peoples in Latium naturally occur in fairly concentrated or linear patches, and geochronological evidence indicates that hominids occupied Moscerini when sea level was high and the shoreline was only a few meters from the cave entrance (see Chapters 3 and 6). Moscerini was the only cave directly adjacent to the sea when utilized by the hominids. Of the four coastal caves, only Moscerini contains shellfish and tortoise remains, suggesting that very small differences in distance to the sea made a big difference in whether mollusks would be carried into a shelter by Mousterian foragers.

Shellfish and tortoise remains in Moscerini provide new information about the strategic and economic contexts of food procurement by Mousterian foragers. Hominids returned to this site many times over thousands of years, and they appear to have used it in a relatively ephemeral manner throughout that time. The rates of lithic artifact accumulation through the stratigraphic sequence show no close relationship to rates of bone or shell accumulation. Like foragers of the later Pleistocene and Holocene, Mousterian hominids may have turned to shellfish and (hibernating?) tortoises in late winter through spring, due to seasonal scarcity of other types of foods. However, Mousterian hominids exploited shellfish much less intensively than is indicated by the shell middens of many modern human cultures.

The convergence of selective transport of ungulate head parts, apparently from scavenged carcasses of old animals, and the gathering of shellfish and tortoises may point to a single foraging mode by the human occupants of Moscerini: the two foraging practices may have been united by an emphasis on opportunism, probably in the context of gathering a variety of small-package resources. The ungulate head-collecting phenomenon actually appears in two coastal sites (Moscerini and Guattari G4–5), whereas shellfish were carried only into one (Moscerini). The search and procurement logistics of both nonconfrontational scavenging and gathering of small sessile prey tend to yield relatively small food packages that could be collected rather than subdued. Because of the inclusion of shellfish in its faunas, the Moscerini case nonetheless reveals significant differences in hominids' willingness to transport certain kinds of small packages over any

distance. Ungulate head parts are likely to have come from scattered localities, requiring appreciable amounts of searching, whereas shellfish normally occur in patches along the coast. Technological evidence associated with scavenging and shellfish harvesting also implies extensive or frequent movement by hominids, based on somewhat higher frequencies of transported tools, core reduction tactics that emphasized production of large flakes and tool blanks, and heavy resharpening of tools (Chapter 14; see also Kuhn 1990a, 1991, n.d.). Holding raw material availability constant, we generally expect more economic use of stone in high mobility situations (Kuhn 1991, 1992).

The seasons in which archaic humans collected aquatic resources may have been the same times of year that modern humans turned to foods from the sea. Shellfish were significant additions to the diets of later peoples living along the Mediterranean coast when plant and animal sources of food energy were scarce in spring (e.g., Deith 1983a, 1983b, 1986, 1989; Deith and Shackleton 1986). Transporting scavenged head parts to sites such as Moscerini may have supplemented a diet otherwise poor in fat; many (not all) species of Mediterranean littoral bivalves contain some fats, but not in amounts that could supplement other deficient foods. Likewise, plant sources other than seaweed (an important winter and spring food to many mammals) may have been in short supply for at least part of the time that hominids used the Moscerini cave for shelter, making animal fat all the more precious for enhancing the nutritional value of other proteinaceous foods (see Speth and Spielmann 1983). The data on shellfish use at Moscerini have parallels in Middle Stone Age caves on the southern coast of Africa (Voigt 1973, 1982) such as Klasies River Mouth (Singer and Wymer 1982). Recent reviews of the ungulate faunas have emphasized the possibility of some scavenging by hominids there as well (Binford 1984; Turner 1989; cf. Klein 1976, 1978, 1979). Direct comparisons of the Moscerini case to published South African MSA faunas are prohibited, however, by inconsistencies in the recovery of bones (Turner 1989) and shells (Elizabeth Voigt, p.c.), particularly in the case of Klasies River Mouth.

LAND USE AND RANGING PATTERNS

Theoretically, the conspicuous variation in the Italian Mousterian cave faunas might be explained by seasonal shifts in hominid foraging habits, *or* by local changes in foraging opportunities in the vicinity of each cave due to regressing sea level, *or* by linear changes in hominid adaptations. The contrasting patterns of lithic artifact transport by Mousterian and late Upper Paleolithic peoples in coastal Italy are a crucial aid for addressing these questions. The level of resolution offered by the seasonality data for ungulate remains is relatively crude, yet the results in some sense support a season-based explanation for the intersite variation in the faunas. The full cycle of seasons is represented by the total Mousterian sample, whereas data on the late Upper Paleolithic suggest fall, winter, and early spring occupations only. This contrast is made interesting by the fact that the study sample encompasses only a small area of Italy. The full range of seasons evident for the Mousterian sample in no way indicates sedentism, since strata indicating different seasons of use were formed many thousands of years apart. The contrast could imply significant differences in the scale and pattern of territory use between the Mousterian and the late Upper Paleolithic. There is a problem with fauna-based interpretations, however, in that people may not necessarily depend on natural shelters throughout the year, even if they remain in an area. As argued above, responses to local restructuring of the coastal habitats as sea level changed is also likely, but there seems to be more behind the variation that we see in the Latium case.

Data on lithic raw material transport are an important source of independent information on the question of territory use by humans; they have the potential to tell us far more than can faunal data about where or how far people might have traveled just prior to their arrival at the coastal shelters. Stone raw materials and the tools manufactured from them can, in principle, be transported extensively and for much longer spans of time than can most foodstuffs (Chapter 8).

Kuhn's data on lithic raw material transport indicate more extensive geographical movements by late Upper Paleolithic peoples than was true in the Mousterian. Late Upper Paleolithic humans arrived in the same area with more tools made of nonlocal flints, apparently in anticipation of an extended (cold season) stay. Late Upper Paleolithic foragers also made use of local lithic raw materials during the time spent along the coast, perhaps as the previously transported tools were exhausted and replaced, but clearly they were not limited to pebble sources all of the time. The Pontinian Mousterian, in contrast, shows little if any evidence of transport of raw material over long distances. Mousterian peoples invariably made do with local flint pebble sources obtained in the immediate vicinity of the coastal caves, instead varying their strategies of core and tool reduction while at the caves (summarized in Table 15.2). Put another way, Mousterians altered their methods of lithic reduction to cope with raw material availability in a more confined area, whereas late Upper Paleolithic peoples enjoyed the advantages of collecting high-quality raw material in the context of movement across larger distances.

The cost of obtaining lithic raw material in either culture period was probably a function of the predominant foraging patterns and the scale of mobility within an annual cycle. Given that coastal Italy is naturally poor in raw materials other than small flint pebbles, traveling long and far would create opportunities to pick up small quantities of stone from distant, restricted sources and move them to places where such raw materials were lacking. A system in which foragers normally move shorter distances and more frequently within the annual round would reduce or even eliminate opportunities to obtain certain larger, high-quality raw materials and move them to distant points in their territory. If people's return to a particular place is not predictable except with respect to regeneration of food patches where the foragers had not been in recent years, then we can expect less evidence of long-distance transport of lithic raw material or tools. Shifts in the frequency of residential movement and duration of particular occupations therefore would have resulted in changing constraints over where and when lithic raw materials could be gathered and where tools could be made and maintained. The advantages of alternative tactics of tool manufacture and renewal would vary accordingly.

Contrasting technological patterns in the Italian Mousterian
paralleling game exploitation

a. Observed points of contrast

	Set 1	Set 2
core reduction techniques:		
flakes produced per pebble	FEW	MANY
blank size and shape	LARGE AND THIN	SMALL
tool use:		
modification/renewal	HEAVY	MODERATE
transport frequency	MODERATE	LOW

b. Inferred points of contrast

	Set 1	Set 2
focus of production	TOOLS	CORES
main source of fresh edges	RENEWAL	REPLACEMENT
main technological "provisioning" strategy	INDIVIDUALS	ACTIVITIES AT PLACES

Note: Set 1 refers to hominid-collected assemblages from Moscerini and Guattari; Set 2, to assemblages from Sant'Agostino and Breuil.

The greater behavioral variation apparent in the Mousterian of Latium with respect to place should not be confused with organizational or logistical complexity. A long time is represented by the Mousterian sample, and the lithic data suggest that the variation we see throughout that time represents a single technological system. One could argue from the lithic and most of the faunal data that Mousterians used the same places more often by sampling foraging opportunities within an area with greater frequency, and perhaps by using patches less intensively on the average. The principles governing Mousterian foraging decisions may have been quite straightforward, with environmental patchiness and local situations conditioning hominid responses in a direct way. Such a system would place a high value on foragers' abilities to improvise in response to fine-grained variation in food availability. This kind of foraging pattern might involve a smaller annual range, but need not imply that Mousterian foragers never ventured outside the coastal area covered by this study. Instead, Mousterian subsistence patterns and scales of social interaction may have allowed the hominids to move through these lands at a different rate than the late Upper

Paleolithic humans with respect to the annual cycle and across years.

The observed differences between the composite patterns of resource use by Mousterian and late Upper Paleolithic peoples in west-central Italy might be contrasted in terms of improvisation versus the incorporation of some longer-range planning. Though simplistic, the concepts are heuristically useful for what they imply about changes in the *scale* of hominid foraging responses, and because we are able to recognize the value of both as skills for living. Given all that has been written between the lines about the behavioral capacities of Neandertals and other archaic hominids—arguments that almost invariably equate "smartness" with adaptive advantage—a way of envisioning evolutionary differences without judgments of less versus more and progressions from incompetence to facility could be liberating.

Differing scales and rates of land use distinguish the adaptations of carnivores to a large extent (such as between wolves and brown bears, or cats and wild dogs), and, in a general sense, might also serve to distinguish important evolutionary changes in hominid adaptations. If the strategic variation within a Mousterian system were conditioned largely by immediate opportunities, then that variation naturally would be expressed at a smaller geographical scale. A more diverse foraging regimen can also be expected as territory size decreases, and foraging decisions responsive to local conditions could seem less specialized overall. Further, even if what Mousterian hominids did in one region was not tactically identical to what they did in the next, the range of variation in foraging practices could be high in both regions. The scale of land use within the annual cycle was probably much larger in the late Upper Paleolithic times, with people coming into an area from farther away for some precon-

ceived purpose. Hence, one sees less variation in Upper Paleolithic exploitation *within* a relatively small geographical area, because fewer seasonal phases of a larger system of land use may be represented. Adjusting the geographical scale to a larger, more regional level might increase the perceived variation in the Upper Paleolithic record, whereas the *range of variation* in the Mousterian would level off sooner, regardless of inter-regional differences in the kinds of tactics emphasized or the species consumed. The faunal and technological data therefore raise new, more specific questions that can be tested by broadening the geographical scope of the kind of research outlined here.

On the Role of Technology in Mousterian Subsistence: Procurement versus Processing

Collaborative research on technology and subsistence in the Latium Mousterian reveals far more about human resource use than either branch of study could have accomplished alone. An explicitly economic perspective on changes in stone technology is a significant departure from the traditional emphasis on tool forms and functions, or *typology*. Recall that tool type frequencies are the principal bases for distinguishing the Middle and Upper Paleolithic in Eurasia and the Middle and Late Stone Age in Africa, dividing up time for zooarchaeologists as well. Yet few direct or obvious functional links exist between the formal components of technology and subsistence in the Latium Mousterian, or elsewhere in Eurasia for that matter. In Italy there are no substantial changes in the frequencies of putative spear points in relation to the differing emphases on hunting and scavenging or gathering among the Mousterian assemblages. We instead find strong correspondences between foraging strategies and the life histories of artifacts, ultimately relating to differing ways of searching for resources in time and space.

It is interesting that archaic humans in Italy successfully hunted large mammals well before sophisticated bone- or stone-tipped projectile weapons were in regular use (Chapter 14; see also Kuhn 1993). Indeed, the prime adult focus in hunting, so important to the discussions above, emerged before

these kinds of weapons appeared in cultural records, a time when animals probably were hunted with simple wooden spears (see Gamble 1986; also Jacob-Friesen 1956). The Upper Paleolithic contrasts with earlier hominid cultures in that it sports a wide variety of nonperishable weapon heads and related paraphernalia. These artifacts are, without question, among the more visually striking elements of hunter-gatherer technologic systems. While such tools can facilitate the food quest, it is unclear whether they were pivotal to human evolutionary history.

Humans' (including archaeologists') fascination with tools is both natural and perennial, because this is the kind of animal that we are. However, the idea that weapons, in particular, conferred a reproductive advantage to certain human populations or, metaphorically, dragged some of them by the wrists faster over the course of evolution is, for the moment at least, little more than a long-standing fantasy. The fact that two variants of *H. sapiens* are found in association with Middle Paleolithic industries in western Asia (compare, for example, Arensburg 1989; Bar-Yosef 1989; Tchernov 1992; Valladas et al. 1987; Vandermeersch 1989) and, now, economic evidence from Italy stand directly in the way of weapon-driven interpretations of the evolutionary process. There is some evidence for a trend toward greater hunting specialization during the Upper Pleistocene, but it is apparent in the faunal record long before we see any substantial changes in stone weaponry or the appearance of bone points and related gear. Counter our intuitions, evidence from the Levant and from Italy have effectively placed the cart where we thought our favorite horse ought to be.

Other, more prevalent, facets of modern and ancient stone technologies—here collectively termed *processing implements*—allow people to get more out of food than their digestive systems can accomplish alone. The absolute limits of processing capabilities, as a function of technology, personnel, and time, therefore can describe important features of subsistence adaptations and their organization. As concerns the Mousterian, we are confronted with industries nearly bereft of stone weapons, but rich in tools apparently associated with processing tasks. Yet Middle Paleolithic, Middle Stone Age, and earlier technologies on the whole display a strange lack of *elaborate* processing tools or complex hearths suitable for intensifying or containing heat (see reviews by James 1989; Perles 1977). Some of the perceived absences of these phenomena are almost certainly because our information is incomplete, but even as more dependable archaeological data become available, absences of many of the processing-related facilities commonly associated with modern hunter-gatherer camps may persist. Archaeological data presently suggest that hominid technologies embodied a more limited set of food-processing options prior to sometime in the early Upper Paleolithic and Late Stone Age, even when battered stones of the African MSA are taken into account. Scraping tools, cutting tools, and shallow hearths are prevalent in many Middle Paleolithic sites, though always of simple design, whereas grinding and pounding implements and evidence of stone boiling are hard to find and may not exist.

Because processing activities represent some of the more time-consuming aspects of the food quest, significant ecological shifts are possible simply by heightening the realized nutritional yield per unit of food obtained. Within any one system, humans' choices of which and how many prey body parts to move will certainly depend upon the kinds of technical support available. We know that technical infrastructures varied between cultural periods, and there is a general trend toward increasing complexity and diversity in processing techniques over the course of the Paleolithic. Specifically, some shifts in humans' ability or need to render key nutrients from animal carcasses may have occurred sometime between the later part of the Middle Paleolithic and the early part of the Upper Paleolithic. As recent discussions by Speth (1989, 1991) and Metcalfe and Barlow (1992) might anticipate, the Mousterian situation in coastal Italy suggests that certain food choice and transport decisions were limited by the processing technology in existence at that time, as well as by the nutritional assets of prey body parts in seasons of fat/carbohydrate scarcity.

Head-collecting and -processing technology

Of especial interest among Mousterian processing techniques in Italy was the treatment of ungulate head parts in the context of scavenging. Mousterians' exceptional interest in head parts when (apparently) scavenging is unexpected, as it is difficult to find evidence of this particular foraging pattern among modern hunter-gatherers. People make use of head parts in modern situations, but not such that the practice would dominate entire faunal sequences in shelters formed over thousands of years. To understand what head collecting in the Mousterian might have been about, it is necessary to turn to other sources of information, such as the habits of nonhuman predators, details of the ungulate anatomy, and, of course, technology. Among the carnivores, a preference for head parts (of medium-sized ungulates) often emerges in the context of scavenging (Chapter 9), especially where food supplies are relatively dispersed. The preference is partly explained by the relative persistence of crania at find sites and the ease with which heads (including the mandible) can be removed from carcasses; the head bias is not altogether a matter of deliberation by foragers.

There are processing and energetic incentives behind head collecting as well. The skull of a large mammal is a complex bony container and requires considerable processing effort and time by humans and carnivores alike. Moving heads of larger prey to a secure place can be worthwhile if these body parts can be processed more effectively by doing so. Equally important anywhere food energy sources are periodically or perennially scarce is the uniquely high fat content of soft tissues of the head; fat persists in these tissues, even in prey that are severely malnourished. As pointed out in Chapter 8, the fat-rich myelin sheaths enclosing the cranial nerves cannot be metabolized, and the yellow marrow reserves in the adult ungulate mandible are among the last to be drained by the metabolic system under conditions of food stress. Because plant production waxes and wanes with the seasons, animal fat will be most valuable to humans whenever plant energy sources decline, and Neandertals would have been no exception in this regard. Under conditions of scarcity, then, the nutritional state of the animal at the time of death should strongly influence humans' (and other predators') decisions about what prey body parts are worthy of transport to, and more extensive processing at, a rockshelter or cave. Nutritional contingencies are not confined to scavenging situations, however. People, whether hunting or scavenging, should always be interested in head parts of prey if fats and carbohydrates are scarce, and ethnoarchaeological accounts clearly show that people are (e.g., Binford 1978; O'Connell et al. 1988a, 1992; Yellen 1977). Foragers may be less interested in heads if other rich, more favored parts requiring less processing effort are available—a fact that accounts for much of the variation in transport and processing decisions from one month to the next, depending on the amplitude of the seasons.

While human foragers could conceivably choose to take only heads away from starved prey obtained by hunting, the effort to procure them can quickly outweigh the potential returns, because, rich or not, the head is a relatively small package. This reasoning assumes an important strategic difference between nonconfrontational scavenging, on the one hand, and hunting and scavenging by aggressive displacement on the other. The value of either class of strategy depends on the nutritional state and bulk mass of prey in the frequencies that they are most typically encountered in a given foraging system. Although isolated exceptions can come about, there is a significantly lower probability that head-dominated faunas represent hunting by predators overall; this expectation is borne out by what scavenging carnivores do in modern settings. But if car-

nivores and Neandertals often produced strongly head-dominated faunas at shelters in the context of scavenging, why do modern people not produce the same kinds of faunal patterns? Part of the answer is to be found in the extent to which the transported products of hunting and scavenging strategies are intermixed in the bone fallout (refuse) at any given site; if mixed at the same place, products of the more common strategy might simply swamp those of another less common strategy, especially if the former is hunting and the latter scavenging; as discussed in Chapter 8, scavenging involves lower transported volumes on the average.

Another part of the answer hinges upon the range of processing options available to hominids. Here, again, I refer to objects associated with grinding, pounding, and/or boiling animal and plant foods. Most of the evidence in the Paleolithic for food-processing behavior is indirect, such as fire-cracked cobbles that might have been used for stone boiling (in the UP). In times of fat scarcity, bone trabeculae of the spinal column of adult prey also represent potentially rich sources of fats, and could have been processed by grinding them up and boiling them, as they are in some modern human situations (e.g., Binford 1978; Yellen 1977). For reasons that are not fully understood, research on the Mousterian of Europe has yielded very limited evidence of pounding and grinding technologies. Unlike trabecular bone tissues, heads can be roasted as they are and then picked apart; processing requires time and fire but no additional technology for extracting nutrients. The absence of container technology and grinding/pounding implements in the Mousterian could have made heads even more attractive to foragers in need of fat.

Because both classes of tactics—hunting and nonconfrontational scavenging—existed within the Latium Mousterian, we may conclude (barring sexual divisions of labor) that hunting capability had little or nothing to do with Mousterians' decisions to scavenge. Rather, foraging conditions made scavenging more worthwhile given the ranging patterns and technological support in existence at the time. In the Italian Mousterian, strict choices to take away just about only heads to two of the caves may have been responses to an advanced state of starvation in deer, poor in fat at a time when this nutrient was needed to supplement the human diet. That the opportunities to scavenge were generated primarily by starvation and other nonviolent deaths rather than strictly by hunting carnivores is consistent with fact that the frequencies of crania to mandibles are generally equivalent (or relatively more mandibles, Chapter 9). Scavenging is really a family of tactics whose diversity and economic rules are not well understood, especially in the temperate zone. The

available information on scavenging by nonhuman predators underscores the importance of food dispersion for understanding why scavenging is more profitable in some conditions and less in others. The technological data for the scavenged faunas from Italy indicate more ephemeral uses of caves and somewhat more extensive searches for resources within a relatively small territory.

On the Meaning of Difference in Human Evolution Studies

Current research priorities for the Mousterian and debates about the Middle-Upper Paleolithic transition center on questions about adaptive variation and evolutionary change. The research described here investigates variation in the Italian Mousterian by combining a unique set of variables demonstrably relevant to how hominids used resources. Basic economics probably was not the only thing driving Paleolithic human behavior, but, if only through greater clarification, such an understanding effectively opens doors onto other behavioral domains. The faunal variables were chosen based on cross-species surveys of modern (human and nonhuman) predators. Collaborative research on core reduction and stone tool use and transport is based on expectations about how technology should relate to human foraging practices in relation to the distributions of lithic raw material in the environment. The research reveals considerable variation in patterns of resource use in the Latium Mousterian caves—some of the variation is well in excess of that found for any later humans considered by this study.

It is clear that the trends observed in the Middle Paleolithic of Latium represent shifts in the frequencies of various aspects of foraging and technology, not the appearance of entirely new components of behavior. For example, evidence of both centripetal core reduction and platform core reduction are present throughout the Pontinian sequence; platform core reduction simply overtakes centripetal techniques with time. This is argued to be an adjustment of tool manufacture to the requirements and limitations of foraging and land use, an adaptive frequency shift within an extant range of alternatives. The same must be said for scavenging and hunting. Mousterian scavenging practices appear odd in light of what modern humans do, but there is no reason to

assume that Mousterians never scavenged after 55,000 years ago, nor hunted before this time. Virtually every known predator, including modern people, engages in both; species differ in their emphases on hunting and scavenging in what is best described as a general continuum. Juxtaposing hunting and scavenging as if they represented distinct hominid predatory niches or adaptations, rather than components of any one, is bound to confuse attempts to understand how this omnivorous predator changed over time. Showing that a predator hunts does not necessarily make that predator the same as another. And scavenging should not, at the level of population relationships, be modeled as the last resort of an incompetent species. We should expect to see some combination of these two general strategy classes in hominid adaptations throughout the Upper Pleistocene and perhaps earlier, because we have no ecologically based reasons to expect that predatory adaptations evolve from scavenging, progressively moving toward hunting ever larger prey. Variation in how hunting and scavenging tactics are manifest in foraging adaptations is a problem of a finer order, as research on modern predators attests.

If there is anything distinctive or anomalous about the Mousterian of west-central Italy compared to anatomically modern human lifeways, it is in how alternative tactics of game procurement and tool manufacture were implemented as components in a larger adaptive system. For example, while scavenging is conspicuous in the earlier part of the Italian sequence, it probably was not the only option for these foragers nor their single mainstay. The Mousterian scavenging pattern stands apart from known modern human cases because it was so clearly separated, spatially and temporally, from hunting. It presents a striking contrast to ethnoarchaeological cases in which the products of both strategy classes are pooled at the same residential places (e.g., Binford 1978; O'Connell et al. 1988a, 1988b, 1992; Bunn et al. 1988).

Within the geographical limits imposed by the study sample, all of the observed trends in foraging and technology appear somewhat "progressive." Scavenging appears to be replaced by hunting, and classic Mousterian centripetal reduction techniques are superseded by single- and double-platform approaches reminiscent of Upper Paleolithic blade core reduction techniques. The fact that observed changes appear to point to a stereotypically modern pattern does not constitute an explanation of them, however. The technological changes may indeed represent responses to alterations in foraging patterns, but the ultimate causes of long-term variation in subsistence remain unclear. I argue above that most of the trends in the Mousterian faunas—other than the prime-adult hunting focus—represent simple changes in how these particular cave sites were used. The kinds of trends identified in the Latium industries are not apparent for the European Mousterian as a whole. The Middle-Upper Paleolithic transition by definition took place over a wide area. The French Mousterian, for example, shows neither a consistent decline over time in the frequencies of retouched tools (Rolland 1988:170), nor a clear increase in the production of blade-like flakes and tool blanks (compare Harrold 1989:691; Pelegrin 1990). Most of the variation we observe in Latium seems to reflect hominids' responses to changing resource opportunities in the vicinities of each of the caves due to regressing seas over the course of the Upper Pleistocene, and corresponding changes in how the caves were used. Such an explanation cites adjustments within a single subsistence system—that is, within the Middle Paleolithic—without calling upon evolution.

That the explanation is simply rooted in seasonality is unlikely, however, given the long spans of time each Mousterian strata series represents. Moreover, spring-associated faunas formed tens of thousands of years earlier than the cold-season faunas. Instead, much of the variation reflects local responses to changing sea levels, topography, and concomitant restructuring of local habitats. All of the caves lie at similar elevations, close to the modern Mediterranean shore. With time, sea level lowered more and more, placing the caves containing the younger series somewhat more inland than the older ones would have been when occupied by hominids. This process would certainly lead to subtle but important differences in the settings, foraging opportunities, and the general appeal of each cave to hominids in the past. The prime adult focus in ungulate hunting by humans, on the other hand, is pan-species, and it is ecologically unprecedented among predators. It certainly exists well beyond the region in question and indicates increasing specialization in this regard. A full mapping of this phenomenon in evolutionary time and space remains to be done. It is reasonably clear, however, that this major ecological shift in humans' relationship with ungulate prey populations *prefaced* the widely documented changes in Paleolithic technology, perhaps redefining the selective milieu for developments in technology thereafter.

The methods and bases for interpretation presented in this study help provide means for addressing many hypotheses germane to the origins of modern humans and the fate of the Neandertals, but rigorous testing will require expansion of the geographical scale considered or, at least, examining more finely divided stratigraphic sequences in the study area as presently defined. Now armed with the means, this is an important stimulus for continued research in west-central Italy (e.g., the thick but as yet unexcavated portions of Breuil, see Bietti et al. 1988, 1990–91; Bietti and Kuhn 1990–91; Bietti and Grimaldi 1990–91; Lemorini 1990–91; Stiner 1990–91) and other areas of the Mediterranean.

Selection upon Variation and the Metering of Time

Significant changes in human behavior appear to have taken place in the late Middle and Upper Pleistocene, and archaic and anatomically modern humans appear to differ in some important ways.

Upon finer inspection, however, these changes are expressed primarily as frequency shifts within extant ranges of alternatives, regardless of whether we are talking about game use, certain technologic behaviors, or human skeletal morphology (e.g., F. Smith 1984; Trinkaus 1992). I currently favor a "soft replacement" model of change; some shifts in resource use, in particular, do not seem to have been all that sudden or regionally isolated. More to the point, however, one very significant shift in the human predator niche does not coincide with the classic transition boundary defined from typological studies of stone tools—it precedes the boundary.

The Middle Paleolithic was a period of enormous flux in human lifeways—so much so that further changes thought to have taken place around 35,000 years ago throughout Eurasia may not be as extreme or unique by contrast. Although the goals and points of argument differ, this general conclusion is suggested in recent presentations by Mellars (1989), Soffer (1989), Bar-Yosef (1989), Tchernov (1992), F. Smith (1984), and Stiner (1990a), based on regional evidence from France, eastern Europe, the Levant, and Italy, respectively. For the moment at least, there seems to be more than one place where some behavioral or anatomical traits thought to demarcate modern humans emerge relatively early.

These findings suggest there is need to question the concept of transition itself. The Middle to Upper Paleolithic boundary is merely a heuristic construct: time is just a yardstick that we redefine whenever we set out to study an archaeological problem, and time scale in fact accounts for much of the difference in our perceptions of sudden and gradual change in species. The more expanded the temporal frame, the more variation is exposed and the more gradual the changes are bound to appear—facts that have obvious implications for a debate about modern human origins that hangs on continuity versus replacement or gradual change versus punctuated equilibrium more generally. In light of this, differing views of modern human origins from the eco-

logical (faunal) perspective is presently a debate between advocates for the "diffusion of genius" and advocates of "selection upon variation in the context of widespread environmental (including social) forces." I obviously favor the latter. Learning more about the Middle Paleolithic and Middle Stone Age in economic terms is likely to undermine the clarity and importance of the boundary that once cleanly separated them from us. The continuity-replacement dialectic has been useful, but I think that there are other productive ways of visualizing change in human foraging practices, alternatives that merit exploration in light of what we now know from the faunal perspective.

Zooarchaeologists who study the Paleolithic periods have worked long and hard under the yoke of tool-based and human paleontological chronologies. We can learn more, in fact, by communicating with technologists on topics of raw material economy and food-processing gear. It is crucial that zooarchaeologists also experiment with the time frames of foraging practice comparisons. By focusing on the places where, and the times when, we expect to find sudden change or points of origin, we deny ourselves the opportunity to witness contradictions—and contradictions do exist in Italy and elsewhere. It does not matter how much one person's opinions or hunches differ from another's about the nature of the human evolutionary sequence, because as scientists we are all equally obliged to challenge what we prefer to believe. Zooarchaeologists are in an auspicious position to do this by examining the biological bases of what the variables chosen for study really mean, making sure that the signatures of human behaviors are clear, and deliberately manipulating the temporal and spatial scales of comparison as a normal part of research design and practice. These procedures safeguard our capacity to be surprised by our own research, allowing ecological transitions in prehistory to fall where they may.

Appendix

APPENDIX 1.1
Grotta dei Moscerini: Standardized anatomical data for large mammals by taxon and vertical provenience

Taxon	MNI[a]	tMNE	Antler or horn	Head	Neck	Axial	Upper front	Lower front	Upper hind	Lower hind	Feet
Moscerini M1:											
red/fallow	1	2	.0	.0	.0	.0	.0	.0	.0	.0	.08
roe	1	4	.0	.0	.0	.0	.0	.17	.50	.12	.04
aurochs	1	3	.50	.0	.0	.0	.0	.17	.0	.12	.0
Moscerini M2:											
red/fallow	1	7	.0	1.00	.0	.0	.0	.0	.0	.12	.08
roe	1	2	.0	.0	.0	.0	.0	.0	.50	.12	.0
red fox	1	1	.0	.0	.0	.0	.0	.0	.0	.06	.0
bear	1	1	.0	.0	.0	.0	.0	.0	.0	.0	.02
Moscerini M3:											
rhino	1	1	.0	.25	.0	.0	.0	.0	.0	.0	.0
red/fallow	15	76	.0	15.00	.0	.0	.0	1.00	.0	.75	.17
roe	4	30	.0	3.25	.0	.0	.25	1.17	.0	.62	.17
wild boar	1	1	.0	.25	.0	.0	.0	.0	.0	.0	.0
ibex	1	7	.0	.50	.0	.0	.0	.0	.0	.0	.21
bear	1	1	.0	.25	.0	.0	.0	.0	.0	.0	.0
Moscerini M4:											
rhino	1	1	.0	.25	.0	.0	.0	.0	.0	.0	.0
red/fallow	8	30	.0	7.25	.0	.0	.0	.0	.0	.12	.0
roe	2	7	.0	1.25	.0	.0	.0	.33	.0	.0	.0
hippo	1	1	.0	.25	.0	.0	.0	.0	.0	.0	.0
bear	1	1	.0	.25	.0	.0	.0	.0	.0	.0	.0
Moscerini M5:											
horse	1	8	.0	.0	.0	.0	.0	.0	.50	.50	.25
red/fallow	7	94	1.00	7.00	.0	.22	.75	2.00	2.50	3.25	.29
roe	4	72	1.00	4.00	.71	.18	1.50	1.83	1.00	.87	.58
aurochs	1	10	.0	.0	.0	.0	.0	.50	.50	.75	.0
ibex	1	11	.0	.0	.0	.02	.25	.50	.0	.12	.21
s. hyaena	2	48	.0	1.25	.86	.04	.50	.79	.50	.56	.20
wild cat	1	13	.0	.50	.0	.06	.25	.21	.0	.12	.03
red fox	1	9	.0	1.00	.0	.04	.0	.07	.50	.06	.0
bear	1	47	.0	.75	.0	.04	.0	.71	.0	1.00	.27
monk seal	1	1	.0	.25	.0	.0	.0	.0	.0	.0	.0

(*continued*)

APPENDIX 1.1   (*Continued*)

			Anatomical regions								
Taxon	MNI[a]	tMNE	Antler or horn	Head	Neck	Axial	Upper front	Lower front	Upper hind	Lower hind	Feet
Moscerini M6:											
red/fallow	7	51	.50	6.25	.0	.08	.25	.83	.50	.75	.33
roe	1	11	.0	.25	.0	.0	.0	.0	.0	.37	.29
aurochs	1	1	.0	.0	.0	.0	.0	.0	.0	.0	.04
ibex	1	1	.0	.0	.0	.0	.0	.17	.0	.0	.0
bear	1	1	.0	.0	.0	.02	.0	.0	.0	.0	.0

[a] MNI is based on the highest standardized MNE value among the nine anatomical regions, rounded to the next whole number; tMNE refers to total MNE (nonstandardized count) for the designated taxon and provenience. Raw MNE for each anatomical region can be derived from this appendix by multiplying the standardized value (shown) by the expected value for the same region (right half of Table 9.4, noting distinctions among carnivores, artiodactyls, and perissodactyls).

APPENDIX 1.2

Grotta Guattari: Standardized anatomical data for large mammals by taxon and vertical provenience

			Anatomical regions								
Taxon	MNI[a]	tMNE	Antler or horn	Head	Neck	Axial	Upper front	Lower front	Upper hind	Lower hind	Feet
Guattari G0:											
elephant	1	2	.0	.0	.0	.0	.0	.0	.50	.06	.0
horse	2	24	.0	1.50	.14	.02	.0	.14	.0	.44	.12
rhino	1	1	.0	.0	.0	.0	.25	.0	.0	.0	.0
red/fallow	14	186	9.00	13.50	1.43	.08	4.00	5.83	1.00	5.00	.29
aurochs	3	68	.0	2.75	.0	.0	1.75	3.00	1.50	2.50	.37
wild boar	1	7	.0	.50	.0	.02	.25	.0	.50	.12	.04
s. hyaena	4	34	.0	4.00	1.00	.04	.50	.21	.0	.19	.02
lion-leopard	1	5	.0	.75	.0	.0	.0	.0	.0	.06	.02
wolf	1	1	.0	.25	.0	.0	.0	.0	.0	.0	.0
bear	1	5	.0	1.00	.0	.0	.0	.07	.0	.0	.0
Guattari G1:											
horse	1	8	.0	.75	.0	.0	.25	.0	.0	.12	.12
red/fallow	6	81	1.00	6.00	.43	.04	1.25	2.83	.0	2.25	.42
aurochs	2	13	.0	2.00	.0	.0	.0	.0	.0	.37	.08
wild boar	1	2	.0	.0	.0	.0	.0	.33	.0	.0	.0
s. hyaena	1	14	.0	.50	.43	.0	.0	.21	.0	.37	.0
lion/leopard	1	1	.0	.0	.0	.0	.0	.07	.0	.0	.0
wolf	1	1	.0	.0	.0	.0	.0	.0	.0	.06	.0
Guattari G2–3:											
horse	1	2	.0	.25	.0	.0	.0	.0	.0	.0	.04
red/fallow	3	19	.50	2.75	.0	.0	.50	.33	.0	.37	.0
aurochs	1	6	.0	.25	.0	.0	.0	.17	.50	.12	.08
wild boar	1	3	.0	.50	.0	.02	.0	.0	.0	.0	.0
s. hyaena	1	3	.0	.50	.0	.0	.0	.0	.0	.06	.0
bear	1	1	.0	.0	.0	.0	.25	.0	.0	.0	.0

APPENDIX 1.2 (Continued)

			Anatomical regions								
Taxon	MNI[a]	tMNE	Antler or horn	Head	Neck	Axial	Upper front	Lower front	Upper hind	Lower hind	Feet
Guattari G4–7:											
horse	1	3	.0	.0	.0	.0	.0	.0	.0	.06	.08
red/fallow	1	7	.0	1.00	.0	.0	.25	.07	.0	.06	.0
aurochs	2	11	.0	1.75	.0	.02	.50	.0	.0	.06	.0
s. hyaena	1	1	.0	.0	.0	.0	.0	.0	.0	.0	.02

[a] MNI is based on the highest standardized MNE value among the nine anatomical regions, rounded to the next whole number; tMNE refers to total MNE (nonstandardized count) for the designated taxon and provenience. To derive raw MNE for each anatomical region, see note in Appendix 1.1.

APPENDIX 1.3

Grotta di Sant'Agostino: Standardized anatomical data for large mammals by taxon and vertical provenience

			Anatomical regions								
Taxon	MNI[a]	tMNE	Antler or horn	Head	Neck	Axial	Upper front	Lower front	Upper hind	Lower hind	Feet
Sant'Agostino S0:											
horse	1	2	.0	.0	.0	.0	.0	.17	.0	.12	.0
red/fallow	3	55	.50	2.25	.14	.0	.0	1.33	.50	1.62	.92
roe	3	53	.50	2.25	.0	.02	.75	.83	.0	.50	1.25
aurochs	1	14	.0	.50	.28	.0	.25	.17	.0	.12	.29
wild boar	1	17	.0	.50	.0	.0	.0	.50	.0	.37	.37
ibex	1	12	.0	.50	.0	.0	.50	.0	.0	.37	.21
leopard	1	1	.0	.0	.0	.0	.0	.0	.0	.0	.02
wild cat	1	10	.0	.50	.14	.04	.0	.14	.0	.19	.0
wolf	1	5	.0	.50	.0	.02	.0	.07	.0	.0	.02
red fox	1	40	.0	.50	.28	.22	.50	.71	.0	.75	.02
bear	1	4	.0	.50	.0	.0	.0	.0	.0	.0	.03
badger	1	1	.0	.0	.0	.0	.0	.07	.0	.0	.0
Sant'Agostino S1:											
horse	1	7	.0	.0	.0	.06	.0	.0	.50	.12	.08
red/fallow	4	85	.50	3.75	.86	.10	2.25	1.50	2.50	2.87	.46
roe	2	45	.0	1.50	.0	.06	1.00	1.00	.0	.0	1.08
aurochs	1	18	.0	1.00	.28	.04	.0	.17	1.00	.62	.08
wild boar	1	14	.0	.75	.0	.02	.25	.33	.0	.37	.17
ibex	1	19	.50	1.00	.0	.02	.25	.33	.0	.75	.17
leopard	1	1	.0	.25	.0	.0	.0	.0	.0	.0	.0
cat/lynx	1	23	.0	.0	.43	.14	.0	.36	.50	.25	.05
wolf	1	15	.0	.50	.14	.08	.0	.21	.0	.19	.03
red fox	1	44	.0	1.00	.28	.26	.25	.71	.50	.69	.03
bear	1	2	.0	.0	.0	.0	.0	.0	.0	.0	.03
badger	1	2	.0	.0	.0	.0	.0	.14	.0	.0	.0
Sant'Agostino S2:											
wild ass	1	1	.0	.0	.0	.0	.0	.0	.0	.12	.0
red/fallow	3	61	.0	2.00	.28	.10	1.75	1.83	1.50	2.50	.21

(continued)

APPENDIX 1.3   (*Continued*)

Taxon	MNI[a]	tMNE	Antler or horn	Head	Neck	Axial	Upper front	Lower front	Upper hind	Lower hind	Feet
roe	2	24	.0	.75	.0	.02	.75	1.17	.0	.37	.29
aurochs	1	4	.0	.0	.0	.0	.25	.17	.0	.25	.0
wild boar	1	14	.0	.50	.0	.04	.0	.50	.0	.37	.17
ibex	1	12	.50	.50	.14	.02	.25	.33	.0	.12	.12
wild cat	1	29	.0	.50	.14	.12	.0	.64	.50	.31	.08
wolf	1	3	.0	.25	.0	.0	.0	.07	.0	.0	.02
red fox	2	50	.0	1.50	.14	.24	.50	.64	1.00	.56	.15
bear	1	2	.0	.0	.0	.0	.0	.0	.0	.0	.03
badger	1	1	.0	.0	.0	.0	.0	.07	.0	.0	.0
monk seal	1	1	.0	.0	.0	.0	.0	.07	.0	.0	.0
Sant'Agostino S3:											
horse	1	1	.0	.0	.0	.02	.0	.0	.0	.0	.0
red/fallow	2	21	.50	1.25	.14	.06	1.00	.33	.50	.37	.04
roe	1	19	.0	.25	.14	.04	.0	.83	.0	.37	.29
aurochs	1	3	.50	.0	.14	.0	.0	.0	.0	.12	.0
wild boar	1	4	.0	.25	.0	.04	.0	.0	.0	.0	.04
ibex	1	5	.0	.0	.0	.0	.25	.0	.0	.25	.08
leopard	1	2	.0	.0	.0	.0	.0	.07	.0	.06	.0
wild cat	1	12	.0	.25	.0	.08	.0	.28	.0	.19	.0
wolf	1	7	.0	.0	.14	.04	.25	.0	.0	.12	.02
red fox	2	24	.0	1.50	.0	.10	.25	.28	.0	.37	.03
bear	1	1	.0	.0	.0	.0	.0	.07	.0	.0	.0
badger	1	1	.0	.25	.0	.0	.0	.0	.0	.0	.0
Sant'Agostino S4:											
horse	1	1	.0	.25	.0	.0	.0	.0	.0	.0	.0
red/fallow	1	9	.0	.25	.0	.0	.50	.50	.0	.25	.04
roe	1	15	.0	.75	.0	.0	.25	.50	.0	.12	.29
aurochs	1	1	.0	.0	.0	.0	.0	.17	.0	.0	.0
wild boar	1	5	.0	.0	.0	.04	.0	.0	.0	.0	.12
ibex	1	25	.0	.50	.0	.06	1.00	.83	.50	.75	.17
leopard	1	2	.0	.0	.0	.0	.0	.07	.0	.06	.0
wild cat	1	1	.0	.0	.0	.0	.0	.07	.0	.0	.0
wolf	1	12	.0	.50	.28	.02	.0	.14	.50	.12	.03
red fox	1	9	.0	.25	.0	.06	.0	.07	.50	.12	.02
Sant'Agostino SX:											
red/fallow	1	4	.0	.0	.0	.0	.25	.17	.0	.25	.0
roe	5	120	.50	4.25	.86	.22	2.50	2.33	1.00	2.75	1.54
aurochs	1	1	.0	.25	.0	.0	.0	.0	.0	.0	.0
wild boar	1	1	.0	.0	.0	.0	.0	.0	.0	.0	.04
ibex	4	128	1.00	1.25	.86	.28	3.50	2.33	1.50	2.87	1.96
cat/lynx	1	3	.0	.0	.14	.0	.25	.0	.0	.06	.0
wolf	2	47	.0	1.50	.43	.12	.50	.86	.0	.81	.10
red fox	1	16	.0	1.00	.0	.06	.0	.36	.50	.19	.0
bear	1	4	.0	.25	.0	.0	.25	.14	.0	.0	.0

[a] MNI is based on the highest standardized MNE value among the nine anatomical regions, rounded to the next whole number; tMNE refers to total MNE (nonstandardized count) for the designated taxon and provenience. To derive raw MNE for each anatomical region, see note in Appendix 1.1.

Grotta Breuil: Standardized anatomical data for large mammals by taxon and provenience

Taxon	MNI[a]	tMNE	Antler or horn	Head	Neck	Axial	Upper front	Lower front	Upper hind	Lower hind	Feet
Breuil Br:											
SU	2	49	1.00	1.25	.43	.26	1.00	.83	1.00	.37	.50
MU	3	101	.50	3.00	.28	.65	1.25	1.67	2.00	2.00	.79
LU	2	44	.50	1.75	.0	.24	1.75	.67	1.00	.87	.17
s. carnivore	1	21	.0	.75	.28	.22	.25	.21	.0	.06	.0
Breuil B3/4:											
horse	1	3	.0	.25	.0	.0	.0	.17	.0	.12	.0
red/fallow	1	17	.50	1.00	.0	.0	.50	.33	.50	.50	.12
roe	1	2	.0	.0	.0	.0	.0	.0	.0	.12	.04
aurochs	1	4	.0	.0	.0	.0	.0	.0	.0	.37	.04
ibex	1	18	.50	.75	.0	.0	.0	.50	.0	.75	.21
MU	3	114	1.50	2.00	1.57	.82	1.50	2.17	1.50	2.37	.46
LU	1	14	.0	.75	.0	.04	.25	.33	.0	.62	.04
s. carnivore	2	21	.0	1.25	.28	.22	.0	.0	.50	.0	.03
wolf	1	1	.0	.25	.0	.0	.0	.0	.0	.0	.0
bear	1	3	.0	.25	.0	.0	.0	.0	.0	.0	.03

[a] MNI is based on the highest standardized MNE value among the nine anatomical regions, rounded to the next whole number; tMNE refers to total MNE (nonstandardized count) for the designated taxon and provenience; generic taxonomic categories were used for ungulate remains that could not be identified to species, but could be assigned to body size category. To derive raw MNE for each anatomical region, see note in Appendix 1.1.

Late Upper Paleolithic shelters: Standardized anatomical data for large mammals by taxon and vertical provenience

Taxon	MNI[a]	tMNE	Antler or horn	Head	Neck	Axial	Upper front	Lower front	Upper hind	Lower hind	Feet
Palidoro 33–34:											
horse	1	8	.0	.25	.0	.06	.25	.33	.50	.0	.0
wild ass	2	40	.0	1.50	.14	.14	.50	1.33	1.50	.75	.29
red	8	109	.50	7.25	.28	.10	5.25	3.00	.50	3.62	.12
aurochs	3	64	.50	2.25	.0	.08	1.00	2.33	2.00	1.75	.58
wild boar	2	10	.0	.50	.28	.02	1.25	.0	.0	.0	.0
ibex	1	1	.0	.0	.0	.0	.0	.0	.0	.12	.0
MU	10	211	.50	9.25	2.71	1.10	4.00	4.33	2.00	4.50	.42
LU	3	97	.50	2.50	1.43	.44	1.25	2.67	2.50	1.75	.58
badger	1	9	.0	1.00	.0	.02	.0	.21	.50	.0	.0
Salvini 10–15:											
red	4	199	.50	2.50	2.43	1.43	3.25	1.67	3.50	3.50	1.83
SU	1	30	.0	.50	.28	.18	.25	.50	.50	.37	.37
LU	2	67	.0	1.50	.71	.39	1.75	.50	1.50	1.50	.50

(*continued*)

APPENDIX 1.5   (*Continued*)

				Anatomical regions						
Taxon	MNI[a]	tMNE	Antler or horn	Head	Neck	Axial	Upper front	Lower front	Upper hind	Lower hind	Feet
Polesini 1–12, small carnivores only:											
s. carnivore	81	780	.0	79.75	.43	.31	28.50	9.36	10.00	11.00	.03
wild cat	2	39	.0	1.25	.0	.02	1.75	.78	.0	.94	.0
red fox	66	556	.0	65.50	.43	.26	22.00	5.14	7.00	6.37	.03
bear	1	1	.0	.0	.0	.0	.0	.0	.50	.0	.0
badger	13	185	.0	13.00	.0	.02	4.75	3.43	3.00	3.69	.0

[a] MNI is based on the highest standardized MNE value among the nine anatomical regions, rounded to the next whole number; tMNE refers to total MNE (nonstandardized count) for the designated taxon and provenience; generic taxonomic categories were used for ungulate remains that could not be identified to species, but could be assigned to body size category. To derive raw MNE for each anatomical region, see note in Appendix 1.1.

APPENDIX 1.6

Buca della Iena: Standardized anatomical data for large mammals by taxon and vertical provenience

				Anatomical regions						
Taxon	MNI[a]	tMNE	Antler or horn	Head	Neck	Axial	Upper front	Lower front	Upper hind	Lower hind	Feet
Buca della Iena I1:											
horse	1	5	.0	.0	.0	.0	.0	.17	.0	.12	.12
rhino	1	1	.0	.0	.0	.0	.0	.0	.0	.12	.0
red/fallow	2	11	1.50	.50	.0	.06	.25	.0	.0	.25	.0
roe	1	2	.0	.0	.0	.0	.0	.0	.0	.25	.0
aurochs	1	8	.0	.0	.0	.0	.0	.17	.0	.75	.04
s. hyaena	1	5	.0	.75	.14	.02	.0	.0	.0	.0	.0
bear	1	11	.0	.50	.0	.0	.0	.28	.0	.06	.07
Buca della Iena I2:											
horse	1	1	.0	.0	.0	.0	.0	.17	.0	.0	.0
red/fallow	1	3	.0	.0	.0	.02	.25	.0	.0	.12	.0
roe	1	1	.0	.0	.0	.0	.0	.0	.0	.12	.0
aurochs	1	1	.0	.0	.0	.0	.0	.0	.0	.0	.04
s. hyaena	1	3	.0	.0	.0	.02	.0	.0	.0	.06	.02
bear	1	2	.0	.0	.0	.0	.0	.0	.0	.0	.03
Buca della Iena I3:											
red/fallow	1	11	.0	.0	.14	.08	.0	.0	1.00	.0	.17
roe	1	1	.0	.0	.0	.0	.0	.0	.0	.0	.04
aurochs	1	1	.0	.0	.0	.0	.0	.0	.0	.0	.04
wild boar	1	1	.0	.0	.0	.0	.0	.17	.0	.0	.0
s. hyaena	1	9	.0	.0	.0	.0	.0	.28	.0	.12	.05
wild cat	1	1	.0	.0	.0	.0	.0	.07	.0	.0	.0
wolf	1	6	.0	.0	.57	.02	.0	.07	.0	.0	.0
bear	1	12	.0	.0	.0	.0	.0	.07	.0	.06	.17
badger	1	15	.0	.0	.0	.02	.25	.50	1.00	.25	.0

APPENDIX 1.6 (*Continued*)

Taxon	MNI[a]	tMNE	Antler or horn	Head	Neck	Axial	Upper front	Lower front	Upper hind	Lower hind	Feet
Buca della Iena I4:											
horse	1	2	.0	.0	.0	.0	.0	.0	.0	.12	.04
red/fallow	2	19	2.00	.0	.0	.16	.0	.17	1.00	.12	.12
roe	1	7	.0	.25	.0	.0	.0	.17	.0	.50	.04
wild boar	1	1	.0	.0	.0	.02	.0	.0	.0	.0	.0
s. hyaena	1	10	.0	.0	.0	.04	.0	.43	.0	.06	.02
leopard	1	1	.0	.0	.0	.0	.0	.07	.0	.0	.0
wolf	1	4	.0	.25	.28	.0	.0	.0	.0	.0	.02
bear	1	21	.0	.25	.0	.0	.0	.14	.0	.19	.25
badger	2	14	.0	.50	.0	.02	.25	.21	1.50	.25	.0
polecat	1	1	.0	.25	.0	.0	.0	.0	.0	.0	.0
Buca della Iena I5:											
horse	1	4	.0	.0	.0	.02	.0	.33	.0	.0	.04
rhino	1	2	.0	.0	.0	.02	.25	.0	.0	.0	.0
red/fallow	1	19	.0	.0	.14	.16	.0	.67	.0	.25	.17
roe	1	4	.0	.25	.0	.0	.0	.33	.0	.0	.04
aurochs	1	3	.0	.0	.14	.02	.0	.0	.0	.12	.0
wild boar	1	3	.0	.50	.0	.0	.0	.0	.0	.0	.04
s. hyaena	1	15	.0	.50	.57	.04	.25	.21	.50	.0	.03
leopard	1	2	.0	.0	.0	.0	.0	.07	.0	.06	.0
wild cat	1	5	.0	.50	.0	.0	.25	.0	.0	.12	.0
wolf	1	3	.0	.0	.0	.02	.0	.07	.0	.06	.0
bear	1	20	.0	.25	.0	.0	.0	.43	.0	.06	.20
badger	3	24	.0	.75	.0	.0	2.50	.21	.0	.50	.0
Buca della Iena I6:											
elephant	1	1	.0	.0	.0	.0	.0	.17	.0	.0	.0
horse	2	20	.0	.0	.0	.04	.0	.33	.0	1.37	.21
rhino	1	4	.0	.0	.0	.04	.25	.0	.0	.12	.0
red/fallow	5	45	4.50	3.00	.0	.16	.25	.33	.0	.87	.25
roe	1	4	.0	.25	.0	.0	.25	.33	.0	.0	.0
aurochs	1	14	.0	.0	.0	.0	.25	.17	.0	1.00	.17
s. hyaena	3	37	.0	3.00	.0	.08	.25	.71	1.50	.19	.07
wolf	1	2	.0	.25	.0	.0	.25	.0	.0	.0	.0
bear	1	20	.0	.25	.0	.0	.25	.21	.0	.0	.25

[a] MNI is based on the highest standardized MNE value among the nine anatomical regions, rounded to the next whole number; tMNE refers to total MNE (nonstandardized count) for the designated taxon and provenience. To derive raw MNE for each anatomical region, see note in Appendix 1.1.

APPENDIX 1.7
Modern Alaskan wolf den assemblages: Standardized anatomical data for large mammals by taxon

Taxon	MNI[a]	tMNE	Antler or horn	Head	Neck	Axial	Upper front	Lower front	Upper hind	Lower hind	Feet
WD1 (Binford's collection, Stiner's data):											
caribou	6	93	.50	.50	.28	.08	2.00	2.33	.50	5.12	.83
dall sheep	1	7	.50	.25	.14	.0	.0	.17	.0	.37	.0
both taxa	7	100	1.00	.75	.43	.08	2.00	2.50	.50	5.50	.83
WD2 (Binford's data):											
caribou	1	25	.0	.50	.14	.12	.50	.50	.50	.62	.21
WD3 (Binford's data):											
caribou	1	20	.50	.25	.0	.0	.50	.33	.0	1.00	.25

[a] MNI is based on the highest standardized MNE value among the nine anatomical regions, rounded to the next whole number; tMNE refers to total MNE (nonstandardized count) for the designated taxon and provenience. To derive raw MNE for each anatomical region, see note in Appendix 1.1.

APPENDIX 1.8
Modern African spotted, brown, and striped hyaena den assemblages: Standardized anatomical data for large mammals by taxon

Taxon[a]	MNI[b]	tMNE	Antler or horn	Head	Neck	Axial	Upper front	Lower front	Upper hind	Lower hind	Feet
Brown hyaena dens—Kalahari, Binford (1981 field data):											
Class I	1	6	1.00	.0	.0	.0	.0	.0	.0	.25	.08
Class II	4	11	4.00	.0	.0	.06	.0	.0	.0	.0	.0
Class III	1	1	.0	.0	.0	.0	.0	.17	.0	.0	.0
Brown hyaena dens—Kalahari (Mills and Mills 1977):											
Class I	6	43	1.00	5.50	.43	.18	.0	.0	.50	.50	.08
Class II	8	70	8.00	3.50	1.86	.12	1.00	.50	.0	.25	.50
Class III	2	30	1.00	1.75	.57	.12	.50	.67	.50	.50	.0
carnivore	21	109	.0	20.25	.86	.28	.25	.0	.0	.06	.10
Spotted hyaena dens—Kalahari, Binford (1981 field data):											
Class II	4	26	3.50	1.50	.14	.14	.50	.17	.0	.25	.0
Class III	4	49	3.50	1.00	3.00	.04	1.00	.17	.0	.0	.42
Spotted hyaena den (entrance)—Zimbabwe, Haynes' collection:											
pachyderm	1	1	.0	.25	.0	.0	.0	.0	.0	.0	.0
wildebeest	2	12	.0	1.25	.0	.02	.25	.0	.0	.25	.08
buffalo	1	1	.0	.0	.0	.0	.0	.0	.50	.0	.0
warthog	1	2	.0	.25	.0	.0	.0	.0	.0	.12	.0
Spotted hyaena den—Timbavati, South Africa (Bearder 1977; Brain 1981):											
all taxa	10	135	10.00	9.00	.0	1.16	3.25	.0	.0	.0	.37
Spotted hyaena den—Amboseli Basin, Kenya (Potts 1982):											
all taxa	10	279	.0	8.00	.0	1.65	9.75	7.83	1.00	6.12	1.21

APPENDIX 1.8 (*Continued*)

Taxon[a]	*MNI*[b]	*tMNE*	*Antler or horn*	*Head*	*Neck*	*Axial*	*Upper front*	*Lower front*	*Upper hind*	*Lower hind*	*Feet*
			Anatomical regions								
Spotted hyaena den—Natab, Namib Desert (Henschel et al. 1979):											
Class I	1	7	.0	.25	.0	.10	.0	.0	.0	.12	.0
Caprid	1	6	1.00	.0	.0	.0	.0	.0	.0	.0	.17
Class III	7	40	6.50	.25	.43	.0	.75	1.00	.0	1.62	.04
Equus sp.	1	1	.0	.0	.0	.0	.0	.0	.0	.12	.0
all taxa	8	45	7.50	.50	.43	.0	.75	1.00	.50	1.75	.04
Striped hyaena dens—Arad Cave, Israel (Skinner et al. 1980):											
donkey[c]	4	79	.0	2.00	.0	.18	1.25	2.33	3.00	4.00	.21
cattle	1	2	.0	.25	.0	.0	.25	.0	.0	.0	.0
pig	1	3	.0	.50	.0	.0	.0	.17	.0	.0	.0
goat/sheep	10	66	5.50	10.00	.0	.08	1.00	.17	.0	.75	.0
camel	6	112	.0	5.25	.43	.16	4.00	3.00	2.50	4.87	.08
gazelle	1	1	.50	.0	.0	.0	.0	.0	.0	.0	.0
porcupine	1	2	.0	.50	.0	.0	.0	.0	.0	.0	.0
dog	9	50	.0	8.75	.0	.20	1.00	.07	.0	.0	.0
fox	1	2	.0	.50	.0	.0	.0	.0	.0	.0	.0
human	1	2	.0	.50	.0	.0	.0	.0	.0	.0	.0

[a] Body size classes I–IV as defined by Brain (1981:275).

[b] MNI is based on the highest standardized MNE value among the nine anatomical regions, rounded to the next whole number; tMNE refers to total MNE (nonstandardized count) for the designated taxon and provenience; generic taxonomic categories were used for ungulate remains that could not be identified to species, but could be assigned to body size category. To derive raw MNE for each anatomical region, see note in Appendix 1.1.

[c] A few fragments of horse are included in these counts. Also note that the observers sometimes supplemented the striped hyaenas' natural diet by placing whole donkey carcasses near the dens.

Literature Cited

Alados, C. L., and J. Escos. 1988. Parturition dates and mother-kid behavior in Spanish ibex (*Capra pyrenaica*) in Spain. *J. Mamm.* 69:172–175.

Alessio, M., F. Bella, G. Calderoni, C. Cortesi, and S. Improta. 1976–77. Carbon-14 dating of bone collagen from Upper Paleolithic Palidoro deposit. *Quaternaria* 19:181–185.

Altuna, J. 1986. The mammalian faunas from the prehistoric site of La Riera. In *La Riera Cave: Stone Age Hunter-gatherer Adaptations in Northern Spain*, edited by L. G. Straus and G. A. Clark, pp. 237–274 and Append. B 421–479. Arizona State Univ. Anthropol. Res. Paper, no. 36.

Alvard, M., and H. Kaplan. 1991. Procurement technology and prey mortality among indigenous neotropical hunters. In *Human Predators and Prey Mortality*, edited by M. C. Stiner, pp. 79–104. Boulder, Colo.: Westview Press.

Andrews, P. 1990. *Owls, Caves and Fossils.* Chicago: Univ. Chicago Press.

Andrews, P., and A. Turner. 1992. Life and death of the Westbury bears. *Ann. Zool. Fennici* 28:139–149.

Anzidei, A. P., A. Bietti, P. Cassoli, M. Ruffo, and A. G. Segre. 1984. Risultati preliminari dello scavo in un deposito Pleistocenico in localita Rebibbia-Casal de'Pazzi (Roma). *Estr. Atti XXIV Riunione Scientifica dell'Ist. Ital. Preistoria e Protostoria nel Lazio*, Ottobre 1982.

Anzidei, A. P., A. Angelelli, A. Arnoldus-Huyzendveld, L. Caloi, M. R. Palombo, and A. G. Segre. 1989. Le gisement Pléistocène de la Polledrara di Cecanibbio (Rome, Italie). *L'Anthropologie* 93:749–782.

Arensburg, B. 1989. New skeletal evidence concerning the anatomy of Middle Paleolithic populations in the Middle East: The Kebara skeleton. In *The Human Revolution: Behavioural and Biological Perspectives on the Origins of Modern Humans*, Vol. 1, edited by P. Mellars and C. B. Stringer, pp. 164–171. Edinburgh: Edinburgh Univ. Press.

Arnold, E. N., and J. A. Burton. 1978. *A Field Guide to the Reptiles and Amphibians of Britain and Europe.* London: Collins.

Arsebük, G., F. C. Howell, and M. Özbaşaran. 1990. Yarımburgaz 1988. *XI. Kazı Sonuçları Toplantısı, I.* Ankara: Ankara Üniversitesi Basımevi, pp. 9–38.

Arsebük, G., F. C. Howell, and M. Özbaşaran. 1991. Yarımburgaz 1989. *XII. Kazı Sonuçları Toplantısı, I.* Ankara: Ankara Üniversitesi Basımevi, pp. 17–41.

Avellino, E., A. Bietti, L. Giacopini, and A. Lo Pinto. 1989. A new Dryas II site in southern Lazio; Riparo Salvini, thoughts on the late Epigravettian in Middle and Southern Tyrrhenian Italy. In *The Mesolithic in Europe*, edited by C. Bonsall, pp. 516–532. Edinburgh: John Donald.

Bächler, E. 1921. Das Drachenloch dei Vättis im taminatal. *Jahrb. St.-Gall. Naturf. Ges. 1920–21.*

Bächler, E. 1940. *Das alpine Paläolithikum der Schweiz.* Basel.

Baden-Powell, D. F. W. 1964. Gorham's Cave, Gibralter: Report on the climatic equivalent of the marine mollusca. *Bull. Inst. Arch.* (Univ. London) 4:216–218.

Bailey, G. 1975. The role of molluscs in coastal economies: The results of midden analysis in coastal Australia. *J. Archaeol. Science* 2:45–62.

Bailey, G. 1978. Shell middens as indicators of postglacial economies, a territorial perspective. In *The Early Post-glacial Settlement of Northern Europe*, edited by P. Mellars, pp. 37–63. London: Duckworth.

Ballard, W. B. 1982. Gray wolf-brown bear relationships in the Nelchina Basin of south-central Alaska. In *Wolves of the World: Perspectives of Behavior, Ecology, and Conservation*, edited by F. H. Harrington and P. C. Paquet, pp. 71–80. Park Ridge, N.J.: Noyes.

Ballard, W. B., and J. S. Whitman. 1987. Marrow fat dynamics in moose calves. *J. Wildlife Manag.* 51:66–69.

Ballard, W. B., J. S. Whitman, and C. L. Gardner. 1987. Ecology of an exploited wolf population in south-central Alaska. *Wildlife Monogr.*, no. 98.

Banfield, A. W. F. 1974. *The Mammals of Canada.* Toronto: Univ. Toronto Press.

Barker, G. 1974. Prehistoric territories and economies in

central Italy. In *Palaeoeconomy,* edited by E. S. Higgs, pp. 111–175. Cambridge: Cambridge Univ. Press.

Barker, G. 1981. *Landscape and Society: Prehistoric Central Italy.* London: Academic Press.

Bárta, J. 1989. Hunting of brown bears in the Mesolithic: Evidence from the Medvedia Cave near Ruzín in Slovakia. In *The Mesolithic in Europe,* edited by C. Bonsall, pp. 456–460. Edinburgh: John Donald.

Bartmann, R. M., G. C. White, and L. H. Carpenter. 1992. Compensatory mortality in a Colorado mule deer population. *Wildlife Monogr.,* no. 121.

Bar-Yosef, O. 1989. Geochronology of the Levantine Middle Palaeolithic. In *The Human Revolution,* edited by P. Mellars and C. Stringer, pp. 589–610. Princeton: Princeton Univ. Press.

Bar-Yosef, O. 1991. The archaeology of the Natufian layer at Hayonim Cave. In *The Natufian Culture in the Levant,* edited by O. Bar-Yosef and F. Valla, pp. 81–93. Ann Arbor, Mich.: International Monographs in Prehistory.

Bar-Yosef, O., B. Vandermeersch, B. Arensburg, A. Belfer-Cohen, P. Goldberg, H. Laville, L. Meignen, Y. Rak, J. D. Speth, E. Tchernov, A.-M. Tillier, and S. Weiner. 1992. The excavations in Kebara Cave, Mt. Carmel. *Curr. Anth.* 33:497–550.

Baryshnikov, G. 1989. Les mammifères du paléolithique inférieur du Caucase. *L'Anthropologie* 93:813–830.

Batcheler, C. L. 1960. A study of the relations between roe, red and fallow deer, with special reference to Drummond Hill Forest, Scotland. *J. Animal Ecol.* 29:375–384.

Baumler, M. F. 1988. Core reduction, flake production, and the Middle Paleolithic industry of Zobiste (Yugoslavia). In *Upper Plesitocene Prehistory of Western Eurasia,* edited by H. L. Dibble and A. Montet-White, pp. 255–274. Philadelphia: Univ. Mus. Monogr. 54, Univ. Pennsylvania.

Bearder, S. K. 1977. Feeding habits of spotted hyaenas in a woodland habitat. *E. Afr. Wildlife J.* 15:263–280.

Behrensmeyer, A. K. 1976. Fossil assemblages in relation to sedimentary environments in the East Rudolf Succession. In *Earliest Man and Environments in the Lake Rudolph Basin,* edited by Y. Coppens, F. C. Howell, G. L. Isaac, and R. E. F. Leakey, pp. 163–170. Chicago: Univ. Chicago Press.

Behrensmeyer, A. K. 1978. Taphonomic and ecologic information from bone weathering. *Paleobiol.* 4:150–162.

Behrensmeyer, A. K., and S. M. Kidwell. 1985. Taphonomy's contributions to paleobiology. *Paleobiol.* 11:105–119.

Belfer-Cohen, A., and O. Bar-Yosef. 1981. The Aurignacian at Hayonim Cave. *Paléorient* 7:19–42.

Benedict, J. B. 1975. The Murray site: A late prehistoric game drive system in the Colorado Rocky Mountains. *Plains Anthropol.* 20:161–174.

Berger, J. 1986. *Wild Horses of the Great Basin, Social Competition and Population Size.* Chicago: Univ. Chicago Press.

Bergerud, A. T., and W. B. Ballard. 1988. Wolf predation on caribou: The Nelchina herd case history, a different interpretation. *J. Wildlife Manag.* 52:344–357.

Bergerud, A. T., and J. B. Snider. 1988. Predation in the dynamics of moose populations: A reply. *J. Wildlife Manag.* 52:559–564.

Bertram, B. C. R. 1979. Serengeti predators and their social systems. In *Serengeti: Dynamics of an Ecosystem,* edited by A. R. E. Sinclair and M. Norton-Griffiths, pp. 221–248. Chicago: Univ. Chicago Press.

Bibikov, D. I. 1982. Wolf ecology and management in the USSR. In *Wolves of the World: Perspectives of Behavior, Ecology, and Conservation,* edited by F. H. Harrington and P. C. Paquet, pp. 120–133. Park Ridge, N.J.: Noyes.

Biddittu, I., P. Cassoli, F. Radicati di Brozcío, A. G. Segre, E. Segre Naldini, and I. Villa. 1979. Anagni, a K-Ar dated Lower and Middle Pleistocene site, central Italy: A preliminary report. *Quaternaria* 21:53–71.

Bietti, A. 1969. Due stazione di superficie del Paleolitico Superiore nella Pianura Pontina. *Bull. Paletnologia Italiana* 78:7–39.

Bietti, A. 1976–77a. Analysis and illustration of the Epigravettian industry collected during the 1955 excavations at Palidoro (Rome, Italy). *Quaternaria* 19:197–215.

Bietti, A. 1976–77b. The excavation 1955–1959 in the Upper Paleolithic deposit of the rockshelter at Palidoro (Rome, Italy). *Quaternaria* 19:149–155.

Bietti, A. 1980. Un tentativo di classificazione quantitiva del 'Pontiniano' Laziale nel quadro delle industrie musteriane in Italia: problemi di derivazione e di interpretazione culturale. *Rivista di Antropologia* 61:161–202.

Bietti, A. 1982. The Mousterian complexes of Italy: A search for cultural understanding of the industrial assemblages. *Anthropos* 27:231–251.

Bietti, A. 1984. Primi risultati dello scavo nel giacimento Epigravettiano finale di Riparo Salvini (Terracina, Latina). *Atti XXIV Riunione Scientifica Ist. Ital. Preistoria e Protostoria,* pp. 195–205.

Bietti, A. 1986. Problemi di metodologia nello studio antropologico delle società di cacciatori e raccoglitori preistorici. *Dialoghi d'Archeologia, N.S.* 1:9–26.

Bietti, A. 1990. The late Upper Paleolithic in Italy: An overview. *J. World Prehistory* 4:95–155.

Bietti, A., and S. Grimaldi. 1990–91. Patterns of reduction sequences at Grotta Breuil: Statistical analyses and comparisons of archaeological vs. experimental data. *Quaternaria Nova* (Nuova Serie) 1:379–406.

Bietti, A., and S. L. Kuhn. 1990–91. Techno-typological studies on the Mousterian industry of Grotta Guattari. *Quaternaria Nova* (Nuova Serie) 1:193–211.

Bietti, A., S. L. Kuhn, A. G. Segre, and M. C. Stiner. 1990–91. Grotta Breuil: A general introduction and stratigraphy. *Quaternaria Nova* (Nuova Serie) 1:305–323.

Bietti, A., and M. C. Stiner. 1992. Les modèles de la subsistance et de l'habitat de l'Épigravettien Italien: l'example de Riparo Salvini (Terracina, Latium). In *Colioque International, Le Peuplement Magdalenien,* edited by H. Laville, J.-F. Rigaud, and B. Vandermeersch, pp. 137–152. Paris: Edition C.T.H.S.

Bietti, A., G. Manzi, P. Passarello, A. G. Segre, and M. C. Stiner. 1988. The 1986 excavation campaign at Grotta Breuil (Monte Circeo LT). *Quaderno Archeologico Laziale* 16:372–388.

Bietti, A., P. Rossetti, and G.-L. Zanzi. 1989. Cultural adaptations and environment: Two test cases from southern central Tyrrhenian Italy. *Rivista di Antropologia* 67:239–264.

Bigalke, E. H., and E. A Voigt. 1973. The interdisciplinary aspect of a study of shellfish-exploitation by indigenous coastal communities. *SAMAB* 10:256–261.

Binford, L. R. 1972. *An Archaeological Perspective.* New York: Seminar Press.

Binford, L. R. 1977. Forty-seven trips: A case study in the character of archaeological formation processes. In *Stone Tools as Cultural Markers,* edited by R. V. S. Wright, pp. 24–36. Canberra: Australian Institute of Aboriginal Studies.

Binford, L. R. 1978. *Nunamiut Ethnoarchaeology.* New York: Academic Press.

Binford, L. R. 1979. Organization and formation processes: Looking at curated technologies. *J. Anthropol. Res.* 35:255–273.

Binford, L. R. 1980. Willow smoke and dog's tails: Hunter-gatherer settlement systems and archaeological site formation. *Amer. Antiq.* 45:4–20.

Binford, L. R. 1981. *Bones: Ancient Men and Modern Myths.* New York: Academic Press.

Binford, L. R. 1982. The archaeology of place. *J. Anthropol. Arch.* 1:5–31.

Binford, L. R. 1983. *In Pursuit of the Past.* London: Thames and Hudson.

Binford, L. R. 1984. *Faunal Remains from Klasies River Mouth.* New York: Academic Press.

Binford, L. R. 1987. Researching ambiguity: Frames of reference and site structure. In *Method and Theory for Activity Area Research,* edited by S. Kent, pp. 449–512. New York: Columbia Univ. Press.

Binford, L. R. 1988. Etude taphonomique des restes fauniques de la Grotte Vaufrey, Couche VII. In *La Grotte Vaufrey: Paléoenvironnement, Chronologie, Activités Humaines,* edited by J.-P. Rigaud, pp. 535–563. C.N.R.S.: Mémmoires de la Societé Préhistorique Française, Tome 19.

Binford, L. R. 1990. Isolating the transition to cultural adaptations: An organizational approach. In *The Emergence of Modern Humans: Biocultural Adaptations in the Later Pleistocene,* edited by E. Trinkaus, pp. 18–41. New York: Cambridge Univ. Press.

Binford, L. R. 1991. When the going gets tough, the tough get going: Nunamiut local groups, camping patterns and economic organization. In *Ethnoarchaeological Approaches to Mobile Campsites: Hunter-Gatherer and Pastoralist Case Studies,* edited by C. Gamble and W. A. Boismer, pp. 25–137. Ann Arbor, Mich.: International Monographs in Prehistory.

Binford, L. R., and Bertram. 1977. Bone frequencies and attritional processes. In *For Theory Building in Archaeology,* edited by L. R. Binford, pp. 77–156. New York: Academic Press.

Binford, L. R., and C. K. Ho. 1985. Taphonomy at a distance: Zhoukoudian, "the cave home of Beijing Man"? *Curr. Anth.* 26:413–442.

Bischoff, J. L., R. Julia, and R. Mora. 1988. Uranium series dating of Mousterian occupations at Abric Romani, Spain. *Nature* 332:68–70.

Blanc, A. C. 1935a. Saccopastore II. *Rivista di Antropologia* 30:3–5.

Blanc, A. C. 1935b. Lo studio stratigrafico di Pianure costiere. *Boll. Società Geologica Italiana* 54:277–288.

Blanc, A. C. 1935c. Sulla fauna Quaternaria dell'Agro Pontino. *Atti Società Toscana di Scienze Naturali* 44:108–110.

Blanc, A. C. 1936a. Sulla stratigrafia quaternaria dell'Agro Pontino e della bassa Versilia. *Boll. Società Geologica Italiana* 60:375–396.

Blanc, A. C. 1936b. Le groupe volcanique Latial et ses relations stratigraphiques avec le Quaternaire marin. *Rev. Géog. Phys. et Géol. Dynamique* 9:57–75.

Blanc, A. C. 1937a. Fauna a Ippopotamo ed industrie paleolitiche nel riempimento delle grotte litoranee del Monte Circeo: I La Grotta delle Capre, II La Grotta del Fossellone. *Rendiconti R. Accademia Nazionale Lincei* 25:88–93.

Blanc, A. C. 1937b. Nuovi giacimenti paleolitici del Lazio e della Toscana. *Studi Etruschi* 11:273–304.

Blanc, A. C. 1937c. Low levels of the Mediterranean Sea during the Pleistocene Glaciation. *Quart. J. Geol. Soc. (London),* no. 93.

Blanc, A. C. 1938. Una serie di nuovi giacimenti pleistocenici e paleolitici in grotte litoranee del Monte Circeo. *Rendiconti R. Accademia Nazionale Lincei* 17:201–209.

Blanc, A. C. 1939a. L'homme fossile au Monte Circé. *L'Anthropologie* 49:254–264.

Blanc, A. C. 1939b. Il Monte Circeo: le sue grotte paleolitiche ed il suo uomo fossile. *Boll. Reale Società Geografica Italiana* 17:485–493.

Blanc, A. C. 1939c. L'uomo fossile del Monte Circeo, un cranio neandertaliano nella Grotta Guattari a San Felice Circeo. *Rivista di Antropologia* 23:1–18.

Blanc, A. C. 1939d. L'uomo fossile del Monte Circeo ed il suo ancora ignoto successore. *Società Italiana per il Progresso delle Scienze, Roma* 17:335–353.

Blanc, A. C. 1940. The fossil man of Circe's mountain. *Natural Hist.* (May):280–287.

Blanc, A. C. 1954. Reperti fossili Neandertaliani della Grotta del Fossellone al Monte Circeo: Circeo IV. *Quaternaria* 1:171–175.

Blanc, A. C. 1955a. Ricerche sul Quaternario Laziale. *Quaternaria* 2:187–200.

Blanc, A. C. 1955b. Scavi e ricerche al Monte Circeo e nella regione di Roma. *Quaternaria* 2:287–291.

Blanc, A. C. 1955c. Relazione sull'attività della sezione di Roma dell'Istituto Italiano di Paleontologia Umana nell'anno 1941–42. *Quaternaria* 2:270–272.

Blanc, A. C. 1957. On the Pleistocene sequence of Rome: Paleoecologic and archaeologic correlations. *Quaternaria* 4:1–17.

Blanc, A. C. 1958. Torre in Pietra, Saccopastore, Monte Circeo, on the position of the Mousterian in the Pleistocene sequence of the Rome area. In *Hundert Jahre Neanderthaler (Neanderthal Centenary),* edited by G. H. R. von Koenigswald, pp. 167–174. Utrecht, Netherlands: Wenner-Gren Foundation.

Blanc, A. C. 1958–61. Industria musteriana su calcare e su valve di *Meretrix chione* associata con fossili di elefante e rinocerante, in nuovi giacimenti costieri del Capo de Leuca. *Quaternaria* 5:308–313.

Blanc, A. C. 1961. Some evidence for the ideologies of early man. In *The Social Life of Early Man,* edited by S. L. Washburn, pp. 119–136. Chicago: Aldine.

Blanc, A. C., and A. G. Segre. 1947. Nuovi giacimenti tirreniani e paleolitici sulla costiera tra Sperlonga e Gaeta. *Historia Naturalis* 2:1–2.

Blanc, A. C., and A. G. Segre. 1953. Excursion au Mont Circé. *INQUA IVe Congres International,* Roma, Pisa.

Blanc, E. 1974–75. Mariella Taschini. *Quaternaria* 18:1–7.

Bleed, P. 1986. The optimal design of hunting weapons. *Amer. Antiq.* 51:737–747.

Blumenschine, R. J. 1986. *Early Hominid Scavenging Opportunities: Implications of Carcass Availability in the Serengeti and Ngorongoro Ecosystems.* Oxford: BAR International Series 283.

Blumenschine, R. J. 1987. Characteristics of an early hominid scavenging niche. *Curr. Anth.* 28:383–407.

Blumenschine, R. J. 1991. Prey size and age models of prehistoric hominid scavenging: Test cases from the Serengeti. In *Human Predators and Prey Mortality,* edited by M. C. Stiner, pp. 121–147. Boulder, Colo.: Westview Press.

Blurton Jones, N., K. Hawkes, and J. O'Connell. 1989. Studying costs of children in two foraging societies: Implications for schedules of reproduction. In *Comparative Socioecology of Mammals and Man,* edited by V. Standon and R. Foley, pp. 365–390. London: Blackwell.

Boëda, É. 1986. Approche technologique du concept Levallois et évaluation de son champ d'application. Thèse de doctorat, Université de Paris 10.

Boëda, É. 1988. Le concept laminaire: rupture et filiation avec le concept Levallois. In *L'Homme de Néandertal,* Vol. 8: *La Mutation,* edited by M. Otte, pp. 41–59. Liège: ERAUL 35.

Boer, A. H. 1988. Mortality rates of moose in New Brunswick: A life table analysis. *J. Wildlife Manag.* 52:21–25.

Bordes, F. 1961a. Mousterian cultures in France. *Science* 134(3482):803–810.

Bordes, F. 1961b. Typologie du paléolithique ancien et moyen. *Cahiers du Quaternarie* no. 1. Bordeaux: Institut du Quaternarie, Université de Bordeaux.

Bordes, F. 1968. *The Old Stone Age.* New York: McGraw Hill.

Boscagli, G. 1985. Attuale distribuzione geografica e stima numerica del lupo (*Canis lupus* Linneaus, 1758) sul territorio Italiano. *Natura* (S. I. S. N., Museo Civico di Storia Naturale e Acquario Civico, Milano) 76:77–93.

Boutin, S. 1992. Predation and moose population dynamics: A critique. *J. Wildlife Manag.* 56:116–127.

Brain, C. K. 1969. The contribution of Namib Desert Hottentots to an understanding of Australopithecine bone accumulations. *Scien. Papers Namib Desert Res. Station* 39:13–22.

Brain, C. K. 1980. Some criteria for the recognition of bone-collecting agencies in African caves. In *Fossils in the Making: Vertebrate Taphonomy and Paleoecology,* edited by A. K. Behrensmeyer and A. P. Hill, pp. 107–130. Chicago: Univ. Chicago Press.

Brain, C. K. 1981. *The Hunters or the Hunted?* Chicago: Univ. Chicago Press.

Braza, R., C. San Jose, and A. Blom. 1988. Birth measurements, paturition dates and progeny sex ratio of *Dama dama* in Doñana, Spain. *J. Mamm.* 69:607–610.

Brugal, J.-P., and J. Jaubert. 1991. Les gisements paleontologiques Pleistocenes a indices de frequentation humaine: un nouveau type de comportement de predation? *Paléo* 3:15–41.

Bucquoy, E., P. Dautzenberg, and G. Dollfus. 1882. *Les mollusques marins du Roussillon,* Vols. 1–3. Paris: J.-B. Baillière & Fils.

Bullock, D., and J. Rackham. 1982. Epiphysial fusion and tooth eruption of feral goats from Moffatdale, Dumfries and Galloway, Scotland. In *Aging and Sexing Animal Bones from Archaeological Sites,* edited by B. Wilson, C. Grigson, and S. Payne, pp. 73–90. Oxford: BAR British Series 109.

Bunn, H. T. 1981. Archaeological evidence for meat-eating by Plio-Pleistocene hominids from Koobi Fora and Olduvai Gorge. *Nature* 291:574–577.

Bunn, H. T. 1983. Comparative analysis of modern bone assemblages from a San hunter-gatherer camp in the Kalahari Desert, Botswana, and from a spotted hyaena den near Nairobi, Kenya. In *Animals and Archaeology: 1. Hunters and Their Prey,* edited by J. Clutton-Brock and C. Grigson, pp. 143–148. Oxford: BAR International Series 163.

Bunn, H. T., and R. J. Blumenschine. 1987. On "theoretical framework and tests" of early hominid meat and marrow acquisition: A reply to Shipman. *Amer. Anthropol.* 89:444–448.

Bunn, H. T., J. Harris, G. Isaac, Z. Kaufulu, E. Kroll, K. Schick, N. Toth, and A. K. Behrensmeyer. 1980. FxJj50, an early Pleistocene site in northern Kenya. *World Arch.* 12:109–136.

Bunn, H. T., and E. M. Kroll. 1988. *Reply to* Binford 'Fact and fiction about the *Zinjanthropus* floor: Data,

arguements, and interpretations.' *Curr. Anth.* 29:135–149.

Bunn, H. T., L. E. Bartram, and E. M. Kroll. 1988. Variability in bone assemblage formation from Hadza hunting, scavenging, and carcass processing. *J. Anthropol. Arch.* 7:412–457.

Bunnell, F. L., and D. E. N. Tait. 1981. Population dynamics of bears—implications. In *Dynamics of Large Mammal Populations,* edited by C. W. Fowler and T. D. Smith, pp. 75–98. New York: John Wiley and Sons.

Burton, R. 1979. *The Carnivores of Europe.* London: B. T. Batsford.

Butynski, T. M. 1982. Vertebrate predation by primates: A review of hunting patterns and prey. *J. Human Evol.* 11:421–430.

Callow, P. 1986a. Concluding discussion. In *La Cotte de St. Brelade 1961–1978,* edited by P. Callow and J. M. Cornford, pp. 389–390. Norwich: Geo Books.

Callow, P. 1986b. Pleistocene landscapes and the paleolithic economy. In *La Cotte de St. Brelade 1961–1978,* edited by P. Callow and J. M. Cornford, pp. 365–376. Norwich: Geo Books.

Caloi, L., and M. R. Palombo. 1978. Anfibi, rettili e mammiferi di Torre del Pagliaccetto (Torre in Pietra, Roma). *Quaternaria* 20:315–428.

Caloi, L., and M. R. Palombo. 1988. Large Paleolithic mammals of Latium (central Italy): Palaeoecological and biostratigraphic implications. In *L'Homme de Néandertal,* Vol. 2, *L'Environnement,* edited by M. Otte, pp. 21–44. Liège: ERAUL.

Caloi, L., and M. R. Palombo. 1990–91. Les grands mammifères du pleistocène supérieur de Grotta Barbara (Monte Circeo, Latium méridional): encadrement biostratigraphique et implications paleoecologiques. *Quaternaria Nova* (Nuova Serie) 1:267–276.

Canavari, M. (and edited by S. Cerulli-Irelli). 1916. Fauna malacologica mariana. *Paleontolographica Italica, Memorie di Paleontologia.* Pisa: Museo Geologico della Università di Pisa.

Cardini, L., and I. Bidditu. 1967. L'attività scientifica dell'Istituto Italiano di Paleontologia Umana dalla sua fondazione. *Quaternaria* 9:353–383.

Cassoli, P. 1976–77. Upper Paleolithic fauna at Palidoro (Rome): 1955 excavations. *Quaternaria* 19:187–195.

Cassoli, P., and F. Guadagnoli. 1987. Le faune del Riparo Salvini: analisi preliminare. In *Riparo Salvini a Terracina, Una Stazione di Cacciatori-raccoglitori del Paleolitico Superiore,* pp. 43–48. Roma: QUASAR.

Caughley, G. 1966. Mortality patterns in mammals. *Ecology* 47:906-917.

Caughley, G. 1977. *Analysis of Vertebrate Populations.* London: John Wiley and Sons.

Cederlund, G. N., H. K. G. Sand, and A. Pehrson. 1991. Body mass dynamics of moose calves in relation to winter severity. *J. Wildlife Manag.* 55:675–681.

Chapman, D. 1975. Antler—bones of contention. *Mammal Rev.* 5:121–172.

Chapman, D., and N. Chapman. 1975. *Fallow Deer: Their History, Distribution and Biology.* Lavenham, Suffolk: Terence Dalton.

Charnov, E. L. 1976. Optimal foraging: Attack strategy of a mantid. *Amer. Naturalist* 110:141–151.

Chase, P. G. 1986. *The Hunters of Combe Grenal: Approaches to Middle Paleolithic Subsistence in Europe.* Oxford: BAR International Series 286.

Chase, P. G. 1987. Spécialization de la chasse et transition vers le Paléolithique supérieur. *L'Anthropologie* 91:175–188.

Chase, P. G., and H. Dibble. 1987. Middle Paleolithic symbolism: A review of current evidence and interpretations. *J. Anthropol. Arch.* 6:263–293.

Chiappella, V. 1956. Scavo nel giacimenta Paleolitico superiore di Palidoro (Roma). *Quaternaria* 3:263–264.

Chiappella, V. 1959. Scavi del 1959 nel giacimento di Palidoro (Roma), relazioni attività scientifica dell'Istituto Italiano Paleontologia Umana dal 1957 al 1961. *Quaternaria* 5:338.

Chiappella, V. 1965. Gli scavi nel giacimento di Palidoro (Roma). *Quaternaria* 7:307–308.

Clark, G. A. 1983. Boreal phase settlement/subsistence models for Cantabrian Spain. In *Hunter-gatherer Economy in Prehistory,* edited by G. Bailey, pp. 96–110. Cambridge: Cambridge Univ. Press.

Clark, G. A., and L. G. Straus. 1986. Synthesis and conclusions Part I: Upper Paleolithic and Mesolithic hunter gatherer subsistence in Northern Spain. In *La Riera Cave: Stone Age Hunter-gatherer Adaptations in Northern Spain,* edited by L. G. Straus and G. A. Clark, pp. 351–365. Arizona State Univ. Anthropol. Res. Paper, no. 36.

Clark, G. A., and J. M. Lindly. 1989a. Modern human origins in the Levant and Western Asia. *Amer. Anthrologist* 91:962–985.

Clark, G. A., and J. M. Lindly. 1989b. The case for continuity: Observations on the biocultural transition in Europe and Western Asia. In *The Human Revolution,* Vol. 1, edited by P. Mellars and C. Stringer, pp. 626-676. Princeton: Princeton Univ. Press.

Clark, J. D. 1981. New men, strange faces, other minds: An archaeologist's perspective on recent discoveries relating to the origins and spread of modern man. *Proc. British Academy* 67:163–192.

Clevenger, A. 1990. Biologia del oso pardo (*Ursus arctos*) en la cordillera Cantabrica. Memoria de Tesis Doctoral, Universidad de León.

Clevenger, A. 1991. The phantom bear of the Spanish Sierras. *Wildlife Conserv.* 94:34–45.

Clevenger, A. P., and F. J. Purroy. 1991. *Ecologia del Oso Pardo en España,* Madrid: Monogr. Museo Nacional de Ciencias Naturales.

Clevenger, A., F. J. Purroy, and M. Saenz de Buruaga. 1987. Status of the brown bear in the Cantabrian Mountains, Spain. *International Conference on Bear Res. and Manag.* 7:1–8.

Clevenger, A., F. J. Purroy, and M. R. Pelton. 1988. Movement and activity patterns of a European brown bear in the Cantabrian Mountains, Spain. *Internat. Conf. Bear Res. and Manag.* 8:205–211.

Clevenger, A., F. J. Purroy, and M. R. Pelton. 1992. Food habits of brown bears (*Ursus arctos*) in the Cantabrian Mountains, Spain. *J. Mamm.* 73:415–421.

Clutton-Brock, T. H., F. E. Guinness, and S. D. Albon. 1982. *Red Deer: Behavior and Ecology of Two Sexes.* Chicago: Univ. Chicago Press.

Cody, M. L. 1986. Diversity, rarity, and conservation in Mediterranean-climate regions. In *Conservation Biology: The Science of Scarcity and Diversity,* edited by M. E. Soulé, pp. 122–152. Sunderland, Mass.: Sinauer Associates.

Corriere Salute. 1992. Il nuovo colesterolo, L. Bazzoli, G. Cadoria, and R. Renzi, coordinati. Supplemento al *Corriere della Sera,* 21 Settembre.

Cowgill, G. L. 1990. Why Pearson's *r* is not a good similarity coefficient for comparing collections. *Amer. Antiq.* 55:512–521.

Crew, H. 1975. An evaluation of the relationships between Mousterian complexes of the eastern Mediterranean: A technological perspective. In *Problems in Prehistory: North Africa and the Levant,* edited by F. Wendorf and A. Marks, pp. 317–350. Dallas: Southern Methodist Univ. Press.

Cribb, R. L. D. 1987. The logic of the herd: A computer simulation of archaeological herd structure. *J. Anthropol. Arch.* 6:376–415.

Crouch, J. E. 1972. *Functional Human Anatomy.* Philadelphia: Lea and Febiger.

Danner, D. A., and N. S. Smith. 1980. Coyote home range, movement, and relative abundance near a cattle feedyard. *J. Wildlife Manag.* 44:484–487.

David, F., and T. Poulain. 1990. La faune de grands

mammifères des niveaux XI et XC de la Grotte du Renne a Arcy-sur-Cure (Yonne): etude préliminaire. In *Paléolithique Moyen Récent et Paléolithique Supérieur Ancien en Europe,* edited by C. Farizy, pp. 319–323. Ile de France: Mémoires du Musée de Préhistoire, no. 3.

Davidson, I., and W. Noble. 1989. The archaeology of perception: Traces of depiction and language. *Curr. Anth.* 30:125–155.

Davies, N. B., A. F. G. Bourke, and M. de L. Brooke. 1989. Cuckoos and parasitic ants: Interspecific brood parasitisms as an evolutionary arms race. *Trends in Ecol. and Evol.* 4:274–278.

Davis, M. B. 1969. Palynology and environmental history during the Quaternary period. *Amer. Scientist* 57:317–332.

Dayan, T., D. Simberloff, E. Tchernov, and Y. Yom-Tov. 1989. Inter- and intraspecific character displacement in mustelids. *Ecology* 70:1526–1539.

Dayan, T., D. Simberloff, E. Tchernov, and Y. Yom-Tov. 1991. Calibrating the paleothermometer: Climate, communities, and the evolution of size. *Paleobiol.* 17:189–199.

Deacon, J. 1984. Later Stone Age people and their descendants in southern Africa. In *Southern African Prehistory and Paleoenvironments,* edited by R. G. Klein, pp. 221–328. Rotterdam: A. A Balkema.

Deal, M. 1985. Household pottery disposal in the Maya highlands: An ethnoarchaeological interpretation. *J. Anthropol. Arch.* 4:243–291.

Deith, M. R. 1983a. Molluscan calendars: The use of growth-line analysis to establish seasonality of shellfish collection at the Mesolithic site of Morton, Fife. *J. Archaeol. Science* 10:423–440.

Deith, M. R. 1983b. Seasonality of shell collecting, determined by oxygen isotope analysis of marine shells from Asturian sites in Cantabria. In *Animals and Archaeology: 2. Shell Middens, Fishes and Birds,* edited by C. Grigson and J. Clutton-Brock, pp. 67–76. Oxford: BAR International Series 183.

Deith, M. R. 1986. Subsistence strategies at a Mesolithic camp site: Evidence from stable isotope analyses of shells. *J. Archaeol. Science* 13:61-78.

Deith, M. R. 1989. Clams and salmonberries: Interpreting seasonality data from shells. In *The Mesolithic in Europe,* edited by C. Bonsall, pp. 73–79. Edinburgh: John Donald.

Deith, M. R., and N. Shackleton. 1986. Seasonal exploitation of marine molluscs: Oxygen isotope analysis of shell from La Riera Cave. In *La Riera Cave: Stone Age Hunter-Gatherer Adaptations in Northern Spain,* edited by L. G. Straus and G. A. Clark, pp. 299–313.

Anthropol. Res. Papers of Arizona State Univ., no. 36.

DelGiudice, G. D., L. D. Mech, and U.S. Seal. 1990. Effects of winter undernutrition on body composition and physiological profiles of white-tailed deer. *J. Wildlife Manag.* 54:539–550.

DelGiudice, G. D., F. J. Singer, and U. S. Seal. 1991. Physiological assessment of winter nutritional deprivation in elk of Yellowstone National Park. *J. Wildlife Manag.* 55:653–664.

Dennell, R. 1983. *European Economic Prehistory: A New Approach.* London: Academic Press.

Diamond, J. M. 1975. The assembly of species communities. In *Ecology and Evolution of Communities,* edited by M. L. Cody and J. M. Diamond, pp. 342–444. Cambridge, Mass.: Belknap Press.

Diamond, J. M. 1978. Niche shifts and the rediscovery of interspecific competition. *Amer. Scientist* 66:322–331.

Diamond, J. M. 1989. Quaternary megafaunal extinctions: Variations on a theme by Paganini. *J. Archaeol. Science* 16:167–175.

Dittrich, L. 1960. Milchgebißentwicklung und Zahnwechsel beim Braunbären (*Ursus arctos* L.) und anderen Ursiden (Dissertation). *Morph. Jahrb.* 101(1):1–141.

Donahue, R. 1988. Microwear analysis and site function of Paglicci Cave, level 4a. *World Arch.* 19:357–375.

Durante, S. 1974–75. Il Terreniano e la malacofauna della Grotta del Fossellone (Circeo) *Quaternaria* 18:331–345.

Durante, S., and F. Settepassi. 1972. I molluschi del giacimento Quaternario della Grotta della Madonna a Praia a Mare (Calabria). *Quaternaria* 16:255–269.

Durante, S., and F. Settepassi. 1976–77. Malacofauna e livelli marini tirreniani a Grotta Guattari, Monte Circeo (Latina). *Quaternaria* 19:35–69.

Durham, W. H. 1981. Overview: Optimal foraging analysis in human ecology. In *Hunter-Gatherer Foraging Strategies,* edited by B. Winterhalder and E. A. Smith, pp. 218–231. Chicago: Univ. Chicago Press.

During, E. 1986. The fauna of Alvastra: An osteological analysis of animal bones from a Neolithic pile dwelling. *Stockholm Studies in Archaeology,* no. 6.

Eberhardt, L. E., and A. B. Sargeant. 1977. Mink predation in prairie marshes during the waterfowl breeding season. In *Proc. 1975 Predator Symposium,* edited by R. L. Philips and C. Jonkel, pp. 33–38. Missoula: Montana Forest and Conservation Experiment Station, Univ. Montana.

Egan, Maj. H., editor. 1917. *Pioneering the West.* Salt Lake City.

Eisenberg, J. F. 1981. *The Mammalian Radiations: An Analysis of Trends in Evolution, Adaptation, and Behavior.* Chicago: Univ. Chicago Press.

Estes, R. D., and J. Goddard. 1967. Prey selection and hunting behavior of the Africa wild dog. *J. Wildlife Manag.* 31:52-70.

Evans, J. G. 1972. *Land Snails in Archaeology, with Special Reference to the British Isles.* London: Seminar Press.

Ewer, R. F. 1973. *The Carnivores.* London: Weidenfeld and Nicholson.

Farizy, C., editor. 1990. *Paléolithique Moyen Récent et Paléolithique Supérieur Ancien en Europe.* Ile de France: Mém. Musée Préhist., no. 3.

Feinberg, H. S./B. Sabelli. 1980. *Simon and Schuster's Guide to Shells.* New York: Simon and Schuster.

Fentress, J. C., and J. Ryon. 1982. A long-term study of distributed pup feeding in captive wolves. In *Wolves of the World: Perspectives of Behavior, Ecology, and Conservation,* edited by F. H. Harrington and P. C. Paquet, pp. 238–260. Park Ridge, N.J.: Noyes.

Festa-Bianchet, M. 1988. Age-specific reproduction of bighorn ewes in Alberta, Canada. *J. Mamm.* 69:157–160.

Fisher, R. A., A. S. Corbet, and C. B. Williams. 1943. The relation between the number of species and the number of individuals in a random sample of an animal population. *J. Animal Ecol.* 12:42–58.

Foley, R. 1984a. Putting people into perspective: An introduction to community evolution and ecology. In *Hominid Evolution and Community Ecology,* edited by R. Foley, pp. 1–24. London: Academic Press.

Foley, R. 1984b. Early man and the Red Queen: Tropical African community evolution and hominid adaptation. In *Hominid Evolution and Community Ecology,* edited by R. Foley, pp. 85–110. London: Academic Press.

Foley, R. 1987. *Another Unique Species: Patterns in Human Evolutionary Ecology.* New York: Longman Scientific and Technical.

Follieri, M., D. Magri, and L. Sadori. 1988. 250,000-year pollen record from Valle di Castiglione (Rome). *Pollen et Spores* 30:329–356.

Fornaca Rinaldi, G., and A. Radmilli. 1968. Datazione con il metodo Th230/U238 di stalagmiti contenute in depositi musteriani. *Atti Società Toscana Scienza Naturale,* Memorie, Serie A 75(2), Pisa.

Fox, M. W. 1984. *The Whistling Hunters: Field Studies of the Asiatic Wild Dog (Cuon alpinus).* Albany: State Univ. New York Press.

Frank, A. H. E. 1969. Pollen stratigraphy of the Lake of Vico (Central Italy). *Paleogeography, Palaeoclimatology, Palaeoecology* 6:67–85.

Frank, L. G. 1986. Social organization of the spotted hyaena *Crocuta corcuta.* II. Dominance and reproduction. *Animal Behavior* 34:1510–1527.

Freeman, L. G. 1981. The fat of the land, notes on Paleolithic diet in Iberia. In *Omnivorous Primates, Gathering and Hunting in Human Evolution,* edited by R. S. O. Harding and G. Teleki, pp. 104–165. New York: Columbia Univ. Press.

Frison, G. C. 1970. The Glenrock Buffalo Jump, 48CO304. *Plains Anthropol. Memiors,* no. 7.

Frison, G. C. 1978. *Prehistoric Hunters of the High Plains.* New York: Academic Press.

Frison, G. C. 1984. The Carter/Kerr-McGee Paleoindian site: Cultural resource management and archaeological research. *Amer. Antiq.* 49:288–314.

Frison, G. C. 1991. Hunting strategies, prey behavior and mortality data. In *Human Predators and Prey Mortality,* edited by M. C. Stiner, pp. 15–30. Boulder, Colo.: Westview Press.

Fuller, T. K. 1991. Effect of snow depth on wolf activity and prey selection in north central Minnesota. *Can J. Zool.* 69:283–287.

Fuller, T. K., and L. B. Keith. 1980. Wolf predation dynamics and prey relationships in northeastern Alaska. *J. Wildlife Manag.* 44:583–602.

Gaillard, J. M., D. Delorme, J. M. Jullein, and D. Tatin. 1993. Timing and synchrony of births in roe deer. *J. Mamm.* 74:738–744.

Gamble, C. 1983. Caves and faunas from Last Glacial Europe. In *Animals and Archaeology: 1. Hunters and Their Prey,* edited by J. Clutton-Brock and C. Grigson, pp. 163–172. Oxford: BAR International Series 163.

Gamble, C. 1984. Regional variation in hunter-gatherer strategy in the Upper Pleistocene of Europe. In *Hominid Evolution and Community Ecology,* edited by R. Foley, pp. 237–260. London: Academic Press.

Gamble, C. 1986. *The Paleolithic Settlement of Europe.* Cambridge: Cambridge Univ. Press.

Gamble, C. 1987. Man the shoveler: Alternative models for Middle Pleistocene colonization and occupation in northern latitudes. In *The Pleistocene Old World: Regional Perspectives,* edited by O. Soffer, pp. 81–98. New York: Plenum Press.

Garrod, D. A. E., L. H. Buzton, G. E. Smith, and D. M. A. Bate. 1928. Excavation of a Mousterian rock-shelter at Devil's Tower, Gibralter. *J. Royal Anthropol. Inst.* 58:33–114.

Garrott, R. A., L. E. Eberhardt, and W. C. Hanson.

1983. Summer food habits of juvenile arctic foxes in northern Alaska. *J. Wildlife Manag.* 47:540–545.

Garrott, R. A., G. C. White, R. M. Bartmann, L. H. Carpenter, and A. W. Alldredge. 1987. Movements of female mule deer in northwest Colorado. *J. Wildlife Manag.* 51:634–643.

Garshelis, D. L., and M. R. Pelton. 1980. Activity of black bears in the Great Smokey Mountains National Park. *J. Mamm.* 61:8–19.

Gasaway, W. C., R. D. Boertje, D. V. Grangaard, D. G. Kelleyhouse, R. O. Stephenson, and D. G. Larsen. 1992. The role of predation in limiting moose at low densities in Alaska and Yukon and implications for conservation. *Wildlife Monogr.*, no. 120.

Gautier-Hion, A., L. H. Emmons, and G. Dubost. 1980. A comparison of the diets of three major groups of primary consumers of Gabon (primates, squirrels and ruminants). *Oecologia* 45:182–189.

Gavin, A. 1991. Why ask "why": The importance of evolutionary biology in wildlife science. *J. Wildlife Manag.* 55:760–766.

Geist, V. 1971. *Mountain Sheep: A Study of Behavior and Evolution.* Chicago: Univ. Chicago Press.

Geneste, J.-M. 1985. *Analyse lithique d'industries moustériennes du Périgord: une approche technologique du comportement des groupes humains au Paléolithique moyen.* Thèse de Doctorat de l'Université de Bordeaux I.

Geneste, J.-M. 1989. Les industries de la Grotte Vaufrey: Technologie du débitage, économie et circulation de la materière premìer. In *La Grotte Vaufrey a Cenac et Saint-Julien (Dordogne), Paléoenvironnement, chronoloie et activités humaines,* edited by J.-P. Rigaud, pp. 441–519. Paris: Mémoires de la Societé Préhistorique Française, Tome 19.

Gifford, D. P. 1977. *Observations of Modern Human Settlements as an Aid to Archaeological Interpretation.* Ph.D. dissertation, Univ. California, Berkeley.

Gifford, D. P. 1978. Ethnoarchaeological observations of natural processes affecting cultural materials. In *Explorations in Ethnoarchaeology,* edited by R. P. Gould, pp. 77–101. Albuquerque: Univ. New Mexico Press.

Gifford, D. P. 1980. Ethnoarchaeological contributions to the taphonomy of human sites. In *Fossils in the Making, Vertebrate Taphonomy and Paleoecology,* edited by A. K. Behrensmeyer and A. P. Hill, pp. 93–106. Chicago: Univ. Chicago Press.

Gifford, D. P. 1981. Taphonomy and paleoecology: A critical review of archeology's sister discipline. In *Advances in Archaeological Method and Theory,* Vol. 4, edited by M. B. Schiffer, pp. 365–438. New York: Academic Press.

Gifford-Gonzalez, D. P. 1989. Ethnographic analogues for interpreting modified bones: Some cases from East Africa. In *Bone Modification,* edited by R. Bonnichsen and M. H. Sorg, pp. 179–246. Orono, Maine: Center for the Study of the First Americans.

Gifford-Gonzalez, D. P. 1991. Examining and refining the quadratic crown height method of age estimation. In *Human Predators and Prey Mortality,* edited by M. C. Stiner, pp. 41–78. Boulder, Colo.: Westview Press.

Gifford-Gonzalez, D. P. 1993. Gaps in the zooarchaeological analyses of butchery: Is gender an issue? In *From Bones to Behavior: Ethnoarchaeological and Experimental Contributions to the Interpretation of Faunal Remains,* edited by J. Hudson, pp. 181–199. Carbondale: Southern Illinois Univ. Press, Occasional Paper no. 21.

Gifford, D. P., G. L. Isaac, and C. M. Nelson. 1980. Evidence for predation and pastoralism at Prolonged Drift: A pastoral Neolithic site in Kenya. *Azania* 15:57–108.

Goodale, J. C. 1957. "Alonga bush": A Tiwi hunt. *Univ. Mus. Bull. (Univ. Pennsylvania)* 21:3–38.

Goodale, J. C. 1971. *Tiwi Wives: A Study of the Women of Melville Island, North Australia.* Seattle: Univ. Washington Press.

Grant, A. 1982. The use of tooth wear as a guide to the age of domestic animals. In *Aging and Sexing Animal Bones from Archaeological Sites,* edited by B. Wilson, C. Grigson, and S. Payne, pp. 91–108. Oxford: BAR British Series 109.

Grayson, D. K. 1978. Minimum numbers and sample size in vertebrate faunal analysis. *Amer. Antiq.* 43:53–65.

Grayson, D. K. 1981. The effects of sample size on some derived measures in vertebrate faunal analysis. *J. Archaeol. Science* 8:77–88.

Grayson, D. K. 1984. *Quantitative Zooarchaeology.* Orlando: Academic Press.

Grayson, D. K. 1991. Alpine faunas from the White Mountains, California: Adaptive change in the late Prehistoric Great Basin? *J. Archaeol. Science* 18:483–506.

Graziosi, P. 1960. *Palaeolithic Art.* London: Faber and Faber.

Groves, C. P. 1974. *Horses, Asses and Zebras in the Wild.* London: David and Charles, Newton Abbot.

Grün, R. 1988. The potential of ESR dating of tooth enamel. In *L'Homme de Néandertal,* vol. 1. *La Chro-*

nologie, edited by M. Otte, pp. 37–46. Liège: ERAUL 28.

Grün, R., H. P. Schwarcz, and S. Zymella. 1987. ESR dating of tooth enamel. *Canadian J. Earth Sciences* 24:1022–1037.

Grün, R., and C. B. Stringer. 1991. Electron spin resonance dating and the evolution of modern humans. *Archaeometry* 33:153–199.

Guilday, J. E., P. Parmalee, and D. Tanner. 1962. Aboriginal butchering techniques at the Eschelman site (36LA12), Lancaster County, Pennsylvania. *Pennsylvania Archaeol.* 32:59–83.

Gusinde, M. 1961. *The Yamana* (translated from the German by F. Schutze), Vols 1–5 (1918–24). New Haven: HRAF.

Guthrie, R. D. 1990. *Frozen Fauna of the Mammoth Steppe: The Story of Blue Babe.* Chicago: Univ. Chicago Press.

Guthrie, R. D., and R. L. Smith. 1990. A comparison of wolf and spotted hyaena dietary strategies in bone use and the production of pseudoartifacts. Paper presented at the International Council for Archaeozoology, Washington, D.C., May 1990.

Hamilton, W. J. III, and C. D. Busse. 1978. Primate carnivory and its significance to human diets. *Bioscience* 28:761–766.

Hamilton, W. J. III, R. E. Buskirk, and W. H. Buskirk. 1978. Omnivory and utilization of food resources by chacma baboons, *papio ursinus. Amer. Naturalist* 112:911–924.

Hardesty, D. L. 1977. *Ecological Anthropology.* New York: John Wiley and Sons.

Harding, R. S. O. 1973. Predation by a troop of olive baboons (*Papio anubis*). *Amer. J. Phys. Anth.* 38: 587–592.

Harding, R. S. O. 1974. The predatory baboon. *Expedition* 16:30–39.

Harding, R. S. O., and S. C. Strum. 1976. The predatory baboons of Kekopey. *Natural Hist.* 85:46–53.

Harrison, D. J., and J. R. Gilbert. 1985. Denning ecology and movements of coyotes in Maine during pup rearing. *J. Mamm.* 66:712–719.

Harrold, F. B. 1989. Mousterian, Chatelperronian and early Aurignacian in western Europe: Continuity or discontinuity? In *The Human Revolution,* Vol. 1, edited by P. Mellars and C. Stringer, pp. 677–713. Princeton: Princeton Univ. Press.

Hauge, T. M., and L. B. Keith. 1981. Dynamics of moose populations in northeastern Alaska. *J. Wildlife Manag.* 45:573–597.

Hausfater, G. 1976. Predatory behavior of yellow baboons. *Behaviour* 56:440–468.

Hawkes, K. 1987. Limited needs and hunter-gatherer time allocation. *Ethology and Sociobiology* 8:87–91.

Hawkes, K. 1992. Sharing and collective action. In *Evolutionary Ecology and Human Behavior,* edited by E. Smith and B. Winterhalder, pp. 269–300. Chicago: Aldine de Gruyter.

Hayden, B., and A. Cannon. 1983. Where the garbage goes: Refuse disposal in the Maya highlands. *J. Anthropol. Arch.* 2:117–163.

Haynes, G. 1980. Prey bones and predators: Potential ecologic information from analysis of bone sites. *Ossa* 7:75–97.

Haynes, G. 1982. Utilization and skeletal disturbances of North American prey carcasses. *Arctic* 35:266–281.

Haynes, G. 1983a. A guide for differentiating mammalian carnivore taxa responsible for gnaw damage in herbivore limb bones. *Paleobiol.* 9:164–172.

Haynes, G. 1983b. Frequencies of spiral and green-bone fractures on ungulate limb bones in modern surface assemblages. *Amer. Antiq.* 48:102–114.

Haynes, G. 1985. Age profiles in elephant and mammoth bone assemblages. *Quaternary Res.* 24:333–345.

Haynes, G. 1987. Proboscidean die-offs and die-outs: Age profiles in fossil collections. *J. Archaeol. Science* 14:659–668.

Haynes, G. 1988. Longitudinal studies of African elephant death and bone deposits. *J. Archaeol. Science* 15:131–157.

Hearty, P. 1986. An inventory of Last Glacial (sensu lato) age deposits from the Mediterranean Basin: A study of isoleucine epimerization and U-series dating. *Zeitschrift für Geomorphologie N. F. Suppl. Bd.* 62:51–69.

Hecker, H. M. 1982. Domestication revisited: Its implications for faunal analysis. *J. Field Arch.* 9:217–236.

Hellgren, E. C., M. R. Vaughan, R. L. Kirkpatrick, and P. R. Scanlon. 1990. Serial changes in metabolic correlates of hibernation in female black bears. *J. Mamm.* 71:291–300.

Henri Martin, H. 1907–10. *Recherches sur l'evolution du Mousterien dans le gisement de la Quina (Charente), Vol. Industrie Osseuse.* Paris: Schleicher Freres.

Henschel, J. R., R. Tilson, and F. von Blottnitz. 1979. Implications of a spotted hyaena bone assemblage in the Namib Desert. *S. Afr. Archaeol. Bull.* 34:127–131.

Higgs, E. S., and M. R. Jarman. 1972. The origins of animal and plant husbandry. In *Papers in Economic Prehistory,* edited by E. S. Higgs, pp. 3–13. Cambridge: Cambridge Univ. Press.

Hill, A. P. 1978. Hyaenas, bones and fossil man. *Kenya, Past and Present* 9:8–14.

Hill, A. P. 1980a. Hyaena provisioning of juvenile offspring at the den. *Mammalia* 44:594–595.

Hill, A. P. 1980b. A modern hyaena den in Ambroseli National Park, Kenya. *Proc. 8th Panafrican Congress of Prehistory and Quaternary Studies,* pp. 137–138. Nairobi, Kenya.

Hill, A. P. 1983. Hyaenas and early hominids. In *Animals and Archaeology: 1. Hunters and Their Prey,* edited by C. Grigson and J. Clutton-Brock, pp. 87–92. Oxford: BAR International Series 183.

Hill, A. P. 1984. Hyaenas and hominids: Taphonomy and hypothesis testing. In *Hominid Evolution and Community Ecology,* edited by R. Foley, pp. 111–128. London: Academic Press.

Hillson, S. 1986. *Teeth.* Cambirdge: Cambridge Univ. Press.

Hoffecker, J. F., G. Baryshnikov, and O. Potapova. 1991. Vertebrate remains from the Mousterian site of Il'skaya I (northern Caucasus, U.S.S.R.): New analysis and interpretation. *J. Archaeol. Science* 18:113–147.

Holdaway, S. 1989. Were there hafted projectile points in the Mousterian? *J. Field Arch.* 16:79–85.

Holmes, R. T., R. E. Bonney, and S. W. Pacala. 1979. Guild structure of the Hubbard Brook bird community: A multvariate approach. *Ecology* 60:512–520.

Horwitz, L. K., and P. Smith. 1988. The effects of striped hyaena activity on human remains. *J. Archaeol. Science* 15:471–481.

Houston, D. C. 1979. The adaptations of scavengers. In *Serengeti: Dynamics of an Ecosystem,* edited by A. R. E. Sinclair and M. Norton-Griffiths, pp. 263–286. Chicago: Univ. Chicago Press.

Howell, F. C. 1962. Alberto Carlo Blanc 1906–1960. *Quaternaria* 6:3–9.

Howell, F. C. 1984. Introduction. In *The Origins of Modern Humans: A World Survey of the Fossil Evidence,* edited by F. H. Smith and F. Spencer, pp. xiii–xxii. New York: Alan R. Liss.

Howell, F. C., and G. Arsebük. 1989. Report on the 1988 investigations in the Cave of Yarımburgaz (Marmara, Turkey). Unpublished manuscript submitted to the National Geographic Soc., Washington, D.C.

Howell, F. C., and G. Arsebük. 1990. Report on the current status of research on the Cave of Yarımburgaz (Marmara, Turkey). Unpublished manuscript submitted to the National Geographic Soc., Washington, D.C.

Hudson, J. 1990. *Advancing Methods in Zooarchaeology, an Ethnoarchaeological Study among the Aka Pyg-* *mies.* Unpublished Ph.D. dissertation, Univ. California, Santa Barbara.

Hudson, J. 1991. Nonselective small game hunting strategies: An ethnoarchaeological study of Aka Pygmy sites. In *Human Predators and Prey Mortality,* edited by M. C. Stiner, pp. 105–120. Boulder, Colo.: Westview Press.

Huggard, D. J. 1993. Effect of snow depth on predation and scavenging by gray wolves. *J. Wildlife Manag.* 57:382–388.

Hurtado, A. M., K. Hawkes, K. Hill, and H. Kaplan. 1985. Female subsistence strategies among Ache hunter-gatherers of eastern Paraguay. *Human Ecol.* 13:1–28.

Hutchinson, G. E. 1957. Concluding remarks. *Niche: Theory and Application, Cold Spring Harbor Symposium In Quantitative Biology* 22:415–427.

Ikeya, M. 1978. Electron spin resonance as a method of dating. *Archaeometry* 20:147–158.

Isaac, G. L. 1971. The diet of early man: Aspects of archaeological evidence from Lower and Middle Pleistocene sites in Africa. *World Arch.* 2:278–298.

Isaac, G. L. 1978. The food-sharing behavior of protohuman hominids. *Scientific Amer.* 238:90–106.

Isaac, G. L. 1984. The archaeology of human origins: Studies of the Lower Pleistocene in East Africa 1971–81. *Advances in World Archaeol.* 3:1–87.

Isaac, G. L., and D. Crader. 1981. To what extent were early hominids carnivorous? An archaeological perspective. In *Omnivorous Primates: Gathering and Hunting in Human Evolution,* edited by R. S. O. Harding and G. Teleki, pp. 37–103. New York: Columbia Univ. Press.

Jackson, D. L., E. A. Gluesing, and H. A. Jacobson. 1988. Dental eruption in bobcats. *J. Wildlife Manag.* 52:515–517.

Jacob-Friesen, K. H. 1956. Eiszeitliche Elephantenjäger in der Lüneburger Heide. *Jarbüch des Römisch-Germanischen Zentralmuseums Mainz* 3:1–22.

Jaksić, F. M. 1981. Abuse and misuse of the term "guild" in ecological studies. *Oikos* 37:397–400.

Jaksić, F. M., H. W. Greene, and J. L. Yañez. 1981a. The guild structure of a community of predatory vertebrates in central Chile. *Oecologia (Berlin)* 49:21–28.

Jaksić, F. M., J. L. Yañez, and E. R. Fuentes. 1981b. Assessing a small mammal community in central Chile. *J. Mamm.* 62:391–396.

James, S. R. 1989. Hominid use of fire in the Lower and Middle Pleistocene: A review of the evidence. *Curr. Anth.* 30:1–11.

Jarman, M. R., and P. F. Wilkinson. 1972. Criteria of animal domestication. In *Papers in Economic Prehis-*

tory, edited by E. S. Higgs, pp. 83–96. Cambridge: Cambridge Univ. Press.

Jaubert, J., M. Lorblanchet, H. Laville, R. Slott-Moller, A. Turq, and J.-P. Brugal. 1990. *Les chasseurs d'Aurochs de La Borde.* Paris: Editions de la Maison des Sciences de L'Homme, Documents d'Archéologique Français, no. 27.

Jefferys, W. H., and J. O. Berger. 1992. Ockham's razor and Bayesian analysis. *Amer. Scientist* 80:64–72.

Jenkinson, R. D. S. 1984. *Creswell Crags, Late Pleistocene Sites in the East Midlands.* Oxford: BAR British Series 122.

Joern, A., and L. R. Lawlor. 1981. Guild structure in grasshopper assemblages based on food and microhabitat resources. *Oikos* 37:93–104.

Johnson, R. A., S. W. Carothers, and T. J. McGill. 1987. Demography of feral burros in the Mohave Desert. *J. Wildlife Manag.* 51:916–920.

Johnson, K. G., and M. R. Pelton. 1980. Environmental relationships and the denning period of black bears in Tennessee. *J. Mamm.* 61:653–660.

Jolly, C. J. 1970. The seed-eaters: A new model of hominid differentiation based on a baboon analogy. *Man* 5:5–26.

Jolly, C. J. 1972. Changing views of human origins. *Yearbook of Phys. Anth.* 16:1–17.

Jones, K. T. 1984. *Hunting and Scavenging by Early Hominids: A Study in Archaeological Method and Theory.* Ph.D. dissertation, Univ. Utah, Salt Lake City.

Jones, K. T., and D. Metcalfe. 1988. Bare bones archaeology: Bone marrow indices and efficiency. *J. Archaeol. Science* 15:415–423.

Jones, R. 1989. East of Wallace's Line: Issues and problems in the colonisation of the Australian continent. In *The Human Revolution,* edited by P. Mellars and C. Stringer, pp. 743–782. Princeton: Princeton Univ. Press.

Kaplan, H., and K. Hill. 1985. Food sharing among Ache foragers: Tests of explanatory hypotheses. *Curr. Anth.* 26:223–246.

Kerney, M. P., and R. A. D. Cameron. 1979. *A Field Guide to the Land Snails of Britain and North-west Europe.* London: Collins, St. James' Place.

Kimber, D. C., C. E. Gray, C. E. Stackpole, and L. C. Leavell. 1961. *Anatomy and Physiology.* New York: Macmillan.

Kitchener, A. 1991. *The Natural History of the Wild Cats.* Ithaca: Comstock Publishing Associates.

Klein, R. G. 1975. Palaeoanthropological implications of the nonarchaeological bone assemblage from Swart-

klip 1, south-western Cape Province, South Africa. *Quaternary Res.* 5:275–288.

Klein, R. G. 1976. The mammalian fauna of the Klasies River Mouth sites, southern Cape Province, South Africa. *S. Afr. Archaeol. Bull.* 31:75–98.

Klein, R. G. 1978. Stone Age predation of large African bovids. *J. Archaeol. Science* 5:195–217.

Klein, R. G. 1979. Stone Age exploitation of animals in southern Africa. *Amer. Scientist* 67:151–160.

Klein, R. G. 1980a. The interpretation of mammalian faunas from Stone Age archaeological sites, with special reference to sites in the southern Cape Province, South Africa. In *Fossils in the Making,* edited by A. K. Behrensmeyer and A. Hill, pp. 223–246. Chicago: Univ. Chicago Press.

Klein, R. G. 1980b. Environmental and ecological implications of large mammals from Upper Pleistocene and Holocene sites in southern Africa. *Annals S. Afr. Mus.* 81:223–283.

Klein, R. G. 1981a. Ungulate mortality and sedimentary facies in the later Tertiary Varswater Formation, Langebaanweg, South Africa. *Annals S. Afr. Mus.* 84:233–254.

Klein, R. G. 1981b. Stone Age predation on small African bovids. *S. Afr. Archaeol. Bull.* 36:55–65.

Klein, R. G. 1982a. Age (mortality) profiles as a means of distinguishing hunted species from scavenged ones in Stone Age archaeological sites. *Paleobiol.* 8:151–158.

Klein, R. G. 1982b. Patterns of ungulate mortality and ungulate mortality profiles from Langebaanweg (Early Pliocene) and Elandsfontein (Middle Pleistocene), south-western Cape Province, South Africa. *Annals of the S. Afr. Mus.* 90:49–94.

Klein, R. G. 1987. Reconstructing how early people exploited animals: Problems and prospects. In *The Evolution of Human Hunting,* edited by M. H. Nitecki and D. V. Nitecki, pp. 11–45. New York: Plenum Press.

Klein, R. G. 1989a. Biological and behavioural perspectives on modern human origins in southern Africa. In *The Human Revolution,* edited by P. Mellars and C. Stringer, pp. 529–546. Princeton: Princeton Univ. Press.

Klein, R. G. 1989b. Why does skeletal part representation differ between smaller and larger bovids at Klasies River Mouth and other archaeological sites? *J. Archaeol. Science* 16:363–381.

Klein, R. G., and K. Cruz-Uribe. 1984. *The Analysis of Animal Bones from Archaeological Sites.* Chicago: Univ. Chicago Press.

Klein, R. G., and K. Scott. 1986. Re-analysis of faunal assemblages from the Haua Fteah and other Late Quaternary archaeological sites in Cyrenaican Libya. *J. Archaeol. Science* 13:515–542.

Knick, S. T. 1990. Ecology of bobcats relative to exploitation and a prey decline in southeastern Idaho. *Wildlife Monogr.,* no. 108.

Koehler, G. M., and M. G. Hornocker. 1991. Seasonal resource use among mountain lions, bobcats, and coyotes. *J. Mamm.* 72:391–396.

Koike, H. 1979. Seasonal dating and the valve-pairing technique in shell midden analysis. *J. Archaeol. Science* 6:63–74.

Koike, H., and N. Ohtaishi. 1985. Prehistoric hunting pressure estimated by the age composition of excavated Sika deer (*Cervus nippon*) using the annual layer of tooth cement. *J. Archaeol. Science* 12:443–456.

Koike, H., and N. Ohtaishi. 1987. Estimation of prehistoric hunting rates based on the age composition of Sika deer (*Cervus nippon*). *J. Archaeol. Science* 14:251–269.

Kortlandt, A. 1965. A comment on 'On the essential morphological basis for human culture.' *Curr. Anth.* 6:320–326.

Kotsakis, T. 1990–91. Late Pleistocene fossil microvertebrates of Grotta Breuil (Monte Circeo, Central Italy). *Quaternaria Nova* (Nuova Serie) 1:325–332.

Kozłowski, J. K. 1990. A multiaspectual approach to the origins of the Upper Palaeolithic in Europe. In *The Emergence of Modern Humans,* edited by P. Mellars, pp. 419–437. Ithaca: Cornell Univ. Press.

Kramer, C. 1982. *Village Ethnoarchaeology: Rural Iran in Archaeological Perspective.* New York: Academic Press.

Kruuk, H. 1972. *The Spotted Hyaena.* Chicago: Univ. Chicago Press.

Kruuk, H. 1978. Spatial organisation and territorial behaviour of the European badger, *Meles meles. J. Zool.* 184:1–19.

Kuhn, S. L. 1989a. Projectile weapons and investment in food procurement technology during the Middle Paleolithic (abstract). *Amer. J. Phys. Anth.* 78:257.

Kuhn, S. L. 1989b. Hunter-gatherer foraging organization and strategies of artifact replacement and discard. In *Experiments in Lithic Technology,* edited by D. Amick and R. Mauldin, pp. 33–48. Oxford: BAR International Series 528.

Kuhn, S. L. 1990a. *Diversity Within Uniformity: Tool Manufacture and Use in the Pontinian Mousterian of Latium (Italy).* Ph.D. dissertation (Univ. New Mexico, Albuquerque). Ann Arbor: UMI.

Kuhn, S. L. 1990b. A geometric index of reduction for unifacial stone tools. *J. Archaeol. Science* 17:583–593.

Kuhn, S. L. 1990–91a. Functional variability and chronological change in Pontinian Mousterian assemblages. *Quaternaria Nova* (Nuova Serie) 1:529–548.

Kuhn, S. L. 1990–91b. Preliminary observations on tool manufacture and use histories at Grotta Breuil. *Quaternaria Nova* (Nuova Serie) 1:367–378.

Kuhn, S. L. 1991. 'Unpacking' reduction: Lithic raw material economy in the Mousterian of west-central Italy. *J. Anthropol. Arch.* 10:76–106.

Kuhn, S. L. 1992. On planning and curated technologies in the Middle Paleolithic. *J. Anthropol. Res.* 48:185–214.

Kuhn, S. L. 1993. Mousterian technology as adaptive response: A case study. In *Hunting and Animal Exploitation in the Later Palaeolithic and Mesolithic of Eurasia,* edited by G. L. Peterkin, H. Bricker, and P. Mellars, pp. 20–26. Archaeol. Papers Amer. Anthropol. Assoc., Vol. 4.

Kuhn, S. L. (n.d.). *Mousterian Lithic Technology and Raw Material Economy: A Case Study.* Princeton: Princeton Univ. Press. In press.

Kurtén, B. 1958. Life and death of the Pleistocene cave bear: A study in paleoecology. *Acta Zoologica Fennica* 95:4–59.

Kurtén, B. 1968. *Pleistocene Mammals of Europe.* Chicago: Aldine.

Kurtén, B. 1971. *The Age of Mammals.* London: Weidenfeld and Nicolson.

Kurtén, B. 1976. *The Cave Bear Story.* New York: Columbia Univ. Press.

Laj Pannocchia, F. 1950. L'industria Pontiniana della Grotta di S. Agostino (Gaeta). *Rivista di Scienze Preistoriche* 5:67–86.

Landres, P. B. 1983. Use of the guild concept in environmental impact assessment. *Environmental Manag.* 7:393–398.

Lemorini, C. 1990–91. Prospects for a functional evaluation of the Mousterian site of Grotta Breuil (Monte Circeo, Italy). *Quaternaria Nova* (Nuova Serie) 1:407–428.

Leonardi, P. 1935. *I Balzi Rossi: le faune, 1. I molluschi pleistocenici della Barma Grande.* Firenze: Istituto Italiano di Paleontologia Umana, Anno 13.

Leopold, B. D., and P. R. Krausman. 1986. Diets of 3 predators in Big Bend National Park, Texas. *J. Wildlife Manag.* 50:290–295.

Leslie, D. M., and C. L. Douglas. 1979. Desert bighorn sheep of the River Mountains, Nevada. *Wildlife Monogr.*, no. 66.

Levine, M. A. 1982. The use of crown height measurements and eruption-wear sequences to age horse teeth. In *Aging and Sexing Animal Bones from Archaeological Sites,* edited by B. Wilson, C. Grigson, and S. Payne, pp. 223–250. Oxford: BAR British Series 109.

Levine, M. A. 1983. Mortality models and the interpretation of horse population structure. In *Hunter-gatherer Economy in Prehistory,* edited by G. Bailey, pp. 23–46. Cambridge: Cambridge Univ. Press.

Leyhausen, P. (translated by B. A. Tonkin). 1979. *Cat Behavior: The Predatory and Social Behavior of Domestic and Wild Cats.* New York: Garland STPM Press.

Lindly, J. M. 1988. Hominid and carnivore activity at Middle and Upper Paleolithic cave sites in eastern Spain. *Munibe* 40:45–70.

Lindly, J. M., and G. A. Clark. 1990. Symbolism and modern human origins. *Curr. Anth.* 31:233–240.

Lopez, B. H. 1978. *Of Wolves and Men.* New York: Charles Scribner's Sons.

Lourandos, H. 1987. Pleistocene Australia: Peopling a continent. In *The Pleistocene Old World: Regional Perspectives,* edited by O. Soffer, pp. 147–165. New York: Plenum Press.

Lovejoy, C. O. 1981. The origin of man. *Science* 211(4480):341–350.

Loving, S., H. Kamermans, C. W. Koot, and A. Voorrips. 1990–91. The Pontinian on the plain: Some results from the Agro Pontino survey. *Quaternaria Nova* (Nuova Serie) 1:453–477.

Lowe, V. P. 1967. Teeth as indicators of age with special reference to red deer (*Cervus elaphus*) of known age from Rhum. *J. Zool., London* 152:137–153.

Lumley, H. de 1972. *La Grotte Moustérienne de l'Hortus.* Marseille: Études Quaternaires, 1.

Lyman, R. L. 1984a. Bone density and differential survivorship of fossil classes. *J. Anthropol. Arch.* 3:259–299.

Lyman, R. L. 1984b. Broken bones, bone expediency tools, and bone pseudotools: Lessons from the blast zone around Mount St. Helens, Washington. *Amer. Antiq.* 49:315–333.

Lyman, R. L. 1985. Bone frequencies: Differential transport, *in situ* destruction, and the MGUI. *J. Archaeol. Science* 12:221–236.

Lyman, R. L. 1987a. Hunting for evidence of Plio-Pleistocene hominid scavengers. *Amer. Anthropol.* 89:710–714.

Lyman, R. L. 1987b. On the analysis of vertebrate mortality profiles: Sample size, mortality type, and hunting pressure. *Amer. Antiq.* 52:125–142.

Lyman, R. L. 1991a. Subsistence change and pinniped hunting. In *Human Predators and Prey Mortality,* edited by M. C. Stiner, pp. 187–199. Boulder, Colo.: Westview Press.

Lyman, R. L. 1991b. Taphonomic problems with archaeological analyses of animal carcass utilization and transport. In *Beamers, Bobwhites, and Blue-Points: Tributes to the Career of Paul W. Parmalee,* edited by J. R. Prudue, W. E. Klippel, and B. W. Styles, pp. 125–138. Springfield: Illinois State Mus. Scientific Papers, no. 23.

Lyman, R. L. 1992. Anatomical considerations of utility curves in zooarchaeology. *J. Archaeol. Science* 19:7–22.

Lyman, R. L., J. M. Savelle, and P. Whitridge. 1992. Derivation and application of a meat utility index for phocid seals. *J. Archaeol. Science* 19:531–555.

MacArthur, R. H. 1968. The theory of niche. In *Population Biology and Evolution,* edited by R. C. Lewontin, pp. 159–176. Syracuse: Syracuse Univ. Press.

MacArthur, R. H. 1970. Species packing and competitive equilibrium for many species. *Theoretical Population Biology* 1:1–11.

MacArthur, R. H., and R. Levins. 1967. The limiting similarity, convergence, and divergence of coexisting species. *Amer. Naturalist* 101:377–385.

Macdonald, D. W. 1979. "Helpers" in fox society. *Nature* 282:69–71.

MacMahon, J. A., D. J. Schimpf, D. C. Anderson, K. G. Smith, and R. L. Bayn. 1981. An organism-centered approach to some community and ecosystem concepts. *J. Theoretical Biology* 88:287–307.

Major, J. T., and J. A. Sherburne. 1987. Interspecific relationships of coyotes, bobcats and red foxes in western Maine. *J. Wildlife Manag.* 51:606–616.

Mallegni, F., R. Mariani-Costantini, G. Fornaciari, E. T. Longo, F. Giacobini, and A. M. Radmilli. 1983. New European fossil hominid material from an Acheulean site near Rome (Castel di Guido). *Am. J. Phys. Anthro.* 62:263–274.

Manzi, G., and P. Passarello. 1989. From Casal de'Pazzi to Grotta Breuil: Fossil evidence from Latium before the appearance of modern humans. *Animal and Human Biology, Annual Report of the Dipartimento di Biologia Animale e dell'Uomo.* Roma: Università di Roma, pp. 111–143.

Manzi, G., and P. Passarello. 1990–91. The human remains from Grotta Breuil (M. Circeo, Italy). *Quaternaria Nova* (Nuova Serie) 1:429–439.

Marean, C. W. 1986. Seasonality and seal exploitation in the southwestern Cape, South Africa. *Afr. Archaeol. Rev.* 4:135–149.

Marean, C. W., and L. M. Spencer. 1991. Impact of carnivore ravaging on zooarchaeological measure of element abundance. *Amer. Antiq.* 56:645–658.

Marean, C. W., L. M. Spencer, R. J. Blumenschine, and S. D. Capaldo. 1992. Captive hyaena bone choice and destruction, the Schlepp effect and Olduvai archaeofaunas. *J. Archaeol. Science* 19:101–121.

Marshack, A. 1989. Evolution of the human capacity: The symbolic evidence. *Yearbook Phys. Anth., Suppl. 10* 32:1–34.

Mattson, D. J., R. R. Knight, and B. M. Blanchard. 1992. Cannibalism and predation on black bears by grizzly bears in the Yellowstone ecosystem, 1975–1990. *J. Mamm.* 73:422–425.

May, R. M., and R. H. MacArthur. 1972. Niche overlap as a function of environmental variability. *Proc. National Acad. Science* 69:1109–1113.

Maynard Smith, J. 1974. *Models in Ecology.* Cambridge: Cambridge Univ. Press.

Maynard Smith, J. 1982. *Evolution and the Theory of Games.* Cambridge: Cambridge Univ. Press.

Mayr, E. 1963. *Populations, Species, and Evolution* (an abridgement of *Animal Species and Evolution*). Cambridge, Mass.: Belknap Press.

McBurney, C. B. M. 1967. *The Haua Fteah (Cyrenaica) and the Stone Age of the South-east Mediterranean.* Cambridge: Cambridge Univ. Press.

McCullough, D. R. 1981. Population dynamics of Yellowstone grizzly bear. In *Dynamic of Large Mammal Populations*, edited by C. W. Fowler and T. D. Smith, pp. 173–196. New York: John Wily and Sons.

McCullough, D. R., D. S. Pine, D. L. Whitmore, T. M. Mansfield, and R. H. Decker. 1990. Linked sex harvest strategy for big game management with a test case on black-tailed deer. *Wildlife Monogr.*, no. 112.

McGrew, W. 1987. Tools to get food: The subsistants of Tasmanian aborigines and Tanzanian chimpanzees compared. *J. Anthropol. Res.* 43:247–258.

Mech, L. D. 1970. *The Wolf: The Ecology and Behavior of an Endangered Species.* Garden City: Natural Hist. Press.

Mech, L. D. 1977. Wolf pack buffer zones as prey reservoirs. *Science* 198:320–321.

Mech, L. D. 1988. Longevity in wild wolves. *J. Mamm.* 69:197–198.

Medin, D. E., and A. E. Anderson. 1979. Modeling the dynamics of a Colorado mule deer population. *Wildlife Monogr.*, no. 68.

Meehan, B. 1982. *Shell Bed to Shell Midden.* Canberra: Australian Inst. of Aboriginal Studies.

Meehan, B. 1983. A matter of choice? Some thoughts on shell gathering strategies in northern Australia. In *Animals and Archaeology: 2. Shell Middens, Fishes and Birds*, edited by C. Grigson and J. Clutton-Brock, pp. 3–17. Oxford: BAR International Series 183.

Meehan, B. 1988. The "dinnertime camp". In *Archaeology with Ethnography: An Australian Perspective*, edited by B. Meehan and R. Jones, pp. 171–181. Canberra: Research School of Pacific Studies, The Australian National Univ.

Mellars, P. 1973. The character of the Middle-Upper Paleolithic transition in southwest France. In *The Explanation of Culture Change*, edited by C. Renfrew, pp. 255–276. London: Duckworth.

Mellars, P. 1989. Major issues in the emergence of modern humans. *Curr. Anth.* 30:349–385.

Mellars, P., editor. 1990. *The Emergence of Modern Humans.* Ithaca: Cornell Univ. Press.

Mellars, P., and C. B. Stringer, editors. 1989. *The Human Revolution.* Princeton: Princeton Univ. Press.

Mendelssohn, H. 1982. Wolves in Israel. In *Wolves of the World: Perspectives of Behavior, Ecology, and Conservation*, edited by F. H. Harrington and P. C. Paquet, pp. 173–195. Park Ridge, N.J.: Noyes.

Metcalfe, D. 1989. A general cost/benefit model of the trade-off between transport and field processing. Paper presented at the 54th Annual Meeting of the soc. for Amer. Arch., Atlanta.

Metcalfe, D., and K. R. Barlow. 1992. A model for exploring the optimal trade-off between field processing and transport. *Amer. Anthropol.* 94:340–356.

Metcalfe, D., and K. T. Jones. 1988. A reconsideration of animal body-part utility indices. *Amer. Antiq.* 53:486–504.

Miller, D. R. T. 1975. Observations of wolf predation on Barren Ground caribou in winter. In *Proc. 1st International Reindeer and Caribou Symposium*, edited by J. R. Luick, P. C. Lent, D. R. Klein, and R. G. White, pp. 209–220. Fairbanks: Biolog. Papers Univ. Alaska, Special Report no. 1.

Miller, F. L., F. W. Anderka, C. Vithayasai, and R. L. McClure. 1975. Distribution, movements and socialization of Barren Ground caribou radio-tracked on their calving and post-calving areas. In *Proc. 1st International Reindeer and Caribous Symposium*, edited by J. R. Luick, P. C. Lent, D. R. Klein, and R. G. White, pp. 423-435. Fairbanks: Biolog. Papers Univ. Alaska, Special Report no. 1.

Miller, S. D. 1985. An observation of inter- and intra-specific aggression involving brown bear, black bear, and moose in southcentral Alaska. *J. Mamm.* 66:805–806.

Mills, M. G. L. 1984a. The comparative behavioural ecology of the brown hyaena (*Hyaena brunnea*) and the spotted hyaena (*Crocuta crocuta*) in the southern Kalahari. *Koedoe, Supplement* 237–247.

Mills, M. G. L. 1984b. Prey selection and feeding habits of the large carnivores in the southern Kalahari. *Koedoe, Supplement* 281–294.

Mills, M. G. L. 1985. Related spotted hyaenas forage together but do not cooperate in rearing young. *Nature* 316(6023):61–62.

Mills, M. G. L. 1989. The comparative behavioral ecology of hyenas: The importance of diet and food dispersion. In *Carnivore Behavior, Ecology, and Evolution,* edited by J. L. Gittlemen, pp. 125–142. Ithaca: Cornell Univ. Press.

Mills, M. G. L., and M. E. J. Mills. 1977. An analysis of bones collected at hyaena breeding dens in the Gemsbok National Parks. *Annals Transvaal Mus.* 30:145–156.

Milton, K., and M. L. May. 1976. Body weight, diet and home range area in primates. *Nature* 259:459–462.

Miracle, P., and D. Sturdy. 1991. Chamois and the karst of Herzegovina. *J. Archaeol. Science* 18:89–108.

Moehlman, P. D. 1989. Intraspecific variation in canid social systems. In *Carnivore Behavior, Ecology, and Evolution,* edited by J. L. Gittlemen, pp. 143–163. Ithaca: Cornell Univ. Press.

Morris, K., and J. Goodall. 1977. Competition for meat between chimpanzees and baboons of the Gombe National Park. *Folia Primatologica* 28:109–121.

Moulin, H. 1986. *Game Theory for the Social Sciences.* New York: New York Univ. Press.

Murie, A. 1944. *The Wolves of Mt. McKinley.* Washington, D.C.: U.S. National Par Service, Fauna Series 5.

Mussi, M. 1977–82. Musteriano a denticolati du ciottolo in località S. Andreadi Sabaudia (Prov. di Latina). *Origini* 11:45–70.

Mussi, M., and D. Zampetti. 1990–91. Le site Moustérien de Grotta Barbara. *Quaternaria Nova* (Nuova Serie) 1:277–287.

Nelson, M. 1991. The study of technological organization. In *Archaeological Method and Theory,* Vol. 3, edited by M. Schiffer, pp. 57–100. Tucson: Univ. Arizona Press.

Nelson, T. A., and A. Woolf. 1987. Mortality of white-tailed deer fawns in southern Illinois. *J. Wildlife Manag.* 51:326–329.

Nievergelt, B. 1981. *Ibexes in an African Environment: Ecology and Social System of the Walia Ibex in the Simen Mountains, Ethiopia.* Berlin: Springer-Verlag.

National Live Stock and Meat Board. 1988. *Nutrient Values of Muscle Foods,* Edition 1. Publication of the National Live Stock and Meat Board.

Nudds, T. D., and M. L. Morrison. 1991. Ten years after "reliable knowledge": Are we gaining? *J. Wildlife Manag.* 55:757–760.

O'Brien, S. J., and E. Mayr. 1991. Bureaucratic mischief: Recognizing endangered species and subspecies. *Science* 251:1187–1188.

O'Connell, J. F. 1987. Alyawara site structure and its archaeological implications. *Amer. Antiq.* 52:74–108.

O'Connell, J. F., K. Hawkes, and N. Blurton Jones. 1988a. Hadza hunting, butchering, and bone transport and their archaeological implications. *J. Anthropol. Res.* 44:113–161.

O'Connell, J. F., K. Hawkes, and N. Blurton Jones. 1988b. Hadza scavenging: Implications for Plio/Pleistocene hominid subsistence. *Curr. Anth.* 29:356–363.

O'Connell, J. F., K. Hawkes, and N. Blurton Jones. 1991. Distribution of refuse-producing activities at Hadza residential base camps: Implications for analyses of archaeological site structure. In *The Interpretation of Archaeological Spatial Patterning,* edited by E. Kroll and T. D. Price, pp. 61–76. New York: Plenum Press.

O'Connell, J. F., K. Hawkes, and N. G. Blurton-Jones. 1992. Patterns in the distribution, site structure and assemblage composition of Hadza kill-butchering sites. *J. Archaeol. Science* 19:319–345.

O'Connell, J. F., and B. Marshall. 1989. Analysis of kangaroo body part transport among the Alyawara of central Australia. *J. Archaeol. Science* 16:393–405.

Ortea, J. 1986. The malacology of La Riera Cave. In *La Riera Cave: Stone Age Hunter-gatherer Adaptations in Northern Spain,* edited by L. G. Straus and G. A. Clark, pp. 289–298. Anthropol. Res. Papers Arizona State Univ., no. 36.

Otte, M., editor. 1988–89. *L'Homme de Néandertal.* Vols. 1–8. Liège: ERAUL.

Otte, M. 1991. Evolution in the relationship between raw materials and cultural tradition in the European Paleolithic. In *Raw Material Economy among Prehistoric Hunter-Gatherers,* edited by A. Montet-White and S. Holen, pp. 161–168. Lawrence, Kansas. Univ. Kansas Press.

Owens, D., and M. Owens. 1979. Notes on social organization and behavior in brown hyaenas (*Hyaena brunnea*). *J. Mamm.* 60:405–408.

Owens, D., and M. Owens. 1984. Helping behaviour in brown hyenas. *Nature* 308:843–845.

Owens, M., and D. Owens. 1985. *Cry of the Kalahari.* Glasgow: Fontana/William Collins Sons and Co.

Ozoga, J. J. 1988. Incidence of "infant" antlers among supplementally-fed white-tailed deer. *J. Mamm.* 69: 393–395.

Ozoga, J. J., C. S. Bienz, and L. J. Verme. 1982. Red fox feeding habits in relation to fawn mortality. *J. Wildlife Manag.* 46:242–243.

Özdoğan, M., and A. Koyunlu. 1986. Yarımburgaz Mağarası: 1986 Yılı Çalışmalarının Ilk Sonuçları ve Bazı Gözlemler. *Arkeoloji ve Sanat (Istanbul)* 32/33:4–14.

Packard, J. P., and L. D. Mech. 1980. Population regulation in wolves. In *Biosocial Mechanism of Population Regulation,* edited by M. N. Cohen, R. S. Malpass, and H. G. Klein, pp. 135–150. New Haven, Yale Univ. Press.

Palma di Cesnola, A. 1965. Notizie preliminari sulla terza campagna di scavi nella Grotta del Cavallo (Lecce). *Rivista di Scienze Preistoriche* 25:3–87.

Palma di Cesnola, A. 1969. Il Musteriano della Grotta del Poggio a Marina di Camerota (Salerno). *Estratto dagli Scritti sul Quaternario in onore di Angelo Pasa, Museo Civico di Storia Naturale,* pp. 95–135. Verona.

Palmieri, A. M. 1976–77. Sedimentological study of the Upper Paleolithic site of Palidoro (Rome, Italy). *Quaternaria* 19:163–179.

Paquet, P. C. 1992. Prey use strategies of sympatric wolves and coyotes in Riding Mountain National Park, Manitoba. *J. Mamm.* 73:337–343.

Parkington, J. 1990. A critique of the concensus view of the age of Howieson's Poort assemblages in South Africa. In *The Emergence of Modern Humans,* edited by P. Mellars, pp. 34–55. Ithaca: Cornell Univ. Press.

Payne, S. 1973. Kill-off patterns in sheep and goats: The mandibles from Asvan Kale. *Anatolian Studies* 23:281–303.

Pelegrin, J. 1990. Observations technologiques sur quelques séries du Chatelperronien et du MTA B du sudouest de la France. Un hypothèse d'évolution. In *Paléolithique Moyen Récent et Paléolithique Supérieur Ancien en Europe,* edited by C. Farizy, pp. 195–202. Nemours: Ed. A.P.R.A.I.F.

Perlès, C. 1977. *Préhistoire du Feu.* Paris: Masson.

Peterson, R. O., and R. E. Page. 1988. The rise and fall of Isle Royale wolves, 1975–1986. *J. Mamm.* 69:89–99.

Peterson, R. O., J. D. Wollington, and T. N. Bailey. 1984. Wolves of the Kenai Peninsula, Alaska. *Wildlife Monogr.*, no. 88.

Pianka, E. R. 1976. Competition and niche theory. In *Theoretical Ecology: Principles and Applications,* edited by R. M. May, pp. 114–141. Philadelphia: W. B. Saunders Co.: Blackwell.

Pianka, E. R. 1978. *Evolutionary Ecology.* New York: Harper and Row.

Pimlott, D. H., J. A. Shannon, and G. B. Kolenosky. 1969. *The Ecology of the Timber Wolf in Algonquin Park, Ontario.* Department of Lands and Forests.

Piperno, M. 1976–77. Analyse du sol Mousterien de la Grotte Guattari au Mont Circé. *Quaternaria* 19:71–92.

Piperno, M. 1984. L'Acheuleano e il Musteriano del Lazio. *Atti XXIV Riunione Scientifica Ist. Ital. Preistoria e Protostoria,* pp. 39–53.

Piperno, M., and I. Biddittu. 1978. Studio tipologico ed interpretazione dell'industria acheuleana e premusteriana dei livelli *m* e *d* di Torre in Pietra (Roma). *Quaternaria* 20:441–535.

Pitti, C., and C. Tozzi. 1971. La Grotta del Capriolo e la Buca della Iena presso Mommio (Camaiore, Lucca). *Rivista di Scienze Preistoriche* 26:213–258.

Potts, R. 1982. *Lower Pleistocene Site Formation and Hominid Activities at Olduvai Gorge, Tanzania.* Unpublished Ph.D. dissertation, Harvard Univ.

Potts, R. 1984a. Hominid hunters? Problems of identifying the earliest hunter/gatherers. In *Hominid Evolution and Community Ecology,* edited by R. Foley, pp. 129–166. London: Academic Press.

Potts, R. 1984b. Home bases and early hominids. *Scientific Amer.* 72:338–347.

Potts, R. 1986. Temporal span of bone accumulations at Olduvai Gorge and implications for early hominid foraging behavior. *Paleobiol.* 12:25–31.

Potts, R. 1988. *Hominid Activities at Olduvai.* New York: Aldine de Gruyter.

Prior, R. 1968. *The Roe Deer of Cranborne Chase: An Ecological Survey.* London: Oxford Univ. Press.

Pritchard, P. C. H. 1967. *Living Turtles of the World.* New York: Crown Publishers.

Radmilli, A. M. 1974. *Gli scavi nella Grotta Polesini a Ponte Lucano di Tivoli e la più antica arte nel Lazio.* Firenze: Sansoni Editore.

Radmilli, A. M., F. Mallegni, E. Longo, and R. Mariani. 1979. Reperto umano con industria Acheuleana rinvenuto presso Roma. *Atti Società Toscana di Scienze Naturali, Memorie, Serie A* 86:203–214.

Radmilli, A. M., and E. Tongiorgi. 1958. Gli scavi nella Grotta la Porta di Positano; Contributo allo conoscenza del Mesolitico Italiano. *Rivista di Scienza Preistoriche* 13:91–109.

Regan, A. B. 1934. Some notes on the history of the

Uintah Basin in Northeastern Utah to 1850. *Proc. Utah Acad. Science Arts and Letters* 11:55–64.

Reher, C. A. 1970. Appendix II: Population dynamics of the Glenrock *Bison bison* population. In The Glenrock Buffalo Jump, 48CO304: Late Prehistoric Period Buffalo Procurement and Butchering on the Northwestern Plains, edited by G. C. Frison. *Plains Archaeologist Memoir* 7:51–55.

Reher, C. A. 1973. Appendix II: The Wardell *Bison bison* sample: Population dynamics and archaeological interpretation. In The Wardell Buffalo Trap, 48SH301: Communal Procurement in the Upper Green River Basin, Wyoming, edited by G. C. Frison. *Anthropol. Papers Mus. Anth., Univ. Michigan* 48:89–105.

Reher, C. A. 1974. Population study of the Casper site bison. In *The Casper Site: A Hell Gap Bison Kill on the High Plains*, edited by G. C. Frison, pp. 113–124. New York: Academic Press.

Rensch, B. 1959 (English translation from German 1954). *Evolution above the Species Level*. New York: Columbia Univ. Press.

Richards, G. 1987. *Human Evolution: An Introduction for the Behavioural Sciences*. London: Routledge and Kegan Paul.

Robinson, W. S. 1951. A method for chronologically ordering archaeological deposits. *Amer. Antiq.* 16:293–301.

Roebroeks, W., N. J. Conard, and T. van Kolfschoten. 1992. Dense forests, cold steppes, and the Palaeolithic settlement of northern Europe. *Curr. Anth.* 33:551–586.

Rogers, L. L. 1981. A bear in its lair. *Natural Hist.* 90:64–70.

Rogers, L. L. 1987. Effects of food supply and kinship on social behavior, movements, and population growth of black bears in northeastern Minnesota. *Wildlife Monogr.*, no. 97.

Rogers, L. L., L. D. Mech, D. K. Dawson, J. M. Peck, and M. Korb. 1980. Deer distribution in relation to wolf pack territory edges. *J. Wildlife Manag.* 44:253–285.

Rolland, N. 1981. The interpretation of Middle Paleolithic variability. *Man* 16:15–42.

Rolland, N. 1988. Observations on some Middle Paleolithic time series in southern France. In *The Upper Pleistocene Prehistory of Western Eurasia*, edited by H. Dibble and A. Monte-White, pp. 161–180. Philadelphia: Univ. Pennsylvania.

Rolland, N. 1990. Middle Palaeolithic socio-economic formations in western Eurasia: An exploratory survey. In *The Emergence of Modern Humans*, edited by P. Mellars, pp. 347–388. Ithaca: Cornell Univ. Press.

Rolland, N., and H. Dibble. 1990. A new synthesis of Mousterian variability. *Amer. Antiq.* 55:480–499.

Root, R. B. 1967. The niche exploitation pattern of the blue-gray gnatcatcher. *Ecol. Monogr.* 37:317–350.

Root, R. 1975. Some consequences of ecosystem texture. In *Ecosystems Analysis and Prediction, (Proc. SIAM-SIMS Conf., Alta, Utah, 1974)*, edited by S. Levin, pp. 83–97. Philadelphia: SIAM.

Rosen, A. M. 1989. Ancient town and city sites: A view from the microscope. *Amer. Antiq.* 54:564–578.

Rosenzweig, M. L. 1966. Community structure in sympatric carnivora. *J. Mamm.* 47:602–612.

Rosenzweig, M. L. 1992. Species diversity gradients: We know more and less than we thought. *J. Mamm.* 73:715–730.

Ross, P. I., G. E. Hornbeck, and B. L. Horejsi. 1988. Late denning black bears killed by grizzly bear. *J. Mamm.* 69:818–820.

Rossetti, P., and G. Zanzi. 1990–91. Technological approach to reduction sequences of the lithic industry from Grotta Breuil. Quaternaria Nova (Nuova Serie) 1:351–365.

Roughgarden, J. 1983. Competition and theory in community ecology. *Amer. Naturalist* 122:583–601.

Rowley-Conwy, P. 1981. Mesolithic Danish bacon: Permanent and temporary sites in the Danish Mesolithic. In *Economic Archaeology*, edited by A. Sheridan and G. N. Bailey, pp. 51–55. Oxford: BAR International Series 96.

Rowley-Conwy, P. 1984. The laziness of the short-distance hunter: The origins of agriculture in western Denmark. *J. Anthropol. Arch.* 3:300–324.

Ruffo, M., and A. Zarattini. 1990–91. The Grotta delle Capre (Goat Cave) at San Felice Circeo: Further investigations. *Quaternaria Nova* (Nuova Serie) 1:241–266.

Rutter, R. J., and D. H. Pimlott. 1968. *The World of the Wolf*. Philadelphia: J. B. Lippincott.

Saether, B.-E., and A. J. Gravem. 1988. Annual variation in winter body condition of Norwegian moose calves. *J. Wildlife Manag.* 52:333–336.

Sattenspiel, L. 1986. The influence of infection and predation on early hominid evolution. Poster Session Presentation, Annual Meetings of the Amer. Assoc. Physical Anthropology in Albuquerque.

Sattenspiel, L., and H. Harpending. 1983. Stable populations and skeletal age. *Amer. Antiq.* 48:489–498.

Savage, C. 1988. *Wolves*. San Francisco: Sierra Club Books.

Savelle, J. M., and A. P. McCartney. 1991. Thule Eskimo subsistence and bowhead whale procurement. In *Human Predators and Prey Mortality*, edited by

M. C. Stiner, pp. 201-216. Boulder, Colo.: Westview Press.

Schaller, G. B. 1967. *The Deer and the Tiger, a Study of Wildlife in India.* Chicago: Univ. Chicago Press.

Schaller, G. B. 1972. *The Serengeti Lion.* Chicago: Univ. Chicago Press.

Schaller, G. B. 1977. *Mountain Monarchs, Wild Sheep and Goats of the Himalaya.* Chicago: Univ. Chicago Press.

Schaller, G. B., and G. R. Lowther. 1969. The relevance of carnivore behavior to the study of early hominids. *Southwestern J. Anth.* 25:307–341.

Schiffer, M. B. 1983. Toward the identification of formation processes. *Amer. Antiq.* 48;675–706.

Schoener, T. W. 1974. Resource partitioning in ecological communities. *Science* 185:27–39.

Schoener, T. W. 1982. The controversy over interspecific competition. *Amer. Scientist* 70:586–595.

Schoener, T. W. 1983. Field experiments on interspecific competition. *Amer. Naturalist* 122:240–285.

Schultz, S. R., and M. K. Johnson. 1992. Breeding by male white-tailed deer fawns. *J. Mamm.* 73:148–150.

Schwarcz, H. P., A. Bietti, W. M. Buhay, M. C. Stiner, R. Grün, and A. G. Segre. 1991. On the reexamination of Grotta Guattari: Uranium-series and electron-spin-resonance dates. *Curr. Anth.* 32:313–316.

Schwarcz, H. P., W. Buhay, R. Grün, M. C. Stiner, S. Kuhn, and G. H. Miller. 1990–91. Absolute dating of sites in coastal Lazio. *Quaternaria Nova* (Nuova Serie) 1:51–67.

Schwarcz, H. P., and R. Grün. 1993. Electron spin resonance (ESR) dating of the origin of modern man. In *The Origin of Modern Humans and the Impact of Chronometric Dating,* edited by M. J. Aitken, C. B. Stringer, and P. A. Mellars, pp. 40–48. Princeton: Princeton Univ. Press.

Scott, K. 1986a. The large mammalian fauna. In *La Cotte de St. Brelade 1961–78,* edited by P. Callow and J. M. Cornford, pp. 109–137. Norwich: Geo Books.

Scott, K. 1986b. The bone assemblages of layers 3 and 6. In *La Cotte de St. Brelade,* edited by P. Callow and J. M. Cornford, pp. 159–183. Norwich: Geo Books.

Seal, U. S., and E. D. Plotka. 1983. Age-specific pregnancy rates in feral horses. *J. Wildlife Manag.* 47: 422–429.

Segre, A. G. 1953. Risultati preliminari dell'esplorazione ecometrica del Basso Tirreno. *La Ricerca Scientifica* 29, no. 9.

Segre, A. G. 1967. Gian Alberto Blanc. *Quaternaria* 9:1–7.

Segre, A. G. 1976–77. Quaternary geology of the Palidoro country, Rome. *Quaternaria* 19:157–161.

Segre, A. G. 1982. Elementi archeologico-preistorici per la definizione del Pleistocene medio in Italia: A, il piu antico Paleolitico, B, Nuovi dati sulla stratigrafia pleistocenico del Bacino di Anagni. *Geografia Fisica Dinamica del Quaternario* 5:247–249.

Segre, A. G. 1984. Considerazioni sulla cronostratigrafia del Pleistocene Laziale. *Atti XXIV Riunione Scientifica Ist. Ital. Preistoria e Protostoria nel Lazio,* pp. 23–30.

Segre, A. G., and A. Ascenzi. 1984. Fontana Ranuccio: Italy's earliest Middle Pleistocene hominid site. *Curr. Anth.* 25:230–233.

Segre, A. G., I. Biddittu, and F. Guadagnoli. 1987. Nuovi dati sul giacimento del Paleolitico Inferiore di Anagni-Fontana Ranuccio. *Quaderni del Centro di Studio per L'Archeologia Erusco-Italica* 14:239–243.

Segre, E. 1972. Luigi Cardini. *Quaternaria* 16:3–14.

Sergi, S. 1954. La mandibola neandertaliana Circeo II. *Rivista di Antropologia* 41:305–344.

Sergi, S. 1955. La mandibola neandertaliana Circeo III (mandibola B). *Rivista di Antropologia* 42:337–403.

Sergi, S., and A. Ascenzi. 1974. *Il Cranio Neandertaliano di Monte Circeo (Circeo I).* Rome.

Settepassi, R., and U. Verdel. 1965. Continental Quaternary mollusca of lower Liri Valley (southern Latium). *Geologica Romana* 4:369–452.

Severinghaus, C. W. 1949. Tooth development and wear as criteria of age in white-tailed deer. *J. Wildlife Manag.* 13:195–216.

Sevink, J., A. Remmelzwaal, and O. C. Spaargaren. 1984. The soils of southern Lazio and adjacent Campania. *Publicatie van het Fysisch Geografisch en Bodemkundig Laboratorium van de Universiteit van Amsterdam,* no. 38.

Shackleton, J. C. 1983. An approach to determining prehistoric shellfish collecting patterns. In *Animals and Archaeology: 2. Shell Middens, Fishes and Birds,* edited by C. Grigson and J. Clutton-Brock, pp. 77–85. Oxford: BAR International Series 183.

Shackleton, J. C 1988a. Reconstructing past shorelines as an approach to determining factors affecting shellfish collecting in the prehistoric past. In *The Archaeology of Prehistoric Coastlines,* edited by G. Bailey and J. Parkington, pp. 11–21. Cambridge: Cambridge Univ. Press.

Shackleton, J. C. 1988b. *Marine Molluscan Remains from Franchthi Cave* (Fasc. 4). Bloomington: Indiana Univ. Press.

Shackleton, N. J., and N. D. Opdyke. 1973. Oxygen

isotope and palaeomagnetic stratigraphy of equatorial Pacific core, V28–238. *Quaternary Res.* 3:39–55.

Shea, J. 1989. A functional study of the lithic industries associated with hominid fossils in the Kebara and Qafzeh caves, Israel. In *The Human Revolution*, Vol. 1, edited by P. Mellars and C. Stringer, pp. 611–625. Princeton: Princeton Univ. Press.

Shipman, P. 1984. Scavenger hunt. *Natural Hist.* 93:20–27.

Shipman, P. 1986. Scavenging or hunting in early hominids: Theoretical framework and tests. *Amer. Anthropol.* 88:27–43.

Shott, M. 1986. Settlement mobility and technological organization: An ethnographic examination. *J. Anthropol. Res.* 42:15–51.

Siegel, P. E., and P. G. Roe. 1986. Shipibo archaeo-ethnography: Site formation processes and archaeological interpretation. *World Arch.* 18:96–115.

Simberloff, D. 1983. Competition theory, hypothesis-testing, and other community ecological buzzwords. *Amer. Naturalist* 122:626–635.

Simek, J. F., and L. M. Snyder. 1988. Changing assemblage diversity in Perigord archaeofaunas. In *Upper Pleistocene Prehistory of Western Eurasia*, edited by H. L. Dibble and A. Montet-White, pp. 321–332. Philadelphia: Univ. Mus. Monogr. no. 54.

Sinclair, A. R. E. 1977. *The African Buffalo: A Study of Resource Limitation of Populations*. Chicago: Univ. Chicago Press.

Sinclair, A. R. E. 1991. Science and the practice of wildlife management. *J. Wildlife Manag.* 55:767–773.

Singer, R., and J. Wymer. 1982. *The Middle Stone Age at Klasies River Mouth in South Africa*. Chicago: Univ. Chicago Press.

Skinner, J. D., S. Davis, and G. Llani. 1980. Bone collecting by striped hyaenas, *Hyaena hyaena*, in Israel. *Paleontology in Africa* 23:99–104.

Skinner, J. D., J. R. Henschel, and A. S. van Jaarsveld. 1986. Bone-collecting habits of spotted hyaenas *Crocuta crocuta* in the Kruger National Park. *S. Afr. J. Zool.* 21:303–308.

Skinner, J. D., and R. J. van Aarde. 1991. Bone collecting by brown hyaenas, *Hyaena brunnea*, in the central Namib Desert, Namibia. *J. Archaeol. Science* 18:513–523.

Smith, B. D. 1975. Middle Mississippi exploitation of animal populations. *Anthropol. Papers Mus. Anth.*, no. 57. Ann Arbor, Mich.: Univ. Michigan.

Smith, C. A. 1986. Rates and causes of mortality in mountain goats in southeast Alaska. *J. Wildlife Manag.* 50:743–746.

Smith, E. A., and B. Winterhalder. 1981. New perspectives on hunter-gatherer socioecology. In *Hunter-Gatherer Foraging Strategies*, edited by B. Winterhalder and E. A. Smith, pp. 1–12. Chicago: Univ. Chicago Press.

Smith, F. H. 1984. Fossil hominids from the Upper Pleistocene of central Europe and the origin of modern Europeans. In *The Origins of Modern Humans: A World Survey of the Fossil Evidence*, edited by F. H. Smith and F. Spencer, pp. 137–210. New York: Alan R. Liss.

Soffer, O. 1985. *The Upper Paleolithic of the Central Russian Plain*. San Diego: Academic Press.

Soffer, O. 1989. The Middle to Upper Palaeolithic transition on the Russian Plain. In *The Human Revolution*, edited by P. Mellars and C. Stringer, pp. 714–742. Princeton, N.J.: Princeton Univ. Press.

Sowls, L. K. 1984. *The Peccaries*. Tucson: Univ. Arizona Press.

Speth, J. D. 1977. Experimental investigations of hard-hammer percussions flaking. In *Experimental Archaeology*, edited by D. Ingersoll, J. E. Yellen, and W. MacDonald, pp. 3–37. New York: Columbia University Press.

Speth, J. D. 1983. *Bison Kills and Bone Counts: Decision Making by Ancient Hunters*. Chicago: Univ. Chicago Press.

Speth, J. D. 1987. Early hominid subsistence strategies in seasonal habitats. *J. Archaeol. Science* 14:13–29.

Speth, J. D. 1989. Early hominid hunting and scavenging: The role of meat as an energy source. *J. Human Evol.* 18:329–343.

Speth, J. D. 1990. Seasonality, resource stress, and food sharing in so-called "egalitarian" foraging societies. *J. Anthropol. Arch.* 9:148–188.

Speth, J. D. 1991. Taphonomy and early hominid behavior: Problems in distinguishing cultural and non-cultural agents. In *Human Predators and Prey Mortality*, edited by M. C. Stiner, pp. 31–40. Boulder, Colo.: Westview Press.

Speth, J. D., and K. A. Spielmann. 1983. Energy source, protein metabolism, and hunter-gatherer subsistence strategies. *J. Anthropol. Arch.* 2:1–31.

Spiess, A. E. 1979. *Reindeer and Caribou Hunters, an Archaeological Study*. New York: Academic Press.

Stephens, D. W., and J. R. Krebs. 1986. *Foraging Theory*. Princeton: Princeton Univ. Press.

Steward, J. 1938. Basin-plateau aboriginal sociopolitical groups. *Bureau of Amer. Ethnology Bull.*, no. 120.

Stiner, M. C. 1986. Analysis of faunal remains from six sites near Low Mountain, Arizona. In *Economic Re-*

sponsiveness: The Changing Role of Small sites in Subsistence Strategies, edited by C. L. Scheick, pp. 329–349. Zuni Arch. Program and Southwest Archaeol. Consultants. Prepared for the Bureau of Indian Affairs, Branch of Roads, New Mexico.

Stiner, M. C. 1990a. *The Ecology of Choice: Procurement and Transport of Animal Resources by Upper Pleistocene Hominids in West-central Italy.* Ph.D. dissertation (Univ. New Mexico, Albuquerque). Ann Arbor: UMI.

Stiner, M. C. 1990b. The use of mortality patterns in archaeological studies of hominid predatory adaptations. *J. Anthropol. Arch.* 9:305–351.

Stiner, M. C 1990–91. Ungulate exploitation during the terminal Mousterian of west-central Italy: The case of Grotta Breuil. *Quaternaria Nova* (Nuova Serie) 1:333–350.

Stiner, M. C. 1991a. A taphonomic perspective on the origins of the faunal remains of Grotta Guattari (Latium, Italy). *Curr. Anth.* 32:103–117.

Stiner, M. C. 1991b. Food procurement and transport by human and non-human predators. *J. Archaeol. Science* 18:455–482.

Stiner, M. C. 1991c. Introduction: Actualistic and archaeological studies of prey mortality. In *Human Predators and Prey Mortality,* edited by M. C. Stiner, pp. 1–13. Boulder, Colo.: Westview Press.

Stiner, M. C. 1991d. An interspecific perspective on the emergence of the modern human predatory niche. In *Human Predators and Prey Mortality,* edited by M. C. Stiner, pp. 149–185. Boulder, Colo.: Westview Press.

Stiner, M. C 1991e. The community ecology perspective and the redemption of "contaminated" faunal records. In *Perspectives on the Past: Theoretical Biases in Mediterranean Hunter-Gatherer Research,* edited by G. Clark, pp. 229–242. Philadelphia: Univ. Pennsylvania Press.

Stiner, M. C. 1992. Overlapping species "choice" by Italian Upper Pleistocene predators. *Curr. Anth.* 33:433–451.

Stiner, M. C. 1993a. The place of hominids among predators: Interspecific comparisons of food procurement and transport. In *From Bones to Behavior: Ethnoarchaeological and Experimental Contributions to the Interpretation of Faunal Remains,* edited by J. Hudson, pp. 38–61. Carbondale: Southern Illinois Univ. Press, Occasional Paper no. 21.

Stiner, M. C. 1993b. Small animal exploitation and its relation to hunting, scavenging, and gathering in the Italian Mousterian. In *Hunting and Animal Exploita-*

tion in the Later Palaeolithic and Mesolithic of Eurasia, edited by G. L. Peterkin, H. Bricker, and P. Mellars, pp. 101–119. Archaeol. Papers Amer. Anthropol. Assoc., Vol. 4.

Stiner, M. C. 1993c. Modern human origins—faunal perspectives. *Ann. Rev. Anthropol.* 22:55–82.

Stiner, M. C., S. Weiner, O. Bar-Yosef, and S. L. Kuhn. (n.d.) Differential burning, recrystallization, and fragmentation of archaeological bone. *J. Archaeol. Science.* In press.

Stiner, M. C., and S. L. Kuhn. 1992. Subsistence, technology, and adaptive variation in Middle Paleolithic Italy. *Amer. Anthropol.* 94:12–46.

Straus, L. G. 1979. Caves: A palaeoanthropological resource. *World Arch.* 10:331–339.

Straus, L. G. 1982. Carnivores and cave sites in Cantabrian Spain. *J. Anthropol. Res.* 38:75–96.

Straus, L. G. 1986. An overview of the La Riera chronology. In *La Riera Cave: Stone Age Hunter-gatherer Adaptations in Northern Spain,* edited by L. G. Straus and G. A. Clark, pp. 19–23. Arizona State Univ. Anthropol. Res. Paper, no. 36.

Straus, L. G. 1987. Upper Paleolithic ibex hunting in southwest Europe. *J. Archaeol. Science* 14:163–178.

Straus, L. G. 1990. The early Upper Palaeolithic of southwest Europe: Cro-Magnon adaptations in the Iberian peripheries, 40,000–20,000 BP. In *The Emergence of Modern Humans: An Archaeological Perspective,* edited by P. Mellars, pp. 276–302. Ithaca: Cornell Univ. Press.

Street, D. 1979. *The Reptiles of Northern and Central Europe.* London: B. T. Batsford.

Stringer, C. B. 1988. Palaeoanthropology: The dates of Eden. *Nature* 331:565–566.

Stringer, C. and P. Andrews. 1988. Genetic and fossil evidence for the origins of modern humans. *Science* 239:1263–1268.

Stringer, C. B., J. J. Hublin, and B. Vandermeersch. 1984. The origin of anatomically modern humans in western Europe. In *The Origins of Modern Humans: A World Survey of the Fossil Evidence,* edited by F. H. Smith and F. Spencer, pp. 51–136. New York: Alan R. Liss.

Strum, S. C. 1981. Processes and products of change: Baboon predatory behavior at Gilgil, Kenya. In *Omnivorous Primates: Gathering and Hunting in Human Evolution,* edited by R. S. O. Harding and G. Teleki, pp. 255–302. New York: Columbia Univ. Press.

Stuart, A. J. 1982. *Pleistocene Vertebrates in the British Isles.* London: Longman.

Sutcliffe, A. 1970. Spotted hyaena: Crusher, gnawer, digestor, and collector of bones. *Nature (London)* 227:1110–1113.

Taber, R. D., K. J. Raedeke, and D. A. McCaughran. 1982. Population characteristics. In *Elk of North America: Ecology and Management,* edited by J. W. Thomas and D. E. Toweill, pp. 279–298. Harrisburg: Stackpole Books.

Taramelli, E., C. Chimenz, A. Mussino, G. Battaglini, and F. Bianchi. 1977. I molluschi del porto di Civitavecchia (Roma). *Atti della Società Italiano di Scienze Naturali e del Museo Civico di Storia Naturale di Milano* 118:299–314.

Taschini, M. 1964. Il livello Mesolitico del Riparo Blanc al Monte Circeo. *Bullettino di Paletnologia Italiana* 17:65–88.

Taschini, M. 1968. La datation au C14 de l'abri Blanc (Mont Circé): quelques observations sur le Mésolithicque en Italie. *Quaternaria* 10:137–165.

Taschini, M. 1970. La Grotta Breuil al Monte Circeo, per una impostazione dello studio del Pontiniano. *Origini* 4:45–78.

Taschini, M. 1972. Sur le Palaeolithique de la plaine Pontine (Latium). *Quaternaria* 16:203–223.

Taschini, M. 1979. L'industrie lithique de Grotta Guattari au Mont Circé (Latium): Définition culturelle, typologique et chronologique du Pontinien. *Quaternaria* 12:179–247.

Tassi, F. 1983. L'orso bruno Marsicano. *Panda* 12 (Estratto, Parco Nazionale d'Abruzzo).

Tatum, L. S. 1980. A seasonal subsistence model for Holocene bison hunters on the eastern plains of North America. In *Cherokee Excavations: Holocene Ecology and Human Adaptations in Northwestern Iowa,* edited by D. C. Anderson and H. A. Semken, pp. 149–169. New York: Academic Press.

Tchernov, E. 1981. The biostratigraphy of the Middle East. In *Préhistoire du Levant,* edited by J. Cauvin and P. Sanlaville, pp. 67–97. Paris: Editions du CNRS.

Tchernov, E. 1984. Faunal turnover and extinction rate in the Levant. In *Quaternary Extinctions,* edited by P. S. Martin and R. G. Klein, pp. 528–552. Tucson: Univ. Arizona Press.

Tchernov, E. 1989. The Middle Paleolithic mammalian sequence and its bearing on the origin of *Homo sapiens* in the southern Levant. In *Investigations in South Levantine Prehistory (Préhistoire du Sud-Levant),* edited by O. Bar Yosef and B. Vandermeersch, pp. 25–38. Oxford: BAR International Series 497.

Tchernov, E. 1992. Biochronology, paleoecology, and dispersal events of hominids in the southern Levant.

In *The Evolution and Dispersal of Modern Humans in Asia,* edited by T. Akazawa, K. Aoki, and T. Kimura, pp. 149–188. Tokyo: Hokusen-Sha.

Teleki, G. 1974. Chimpanzee subsistence technology: Materials and skills. *J. Human Evol.* 3:575–594.

Teleki, G. 1975. Primate subsistence patterns: Collector-predators and gatherer-hunters. *J. Human Evol.* 4:125–184.

Terborgh, J. 1977. Bird species diversity on an Andean elevational gradient. *Ecology* 58:1007–1019.

Terborgh, J. 1983. *Five New World Primates: A Study in Comparative Ecology.* Princeton: Princeton Univ. Press.

Terborgh, J., and J. M. Diamond. 1970. Niche overlap in feeding assemblages of New Guinea birds. *Wilson Bull.* 82:29–52.

Thackeray, J. F. 1988. Molluscan fauna from Klasies River, South Africa. *S. Afr. Archaeol. Bull.* 43:27–32.

Thompson, I. D., and R. O. Peterson. 1988. Does wolf predation alone limit the moose population in Pukaskwa Park? A Comment. *J. Wildlife Manag.* 52:556–559.

Tietje, W. D., B. O. Pelchat, and R. L. Ruff. 1986. Cannibalism of denned black bears. *J. Mamm.* 67:762–766.

Tilson, R., F. von Blottnitz, and J. Henschel. 1980. Prey selection by spotted hyaena (*Crocuta crocuta*) in the Namib Desert. *Madoqua* 12:41–49.

Tilson, R. L., and W. J. Hamilton. 1984. Social dominance and feeding patterns of spotted hyaenas. *Animal Behaviour* 32:715–724.

Tixier, J., M. L. Inizian, and H. Roche. 1980. *Préhistoire del pierre taillée.* Vol. 1, *Terminologie et technologie.* Valbonne: C.R.E.P.

Todd, L. C. 1983. *The Horner Site: Taphonomy of an Early Holocene Bison Bonebed.* Unpublished Ph.D. dissertation, Univ. New Mexico, Albuquerque.

Todd, L. C. 1991. Seasonality studies and Paleoindian subsistence strategies. In *Human Predators and Prey Mortality,* edited by M. C. Stiner, pp. 217–238. Boulder, Colo.: Westview Press.

Todd, L. C., and J. L. Hofman. 1987. Bison mandibles from the Horner and Finley sites. In *The Horner Site: The Type Site of the Cody Cultural Complex,* edited by G. C. Frison and L. C. Todd, pp. 493–539. New York: Academic Press.

Todd, L. C., J. L. Hofman, and C. B. Schultz. 1990. Seasonality of the Scottsbluff and Lipscomb bison bonebeds: Implications for modeling Paleoindian subsistence. *Amer. Antiq.* 55:813–827.

Tooby, J., and I. DeVore. 1987. The reconstruction of

hominid behavioral evolution through strategic modeling. In *The Evolution of Human Behavior: Primate Models,* edited by W. G. Kinsey, pp. 183–237. Albany: State Univ. New York Press.

Torrence, R. 1983. Time budgeting and hunter-gatherer technology. In *Hunter-gatherer Economy in Prehistory: A European Perspective,* edited by G. Bailey, pp. 11-22. Cambridge: Cambridge Univ. Press.

Torrence, R. 1989. Re-tooling: Towards a behavioral theory of stone tools. In *Time, Energy and Stone Tools,* edited by R. Torrence, pp. 57–66. Cambridge: Cambridge Univ. Press.

Torres, T. J. 1988. *Osos (Mammalia, Carnivora, Ursidae) del Pleistoceno de la península Ibérica.* Publicaciones especiales de boletín geologica y minero (reimpresión del I–VI, T. XCIX), 1988.

Tozzi, C. 1970. La Grotta di S. Agostino (Gaeta). *Rivista di Scienze Preistoriche* 25:3–87.

Tozzi, C. 1974. L'industria musteriana della Grotta di Gosto sulla Montagna di Cetona (Siena). *Rivista di Scienze Preistoriche* 29:271–304.

Tozzi, C. 1976. Il Mesolitico della Campania. *Atti della 17 Riunione Scientifica, Istituto Italiano per la Preistoria e Protostoria,* pp. 33–49. Firenze: Parenti.

Trinkaus, E. 1983a. *The Shanidar Neandertals.* New York: Academic Press.

Trinkaus, E. 1983b. Neandertal postcrania and the adaptive shift to modern humans. In *The Mousterian Legacy,* edited by E. Trinkaus, pp. 165–200. Oxford: BAR International Series 164.

Trinkaus, E. 1986. The Neandertals and modern human origins. *Ann. Rev. Anth.* 15:193-218.

Trinkaus, E., editor. 1989. *The Emergence of Modern Humans.* Cambridge: Cambridge Univ. Press.

Trinkaus, E. 1992. Paleontological prespectives on Neandertal behavior. In *Cinq millions d'années, l'aventure humaine,* edited by M. Toussaint, pp. 151–176. Liège: ERAUL. 56.

Turner, A. 1984. Hominids and fellow-travellers: Human migration into high latitudes as part of a large mammal community. In *Hominid Evolution and Community Ecology,* edited by R. Foley, pp. 193–218. London: Academic Press.

Turner, A. 1986. Correlation and causation in some carnivore and hominid evolutionary events. *S. Afr. J. Science* 82:75–76.

Turner, A. 1989. Sample selection, Schlepp effects and scavenging: The implication of partial recovery for interpretations of the terrestrial mammal assemblage from Klasies River Mouth. *J. Archaeol. Science* 16:1–11.

United States Department of Agriculture. 1986. *Compo-sition of Foods: Beef Products.* Washington, D.C.: United States Department of Agriculture, Human Nutrition Information Service, Agriculture Handbook no. 8-13.

Valladas, H., J. L. Horon, G. Valladas, B. Arensburg, O. Bar-Yosef, A. Belfer-Cohen, P. Goldberg, H. Laville, L. Meignen, Y. Rak, E. Tchernov, A.-M. Tillier, and B. Vandermeersch. 1987. Thermoluminescence dates for the Neanderthal burial sites at Kebara (Mount Carmel), Israel. *Nature* 330:159–160.

Valladas, H., J. L. Reyss, J. L. Horon, G. Valladas, O. Bar-Yosef, and B. Vandermeersch. 1988. Thermoluminescence dating of Mousterian "Proto-Cro-Magnon" remains from Israel and the origin of modern man. *Nature* 331:614–616.

Van Ballenberghe, V. 1983. Two litters raised in one year by a wolf pack. *J. Mamm.* 64:171–172.

Van Ballenberghe, V., and L. D. Mech. 1975. Weights, growth, and survival of timber wolf pups in Minnesota. *J. Mamm.* 56:44–63.

Vandermeersch, B. 1989. The evolution of modern humans: Recent evidence from southwest Asia. In *The Human Revolution: Behavioural and Biological Perspectives on the Origins of Modern Humans,* Vol. 1, edited by P. Mellars and C. B. Stringer, pp. 155–164. Edinburgh: Edinburgh Univ. Press.

Van Valkenburgh, B. 1989. Carnivore dental adaptations and diet: A study of trophic diversity within guilds. In *Carnivore Behavior, Ecology, and Evolution,* edited by J. L. Gittleman, pp. 410–436. Ithaca: Cornell Univ. Press.

Villa, P., and E. Mahieu. 1991. Breakage patterns of human long bones. *J. Human Evol.* 21:27–48.

Vincent, A. 1988. Remarques preliminaires concernant l'outillage osseux de la Grotte Vaufrey. In *La Grotte Vaufrey: Paléoenvironnement, Chronologie, Activités Humaines,* edited by J.-P. Rigaud, pp. 529–533. C.N.R.S.: Mémmoires de la Société Préhistorique Française, Tome 19.

Vitagliano, S. 1984. Nota sul Pontiniano della Grotta dei Moscerini, Gaeta (Latina). *Atti della XXIV Riunione Scientifica dell'Istituto Italiano di Preistoria e Protostoria nel Lazio,* 8–11 Ottobre 1982, pp. 155–164.

Vitagliano, S., and M. Piperno. 1990–91. Lithic industry of level 27 *beta* of the Fossellone Cave (S. Felice Circeo, Latina). *Quaternaria Nova* (Nuova Serie) 1:289–304.

Voigt, E. A. 1973. Stone Age molluscan utilization at Klasies River Mouth Caves. *S. Afr. J. Science* 69:306–309.

Voigt, E. A. 1982. The molluscan fauna. In *The Middle*

Stone Age of Klasies River Mouth in South Africa, edited by R. Singer and J. Wymer, pp. 155–186. Chicago: Univ. Chicago Press.

Voorhies, M. R. 1969. *Taphonomy and Population Dynamics of an Early Pliocene Vertebrate Fauna, Knox County, Nebraska.* Contributions to Geology, Special Papers, no. 1. Laramie: Univ. Wyoming.

Voorrips, A., S. Loving, and H. Kamermans. 1983. An archaeological survey of the Agro Pontino (Province of Latina). In *Archaeological Survey in the Mediterranean Area,* edited by D. Keller and D. Rupp. Oxford: BAR International Series 283.

Vrba, E. S. 1992. Mammals as a key to evolutionary theory. *J. Mamm.* 73:1–28.

Walter, G. H., P. E. Hulley, and A. J. F. K. Craig. 1984. Speciation, adaptation and interspecific competition. *Oikos* 43:246–251.

Walters, I. 1988. Fire and bones: Patterns of discard. In *Archaeology with Ethnography: An Australian Perspective,* edited by B. Meehan and R. Jones, pp. 215–221. Canberra: Australian National Univ.

Watts, P. D., and C. Jonkel. 1988. Energetic cost of winter dormancy in grizzly bear. *J. Wildlife Manag.* 52:654–656.

Watts, P. D., N. A. Øritsland, and R. J. Hurst. 1987. Standard metabolic rate of polar bears under simulated denning conditions. *Physiological Zool.* 60:687–691.

Whallon, R. 1989. Elements of cultural change in the later Palaeolithic. In *The Human Revolution,* edited by P. Mellars and C. Stringer, pp. 433–454. Princeton: Princeton Univ. Press.

White, G. C., R. A. Garrott R. M. Bartmann, L. H. Carpenter, and A. W. Alldredge. 1987. Survival of mule deer in northwest Colorado. *J. Wildlife Manag.* 51:852–859.

White, R. 1982. Rethinking the Middle/Upper Paleolithic transition. *Curr. Anth.* 23:169–192.

White, T. D., and N. Toth. 1991. The question of ritual cannibalism at Grotta Guattari. *Curr. Anth.* 32:118–124.

Wiens, J. A. 1977. On competition and variable environments. *Amer. Scientist* 65:590–597.

Wiens, J. A. 1983. Competition or peaceful coexistence? *Natural Hist.* 92:30–34.

Wilcove, D. S., C. H. McLellan, and A. P. Dobson. 1986. Habitat fragmentation in the temperate zone. In *Conservation Biology: The Science of Scarcity and Diversity,* edited by M. E. Soulé, pp. 237–256. Sunderland, Mass.: Sinauer Associates.

Wilkinson, P. F. 1976. "Random" hunting and the composition of faunal samples from archaeological excavations: A modern example from New Zealand. *J. Archaeol. Science* 3:321–328.

Winterhalder, B. 1986. Diet choice, risk, and food sharing in a stochastic environment. *J. Anthropol. Arch.* 5:369–392.

Wirtz, W. O. 1968. Reproduction, growth and development, and juvenile mortality in the Hawaiian monk seal. *J. Mamm.* 49:229–238.

Wiszniowska, T. 1982. Carnivora. In *Excavation in the Bacho Kiro Cave (Bulgaria), Final Report,* edited by J. K. Kozłowski, pp. 52–55. Warsaw: Państwowe Wy Dawnictwo Naukowe.

Wolpoff, M. 1989. Multiregional evolution: The fossil alternative to Eden. In *The Human Revolution,* edited by P. mellars and C. Stringer, pp. 62–108. Princeton: Princeton Univ. Press.

Wooding, J. B., and T. S. Hardisky. 1992. Denning black bears in northcentral Florida. *J. Mamm.* 73:895–898.

Woolf, A., and J. D. Harder. 1979. Population dynamics of a captive white-tailed deer herd with emphasis on reproduction and mortality. *Wildlife Monogr.,* no. 67.

Wrangham, R. 1977. Feeding behaviour of chimpanzees in Gombe National Park, Tanzania. In *Primate Ecology: Studies of Feeding and Ranging Behaviour in Lemurs, Monkeys and Apes,* edited by T. H. Clutton-Brock, pp. 504–538. New York: Academic Press.

Wynn, T., and W. McGrew. 1989. An ape's view of the Oldowan. *Man* 24:383–398.

Yellen, J. E. 1977. Cultural patterning in faunal remains: Evidence from the !Kung Bushmen. In *Experimental Archaeology,* edited by D. Ingersoll, J. E. Yellen, and W. Macdonald, pp. 271–331. New York: Columbia Univ. Press.

Yellen, J. E. 1991a. Small mammals: !Kung San utilization and the production of faunal assemblages. *J. Anthropol. Arch.* 10:1–26.

Yellen, J. E. 1991b. Small mammals: Post-discard patterning of !Kung San faunal remains. *J. Anthropol. Arch.* 10:152–192.

Yesner, D. R. 1981. Archaeological applications of optimal foraging theory: Harvest strategies of Aleut hunter-gatherers. In *Hunter-gatherer Foraging Strategies,* edited by B. Winterhalder and E. A. Smith, pp. 148–170. Chicago: Univ. Chicago Press.

Zei, M. 1970. Ricerche nel Lazio meridionale. *Rivista di Scienze Preistoriche* 25:323–325.

Index

abrasion, 104–105, 108, 110, 112, 114–115, 122, 125; definition of (on bone), 104–105; quantitative accounts of (on bone), 108–127; surf-induced, 159, 161, 177, 182, 185–187. *See also* geological scratches.

Abri Vaufrey, 8

accumulation rates of lithic artifacts and bones, comparisons of, 366–367, 375, 379

actualistic studies, 67, 96, 145, 168; archaeological records and scaling of, 96; of carcass consumption by predators at death sites, 258; of processing and transport of crania by predators, 241, 266

adaptation, capacity for variable response in, 14; central role of subsistence in, 353; to common prey species, 234–235, 353, 372; definition of niche vs., 15; space- and time-dependent phenomena in human, 373

adaptational change, directions of, 308–315; frequency shifts in, 369, 385–387

adaptive potential in *Homo sapiens*, 15

adaptive radiations in Miocene-Pliocene carnivores, 16

adaptive variation in large predators, dimensions of, 372; measures of, 201, 385

Adriatic Sea, 180

Africa, 237, 377; coexistence of hominids and carnivores in, 309

African cape buffalo. *See* cape buffalo.

African lions. *See* lions.

African wild dogs. *See* wild dogs.

Agate Basin site, bison mortality patterns in, 301–304

age classifications of isolated teeth, 289

age cohorts, of equal vs. unequal duration, 275, 282; keyed to life history characteristics, 282, 321, 355; mortality pattern types and numbers of, 289

age frequency counts for consecutive cohorts, definition of, 275

AGEpel as age structure parameter, 281–282

age-specific vulnerability to death factors, 275, 278–281

age structures of living populations, natural variation in, 274. *See also* mortality analysis, mortality models, mortality patterns.

AGE variable, 18–21

agencies of bone collection in Italian caves, 95–157

aggregation errors in data analysis, issue of, 69, 202

agrarian economies, processing of ungulate parts in, 230

Agro Pontino. *See* Pontine Plain, Pontine Marshes.

Akp dogyard, caribou mortality patterns in, 301–304; seasonality data for Nunamiut-killed caribou in, 337–338

Alaska, 136; caribou mortality in, 278, 280; caribou mortality patterns caused by Nunamiut hunters, 301–304; carnivore reproductive schedules in, 319; mortality patterns in wolf-killed moose in, 298–300; seasonality data for Nunamiut-killed caribou in, 334, 336; wolf den faunas from, 248, 251–266, 348, 396

Alban Hills, 33

Alberta (Canada), 226, 285; mortality patterns in wolf-killed moose in, 298–300

alternating cave occupations by hominids and carnivores, 28, 150–153, 206, 317, 343, 373–374; tempo of, 330–331

altricial infants of bears, 325

Alvard, M., 368

ambiguous signatures of hunting and scavenging, 354

Amboseli spotted hyaena den assemblage, 248–266, 396

ambush hunting strategies of carnivores, 296–300; mortality patterns resulting from, 296–300; use of landscape features in, 296

ambush hunting strategies of humans, 301–308, 372; communal vs. solo, 286; and prime adult harvesting, 355–356, 372; selective, 279

ambush predators, humans as, 301–308, 375; niche divergence among, 308–312, 314

Amsterdam, University of, 30

analytical approach. *See* research design.

anatomical bar charts for medium-sized ungulates, 240, 242, 245–257

anatomical completeness (tMNE/MNI), index of, 242, 245, 355; trends in, 359–361

anatomical indexes, 242–245; HEAD/L, 20, 242, 245; (H+H)/L, 242, 245, 355; HORN/L, 242, 245; method for counting head parts and, 20, 238; regression analyses of, 240, 361; tMNE/MNI, 242, 245, 355

anatomical regions, definition of nine, 240–242; standardized MNEs for, 389–397

anatomical representation. *See* body part representation, food transport.

anatomically modern humans, origins of 3–5

Anbarra, 193, 196

Andrews, P., 96, 321

angle of retouch on stone tools, 356

angular splits on mandibles, 140–145

Aniene River, 27, 66, 86, 202

animal communities, 7–9; biased cave faunas derived from, 14, 68; concepts about the nature of, 14–17; effects of climate on, 68, 73–77; effects of history on, 15–16; latitudinal variation in, 68, 73–77, 92–93; marine, 159; of Pleistocene British Isles, 68, 74–77; of Pleistocene Israel, 68, 75–76; of Pleistocene Italy, 17, 68–94, 374; species recruitment and loss rates in, 16, 68, 73–77; species sampling in, 199–201; structures of, 14, 18, 68–94, 92; variation in species richness in, 14, 68, 73–77, 92–93

antlers, in carnivore dens, 224, 259–260, 269, 343, 345–349; expectations for, 343–345; as food supplement, 345; frequencies of shed vs. unshed, 259–260, 332, 343, 345–349; growth and shedding cycles of, 259, 332, 343–345; in Guattari, 41, 259–260, 345–349; in Paleolithic faunas, 247, 345–349; in Pleistocene hyaena dens, 343, 345–349; in Nunamiut kill sites, 232; seasonality determinations from, 21, 343–351, 378

China, 130

Chiroptera, 70, 160, 202

chital, tiger-caused mortality in, 298–300

choice, concepts of prey age, 314; versus standing species abundance, 199–200

cholesterol, humans' needs for dietary, 230; in shellfish, 196; in ungulate brain tissues, 229–230

Choronia lampas, 160, 180

chronology, 33–37; of cave sites in west-central Italy, 30, 33–37; geology-based, 5, 10, 33–37, 45–46, 359, 379; glaciation-deglaciation cycles and, 3–4, 8, 18, 45–46, 68, 73–77; of hominid fossils, 8, 33, 387; oxygen isotope, 46–47, 59, 75, 193; pollen, 34, 76; radiometric, 10, 33–37, 41, 49, 58, 60, 64, 66–67, 359; rank-ordering of Mousterian assemblages by, 358–365; relative, 36, 359; species-based (bio-), 33–37, 45–46, 66, 73–77, 85, 87–88, 92–93, 387; stone tool typologies and, 3–4, 8, 24, 33, 177, 373, 382, 386–387; time boundaries and, 8, 371, 373, 382, 386–387

Chucalissa site, white-tailed deer mortality in, 301–304

Circeo (Guattari) I, 32–33, 41, 43, 216, 356; circumstances of discovery of, 29, 152

Circeo (Guattari) II, 32, 41

Circeo (Guattari) III, 32, 41

clams, in Moscerini, 46, 159–161, 175, 178–180, 189–195, 197, 350–351; Mousterian tools made from, 32; nutritional value of, 189, 192, 196–197; sand-dwelling, 160. *See also* shellfish.

Class I-IV bovids, 249, 397

Clethrionomys glareolus, as climatic indicator, 74

Clevenger, A., 80, 285

climate, glaciation-deglaciation cycles and global, 3–4, 8, 63, 68, 73–77, 190; local consequences of changes in, 28, 190–191, 372; mammal community turnover and, 73–77, 92–93; maritime-regulated, 25, 319; pollen data and Middle-Upper Pleistocene, 34, 76, 372; species sensitivity to, 73–77, 92–93, 177, 202; trend in prime adult harvesting and deterioration of Pleistocene, 377

clines, latitudinal, 8, 74; maritime-continental, 8, 74; seasonality determinations and variation in prey growth and development schedules along, 332–336, 343; spotted hyaena food transport patterns as function of latitudinal, 263, 377

coastal plains of Latium, 24–25, 32, 57; marshes of, 26; Pleistocene breadth of, 28. *See also* Pontine Plain, Fondi Basin.

coastal sites, inundation of, 215–216

cockles, 160, 180

coevolution, of hominids and canids, 170; of predators, 9, 16, 374

coexistence, 201; hominid-carnivore, 273; paleontological legacy of predator, 6–9, 373–374; patterns of, 10; scales of relationship in, 14; species data and hominid-carnivore, 218; of "warm" and "cold" mammalian species, 76–77

collaborative research on Paleolithic subsistence and technology, 21–22, 32, 352–370, 382, 385

collared peccaries, mortality in trophy-hunted, 298–300

Colle Albani, 33

colonization by hominids, 16; by shellfish, 191

Colorado, deer mortality patterns in, 283, 285

columbella, 161

communal denning, 80–81; juvenile-biased carnivore mortality and, 317

communities. *See* animal communities.

community ecology, definitions from, 14–15; perspectives from, 6–7

comparative faunal collections, 69, 159

competition, 6–7, 13, 218; and cave use, 287; character displacement in prey age selection due to, 308–315, 374; continuous versus periodic, 201; evolutionary arenas or forums of, 7, 13; at feeding sites, 219, 222–224, 318; at food procurement sites, 251–252; food transport for reducing, 219; interference, 6–7; limiting similarity and, 15–16, 236, 309; for mates and seasonal mortality in ungulates, 283–287; resource partitioning as relief from, 201, 214, 374; among social predator species, 10; and tenets of niche theory, 308–309, 312–315

competition avoidance, 13–14, 16, 287, 308–309, 312–315

competitive (mutual) exclusion, 15–16, 208

complex strategists, humans as, 351

composite weapons, 61

conch shell, 160, 180, 183

cone fractures, 105–115, 122, 125, 129–132, 136–137, 146, 154–156, 161, 174–176; definition of, 105–107; potential causes of, 106; quantitative accounts of (on large mammal bones), 108–127; summary of data on, 130–132, 154–156; on tortoise shells, 161, 174–176

confrontational scavenging, ethnographically based definition of, 266; strategic contrast between nonconfrontational and, 384

constants as comparative baselines, 7–8. *See also* reference cases.

container technology, food transport decisions and, 219, 225, 228, 234, 384, 387; stone-boiling and, 383

continental shelf of Latium coast, 26–28. *See also* topography.

continuity-replacement dialectic, 387

control data. *See* reference cases.

controlled comparisons of predators, 7–8, 57, 61, 220–221, 355–356; in relation to genus-specific prey behavior, 301. *See also* reference cases, research design.

cooperative ambush hunting, 7, 307–308, 375; concepts about, 314; and technological sophistication, 368

cooperative carcass processing, 307

cooperative infant care, 7

coprolites (carnivore), 43, 151, 154–156, 202; in Buca della Iena, 151; in Breuil, 86; as diagnostic of den faunas, 317; in Fossellone, 129; in Guattari, 43, 45, 84, 151

core reduction techniques (tactics), economic properties of, 365; maximizing blank size vs. numbers of flakes in, 358; Mousterian, 5, 21, 32, 352, 356–358, 379–382; study of, 49; trends in Mousterian, 362–366; Upper Paleolithic blade, 5. *See also* technology.

core use-life in relation to reduction technique, 357–358; contexts of variation in, 362

cortical stripping of long bones by carnivores, 105, 136

costs, of food handling, 221; of food procurement and processing, 221, 227, 234; of food transport, 221, 225, 227, 232

counting faunal remains. *See* MNE, MNI, NISP, N-taxa.

coyotes, 136–138; digestive etching by, 168; predation on deer fawns by, 283–284, 308; scatologic bone samples from, 67

crania, nutritional contents of, 227–230, 369, 350–351, 383–385; prey death sites and persistence of, 266

cranial and mandibular MNEs in Mousterian faunas, comparisons of, 260, 266, 355; and nonviolent sources of scavenging opportunities, 385

crater lakes, pollen cores from Italian, 34

crenelation of bone fracture edges, 105–106. *See also* gnawing.

crested blade technique of Upper Paleolithic, 357

Cretaceous limestone, 24, 33

Cricetus cricetus, 70

food processing, 7, 13, 17, 95–157; as adaptation, 220; carnivores' capabilities for, 127, 221, 223, 240; costs of, 221, 227, 234, 383–385; evolutionary implications of, 13, 17; fat and, 146–147, 226, 383–385; humans' capabilities for, 7, 219, 224–225, 382–385; labor-intensive, 225; by Pleistocene hominids, 62, 66, 103–150, 192, 383–387; reference data on, 66; role of technology in food procurement vs., 382–385, 387; seasonal patterns in, 230; of shellfish with the aid of fire, 192; technical support for, 219, 221, 225, 228–229, 382–385, 387; transport to enhance opportunities for, 219, 221, 223; women's labor and cooperative, 220–221. *See also* bone modification, marrow processing.

food procurement vs. processing, role of technology in, 383–385

food producers, as trophic level, 14

food provisioning of dependents, 7, 221–223; at maternity dens, 223; spatial constraints on, 222

food quality, 17; effects on prey age selection by humans, 308, 376–377; effects on transport decisions of humans, 20, 189–197, 219–230, 234–235, 266–268; as function of season, 332

food scarcity, predators' responses to, 225, 235–270, 379

food search tactics, 158–159, 365–370, 375–376; covariation between Mousterian core reduction techniques and, 352–370, 375–376, 379–382; dispersed food supplies and, 222–224, 377; modeling of, 223; of Mousterian hominids, 353–354, 372, 374–376, 379–382; potential incompatability between hunting and gathering in human, 268; as reflected by ungulate mortality data, 271, 273, 283, 315, 376; scales of territory use and Paleolithic, 365–366; 369–370, 379–382; sociality and, 268, 351, 376–377, 380–382; uncertainty in locating resource patches and, 237

food sharing, 220–222, 225; to reduce foraging risk, 221, 223

food storage, 231

food stress, inter- and intraspecific violence triggered by, 318

food supply, limitations set by, 16, 272–273

food transport, analytical approach to, 219–242; of aquatic versus terrestrial prey, 192–198, 378–379; archaeological expectations for, 220, 230–235; behavioral and ecological bases of, 20, 219–236, 378–379, 383–385; behavioral tendencies in, 220, 248–270; and cave sites, 10; choices (takeaway options), 20, 222–223, 257–259, 355; container technology and, 219, 225, 228, 234, 383–385; contexts of food consumption and, 219–235, 378–379; controlled interspecific comparisons of, 20, 236–270; costs of, 221, 225, 227, 232; energetic conditions of, 191, 197–198, 378–379; evolutionary perspective on, 219; expectations for, 20, 230–236; to foraging hubs, 10, 231; and foraging niche, 7; of hard parts by mouth, 223; motives for, 221; nonhuman primates and the question of, 220–221; nutrition-based decisions about, 189–197, 219–230, 234, 266–267, 355, 383–385; as parts of predatory adaptations, 13, 17, 220; processing capabilities and, 20, 219–235, 283–285; and procurement strategies, 10, 20–21, 236–270; rates and volumes as function of distance, 219–220, 224, 231–233, 257–266, 378–379; to reduce risk of interference competition, 219; in response to food scarcity, 225, 235–270, 383–385; sociality and, 192–194, 222; of soft parts in stomach, 220, 223; strategies of, 17, 158–159, 189–192; trajectories, 231–233, 236; trends in Mousterian, 353, 359–361, 372, 375, 377–378; variation in strategies of, 248–270; volumes, 7, 236–270, 384. *See also* anatomical indexes, body part representation, ratio of.

food web, 7, 15

foraging behavior, aquatic resources and hominid, 189–196, 378–379; basic components of, 9; decision repetition rates in, 11, 273; food transport as, 219–235; gathering as, 7, 158–159, 186; of resource generalists, 16; organization of, 17, 22, 268, 371, 373; of resource specialists, 16

foraging hubs, food pooling at, 231; "home base" hypothesis and, 221; processing facilities and, 219–235; shoreline day camps as, 193, 196

foraging logistics, in Mousterian, 369, 381–382; and small game use, 198, 378–379

foraging models from population ecology, 221

foraging modes in Latium Mousterian, 369, 375, 379–382

foraging radii of hominids, and scavenging opportunities, 366–367; and shellfish procurement, 189–192

foraging returns from nonconfrontational scavenging, 354, 366, 369, 375, 379

foraging specialization. *See* specialization.

foraging strategies. *See* strategies.

formal tool types, 352, 365–366; hunting success and, 368; lack of variation in Mousterian, 46, 356–357, 366, 372, 374

formation histories of faunas. *See* taphonomic histories.

Fornaca Rinaldi, G., 36

Forsyt-Mayor, collaboration with G. A. Blanc, 29

Fossellone, Grotta del, Aurignacian industries from, 26; excavations of, 56; hyaena coprolites in, 129; hyaena mortality pattern in, 327–331; infant hyaena remains in, 129, 323; location of, 26; Mousterian industries from, 32

fossil hominids. *See* hominids.

fossiles directeurs, use of, 33; *Lithodomus* as, 33; Paleolithic stone tool industries as, 33; *Strombus bubonius* as, 33, 177

foxes, 19, 66; deciduous tooth shedding schedule of red, 320–321; mortality patterns in Latium, 327–331; permanent tooth morphologies of, 322; predation on snails by red, 161, 172–174; reproductive schedules of red, 319; in Sant'Agostino, 166, 330; scatologic bone samples from modern, 67; as scavengers, 117; tooth eruption and occlusal wear scheme for, 322–324

fracture complexes on large mammal remains, 140–147

fracture forms on bones, definitions of, 104–106; quantitative accounts of, 108–127, 154–156, 161

fragment lengths of bones, comparisons of medians and ranges of, 98–99, 154–156

fragmentation of bone, evaluations of biases in identifiability caused by, 95, 98–100, 147–150, 154–156, 202; in hyaena dens vs. human sites, 239–240; due to ingestion by carnivores, 167, 173; NISP and, 69–73

fragmentation of marine shells, 161, 182, 184, 186–188, 190

France, Dordogne Cliffs of, 24, 307; hippopotamus in, 76; Middle Paleolithic of, 386–387; ungulate reproductive schedules in, 333

Franchthi Cave, 193

freeze-thaw cycles and ungulate carcass availability. *See* snow accumulation, winter-killed ungulates.

Frison, G. C., 307

frugivores, as trophic level, 200

fulcrum of wear in mammalian cheek tooth rows, 289, 320, 322

furs, Upper Paleolithic hunting to obtain carnivore, 317

Gaeta, cliffs of, 25, 47, 57; coastal surveys near, 46; modern town of, 24–25

Gamble, C., 8, 10, 206, 218, 317

game drives, 307

Game Theory, 13

maximum potential lifetime of population (MPL), as age structure parameter, 281–282, 316; based on destruction of cheek tooth crowns, 321–327

Maynard Smith, J., 13

McMaster University (Canada), 35, 196

mean age of death (mean lifespan), 315

"meaty" ungulate body part profiles, hunting and, 258–270, 377; in Middle Paleolithic, 242–243, 365, 375–377; seasonality of Paleolithic, 349–351; in Upper Paleolithic, 243

mechanics of stone fracture, tool forms and, 353

medial thickness of stone tool blanks, 356

median reduction index for single-edged stone tools, 356, 362; trend in, 364–365

Mediterranean provinces, 9; species richness in, 18, 68, 73–77, 92–93

Mediterranean rim, carnivore representation in cave faunas of, 316–317

medium-sized ungulates, bone-based MNEs for, 243, 249–270, 334, 355, 389–397; as central food resources for large predators, 234, 245, 249, 256, 267; definition of, 245, 249

medullae, hemopoietic zones in bone, 291–292

Meehan, B., 193, 196

Megaceros giganteus, 70, 84

Meles meles, 70

Mellars, P., 387

Melville Island, 186

Meretrix. See *Callista*.

Mesolithic, cultural complexes, 61; shellfish harvesting during, 193–194, 196, 198; shelters in Latium, 26; Spanish, 248–249; use of shells as ornaments during, 182

metabolizable fats in mammals, 227–230

metal containers, food transport decisions and availability of, 219, 225, 228, 234

Metcalfe, D., 383

methodology and analytical approaches, 3, 17–23, 95–97, 221, 236–242, 248–249, 320–327, 332–337, 343–345, 353–358. See also research design.

Microtus arvalis, 70

Middle Paleolithic of Latium, 352; anomalous ungulate body part representation in, 228, 231, 245, 266–267, 345–349; flexibility in hominid behavior during, 371, 380–382, 387; food transport patterns during, 189–193, 197–198, 242–270; hominid diet during, 199–218, 374; hunting-scavenging during, 268, 371–378, 385–387; processing options in, 383–385; seasonal site use during, 332–351, 380–382; ungulate mortality patterns generated during, 288–315. See also Mousterian cave sites, Mousterian industries.

Middle Paleolithic technology. See Mousterian industries, technology.

Middle Pleistocene, 33, 273; Latiale volcanic eruptions during, 33

Middle Stone Age (MSA), 3–5, 382, 387; processing options during, 383; shellfish exploitation during, 46, 176, 194, 197, 379

Middle-Upper Paleolithic transition, 4–5, 8, 22, 36, 201, 374, 382; debates about, 385–387; lack of synchrony in biological and behavioral changes relative to, 374, 387

Mienis, H. K., 159

milk teeth. See deciduous teeth.

Mills, M. E. J., 348

Mills, M. G. L., 67, 224, 300, 348

minerals in food, 225

Miniopterus schreibersii, 70, 160

Minnesota, black bear reproductive schedule in, 319

Miocene, adaptive radiations in carnivores during, 16–17, 309

Mississippian deer hunting and mortality patterns, 301–306, 310–312

MNE, 18–21; antler, 343–349; bone-based, 19, 237–240, 243, 354–355; comparisons of bone-based vs. tooth-based cranial and mandibular, 238; cross-element comparisons and, 100; data for ungulates, 243–270, 389–397; differential preservation of skeletal tissue classes and, 233, 236–238; epiphysis-based vs. shaft-based limb, 238–240; expected values for artiodactyls, carnivores, and perissodactyls, 244; generic vs. species-level determinations of, 245–247; instructions for deriving raw, 390; raw counts of, 19, 242; red deer canine, 345–349; standardized bone-based, 19, 100, 240–242, 389–397; tooth-based, 19

MNI, 18–21; aggregation errors associated with, 69; antler, 343–348; assumptions about, 69; bone-based, 19, 241–242, 245, 248, 320, 355, 389–397; cranial, 97–103, 343–348; definitions of, 99–100; double counting errors associated with, 320–327; red deer canine, 345–349; shell-based, 161; tooth-based, 19, 289, 320–327

mobile human societies, 351, 372

mobility, Binford's model of hunter-gatherer, 232; differing scales of Middle and Upper Paleolithic, 351, 365–367, 372, 379–382

models, body part choice and transport, 219–235, 266–269, 354; carnivore-based, 6–8, 354; economic, 6; hunter-gatherer mobility, 232; primate-based, 6–8, 220–221; of scavenging, 232–234, 266, 300, 354; "soft replacement" human evolution model, 387; technology driven evolution, 382–383

modern human origins, 5, 22

Mohave Desert, 278; burro reproductive schedule in, 333; instantaneous age structure of burros from, 294–295

moles, 70, 160

mollusks. See land snails, shellfish.

Monachus monachus, 70

Monachus schauinslandi, 81

Mongolia, wild ass reproductive schedule in, 333

monk seals, 46, 70; denning behavior and associated mortality in, 81; hominid predation on, 133, 197; in Latium Pleistocene caves, 81, 133, 327–330

Monodonta turbinata, 160, 178, 180

monopolization behavior, in context of den use, 79, 133, 208–210, 287; in context of feeding, 221, 264

monospecific carnivore faunas in den sites, palimpsest accumulations and, 210

monospecific ungulate faunas in Paleolithic sites, potential implications of, 217–218

Monte Agmemone, 46

Monte Circeo, 24–29, 327; hominid fossils from, 32–33, 41–44; tectonic uplift of, 28, 33

moose, seasonal mortality patterns in, 283; U-shaped mortality patterns in wolf-killed, 278–280, 298–300

Morocco, 179

mortality (age structure) analysis, baseline expectations for nonselective harvesting, 360; choice of tooth elements for, 281; effects of skeletal preservation biases in, 277; prior applications of, 273–274; scales of human perception and, 273; spatial and temporal scales of, 271, 274, 277, 292; taphonomy and, 277; theory and method in, 271–287; three-age system of, 21, 289–315, 320–327; tooth eruption and occlusal wear schemes for studying, 18, 288–292, 320–327; use of data distributions in, 293

mortality cases, definition of, 288–289

terns in Upper Paleolithic, 248–266; ungulate reproductive schedules in, 333

spatial contingencies and models of food transport, 231–233

Spearman's rank order correlation of, dMNI and numbers of juvenile age cohorts filled, 334; Mousterian, faunal data by increasing age, 360; lithic data by increasing age, 364

spears, hunting with, 307, 382. *See also* projectile points.

special-purpose sites, body part profiles in, 232; multi-site archaeological investigations and, 286

specialist feeders, 16

specialization, 201; as evidenced by food transport data, 261–266; as evidenced by ungulate mortality patterns, 288–315, 386; implications of species data for resource, 217–218; prime adult ungulate harvesting and trend toward hominid predatory, 22, 313–314, 371–376, 382–383, 386; scales of observation in studies of hominid foraging, 382

specialized predation vs. seasonal foraging opportunities, 283–287

speciation and subspecies, 9

species abundance. *See* species representation.

species choices by predators, responses to local abundance and, 192–193, 199–200; shellfish distributions and, 189–193

species consumed, by Mousterian hominids, 352, 354, 362, 368, 374; by predators, 19–21, 158–218, 353, 362, 374; diversity in, 18, 199, 201; ecological and evolutionary significance of, 200–201

species counting methods. *See* NISP, N-taxa.

species diversity, 18; living, 374; in Mediterranian mollusks, 159; in shell middens, 196

species lists, for mammals in Upper Pleistocene Italy, 70; for small animals, 160–161; taphonomy and reevaluations of, 6, 8

species in Pleistocene, British Isles, 74–77; France and Belgium, 74; Israel, 75–76; Italy, 73–77, 92–93, 160–161

species representation 17–20, 23; in Breuil, 85–86, 163–164; in Buca della Iena, 86–87, 163–164; in Guattari, 83–84, 161, 163; identifying potential bone collectors in caves from, 77–94; for large mammals in west-central Italy, 77–94; in Moscerini, 82–83, 161–163, 166–176; in Palidoro, 86–88, 163, 165; in Polesini, 86, 88, 90–91, 163, 165–166; in predator diets, 19–21, 158–218, 353, 362, 374; in Riparo Salvini, 86–89, 163; in Sant'Agostino, 84–85, 161–162, 164, 166–171; for small animals in west-central Italy, 160–166; taphonomy and reevaluations of, 6, 8

species richness (numbers of species), changes in global climate and, 18, 68, 73–77, 92–93; effects of scavenging on, 208; regression analysis of, 205–210

species-specific development rates and inherent suitability for seasonality analyses, 335

Sperlonga, coastal surveys near, 27, 29, 46; modern town of, 27

Speth, J. D., 227, 266, 383

spinal parts of prey. *See* axial body parts.

spleen, nutritional value of cattle, 229

sponges (marine), 160–161, 180, 183, 189, 194–196

spongy bone. *See* trabecular bone.

spotted hyaena (species), 70

spotted hyaena dens, in Buca della Iena, 30, 35–38, 66–67, 108–110, 151, 154–157; deer antler in, 224, 259–260, 269, 343, 345–349; in Fossellone, 129; in Guattari, 84, 93, 125, 127, 129, 152; modern examples of, 67, 224, 396–397; in Moscerini, 93, 123; Pleistocene examples of, 66, 151, 224. *See also* body part representation.

spotted hyaenas, 3–4, 7, 10, 15–16, 20, 316; aseasonal birthing in, 318–319, 330; bone collecting by, 80, 93, 95, 222–225, 355; cave use by, 16–18; consumption of tortoises by, 215; coprolites of, 43, 45, 84, 129, 151; cross-environmental variation in food transport by, 223, 263, 355; deciduous tooth shedding schedule of, 320–321, 323; den faunas collected by, 248–266, 389–390, 394–397; denning seasons of modern, 212, 319, 347; denning seasons of Pleistocene Latium, 332–351; diets of modern and Pleistocene, 199–218, 362, 374; feeding competition at kill sites among, 318; as hunter-scavengers, 223–224, 248–270, 355; infant mortality in, 129; maternity dens of, 21, 80, 151–152; modern and Pleistocene distributions of, 76, 223, 263, 318–319, 330, 346; mortality patterns in, 327–331; old-biased ungulate mortality patterns and scavenging by modern, 300, 355; processing and digestion of bone by, 127, 169, 212, 223; tooth eruption and occlusal wear scheme for, 323–325; juvenile-biased ungulate mortality pattern caused by Pleistocene, 296–300, 310–312

spur-thighed tortoise, 160, 174–175

St. Césaire, 4

stable isotope (^{18}O) analysis of shells, 196

staging of food transport and processing, 231

stalagmite, U-series dating of, 33–37. *See also* flowstones.

standardization of body part data (MNE), method for, 240–242, 245

standardized MNE data for ungulates and carnivores, complete, 389–397

starvation, as foremost cause of fawn deaths in absence of predators, 283–284; seasonal death patterns caused by, 266–267; as ultimate cause of bear hibernation deaths, 318

stone-boiling, 383

stone-tipped projectile weapons, 368; prime-dominated ungulate mortality and hunting with, 314, 368

stone tools. *See* technology.

storage of food, 231

strategic variation in Paleolithic subsistence systems, 198, 312–313, 351

strategies, contrast between confrontational and nonconfrontational scavenging, 384; covariation between Mousterian technologic and foraging, 352–370, 369, 379–385; methods for identifying, 17; rules for combining, 10, 269, 351, 372, 385; of stone tool and blank production, 356, 372, 380–385; as variable response, 14. *See also* food transport, mortality patterns, resource switching behavior.

stratigraphy, chronologic ordering of Mousterian assemblages by, 359, 364; site-by-site accounts of, 37–67

stress, seasonal mortality and periodic food, 283–287

striped hyaenas, den faunas collected by, 248–266, 355, 397; food transport behavior by, 222–223, 355; horns and heads in den of, 348–349; nonconfrontational scavenging by, 266, 355; as obligate scavengers, 223, 250–270

Strombus bubonius, 33, 56, 177–179, 182

structural fats in head and spinal cord of mammalian prey, 227–229

Stuart, A. J., 74–75, 344

subadult helpers at dens, 222, 317

subcutaneous fat in ungulate prey, availability of, 226–227

subordinate competitors, foraging strategies of, 222–223

subsistence, as core of human adaptations, 353; covariation in Mousterian technology and, 365–370; organization of, 5, 198, 312–313, 371–373, 385; role of Mousterian technology in, 382–385; shared time and energy budget of technology and, 353, 356, 368

three-age system of mortality analysis, 288–289, 321; applications of, 288–315, 320–330; for carnivores, 320–327; keyed to life history characteristics of females, 321; for ungulates, 288–292

throwing boards, Upper Paleolithic, 5

thymus, nutritional value of cattle, 229, 266

tigers, old-biased mortality patterns and scavenging by, 300; as solitary ambush predators, 296; ungulate mortality patterns caused by, 296–300, 310–312

Tilson, R., 224, 300

Timbavati spotted hyaena den fauna, 248–266, 396; horns and heads in, 348–349

time, geologic and radiometric, 5, 10, 33–37, 359; human evolution studies and intervals of, 373, 382, 386–387; markers of, 8, 33, 177, 382; use of Paleolithic industry types for dividing, 382, 386–387. *See also* chronology.

Tivoli, modern town of, 66

Tiwi of Melville Island, 186

tLITHICS (tools, flakes, and cores combined), 367

tMNE, 242, 245, 355; for cervids, bovids, and equids combined, 367; raw (nonstandardized), 389–397

tMNE/MNI, 242, 245, 253–262, 355; trend in, 359–361

toe bones, damage to, 145–147, 154–156; scarcity of, 246

Tongiorgi, A., excavations by, 30, 58

tongue, nutritional value of ungulate, 229–230, 266

Tooby, J., 220

tool forms, 353, 368, 372, 374; and functions, 353, 382; mechanics of stone fracture and, 353

tool "life histories," Mousterian, 352, 364–366, 369; persistent resharpening in, 366

tool marks, 138–140, 161; earliest known, 273. *See also* cut marks.

tool reduction histories. *See* technology.

tool sizes and tool marks, 138–140

tool transport in Latium Paleolithic, 32, 231–233, 351, 356, 364–366, 379–382; contrasts between Middle and Upper Paleolithic, 380–382

tool types, hunting success and Paleolithic, 368

tool typology, Bordes' Paleolithic, 5–6, 10, 31, 46, 49, 356, 368, 382; LaPlace's Paleolithic, 49; and partitioning of time in human evolution research, 8, 33, 177, 382, 386–387

tooth development, carnivores and precocious permanent, 320; root growth in relation to, 322–327

tooth eruption and occlusal wear, assumptions about rates of, 336; as basis for aging mammals, 21, 281; as basis for seasonality determinations, 332–336; deciduous-permanent replacement boundary and, 289; inherent (biologically-based) errors in, 291, 334–335, 337, 341; and longevity in species, 335–336, 341; methods for studying, 288–292, 332–336, 320–327, 354; nonlinear rates of, 281, 291; root development in relation to, 322–327; sample size effects and analyzing, 289; scheme for carnivores, 320–327; scheme for ungulates 289–292; significance of empty cohorts in seasonality analyses of, 334–335

tooth punctures in bone, 106, 133–134; carnivore body sizes and, 133–134; definition of, 106; digestive etching and, 167–168

tooth punctures in land snail shells, 161, 172–174

topography, distances of caves from shoreline and, 27–28, 353, 370; of Latium, 24–29; Paleolithic hunters use of, 375; and sea level changes, 27–28, 190–191; subaqueous, 28; wolves use of, 297

Torre in Pietra, fossil tortoise from, 175–176

Torres, T. J., 321

torso parts of ungulates, 227; ratios of peripheral parts to, 233. *See also* axial body parts.

tortoises, 19, 46, 160, 158–159, 174–176, 197; as climatic indicators, 74; European pond, 74, 160; hibernation and fossil, 159, 175–176; Mousterian scavenging of ungulates and gathering of, 343, 350–351, 362, 365–367, 371, 375, 378–379; in spotted hyaena den fauna, 215; spur-thighed, 160

Toth, N., 127

Tozzi, C., 49, 56, 66–67, 85–86

trabecular bone, body part profiles and destructibility of, 69, 98, 231, 355; hemopoietic zones in, 291–292; processed as food, 228, 234–235, 259, 384

trampling damage to marine shells, 188

transition. *See* Middle-Upper Paleolithic transition.

Transkei Coast, shellfish exploitation on, 193

transport behavior. *See* food transport.

transport choices. *See* body part choices, food choices.

transport costs. *See* costs.

transport of stone tools and raw material. *See* raw material economy, tool transport.

transverse dents in bone, definition of, 104–105; quantitative accounts of, 108–127

travertine formation, at Palidoro, 61–63; at Ponte Lucano, 66

trends in Latium Mousterian foraging and technology, 245, 269–270, 310–315, 352–370; local nature of, 372

triangular graphs for mortality analyses, definition and uses of, 288–315, 320–330

trophic level, 14, 199–200, 216–217

trophy hunting, 298–300, 310–312. *See also* hunting.

tropical environments, foraging in, 225–226, 230; ungulate fat build-up in, 226

t-test of relationship between burning and bone fragment size, 148–149

Tulekana site, caribou mortality pattern in, 301–304; seasonality data for juvenile caribou in, 337–338

turbin shells, 160, 178, 180, 184, 189; hominid modification of, 178, 180

Turkey, paleontological reference case on bears from, 321, 325–326, 330

Turkmenia, wild ass reproductive schedule in, 333

Turner, A., 16, 239, 321

Turner site, white-tailed deer mortality pattern in, 301–304

turret shells, 160, 180, 184

Turritella, 160, 180

Tuscany (Toscano), excavations and geochronologic studies in, 30, 33; karst formations of coastal, 66; province of, 10

typology. *See* tool typology.

Tyrrhenian Seacoast, 24–25, 27, 33; interglacial beaches of, 33–37, 45–47, 52, 56, 59–60, 177, 190, 193

umbo breaks on marine shells, 182, 186

ungulate biomass and foraging opportunities for predators, 224

ungulate body size categories, 20, 68, 145, 249, 397

ungulate mortality patterns. *See* mortality patterns of ungulates.

ungulates, birthing synchrony in, 332–336; hard vs. soft tissue anatomy of, 355; as investigator-defined resource class, 15–16, 202, 268; latitudinal variation in birthing and development in, 332–336; life history characteristics of, 282, 291–292; in predator diets in Latium, 199–218; predator guild centering on, 268, 374; seasonal deaths in Paleolithic Latium, 18, 21, 284, 336–351, 354, 361–362, 365–366, 378; standardized MNE data for, 248–256, 389–397

University of Amsterdam, surveys sponsored by, 30

by, 133, 135; hominid predation on, 133; lagomorphs in diets of denning, 167, 212; mortality patterns in Pleistocene, 327–331; as obligate hunters, 202, 250–270, 273; prey body part profiles generated by denning, 248–266, 396; reproductive schedules of modern, 152, 319, 330; scavenging by, 226, 251, 264, 285; tooth eruption and occlusal wear scheme for, 322–324; ungulate mortality patterns caused by, 295–300, 310–312, 377; use of caves by, 16, 18, 206
wood mouse, 70, 160
World Wars, research in west-central Italy between, 29
worm shells (marine worms), 160, 180, 184
wrenches, Upper Paleolithic bone, 5
Wretton fauna, 74
Wurm I, 60
Wyoming, bison jump and trap sites in, 307

xeric environments, ungulate fat build-up in, 226

Yarimburgaz Cave (Turkey), 324–326; cave bear mortality pattern in, 330

Yellen, J., 103, 228
yellow marrow, 291–292, 384

Zanone, Island of, 27
zebras, as large-sized ungulates, 249; lion-caused mortality pattern in, 298–300; mortality pattern in trophy-hunted, 298–300; spotted hyaena-caused mortality pattern in, 298–300
Zhoukoudien Cave, 130
Zimbabwe spotted hyaena den fauna, 248–266, 396; horns and heads in, 348–349
zooarchaeological variables. *See* variables for study.
zooarchaeology, human evolution research and, 5–6, 9, 387; lithic industry chronologies and, 387
Zoological Museum of Rome, comparative skeletal collections of, 69
Zululand, spotted hyaena reproductive schedules in, 319
Zuni Pueblo, canid gnawing damage in historic bone midden fauna from, 136–137, 141
Zymella, S., 36